EUROPEAN HISTORICAL DICTIONARIES
Edited by Jon Woronoff

Historical Dictionary of Turkey

Second Edition

Metin Heper

European Historical Dictionaries, No. 38

The Scarecrow Press, Inc.
Lanham, Maryland, and London
2002

SCARECROW PRESS, INC.

Published in the United States of America
by Scarecrow Press, Inc.
A Member of the Rowman & Littlefield Publishing Group
4720 Boston Way
Lanham, Maryland 20706
www.scarecrowpress.com

4 Pleydell Gardens, Folkestone
Kent CT20 2DN, England

British Library Cataloguing in Publication Information Available

Library of Congress Cataloging-in-Publication Data

Heper, Metin.
    Historical dictionary of Turkey / by Metin Heper.—2nd ed.
        p. cm. — (European historical dictionaries ; no. 38)
    Includes bibliographical references (p.)
    ISBN 0-8108-4133-9 (alk. paper)
        1. Turkey—History—Dictionaries. I. Title. II. Series.

    DR436 .H47 2002
    956.1'003—dc21

                                        2001057615

First edition by Metin Heper, European Historical Dictionaries, No. 2,
Scarecrow Press, Metuchen, N.J., 1994   ISBN 0-8108-2817-0

Contents

Editor's Foreword

Turkey, not so long ago dismissed as the "end" of Europe, has increasingly become a center of regional affairs. After decades as a bastion against the Soviet Empire, it can finally deal normally with Eastern European countries and the successor states of the Soviet Union. Some of these, by the way, were previously part of the Turkish sphere; several still share the same religion and ethnic roots. Contacts with the Middle East are much closer now, facilitated by a common religion and mutual economic interests. Yet, while restoring and intensifying these relations, Turkey has not turned away from the West. To the contrary, it is seeking closer economic and political links and aspires to membership in the European Union while remaining a staunch ally of the United States.

This realignment is making Turkey considerably more significant and influential. Its primary role is no longer military, to contain the Soviet threat. It can thus expand its political, economic, social, and cultural activities in the former Soviet Union and elsewhere. For some nearby countries, it can even become a leader and role model, offering a secular, democratic, and modern alternative to the fundamentalism preached in Iran and elsewhere. Despite difficulties and setbacks, Turkey has developed a working political party system and has considerably improved its economic performance. Its foreign policy and diplomacy are already bearing fruit. And, as ever, it boasts important assets, including a large but productive population, a strong military, and an exceptional strategic location where Europe, Africa, and Asia come together.

While considering Turkey's present resurgence, however, we should not forget its long and sometimes troubled past. It has had moments of glory, extraordinary moments, when it ruled one of the world's largest empires. It has also had moments of decline and near disaster, when that empire came apart and it was uncertain whether even the core might survive. Thanks to Atatürk, the nation's great modern leader, it did. These stories—those moments of glory and of decline—are all traced in this book, which starts with the rise of the Ottoman Empire in the 13th century and concludes with the present day. It presents many significant persons, places, and events as well as important aspects of the economy, culture, and society. The chronology and appendices clarify this long history as well as provide an overall picture of the present. An exceptionally complete bibliography directs interested readers to more specialized sources.

It would be hard to find a more suitable author for this volume than Metin Heper. Born in Turkey and educated in that country, the United States, and the United Kingdom, Dr. Heper is presently a professor of political science at Bilkent University in Ankara, director of the Center for Turkish Politics and History there, and a founding member of the Turkish Academy of Sciences. He has also lectured and taught abroad. Professor Heper has written widely on the subjects covered here and his articles have appeared in leading scholarly journals. In addition, he has authored *The State Tradition in Turkey* and *İsmet İnönü: The Making of a Turkish Statesman*, and has edited or co-edited a dozen other books. Having produced an already informative first edition of this *Historical Dictionary of Turkey*, he now offers an even more extensive work that will help us better understand this important and often neglected country.

—Jon Woronoff
Series Editor

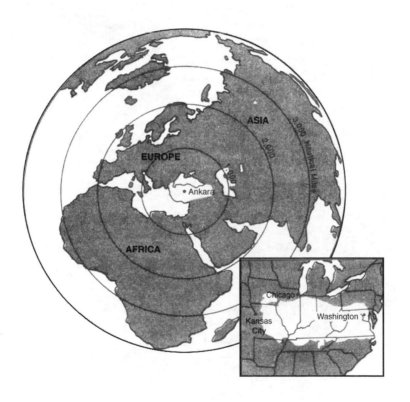

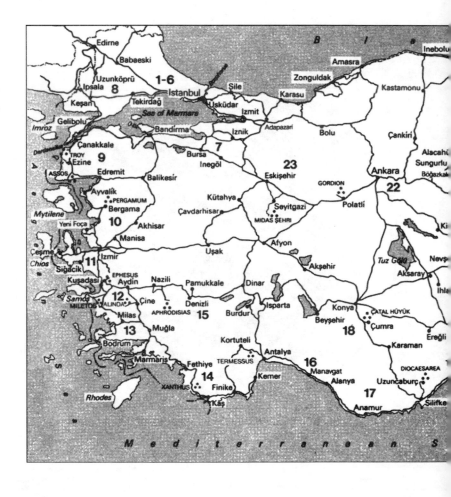

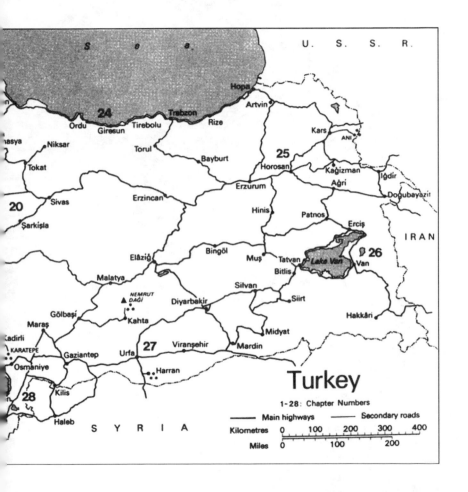

Turkey

1-28: Chapter Numbers

Main highways ———   Secondary roads ———

Kilometres	0	100	200	300	400
Miles	0		100		200

S   e   a

U.   S.   S.   R.

Hopa

Artvin

Ordu   Giresun   Trabzon   Rize

Kars   ANI

Niksar   Torul   Bayburt   Horosan   Kağizman   Iğdir

Tokat   Erzincan   Erzurum   Ağri   Doğubayazit

Sivas   Hinis   Patnos   Erciş   IRAN

Şarkişla   Elâziğ   Bingöl   Muş   Tatvan   Lake Van   Van   26

Malatya   Bitlis

NEMRUT DAĞI   Silvan

Gölbaşi   Diyarbakir   Siirt

Maraş   Kahta   Midyat   Hakkâri

Kadirli   KARATEPE   Viranşehir   Mardin

Osmaniye   Gaziantep   Urfa   27

Kilis   Harran

Haleb   S   Y   R   I   A

20   24   25   28

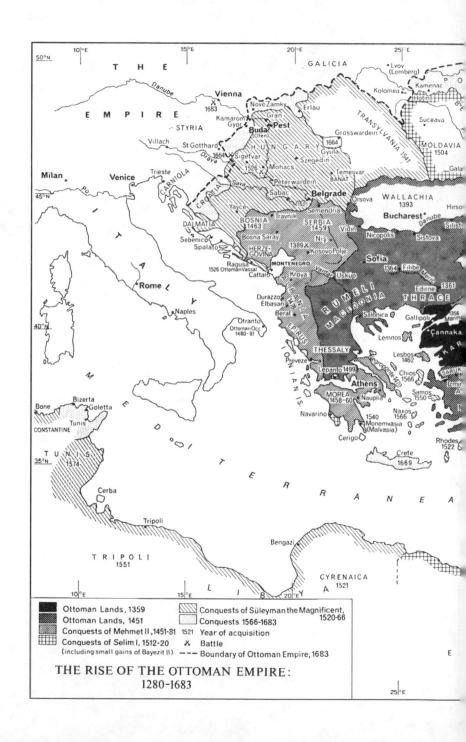

THE RISE OF THE OTTOMAN EMPIRE:
1280-1683

Legend:

- Ottoman Lands, 1359
- Ottoman Lands, 1451
- Conquests of Mehmet II, 1451-81
- Conquests of Selim I, 1512-20 (including small gains of Bayezit II)
- Conquests of Süleyman the Magnificent, 1520-66
- Conquests 1566-1683
- 1521 Year of acquisition
- ✕ Battle
- --- Boundary of Ottoman Empire, 1683

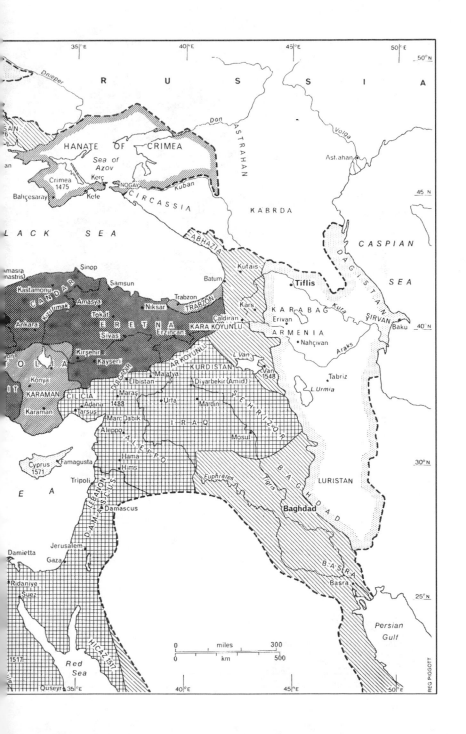

■	Losses 1683–99 (*Treaty of Karlowitz*)	Turkey in 1923	
■	Losses 1700–18 (*Treaty of Passarowitz*)	1878	Date or period of autonomy
▥	Losses 1719–74 *Treaty of Küçük Kaynarca*	1830	Date of independence
▨	Losses 1775–1812 *Treaty of Bucharest*	—·—·	Boundaries of spheres of influence in Anatolia after the 1914–18 War
▩	Losses 1813–29/30 *Treaty of Edirne*	········	Boundary after Treaty of Sèvres 1920
▦	Losses 1830–78 *Treaty of Berlin*	————	Boundary after Treaty of Lausanne 1923
▧	Losses 1879–1915 *Treaties of London & Bucharest*		
▤	Losses 1916–23 *Treaty of Lausanne*		

DECLINE OF THE
OTTOMAN EMPIRE
AND RISE OF THE TURKISH REPUBLIC
1683–1975

Acknowledgments

Map "Turkey, Europe, Asia, and Africa/Turkey in Scale" has been adopted from Paul M. Pitman III, ed. *Turkey: A Country Study*, Washington, D.C.: Library of Congress, 1988, p. xv; maps "The Rise of the Ottoman Empire, 1280–1683" and "Decline of the Ottoman Empire and Rise of the Turkish Republic, 1683–1975" from Stanford J. Shaw and Ezel Kural Shaw, *History of the Ottoman Empire and Modern Turkey,* volume II, Cambridge: Cambridge University Press, 1977, pp. xxii–xxiii and xxxiv–xxxv, respectively; and map "Turkey" from John Freely, *Turkey*, London: Collins (now HarperCollins), 1986, pp. 13–14. Permissions given are gratefully acknowledged.

Reader's Notes

The modern standard Turkish spelling system has been adopted in this book. There are only a few exceptions to indicate pronunciation for the English reader—for example, pasha, instead of paşa. I have conformed to the frequent Turkish practice of changing the final Ottoman letters *d* and *b* into *t* and *p*, thus Mehmet, Bayezit, and *mektep*. Arabic words used in Turkish have been given their Turkish spellings, thus *mültezim* and *medrese* rather than *multazim* and *madrasa*.

Turkish letters not pronounced like their English equivalents and their rough English, French, and/or German equivalents are:

a: *u* as in *cut* (French *a*, as in *avec*)
c: *j* as in *jet*
ç: *ch* as in *chart*
g: hard *g* as in *get*
ğ: usually silent; lengthens a preceding *a* or *ı* (the undotted *i*); *y* after *e* and *i*
ı: (the undotted) *i* as in *soldier*
i: *i* as in *bit*
j: *si* as in *cohesion* (French *j* as in *jour*)
ö: French *eu* as in *deux*; same as German *ö*
ş: *sh* as in *shell*
ü: same as German *ü*; French *u* as in *tu*

Turks took family names from 1935 onward. Those persons who did not live beyond 1934 are mentioned in the dictionary by their given names only. Also, if a person has always been referred to by both given and family names, that person's name was presented in that manner in the dictionary, that is, given name preceding the family name and not the other way around, as in the case of other persons discussed in the dictionary.

All dollar figures are in U.S. dollars unless otherwise noted.

Bold letters are used to indicate that a given topic has its own entry in the dictionary.

Abbreviations and Acronyms

ENGLISH

BSEC	Black Sea Economic Cooperation
BSF	Black Sea Force
CUP	Committee for Union and Progress
DCP	Democratic Center Party
DECA	Defense and Economic Agreement
DEP	Democracy Party
DLP	Democratic Left Party
DTP	Democratic Turkey Party
DP	*Demokrat* Party
DP	*Demokratik* Party
DTP	Democratic Turkey Party
EC	European Community
EEC	European Economic Community
EOKA	National Organization of [Greek] Cypriot Fighters
EU	European Union
FAO	United Nations Food and Agriculture Organization
FP	Freedom Party
FSP	Freedom and Solidarity Party
GAP	Southeastern Anatolia Project
GDS	General Directorate of Security
GEC	Gendarmerie General Command
GNP	Gross National Product
GSM	Global System for Mobile Communications
GTP	Grand Turkey Party
ISE	Istanbul Stock Exchange
JP	Justice Party
METU	Middle East Technical University
MHA	Mass Housing Administration
MP	Motherland Party
NAP	Nationalist Action Party
NATO	North Atlantic Treaty Organization

NDP	Nationalist Democracy Party
NLP	Nationalist Labor Party
NP	Nation Party
NSC	National Security Council
NSP	National Salvation Party
NTP	New Turkey Party
NUC	National Unity Committee
OSCE	Organization for Security and Cooperation in Europe
PDP	People's Democracy Party
PKK	Kurdistan Worker's Party
PLP	People's Labor Party
PP	Populist Party
PPA	Public Participation Agency
PPF	Public Participation Fund
PRP	Progressive Republican Party
RDP	Reformist Democracy Party
RFP	Republican Free Party
RNP	Republican Nation Party
RPNP	Republican Peasant's Nation Party
RP	Republican Party
RP	Resurrection Party
RPP	Republican People's Party
RRP	Republican Reliance Party
RF	Retirement Fund
SSA	Social Security Administration
SDP	Social Democracy Party
SDPP	Social Democratic Populist Party
SEE	State Economic Enterprise
SP	Socialist Party
SSK	Social Security Administration
TCP	Turkish Communist Party
TLP	Turkish Labor Party
TPP	True Path Party
US/AID	United States Aid Agency
UN	United Nations
VP	Virtue Party
WP	Welfare Party

TURKISH

AA	Anadolu Ajansı [Anatolian News Agency]
ANAP	Anavatan Partisi [Motherland Party]
AP	Adalet Partisi [Justice Party]

BTP	Büyük Türkiye Partisi [Grand Turkey Party]
CGP	Cumhuriyetçi Güven Partisi [Republican Reliance Party]
CHP	Cumhuriyet Halk Partisi [Republican People's Party]
CKMP	Cumhuriyetçi Köylü Millet Partisi [Republican Peasant's Nation Party]
CP	Cumhuriyetçi Parti [Republican Party]
CSF	Cumhuriyetçi Serbest Fırka [Republican Free Party]
DEP	Demokrasi Partisi [Democracy Party]
DİSK	Devrimci İşçi Sendikaları Konfederasyonu [Confederation of Revolutionary Trade Unions]
DMP	Demokrat Merkez Partisi [Democratic Center Party]
DP	Demokrat Parti [*Demokrat* Party]
DP	Demokratik Parti [*Demokratik* Party]
DSP	Demokratik Sol Parti [Democratic Left Party]
DTP	Demokratik Türkiye Partisi [Democratic Turkey Party]
DYP	Doğru Yol Partisi [True Path Party]
FP	Fazilet Partisi [Virtue Party]
GAP	Güneydoğu Anadolu Projesi [Southeastern Anatolia Project]
HADEP	Halkın Demokrasi Partisi [People's Democracy Party]
HEP	Halkın Emekçi Partisi [People's Labor Party]
HP	Halkçı Parti [Populist Party]
HP	Hürriyet Partisi [Freedom Party]
IDP	Islahatçı Demokrasi Partisi [Reformist Democracy Party]
MÇP	Milliyetçi Çalışma Partisi [Nationalist Labor Party]
MDP	Milliyetçi Demokrasi Partisi [Nationalist Democracy Party]
MHP	Milliyetçi Hareket Partisi [Nationalist Action Party]
MİT	Milli İstihbarat Teşkilatı [National Intelligence Agency]
MP	Millet Partisi [Nation Party]
MSP	Milli Selamet Partisi [National Salvation Party]
OYAK	Ordu Yardımlaşma Kurumu [Army Mutual Assistance Association]
ÖDP	Özgürlük ve Dayanışma Partisi [Freedom and Solidarity Party]
PKK	Kürdistan İşçi Partisi [Kurdistan Workers Party]
RP	Refah Partisi [Welfare Party]
SHP	Sosyal Demokratik Halkçı Parti [Social Democratic Populist Party]
SODEP	Sosyal Demokrasi Partisi [Social Democracy Party]
SP	Sosyalist Parti [Socialist Party]
TCF	Terakkiperver Cumhuriyet Fırkası [Progressive Republican Party]
TESEV	Türkiye Ekonomik ve Sosyal Araştırmalar Vakfı [Turkish Economic and Social Studies Foundation]
TİP	Türkiye İşçi Partisi [Turkish Labor Party]
TİSK	Türkiye İşverenler Sendikaları Konfederasyonu [Confederation of Turkish Employers' Union]
TKP	Türkiye Komünist Partisi [Turkish Communist Party]
TÜRK-İŞ	Türkiye İşçi Sendikaları Konfederasyonu [Confederation of Turkish Trade Unions]

TÜSİAD	Türkiye Sanayiciler ve İşadamları Derneği [Turkish Industrialists' and Businessmen's Association]
TOBB	Türkiye Odalar ve Borsalar Birliği [Turkish Union of Chambers of Commerce and Stock Exchanges]
YDP	Yeniden Doğuş Partisi [Resurrection Party]
YÖK	Yüksek Öğretim Kurumu [Council of Higher Education]
YTP	Yeni Türkiye Partisi [New Turkey Party]

Chronology*

Ottoman Period

1261–1310	Foundation of ghazi principalities, including that of Ottoman.
1326	Ottoman conquest of Bursa.
1327	First Ottoman silver coin [akçe] printed in Bursa.
1352	Orhan grants capitulations to the Genoese.
1361	Murat I conquers Adrianople (Edirne).
1385	Ottoman conquest of Sofia.
1389	Battle of Kossovo; Ottomans victorious, but Murat I slain.
1394–1402	Ottoman blockade of Constantinople.
1402	Battle of Ankara; Timur captures Bayezıt I.
1413	Mehmet I unifies Ottoman territories.
1424	Peace treaty between Ottomans and Byzantines.
1453	Siege of Constantinople; fall of Pera.
1460	Conquest of the Morea.
1475	Ottoman suzerainty over the khanate of the Crimea.
1475	Battle of Çaldıran; Selim I defeats Shah Ismail.
1516–1517	Syria and Egypt taken.
1521	Belgrade falls.
1529	First siege of Vienna.
1571	Formation of Holy League against the Ottomans.
1578	Annexation of Georgia.
1595–1610	Celali revolts.

* Not all elections and governments are presented here; some are fully covered elsewhere in this volume.

1669   Crete falls.

1683   Second siege of Vienna.

1699   Treaty of Karlowitz.

1711   Peter the Great defeated.

1715   Morea retaken.

1718–1730   The Tulip Period.

1736–1739   Belgrade retaken.

1765–1774   War with Russia.

1774   Treaty of Küçük Kaynarca.

1789–1807   Era of reforms initiated by Selim III.

1826   Greece proclaims independence.

1839   Gülhane Imperial Rescript; beginning of the *Tanzimat* (Reform) Period.

1854–1856   Crimean War.

1856   Reform Edict proclaimed.

1858   Land Code enacted.

1859   Ambassador sent to United States.

1867   First Ottoman sultan (Abdülaziz) in Europe.

1876   Proclamation of the First Constitutional Period.

1878   Parliament prorogued indefinitely.

1900   Istanbul University opens.

1908   Second Constitutional Period begins; Liberal Union formed.

1909   Abdülhamit II deposed.

1911   Freedom and Accord Party established.

1912–1913   First Balkan War.

1913   Committee of Union and Progress in power; Second Balkan War.

1914   Ottomans enter the First World War on the side of Axis powers.

1918   Mondros Armistice.

War of Independence and Its Aftermath

1919 **May 19:** Mustafa Kemal lands in Samsun to start the national liberation movement. **June 22:** Amasya Circular Letter. **July 23–August 7:** Erzurum Congress. **September 4–11:** Sivas Congress.

1920 **February 19:** National Pact. **March 16:** Istanbul under Allied military control. **April 23:** Grand National Assembly convenes. **June 22:** Greek army advances against the Nationalists. **August 10:** Treaty of Sèvres, parceling Turkey among the Allied powers.

1921 **January 20:** Constitutional Act enacted. **March 16:** Treaty of Moscow with Soviet Union.

1922 **August 30:** Decisive victory over invading Greek forces. **October 11:** Mudanya Armistice. **November 1:** Sultanate abolished.

1923 **February 17:** İzmir Economic Congress. **July 24:** Treaty of Lausanne essentially determines Turkey's present boundaries. **August 9:** People's Party founded, to become the Republican People's Party on November 10, 1924. **October 23:** Ankara becomes capital city.

First Turkish Republic

1923 **October 29:** Turkish Republic proclaimed.

1924 **March 3:** Caliphate abolished. **April 8:** Religious courts abolished. **August 26:** İş-Bank set up. **November 17:** Progressive Republican Party formed.

1925 **February 11–June 29:** First Kurdish insurrection. **June 5:** Progressive Republican Party dissolved by the government. **September 30:** Religious orders suppressed. **November 25:** Wearing of the fez forbidden by law. **December 26:** International calendar and international system of time adopted.

1926 **February 17:** New civil code (based on the Swiss code) adopted, effective October 4. **March 1:** New criminal code (based on the Italian code) adopted, effective July 1. **June 5:** Anglo-Turkish Treaty. **June 28:** New commercial code (primarily based on the German code) adopted.

1927 **March 7:** Kurdish revolt under Sheikh Said breaks out; intermittent insurrections brought under virtually complete control in 1938.

1928 **April 10:** State declared secular. **November 3:** Latin alphabet adopted, effective December 1, 1928.

1929 **June 17:** Suppression of communist propaganda in Turkey.

1930 **April 16:** Women given the right to vote in municipal elections. **August 12:** Republican Free Party formed. **November 17:** Republican Free Party dissolves itself.

1931 **April 20:** Republican People's Party declared republican, nationalist, populist, statist, secular, and revolutionary-reformist.

1932 **February 19:** People's Houses opened. **August 12:** Turkey joins League of Nations.

1934 **February 9:** Balkan Pact with Greece, Yugoslavia, and Romania. **June 21:** Law requiring all citizens to adopt family names adopted, effective January 1, 1935. **November 26:** Mustafa Kemal bestowed family name of "Atatürk" (Father of Turks) by National Assembly. **December 8:** Women eligible to vote in national elections and to become members of the National Assembly.

1935 **May 27:** Sunday, rather than Friday, becomes the day of rest.

1936 **July 20:** Montreux Convention signed.

1937 **July 9:** Saadabad Pact with Iraq, Iran, and Afghanistan.

1938 **November 10:** Atatürk dies. **November 11:** İsmet İnönü becomes president of republic.

1939 **June 29:** Alexandretta (Hatay) Assembly votes for union with Turkey. **October 19:** Ankara Pact with Great Britain and France.

1941 **June 18:** German-Turkish Friendship and Non-aggression Pact.

1942 **November 11:** Wealth Tax enacted.

1943 **December 4–6:** Cairo Conference; Winston Churchill, Franklin D. Roosevelt, and İnönü participate.

1945 **February 24:** Turkey signs United Nations charter, ratified by National Assembly on August 15. **June 7:** Soviet ultimatum; Turkey rejects territorial demands.

1946 **January 7:** *Demokrat* Party (DP) founded. **May 31:** New electoral law enacted, providing for direct and secret ballot.

1947 **March 12:** President Harry S. Truman announces program of U.S. aid to Greece and Turkey. **July 12:** İnönü's declaration paves the way for an unhampered opposition and, eventually, multiparty politics.

1948 **July 20:** Nation Party founded.

1949 **March 24:** Turkey grants de facto recognition to Israel. **August 8:** Turkey admitted to Council of Europe.

1950 **February 16:** Judiciary given responsibility for the administration of electoral law. **May 14:** *Demokrat* Party (DP) wins general elections; end of 27-year-old

Republican People's Party rule. **July 4:** Israel and Turkey sign trade agreement. **July 25:** Turkey decides to send troops to Korean War.

1952   February 18: Turkey and Greece become full-fledged members in NATO.

1953   February 25: Non-aggression and Friendship Pact signed with Greece and Yugoslavia.

1954   January 27: Nation Party dissolved by court order on grounds that it seeks to use religion for political purposes. **February 2:** Republican Nation Party founded, successor to Nation Party. **April 2:** Treaty of Mutual Friendship with Pakistan. **August 9:** Balkan Pact signed with Greece and Yugoslavia.

1955   February 24: Baghdad Pact with Iraq, becoming operative April 15, joined by Great Britain on April 4, Pakistan on September 23, and Iran on October 11. **September 6:** Anti-Greek rioting in Istanbul, İzmir, Ankara. **December 20:** Freedom Party established by dissidents in *Demokrat* Party.

1956   June 6: Press Law amended, increasing the government's powers over the press. **June 27:** Law limiting the holding of public political meetings is enacted. **November 26:** Turkey withdraws its ambassador to Israel until such time as Israel is willing to resolve its differences with the Arabs.

1957   January 15: U.S.-Turkish agreement, Turkey undertakes to guarantee the convertibility and transfer of capital and earnings of approved U.S. private investment in Turkey. **March 6:** Schools for preachers and prayer leaders given official status.

1958   January 16: Nine army officers arrested for plotting against the government. **November 24:** Freedom Party dissolves itself to merge with Republican People's Party.

1959   February 19: Greece, Turkey, and Britain agree to establish an independent Cyprus Republic on a communal basis. **March 5:** Turkey and United States sign bilateral defense agreement, ratified by Turkey in May 1959. **July 31:** Turkey applies for associate membership in European Economic Community.

1960   March 19: Israel and Turkey sign trade and payments agreement. **April 18:** All party political activity suspended for three months, pending an investigation of Republican People's Party by an Assembly commission. **April 28, 30, May 2, 14:** Student demonstrations against government. **May 21:** Army War College cadets march in Ankara in support of antigovernment demonstrations. **May 27:** Officer coup seizes power; General Gürsel co-opted as its leader. **September 21:** *Demokrat* Party abolished by court order. **October 14:** Leaders and parliamentarians of DP go on trial for unconstitutional acts as well as corruption. **November 13:** Gürsel dismisses 14 of the 37 members of National Unity Committee for their radical views.

1961 January 6: Constituent Assembly convenes. **February 11:** Justice Party (JP) established, also New Turkey Party.

Second Turkish Republic

1961 July 9: New Constitution ratified in nationwide referendum. **September 15:** Celal Bayar (former president), Adnan Menderes (former prime minister), Fatin Rüştü Zorlu (former foreign minister), Hasan Polatkan (former finance minister), and 11 other members of *Demokrat* Party sentenced to death. The sentences of Bayar and the 11 commuted to life imprisonment. Death sentences executed. **October 25:** New, two-house Grand National Assembly convenes.

1962 February 22: Coup attempt led by Colonel Talat Aydemir fails. **August 26:** U.S. Vice President Lyndon Johnson visits Turkey.

1963 May 21: Another coup attempt by Aydemir and fellow officers put down. **September 12:** Turkey becomes an associate member of European Economic Community. **December 25:** Turkish warplanes fly over Nicosia as warning against massacre of Turks on Cyprus.

1964 March 12: Turkey warns Archbishop Makarios to stop Greek community's atrocities toward the Turkish community on the island. **June 6:** U.S. President Johnson dissuades the Turkish government from military intervention in Cyprus.

1965 December 3: Soviet Union decides to contribute to construction of Turkey's third steel plant.

1966 January 14: U.S. President Johnson sends terse letter to İnönü, asking Turks not to launch a military operation in Cyprus. **January 31:** İnönü's firm reply to Johnson, while resentment against U.S. influence in Turkey grows. **July 8:** President Cevdet Sunay pardons Celal Bayar, former president of republic.

1967 April 30: Reliance Party formed.

1968 June 24: Istanbul University closed until July 15, following student unrest. **October 25–30:** French President General Charles de Gaulle visits Turkey.

1969 January 6: U.S. Ambassador Robert Komer's car burnt by leftist students. **February 9:** Alparslan Türkeş elected chairman of newly established Nationalist Action Party. **May 3:** Extreme rightists disrupt funeral ceremony of the late president of High Court of Appeals. **May 31:** Istanbul University closed, following student siege.

1970 January 23: Pro-Islamic National Order Party formed. **June 15–16:** Workers demonstrate in Istanbul and Kocaeli; martial law proclaimed. **July 22:** Turkey and European Community sign agreement after Ankara's completion of the first phase of preparation for future membership. **December 18:** Ferruh

Bozbeyli and 26 other JP deputies expelled from their party, form *Demokratik Party*.

1971 January 20: Middle East Technical University closed, following student unrest. **March 3:** Four American NCOs kidnapped, released five days later by urban leftist guerillas. **March 12:** Chief of general staff and commanders of three forces issue memorandum calling for strong government to fight anarchy and inflation and implement social reforms, or else the military will intervene; Prime Minister Süleyman Demirel resigns. **April 7:** Nihat Erim's above-parties government formed at the behest of the military. **April 27:** Martial law declared, all student associations banned. **May 21:** Constitutional Court closes down National Order Party for antisecular propaganda. **July 20:** Constitutional Court closes down Labor Party of Turkey for making communist propaganda and encouraging separatist movements. **September 20:** Constitutional amendments adopted by Parliament. **October 12:** U.S. Vice President Spiro Agnew visits Ankara. **October 18:** Queen Elizabeth II in Ankara.

1972 January 10: Military High Court of Appeals upholds death sentences against three members of Turkish People's Liberation Army; executions on May 6. **March 8:** Autonomy of Turkish Radio and TV curtailed. **May 4:** General Kemalettin Eken, head of the Gendarmerie, wounded by young terrorists. **May 8:** İsmet İnönü, chairman of Republican People's Party (RPP), resigns after defeat of his followers at RPP convention. **May 14:** Bülent Ecevit becomes chairman of Republican People's Party, succeeding İnönü who was chairman for the past 34 years. **September 4:** Republican Party formed. **December 5:** First Turkish ambassador to Peking (now Beijing) presents his credentials.

1973 March 3: Republican Party unites with Reliance Party, to become Republican Reliance Party. **April 6:** Senator and retired Admiral Fahri Korutürk elected president of republic. **June 31:** Turkey and European Community sign a supplementary protocol regulating Turkey's associate membership. **October 26:** Turkey and Soviet Union sign an agreement to jointly build a dam in Turkey. **December 25:** İsmet İnönü dies.

1974 April 22: Law that restores political rights of former *Demokrat* Party members in force. **June 22:** Socialist Labor Party of Turkey formed. **July 15:** Athens-led Cypriot Army takes over government on Cyprus. **July 20:** Turkish armed forces intervene to restore peace and stability on Cyprus. **July 31:** Turkey, Greece, and Britain sign cease-fire accord on Cyprus. **August 14:** Turkish forces in Cyprus hit east and west of Nicosia, the capital, and enter Famagusta, as Geneva peace talks fail. **October 15:** U.S. President Gerald Ford vetoes a bill that proposed to cut military aid to Turkey.

1975 February 6: Turkey suspends talks on the implementation of bilateral accords with United States. **February 13:** Turkish Federated State of Cyprus proclaimed. **March 31:** Six-month-old government crisis ends as Prime Minister Süleyman

Demirel announces "nationalist front" government of Justice Party, National Salvation Party, Nationalist Action Party, and Republican Reliance Party. **July 26:** Activities of U.S. military bases in Turkey suspended. Turkish army to take over full control of the bases. **October 3:** U.S. House of Representatives to partially lift arms embargo on Turkey. **December 25:** Soviet Premier Aleksey Kosygin visits Ankara.

1976 March 28: Turkey and United States sign new military accord, which restores American privileges at defense facilities in Turkey. **May 12:** Seventh Islamic Conference opens in Istanbul. **August 9:** Ankara sends tough reply to Greece's note claiming Turkey violated Aegean continental shelf with Seismic I research. **September 17:** Tens of thousands of leftist Confederation of Revolutionary Trade Unions (DISK) member-workers go on strike to protest government efforts to extend the lifespan of the State Security Courts.

1977 January 3: Kirkuk-Iskenderun pipeline inaugurated. **May 1:** 37 dead in May Day rally in Istanbul. **August 14:** Turkey claims Greece violated international treaties by militarizing Aegean islands. **August 30:** In Great Victory Day message, President Fahri Korutürk says, "Keep army out of politics." **October 6:** Türk-İş (largest labor confederation in Turkey) presents memorandum to government, Parliament, and political parties and demands reforms; threatens general strike.

1978 January 30: Rightist youths stage illegal demonstration in Ankara. **March 17:** Turkey strongly criticizes Israeli invasion of Lebanon. **May 31:** Prime Minister Ecevit meets U.S. President Carter. **June 10:** Chief of general staff General Kenan Evren reacts to wave of violence engulfing Turkey, saying the armed forces will not allow anyone to divide the country. **June 23:** Turkey and Soviet Union sign "political document." **July 11:** Gunmen kill Professor Bedrettin Cömert of Hacettepe University in an ambush. **September 27:** United States formally lifts embargo on aid to Turkey. **December 24:** Sectarian clashes in Kahramanmaraş in southeastern Turkey leave 117 dead and over 1,000 wounded.

1979 March 8: President Korutürk once more warns political leaders: "Keep armed forces out of your conflict." **March 29:** U.S. Congress approves $200-million military aid to Turkey. **April 12:** One American serviceman killed, another seriously wounded by gunmen in İzmir. **May 4:** U.S. Senate turns down $50-million aid grant proposal to Turkey. **May 11:** Gunmen kill one American serviceman and injure another; outlawed Marxist-Leninist Armed Propaganda Union claims responsibility. **May 22:** U.S. Senate approves $50-million grant to Turkey. **June 15:** Turkish and Greek officials open intercommunal talks on Cyprus. **June 23:** Turkey cannot permit U-2 flights over its airspace under present circumstances, chief of general staff General Evren says. **August 8:** Some students at the opening ceremony of Middle East Technical University refuse to stand to attention and force others to sit down when Turkish National Anthem is sung. Instead, they sing the communist "International" and take oath of revolution. **October 5:** Palestinian Liberation Organization (PLO) Chief Yasser Arafat inaugurates permanent PLO Office in Ankara. **October 9:** Government extends the (temporary) status of U.S. bases in Turkey. **November 20:** Professor Ümit Doğanay, deputy dean of the Istanbul University's political sciences faculty, assassinated by terrorists.

1980 January 2: Letter of warning by the chief of general staff and other top army generals calling for urgent action by all "constitutional institutions" and political parties against terrorism, handed over by President Korutürk to ruling Justice Party leader Demirel and opposition Republican People's Party Chairman Ecevit. **February 2:** DISK takes general strike decision against government's economic measures, which it calls "fascist pressure on labor." **February 22:** Turkey unilaterally opens Aegean airspace to air traffic. **February 28:** Martial Law Commander General Nevzat Bölügiray says there is "an undeclared civil war in Turkey." **April 18:** Turkey signs nuclear nonproliferation accord. **May 8:** Labor Party of Turkey closed down by the Constitutional Court. **May 13:** General Evren urges political parties to elect new president without delay. **May 26:** General Evren says Turkish armed forces will continue to follow the path drawn by Atatürk. **July 1:** Turkey and European Community conclude a new association agreement. **July 9:** Police forces reported ineffective in Fatsa Township, which is under control of extreme leftist factions and "people's committees." **July 19:** Former Premier Nihat Erim assassinated by four terrorists in Istanbul. **August 30:** Angered by National Salvation Party chief Necmettin Erbakan's absence at the Victory Day celebrations, General Evren asks, "Is he against the August 30 Victory?" (August 30, 1922, was the date of decisive victory over invading Greek forces.) **September 6:** Group of fanatics refuses to sing national anthem in National Salvation Party rally in Konya. **September 12:** Turkish armed forces, headed by General Evren, take over the administration. **September 16:** Head of State General Evren holds his first press conference and says, "Our aim is to protect and safeguard democracy." **October 11:** Ankara military court decides to arrest National Action Party leader Alparslan Türkeş and 36 party members for "instigating civil war." **October 15:** National Salvation Party Chairman Necmettin Erbakan and 21 party members arrested for acting against secular principles of Republic. **October 27:** Provisional constitution announced; 1961 constitution to remain in force until a new constitution is drafted. **December 2:** Turkey decides to downgrade its relations with Israel to minimum. **December 4:** Turkey signs $200-million aid agreement with United States.

1981 January 23: Premier Bülend Ulusu attends Islamic summit in Jidda, Saudi Arabia. **February 14:** National Security Council reminds nation that all political activities have been banned in the country. **June 15:** Turkey and Syria sign juridical agreement. **October 1:** Political Affairs Committee of Council of Europe recommends continuation of Turkish membership. **October 16:** National Security Council dissolves all political parties. **October 23:** Consultative Assembly inaugurated. Head of State Evren outlines the task of new assembly—to reinstate democracy. **November 3:** Martial law court sentences Bülent Ecevit to four months in prison for engaging in political activity.

1982   April 8: Turco-Romanian Economic Cooperation protocol signed. **April 10:** Ecevit in custody for article he wrote in a Norwegian paper; acquitted on June 2. **April 26:** Second arrest order for Ecevit for letter he allegedly wrote to a Dutch journalist, later broadcast by BBC. **July 23:** Moratorium announced between Turkey and Greece, which calls on the two countries to refrain from provocative acts and statements. **August 4:** National Security Council lifts restrictions on expression of political views; ban on political comments by former political leaders remain in force.

Third Turkish Republic

1982   November 7: National referendum on draft constitution held, 91 percent of those who voted (also 91 percent) approve new constitution; together with the constitutional referendum General Evren is elected Turkey's president. **November 16:** Prime Minister Bülend Ulusu meets Soviet Prime Minister Nikolai Tikhonov in Moscow. **November 29:** Turkey and United States to sign Memorandum of Understanding for modernization of more than 10 airfields in Turkey. **December 15:** Turkey and People's Republic of China sign accord stipulating increase in economic cooperation.

1983   January 28: Parliamentary Assembly of Council of Europe votes to give "serious consideration" to Turkey's expulsion from the council because of alleged human rights violations. **February 24:** Ankara martial law court sentences Necmettin Erbakan to four years in prison for attempting to establish state based on Islam. **April 24:** Ruling National Security Council lifts ban on political activities. **May 4:** Ankara martial law court sentences defunct Workers and Peasants Party of Turkey Chairman Doğu Perinçek to 12 years imprisonment. **May 16:** Nationalist Democracy Party becomes first political party to be set up following September 12, 1980, military takeover. **May 19:** Populist Party formed. **May 20:** Turgut Özal forms Motherland Party. Grand Turkey Party is established by those close to defunct Justice Party. **May 29:** Professor Erdal İnönü (son of late İsmet İnönü) announces establishment of Social Democracy Party. **May 31:** Military administration closes down Grand Turkey Party, claiming it is a continuation of defunct Justice Party. **June 23:** True Path Party, filling the vacuum created by the closure of Grand Turkey Party, is established. Military administration vetoes top brass of Social Democracy Party, including its chairman, Erdal İnönü. **July 7:** National Security Council vetoes 30 founders of True Path Party. **August 24:** National Security Council gives approval to participation of Motherland Party in November 6 elections. The Council does not approve the list of founding members of True Path Party and Social Democracy Party, thus disqualifying them from taking part in the elections. **November 6:** Motherland Party wins elections by a majority. **November 15:** Turkish Cypriots announce establishment of Turkish Republic of Northern Cyprus; Turkey recognizes new state. **December 29:** Prime Minister Özal unveils package of radical economic measures liberalizing imports and taking steps toward full convertibility of Turkish lira.

1984 **March 13:** President Li Xiannian arrives in Ankara to become first Chinese head of state to visit Turkey. **May 2:** Turkey and West Germany sign cooperation agreement for peaceful use of nuclear energy. **November 13:** Permanent Economic Committee of Islamic Conference Organization opens three days of meetings with an inaugural speech by President Kenan Evren, the committee's chairman. **December 25:** Soviet Premier Tikhonov arrives in Ankara for official visit.

1985 **February 13:** Martial law tribunal acquits leaders of defunct National Salvation Party of charges of attempting to set up state based on Islam. **April 2:** Prime Minister Özal meets U.S. President Ronald Reagan. **July 9:** Helmut Kohl, chancellor of Federal Republic of Germany, arrives in Turkey for official visit. **November 3:** Populist Party and Social Democracy Party merge, to form Social Democratic Populist Party. **November 14:** Democratic Left Party (DLP) founded by Rahşan Ecevit (wife of Bülent Ecevit).

1986 **May 4:** Opposition Nationalist Democracy Party extraordinary convention decides to dissolve the party. **May 9:** Former Turkish Union of Chambers President Mehmet Yazar establishes Free Democratic Party, along with 22 former Nationalist Democracy Party deputies. **May 16:** True Path Party forms parliamentary group after 20 former independent deputies join the party. **May 18:** Former Prime Minister Bülent Ecevit returns to political scene. **May 30:** Erdal İnönü elected new chairman of Social Democratic Populist Party. **August 15:** Turkish warplanes bomb separatist rebel hideouts in Northern Iraq four days after 12 Turkish soldiers are killed near the border. **October 24:** Prime Minister Özal breaks ground for 847-kilometer pipeline that will bring Soviet natural gas to Turkey. **November 30:** Free Democratic Party dissolves itself after by-election defeat. **December 19:** Turkish and Greek soldiers clash at border. **December 26:** People's Party established by 20 former Social Democratic People's Party deputies. **December 29:** People's Party dissolves itself; 19 of its deputies join DLP.

1987 **January 8:** President Evren in speech says Muslim fundamentalism has been resurrected in Turkey, and calls on state officials and people to struggle against all kinds of extremism. **January 10:** Former Prime Minister Bülent Ecevit sentenced to prison term of 11 months for speech he made during September (1986) election campaign in which he allegedly violated political ban against former political leaders. **January 25:** President Evren flies to Kuwait to attend two-day summit of heads of Islamic countries. **January 26:** Turkey recognizes individual rights of Turkish citizens to apply to European Human Rights Commission. **March 4:** Turkish jet fighters bomb separatist rebel camps and ammunition depots in southern Iraq in retaliation for separatist killings of civilians in Turkey. **March 16:** Turkey and United States extend 1980 Turkish-American Defense and Economic Cooperation Agreement until December 18, 1990. **March 26:** Turkey decides to counter Greek decision to explore for oil in disputed areas of Aegean Sea. **March 27:** Turkish armed forces are placed in state of readiness as tensions mount between Turkey and Greece. **March 28:** Turkey receives assurances from Greece that it will not explore for oil in disputed waters of Aegean Sea. **April 7:** Former Nationalist Action Party chairman Alparslan Türkeş sentenced to prison term of 11 years; party leadership accused of plotting ultranationalist armed revolt in the country. **April 14:** Turkey applies to European Community for full membership. **June 29:** Prime Minister Turgut Özal announces that General Necip Torumtay will become Turkey's chief of general staff to replace General Necdet Öztorun, widely believed to be the army's choice. **July 14:** Government establishes office of emergency rule regional governor to coordinate fight against terrorism in eight eastern and southeastern provinces. **September 6:** National referendum lifts bans against political leaders who ruled the country before the 1960 military intervention, with a razor-thin majority. **September 13:** Bülent Ecevit becomes chairman of Democratic Left Party. **September 24:** Süleyman Demirel becomes chairman of True Path Party. **October 4:** Alparslan Türkeş becomes chairman of Nationalist Work Party. **October 11:** Necmettin Erbakan becomes chairman of Welfare Party. **November 29:** General elections held; Motherland Party retains majority of seats in Parliament.

1988   January 11: Turkey signs Council of Europe's convention on the "Prevention of Torture and Inhuman or Degrading Treatment or Punishment." **January 25:** Turkey signs United Nations' international convention against inhuman treatment and torture. **February 1:** Socialist Party founded. **April 6:** British Prime Minister Margaret Thatcher arrives for three-day official visit. **June 26:** President Evren begins five-day state visit to United States. **July 12:** President Evren starts three-day visit to Britain. **October 11:** Government liberalizes bank interest rates. **October 16:** President Evren flies to Federal Republic of Germany for five-day official visit; he tells journalists that articles of Penal Code dealing with communism should be scrapped to open the way for the establishment of a Communist Party in Turkey. **December 3:** Council of Higher Education, the highest body of Turkish universities, decides to lift ban against Islamic-style head scarves for women university students. **December 8:** Constitutional Court rejects request by chief prosecutor to close down Socialist Party. **December 16:** Prime Minister Özal meets with U.S. President Reagan and President-elect George H. W. Bush at White House.

1989   February 2: Turkey and Iran sign agreement in Ankara, reviving a 52-year-old border security pact, which aims to curb drug smuggling and rebel activity. **March 7:** Constitutional Court annuls law allowing women students to wear Islamic-style head scarves at universities. **April 11:** Labor unrest spreads throughout Turkey after government and trade union negotiators fail to agree on pay hike for 600,000 workers employed by state. **April 13:** Konya municipality lifts its previous decision to segregate male and female students on buses after wide-scale student protests. **May 16:** Turkey gives United States permission to modernize Pirinçlik listening station in southeastern coastal town of Fethiye. **August 17:** In an unprecedented move, the armed forces issue statement declaring they "will do everything to combat separatist terrorism that aimed at destroying the national existence and territorial integrity of the country," following a sudden escalation in separatist incidents in southeastern Turkey. **September 17:** Central Bank announces it has completed payment of country's rescheduled foreign debts, introduced 22 years ago under the name of "Convertible Turkish Lira Accounts." **October 31:** Parliament elects Prime Minister Turgut Özal as president. **November 17:** Yıldırım Akbulut elected chairman of Motherland Party. **November 29:** Turkey approves European Social Charter. **December 8:** After 60 years of illegality, the clandestine Turkish United Communist Party announces its decision to end its "illegal" status and establish a legal Communist Party in Turkey.

1990   January 31: Professor Muammer Aksoy assassinated. Two separate unknown Islamic fundamentalist groups claim responsibility for killing ardently secularist professor. **February 4:** European Community foreign ministers agree to delay negotiations with Turkey on its full membership request; however, all members with the exception of Greece say they wish closer relations with Turkey. **April 5:** International Monetary Fund designates Turkish lira fully convertible currency. **May 1:** May Day turns sour as left-wing supporters try to stage mass rallies in Istanbul and clash with police; 1,100 taken into custody. **May 17:** Democratic Center Party of Bedrettin Dalan established. **June 4:** Turkish United Communist Party founded. **June 7:** Independent deputies who quit the main opposition Social Democratic Populist Party establish People's Labor Party. **August 2:** Turkey voices deep concern as Iraq invades Kuwait, and asks Baghdad to restore Kuwaiti territorial integrity and sovereignty. **August 8:** Turkey joins United Nations Security Council sanctions against Iraq and closes down the twin pipeline carrying Iraqi crude oil exports to its Mediterranean terminal at Yumurtalık. **August 12:** Parliament gives government permission to send troops abroad and allows foreign forces to be stationed on Turkish soil only if Turkey is attacked. **September 5:** Parliament gives authority to the government to send Turkish troops abroad and allow foreign troops to be stationed in Turkey without restrictions. **September 18:** Defense and Economic Cooperation Agreement between Turkey and United States extended for another year. **September 23:** President Özal goes to United States to meet President Bush. **October 6:** Professor Bahriye Üçok, known for her strong prosecular views, killed in a parcel bomb attack. **November 19:** President Özal and Prime Minister Yıldırım Akbulut sign historic treaty that cuts conventional forces in Europe and ends cold war. **December 3**: Chief of general staff General Necip Torumtay resigns, saying the principles he believes in and his understanding of government render it impossible for him to continue in office. **December 5:** Parliament votes to establish Parliamentary Human Rights Commission. **December 19:** Government asks NATO to deploy Allied mobile forces in southeastern Turkey against possible Iraqi attack.

1991   January 17: Parliament gives added war powers to government, including permission for United States to use Turkish air bases. **March 12:** Turkey and the Soviet Union sign Friendship and Cooperation Treaty. **March 23:** At joint White House press conference with U.S. President Bush, President Özal says Turkey will not allow the creation of a Kurdish state in northern Iraq. **April 12:** Bill lifts ban on speaking in Kurdish. **May 13:** Unidentified terrorists fatally shoot retired Lt. Gen.

İsmail Selen in Ankara and Gendarmerie Commander Brig. Gen. Temel Cingöz in Adana. **June 5:** President Özal says it is unthinkable that Turkey will shoulder its share of the military burden of European security while being left out of other areas in the "new Europe." **July 6:** Turkey's first woman governor appointed to Muğla province. **July 20:** U.S. President Bush arrives in Turkey for two-day visit. **July 29:** Turkey forbids allied forces to launch future punitive air strikes against Iraq from Turkish air bases. **August 15:** In İzmir, police arrest at least 44 Kurdish rebels who were participating in celebrations of seventh anniversary of Kurdish separatist struggle in Turkey. **August 19:** In Istanbul, British businessman Andrew Blake killed. Left-wing and Islamic groups both claim responsibility for the assassination. **September 14:** Democratic Center Party merges with True Path Party. **September 17:** In Ankara, Patriotic Union of Kurdistan leader Talabani asks President Özal to lobby for continued presence of allied force in Turkey to protect Kurds in Iraq from possible attacks by that government. **October 1:** Saudi King Fahd informs President Özal that his country would donate $1 billion to Turkish Defense Fund, by providing Turkey with $200 million in crude oil each year for five years. **October 21:** Prime Minister Mesut Yılmaz resigns as his Motherland Party trails behind True Path Party at October 20 general elections. **October 24–26:** Turkish jets raid Kurdish rebel camps in northern Iraq. **November 19:** True Path Party leader Demirel signs pact with Social Democratic Populist Party leader Erdal İnönü to form coalition government. The coalition controls 266 of 450 seats. **December 25:** In Istanbul, firebombs are thrown at department store owned by brother of Necati Çetinkaya, the recently appointed governor-general of Turkey's southeastern provinces. **December 26:** In Paris, previously unknown group called Kurdistan Committee seizes Turkish Embassy to protest alleged assassination of 30 people in Kulp and Lice (both in southeastern Turkey) by Turkish army. **December 29:** Nationalist Action Party merges with Nationalist Labor Party. Nationalist Labor Party then elects former Nationalist Action Party leader Alparslan Türkeş as its leader.

1992   January 15: Parliamentary Human Rights Commission presents a report proposing stringent security measures combined with religious propaganda to combat the spread of Kurdish nationalism. **January 19:** Speaker of Parliament rejects request by Ankara State Security Court to lift the parliamentary immunity of 22 former members of Kurdish-backed People's Labor Party, who entered Parliament on Social Democratic Populist Party ticket. **February 2:** Prime Minister Süleyman Demirel and Greek Prime Minister Constantine Mitsotakis agree to prepare accord of "friendship, good-neighborliness and cooperation" and to back UN-sponsored efforts to reunite Cyprus. **February 3:** Black Sea Economic Cooperation Project is initialed by foreign ministers of nine countries in Istanbul. **February 11:** In talks in Washington, U.S. President Bush and Prime Minister Demirel agree to increase aid to Central Asian and Transcaucasian republics. **February 16:** Government decides to increase customs duties and/or special fund provisions on more than 70 key import commodities while denying return to protectionism. **February 21:** Turkey conducts military exercises near Armenian border against background of growing tension between Azerbaijan and Armenia over the disputed enclave of Nagorno-Karabakh. **February 26:** Parliamentary Human Rights Commission concludes that ban on head scarves in universities is an infringement of human rights. **March 3:** Prime Minister Süleyman Demirel calls on United States and Russia not to arm Armenia amid growing fears that conflict over Nagorno-Karabakh could drag in neighboring countries. **March 9:** Prime Minister Demirel announces that Kurds will be able to celebrate Newroz (Kurdish New Year) on March 21. **March 13:** European Parliament condemns Kurdish PKK but calls for a halt to cross-border operations because civilians are being killed. **March 18:** Prime Minister Demirel asks United States to seek diplomatic solution to fighting between Armenians and Azerbaijanis over Nagorno-Karabakh, and says Turkey is being forced to get involved. **March 21–22:** Clashes erupt between army and Kurds following Kurdish rebels' call on supporters to stage demonstrations during the Newroz (Kurdish New Year). **March 26:** Turkey and United States sign agreement enabling Turkey to produce 40 additional F-16 fighter planes. Germany announces plans to suspend all arms shipments to Turkey until Ankara guarantees that the weapons are not being used against population in southeast. **March 30:** Prime Minister Demirel warns Syria to stop supporting PKK rebels. **April 26:** Prime Minister Süleyman Demirel begins a trip to Azerbaijan, Kazakhstan, Kyrgyzistan, Tajikistan, Turkmenistan, and Uzbekistan in an effort to further develop Turkey's relations with newly established central Asian countries. **May 5:** Germany lifts ban on military aid to Turkey. **June 7:** Local by-elections held: True Path Party wins 173 municipalities; Social Democratic Populist Party, 70; Motherland Party, 52; Welfare Party, 15; and Democratic Left Party, 1. **June 13:** Tansu Çiller becomes True Path Party leader. **July 2:** Ban lifted on political parties closed down by 1980 military intervention. **July 5:** Tansu Çiller becomes prime minister, to lead True Path Party-Social Democratic Populist Party coalition. **July 10:** Constitutional Court bans Socialist Party on charges of engaging in separatist activity. **July 14:** Constitutional Court closes pro-Kurdish People's Labor Party. **August 27:** Turkey establishes diplomatic relations with Bosnia-Herzegovina, Croatia, Macedonia, and Slovenia. **September 9:** Republican People's Party, banned after 1980 military intervention, reopens. Deniz Baykal elected chairman. **September 10:** Democratic Party, closed by military after 1960 coup, reopens after 32 years. Former Foreign Minister Hayrettin Erkmen becomes chairman. **September 14:** Iran agrees to cooperate with Turkey in efforts to fight PKK. **September 19:** Party members raise Kurdish flag and sing their national anthem during second People's Labor Party extraordinary convention in Ankara. **October 7:** New Party established. **October 14:** *Financial Times* survey ranks Turkey among the top 30 countries in the world in terms of creditworthiness and ability to pay. **November 6:** Socialist Turkey Party founded. **November 15:** Turkey and Israel sign a treaty of friendship. **November 19:** Criminal Trials Procedure Act amended in more liberal direction. **November 23:** Hasan Celal Güzel founds Resurrection Party and becomes its chairman. **December 19:** Justice Party convention closes the party and hands over all property and original emblem to True Path Party. **December 24:** Parliament renews mandate for Operation Provide Comfort for protecting the northern Iraqis.

1993 **January 14:** Turkish armed forces put on red alert following allied air strikes on Iraq. Prime Minister Süleyman Demirel visits Syria where he is told that Syria will not back PKK rebels. **January 23:** A secret report submitted to National Security Council accuses Hizbullah (Party of God) of committing unsolved murders in the southeast and seeking to introduce Sharia law in the country. **January 29:** Great Unity Party established. **January 30:** All European Union countries except Great Britain, Denmark, and Ireland to issue "joint visas" to Turkish citizens. **February 9:** Prime Minister Süleyman Demirel states Islamic Action group that claimed responsibility in the murder of journalist Uğur Mumcu had been trained in Iran. **February 23:** National Security Council proposes an economic package for the southeast since "recent military operations have broken the back of PKK." **March 3:** Turkey and European Union are to establish a commission to oversee transition to customs union due in 1995. **March 15:** Government refuses to negotiate with PKK because it is a "terror organization." **March 17:** PKK leader Abdullah Öcalan unilaterally declares a 25-day cease-fire; PKK fighters will not disarm until peace accord is reached with government. **April 16:** At press conference in Bar İlyas, Lebanon, Abdullah Öcalan, leader of PKK, announces indefinite extension of cease-fire begun on March 20. **April 17:** President Özal dies of heart attack. **May 16:** Parliament elects Süleyman Demirel president of Republic. Erdal İnönü becomes caretaker prime minister. **June 12:** U.S. Secretary of State Warren Christopher asks Turkish government for compliance with U.S. proposal to reduce human rights violations. **June 13:** True Path Party elects Tansu Çiller as party leader. **June 14:** President Demirel appoints Çiller prime minister. **July 2:** Islamic rioters set fire to a hotel in Sivas that accommodated leftist writers and intellectuals, whom they accuse of spreading atheism. Forty people die while Aziz Nesin, who had published Salman Rushdie's *Satanic Verses* and who apparently was the primary target, survives. **July 15:** Constitutional Court bans Kurdish-backed People's Labor Party. **August 16:** Foreign Minister Hikmet Çetin urges U.S. Secretary of State Warren Christopher to help lift UN oil sanctions against Iraq, pointing out that sanctions not only hurt Iraqi government but also Iraqi and Turkish peoples. **September 11:** Ankara Mayor Murat Karayalçın elected Republican People's Party leader. **October 14:** Prime Minister Çiller arrives in United States for meetings with U.S. President Bill Clinton and other U.S. officials. **October 22:** Rebels kill Brigadier General Bahtiyar Aydın in Lice. **November 29:** Prime Ministry announces that air strikes were carried out against nine separatist targets in Northern Iraq, with the knowledge of Iraqi authorities. **December 12:** Hatip Dicle becomes pro-Kurdish Democracy Party leader. **December 23:** Four pro-Kurdish Democracy Party deputies' parliamentary immunity is lifted, making them liable for prosecution by Ankara State Security Court.

1994 **February 28:** Prime Minister Çiller calls for a public rally at Istanbul's Taksim Square to defend secularism against fundamentalist attacks symbolically aimed at Atatürk's memory. **March 21:** Government adopts a flexible attitude toward celebration of Newroz. **March 27:** At local elections, the municipalities of Istanbul and Ankara go to Welfare Party. **April 14:** Washington announces that International Monetary Fund (IMF) will support the government's stabilization program. **April 15:** First meeting of Welfare Party-controlled Istanbul Municipality's Council starts with Welfarists praying while secular members sing the national anthem. **May 4:** World Bank approves a $100-million credit to support government's privatization plans. **May 12:** People's Democracy Party founded by members of Democracy Party; government authorizes preliminary work on first nuclear power plant in Akkuyu. **May 18:** Government announces "democratization package." **June 7:** Turkey warns Greece that any attempt to extend its territorial waters to 12 miles will be tantamount to declaration of war. **June 16:** Twelve leading deputies of Democracy Party resign from their party. **June 17:** Constitutional Court bans Democracy Party. **July 1:** Turkey unilaterally imposes new shipping regulations for the straits of Bosporus and Dardanelles, including requiring Turkish permission for the passage of ships over 150 meters long. **July 26:** Liberal Party formed by Besim Tibuk. **August 10:** Turkey's second communications satellite Türksat 1B on course. **August 27:** Government rejects a plan for U.S. military aid, requiring favorable report on human rights in Turkey and on Greek-Turkish negotiations over Cyprus, before the release of aid. **September 1:** European Union raises its quotas for imports of Turkish textiles by an average of 35 percent. **September 9:** Turkey and Greece agree to start up regular talks as a means of solving their differences. **October 16:** Doğu Perinçek reelected Labor Party leader. **October 19:** President Süleyman Demirel refutes Russian charges that Turkey is trying to create an ethnically based sphere of influence within the Commonwealth of Independent States. **November 3:** Turkey and Israel sign agreements on joint struggle against drug trafficking, terrorism, and other crimes, and on communications and postal services. **November 6:** Social Democratic Populist Party and (new) Republican People's Party decide to merge. **November 9:** President Demirel launches Southeast Anatolia Project—a hydroelectric and irrigation project consisting of a complex of 22 dams on Euphrates and Tigris rivers. As it could reduce water supplies to Syria and Iraq, both countries oppose the plan. **December 8:** Five Kurdish members of Parliament—Hatip Dicle, Orhan Doğan, Selim Andak, Ahmet Türk, and Leyla Zana—are convicted of supporting PKK and sentenced to fifteen years in prison. **December 21:** High Military Court dismisses six officers from army because of their fundamentalist Islamic activities within ranks. **December 22:** Rich textile heir Cem Boyner's New Democracy Movement transformed into a political party. **December 24:** Republican People's Party and Social Democratic People's Party decide to merge.

1995 January 10: Prime Minister Çiller announces that Newroz will become an official holiday in Turkey. **January 15:** Greece agrees to withdraw its veto against Turkey's entry to Customs Union. **February 19:** Republican People's Party (RPP) and Social Democratic People's Party merge under RPP roof; Hikmet Çetin becomes leader of new party. **March 6:** Turkey's entry into customs union with European approved. **March 12:** After an unidentified group opens automatic gunfire on a neighborhood coffeehouse, riots by Alevite community break out in poor districts of Istanbul, leading to clashes with police; life and property lost; army units step in and curfew imposed. **March 18:** Germany bans all PKK activities within its borders and starts to deport illegal activists back to Turkey. **March 20:** Government forces numbering 35,000 enter northern Iraq to conduct operations against PKK rebels, with armored battalions. **April 2:** U.S. Deputy Secretary of State Richard Holrooke supports Turkey's operation in northern Iraq, adding that security of Turkey's borders affects the security of Europe. **April 11:** PKK leader Abdullah Öcalan says he is prepared to negotiate a political solution to the conflict in the southeast; government not willing to negotiate with a "terrorist." **April 19:** Prime Minister Tansu Çiller meets with U.S. President Clinton in Washington, D.C.; Clinton urges Çiller to pull Turkish forces out of northern Iraq. **April 21:** Turkey and Armenia agree to reopen an air route between between Erzurum in eastern Turkey and Yerevan in Armenia. **April 26:** The Netherlands refuses to ban Kurdish Parliament in exile at the Hague; in return, Turkish government bars the Netherlands from bidding in defense contracts. **April 27:** United States and Japan come up with a $500-million loan for Turkey. **April 30:** President Demirel refuses to go to Moscow to attend celebrations marking 50th anniversary of ending of World War II in protest of Russian aggressions against Chechens in that federation. **May 8:** Nationalistic Action Party Leader Türkeş says Turks and Kurds lived together for 900 years and, consequently, he cannot imagine Turk being an enemy of Kurd. **May 13:** Russia promises to exclude PKK activities from Russia. **June 1:** Despite Turkish protests, Greece extends its territorial waters to 12 miles. **July 9:** Accord with Uzbekistan for the transport of Uzbek natural gas to Turkey via Turkmenistan-Georgia line. **July 23:** Parliament lowers voting age from 21 to 18 and allows political participation by unions; in Istanbul, International Securities Free Zone established. **July 28:** Istanbul Gold Exchange inaugurated. **August 10:** Accord between Turkey and Bosnia-Herzegovina; Turkey will train Bosnian troops and aid Bosnian defense industry. **September 10:** Deniz Baykal becomes Republican People's Party leader. **September 20:** Prime Minister Çiller resigns, following withdrawal of Republican People's Party from its coalition with Çiller's True Path Party. **November 5:** Tansu Çiller's True Path Party and Deniz Baykal's Republican People's Party form coalition government. **December 2:** Religiously oriented Welfare Party declares it is not against taking of interest. **December 13:** European Parliament admits Turkey into customs union with EU, effective January 1, 1996. **December 14:** PKK leader Abdullah Öcalan declares a unilateral cease-fire. **December 24:** General elections held. Religiously oriented Welfare Party obtains plurality of votes, followed by True Path Party, Motherland Party, Democratic Left Party, and Republican People's Party.

1996 January 27: Political crisis over Kardak islets on the Aegean Sea amid Turkish and Greek claims of sovereignty over islets. **February 13:** Turkey and Turkmenistan sign accord for supply of natural gas to Turkey. **March 3:** True Path Party (TPP) and Motherland Party (MP) form coalition government; Mesut Yılmaz of MP will become prime minister for one year, Tansu Çiller of TPP will take over prime ministry from Yılmaz for two years, and an unnamed member of MP will serve as prime minister during the last two years of the parliamentary term. **March 21:** Prime Minister Yılmaz celebrates Newroz in southeastern town of Iğdır. **March 24:** Parliament votes to conduct investigation into charges that former Prime Minister Tansu Çiller manipulated government contracts for personal gain. **April 8:** Arab League pronounces signing of military cooperation agreement between Turkey and Israel as "show of ill-will" and an "act of aggression." **April 10:** Tension between Turkey and Iran mounts over countercharges of spying. **April 23:** Parliament approves Welfare Party motion to open investigation on former Prime Minister Çiller for her part in mishandling of privatization bid; Athens vetoes $3.4 billion earmarked for Turkey by EU. **May 25:** True Path Party leader Tansu Çiller withdraws her party from coalition. **May 26:** Council of Ministers meets in southeastern city of Diyarbakır, underlining the importance of the region. **June 2:** Local elections held; Welfare Party garners plurality of votes, followed by Motherland Party, True Path Party, Democratic Left Party, Grand Turkey Party, Republican People's Party, Nationalist Action Party, and People's Democracy Party, in that order. **June 6:** Prime Minister Yılmaz resigns, ending TPP-MP coalition. Welfare Party leader Necmettin Erbakan assures that his party is not antidemocratic; it has no plans to relinquish Turkey's membership in NATO; and it backs customs union with EU. Government rejects $22-million U.S. economic aid package because of stipulations calling for Turkey to cease its blockade of humanitarian aid package to Armenia. **June 12:** President Demirel responds harshly to claims by Saudi Arabia that Turkey's cooperation pact with Israel could deteriorate relations with Arab world. **June 13:** Government armed forces launch a new offensive into northern Iraq; 5,000 troops go seven kilometers into territory. **June 19:** Turkey and Crotia sign agreement on military cooperation. Welfare Party (WP) votes with True Path Party to turn down a former WP motion to hold parliamentary investigations into charges that TPP leader Çiller misused discretionary funds that were at her disposal as then prime minister. **June 23:** In Ankara, 30 leading members of pro-Kurdish People's Democracy Party arrested, after party convention where Turkish flag was brought down by masked militans. **June 28:** Welfare Party and True Path Party form coalition government. WP leader Necmettin Erbakan is prime minister and TPP leader Çiller deputy prime minister and foreign minister. **July 11:** Government warplanes hit PKK base on Iraqi border. **October 19:** Deputy Prime Minister Çiller announces new democratization and human rights package, in response to criticism from Europe. **November 25:** Prime Minister Erbakan announces he will not attend EU conference in Dublin. Parliamentary committee investigating charges of corruption against former Prime Minister Çiller declares charges unsubstantiated. **November 28:** Parliamentary commission studying corruption charges against Deputy Prime Minister and Foreign Minister Çiller decides against sending her to High Court.

1997 **January 20:** Turkey and Turkish Republic of Northern Cyprus (TRNC) sign historic declaration: any attack on TRNC is tantamount to attack on Turkey itself.

January 23: Prime Minister Necmettin Erbakan heavily criticized for inviting leaders of religious orders to dinner at his official residence. **February 28:** National Security Council states that "secularism is not only a form of government but also a way of life and the guarantee of democracy and social peace," a warning to Erbakan government to refrain from efforts to Islamize society and polity. The council recommends to government 20 specific measures to combat "reactionary Islam." **April 15:** Turkey becomes a full member of Western European Union. **April 28:** Black Sea Economic Cooperation Conference held in Istanbul. **April 30:** Greece and Turkey agree to establish a group of "wise men" to help resolve their differences. **May 5:** Turkey, United States, and Israel to conduct joint naval exercises in the Mediterranean at the end of summer; strong reactions from Arab countries. **May 28:** Major unions and business representatives agree to hold a huge protest rally against Erbakan government. **May 30:** U.S. President Clinton opens the way for Turkey to receive $22 million from Economic Support Fund in 1997. **June 12:** Office of chief of general staff announces it has set up a West Study Group to better monitor Islamic fundamentalism in the country. **June 18:** Prime Minister Erbakan resigns, and calls on President Demirel to appoint Çiller prime minister. **June 30:** Motherland Party of Yılmaz, Democratic Left Party of Bülent Ecevit, and Democratic Turkey Party of Hüsamettin Cindoruk form coalition government; Yılmaz is prime minister. **July 6:** Nationalist Action Party elects Devlet Bahçeli as its new leader. **July 8:** President Demirel and Greek Prime Minister Costas Simitis pledge to reconcile differences without use of force and to recognize each country's legitimate interests in Aegean Sea. **August 16:** Parliament adopts eight-year compulsory secular education. **September 30:** Prime Minister Yılmaz obtains German Chancellor Kohl's support for Turkey's EU candidacy. **November 10:** In a change of policy encouraged by French President Jacques Chirac and German Chancellor Helmut Kohl, EU foreign ministers agree in principle to invite Turkey to European Union conference. **December 4:** Government issues a set of directives intended to curb police brutality of suspects, including surprise visits to police stations. **December 13:** EU decides to exclude Turkey in membership talks for the first and second wave of Union expansion; Ankara resolves to suspend relations with EU. **December 19:** Prime Minister Yılmaz threatens to withdraw Turkey's application to join EU if the Union does not reverse its decision to exclude Turkey from the next wave of expansion.

1998   January 16: Constitutional Court closes Welfare Party (WP) "because of evidence confirming its actions against the principles of the secular Republic." **February 8:** 50,000 government soldiers enter a 240-kilometer-long "buffer zone" in northern Iraq to prevent an influx of Kurdish refugees to Turkey in the event of war. **March 7:** Prime Minister Mesut Yılmaz accuses Germany of following a policy of *lebensraum* (creating a living space for Germany) in order to block Turkey's membership in European Union. **March 17:** Appeals Court acquits former Prime Minister Çiller on one of a series of charges made against her, on the grounds that there was no evidence Çiller knowingly misused government funds. **March 27:** National Security Council recommends to Yılmaz government a list of steps to "curb the influence of those who wish to condemn the Turkish people to a backward way of life." **April 16:** Parliament votes to open new investigation into former Prime Minister Çiller's accumulation of wealth between 1991 and 1996. **April 22:** Parliament votes to investigate personal finances of Prime Minister Yılmaz. **April 29:** Court orders former Prime Minister Erbakan to stand trial for insulting judiciary. **May 10:** Reformist group in Virtue Party, led by Recep Tayyip Erdoğan, Abdullah Gül, and Bülent Arınç, wishes to democratize the party and pull it closer to the center of political spectrum. **May 12:** Parliament votes to open new investigations against Prime Minister Yılmaz over allegations that he improperly awarded a contract to supporters to build an airport in Istanbul. **May 15:** Virtue Party (VP), successor party to Welfare Party, elects Recai Kutan as its leader. **May 20:** Chief of General Staff Hakkı Karadayı officially warns Russian government regarding their plans to sell S-300 missiles to the Republic of Cyprus. **July 7:** Turkey protests Greek militarization of islands in Aegean Sea, near Turkey's coast. **September 7:** Turkish and Israeli Prime Ministers meet in Israel to discuss ways in which they can develop trade between the two countries. Virtue Party parliamentarian Ersönmez Yarbay states that new VP would have a less dogmatic and more contemporary image than its predecessor, Welfare Party. **October 6:** Government announces a 10-day ultimatum: if Syria does not curb its support of PKK, then the military will start cross-border operations to PKK targets in Syria. **November 6:** Turkey imposes new navigation rules for Bosporus Strait, including the ability to stop traffic when currents are unfavorable, the ability to stop any ship on legal grounds, and the right to require more ships to use local pilots. **November 8:** Military pursues PKK rebels into northern Iraq. **November 19:** Authorities arrest People's Democracy Party chairperson Murat Bozlak for referring to Abdullah Öcalan in public as a "party leader" rather than a "terrorist." **November 23:** True Path Party and Motherland Party cooperate to save their leaders Çiller and Yılmaz, respectively. In the voting, the parliamentary commission investigating their cases decides against sending the leaders to High Court. **November 25:** Prime Minister Yılmaz's government loses a vote of confidence due to corruption allegations.

1999   January 17: Minority government formed by Democratic Left Party leader Bülent Ecevit receives vote of confidence; government is supported from outside by TPP and MP. **February 16:** Greek Embassy in Nairobi, Kenya, hands over PKK leader Öcalan to Kenyan authorities; while on his way to an unspecified destination in Nairobi, Öcalan is captured by Turkish commando units and flown to Turkey on a Turkish plane sent for this operation to Kenya. **March 15:** 15,000 members of government forces enter Iraq in hot pursuit of PKK rebels. **April 18:** General elections held; Democratic Left Party of Bülent Ecevit obtains plurality of votes, followed by Nationalist Action Party of Devlet Bahçeli, Virtue Party of Recai Kutan, Motherland Party of Mesut Yılmaz, and True Path Party of Tansu Çiller. Republican People's Party and People's Labor Party votes remain below 10 percent threshold. **April 30:** U.S. State Department report criticizes Germany, Italy, and Greece for their lack of conviction in Turkey's fight against one of the world's major terror and drug-smuggling organizations, namely PKK. **May 2:** President Demirel says head scarf is a symbol of political Islam; Virtue Party's newly elected deputy Merve Kavakçı is prevented from taking oath of office when she refuses to remove her head scarf. Prime Minister Ecevit emphatically declares, "Parliament is not a place to defy the state." **May 28:** Coalition government among Democratic Left Party (DLP), Nationalist Action Party (NAP) and Motherland Party (MP) formed. DLP leader Bülent Ecevit is prime minister. **June 18:** Military judges removed from State Security Courts. **June 26:** Prime Minister Ecevit releases a circular on human rights and freedom of thought, asking that directives issued to date be strictly adhered to. Republican People's Party chooses Altan Öymen as its new leader. **June 29:** Court sentences PKK leader Öcalan to death for treason. **September 26:** Turkey to be included in newly formed G-20 countries, which comprise G-7 countries, 10 large developing countries, and representatives from EU, IMF, and World Bank. **September 28:** Prime Minister Ecevit meets U.S. President Clinton at White House. Clinton expresses active U.S. interest in finding a solution to lingering Cyprus crisis, says improvements in human rights and Greek-Turkey relations will reflect in the process of Turkey's full membership in European Union, and gives assurances that a Kurdish state will not be established in northern Iraq. **November 3:** During state visit in Moscow, Prime Minister Ecevit says Turkey respects territorial integrity of Russia. However, he adds, Turkey is concerned about civilian casualties in Chechenya. **November 14:** U.S. President Clinton comes to Turkey to attend the Organization of Security and Cooperation in Europe summit in Istanbul. **November 15:** In a speech he made at Turkish National Assembly, President Clinton says Turkey plays a critical role in the development of the region, and that in the 21st century it should take courageous steps so that it would continue to have such an impact. **November 17:** Black Sea Economic Cooperation summit convenes in Istanbul. In his opening speech, President Demirel says Black Sea Economic Community will serve to link Europe and Asia, on one hand, and Caspian Sea, Black Sea, and Mediterranean basins on the other and promote peace and prosperity in this region. **November 18:** European Security and Cooperation Organization summit opens in Istanbul. In his opening speech, President Demirel says everybody failed to adopt timely measures to stem recent conflicts arising out of ethnic problems. President Süleyman Demirel, Azerbaijani President Aliyev, and Georgian President Şevardnadze sign package agreements on Bakü-Tiblisi-Ceyhan cross-border pipeline. **December 10:** At Helsinki summit, Turkey named candidate country for EU. **December 22:** Turkey and IMF sign a stand-by agreement; government promises to launch a series of economic reforms over the next three years in exchange for IMF loans totaling $4 billion. **December 27:** President Demirel wishes Christian citizens of Turkey a Merry Christmas, first official state recognition of the holiday.

2000 January 13: Prime Minister Ecevit, Deputy Prime Minister Bahçeli, and MP leader Yılmaz decide to delay the execution of the PKK leader Öcalan until the European Court of Human Rights rules on his appeal. **January 17:** In a raid on their new headquarters in Istanbul, police kill Hizbullah leader Hüseyin Velioğlu and capture number two and three leaders, opening the way to the collapse of the bloodthirsty Islamic group. **January 26:** The office of chief of the general staff holds the Virtue Party responsible for Hizbullah murders. **February 3:** In a first visit to Greece by a Turkish foreign minister, Ismail Cem arrives in Athens to sign five accords ranging from culture to maritime transit. **February 9:** The PKK announces that it has ended its armed struggle against the government forces and will pursue its efforts "within the framework of peace and democracy." **February 10:** Virtue Party breaks a taboo and celebrates Valentine's Day. **February 24:** Court charges the mayors of the southeastern cities of Diyarbakır, Siirt, and Bingöl—all three members of HADEP—with conspiring to aid the PKK. **March 4:** Court of Appeals allows the use of Kurdish names. **March 10:** Former Prime Minister Erbakan is given one-year prison sentence on the grounds that a speech he made in 1994 incited hatred and enmity in people. **May 5:** Parliament elects Ahmet Necdet Sezer, former chairman of the Constitutional Court, Turkey's tenth president. **May 14:** Virtue Party leader Kutan reelected party's chairman. His reformist rival Abdullah Gül garners 521 of the 1154 votes cast. **July 12:** MP leader Yılmaz joins the cabinet as minister of state and deputy prime minister. **July 17:** The European Union asks Turkey to allow for broadcasting and education in Kurdish as conditions for inclusion in the EU as a full member. **July 21:** Turkish Petroleum Agency privatized; it goes to İş-Bank-Doğan Holding consortium for $1,260 billion. **August 15:** Turkey signs United Nations' Civil and Political Rights Charter, and Economic, Social, and Cultural Rights Charter. **August 30:** Public prosecutor files a suit against Fethullah Gülen, leader of Islamic *Fethullahçılar,* for "activities directed toward the establishment of a state based on Islam." **September 30:** Deniz Baykal is elected chairman of the RPP, after a 15-month interval. **November 4:** Devlet Bahçeli reelected chairman of the Nationalist Action Party. **November 24:** Government decides to privatize three major state banks—Ziraat Bank, Emlak Bank, and Halk Bank—as part of a plan to withdraw from the financial sector. **November 27:** Director of National Intelligence Agency Şenkal Atasagun says he is against the execution of Öcalan and supports television broadcasts in Kurdish.

2001 January 1: President Sezer says Turkey needs to improve its human rights and democratization records and remove financial irregularities. **February 21:** Critical confrontation between President Sezer and Prime Minister Ecevit leads to the most critical financial crisis during the Republican period. **February 22:** Transition to fluctuating rate (within limits) in foreign exchange. **March 2:** Kemal Derviş, former deputy director of the World Bank, becomes state minister responsible for the economy. **March 14:** New economic program disclosed: the banking sector will be overhauled, the interest and foreign exchange rates stabilized, populism will be avoided. **April 22:** Minister of Energy and Natural Resources Cumhur Ersümer resigns upon accusations of misuse of office and financial irregularities. **April 29:** At the CHP Fifth Congress, Ecevit is again elected the chairperson of the party. **May 12:** Parliament passes law to privatize the

Telecommunications Agency. **May 15:** The International Monetary Fund (IMF) approves augmentation of Turkey's stand-by credit to $19 billion. **June 26:** The Constitutional Court closes the Virtue Party on the grounds that it acted against the secular premises of the Republic.

Introduction: Turkey—An Overview

Turkey is both an old and a new country. The Turks have been living in Anatolia for the last millennium. During those long centuries, they have experienced mutual ac-culturation vis-à-vis several peoples. Furthermore, since the end of the 18th century, the country has gone through extensive **Westernization**. These developments led to an inevitable clash between tradition and modernity.

However, in the case of Turkey, tradition has not arrested modernization; rather, the traditional has adapted itself to the modern. The revival of Islam and the emergence of certain ethnic identities during the recent decades have not led to the reversal of progress in the economy and democracy. There is a thriving pri-vate sector. Turkey has resolved its chronic balance of payments. Not unlike the situation in several other countries, the economy faced crises from time to time; however, Turkey managed to set it right each time. At the turn of the 21st century, Turkey is the only Muslim country with a democratic political system. Modern neighborhoods in urban centers resemble their counterparts in advanced Western countries.

Consequently, although Turkey belongs to both the West and the East, its West-ern credentials are more marked. It is a member of the Council of Europe, **North Atlantic Treaty Organization** (NATO), and Organization for Economic Coopera-tion and Development (OECD), and is a candidate country for accession to the **Eu-ropean Union** (EU).

Travelers from the African and Asian continents have often remarked that Europe starts in Turkey. The Turks are a hospitable people. Both of these factors, plus the fact that the country has beautiful and sunny coastlines, played a role in Turkey's successful development of **tourism**. Yet, compared to other countries of similar size and importance, Turkey is one of the least-known countries.

LAND AND PEOPLE

Turkey is in the Northern Hemisphere, midway between the North Pole and the equator in the Temperate Zone. It is surrounded on three sides by seas—to the north, the **Black Sea**; to the northwest, the **Marmara Sea**; to the West, the **Aegean Sea**; and to the south, the **Mediterranean**.

Turkey occupies the compact landmass of the Anatolian Peninsula together with the city of **Istanbul** and its Thracian hinterland. The country is a natural passage between Europe and Asia; it has a territory of 779,452 square kilometers (755,688 sq. kms. in Anatolia and 23,764 sq. kms. in Europe-Thrace). Turkey has borders with **Armenia**, Georgia, **Greece**, **Bulgaria**, the **Russian Federation**, **Iran**, **Iraq**, and **Syria**.

The country has a greatly diversified terrain, which includes the vast Anatolian plain, the rugged forested regions of the Black Sea, the semiarid land of the southwest, the natural lakes of Van in eastern Anatolia (3,713 sq. kms.) and Tuz [Salt] in central Anatolia (1,500 sq. kms.), and the distinctive coastlines of the Mediterranean and Aegean. The average altitude of Turkey is 1,132 meters. Only one-fifth of the country lies below 500 meters in altitude. The high Anatolian plain is separated in the north from the Black Sea by a mountain range, the **Pontus chain**, which is 700 meters high on the west and over 3,300 meters high on the east. Lying across southern Anatolia is a second mountain range, the **Taurus chain**, parallel to the one in the north. The highest peak of this chain, Erciyes Mountain, soars to a lofty 4,000 meters. These two mountain systems merge to form an imposing complex in northeastern Anatolia, the topmost point of which is **Mt. Ararat** (5,500 meters)—according to legend, the spot where Noah safely brought his Ark to rest on dry land after the deluge. Through the northwestern edge of Anatolia pass the Dardanelles and Bosporus **Straits**, which are the southern and northern gateways to the Sea of Marmara respectively. The portion of Turkey that lies in Europe, (Eastern) Thrace, begins on the western side of these straits, and includes a portion of the city of Istanbul.

Because Turkey is surrounded on three sides by seas and because of significant topographical variance from one region to another, Turkey enjoys a variety of climates. The average annual temperature varies between 18 and 20°C (64–68°F) on the Mediterranean coast, drops to 14–15°C (57–59°F) on the Aegean coast, and in most of the interior areas (depending on the location and altitude), fluctuates between 4–18°C (39–64°F). Eastern Anatolia and some interior parts of the country are subject to extremely cold winters; average temperatures in these areas are -10°C to 0° (14° to 32°F) in winter.

Turkey also experiences differing degrees of rainfall. Generally, heavy precipitation is observed on the slopes of mountains facing the sea, the most notable area being the eastern Black Sea coast. Rainy season starts in the autumn and continues until late spring on the Marmara, Mediterranean, and Aegean coasts. The Black Sea coast has heavy precipitation throughout the year. In the internal areas and southeast Turkey, rainfall is heaviest in the spring, with snow in the winter. In the east, the winters are quite cold with heavier snowfall and rainy springs.

Along with the topography and climate, flora and fauna also vary greatly in Turkey. In the western Mediterranean, Aegean, and Marmara coasts, maquis, olive, and citrus are found; mountains are covered with pine trees. The Black Sea region is famous for its forests of deciduous and coniferous trees as well as apples, pears, cherries, hazelnuts, mandarins, oranges, and tea. Along the eastern Mediterranean shores, vegetation is tropical, with banana, palm, and citrus trees. In this region, too, pine trees cover mountains. On the steppes of Central Anatolia are found natural pastures and scattered forests.

Turkey is the habitat of the same animals found in European countries—deer, bear, lynx, wolf, fox, wild boar, nearly all species of rodents, plus buffalo. Turkey is also home to birds of many kinds, especially in the "Bird's Paradise," the national park on Lake Manyas near **Balıkesir** province in northwestern Turkey.

According to the November 1997 census, Turkey's population is 62,865,574. From 1990 to 1997, the average annual rate of increase was 1.53 percent. In Turkey, based on the experience of recent decades, it takes about 30 years for the total population to double.

In 1997, the urban share of the population was 61 percent and the rural share 39 percent. In 1997, there were 17 cities with a population of more than one million. They were led by **Istanbul** (9.1 million), **Ankara** (3.5 million), **İzmir** (3.1 million), and **Adana** (2.1 million). The 1997 census indicated that from 1990 to 1997, the average annual urban growth was 2.8 percent and the depreciation of the rural population was 0.67 percent; in other words, there has been a high rate of migration from rural to urban areas. The Marmara and Aegean regions have received migration during all intercensal periods. The highest out-migration has taken place in the Black Sea, eastern, and southeastern regions.

During the Republican period (from 1923 to the present), Turkey has received waves of immigrants from Greece, Yugoslavia, Romania, and, in particular, Bulgaria. The mother tongue of 98 percent of the immigrants in question is Turkish. Turkey has a rather homogeneous population structure. One important reason was the loss of the Ottoman Empire. The deportation of Armenians during World War I and the population exchange with Greece following the **Turkish War of Independence** (1920–1922) also played a role. Today's population is almost entirely Muslim, of whom the majority (about four-fifths) are of **Sunni**, or Orthodox, belief, the remainder being Shi'a or, in Turkish, Alevis. The only significant division is between Turkish and Kurdish citizens of the republic. The **Kurds** are estimated minimally at 10 million and maximally at 20 million. However, they, too, are Sunni Muslims.

Industrialization and the expansion of services have not keep up with high rates of urbanization over the years, and the quality of life in large urban centers has therefore declined. Overall, half the city population lives in squatter areas. City amenities often cannot cope with the new influx of people. This is despite the fact that, from the early 1980s onwards, local governments were provided with ample funds and a great deal of authority, which led to greater amounts of services in urban areas.

HISTORY

The Turks, along with the Mongols, Manchus, Bulgarians, and others, once constituted a group of Altaic peoples in Outer Mongolia in Central Asia (around the second millennium B.C.E.). Inscriptions from the first Turkish kingdom, situated along the Orkhon River in Siberia, date back to the early seventh century.

In the same century, the Turks had their first encounter with **Islam** when the Arab conquest of **Iran** had its impact in Central Asia as well, and the bulk of the Turks became Muslims by the 10th century. In the following 10 centuries, Islam significantly shaped Turkish states, society, and culture. The Turks' second critical encounter was with the Byzantine Empire following the Turks' migration to the Middle East, when they began fighting for Islam against the nonMuslims in Anatolia in the mid-11th century. The Byzantine Empire left a deep imprint on the Turks, particularly on the state, religion, and the society of the Ottoman Empire (1299–1922).

The Ottoman Empire

The Ottoman Empire grew out of a Turkish emirate centered north of the modern city of Eskişehir in northwestern Anatolia and was led by **Osman I** (1299–1324). Faced with a disunited opposition—Serbs, Bulgarians, Byzantines, and the Latin West—and led until the second part of the 16th century by able sultans, the Ottomans expanded their tiny state into a full-fledged empire. At its zenith in the 16th century, the empire stretched from Hungary in the north to the Arabian Peninsula in the south and from Algiers in the west to modern western Iran in the east. During this evolution, the Ottoman conquest of **Istanbul** (known at the time as Constantinople) in 1453 symbolized the passage from a frontier state to an empire.

The period extending from the conquest of Istanbul to the death of Sultan **Süleyman I (the Magnificent)** in 1566 (who came to the throne in 1520) was the golden age of the Ottoman Empire. As the empire expanded on three continents, the Turks found themselves in the middle of European politics. Francis I of France and a candidate for the Hungarian throne requested Süleyman the Magnificent's help against the Hapsburgs several times. In the east, the Ottomans conquered the historic Muslim capitals, Damascus and Cairo, and the three sacred cities of Islam, Jerusalem, Mecca, and Medina. The Ottoman sultans began using the title of **caliph**.

It was also during this period that the Ottoman government developed fully into its classical pattern. At the head of the system stood the **sultan**, who in theory had the ultimate title to all land. Most arable land was temporarily allocated to cavalrymen who as fief-holders supervised agricultural activities, collected taxes, and, when the need arose, provided armed fighting men. The army was organized on a system of levying a tribute of boys from Christian subjects. The Ottoman civil service was staffed through the same method. Having no strong roots in society and having gone through long periods of training and/or education at state institutions, the Ottoman officers and officials became the loyal servants of the sultan. Along with the members of (**Sunni**) religious institutions, they made up the ruling stratum. This group did not pay taxes and, as such, constituted a distinct class from other peoples in the empire who paid taxes, no matter whether Muslim, Christian, or Jew.

The major non-Muslim religious groups in the empire were the Greek Orthodox, Gregorian Armenian, and Jews. Non-Muslims did not serve in the army; instead, they paid a special head-tax (**cizye**). Non-Muslim religious communities, or *millet*s, were essentially administered through their lay heads and clergy, who had authority concerning not only church administration, worship, education, and charity but also supervision of the civil status of their co-religionists.

The Ottoman decline started toward the end of the 16th century and lasted close to three centuries. There were two basic reasons for this decline. One cause was the agricultural, commercial, industrial, and technological developments in the Atlantic states, as a consequence of which the Turks began to lose consistently in war against their now fairly strong European adversaries. The second cause was the collapse of the governmental machinery in the Ottoman Empire itself. For one thing, the caliber of rulers declined. This led to the emergence of palace cliques and intrigues to advance favorites in public office. The atmosphere of weak sultans and palace intrigue encouraged bribery and the purchase of offices. In the process, both the civil bureaucracy and the military ranks were adversely affected. Some former fiefs were leased as tax-farms, which produced less revenue than desired. Tax-farmers developed into petty local lords with considerable de facto autonomy. Agricultural production suffered. Under the Treaty of **Karlowitz** in 1699, the Ottomans lost Podolia to Poland, Hungary and Transylvania to Austria, and the Morea to Venice. The Ottoman losses of territory continued during the following decades. By the middle of the 18th century, the Ottoman Empire was no longer a great power.

These developments brought to the forefront the issue of reform. Until the 18th century, reformers pointed to the need to revive the golden age. From the early 18th century onward, however, they turned their gaze to the West, although during that century they wavered in taking significant steps, in spite of the fact that Ottoman reverses at the hands of their European enemies continued. A humiliating defeat to Russia in 1774 clearly showed the superiority of Western arms. The Ottomans had become helpless in the face of spreading nationalism (first the Greeks and then the Serbs and Romanians) and the attacks of European powers. Finally, in 1826, the traditional **Janissary Corps** was abolished and a better-trained corps was created in its place. The navy, too, was refurbished. Efforts were made to create a new bureaucracy along Western lines; bureaucrats were offered education in French and other secular subjects. Steps were taken to centralize the system of **taxation**. The bureaucrats, in particular the "French-speakers," dominated the *Tanzimat* **(Reform) Period**, which started with the **Imperial Rescript of Gülhane** in 1839, continued with the **Reform Decree** of 1856, and lasted until 1876. The Rescript and the reform measures that followed combined old and new, both in governmental structure and thought patterns. No radical reform was accomplished but old habits were badly shaken, paving the way for more comprehensive reforms during the next century. In this respect, the degree of **Westernization** in law, **civil bureaucracy**, diplomacy, and **education** was significant. Furthermore, the Ottoman Empire lost no territory during the Reform period.

Toward the end of the 1860s, the so-called **Young Ottomans**, comprising some bureaucrats at the middle echelons of the civil service, began agitating for "constitutional government." They first opposed the authoritarianism of some leading bureaucrat-statesmen and then "the personal rule" of Sultan Abdülaziz (1861–1876). They based their argument on "the tradition of consultation in

Islam," longed for a representative assembly, and formulated **Ottomanism** to hold the realm together. On December 23, 1876, the First Constitutional Period started in the Ottoman Empire.

The regime was, in fact, a narrowly circumscribed political regime, for the sultan retained extensive powers including those of approving legislation, appointing ministers, convening and dissolving the Parliament, and exiling people "who endangered state security." On the other hand, the 1876 **Constitution** emphasized the equality of all Ottoman subjects. But the members of the Parliament proved to be too independent-minded for the new Sultan **Abdülhamit II** (1876–1909), who, by using the Russo-Turkish war as an excuse, prorogued the chamber in February 1878 for the next 30 years.

Abdülhamit II perfected the regime of personal rule that had been started by Abdülaziz II. His opponents were kept in exile. Early in his reign, Romania, Serbia, and Montenegro gained their independence. In addition, Austria occupied Bosnia-Herzegovina, and **Great Britain** took over **Cyprus**. The sultan used these developments as an excuse to centralize rule. The power shifted back from the bureaucratic elite to the sultan. Abdülhamit II cast aside the notion of Ottomanism and placed emphasis on Islamic solidarity and **Pan-Islamism**. There was an increase in anti-Westernism.

Opposition arose against Abdülhamit II from two different quarters. Educated Turks (army officers, bureaucrats, and some professional men) did not approve of the sultan's repressive rule. These constituted the **Young Turk** group, which formed the **Committee for Union and Progress** (CUP). Some non-Turkish groups, including the Arabs, opposed the sultan on nationalist lines and initiated separatist movements. By the end of the 1890s, the separatist movements were brought under control, but members of the Young Turk group intensified their opposition to the sultan both within and particularly outside of the country. The disaffection of army officials proved decisive. As a last resort, Abdülhamit II reinstated constitutional government on July 24, 1908. The regime was considerably liberalized. On April 13, 1909, however, a violent conservative reaction took place. In response, General **Mahmut Şevket Pasha** and his Third Army secured control of **Istanbul**. The Young Turks returned to power and Abdülhamit II was sent into exile. The new sultan's powers were curtailed and the cabinet was made collectively responsible to Parliament.

A lively political era followed. However, the CUP dominated the political scene, particularly after the April 1912 elections, which were rigged by the Committee. A year later, the Committee turned into a party. During the Young Turk era (1909–1918), three trends of thought as to the essence of political unity and social solidarity vied against one another. The first was Ottomanism, which postulated the equality of all Ottoman subjects (of whatever religion or language) and their loyalty to a common government. The second was **Islamism**, which opposed rapid Westernization and promoted the doctrine of Pan-Islam. The third was **Turkism**, which emphasized Turkish language and culture. Growing nationalism among the Christians in the Balkans and the development of Arab and Albanian self-awareness led to the gradual waning of Ottomanism and Islamism while the feeling of Turkishness grew. One of its forms,

Pan-Turanism, aimed at the unification of all Turkic-speaking peoples living mostly in the Caucasus and Central Asia. The leading proponent of Turkism devoid of Pan-Turanism, **Ziya Gökalp**, opted for Islamization and modernization alongside Turkification; his ideal was a marriage between Western civilization and Turkish culture. The Young Turk era was also characterized by considerable Westernization efforts with regard to political parties, government, press, finance, bureaucracy, **military**, and law.

In 1914, the Ottoman Empire entered **World War I** on the German side. Traditional hostility to Russia and the Pan-Turanistic ideals of **Enver Pasha**, the war minister and most influential member of the triumvirate that ruled the empire at the time, played a crucial role here. The eventual defeat of the Ottoman armies destroyed the CUP government. The war, on the other hand, served to further reinforce Turkish national sentiment. Efforts were made to train more Turks for commercial and technical jobs.

The Treaty of **Sèvres**, handed down to the Ottoman government in May 1920 by the Allied side, proclaimed the death warrant of Turkey; it aimed at the partition of Anatolia—the homeland of Turks. In response, Turks started a nationalist struggle led by Mustafa Kemal (later, **Atatürk**). The **Turkish War of Independence** was carried out by the government of the Grand National Assembly convened in Ankara on April 23, 1920, with Atatürk acting as the president of the assembly. On September 9, 1922, the war ended with total Turkish victory. On November 1, 1922, the sultanate was abolished and the Ottoman Empire passed into history. The **Treaty of Lausanne**, signed on July 24, 1923, met the essential Turkish demands; Turks regained their homeland in Anatolia and part of Thrace. On October 29, 1923, the Turkish Republic was proclaimed and Atatürk was elected president.

The Turkish Republic

The first decade of the Republic was characterized by radical social and cultural change. The principal objective was secularization of polity and society. On March 3, 1924, the **caliphate** was abolished; the closing down of religious schools and courts followed this move. The **Republican People's Party** was instrumental in carrying out the reforms, including the adoption of law codes from different European countries and the Latin alphabet. In 1924 and 1930, experiments were made in multiparty political regimes—though both turned out to be short-lived: the **Progressive Republican Party** established in 1924 and the Free Republican Party set up in 1930 were seen by the regime as obstacles to **Westernization** and summarily closed. The regime adopted republicanism, nationalism, populism, statism, **secularism,** and reformism as its basic aims. In foreign relations, the regime's motto was "peace at home, peace abroad"; by the 1930s, Turkey had cordial relations with all its neighbors. **Atatürk**, the savior of the country, founder of the Turkish Republic and architect of extensive Westernizing reforms, passed away on November 10, 1938.

Turkey managed to stay out of **World War II**, despite pressures from both sides. Following the war, Turkey faced a threat from the Soviet Union (*see* RUSSIA) to its territorial integrity. In 1947, under the Truman Doctrine, the **United States** began to supply Turkey with military and economic aid.

In 1945, Turkey made a transition to multiparty politics. In January 1946, the *Demokrat* **Party** was founded, which in 1950 formed the government. In 1952, Turkey became a member of the **North Atlantic Treaty Organization**(NATO). Earlier, starting in 1950, a Turkish brigade had fought in the Korean War on the side of the United Nations' forces. In 1954, Turkey signed a defensive treaty with **Greece** and Yugoslavia, and in 1955 entered the **Baghdad Pact** that included **Iraq, Iran**, Pakistan, and **Great Britain**. Because Turkey recognized **Israel**, its relations with Arab countries other than Iraq were and continue to be strained. From 1955 on, Turkish-Greek relations became tense over the **Cyprus** issue. The London agreement of 1959 made Cyprus independent; military garrisons from Greece and Turkey were stationed on the island.

In the early 1950s, the economy prospered. In the second part of the decade, however, the country faced serious economic difficulties, including trade deficits and inflation. The latter led to a drastic reduction in the purchasing power of the bureaucratic middle classes.

The Democrats relaxed government controls on the influence of **Islam** in the polity and society. The consequence was the emergence of a reactionary tendency as manifested particularly in activities of the **Ticani** religious order, the members of which destroyed a few statues of Atatürk in their fight against "idolatry." Also, there was an open reappearance of religious sentiment that had earlier been repressed under the rigidly secularist one-party regime.

The Republican People's Party's relentless criticism of "the Democrats' disregard of Atatürkist principles," in particular their "anti-secularist policies," and the worsening economic situation from the mid-1950s on led the Democrats to adopt an authoritarian stance toward the intellectual-bureaucratic elite in general and the opposition party in particular. Perceiving a civil war in the cards, the **military** intervened on May 27, 1960. The National Unity Committee, as the junta was known, arranged the convening of a **Constituent Assembly**, which prepared a new (1961) **constitution**. This constitution, among other things, expanded the scope of individual rights and liberties and set up a constitutional court, the **National Security Council** (the membership of which included the chief of the general staff and the army, navy, air force, and gendarmerie commanders), and the State Planning Organization. The constitution bolstered the powers of the Council of State (the Turkish version of **France's** *Conseil d'Etat*), with a view to placing checks on the political executive. The ultimate aim was to prevent "the tyranny of the majority."

Another step along the same lines was the introduction of proportional representation in elections instead of majority vote. Partly as a result of this last measure, Turkey was ruled from 1961 to 1965 by coalition governments, during which time two aborted coup attempts were made (in 1962 and 1963). In the 1965 general elections, the **Justice Party**, heir to the *Demokrat* **Party** and led by **Süleyman Demirel**, captured the majority of seats in the Parliament; Justice Party governments ruled the country from 1965 until 1971. Political life during these years was characterized by constant clashes between the state elite based in the Republican People's Party and universities and the political (read "populist") elite of the Justice Party.

A renewed crisis over Cyprus developed late in 1963. Cypriote Greeks attempted to diminish the political rights of their Turkish countrymen and to engineer Cyprus's union with Greece, which led to prolonged fighting between the two communities. In March 1964, a United Nations peace force was stationed on the island. On more than one occasion, Turkey was on the verge of sending its forces to the island. Meanwhile, U.S. President Lyndon Johnson asked both Greece and Turkey to refrain from military action, which led to anti-Americanism in Turkey. The **Ankara** government began to pursue a somewhat more independent line in foreign policy.

The 1960s in Turkey were characterized not only by intense conflict between the state elite and political elite but also growing fragmentation and polarization of the polity and society. In the liberal atmosphere brought about by the 1961 constitution, neofascist, Marxist, and Islamic **fundamentalist** groups came into head-on confrontations, which frequently led to violence. On March 12, 1971, the military intervened a second time in Turkish politics. The freedom of the press and the autonomy of the Radio and Television Authority and the universities were curtailed. The National Security Council was now to "advise" the Council of Ministers, not just to "offer information" on request.

Turkey returned to multiparty politics in 1973. From 1973 to 1980, either coalition or minority governments ruled Turkey. The first coalition government was that between the left-of-center Republican People's Party and the religiously oriented **National Salvation Party**. After the collapse of this coalition in 1974, the country was, for the most part, ruled by center-right coalitions.

The 1970s were characterized by a deteriorating economic situation, the growth of political violence, and difficulties in foreign affairs. Coming to the aid of the Turkish Cypriots, Turkey invaded the northern part of Cyprus in 1974. The United States responded by imposing an arms embargo. Turkey also had its differences with Greece over the extent of the territorial waters of the two countries in the **Aegean** and the related issue of airspace. Toward the end of the decade, escalating violence, which included the assassination of some prominent national figures and communal clashes, led the governments to declare martial law. The militant left and right as well as the Islamic fundamentalists were again in the ascendancy. These developments were paralleled by a deep recession. Thinking that constant bickering among the political parties aggravated the situation, on September 12, 1980, the **military** once again took the government into its own hands.

The military perceived its immediate task as that of restoring law and order. The extremist trade union federations on the left and associations of the ethnic and religious right were banned, as were all political parties. Violence was largely stopped. A new constitution (1982) was prepared that created a strong presidency and further bolstered the powers of the National Security Council. The universities were brought under the supervision of a newly created **Council of Higher Education**.

The military backed the economic measures adopted just before the intervention, which placed more emphasis on market forces. Strikes and lockouts were banned. Soon, there was a considerable decline in inflation and Turkey's balance of payments showed a remarkable improvement.

Turkey came under increasing foreign pressure because of military rule (1980–1983). The Council of Europe censured political repression. The **Human Rights** Commission (in Strasbourg, France) pressed for the improvement of human rights in Turkey. The **European Community** tied its aid to Turkey to the restoration of democracy. These pressures, plus the fact that the military had not intervened to stay in power indefinitely, led to Turkey's return to multiparty politics in 1983.

From 1983 to 1991, **Motherland Party** (MP) governments governed Turkey. These governments aimed at freeing the economy from the dominance of the bureaucratic state. They adopted measures to replace the import-substitution economic strategy with an export-oriented one. The private sector was supported, although it was subjected to market forces and international competition. Turkey's export earnings increased considerably; inflation, however, could not be brought under control.

The governments of 1991–1999 did not abandon the market-oriented economic policies of the Motherland Party governments; however, they also aimed to improve the income distribution, which had worsened under the Motherland governments. The successes concerning both of these goals were limited. The major culprits here were such visionless, if not opportunistic, politicians as **Tansu Çiller**, **Mesut Yılmaz**, and **Deniz Baykal** and the weak coalition governments that they led. Çiller started her years as prime minister with an ambitious economic program, but soon backtracked under popular pressure. In the preceding 1991–1993 period, **Süleyman Demirel** governments had also subscribed to patronage policies; however, Demirel had always had the grand project of Great Turkey. In his turn, Yılmaz could not maintain himself in power when twice he became prime minister and, in any case, when in power, could not take the initiative on any policy front. Baykal was no different from Yılmaz; worse still, when in opposition, he was the least constructive critic of the policies of the governments in power.

One of the few economic achievements of these years was a reformist **tax** law enacted during the June 1997–December 1998 coalition government of the Motherland Party of Mesut Yılmaz, the **Democratic Left Party** of **Bülent Ecevit**, and the **Democratic Turkey Party** of **Hüsamettin Cindoruk**. This coalition government also managed to pull the inflation rate below the 60 percent mark, introduced the compulsory eight-year secular education that the National Security Council had recommended to the previous (religiously oriented) **Welfare Party**-(secularly oriented) **True Path Party** coalition government, and was successful in its fight against the criminal underworld. In the 1991–1998 period, on the economic front, there was a constant clash among the unprincipled liberalism of Çiller, the liberalism-conservatism-nationalism of Yılmaz, and the nationalist-left viewpoint of Ecevit. On the left of the political spectrum, there was a personal clash between Ecevit and Baykal; on the right, a similar situation occurred between Yılmaz and Çiller. The fragmentation both on the right and the left played into the hands of the Welfare Party, and its leader **Necmettin Erbakan**, the first-ever almost primarily religiously oriented prime minister of Turkey (June 1996–June 1997).

During Erbakan's prime ministry, Turkey experienced what was popularly called a "postmodern coup." Alarmed by what it perceived as the critical rise of reactionary Islam in Turkey, the military, through the National Security Council (NSC), urged the government to adopt a series of reforms. When the Welfare Party-True Path Party coalition showed signs of reluctance to enact into law the recommendations made by the NSC, the commanders repeated their demands through the council. At the same time, they gave briefings to several groups, including journalists, judges of high tribunals, and university chancellors, about the grave threat facing the country. The military received support from the top associations of employers and labor, which called for the resignation of the government, and from the people at large, who every evening at 9.00 P.M. sharp began to turn off and on their lights in protest of the government. Under such pressure, the government resigned (June 1999).

The post–April 18, 1999, general elections period promised a new page in Turkish politics. At the 1999 elections, the Democratic Left Party (DLP) of Ecevit and the **Nationalist Action Party** (NAP) of **Devlet Bahçeli** came in first and second, respectively. Both parties displayed characteristics of a center party. The success of these two parties at the polls reflected rising values in the Turkish polity: clean politics, absence of political bickering, emphasis on national unity in and territorial integrity of the country, coupled with genuine interest in the welfare of the people, accountability and transparency, and consensual politics. The coalition government of the DLP, NAP, and MP functioned in harmony and in a responsive and responsible manner, and began to tackle most of the critical and lingering problems of the country. From the enactment of the new banking law and corrective amendments to it, to the reform of the **Social Security** system, which raised the retirement age, and the adoption of international arbitration, the government acted in a decisive manner. Its resolute stance against reactionary Islam, while remaining sympathetic to the religious sensitivities of the people, had the potential of further moving the religiously oriented parties in Turkey to the sidelines. By bringing a long-forgotten stability and seriousness to Turkish politics, it made occasional military incursions into governmental affairs even less probable.

In the 1990s, Turkey continued to face the armed struggle for **Kurdish** separatism in its southeastern region. The government pursued a three-pronged policy of establishing law and order, developing the region economically, and granting some degree of cultural autonomy. The government recognized the distinctive "Kurdish identity" and allowed singing and publication in Kurdish. The capture of **Abdullah Öcalan**, the leader of terrorist Kurdistan Worker's Party (PKK), in February 16, 1999, marked the end of the latest phase of Kurdish separatism, and perhaps opened the way to a peaceful settlement of that issue.

According to Article 10 of the (1982) Turkish constitution, "all individuals are equal without any discrimination before the law, irrespective of language, race, color, sex, political opinion, philosophical belief, religion or sect, or any such considerations." The Turkish citizens of Kurdish origin could live in any part of Turkey, have any job or profession, use their right to elect and be elected, work in public services, and be active in politics not unlike other citizens. Almost one-third of the parliamentarians in the Parliament representing various parts of the country are of Kurdish origin. It should be noted in passing that the European Framework Convention on National Minorities drawn up by the **European Union** (EU) as part of the Copenhagen Criteria leaves the issue of who should be considered a minority to the discretion of individual countries. According to the 1923 **Lausanne Treaty** made between Turkey and the Allied powers, only non-Muslims are designated as minorities in Turkey. Neither in the Ottoman Empire nor in the Turkish Republic has there been a tradition of designating Muslim groups as minorities.

In addition, such freedoms as the freedom of using Kurdish in daily and cultural activities and in publishing books, magazines, and newspapers, including the pro-Kurdish ones, were granted to Turkish citizens of Kurdish origin. This was part and parcel of the general "democratization" process that had been going on for some time in Turkey. Indeed, during recent years, there have been efforts to bring Turkish democracy to the level of the democracies of the EU (to which Turkey applied in 1987 for full membership, then called the European Community). Among other things, Turkey tried hard to improve its human rights' record. To this end, Turkey recognized the individual right of its citizens to apply to the European Human Rights Commission, and signed the conventions of the Council of Europe and United Nations on the prevention of torture and inhuman treatment. In addition, it adopted the charter of the **Conference on Security and Cooperation in Europe** (CSCE) and set up a parliamentary human rights commission. Turkey also amended its 1982 constitution in a more liberal direction.

Over the years, several cases of human rights violations have been filed at the European Human Rights Commission against Turkey; in several instances, the commission upheld the applications. Almost all cases arose out of certain acts carried out during the heat of the armed struggle in the southeast. For all practical purposes, that confrontation is now dying out. A second category of applications to the commission had to do with torture and inhuman treatment. Throughout the 1990s, there has been a determined campaign in Turkey against torture. This campaign has been conducted through the media by forming a special commission in the Parliament, adopting the necessary legal measures, and including the issue in school curricula.

In the 1990s, Turkey further diversified its foreign relations. Until the Cyprus crisis and the American arms embargo, Turkey's foreign policy was essentially oriented toward the West. From the mid-1970s on, Turkey sought allies in the Third World essentially for its diplomatic struggle against Greece in the United Nations. During the 1980s, for economic reasons, Turkey wished to improve its relations with several countries, including neighbors like **Bulgaria**, Syria, and Iran, with which its relations were strained in the past. With the collapse of the **Soviet Union** and the emergence of Muslim **Turkic republics** in Central Asia, Turkey's geostrategic position became even more important. The West counted on secular Turkey to act as a bulwark against the spread of Islamic fundamentalism in these newly established republics and, to some extent, play the role of intermediary in Western economic ventures there. Turkey itself sought close cultural and economic relations with the republics and began broadcasting a television program there.

During the same period, Turkey began to adopt a more active posture in other areas. During the 1990–1991 **Gulf War**, for instance, Turkish President **Turgut Özal** engaged in intense telephone diplomacy with both the Western leaders, in particular with U.S. President George H. W. Bush, and leaders in the Middle East. In June 1992, Turkey initiated and successfully established the **Black Sea Economic Cooperation Region/Organizaton**, which includes the entire Black Sea region, Caucasia, and the Balkans. It envisaged economic, commercial, and eventually political cooperation among the countries. Turkey played an active role in the peace operations in Bosnia-Herzegovina and Somalia. Following the attack on the twin towers in New York City, Turkey took its place on the side of those who aimed at climinating international terrorism.

Turkey also made some progress toward becoming a full member of the European Union. On January 1, 1996, a **Customs Union** between Turkey and the EU came into effect. On December 4, 1997, in its "Agenda 2000," the European Commission left Turkey out of the first and the second waves of EU integration process. Then, at the EU summit meeting on June 5 1998, a program of total integration between Turkey and the EU was devised. On December 10, 1999, Turkey was declared "a candidate state" destined to join the EU on the basis of the same criteria as applied to the other candidate states.

In addition to the United Nations and NATO, Turkey has memberships in the Council of Europe, the Organization for Economic Cooperation and Development (OECD), the Organization for Security and Cooperation in Europe (OSCE), and partnership status in the Western European Union. Turkey's post-1980 promarket economy has had a positive impact on its economic and political relations with Europe. More than 50 percent of Turkey's foreign trade is realized with the European countries. Furthermore, more than 60 percent of foreign investments in Turkey originate from EU countries. Still, EU's affirmation of Turkey's "Europeanness," even if in a roundabout way, constituted another important milestone in Turkey's two-century-old project of Westernization. More immediately, it provided a further boost to Turkey's efforts to adjust its politics and economy to the Copenhagen criteria, which is necessary for Turkey's accession to the EU as a full member.

ECONOMY

During the 19th century, of all branches of the economy, traditional **agriculture** changed least. Even during the years of cotton boom (for instance, 1863), the land was planted to wheat, barley, and other grains, which were consumed on the farm. Erratic rain exposed the farmers to great risks. The **taxation** on agricultural products was heavy. The governments' attempts to improve agricultural practices and to raise the quality of crops began early in the century but registered no success until the last quarter of the century. The most important improvement achieved toward the end of the century was in irrigation.

In the Ottoman period, it was only during the two or three decades preceding **World War I** that factory **industry** started to take the place of the traditional handicraft industries. At about the same time, the development of mineral resources began to take place. In the decades proceeding the founding of the Republic (1923), Turkey had a sufficiently large and not very poor population. There was an abundance of coal, iron, copper, lead, and other minerals as well as a wide range of agricultural raw materials, in particular, cotton, silk, wool, wood, leather, tobacco, fruits, and oilseeds. There was, however, a lack of a Turkish middle class with the necessary capital, enterprise, and managerial skills. This was coupled with the disinterest of governments in economic development in general and industry in particular.

During the 1920s, Turkey experimented with economic liberalism. This was followed by the Statist Era of 1930–1950. During the Democrats' decade of 1950–1960, a less *dirigiste* approach to the economy was adopted. The emphasis had been on the agricultural sector and private economy. The 1961 **Constitution** introduced a planned period and a State Planning Organization was established. The constitution also stipulated broad economic and social goals—land reform, "a standard of living befitting human dignity," free trade unionism, a universal **social security system**, and medical care. From 1960 until the end of the 1970s, the dominant economic policy was that of import substitution. During the 1980s and the early 1990s, Turkey pursued an export-oriented economic policy with greater emphasis on market forces.

At the inception of the Republic (1923), annual per capita income in Turkey was $35; in 1998, it stood at $6,486. The growth in per capita income was not consistent. It did not reach the $100 mark before 1940, when it became $103. Then, during the **World War II** years, per capita income tripled, reaching $386 in 1943. Per capita income in Turkey did not surpass this figure before 1957, in which year it became $415. There were significant fluctuations during the later years, however, and in 1961, the figure was down to $194. The increase in per capita income as of the later 1960s, however, became relatively more consistent. The per capita income was $271 in 1965, $523 in 1970, $1,164 in 1975, $1,556 in 1980, $1,353 in 1985, $2,706 in 1990, and $5,691 in 1995.

Gross National Product (GNP) growth rates, too, displayed an inconsistent pattern. The 1920s were boom years, with 15, 13, 18, 11, and 22 percent growth rates in 1924, 1925, 1926, 1928 and 1929, respectively. During the world financial crisis of the early 1930s, the growth rate dipped as low as -11 percent (1932). It also remained negative during the World War II period, yet it shot up to 16 percent in 1933, 23 percent in 1936, and 32 percent in 1946. The first three years of the 1950s also witnessed high growth rates—13, 12, and 11 percent. Since then, the growth rate has displayed a more even pattern. In only three years was it negative (1954, 1979, and 1980); otherwise, it fluctuated between 2 and 10 percent. The growth rate was 4 percent in 1982, 8 percent in 1984, 8 percent in 1986, 2 percent in 1988, 10 percent in 1990, and 8 percent in 1997.

In 1923, the share of agriculture in GNP was 43 percent while those of industry and services were 11 and 46 percent, respectively. This ratio remained more or less the same until 1960, when the corresponding figures were 37, 16, and 47, respectively. With the adoption of the industrialization policy in the post-1960 planned period, the share of agriculture in GNP fell while those of industry and services went up. Agricultural products made up 29, 23, 16, and 16 percent of GNP in 1970, 1980, 1990, and 1997 respectively; the corresponding figures for industry and services during those years were 19, 22, 26, and 22, and 52, 55, 58, and 62, respectively.

The post-1980 emphasis on market forces, which paralleled an export-oriented economic policy, was maintained throughout the 1980s and the early years of the 1990s. As of the early 1980s, imports were almost completely liberalized and the Turkish lira was strengthened against major foreign currencies. Both domestic demand and public consumption expanded vigorously. From 1986 onwards, total investment was always at least 2.2 percent of GNP. (That figure was 1.4 in 1950, 1.3 in 1960, 1.7 in 1970, 2.0 in 1980, 1.3 in 1994, and 1.7 in 1999.)

The financing of the significant increase in demand posed an important problem. Public savings had not kept pace with public investments. In 1993, the ratio of budgetary deficit to GNP was 6.7 percent; in 1994, 3.9 percent; in 1995, 4.0 percent; in 1996, 8.3 percent; in 1997, 7.6 percent; in 1998, 7.1 percent; and in 1999, 7.0 percent.

Due to the strong growth in consumption, the share of total fixed investment in GNP fell to 20 percent in 1998. That share was 23 percent in 1986, 24 percent in 1988, and 22 percent in 1989. The share of the private sector in total fixed investment stood at 5.2 percent in 1998, a slightly lower figure than that for 1989 of 5.5 percent, but higher than or equal to those since 1962. The share of private manufacturing investment was 7.7 percent in 1998.

In April 1999, the civilian labor force was 23.78 million; civilian employment was 22.05 million, of which 10.05 million worked in agriculture, 3.33 million in industry, and 8.63 million in services. This left 1.73 million unemployed with an official unemployment rate of 7.3 percent. In April 1994, the unemployment rate was 8.4 percent; in April 1996, 6.3 percent; and in April 1998, 6.4 percent.

In January 1999, Turkey's balance of trade stood at $-10.4 billion (compared to $-7.3 billion in 1991), private unrequited transfers at $4.8 billion (compared to $2.9 billion in 1991), official unrequited transfers at $4.8 billion (compared to $2.2 billion in 1991), current account balance at $-1.4 billion (compared to $250 million in 1991), and its overall balance at $5.2 billion (compared to $-1 billion in 1991). That same year, Turkey imported $39.7 billion worth of goods, and exported $29.3 billion worth of goods. Comparable figures in 1991 were $947 million and $588 million, respectively. In 1991, investment goods made up 28.8 percent, consumer goods 13.8 percent, and raw material 57.4 percent of the imports. Comparable figures in 1996 were 29.9, 14.4, and 55.7. In 1991, 20.1 percent of exports were from agriculture and livestock, 77.8 percent from industry, and 2.1 percent from mining and quarrying sectors. The ratio of imports to exports sustained an average level of 60 percent in the 1980 to 1997 period.

The GNP achieved an average increase of 5.3 percent per annum between 1980 and 1990, 3.2 percent between 1990 and 1995, and 7.7 percent between 1995 and 1997. In 1960, the share of agriculture in GNP was 37.9 percent. It dropped to 15.8 in 1997. In the same period, the share of industry remained almost the same—21.7 percent in 1960 and 21.9 in 1997. The share of the service sector in GDP was under 50 percent in 1980, 59.4 percent in 1995, and 62.4 percent in 1997. Within the service sector, the trade sector is the fastest growing subsector, which increased by 11.2 percent in 1997 alone. Although in 1990 the GNP per capita (according to the purchasing power parity) was $4,699, in 1998 it went up to $6.5 billion. In 1999, tourism revenues were $5.2 billion, and expenditures $1.5 billion. In 1990, the comparable figures were $52 million and $48 million.

In 1993, Turkey had $1.5 billion worth of gold and $16.3 billion in convertible foreign exchange while its foreign debt was $67.4 billion. Comparable figures in 1998 were $1.2 billion, $30 billion, and $97.2 billion. In 1993, the ratio of foreign debt to GNP was 37.3 percent, in 1998 it went up to 47.5 percent. In 1990, **inflation** according to consumer prices was 60.4 percent; in 1994, it shot up to 125.5 percent; in 1998, it receded to 69.7 percent.

SOCIETY

During Ottoman times, society in Turkey was a mosaic of numerous religious communities with the Muslim community as the core community. An omnipresent as well as a relatively omnipotent state was superimposed upon this mosaic of communities. In the absence of politically effective aristocratic and bourgeois classes, the family and mosque were the basic institutions of civil society-as-community. **Islam** and other communitarian and familial values shaped the mind-set of the Muslim community; the Muslim community later constituted the essential element of society in Republican times (from 1923 to the present).

Modernization efforts, seriously undertaken first during the 19th century and given far greater impetus following the establishment of the Republic, aimed at eliminating the impact of Islam, seen as a retrogressive force on society as well as polity. **Education** was conceived as the principal means to that end. Particularly during the Republican period, an effort was made to create a Turk who would think logically. Heavily influenced by the Enlightenment tradition, the founders of the Republic led by **Atatürk** tried to use **literature**, **theater**, and the like alongside education to inculcate secularist values on people. As proponents and implementers of the so-called Turkish Revolution, the intellectual-bureaucratic elite attempted a radical reform from above. Viewing themselves as tutors, these elites endeavored to dominate **civil societal** elements to "elevate them to the level of contemporary civilization." Following the demise of Atatürk (1938), the intellectual-bureaucratic elite took Atatürkism, with its core principle of secularism, as a political manifesto and did their best to suppress the demands of civil societal elements such as a greater freedom of conscience. They tried to keep civil societal elements under control even after the transition to the multiparty period in 1945.

The modernization efforts in question left a deep imprint in Turkey; to a great extent, a Muslim community socialized into Muslim and other communitarian values was replaced by a secularly oriented society. The transformation, however, has essentially taken place at the cognitive level, for Atatürkism has not provided a cultural compass for the everyday behavior of the man in the street. Also, there were no well-developed and widely accepted aristocratic and/or bourgeois values (because the corresponding classes could not have developed in a society dominated by a state-oriented intellectual-bureaucratic elite) that could be an alternative to the Muslim and other communitarian values. The consequence was a bifurcated society of cognitively **Westernized** elites who despised people's "traditional" values on the one hand, and a people cognitively Westernized yet clinging to their Muslim and other communitarian values on the other

Following the transition to multiparty politics, this deeply divided society began to undergo a mutation. For one thing, populist elites, operating in such center-right political parties as the ***Demokrat* Party, Justice Party, True Path Party,** and **Motherland Party,** and such religiously-oriented political parties as the **National Salvation Party** and **Welfare Party,** began to more closely represent the people and articulate their interests. In addition, such post–**World War II** developments as urbanization, industrialization, increased literacy, and the like enabled civil societal elements to participate in politics more effectively. The upshot, among other things, was relative ruralization of the urban scene, retraditionalization of social life, and occasional displays of **fundamentalist** tendencies.

The 1960 and 1971 military interventions emerged, among other things, as efforts to stem such "reversals from a Western way of life." The interventions were successful in suppressing the fundamentalist movements; this was not too difficult a task as cognitive secularism had to a great extent taken root in society. The intervenors' attempts to suppress religious and other communitarian values, however, did not turn out as successfully, because Atatürkism, as noted, did not provide an alternative cultural system for most people.

As of the early 1980s, the **military** officers reversed their earlier position and began to perceive **religion** as an important element of social unity and as a source of arguments to persuade the masses to lead a modern way of life. Consequently, in the eyes of military officers, it became quite legitimate for people not only to personally lead a Muslim way of life but to make political demands of a religious nature as long as they did not border on religious fundamentalism.

On a broader plane, efforts were made to reconcile traditional values with progress in the economy and technology. The so-called technical elites—Muslim engineers—of the Motherland Party played a critical part here. **Turgut Özal**, prime minister from 1983 to 1989 and president from the latter date until 1993, was, on the one hand, initiator of a significant economic transformation in Turkey and, on the other, an earnest defender of freedom of conscience.

Özal was also a strong proponent of freedom of thought and freedom of entrepreneurship. He aimed to roll back the frontiers of the state and create an atmosphere of toleration for different views and tendencies. Under the circumstances, from the early 1980s onward, intellectuals of different persuasions paid increasing attention to the role **civil society** should have in Turkey. For various reasons, all wanted civil society to play a more prominent part vis-à-vis the state. Civil societal actors, including veiled college students, Muslim intellectuals, environmentalists, as well as homosexuals, transsexuals, and transvestites, appeared on the public scene, expressing their views and articulating their demands. **Women's** issues took on a truly feminist color. Women no longer demanded equality only, but also stressed their difference and called for the realization of their autonomy.

Turkish **literature** paid greater attention to the individual, paralleling the growth of urban professional classes. Social realism, which had long reflected the Turkish writers' concern with issues of development, began to be replaced by explorations in psychology, surrealism, and even postmodernism, while novelists came to place greater stress on art for its own sake and correspondingly reduced their social and ideological engagement. **Music** provided an arena where the elite and popular tastes on the one hand, and regional tradition and classical music on the other, became intermixed. Eventually, popular musicians and entertainers came to have the largest following. Toward the end of the 1990s, Turkish society showed ever-increasing levels of diversity as well as glimmers of toleration of the "other."

TURKEY AT THE TURN OF THE CENTURY

The Turks look with optimism to the future. They have made considerable progress toward the consolidation of their democracy. Another overt military intervention is not in the cards. There has been a continuous democratization of the regime. This was coupled with an emphasis on consensus and political realism.

The Turks also managed to roll back, to some extent, the frontiers of the state and to substitute an export-oriented economy for an import-substitution one. This feat extricated them from their lingering economic dependence on other countries. Barring occasional economic crises, they now seek outlets for their economic goods and services in place of loans and grants from other countries. They are even able to extend credits to others, even though at modest levels.

The Turks' newly gained economic self-sufficiency returned to them their self-confidence. It also enabled them to further diversify their foreign relations and play an active part in world affairs. Their increasingly significant role in international relations also derives from their country's strategic importance, as was proven during the **Gulf War**, the war against terrorism in Afghanistan, and their potential role as a bulwark to the spread of religious **fundamentalism** in the new **Turkic republics** in Central Asia and as a partner in the Western countries' economic ventures there.

To many countries, Turkey is a dependable and staunch ally or a peace-seeking neighbor with a flourishing economy and a well-established democracy, the two characteristics of the country making it politically stable and free from irredentist aspirations. The Turks have adopted a territorial rather than a religious notion of nationalism, which enables them to pursue a foreign policy not burdened by religious considerations. They made a categorical decision to adopt a Western way of life, a basic dimension of which is, of course, a liberal-democratic state.

The major problems the Turks faced in the late 1990s were **inflation** and **Kurdish** separatism in southeastern Turkey. Their growing economy has enabled the Turks to prevent inflation from having disruptive social effects in society. Recent governments have been determined to solve the problem once and for all by eliminating unproductive public spending—in particular, by privatizing the bulk of the state economic enterprises, and eliminating political patronage. The recognition of Turkey as a candidate country for the **European Union** provided fresh incentives to succeed in this goal.

The Turks wish to handle Kurdish separatism with a velvet glove. On the one hand, they have been adamant to maintain the unitary nature of their state and are determined to suppress terrorism. On the other, they sincerely want to further develop the region where Turkish citizens of Kurdish origin live in great numbers. For a long time, such efforts were frustrated by the lingering hostilities. Recently, those hostilities seem to have ended. The Turks view the Kurds as no different from themselves, that is, as "first-class citizens." They argue that as long as the Kurds identify themselves politically with the unitary state they should be free to maintain their cultural identity and enjoy their cultural traditions.

During the 19th century, Turkey was referred to as the "sick man of Europe." Turkey is no longer "sick." Yet Europeans have tended to consider Turkey not "of Europe," despite the Turks' centuries-old efforts and considerable success in **Westernization**. However, the long unwillingness of the European Community/Union to admit Turkey as a full member did not depress many Turks because of their newly gained self-confidence and diversified international relations. They also were not worried that this rejection might have played into the hands of the relatively few fundamentalists in the country. Those Turks who did resent the European attitude toward Turkey did so because Europeans kept overlooking the Turks' European credentials. Now that Turkey is finally a candidate country for the European Union, the Turks are pleased that a goal they have cherished for two centuries may soon be fulfilled.

The Dictionary

– A –

ABADAN-UNAT, NERMİN (1921–). Professor of political science. From 1978–1980, she served as a member of the Senate. In 1984, Abadan-Unat received the *Das Grosse Verdienstkreuz* high merit decoration from the German president. Her books include *Public Opinion: The Concept and Its Sphere of Influence* [Kamuoyu: Kavram ve Etki Alanı], *Bureaucracy* [Bürokrasi], *Problems of Turkish Workers in West Germany* [Batı Almanya'da Türk İşçilerinin Sorunları], *An Analysis of the 1965 (Parliamentary) Elections from the Perspective of Political Science and Constitutional Law* [Siyaset Bilimi ve Anayasa Hukuku Açısından 1965 Seçimlerinin Tahlili], *Turkish Workers in Germany, Migration and Development,* and *Women in Turkish Society.*

ABASIYANIK, SAİT FAİK (1906–1954). A leading writer of short stories. He depicted in particular the life of fishermen and the inhabitants of slum neighborhoods. He also produced surrealistic works dealing with associations expressing the subconscious. Abasıyanık was elected an honorary member of the Mark Twain Society in 1953 for his contributions to modern **literature**. His short story collections include "Samovar" [Semaver], "The Cistern" [Sarnıç], "The Pile-Driver" [Şahmerdan], "The Unneeded Man" [Lüzumsuz Adam], "The Neighborhood Coffeehouse" [Mahalle Kahvesi], "Cloud in the Sky" [Havada Bulut], "Company" [Kumpanya], "At the Pond" [Havuzbaşı], "The Last Birds" [Son Kuşlar], "There Is a Snake at Mount Alem" [Alemdağ'da Var Bir Yılan], "Lightly Sugared" [Az Şekerli], and "The Child in the Tunnel" [Tüneldeki Çocuk]. Abasıyanık also tried his hand at novel writing—*The Life Sustaining Motor* [Medar-ı Maişet Motoru] reprinted as *A Bunch of People* [Birtakım İnsanlar]—and at poetry—*Now Is the Time for Love* [Şimdi Sevişme Vakti].

ABDULLAH CEVDET (1869–1932). Ottoman intellectual and journalist. Cevdet was one of the pioneers of the **Westernization** movement during the Second Constitutional Period (1908–1918). While at the School of Medicine, he participated in the establishment of the Association for the Union of Ottomans. In 1897, he was one of the cofounders of the journal *Ottoman* [Osmanlı], which was published in

Geneva and which called for armed rebellion against **Abdülhamit II's** authoritarian rule. In 1904, he started to publish *Opinion* [İçtihad]; the mission of this journal was to educate people in Western culture. Cevdet was a defender of **secularism**, private enterprise, and decentralized rule. He thought that biological materialism, by bringing about an elite community, would replace **religion** in the long run. *See also* YOUNG TURKS.

ABDÜLHAK HAMİT (1852–1937). Poet and playwright. A prominent member of the late 19th-century *Servet-i Fünun* [Treasure of the Sciences] movement in literature (on this movement, *see* LITERATURE). Hamit took his inspiration from the poets and writers of the classical period. At the time he lived, he was referred to as the "Greatest Poet" [Şair-i Azam]. His most celebrated collection of poems is *Tomb* [Makber] (title poem) and his most important play is *Mrs. Finten* [Finten].

ABDÜLHAMİT II (1842–1918). The Ottoman **sultan** who was on the throne from 1876 until 1909. In 1878, he prorogued the (first Ottoman) Parliament, which had been convened the year before, and resorted to personal rule. Abdülhamit adopted a neutralist foreign policy and made efforts to develop the country economically. He placed emphasis on modern **education** and set up many new schools of higher learning. He also pursued **Pan-Islamism** to hold what remained of the empire intact. Abdülhamit was removed from power by the **Young Turks**, mostly products of the new schools he had opened.

ABDÜLMECİT EFENDİ (1868–1941). Last **caliph** (1922–1924). He supported the nationalists during the **Turkish War of Independence**. As part of the Republic's secularization policies, he was deposed and banned from the country in 1924. Abdülmecit Efendi was known for intellectual and artistic gifts.

ADALETNAMES [Justice Decrees]. Issued during the 17th and 18th centuries to prohibit actions that violated the law and were contrary to the justice inherent in the concept of the **sultan**. These decrees had to be repeatedly reissued because the abuses that they aimed to eliminate lingered on.

ADANA. Turkey's fourth largest city after **Istanbul, Ankara**, and **İzmir**, with a population of 2,164,145 (1997). Situated in the fertile lands of the Çukurova Plain in the Mediterranean Region, the city is an important industrial center. In particular, agroindustrial centers are highly developed; in its hinterland, cotton, rice, sesame, and peanuts are grown in great amounts. The Stone Bridge constructed by Emperor Hadrian and the Grand Mosque and the Hasan Kethüda Mosque, both built in the 16th century, are among the most important historic relics.

ADASAL, RASİM (1902–1982). Doctor of medicine. He played an important role in the development of psychiatry as a branch of medical theory and practice in Turkey.

ADIVAR, HALİDE EDİP (1884–1964). Writer who lent moral support to the Turkish **War of Independence** through her fiery oratory and writings as, for instance, in *The Shirt of Flame* [Ateşten Gömlek]. In her novels *Strike the Whore* [Vurun Kahpeye] and *The Clown and His Daughter* (originally written in English and later translated into Turkish as *The Grocery with Flies* [Sinekli Bakkal]), Adıvar depicted political intrigues in a small town and the problems of **Westernization** in Turkey, respectively. Two other novels—*The Sandfly* [Tatarcık] and *The Endless Fair* [Sonsuz Panayır] gave an account of developments in the social and intellectual milieu of the new Turkey. Her other novels include *The Son of Master Kerim* [Kerim Ustanın Oğlu], *The Soother* [Çaresaz], *The Comedy of Longing Street* [Sevda Sokağı Komedyası], *Bits of Life* [Hayat Parçaları], *Mme. Akile Street* [Akile Hanım Sokağı], *The Revolving Mirror* [Döner Ayna], *The Murder at the "Yol" Palace* [Yolpalas Cinayeti], *The Son of Zeyno* [Zeyno'nun Oğlu], *Predestined Sentence* [Mevut Hüküm], *Duffield Heartache* [Kalp Ağrısı], and *Kiepenheuer*. Adıvar, who also wrote plays and short stories, is the author of such memoirs and historical writings as *Memoirs of Halide Edip*, *The Turkish Ordeal*, *Turkey Faces West*, and *The Conflict of East and West in Turkey*.

ADVANCED ISLAMIC INSTITUTE. Opened in 1959. It is part of an effort to train enlightened men of **religion**. *See also* ISLAM.

AEGEAN SEA. It lies to the west of Turkey, between **Greece** and Turkey. It is 214,000 square kilometers. The single most important port city on the Aegean is **İzmir.** The rights to the continental shelf of the Aegean and the territorial waters on that sea have been important matters of dispute between Greece and Turkey.

AGRICULTURE. In the first few decades of the Republic, agriculture had a dominating role in Turkey's national economy. Since 1973, its percentage contribution to gross national product (GNP) has been below those of **industry** and services. Although agriculture's share in GNP was 43 percent in 1927, it dropped to 17 percent in 1991 and to 16 percent in 1998. The decrease in the shares of the agricultural sector in the GNP did not mean a drop in productivity; rather, it was a result of priority being placed on industry. Over the years, the agricultural sector adopted modern technologies and new concepts of management. In 1997, exports of agricultural products increased 10.5 percent compared with the previous year and approached $5.5 billion. In 1940, the cultivated and sown lands were 14.8 million hectares; in 1996, that figure rose to 28 million hectares. In 1996, 78.9 percent of these lands were used for dry agriculture and 21.1 percent for irrigated agriculture. Since 1950, governments supported agriculture by the provision of easy credit facilities, price support, and the extension of irrigation. The Agricultural Bank has been the most significant source of loans to farmers' sales and agricultural credit cooperatives. The Office of Soil Products buys cereals, mainly wheat, at above farm-gate prices. The Sugar Factories Corporation and the State Monopolies Directorate are purchasers of sugar beets, tobacco, and tea.

A number of semipublic sales cooperatives purchase cotton, hazelnuts, pistachios, grapes, dried figs, olive oil, and sunflowers. The General Directorate of State Hydraulic Works has primary responsibility for the extension of irrigation while the General Directorate of Soils and Water builds minor irrigation canals and carries out on-farm development. Between 1950 and 1960, the growth in agricultural output was largely a result of the increase in arable land. During the past three decades, the rise in agricultural output has been due to higher yields obtained through mechanization, use of fertilizer, better seed and land management, and extension of irrigation. In 1960, farmers used less than 300,000 tons of chemical fertilizer; by 1970, the total had risen to around 6.5 million tons and in 1997 to 10 million tons. Between 1962 and 1977, the total irrigated area increased from around 360,000 to about 2.6 million hectares. In 1998, close to 8 million hectares of cropland were irrigated. The number of tractors has grown from around 42,000 in 1960 to 325,000 in 1977 and 875,000 in 1997. In 1960, the number of seed drills was 5,600; in 1997, that number was 12,000. According to the 1995 data, 68.6 percent of agricultural production is vegetable products, 23.2 percent animal husbandry products, 2.8 percent forestry products, and 5.4 percent agriculture products. Turkey produces a variety of agricultural crops. Wheat, barley, and maize are the leading cereals; lentils, chickpeas, and dry beans the leading pulses; sugar beets, cotton, and tobacco the leading industrial crops; cottonseed, sunflower, and groundnut the leading oilseeds; and grapes, figs, citrus fruits, and hazelnuts the leading fruits and nuts.

Agriculture in Turkey is not without problems. Governments have not used their resources to optimum effect. Agricultural credit has expanded rapidly but many strings were attached to it. Price-support policies were motivated by short-term political ends. On the other hand, Turkey's agricultural area is far larger than any of the Western European countries. Furthermore, when the **Southeastern Anatolian Project** is completed, of the total 3.4 million hectares of cultivable agricultural lands in the Harran Plain south of the city of Şanlı Urfa in the southeastern Turkey, 1.7 million hectares (50 percent) will be irrigable.

AĞAOĞLU, ADALET (1929–). Novelist and playwright who dwelt on the reactions of intellectuals to rapid social change, Turkish guest workers abroad, relations between the sexes, and leftist political behavior patterns. Her play *To Live* [Yaşamak] was broadcast by French and German radio stations in 1955 and 1956. Ağaoğlu gained fame with her novel *To Lie Down to Die* [Ölmeye Yatmak]. Other important novels of hers are *The Wedding Night* [Düğün Gecesi] and *High Tension* [Yüksek Gerilim].

AĞAOĞLU, AHMET (1869–1939). Intellectual and politician. He was born in the city of Şuşa in **Azerbaijan** and played an important role in the **Turkism** movement during the period of the **Committee for Union and Progress** (CUP). He also served as a member of the central administrative council of the CUP. During the early Republican period, Ağaoğlu was the chief columnist of the daily

Hakimiyet-i Milliye. He was a member of Parliament between 1923 and 1931. He was one of the founders of the **Free Republican Party** and opposed the "authoritarianism" of the **Republican People's Party**. Ağaoğlu argued that Muslim countries declined because **Islam** failed to adapt itself to changing conditions for a long while. He saw salvation in nationalism that would open the door to Western civilization. In his well-known essay "Three Civilizations" [Üç Medeniyet], he pointed out the futility of trying to prove that Islamic or Buddhist-Brahmanic civilizations were superior to Western civilization.

AĞAOĞLU, SAMET (1909–1982). Politician, memoirist, and short story writer. He held several ministerial posts and sat in Parliament during the 1950s. Ağaoğlu's fiction is characterized by introverted, obsessive personalities. His short stories include "Progeny" [Zürriyet], "Ghafur the Teacher" [Öğretmen Gafur], "An Extended Family" [Büyük Aile], "The Man in the Cell" [Hücredeki Adam], and "The Death of the Mule" [Katırın Ölümü]. Ağaoğlu wrote such political memoirs as *My Father's Friends* [Babamın Arkadaşları], *My Friend Menderes* [Arkadaşım Menderes], and *The Causes for the Birth and Rise of the Demokrat Party* [Demokrat Parti'nin Doğuş ve Yükseliş Sebepleri].

AHİ GUILDS (Brotherhoods). Organized at the time the Ottoman Empire was founded to bring help and relief to people when the defense of the centralized state failed. *Ahi* guilds' revenues came from religious endowments [*vakıf*]. Over the centuries, guilds became secularized. Each guild, which comprised masters, journeymen or master apprentices, and ordinary apprentices, was organized in a rigid hierarchy under a *şeyh*, or head member. Only masters were permitted to open shops. The number of shops sanctioned for each guild was strictly limited. Guilds directed and closely supervised the transactions of their members.

AHMET HAŞİM (1887–1933). Poet and memoirist. He ranks among the principal representatives of the expressionist and symbolist school in Turkey. For Haşim, the intelligibility or "message" of the verse was secondary to the aesthetics and feeling of poetry. In his poetry, Haşim's main concern was with beauty for its own sake. His poems were published in *Hours by the Lake* [Göl Saatleri], *The Wine Cup* [Piyale], *According to Us* [Bize Göre], and *The Home for Homeless Storks* [Gurabahane-i Lâklâkan].

AHMET MİDHAT (1844–1912). Writer, journalist, and instructor. He worked for the spread of literacy and had a widespread impact on the cultural life of the late Ottoman period. A very prolific writer, Midhat used all literary genres except poetry.

AHMET RASİM (1864–1932). Writer of memoirs, Istanbul folklorist, and short story writer. Rasim was a master of personal memoirs, tidbits of Istanbul life, and the kind of anecdotes that Turkish people were fond of recounting to others. He caricatured human foibles in a graceful manner. His memoirs and anecdotes include *City Letters* [Şehir Mektupları], *Forms of Time* [Eşkal-i Zaman], *Harlotry of Olden Times* [Fuhş-i Atik], *The Bastinade* [Falaka], and *After All He Is a Reporter* [Muharrir Bu Ya].

AHMET RIZA (1858–1930). Ottoman intellectual and politician who subscribed to positivism. Rıza joined the **Young Turks** movement against **Abdülhamit II**. On his initiative, the Association for the Union of Ottomans (founded in 1889) assumed the name of **Committee for Union and Progress** in 1895. He became the head of the Committee's Paris branch. In the same year, he began publishing the journal *Consultation* [Meşveret], which dealt with **educational** and cultural issues. The journal called for a synthesis of Western science and Eastern culture. Rıza thought that the (Ottoman) dynasty should be the bond of unity for different ethnic and sectarian groups in the empire but that the authority of the **sultan** should be limited by a **constitution**.

AHMET VEFİK PASHA (1823–1891). Ottoman playwright, linguist, and statesman. He made a significant contribution to the development of Ottoman **theater** by translating several Western plays and adapting them to local traditions. He also served as governor, minister, and speaker of the first Ottoman Parliament (in 1878).

AKAD, LÜTFİ Ö. (1916–). The leading figure among the post–**World War II** "true film producers" who tried to liberate Turkish movies from their "theatrical" features. With Akad, a search for an authentic and original **cinema** truly began. His first film, *Strike the Whore* [Vurun Kahpeye], was a landmark from this perspective. Akad's other important works include *The River* [Irmak], *Heavenly Flower* [Gökçe Çiçek], *The Bride* [Gelin], *The Wedding* [Düğün], and *Ransom* [Diyet].

AKAT, ASAF SAVAŞ (1943–). Professor of economics and columnist. He was one of the founders of the **New Democracy Movement** (later, Party) led by **Cem Boyner**. He is the author of *Agenda of Social Democracy* [Sosyal Demokrasi Gündemi].

AKBULUT, YILDIRIM (1935–). Lawyer and politician. Akbulut was elected to Parliament in 1983 on the **Motherland Party** list. He served as minister of interior from October 26, 1984, to November 6, 1987. Akbulut was Speaker of Parliament from December 25, 1987, until October 20, 1991. He became prime minister on November 9, 1989, in which post he stayed until June 15, 1991. Akbulut served as Speaker of Parliament again from May 20, 1999, until October 18, 2000.

AKÇURA, YUSUF (1876–1935). Intellectual and historian. In his famous work *Three Types of Politics* [Üç Tarz-ı Siyaset], Akçura delineated three alternative policies the Ottoman state could adopt—**Ottomanism**, **Islamism**, and **Turkism**.

His preference was for Turkism, by means of which he hoped that Turks in the Ottoman Empire would form a political nation with Turks outside of the Ottoman Empire by underscoring their common ethnic values.

AKDAĞ, MUSTAFA (1913–1972). Professor of history. Akdağ was one of the first social scientists of significance who did research on the economic and social structure of the Ottoman society. He is best known for his work on the **Celali Revolts** in the Ottoman Empire during the second part of the 17th century.

AKSAL, SABAHATTIN KUDRET (1920–1993). Poet, playwright, and short story writer. Aksal was influenced by the Bohemian school of the *Garip* (*see* LITERATURE); later, he focused his attention on man's place in the universe and eternal values. His poems were published in *Oriental Café* [Şarklı Kahve], *Day Light* [Gün Işığı], *Clear Sky* [Duru Gün], *By Your Hand* [Elinle], *To Wake One Morning* [Bir Sabah Uyanmak], and *The Threshold* [Eşik], and his short stories in *The Soda Pop Three* [Gazoz Ağacı] and *Wounded Beast* [Yaralı Hayvan]. Aksal wrote such plays as "The Joker" [Şakacı], "Three Mirrors in One Room" [Bir Odada Üç Ayna], "The Inside-Out Umbrella" [Tersine Dönmüş Şemsiye], "There's a Celebration at the Café" [Kahvede Şenlik Var], and "The King's Chill" [Kral Üşümesi].

AKSES, NECİL KAZIM (1908–1999). Composer and one of the pioneers in Turkish national opera. Early in his career, Akses arranged monophonic songs with the polyphonic Western techniques. However, he stylized the folkloric and traditional elements instead of harmonizing them directly. Later, he turned to orchestral works and utilized such modern interpretations of contemporary music as indeterminacy. His compositions include *Castle of Ankara*, *Poem,* and *Ballade.* Akses received Germany's Medal of First Class Service and Italy's awards of *Cavaliere Ufficiale* and *Commendatore.*

AKURGAL, EKREM (1911–). Professor of archaeology and honorary member of **Turkish Academy of Sciences**. Akurgal obtained his Ph.D. from Berlin University and received an honorary degree from Bordeaux University. He worked as visiting professor at Princeton University, University of Berlin, University of Vienna, and Scuola Normale Superiore (Pisa). He became a member of the Austrian Archaeological Institute, American Archaeological Institute, Association of the Development of Hellenic Studies (London), German Archaeological Institute, Austrian Academy, British Academy, Swedish Academy, Danish Academy, and French Academy. Akurgal was awarded the German Great Merit Award, the Goethe Medal, and the Turkish Ministry of Culture's Great Award. He is best known for his study of Anatolian civilizations and the mutual interactions in this regard between the West and the East.

ALACA HÜYÜK. A hamlet about 150 kilometers to the east of **Ankara**. It is the site of magnificent works of art from the **Hittite** Empire (1450–1200 B.C.E.).

ALATON, İSHAK (1927–). Alaton, a graduate of Motola Tekniska Höghkola in Sweden, serves as chairman of the Alarko Holding Company.

ALDIKAÇTI, ORHAN (1924–). Professor of constitutional law. He is one of the architects of the 1982 **constitution**. Aldıkaçtı is the author of *Heads of State in Modern Democracies and Turkey* [Modern Demokrasilerde ve Türkiye'de Devlet Başkanlığı].

ALEMDAR MUSTAFA PASHA (1765–1808). Ottoman grand vizier. He played a crucial role in the events leading to and drawing up of the **Deed of Alliance** [Sened-i İttifak] of 1808.

ALEVİS. A heterodox **Islamic** minority in Anatolia that crosses ethnic boundaries. Alevis have no church, no codified doctrine, no accepted clergy, and no school to teach Alevi tenets. The preoccupation with the inner essence of being [*tarikat*] constitutes the basic dimension of their religious life. The great majority of Alevi communities consider **Hacı Bektaş Veli** as their patron saint. The Alevis have no links with **Iran** where Shi'ism is prevalent. For Alevis, Shi'i refers to "those fanatics in Iran." It is estimated that Alevis constitute about 20 percent of Turkey's total population. The Turkish Alevis are loyal citizens of Turkey. *See also* ISLAM; SHI'A.

ALEXANDRETTA (Hatay). *See* FRANCE; SYRIA.

ALİ, SABAHATTİN (1907–1948). A gifted writer in the tradition of Turkish **literature** that deals with village life and village problems. An important work of his is *Yusuf from Kuyucak* [Kuyucaklı Yusuf], which reflects life in the small town of Edremit (in western Turkey) from 1903 to 1915.

ALİ KUŞÇU (15th century). Famous scholar of mathematics and astronomy. Ali Kuşçu worked on the distances of other planets from the Earth and explicated the most advanced mathematical theorems of his age in his works.

ALİ PASHA (1815–1871). The Ottoman grand vizier. He prepared the 1856 **Reform Decree**, which granted religious and sectarian equality to the subjects of the Ottoman state. Ali Pasha was a proponent of prudence in governmental affairs. *See also* TANZİMAT (REFORM) PERIOD.

ALİCAN, EKREM (1916–2000). Politician. Alican served at different times as member of Parliament, minister of finance, and deputy prime minister. He was the founder and first chairman of the **New Turkey Party**, established in 1961.

ALNAR, HASAN FERİD (1906–1978). Composer. He was a student of Joseph Marx and Oswald Kabasta at the Vienna Academy of Music and Performance.

Alnar, who contributed to the realization of the first opera performances in Ankara, conducted the Munich Philharmonic Orchestra and Stuttgart Radio Orchestra. Alnar employed the characteristics of traditional Turkish music. His most famous work is *Concerto for Kanun* [dulcimer] *and Strings*.

ANADOLU AJANSI [Anatolian Agency] (AA). The main news agency in Turkey, which is semiofficial but autonomous. It was founded by **Atatürk** in 1920.

AND, METİN (1927–). Professor of art history and a member of the **Turkish Academy of Sciences**. Served as visiting professor at New York University, Tokyo University, and Giessen Justus Liebig University (**Germany**), and received the French government's *Officier de l'Ordre des Arts et des Lettres*. He is the author of numerous books on Turkish and Islamic culture and art.

ANDAY, MELİH CEVDET (1915–). One of the leading members of the literary movement called *Garip* [Strange] (on the *Garip* movement, *see* LITERATURE). Anday described himself as a "poet of fair, happy days," yet in Turkish literary circles he is best admired for his darker, more reflective moods. His poems were published in *Melancholy* [Melankoli], *Stranger* [Garip], *The Tree That Lost Its Peace* [Rahatı Kaçan Ağaç], *The Telegraph Office* [Telgrafname], *Side by Side* [Yanyana], *Odysseus with Arms Bound* [Kolları Bağlı Odysseus], and *On the Nomad Sea* [Göçebe Denizin Üstünde]. Anday also wrote essays, travel notes, plays, and novels. "The Mikado's Trash" [Mikado'nun Çöpleri] is one of his better-known plays.

ANİ (RUINS OF). Some 50 kilometers to the east of Kars. The former capital of the medieval kingdom of **Armenia**, it dates from the 10th century B.C.E. Ani developed into the "city of a thousand and one churches," particularly during the reigns of the Armenian kings Sembat II the Conqueror (977–989) and Gagik I (989–1020). Today, the site looks like the mirage of a ghostly medieval city; it has remained uninhabited for the last six centuries.

ANKARA. Turkey's capital and second largest city, located in central Anatolia with a population of 3,693,390 (1997). Ankara is situated on a plateau that links the northern Anatolian mountain region to the north with the **Konya** plains to its south. Although a city of civil servants, industries and services have registered significant growth since the 1970s. With its **National Library**, state **theaters**, State **Opera and Ballet**, Presidential Symphony Orchestra, and seven universities, Ankara is a cultural center second only to **Istanbul**. Ankara's history can be traced back to the early Paleolithic Period. The old city is the site of many historic buildings. These include the ancient Roman baths dating back to 212–217 C.E.; the Temple of Augustus, the most impressive of Ankara's ancient monuments, built during the years 25–20 B.C.E. just after Augustus had made Ancyra (as it was then called) the provincial capital of Galatia, and converted into a Christian church in about the fifth century C.E.; the Mosque of Hacı Bayram, originally built in 1427 and named after Hacı Bayram Veli, the founder in Ankara of the Bayrami order of dervishes, who for more than five centuries has been venerated as Ankara's favorite Muslim saint; the medieval citadel whose original fortifications are thought to have been built from 630 C.E. onward; Alâeddin Camii, one of the three surviving Selcukiad mosques in the city dating back to 1178; and Arslanhane Camii, or the Mosque of Lion House, the only Selcukiad-period mosque in Ankara that still retains its original form. In old Ankara, there is also a *Bedesten* (covered market) built during the reign of Sultan **Mehmet II**; it has been restored in recent years and now serves as the famous Museum of Anatolian Civilizations. The museum contains finds starting from the Paleolithic Period (i.e., prior to about 7000 B.C.E.).

ANKARA UNIVERSITY. Turkey's second largest university. The nucleus of the university was the Faculty of Language and History-Geography, which opened in January 1936. Then, the School of Political Sciences (the old Civil Service School recently reorganized) was moved from **Istanbul** to **Ankara**. The university itself was opened on July 6, 1948. *See also* COUNCIL OF HIGHER EDUCATION; EDUCATION; FACULTY OF POLITICAL SCIENCES, ANKARA UNIVERSITY.

ANTALYA. The seaside city on the **Mediterranean** with a population of 1,434,076 (1997). Founded in the second century B.C.E., Antalya, with its Lara beach to the east and the Konyaaltı beach to the west, abounds with tourists at every season. The main historical attractions include the Mosques with Flute Minarets, which is the symbol of the city; Tekeli Mahmut Paşa Mosque; the Kaleiçi [Inner Citadel] District where the old Antalya houses are situated; the Atatürk and Karalıoğlu parks where various exotic Mediterranean plants are grown; Hadrian's Gate, and the **Atatürk** and the Archaeological **Museums**.

ARAS, TEVFİK RÜŞTÜ (1883–1972). Politician. A doctor by profession, he served as minister of foreign affairs from 1923 until 1938. Aras wrote *Ten Years in the Wake of Lausanne* (**Peace Treaty**, 1924) [Lozan'ın İzlerinde 10 Yıl] and *My Views* [Görüşler] as well as three books on medicine.

ARCHITECTURE. The buildings created by Turkish architects since the 11th century have an important place in the heritage of world architecture. The Selimiye and Süleymaniye Mosques built by Mimar [Architect] Sinan reflect the degree of maturity that the Ottoman architecture had reached in the 16th and 17th centuries in dealing with space and mass compositions. During the 19th century, Ottoman architects were heavily influenced by their European counterparts. There is continuity from Ottoman architecture to the First National Architectural Movement, which was dominant until 1930. The movement was led by Kemaleddin Bey and

Vedat Tek, who assigned special importance to façades, which they decorated with stone carvings and ceramic tiles. After 1930, foreign architects brought functional designs and an austere look to buildings. The Second National Architectural Movement of 1940–1950 focused on some of the elements of design. There was a meticulous search for a balance between the architectural concepts and the material chosen. In particular, such structural elements as eaves, wooden latticework, brackets, and windows were used. Sedat Hakkı Eldem and Emin Onat were among the important architects of this period. In the 1950–1960 period, the influence of foreign architecture became stronger. An exploration process in education, organization, and design prepared the ground for the emergence of contemporary Turkish architecture. Since the 1960s, Turkish architects have gone in search of new concepts and aesthetic values in architecture, leading to a dynamic and productive pluralism. Contemporary Turkish architects have tried myriad architectural approaches from the use of fantastic and/or irrational forms to expressive approaches, from creating monumental symbols to the utilization of traditional symbols, and from an arabesque search to postmodernist designs.

AREL, BÜLENT (1919–1990). Composer. At **Ankara** State Conservatory, Arel studied under Pratorious and Zuckmayer. His youthful compositions of the 1950s include *Symphony No. 1*, *Symphony No. 2,* and *Piano Trio*. These pieces create an impressionistic atmosphere. Between 1959 and 1962, Arel worked at the newly created Columbia-Princeton Music Center as instructor and composer. He also taught music at Yale University (1964) and the State University of New York at Stony Brook (1971–1990). Until 1957, he employed conventional methods in his orchestral, chamber, and other kinds of music. In the post-1957 period, electronic elements and the 12-tone technique began to dominate his music. His pieces of electronic music include *Music for String Quartet and Oscillator, Stereo-Electronic Music No. 1, Music for a Sacred Ceremony,* and *Impressions from the Wall Street.*

ARF, CAHİT (1910–1997). Mathematician. He completed his doctoral studies at Göttingen University in **Germany**, working with Helmut Hasse. Arf became famous for the Hasse-Arf theorem. He proved that problems that can be rendered into second-order algebraic equations could be solved by the aid of ruler and compass. He is also known for "Arf circles" in mathematics.

ARMED FORCES. *See* DEFENSE; JANISSARY CORPS; MILITARY AND POLITICS; NİZAM-I CEDİT; TRIUMPHANT SOLDIERS OF MUHAMMAD.

ARMENIA/ARMENIANS. Armenia lies to the east of Turkey. Historically, Armenians (*see* MINORITIES) lived in several parts of Anatolia and in today's Armenia. In the Ottoman Empire, many of the tradesmen and artisans were Armenians. From the

Tanzimat (**Reform**) **Period** onward, several of them became civil servants and some climbed to high ranks. Following the Greek uprising in the 1920s, the Armenians were referred to as "loyal nation" [*millet-i sadıka*] because of their continued allegiance to the Ottoman cause. Toward the end of the 19th century, due to the Russian (*see* RUSSIA) expansion toward the Caucasus and the spread of the Enlightenment in Europe, the Armenian culture went through an invigoration and foreign powers began to interest themselves in the Ottoman Armenians. These developments led to the emergence of the "Armenian question." By the end of the 1880s, partly as a result of Russian and, to lesser extent, British (*see* GREAT BRITAIN) and French (*see* FRANCE), policies weakening the Ottoman Empire, Armenian nationalism began to flourish, particularly among the Armenians living in the eastern provinces of the Ottoman Empire, and ended up in a number of Armenian revolts that began in 1890. **Abdülhamit II** suppressed these revolts by military units made up of Ottoman Kurds (*see* KURDS). The Armenian revolutionary societies presented the armed clashes in question as the killing of Armenians by Turks, but on March 28, 1894, the British ambassador in Istanbul reported to the Foreign Office in London: "The aim of the Armenian revolutionaries is to stir disturbance, to get the Ottomans to react to violence, and thus get the foreign powers to intervene."

In the early stages of **World War I**, Armenians in the Caucasus took their places on the side of the Ottomans against the Russians. In early 1915, however, they turned against the Istanbul government. In order to eliminate the threat from behind their front lines, the Ottoman government decided to deport the Armenians in the eastern provinces to **Syria** and Palestine. During the deportation, a great number of Armenians lost their lives. This led to an ongoing conflict between the Turks and Armenians and between Turkey and Armenia. The Armenians have claimed that it was a case of genocide, and put the number of Armenian losses to more than 1.5 million people. British historian A. J. Toynbee put the figure at 600,000. The Turks have argued that 1,300,000 Armenians lived within the boundaries of the Ottoman Empire in 1914; 200,000 died in the war and 100,000 during the deportation; during those years, due to the "troubles," an equal number of Turks (if not more) lost their lives; and that in the aftermath of the deportations, the British toyed with the idea of trying some members of the last Ottoman government whom they had taken to Malta for war crimes, but could not find evidence in the Ottoman archives, which they controlled (because they were the major occupying power in Istanbul).

The events of the late 19th century and the 1915 deportation of Armenians have adversely affected Turco-Armenian relations to this day. The Armenian diasporas in the West repeatedly brought the issue to the international agenda. In order to draw Western attention to their claims, for a while, the Secret Army for the Liberation of Armenia (ASALA) killed Turkish diplomats in Western capitals. Armenians were also instrumental in getting some Western parliaments, particularly in those countries where there were large communities of Armenian origin, to accept resolutions condemning Turkey of having committed genocide.

In recent years, Turkey has been keen to develop regional cooperation in the Caucasus region, including Armenia. Turkey wishes to develop its economic and cultural relations with the Turkic republics that gained their independence following the collapse of the Soviet Union in 1991. One of those republics is **Azerbaijan**. Armenia poses a barrier to Turkey's transportation lines with Azerbaijan and, through that country, to the other Turkic republics. On the other side of the fence, Armenia is a landlocked country and needs access to the outside world through Turkey. Yet even economic cooperation, which would lessen the tension between the two countries, cannot flourish with the aggression between the two. Relations between the two countries have been further strained because of the Azerbaijan-Armenia conflict over the autonomous Nagorno-Karabakh region in Azerbaijan. In their confrontation over this disputed territory, Azerbaijan expects active support from Turkey.

Turkey recognized the independence of Armenia on December 16, 1991. In times of need, Turkey has extended humanitarian aid to Armenia and facilitated the transit of such aid. Both Armenia and Turkey are founding members of the **Black Sea Economic Cooperation Organization** (BSCE). There are, however, no diplomatic relations between the two countries. Turkey wishes to normalize its relations with Armenia, hoping that one day both countries will leave the judgment of history to history itself.

ARPALIK. Pension or unemployment compensation for high-ranking officials between formal appointments in the Ottoman Empire. In time, it came to mean an additional stipend provided for favorites.

AŞAR [Tithes]. The best known of the taxes authorized by Islamic law during the Ottoman Empire—the canonical one-fifth of agricultural produce.

ASELSAN. Military electronics industries. The major shareholder is the Foundation for Strengthening the Air Force.

ASENA, DUYGU (1946–). Journalist. Asena is Turkey's leading feminist author. Her most important work is *Woman Has No Name* [Kadının Adı Yok].

ASPENDOS. One of the original Pamphylian cities, about 40 kilometers east of **Antalya**. It is famous particularly for its magnificent theater dating back to the Greco-Roman world of the second century C.E.

ATAÇ, NURULLAH (1898–1957). A leading essayist and critic. He was highly influential among the post-1940 generations of literati in developing a plain, expressive narrative style and a rationalistic genre of writing. Ataç was a passionate Turkicist in the linguistic field, and avoided using any words of non-Turkish derivation when possible. He also used an inverted grammatical construction. Ataç's essays include "What the Days Bring" [Günlerin Getirdiği], "Scratch Pad"

[Karalama Defteri], "From One Subject to Another" [Sözden Söze], "While Searching" [Ararken], "Let Us Say" [Diyelim], "By the Way" [Söz Arasında], "Letters to My Readers" [Okuruma Mektuplar], "Diary" [Günce], and "Prospero and Caliban" [Prospero ile Caliban].

ATAMAN, SADİ YAVER (1906–1994). Made significant contributions to the popularizing of folk music. He directed the program "Airs of the Country" [Memleket Havaları] at Radio Istanbul.

ATATÜRK, MUSTAFA KEMAL (1881–1938). Founder of the Turkish Republic and its president from 1923 to 1938. Born in Salonica, in today's **Greece**, he graduated from Army Staff School in 1905 and concerned himself from that time on with the problems the country faced. He first served in Damascus where he established the "Association of Fatherland and Freedom" in 1907. Then he was appointed to the Third Army in Macedonia; he was assigned to the headquarters of the Army in Salonica. During those years, Mustafa Kemal began to work in the **Committee for Union and Progress** (CUP). In 1909, he was on the staff of the army when it quelled a religiously oriented riot in **Istanbul**. It was at this time that Mustafa Kemal concluded that the military should not involve itself in everyday politics. He took part in the victorious battle in 1911 against the Italians in Tripoli. On the eve of **World War I**, Mustafa Kemal served as a military attaché in Sofia.

During the war, he successfully defended the Dardanelles against a large Allied fleet. Following the war that the Ottoman Empire (along with other Central powers) lost, Mustafa Kemal had himself appointed inspector-general in the Third Army in eastern Anatolia. His real aim was to save the country from Allied forces that had invaded parts of the country following the war. On May 19, 1919, Mustafa Kemal arrived in Samsun, a port city on the **Black Sea**, in order to start a national liberation movement. On June 21, 1919, in his Amasya Circular, he called upon disparate Associations for the Defense of Rights, which had been founded in different parts of Turkey, to join their forces to secure the integrity and independence of the country. On July 23, 1919, Mustafa Kemal participated at the **Erzurum Congress** at which a representative group was elected; the congress rejected any formula (mandate) short of total independence for Turkey. On September 4–7, 1919, Mustafa Kemal and the members of the representative group convened the **Sivas Congress**; at the congress, the Association of Rumelia and Anatolia for the Defense of Rights was formed. He had now mobilized various groups around his efforts to save the country from the Allied forces. On April 23, 1920, he convened the Turkish Grand National Assembly in **Ankara**, and became chairman of the Assembly and head of the government. On August 30, 1922, Turkish armies, under Mustafa Kemal's command, won the final victory against the Greek forces. The Ottoman dynasty was dissolved.

On October 29, 1923, the Turkish Republic was proclaimed; Mustafa Kemal became the president. Mustafa Kemal then devoted himself to reforms that would

Westernize the country. **Secularism** constituted the linchpin of these reforms. The **caliphate** was dissolved. **Education** was completely secularized. Dervish convents were closed. The Latin alphabet and Western calendar were adopted. Mustafa Kemal also supported economic reforms; in his opinion, political independence needed to be complemented by economic autonomy. In **foreign policy**, he adopted the motto of "peace at home and peace abroad."

In 1924 and 1930, Mustafa Kemal twice experimented with multiparty democracy; in each case, he put an end to democracy, because in his opinion, a multiparty regime showed signs of reversing the Westernization process. In 1934, the Turkish Grand National Assembly conferred upon Mustafa Kemal the name of "Atatürk," father of Turks. In his later years, Atatürk concentrated more on issues of history and **language**. He tried to show that the Turks were not only warriors but had also contributed to world civilization. In this way, he endeavored to enable the Turks to regain their self-confidence. He also made efforts to liberate the Turkish language from foreign influences and develop a purer Turkish. Atatürk passed away on November 10, 1938, but his ideas have significantly influenced later generations of Turks. *See also* ATATÜRKISM.

ATATÜRK MAUSOLEUM. In **Ankara**. A national shrine honoring the founder of Turkey. A museum on the site houses some photographs and personal memorabilia of **Atatürk**.

ATATÜRKISM. The worldview developed by **Atatürk** and his associates. It was the political philosophy behind the **Westernizing** reforms of the early Republic that aimed at substituting reason for **religion** (tenets of **Islam**); the latter was considered an obstacle to progress. The basic principles of the worldview were republicanism, **secularism**, nationalism, populism, statism, and revolutionism-reformism. Over the years, people of different political persuasions attributed various meanings to these principles. Even the question of whether Kemalism (Atatürkism) was a worldview or an ideology became a matter of contention. The post-Atatürk bureaucratic-intellectual elites and their allies in the **Republican People's Party** and civil bureaucracy took it as an ideology (converted it from a way of rational thinking to a political manifesto) and considered themselves to be its guardian. Such a stance on their part brought them into conflict with antibureaucratic, antistate political leaders, in particular those of the *Demokratik* **Party**, **Justice Party**, and **True Path Party**. These parties emphasized "**national will**," took voting as the sole criterion of political legitimacy, and opposed the view of the former that Atatürkism is the primary source of public policy making. Having initially adopted the ideological version of Atatürkism, the **military** intervened in politics in 1960 and 1971 with the argument, among others, that Atatürkism had come under threat. When the military took power in 1980 for the third time during the Republican period, the military reverted to Atatürkism as a worldview. For them, Atatürkism meant being against Marxism, fascism, and theocracy; in the military's submission, these did not have rational premises and were therefore not in the best interests of the country. *See also* ATATÜRK.

ATAY, FALİH RIFKI (1894–1971). Writer and politician. Through his pen, Atay advocated the principles on which the young Republic was founded. He wrote articles in the newspaper *Akşam*. From 1923 to 1950, he was a member of Parliament. Atay was an unswerving Kemalist (*see* ATATÜRKISM) and **Westernizer**. He is well known for his memoirs of **Atatürk**, which included *Atatürk: From His Birth to His Death* [Atatürk: Doğumundan Ölümüne Kadar], *What Atatürk Told Me* [Atatürk'ün Bana Anlattıkları], *The Armistice Notebook of Mustafa Kemal* [Mustafa Kemal'in Mütâreke Defteri], *Residence of Atatürk* [Çankaya], *Memoirs of Atatürk, 1914–1919* [Atatürk'ün Hatıraları, 1914–1919], and *What Was Atatürk* [Atatürk Ne idi]. Among his travel accounts, *Fascist Rome, Kemalist Tirana, Lost Macedonia* [Faşist Roma, Kemalist Tiran, Kaybolmuş Makedonya] and *Moscow, Rome* [Moskova-Roma] are best known. Atay is also the author of *What Is Kemalism?* [Atatürkçülük Nedir?].

ATLI, NEVZAT (1925–). Doctor of medicine and composer. Atlı was instrumental in reviving the traditional art music in the Republican period. He directed the State Chorus for Classical Turkish Music [Devlet Klâsik Türk Musikisi Korosu].

ATSIZ, NİHAL (1875–1975). Poet and author. Atsız, who in the late 1930s and early 1940s targeted communist writers in Turkey, was an ardent proponent of ethnic nationalism. He rejected the idea of **Islam** constituting an integral part of Turkishness. Atsız publicized his views in such Turkist periodicals as *Atsız Mecmua*, *Orhun*, *Orkun*, and *Ötüken*. *See also* TURKISM.

AVCI, SABİT OSMAN (1921–). Engineer and politician. He served as the Speaker of Parliament from November 26, 1970, until October 24, 1973.

AVCIOĞLU, DOĞAN (1926–1983). Political writer who attributed Turkey's underdevelopment to the "lingering feudalism in Turkey" and "Western imperialism." Among his books are *The Turkish System: Yesterday, Today, and Tomorrow* [Türkiye'nin Düzeni: Dün, Bugünü ve Yarını], *The Foreign Interference in the Incident of March 31* [31 Mart'ta Yabancı Parmağı], *On Revolution* [Devrim Üzerine], and *The History of the National Struggle* [Milli Kurtuluş Tarihi].

AYAN. Local notables in the Ottoman Empire.

AYAZ, MUSTAFA (1938–). Painter. Ayaz won several national awards. Early in his work, he produced abstractions of nature and figure studies. In these works, the impressions of Anatolian folk dances and the figures of villages and their wagons were discernible. In the post-1970 years, Ayaz left behind abstractionism.

He began to divide the surface of the canvas into geometric segments and inserted linear designs into the segments, thereby creating a carpetlike effect devoid of depth or recession.

AYBAR, MEHMET ALİ (1910–1995). Politician, chairman of the **Turkish Labor Party**. A professor of international law by profession, Aybar always sought to develop a particular socialist theory and praxis that would better fit Turkey's specific conditions.

AYDEMİR, ŞEVKET SÜREYYA (1897–1976). Popular historian and public figure. Aydemir was a Pan-Turanist in his youth. Later, he became an ardent Marxist. Finally, he "vowed his strength to the Revolution of **Atatürk.**" Aydemir was one of the founders of *Kadro*, an intellectual and ideological periodical. He wrote somewhat fantasized biographies of Atatürk, **İsmet İnönü, Enver Pasha**, and **Adnan Menderes**. His *The Man in Search of Water* [Suyu Arayan Adam]—a fictionalized autobiography—and *If the Soil Should Awake* [Toprak Uyanırsa]— a fictionalized memoir—are among the best known of his works. He is also the author of the book *Revolution and Cadre* [İnkılâp ve Kadro].

AYDEMİR, TALAT (1917–1964). Officer. From the mid-1950s onward, he was active in plotting against the *Demokratik* **Party** government. He was outside the country at the time of the 1960 military intervention. He himself tried two unsuccessful coups in February 1962 and May 1963. Following the second attempt, he was sentenced to death, which was carried out.

AYKAL, GÜRER (1942–). Conductor. He studied at Academia Chigiani in Siena, Italy, and the Royal Academy of Music in Great Britain. Aykal worked with such conductors as Andre Previn, Rudolf Swartz, and George Hurst. He taught at Indiana University in the **United States**, and gave concerts in **Bulgaria**, Belgium, Colombia, Finland, **France, Germany, Great Britain**, Hungary, Italy, the Netherlands, Northern Ireland, Poland, Romania, the Soviet Union (*see* RUSSIA), Spain, and Venezuela. Aykal is the conductor of the Turkish Presidential Symphony Orchestra.

AZERBAIJAN. Turkey's neighbor to the northeast. Azerbaijan declared its independence on August 30, 1991. Turkey was the first country to recognize Azerbaijan's independence. The two countries share an almost-common language and culture. Turkey has backed Azerbaijan in its efforts to overcome the problems of a newly independent state. Turkey and Azerbaijan signed more than 100 bilateral agreements to cooperate in such fields as economy, **education**, culture, **health**, science, and **tourism**.

Concerning the conflict between **Armenia** and Azerbaijan over the disputed autonomous Nagorno-Karabakh territory in Azerbaijan, which was occupied by Armenia, Turkey supports the United Nations (UN) Security Council resolutions that the territorial integrity of Azerbaijan should be respected by all countries, including Armenia. Turkey thinks that the conflict over the disputed territory should be settled within the framework of the **Organization for Security and Cooperation in Europe** (OSCE) and encourages bilateral talks between Azerbaijan and Armenia.

– B –

BABIÂLİ [Sublime Port]. Executive offices of the grand vizier in the Ottoman Empire. Also called Paşakapısı [Gate of the Pasha]. It later referred to the civil bureaucracy as a whole.

BAGHDAD PACT. Mutual security organization of Turkey, **Iran**, **Iraq**, Pakistan, and **Great Britain**. It ended with the revolution in Iraq in 1958.

BAHÇELİ, DEVLET (1948–). Professor of economics and politician. In 1987, he joined the **Nationalist Labor Party**—the predecessor party to the rightist **Nationalist Action Party** (NAP) and led by **Alparslan Türkeş**. Upon Türkeş' death in April 1997, Bahçeli became the chairman of the NAP. Upon the victory of the NAP in the April 18, 1999, general elections, Bahçeli became minister of state and deputy prime minister. Since 1997, Bahçeli has pulled the NAP toward the center of the political spectrum, a process that was started by Türkeş in the early 1980s.

BAKİ (1528–1600). Developed **Divan** poetry to its zenith at the end of the 16th century. Baki was the greatest master of the lyric poem. He used primarily **Istanbul** Turkish and treated the theme of love in his harmoniously structured poems.

BAKÜ-CEYHAN PIPELINE. With the aim of creating the so-called East-West Energy Corridor, at the November 18–19, 1999, meeting in **Istanbul** of the **Organization for Security and Cooperation in Europe**, **Azerbaijan**, Georgia, Kazakhstan, Turkmenistan, and Turkey signed a number of agreements concerning the Bakü-Ceyhan main oil and natural gas export pipeline. The pipeline will be 1,700 kilometers long, and will pass through Azerbaijan, Georgia, and Turkey. The agreement predicts the pipeline to be operational in 2004, if the construction of the pipeline starts in 2001 as planned.

BALIKESİR. The historic city to the south of **Marmara Sea**, with a population of 1,029,204 (1997). The Zağanos Paşa Mosque, the Yıldırım Mosque, the Clock Tower, and the Karesi Bey Tomb are important historical structures.

BALLET. *See* OPERA AND BALLET.

BALKAN WARS. The First Balkan War (1912–1913): The Ottomans fought against the Greeks, Serbs, and Bulgarians. The war ended with the Treaty of London; the Ottomans gave up most of Thrace, including the city of Edirne. This led to the beginning of the **Committee for Union and Progress**'s authoritarian rule. The Second Balkan War (1913): The disputes among the Greeks, Serbs, and Bulgarians over the division of the spoils of the First Balkan War turned the tables in the Ottomans' favor. The Bulgarians made a surprise attack on their former allies. The Ottomans took advantage of the situation and recovered Eastern Thrace and Edirne. The war ended with the Ottomans signing separate treaties with **Bulgaria**, Serbia, and **Greece**. In the two Balkan wars, the Ottomans lost 83 percent of their land in Europe.

BALTA LİMANI TREATY. Anglo-Ottoman trade agreement signed in 1838. It confirmed and expanded the old British **capitulatory** privileges in the Ottoman Empire.

BANGUOĞLU, TAHSİN (1904–1989). Linguist, author, and politician. Banguoğlu taught linguistics at **Ankara University** and opposed cleansing the Turkish **language** of all loan words. He served as minister of **education** in the 1948–1950 period. He played a significant role in the introduction of courses on **religion** in grade schools, opening of prayer leader-preacher schools, and foundation of a Faculty of Religious Studies. In 1970, Banguoğlu was elected chairman of the **New Turkey Party** and served in that capacity for one year. He wrote several books on Turkish grammar.

BANKING. The Central Bank of Turkey, besides issuing currency, carries out the monetary policy (*see* MONETARY AND FISCAL POLICY), regulates money supply, and gives loan to the banks. The foreign currency exchange rates are formed under free market conditions. When necessary, the Central Bank enters the market.

In the post-1980 period, entrance to the banking sector was liberalized. This led to the decrease in the predominance of the public sector in the system and, consequently, to the development of a competitive environment for banking. Since 1980, the profits of the banking sector have shown a continuous increase both in real terms and in the share of the profits after taxes in the total assets. At the same time, the banks rapidly diversified their services to customers. Among other things, stocks and bonds have shown a considerable increase in bank portfolios. Their ratio in the total assets went up from 3.7 percent to 10 percent between 1980 and 1997.

At the end of 1999, there were 81 banks—excluding the Central Bank—operating in Turkey. There were seven state-owned banks, of which four were commercial and three were development and investment banks. There were 38 private commercial banks, which were either retail banks with numerous branches or specialist banks concentrating on **foreign trade** and corporate banking with few branches. The remaining 19 were foreign banks operating in Turkey, of which 6 are based in Turkey and 13 are branches of foreign banks. The equity of shareholders amounted to $7.7 billion. In 1999, the Banking and Auditing Institution was established. The institution, which has financial and administrative autonomy, has the responsibility of insuring the protection of savings, among other things. The Board of Sworn Bank Auditors, which conducted audits on behalf of the Treasury, started to operate under this institution. However, since 1999, several small banks evinced extremely risky positions and were taken under the control of the newly created Savings Deposits Insurance Fund.

When Turkey was hit by a major financial crisis on February 21, 2001 (*see* MONETARY AND FISCAL POLICY), even the two big state banks were unable to meet their obligations in the markets for a short while. First, the Central Bank came to their aid by providing liquidity. Second, three major state banks were placed under a supervisory board of directors.

BARKAN, ÖMER LÜTFİ (1905–1979). An internationally known pioneer of Turkish economic history. Barkan was one of the first to make systematic use of the Ottoman archives. He made important contributions on the ownership of land, prices and price movements, demographic situation, and colonization in the Ottoman Empire in the 16th century. In 1957, Barkan was awarded an honorary doctorate by Strasbourg University.

BAŞKUT, CEVAT FEHMİ (1905–1971). A popular playwright and journalist. Başkut attracted large audiences with his clear accounts of economic hardships that respected civil servants faced. In his work, he depicted a clash of values. *I Vote for You* [Sana Rey Veriyorum] and *An American in Harput* [Harput'ta Bir Amerikalı] are among the best known of his plays.

BAYAR, CELAL (1883–1985). Third president of the Turkish Republic. He was born on May 16, 1883, in Umurbey village in **Bursa** province. In his youth, Bayar worked at the Bursa branch of the Deutsches Orient Bank, among other jobs. In 1907, he joined the **Committee for Union and Progress** and, after **World War I**, became a member of the Ottoman Association for Defense of Rights. Bayar served in the last Ottoman Parliament and then became a member of the Turkish Grand National Assembly convened in **Ankara** in April 23, 1920. In 1921, he was appointed minister of economy and then, in 1924, minister of reconstruction and resettlement. In the 1924–1932 period, Bayar served as director general of the newly founded **İş-Bank**.

In 1932, he again became minister of economy and stayed in that post until 1937. During those years, Bayar had an important impact on the economy. On the one hand, he placed emphasis on the development of the private sector through state subsidies and, on the other, he was instrumental in the establishment of various state economic enterprises. In 1937 and 1938, for brief periods, Bayar also served as prime minister.

Following the installation of the multiparty regime in 1945, Bayar, with three of his colleagues—**Fuat Köprülü, Adnan Menderes,** and **Refik Koraltan**—resigned from the **Republican People's Party,** the single party of the 1923–1945 period (excepting brief two-party interludes of 1924 and 1930), and formed the *Demokrat* **Party** (DP), becoming its chairman. On May 14, 1950, the DP won the general elections and on May 22, 1950, Bayar became Turkey's third president.

Bayar was Turkey's first president with a civilian background. During his presidency (1950–1960), along with Adnan Menderes—the prime minister of the decade—he played a significant role in public policy making. He elicited sharp criticisms from the opposition for his partisan approach (as president, he had to stay neutral).

In the aftermath of the 1960 **military** intervention, Bayar was tried by the High Court of Justice and faced capital punishment for violating the constitution while president; the National Unity Committee commuted this to life imprisonment. He was freed in late 1964. During his last years, he first gave his moral support to the *Demokratik* **Party** and then to the **Justice Party.**

BAYAR, UĞUR (1964–). Banker and high-ranking civil servant. Bayar has a B.S. degree in applied mathematics and statistics from the State University of New York. He served as an international business consultant, manager at Citibank **(Istanbul),** assistant general manager at Yatırım (Investment) Bank, and as acting chairman of Privatization Administration. Since August 1997, Bayar has been chairman of Privatization Administration. Under his leadership, Turkey's revenues from privatization went up considerably. In 1998, *Euromoney Magazine* selected him as one of 50 top professionals under the age of 40. That same year, the World Economic Forum named Bayar as one of the 100 Global Leaders of Tomorrow; the September 1998 issue of *Global Finance Magazine* included him in the list of world's most powerful 600 people; and, in June 2000, *Business Week* mentioned Bayar as one of the 50 leaders at the forefront of change.

BAYEZIT I [YILDIRIM, THE "THUNDERBOLT"] (1360–1403). The fourth Ottoman **sultan,** who reigned between 1389 and 1403. He captured various principalities in Anatolia and Rumelia and turned the Ottoman *principality* into the Ottoman *state.* Bayezıt I then adopted the title of "sultan" and proclaimed himself the defender of **Islam,** which elicited a European Crusade to the Ottoman realm. Bayezıt I won against the crusaders on September 25, 1396, at the Niğbolu Battle. On July 28, 1402, he lost the battle of Ankara against Timur, the new ruler of Central Asia and **Iran.** Following this defeat, the Ottoman state came to the brink of complete disintegration. The first Imperial School [Enderun-u Hümayun] was established during Bayezıt I's reign.

BAYKAL, DENİZ (1938–). Professor of political science and politician. Baykal did graduate work at Columbia University and the University of Berkeley in

California. He was elected to Parliament in 1973 on the **Republican People's Party** (RPP) ticket. He became minister of finance in 1974 and minister of energy and natural resources in 1978. Following the 1980 **military** intervention, along with other politicians, Baykal was banned from politics for a period of five years. He again became a member of Parliament in 1987 on the **Social Democratic Populist Party** list. He was appointed to the post of secretary-general of the latter party. On September 9, 1992, Baykal was elected chairman of the RPP, which, along with other political parties, had been closed following the 1980 military intervention but was allowed to reopen after July 1992. In the aftermath of the April 18, 1999, general elections, at which the RPP could not clear the nationwide 10 percent electoral quotient, Baykal resigned from the chairmanship of the party. On September 30, 2000, he again became the chairman of the party.

BAYKAM, BEDRİ (1957–). Painter. He obtained a master's degree in economics from Sorbonne University (Paris) in 1983, and did painting at the California College of Arts and Crafts, Oakland. Baykam is an enterprising and audacious artist. His closeness to the representatives of the new expressionist trends in the West in general, and the **United States** in particular, has played an important role in Baykam's half-mocking, half-critical view of the world. He is accepted as one of the Turkish representatives of the new expressionism.

BAYKURT, FAKİR (1929–1999). Novelist. Baykurt served several sentences for political offenses. He described the social milieu into which he was born in vivid detail and by the use of authentic Turkish dialect. His most famous novels are *The Snakes' Revenge* [Yılanların Öcü] and *American Bandage* [Amerikan Sargısı]. Baykurt also wrote short stories, essays, and folktales.

BEKTASHİ MYSTIC ORDER. Founded by **Hacı Bektaş Veli**, circa 13th century. Preachers of the order served as the principal advisers of the **Janissary Corps** in the Ottoman Empire. The order accepted orthodox interpretations of **religion** more than any other mystic order. It spread widely among the nomads in eastern Anatolia and southeastern Europe. The order's formal status, as part of the Janissary Corps, ended with the dissolution of the latter corps in 1826. *See* MAHMUT II.

BELLİ, MİHRİ (1915–). Economist and politician. He was one of the leaders of the outlawed **Turkish Communist Party**. In the 1960s, he became the main exponent of the "national democratic revolution," which held that a revolution in Turkey was only possible through the actions of a progressive elite.

BERAT [diploma, patent]. Ottoman document conferring a rank, position, salary, or privilege.

BERGAMA (PERGAMUM). Ancient Hellenized Anatolian city about 100 kilometers north of **İzmir**. The acropolis rises precipitously on three sides to a height of 300 meters above the plain.

BERK, İLHAN (1918–). Poet of the post–**World War II** "New Movement" (on this movement, see LITERATURE). Books in which his poems were published include *Greetings of Those Who Burned the Sun* [Güneşi Yakanların Selamı], *Song of Turkey* [Türkiye Şarkısı], *Sea of Galilee* [Galile Denizi], *Cuneiform* [Çivi Yazısı], and *Like a Troubador* [Aşıkkane].

BERKER, RATİP (1909–1997). Professor of mathematics and mechanics. He obtained his B.A. and Ph.D. degrees in Nancy and Lille Universities in France, respectively. Berker worked as a visiting professor at Indiana University and Lille University and was conferred two honorary degrees in Turkey. He made important contributions to the Navier-Stokes equations and the d'Alembert Paradox in fluid mechanics.

BERKES, NİYAZİ (1908–1988). Professor of sociology. From 1952 onward, Berkes worked at McGill University in Montreal, Canada. He studied social structure and modernization in general and secularization in particular in the Ottoman-Turkish polity. His most significant work is *The Development of Secularism in Turkey*.

BERMEK, ENGİN (1939–). Professor of molecular biology. Bermek, whose work includes the study of the mechanisms and regulation of gene expression, postsynthetic modifications of proteins, and molecular immunology, is president of the **Turkish Academy of Sciences**.

BEYATLI, YAHYA KEMAL (1884–1958). A leading romantic poet who remained attached to the cultural richness of the Ottoman period and to its **Divan** poetry (on Divan poetry, see LITERATURE). Beyatlı blended neoclassicism, the Parnassian School, and traditional metric poetry. His most famous poem is "The Silent Ship" [Sessiz Gemi], which treats the themes of separation and death. His poems were published, among others, in *24 Poems and Leyla* [24 Şiir ve Leyla], *Our Own Dome of Sky* [Kendi Gök Kubbemiz], *Ancient Poetry with Its Wind* [Eski Şiirin Rüzgarıyla], and *Unfinished Poems* [Bitmemiş Şiirler]. Beyatlı, who also wrote articles, memoirs, and essays, sat in the first Republican Grand National Assembly of 1920–1923, and from 1926 onward served as ambassador to Poland, Spain, Portugal, and Pakistan.

BEYLERBEYİ SARAYI. Ottoman imperial pleasure palace on the shores of Bosporus built by **Mahmut II**, enlarged and modernized in 1865.

BİLGİ UNIVERSITY. Founded in **Istanbul** in 1996. It is a private university where the medium of instruction is English. *See also* EDUCATION.

BİLKENT UNIVERSITY. Founded in 1986 in **Ankara**, it is one of Turkey's leading private universities where the medium of instruction is English. *See also* EDUCATION.

BİRET, İDİL (1941–). Pianist of international fame. She studied with Jean Doyan and Nadia Boulanger at Paris University. She was conferred the Lili Boulanger Foundation (Boston) award and the Polish Achievement Award.

BLACK SEA. It is adjacent to Turkey in the north. It is 422,000 square kilometers. Turkey's most important port cities on the Black Sea are Samsun, Sinop, Rize, **Trabzon**, and Zonguldak.

BLACK SEA ECONOMIC COOPERATION REGION/ORGANIZATION (BSEC). The potential of the countries of the **Black Sea** region to achieve mutually advantageous economic cooperation has been promoted by Turkey. The underlying idea is to ensure that the Black Sea region becomes an area of peace, stability, and prosperity through close economic relations. In December 1990, Turkey, the Soviet Union (*see* RUSSIA), **Bulgaria**, and Romania attended the first preparatory meeting of the Black Sea Economic Cooperation Region (BSEC). The BSEC was founded in Istanbul in 1992. In 1999, Albania, **Armenia**, Bulgaria, Georgia, **Greece**, Moldova, Romania, the Russian Federation (*see* RUSSIA), Turkey, and Ukraine were full members, and Austria, Egypt, **France**, **Germany**, **Israel**, Italy, Poland, Slovak Republic, and Tunisia had observer status. One of the long-term objectives of the BSEC is to gradually establish a **free trade** area, followed by political cooperation among member countries. The BSEC aims to establish cooperation with other international organizations and initiatives. Noteworthy in this context is the developing relationship between the BSEC and the **European Union** (EU).

BLACKSEAFOR AGREEMENT. A **Black Sea** Force (BSF) was set up on April 2, 2001, by the countries around that sea (**Bulgaria**, Georgia, Romania, the Russian Federation [*see* RUSSIA] and Turkey). The BSF will be involved in humanitarian search and rescue operations, mine sweeping, environmental protection, and other activities decided by the parties to the agreement.

"BLOODY SUNDAY" (February 16, 1969). Clashes between leftists and rightists in **Istanbul** that left two dead and sixty injured. This was one of the first concrete indications of the political polarization Turkey was experiencing at the time. Polarization was intensified and clashes became more deadly during the following decade.

BODRUM (Ancient Halicarnassus). Very popular resort town on the Aegean coast in southwest Turkey. It was the site of the Mausoleum of Halicarnassus, listed by Philo of Byzantium among his Seven Wonders of the World, and of the magnificent Castle of St. Peter, the construction of which started sometime after 1402. The Knights of St. John inhabited the castle until 1522.

BOĞAZİÇİ UNIVERSITY. One of Turkey's leading state universities. It was created with the conversion in 1971 of **Robert College** (in **Istanbul**) into a Turkish university. The medium of instruction at the university is English. *See also* EDUCATION.

BOĞAZKALE (Ancient Boğazköy). Ancient capital of the **Hittite Empire**, about 150 kilometers east of **Ankara**. About 300 meters to the east of Boğazkale are found the ruins of the Great Temple, whose construction began in the 14th century B.C.E.

BORAN, BEHİCE (1910–1987). Sociologist and politician. Boran studied Turkish social structure in general and social stratification in particular. She chaired the **Turkish Labor Party** in 1970. Boran subscribed to the idea that socialist theory and praxis have universal characteristics that should not change from one context to another.

BORATAV, PERTEV NAİLİ (1907–1998). Folklorist. From 1952 until 1974, Boratav worked at the Centre National de la Recherche Scientifique in Paris. He pioneered the systematic collection and interpretation of folkloric material in terms of their historical context and vis-à-vis change in that historical environment. Boratav also studied works in folk **literature** in their own right—how a certain genre became diversified in terms of subject matter, types, and motives; what kinds of similarities existed among like genres in terms of expression and shape; and how a certain genre became widespread over time. He published numerous books on folklore both in Turkish and in French.

BOYNER, CEM (1955–). Textile tycoon who led the unsuccessful **New Democracy Movement** (later, Party).

BOZBEYLİ, FERRUH (1927–). Politician. He served as Speaker of Parliament from 1965 to 1970. In 1970, Bozbeyli became chairman of the *Demokratik Party* and stayed in that post until 1979, when he left active politics.

BOZKURT, MAHMUT ESAT (1892–1943). Professor of law and politician. Minister of justice from 1924 until 1930, he introduced the new (Swiss) civil law in 1926 that superseded the Şeriat.

BÖLÜKBAŞI, OSMAN (1913–2002). Politician. In 1948, he founded the **Nation Party**. When the Nation Party was closed in 1953 on the grounds that it acted against **secularism**, Bölükbaşı initiated the establishment of the Republican Nation Party and became its chairman. When, in 1958, the Republican Nation Party merged with the Turkish Peasant Party to form a power block against the government party—the *Demokrat* **Party**—Bölükbaşı became the chairman of the new **Republican Peasant's Nation Party**. In 1961, he became a member of the **Constituent Assembly** that prepared the 1961 constitution. In 1962, Bölükbaşı formed a new Nation Party. In 1972, he resigned from the latter party. Bölükbaşı quit active politics the next year.

BULAÇ, ALİ (1951–). Islamic author and editor. His books include *Contemporary Concepts and Orders* [Çağdaş Kavramlar ve Düzenler], *Turkish Meaning of the Koran* [Kur'an-ı Kerim'in Türkçe Anlamı], *On the Koran and Sunnite* [Kuran ve Sünnet Üzerine], *Problems of Thought in the Islamic World* [Islam Dünyasında Düşünce Sorunları], *Humanity's Search for Freedom* [İnsanın Özgürlük Arayışı], *The Truth about the Middle East* [Ortadoğu Gerçeği], *Issues on the Agenda* [Gündemdeki Konular], *Social Change in the Islamic World* [İslam Dünyasında Toplumsal Değişme], and *An Enlightened Going Astray* [Bir Aydın Sapması].

BULGARIA. Turkey's neighbor to the northwest. Turco-Bulgarian relations have long been dominated by successive waves of forced **emigration** of the Turkish minority in Bulgaria to Turkey. Various treaties obliged Bulgaria to respect the rights and freedoms of the Turkish minority and enabled Turkey to speak on behalf of the Turkish-Muslim minority in Bulgaria. Among the said treaties are the 1878 Berlin Treaty, 1909 Istanbul Protocol and Convention, 1913 Peace Treaty, 1919 Neuilly Peace Treaty, 1925 Turkish-Bulgarian Treaty of Friendship, 1925 Turkish-Bulgarian Convention of Settlement, 1947 Bulgarian Peace Treaty, and 1968 Emigration Agreement.

Initial emigrations took place from Bulgaria to Turkey during the 1930s. They were calm migrations because they were not on a massive scale. After 1944, however, the Bulgarian government, in violation of the agreements, did not allow the voluntary emigration of the Turks in Bulgaria. Then, in 1950, the Bulgarian government suddenly changed its policy and forced the Turks to emigrate. Consequently, in 1950 and 1951, approximately 150,000 Turks immigrated to Turkey under miserable conditions. From November 1951 to 1968, emigration was again prohibited. Following the 1968 agreement, the Turks in Bulgaria once more began to immigrate to Turkey; between 1968 and 1978, about 130,000 immigrants came to Turkey from Bulgaria.

From 1984 on, the Bulgarian government again changed its policy, and this time it resorted to "ethnic cleansing" concerning the Turks in Bulgaria. The latter were deprived of the rights of publishing and receiving education in Turkish, forced to take Bulgarian names, restricted from holding religious ceremonies on such occasions as weddings, subjected to mass deportations, and the like. These developments gave rise to a frenetic diplomatic activity on the part of the Turkish government to persuade the Bulgarian government to put an end to such practices. Turkey delivered several diplomatic notes to Bulgaria, obtained sympathetic declarations from the **Islamic Conference Organization** of which it is a member, applied to the United Nations Security Council, and activated the Human Rights mechanisms of the **Conference on Security and Cooperation in Europe**. These efforts bore fruit. Bulgaria opened its frontiers in 1989 and, in three months, close to 300,000 Turks in Bulgaria literally fled to Turkey. Turkey proposed to Bulgaria the signing of a new Emigration Treaty, as the Turks coming to Turkey were deprived of everything they had left behind. Bulgaria rejected the Turkish proposal. Turkey was forced to close its borders with Bulgaria. The lot of the Turks in Bulgaria improved only after the Todor Zhikov regime collapsed. In March 1990, the Bulgarian National Assembly voted for the free choice of names by the Turkish-Bulgarians living in that country. Turkey and Bulgaria had diplomatic talks. The Movement of Rights and Freedoms, a political party that represents the 1.5 million Turkish minority in Bulgaria, was allowed to participate in the June 1990 elections (and the party won the third-largest number of seats). In the latter part of the 1990s, Bulgaria made efforts to conform to the standards of the **European Union** (EU). Consequently, Turks and Bulgarians have been freely traveling between the two countries.

Despite the long-strained relations between the two countries, trade between Turkey and Bulgaria has never come to a standstill. During the late 1970s, Turkey bought electricity from Bulgaria; in the 1990s, Turkey purchased natural gas from that country. In return, Turkey sold electricity and petroleum and extended loans to Bulgaria.

BUREAUCRACY. See CIVIL BUREAUCRACY.

BURSA. Historic city in northwest Turkey with a population of 1,998,529 (1997). King Prusias of Bithynia founded Bursa in 183 B.C.E. It was the capital of the Ottomans from 1326 to the early 15th century. In the city are found the mosques, mausoleums, and pious foundations of the first Ottoman **sultans**, who are buried there. Among the most outstanding are the Ulucami (Great Mosque), built in the years 1396–1399 by Sultan **Bayezıt I**; the Orhan Gazi Mosque, built in 1336 by Sultan Orhan; the tombs of Sultan **Osman I** and Sultan Orhan; the mausoleums of Sultan Murat II and Sultan Mehmet I; the mosque complexes of Sultans Murat I and Bayezıt I; and Yeşil Cami [Green Mosque], commissioned by Sultan Mehmet I in 1413.

– C –

CALIPH/CALIPHATE. The caliph is the **Islamic** spiritual leader with the right to legislate in areas not covered by the Islamic canonical rules. The caliph sometimes takes his place alongside a temporal ruler—the **sultan**. Under those circumstances, the caliph is at least responsible for regulating matters of personal behavior and individual relationships. Often, one person acts as both caliph and sultan. Ottoman rulers began to use the title of caliph following **Selim I's** conquest of Arab lands from 1512 to 1520, particularly to underline their preeminence in the Islamic realm and their right to promote and safeguard the Muslim religion and law. Real Ottoman claims to the caliphate were made only in periods of weakness, as in the 18th century, or when Ottoman rulers tried to hold together the Muslim peoples of the empire, as in the late 19th century. The Turkish Republic abolished the caliphate on March 3, 1924.

CALP, NECDET (1922–1999). Former private secretary of late Prime Minister **İsmet İnönü** and undersecretary of Prime Minister **Bülend Ulusu**. Calp founded and led the **Populist Party** until June 1985, when he was replaced by **Aydın Güven Gürkan**.

CANSEVER, EDİP (1928–1986). Poet of the post–**World War II** "Second New" existentialist movement (on this movement, *see* LITERATURE). Early in his poetry, Cansever depicted the hedonistic life of a wealthy **Istanbul** youth. Later, he used unaccustomed styles of poetry and surreal forms of expression. Some of the books in which Cansever's poems were published are *Evening* [İkindi Üstü], *The Gravitational Carnation* [Yerçekimli Karanfil], *Petroleum* [Petrol], *Where Is Antigoni?* [Nerede Antigone?], *Dirty August* [Kirli Ağustos], *I Am Ruhi Bey, How Am I?* [Ben Ruhi Bey Nasılım?], and *Poet's Log Book* [Şairin Seyir Defteri].

CAPITAL LEVY [Varlık Vergisi]. Passed on November 11, 1942. The aim was to tax the previously untaxed commercial wealth and to bring under control the inflationary spiral during **World War II**. Among others, some non-Muslim citizens concealed their wealth; instead of trying to catch the real culprits, the assessment committees increased the estimates of non-Muslims' capital wealth. Consequently, some non-Muslims were forced to sell all or part of their businesses or properties to pay the tax. Following the war, many non-Muslims transferred their investment and commercial activities to other countries.

CAPITULATIONS. Commercial treaties going back to 1536 by which Western states were accorded privileges of trading freely in Ottoman ports, their traders coming under the jurisdiction of their own law and consuls rather than of Muslim judges, having freedom of conscience, and being exempt from Ottoman taxes. Granted during the heyday of the empire, capitulations became a great financial burden for the Ottoman state in later centuries. They were abolished at the beginning of **World War I**.

CAPPADOCIA. Area to the west of Great Salt Lake in central Anatolia. Cappadocia was one of the principal centers of the Byzantine Empire. A great number of churches were built here. It is now an internationally focused historical site visited by tens of thousands of tourists annually.

CAVİT BEY, MEHMET (1875–1926). Economist and politician. He twice served as economy minister during the **Committee for Union and Progress** governments. Cavit Bey advised **Ankara** government at the **Lausanne Peace Treaty** (1922–1923) negotiations. He then quit active politics. He was a known critic of **Atatürk.** In 1926, he was tried on grounds that he was one of the organizers of an attempt on Atatürk's life, found guilty, and sentenced to death, which was carried out.

CEBESOY, ALİ FUAT (1882–1968). General and politician. Cebesoy was a classmate of Mustafa Kemal (**Atatürk**) at the War College. He cooperated closely with Mustafa Kemal during the **Turkish War of Independence.** In June 1920, he became commander of the Western Front and served as ambassador in Moscow between November 1920 and March 1921. In November 1924, he became a cofounder of the **Progressive Republican Party.** Between April 1939 and March 1943, he served as minister of public works; between March 1943 and August 1946, as minister of transport; and between January 1948 and November 1948, as Speaker of Parliament. Cebesoy quit active politics in 1960.

CELALİ REVOLTS. A general name given to movements and riots of dissent in Anatolia during the 16th and 17th centuries. The first revolt of this nature broke out in **Tokat** in 1519 against the suppression of the heterodox religious beliefs by the Ottoman state; a man called Celal started the revolt.

CEM, İSMAİL (1940–). Author, journalist, and politician. Cem graduated from Lausanne University Law School and has a M.A. degree from l'Institut d'Etudes Politiques de Paris. He worked as a journalist and chief editor in several newspapers in Turkey. Cem became a member of Parliament in 1995, and has served as foreign minister since 1997. In his capacity as foreign minister, he has been instrumental in realizing dramatic improvements in Turkey's relations with **Greece** in particular and the **European Union** (EU) in general. Cem is the author of *The History of Underdevelopment in Turkey* [Türkiye'de Geri Kalmışlığın Tarihi], *March the 12th* [12 Mart], and *500 Hundred Days at Turkish Radio and Television* [TRT'de 500 Gün].

CEM SULTAN (1459–1495). Ottoman crown prince. Cem Sultan struggled against his older brother Bayezıt II and briefly proclaimed his **sultanate.** Because of his eight-day sultanate, he is known as a "sultan." He is also the only Ottoman crown prince who took refuge in the West, when he finally lost against his brother. The West tried to use him against Bayezıt II. Cem Sultan grew up as an intellectual well versed in philosophy, history, geography, **music**, and Persian. He was an accomplished poet and wrote his best poems in Persian and in lyric style and prosodical meter.

CEMAL PASHA (1872–1922). Ottoman general and politician. At the turn of the century, Cemal Pasha organized the military wing of the **Committee for Union and Progress** (CUP) as well as the Committee's branch in Rumelia. Between 1909 and 1911, he served as governor of **Adana** and Baghdad. In 1913, he acted as minister of public works and then of the navy. Cemal Pasha played a crucial role in the Ottoman Empire's decision to enter **World War I** on the Central powers side. He was then appointed commander of the Fourth Army in Palestine. As one of the leaders of the CUP, he contributed significantly to domestic and **foreign policy** in the 1912–1918 period.

CENTRAL TREATY ORGANIZATION (CENTO). Mutual security organization of Turkey, **Iran**, Pakistan, and **Great Britain**, founded in 1959. CENTO succeeded the **Baghdad Pact**.

CERİDE-İ HAVADİS. The first Ottoman private daily newspaper. It was founded by an English journalist and correspondent, William Churchill, and published between 1840 and 1864.

CEVDET PASHA (1823–1895). Ottoman historian and student of law. He belonged to the group of intellectuals who had grave doubts concerning the adoption of Western codes intact. An association headed by Cevdet Pasha prepared the **Mecelle**, an outcome of the first effort in codification of **Islamic** jurisprudence. The Mecelle contains parts of civil law, torts, and civil procedural law. It was applied by secular rather than Islamic courts. Cevdet Pasha is also author of the well-known *History of Cevdet* [Tarih-i Cevdet], which deals with Ottoman history between 1774 and 1826. He also wrote historical pieces covering the late 19th century as well as a grammar book coauthored by **Fuat Pasha**. Cevdet Pasha was one of the most influential thinkers of the *Tanzimat* **(Reform) Period** (1839–1876). Being a conservative reformer, he tried to reconcile **Westernization** with tradition.

CİNDORUK, HÜSAMETTİN (1933–). Lawyer and politician. He graduated from **Ankara University's** Law School and practiced law. In May 1985, Cindoruk became the chairman of the **True Path Party**, served as the Speaker of Parliament from September 14, 1991, until October 1, 1995. On November 6, 1997, he founded the **Democratic Turkey Party**.

CINEMA. The first Turkish documentaries and newsreels were made in 1914 for the army, the same year the Army Central Cinema Agency was founded. The civilian cinema industry developed separately from the military film industry. *The Demolition of the Russian Monument in Ayestofanos,* filmed in 1914, is the first Turkish documentary. *The Wedding of Himmet Ağa,* the filming of which started in 1914 and was completed in 1919, is the first full-length movie. *Istanbul Sokakları* [The Streets of **Istanbul**] (1931) is the first Turkish film with a soundtrack. The cinema was the cheapest form of public entertainment. The founders of the Turkish Republic were not interested in movies as an instrument for spreading Republican ethics. Political leaders were only interested in keeping the movie industry under their control by enacting a severe censorship system in 1939, and, until the end of **World War II**, they did not support the industry at all. Consequently, the technical equipment remained poor and outdated. Many Turkish films were just adaptations of foreign novels, plays, or movies that had become popular in Turkey. Also, a great number of films, most of which were directed by **theater** actor **Muhsin Ertuğrul**, were heavily influenced by the theaters with long dialogues and theatrical acting.

In 1948, the Turkish Film Producers' Association managed to obtain a discount in the municipality entertainment tax. In the 1917–1948 period, the average number of films per year was two; that number shot up to 43 in the 1949–1956 period, 70 in the 1957–1960 period, 123 in the 1961–1963 period, and 220 in the 1964–1975 period. Filmmakers, however, continued to make inexpensive movies for inexpensive public consumption. On the other hand, from the mid-1950s, the film magazine *Sinema*, although published for only two years, created for the first time in Turkey an awareness of the cinema as art. This had some impact on filmmaking. Among other things, directors began to use cinematographic language. Director **Lütfiö Akad** played a crucial role here. Akad was influenced by the poetic realism of the French cinema and the American film noir as well as Turkey's own traditions. Overall, however, any improvement in the quality of movies was limited, at least until the 1970s. Filmmakers used the most popular themes of a given time until people grew tired of them. They continued to adopt big foreign hits. Escapist movies, or melodramas, and "movies with a social content" were added in the 1970s. Metin Erksan, Halit Refiğ, Ertem Göreç, **Yılmaz Güney**, and Memduh Ün were among the leading directors who made films with implicit social comment. A film of this genre, *Susuz Yaz* [Dry Summer], directed by Erksan in 1964, won an award at the Berlin Film Festival. During the same decade, movies exploiting sex proliferated. These were stopped from being shown by the military government of 1980–1983. The total number of films that had reached 609 (152 per year) in the 1976–1979 period went down to 220 (73 per year) in the period 1980–1983. During the 1980s, younger directors in particular were interested in making movies with a social content but they faced strict censorship. They took as their themes workers' woes, problems faced by urban migrants, and the like.

During the 1970s, more Turkish movies began to win awards in international festivals. Various cinema clubs that were started in the 1960s as well as several film magazines contributed to this accomplishment. Together, they made directors aware of cinema trends in various countries. Film festivals that were held in Turkey since the mid-1960s also had a positive impact on Turkish movies. Another important development was the notable relaxation of censorship on movies from the late 1980s onwards. The 1990s were the most successful years. There was a distinct improvement in the quality of films produced and an increase in the numbers of university departments providing education in this field. A generation of new directors, actors, and actresses who had received high-quality education emerged. The state provided support for the cinema. A competition developed between cinema and **television**. All of these developments contributed to the upgrading of the quality of cinema in Turkey.

In 1990, there were 354 movie houses in Turkey, with a seating capacity of 190,717. A total of 38,326 movies were shown; 18,587 of them were national production and 19,739 foreign production. Moviegoers totaled 19,233,976; of that number, 5,668,705 of them saw national productions and 13,565,271 foreign productions. **Istanbul** had 70 movie houses, **Ankara** 25, **İzmir** 19, and **Adana** 15, followed by **Gaziantep** and Hatay, 12 each, and **Bursa** with 11 movie houses.

CIVIL BUREAUCRACY. During the early Ottoman centuries (14th to 16th), the civil bureaucracy was a relatively insignificant component of the government. During the centuries of disintegration (17th and 18th), it benefited from the power vacuum at the apex. At the time, the civil bureaucratic elite became part of the ruling hierarchy comprising the **military**, Islamic, and civil bureaucracies. They shared norms deriving from neotraditionalism and **Islam**. A set of norms in the form of **Westernization** goals was to develop only when the civil bureaucratic elite began to make contacts with the West from the 18th century onward.

From the end of the 18th century, it was conceived as appropriate to diverge from the old order, which had degenerated anyway, in order to save the empire. In the process, the civil bureaucratic elite assumed the policy-making function. The **sultan** was responsible for promulgation of policy decisions, but more and more, those decisions were developed by the advisory councils of the quasi-autonomous ministries and departments and by advisory councils outside and above the ministries and councils. Sultan **Mahmut II**'s objective was to develop a bureaucracy able to save the empire through political formulae based on "reason." Several schools were established to train students for bureaucratic careers as "enlightened statesmen." This led to the development of a new breed of civil servants who viewed themselves as a cadre apart from social groups, as from the sultan.

The Republic (established in 1923) adopted the strategic decision of wholesale acceptance of Western civilization—a total transformation of the sociocultural, economic, and political life of the nation. A long-range program of educating a new generation of civil servants loyal to the Republican ideals was adopted. The formal education offered in the schools set up for this purpose was conducive for the development of an extremely elitist attitude. The Republican version of bureaucratic ruling tradition reached its zenith in the 1930s when the place of the civil bureaucracy in government rose in prominence and it adopted the Republican ideals.

In the 1950s, the bureaucratic elite unfavorably reacted to the *Demokratik Party* (DP) governments. They thought politics was no longer used to promote the interests of the nation as a whole. They complained that the new political elite dragged politics down into the streets. In reaction, the DP governments dismissed some key bureaucrats and reduced the economic status of the bureaucracy.

The 1961 **constitution** tipped the balance toward the civil bureaucratic elite in their tug-of-war with politicians by strengthening such bureaucratically staffed agencies as the Council of State and creating new agencies such as the Constitutional Court. However, in the next two decades, political governments kept on challenging the jurisdictions of these agencies and packed the bureaucracy with their supporters. These developments led to the politicization of the civil bureaucracy and a substantial decrease in its efficiency and effectiveness.

The **Motherland Party** governments that came to power in 1983 adopted a liberal economic policy, with emphasis on market forces rather than regulation from above. Their goal concerning the civil bureaucracy was to reduce the scope of the bureaucracy in economics and increase its efficiency and effectiveness. Accordingly, four policies were adopted: **privatization** of state economic enterprises, simplification of bureaucratic procedures and other organizational reforms, decentralization of government, and reduced bureaucracy at the center. Then and later, only limited success was achieved concerning these objectives. Consequently, the civil bureaucracy, which in the past was not only *object* but also *subject* of reform and modernization, on the whole remained a politicized as well as an inefficient and ineffective institution. In the 1990s, there were only some isolated pockets of efficiency and effectiveness in civil bureaucracy.

CIVIL SOCIETY. Ottoman-Turkish polity and society was long characterized by a center-periphery cleavage along cultural lines. The state was far more important than society. Political power led to economic wealth, and not vice versa. Under the circumstances, civil society could not flourish. Consequently, civil society in Turkey could begin to take root only from the 1980s onward. At the end of the 1990s, there were three basic developments. First is the rise of **Islamic** groups, which have created many foundations around which they organize for the "Islamization of society from below." Second are secular groups, which in the past had asked for the intervention of the state to block the efforts to Islamize society, and now mobilize considerable resources for democratic struggle against the Islamists. The raison d'être of both of these groups is the place and role of **religion** in society and polity. Third are groups which are organized in almost a hundred nongovernmental organizations (NGOs) and interested in such issues as **women**, the **environment**, **consumer protection**, **human rights**, disabled people, and the like. The latter favor partnerships with local governments to identify, prioritize, and solve problems. The **National Program** (March 2001), devised to conform Turkey's institutions and practices to those of the **European Union** (EU), envisages a number of measures concerning the civil society. They include "enhancing constitutional safeguards for nongovernmental organizations" and "reviewing the legislation on the freedom of association and peaceful assembly."

CİZYE. Head-tax imposed on non-Muslims in the Ottoman Empire in return for protection of their lives, properties, and religions, and for exemption from military service. It was replaced in 1856 by the *bedel-i askeri* [military service tax]. The latter tax continued to be levied until 1909.

COMMITTEE FOR UNION AND PROGRESS (CUP). Organ of the **Young Turks**, which was instrumental in bringing down **Abdülhamit II** and resulted in the proclamation of the Second Constitutional Period. The CUP played a key role from behind the scenes during the authoritarian regime of 1912–1918. **Ahmet Rıza** and **Mehmet Murat** were leading figures in the early years as theoreticians and organizers. Another important theoretician and founder was **Abdullah Cevdet**. The CUP was preceded by the Society of Union and Progress (1887), the Ottoman Union Society (1889), and the Ottoman Society of Union and Progress (1889). The Committee proclaimed itself a party in 1909. The movement developed by calling for constitutionalism, **Ottomanism**, and freedom. Some bureaucrats, army officers, and even members of the *ulema* became "Unionists." While controlling the government, the Unionists opted for central authority (as against decentralization) and the domination of the economy by the Muslim and Turkish elements (in contrast to granting autonomous rights to the religious and national **minorities**). A policy of Turkification was pursued.

The Unionists attempted some important reforms. A new system of provincial and municipal government was put into effect. In **Istanbul**, numerous new municipal services were provided. The first steps were taken in economic nationalism. The **educational** system was revamped and educational opportunities were extended for girls. A new Family Act gave **women** new rights. There emerged a vast surge of ideas and self-expression and the press was considerably expanded.

Although the CUP did not mind criticism in general, it did not tolerate criticism of itself. The leading intellectual currents of the Unionist years were **Islamism** and **Westernism**, both seeking answers to the questions of what they were trying to salvage and who they were—Muslims or Turks. The super-Westernist Abdullah Cevdet's colorfully expressed dictum—"There is no second civilization; civilization means European civilization and it must be imported with both its roses and thorns"—was later adopted by the founders of the Republic. The CUP was dissolved at the end of **World War I**, which the Ottomans along with the other Central powers lost.

COMMUNICATIONS. *See* TRANSPORTATION AND COMMUNICATIONS.

CONFERENCE ON SECURITY AND COOPERATION IN EUROPE. *See* ORGANIZATION FOR SECURITY AND COOPERATION IN EUROPE.

CONSTITUENT ASSEMBLY [Kurucu Meclis]. Established on December 16, 1961, by the National Unity Committee (NUC) of the May 27, 1961, military intervenors. It shared powers with the NUC and, on May 27, 1962, passed the 1961 **constitution**, which was then submitted to a national referendum and accepted.

CONSTITUTIONS. Turkey is presently ruled under the 1982 constitution. Turkey's constitutional history goes back to 1876 when the first Ottoman constitution was drawn up. The 1876 constitution was enacted with the ostentatious aim of limiting the **sultan**'s powers. Parliament had the right to legislate but overwhelming powers remained in the sultan's hands. Parliament could not circumvent the sultan's veto. The sultan himself could legislate by decree and often did so. The sultan appointed his ministers, who were not collectively and individually responsible to Parliament. The sultan could exile any person deemed to be dangerous to the state and prorogue Parliament, which he did in 1878 for 30 years. In 1909, at the beginning of the **Young Turks** era, the sultan was required to swear fidelity to the nation. Political power began to be transferred from the sultan and his ministers to Parliament. The Council of Ministers was made responsible to Parliament. The sultan's power to dissolve Parliament was greatly circumscribed. However, the **Committee for Union and Progress**, which dominated the Young Turk era of 1909–1918 and was influential in government, forced through a constitutional amendment that strengthened the executive over Parliament. The sovereignty of the nation was first accorded its full recognition in a constitutional document in 1921 when the **Turkish War of Independence** (1920–1922) was in full swing. The 1924 constitution, primarily as a reaction to the earlier supremacy of the executive, concentrated all powers in the assembly. During the single-party years (1923–1945), the **Republican People's Party** and, in the 1950–1960 period, the *Demokrat* **Party**, dominated Parliament. Consequently, the 1961 constitution (enacted in the wake of the 1960 military intervention) dispersed powers. A constitutional court, a second chamber, and the **National Security Council** were created.

The powers of the Council of State (the Turkish version of France's *Conseil d'Etat*) were bolstered. The Radio and **Television** Agency was granted autonomy and the scope of basic rights and liberties was significantly expanded. As the new freedoms granted by the 1961 constitution were perceived to be abused following the March 12, 1971, **military** intervention, the constitution was significantly amended to limit liberty and democracy and to promote order. The basic rights and liberties were somewhat curtailed. The National Security Council was now empowered to "advise" the Council of Ministers, not just to provide "information." The Constitutional Court was barred from testing the constitutional validity of constitutional amendments; only procedural aspects of such amendments could be reviewed by the court.

The present 1982 constitution was drafted following the 1980 military intervention. In the eyes of the framers of the 1982 constitution, the Turkish polity was excessively fragmented and polarized and the judicial and bureaucratic arms of government overly politicized during the previous decade. Distrustful of other governmental organs, the framers of the constitution placed the president in the position of guardian of the state. The president is to "ensure the implementation of the Constitution, and the steady and harmonious functioning of the state organs" (Article 4). The president has wide powers of appointment to the Constitutional Court, Council of State, Military Court of Appeals, Supreme Council of Judges and Prosecutors, and High Court of Appeal. The president is also chairman of the National Security Council, which has the right to submit its views on state security to the Council of Ministers, which evaluates them. The 1982 constitution also strengthened the prime minister vis-à-vis the individual ministers and the Council of Ministers over the assembly. The prime minister may now drop a minister from the cabinet without the whole council having to resign; the Council of Ministers' powers to rule by decree-law are widened. In the constitution, basic rights and liberties are hedged about by many qualifications. The State Security Courts were established. The constitution was approved in a referendum (where voting was compulsory) by 91 percent of those who voted (also 91 percent).

The new constitution was formulated with the purpose of preventing the political crises of the 1970s from recurring. It thus placed greater emphasis on prudent leadership than on political participation. After a decade of living with it, from the mid-1980s onward, politicians became in favor of bolstering the liberal and democratic dimensions of the constitution. Intellectuals' constant criticism of the "illiberal" aspects of the constitution and, later, the wish to accede to the **European Union** (EU), were contributory factors. The most important amendments to the constitution included repealing the two paragraphs of the preamble referring to the necessity and legitimacy of the 1980 military intervention, doing away with the bans on political activities of **unions**, associations, **foundations**, **cooperatives**, and public professional associations and allowing cooperation between political parties and these civil societal associations, permitting political parties to establish **women**'s and **youth** branches, foundations, and organizations in other countries, lowering the voting age as well as that of party membership from 21 to 18, recognizing the right to unionize (but not the right to strike or to conclude collective agreements) to public employees, allowing college professors and students to become members of political parties, making it possible for the Constitutional Court to close a political party only if the party as a whole became a *focus* of challenge to the basic characteristics of the Republic (including the principle of secularism), totally civilizing the State Security Courts, providing a legal base for **privatization**, and recognizing the seeking of arbitration in cases involving foreign firms.

CONSULTATIVE ASSEMBLY [Danışma Meclisi]. Set up on July 1, 1981. This body was carefully selected by the 1980 **military** intervenors. The assembly was to prepare the draft of a constitution and perform necessary legislative functions; its draft bills were finalized by the **National Security Council** (NSC) comprising the five generals who had carried out the 1980 military intervention. The

1982 **constitution** prepared by the Consultative Assembly was given its final shape by the NSC.

CONSUMER PROTECTION. In 1994, the Law for the Protection against Unfair Competition went into effect, and the Competition Board was formed. The board takes measures that provide for the operation of the rules of competition in **privatization** applications. In 1996, a consumer council was established, which among other things engages in such activities as educating and informing customers, encouraging them to get organized, and protecting their rights as customers. The state is also obliged to be involved in similar activities. For this purpose, the Ministry of Industry and Trade holds meetings and publishes books and magazines.

COOPERATIVES. Cooperatives in Turkey hark back to the second half of the 19th century. In 1867, the first cooperative law was enacted, and in 1888, the Agricultural Bank was set up. Some regard the establishment of the fig producers union in 1914 as the real beginning of the cooperative movement.

In the post-1923 Republican period, **Atatürk** supported the forming of cooperatives, because, in his opinion, cooperatives could be a means of democratic participation and a more even distribution of economic benefits. In the process, the state became the guide to the movement, which, of course, worked against the ideal of "democratic participation." However, the 1944 National Cooperative Congress, the first of its kind, partially saved the movement from the tutelage of the state. During **World War II** and its aftermath, the movement benefited from the European experience. In 1946, the Possessions Credit Bank of Turkey [Türkiye Emlak Kredi Bankası] (in 1988, Possessions Bank) was established to provide cheap credit to cooperatives and their members. By 1996, there were 50,150 cooperatives with a combined membership of 8,081,100. The sectors into which they were divided included the following: **agriculture**—6,627 associations with 3,001,556 members; consumer—2,077/457,045; credit unions—3,319/2,570,831; fisheries—313/15,783; housing—33,336/1,655,853; independent retailers—124/8,968; insurance—1,215; social care—3/983; and transport—2,184/104,070. Cooperative membership constituted 12.9 percent of the population.

COUNCIL OF HIGHER EDUCATION [Yüksek Öğretim Kurulu]. Better known by the Turkish acronym YÖK. Set up on November 6, 1981, it was empowered to supervise the administration of the universities, including such significant areas as promotions and admissions.

CRIMEAN WAR (1853–1856). Erupted out of a conflict between **Russia** on the one hand, and **Great Britain** and **France** on the other, over the issue of who would dominate the Middle East as the Ottoman Empire declined. The British and French troops fought on the side of the Ottomans and against the Russians. The war ended with the Treaty of Paris in March 1856. All sides agreed to evacuate territory taken during the war. Russia, Great Britain, and France, as well as Austria and Prussia, which also participated at the peace conference, declared their joint guarantee of the territorial integrity and independence of the Ottoman Empire.

CUMALI, NECATİ (1921–). Poet, short story writer, and playwright. Cumalı's work reflects a combination of realism and optimism. The author's style is to describe rather than change the society in which he lives. Cumalı's verse as well as his prose have been written in a simple, nonornamental style and reflect psychological insights. His best-known works are the play *Wooden Shoes* [Nalınlar] and the short story "Dry Summer" [Susuz Yaz], the title story of a collection of eight stories. His play *Buried Treasure* [Gömü] and his novel *Tobacco Time* [Tütün Zamanı] have also attracted widespread attention.

CUMHURİYET [Republic]. The first major newspaper of the Turkish Republic, founded on May 7, 1924. Initially, it espoused the Republican norms formulated by **Atatürk** and his associates. During recent decades, it has become an advocate of leftist views.

CUSTOMS UNION. The Customs Union (CU) with the **European Union** (EU) was concluded on January 1, 1996, following the overhauling by Turkey of its legal system. The CU gives Turkey improved access to the group of countries making up the Common Market. It guarantees the free circulation of goods. Customs duties and charges have been abolished and quantitative restrictions on goods prohibited. Among other policies, the CU involves the harmonization of Turkey's intellectual property laws with those of the EU, and extends market and competition rules to the Turkish economy.

CYPRUS PROBLEM. Between 1571 and 1878, Cyprus was under Ottoman rule. In 1878, the Ottoman Empire, threatened by tsarist **Russia**, gave the island to the British in return for a defense post there and annual payments. In 1914, the British annexed the island. Following **World War II**, the Greek Cypriots wished to obtain independence from **Great Britain** and sought the union of Cyprus with **Greece**, or *enosis*. This was unacceptable to the Turkish Cypriots. In 1960, the island became an independent republic, with governmental powers divided between the two communities, and Turkey, Greece, and Great Britain acting as guarantors of the independence and sovereignty of the Republic of Cyprus. Soon the Greek Cypriots attempted to steer the republic toward *enosis* with Greece. When the Turkish Cypriots opposed these moves, intercommunal strife broke out. EOKA, a Greek Cypriot terrorist organization, led the Greek Cypriot efforts to intimidate the Turkish Cypriots, which included pillage of property and killings. In 1964, the United Nations (UN) sent a peacekeeping force to the island, which remains there to this day. The UN force could not, of course, restore the constitutional system that had collapsed. The Turkish Cypriots could no longer take part in government; the Turkish Cypriots had escaped to safe havens—isolated enclaves on the island—to protect themselves from the numerically superior Greek Cypriots.

On July 15, 1974, a coup was staged on the island against President Archbishop Makarios by the more impatient Greek Cypriot elements who wanted to make the island part of Greece immediately. The fomenters of the coup declared the island the "Hellenic Republic of Cyprus," named EOKA member Nicos Sampson as its president, and started systematic intimidation including the massacre of Turkish Cypriots. Consequently, after consultation with Britain, Turkey used its right of intervention under the 1960 treaty to restore the independence of Cyprus and invaded the northern part of the island. In the months that followed, many Greek Cypriots living in the north moved to the south and many Turkish Cypriots living in the south did the opposite. This was followed by the establishment of the Turkish Federated State of Cyprus in the north. By establishing this state, Turkish Cypriots sought to establish a federation in Cyprus with the Greek Cypriots. The Greek Cypriots opposed the idea. As the two communities could not agree on a federal solution, on November 15, 1983, the Turkish Cypriots proclaimed the Turkish Republic of Northern Cyprus (TRNC). The international community has not recognized the TRNC.

Since 1983, intercommunal negotiations under the UN auspices have been taking place but no substantive agreement has been reached to date. Turkey has been committed to achieving a freely negotiated solution. According to Turkey, an international solution can only bear fruit if it is built on the existing realities on the island. The starting point for properly addressing the Cyprus issue should be the existence of two equal states on the island, sovereign in their internal affairs. Turkey opts for a confederal political structure. Although the Greek Cypriots long for the *status ante*, the Turkish Cypriots reject being once again relegated to a minority status.

Turkey expressed its objections when recently the **European Union** (EU) started accession negotiations with the Greek Cypriot side, arguing that it is against the idea of balance between the two communities on the island set up by the 1960 agreement between Great Britain, Greece, and Turkey. Displeased by this particular development, in July 1999, Turkey and the TRNC decided to deepen their relationships "with the target set at the highest level" and sign a special relationship agreement. Then, in December 1999 when the EU granted Turkey candidate state status, the Union made it clear that it expects the parties to reach a solution by 2004, and that if such a solution is not found until said date, following a review of the situation, it may admit the Greek Cypriot side to the European Union.

Ç

ÇAĞLAR, BEHÇET KEMAL (1908–1969). Poet. A nationalist and fervent admirer of **Atatürk**. He was influenced by folk poetry. A comprehensive poetry anthology of his is *From within Me* [Benden İçeri]. *From Dolmabahçe Palace to* the *Mausoleum* [Dolmabahçe'den Anıt Kabir'e Kadar] is a biography of Atatürk by Çağlar.

ÇAĞLAYANGİL, İHSAN (1908–1993). Politician. He became minister of labor in 1965 and served as minister of foreign affairs in the 1965–1971 and 1975–1977 periods. In 1976, he became Speaker of the Senate, and from April 1980 until September 1980, was acting president. Çağlayangil was basically a Westernist. During the 1970s, however, he contributed to Turkey's efforts to develop closer relations with the Middle Eastern countries.

ÇAKMAK, FEVZİ (1876–1950). General and politician. The Turkish Republic's first chief of the general staff, he served in that capacity from October 1922 until January 1944. From 1946 to 1948, he was a member of Parliament from the *Demokrat* **Party**. In 1948, he became one of the founders of the **Nation Party** and its honorary chairman. Çakmak was later criticized for not making the necessary efforts to modernize the **military** while he had been chief of the general staff.

ÇALLI, İBRAHİM (1882–1960). Leading impressionistic painter. Çallı used warm colors and flickering light effects. The so-called Çallı group formed the Society of Ottoman Painters in 1914. In 1921, the latter's name was changed to the Society of Turkish Artists.

ÇAMLIBEL, FARUK NAFİZ (1898–1973). Patriotic and sentimental poet. Along with others, Çamlıbel gave a sense of novelty to the first decade of poetry in the Republican period. He was considered a master of the meter style. First and foremost a nationalist poet, Çamlıbel often used his poems as didactic vehicles as well as a source of aesthetic enjoyment. "Inn Walls" [Han Duvarları], the title poem of a collection of his poems, is his best-known work. Çamlıbel also wrote plays; *The Beast of Prey* [Canavar], *The Attack* [Akın] and *Native Home* [Özyurt] are some of these plays. *Rain of Stars* [Yıldız Yağmuru] is Çamlıbel's sole novel.

ÇATAL HÜYÜK. Turkey's most important archaeological site. Situated in south central Anatolia about 40 kilometers south of **Konya**, it was discovered in 1958. Dating back to 6800 B.C.E., it is the most ancient Neolithic site yet found in Anatolia. Its discovery led to an enormous increase in our knowledge about the Neolithic and Bronze Age cultures in Anatolia.

ÇAVDAR, AYHAN O. (1930–). Professor of pediatric oncology and hematology. Çavdar, whose work includes the study of malignant lymphomas, acute leukemia, and abnormal hemoglobins, was the president of the **Turkish Academy of Sciences** from 1994 until 2000.

ÇELEBİ. Title of Ottoman prince.

ÇERKEZ ETHEM (1880–1950). Militia leader. Çerkez Ethem took part in the initial struggle against the invading forces following **World War I**. He became a rebel when Mustafa Kemal's (**Atatürk's**) **Ankara** government decided to convert all militia into a regular army. The Ankara government was forced to divert some of its forces from the main goal of liberating Turkey from invading Allied (mainly Greek) forces, in order to quell the Çerkez Ethem rebellion. Ultimately, Çerkez Ethem took refuge with the Greek forces.

ÇİFT BOZAN RESMİ. Ottoman "tax for disrupting cultivation." This tax was paid by the cultivator for permission to abandon his plot. The system was based on the idea that all wealth (though not necessarily all property) belonged to the **sultan**, who had the duty of seeing to it that all the arable lands were fully cultivated.

ÇİLLER, TANSU (1944–). College professor and politician. Çiller came to the public eye by her pointed criticisms of **Turgut Özal's** economic policies. She was recruited to the **True Path Party** (TPP) in November 1990, was elected member of Parliament in the October 1991 general election, and served as the minister of state responsible for economic affairs in the TPP-**Social Democratic Populist Party** (SDPP) coalition government formed following the election. Çiller was elected chairman of the TPP on June 13, 1993, and served as Turkey's first female prime minister from June 1993 until February 1996 in three successive coalition governments that the TPP formed, once with the SDPP and twice with the (new) **Republican People's Party**. In June 1996, Çiller became deputy prime minister in the coalition government that the TPP had formed with the religiously oriented **Welfare Party**. That coalition ended in June 1997. On several occasions, the Parliament accused Çiller of various misdemeanors while prime minister, but in each case, she was saved by parliamentary arithmetic of coalition formation and/or maintenance.

– D –

DAĞLARCA, FAZIL HÜSNÜ (1914–). Poet. In his most important poems, he addressed himself to social contradictions and the lot of the workers. Dağlarca also produced work that took as its subject matter humankind, nature, and the supernatural. Dağlarca, who won international awards, is considered to have written some of the most vigorous Turkish poetry of the mid-20th century. His complete works to 1979 are found in the *Dağlarca Series* [Dağlarca Dizisi] (13 volumes.)

DALAN, BEDRETTIN (1941–). Engineer, bureaucrat, industrialist, and politician. He was one of the founders of the **Motherland Party**, served as metropolitan mayor of **Istanbul**, and formed the **Democratic Center Party** (DCP). The DCP did not make an impact on Turkish politics. Dalan is best known as an activist and successful mayor.

DAMAT FERİT PASHA (1853–1923). Grand vizier. He was son-in-law of Sultan **Abdülmecit**. Damat Ferit was a founder of the Freedom and Concord Party, which was formed as a rival party to the **Committee for Union and Progress** in 1911. He formed five governments when **Istanbul** was under Allied occupation following **World War II**. Trusting in the British, Damat Ferit tried to suppress the national resistance movement in Anatolia.

DEDE. In the **Alevi** community, the dedes are the leaders of religious ceremony and the transmitters of sacred knowledge to the community. Being a dede is inherited through patrilineage.

DEDE KORKUT STORIES. Tales in the line of old epic literature (on this literature, *see* LITERATURE). They were converted into written form about the end of the 14th and beginning of the 15th centuries. In places, the tales resemble Greek mythology.

DEED OF ALLIANCE [Sened-i İttifak]. Signed in 1808 by four leading local notables and the **sultan**. The local notables promised to help the sultan with collection of taxes, recruitment to the army, and maintenance of law and order. The sultan gave his official recognition to the local notables.

DEFENSE. According to the **constitution**, the president is the commander-in-chief of the **armed forces**. The chief of general staff is the commander of the armed forces; in times of war, he performs the duties of the commander-in-chief on behalf of the president. The chief of general staff is nominated by the cabinet and appointed by the president. The chief of general staff determines the principles and priorities in **military** education and training, personnel deployment, organization, strategic planning and logistical services; insures that the army, navy, and air force comply with those principles; and prioritizes and exercises overall operational control over the three forces. The decisions related to the form and the application of the national defense policy are discussed at the **National Security Council** and then recommended to the government.

The Ministry of Defense is a parallel organization. The minister is a member of the cabinet. However, many, including the top staff members of the ministry, are military officers. The tasks of the ministry are conscription to services; supply of weapons, material and equipment; logistical services; health and veterinary services; construction, real estate, settlement, and infrastructure services; and financial and auditing services. By drawing upon domestic resources, the Turkish defense industry companies produce and develop the systems and equipment needed by the Turkish Armed Forces in such fields as aviation, missiles and rockets, military electronics, military shipbuilding, armored vehicles, and the ammunition for weapons.

Turkey's defense policy is based on **Atatürk**'s principle of "peace at home and peace abroad." Turkey is a member of the **North Atlantic Treaty Organization**

(NATO). The responsibilities and commitments resulting from NATO membership form the mandatory principles of Turkish security policy. Turkey attributes great importance to the arrangement of peacekeeping activities under the control of the United Nations (UN) and the **Organization for Security and Cooperation in Europe** (OSCE). It sent troops to Korea under the UN umbrella in 1950, participated in humanitarian aid activities in Somalia in 1993, and undertook active duties in providing peace in Bosnia-Herzegovina and Afghanistan.

The **Gulf crisis** and the ensuing war erupted at a time when some Western countries were raising questions about whether Turkey was still a strategically important country, in view of the dramatic changes in the Soviet Union (*see* RUSSIA) and Eastern Europe, which led to the demise of the Warsaw Pact. In the post–Gulf War era, the NATO countries once again perceive Turkey as a key ally for maintaining stability in the Middle East.

The land forces comprise four armies. The air force consists of the First Tactical Air Force, Second Tactical Airforce, Air Training Command, and Supply Units and Establishments. The navy consists of the Northern Area Sea Command, Southern Area Sea Command, Naval Training Command, War Fleet Command, Submarine Fleet Command, Mine Fleet Command, and one Landing Units Command. As of 1998, Turkey had 639,000 active troops and 378,000 reserve troops, 4,205 tanks, 21 frigates, 15 submarines, and 18 combat aircraft squadrons. That year the defense budget stood at $8.2 billion. *See also* MILITARY AND POLITICS.

DEMİREL, SÜLEYMAN (1924–). Politician. Demirel graduated from **Istanbul Technical University** in 1949 as a civil engineer and worked as a civil servant until 1960. During those years, he twice spent brief periods in the **United States**. In 1962, he joined the **Justice Party** (JP) and in November 1964, he became its chairman. In February 1965, Demirel was made minister of state and deputy prime minister in the **Suat Hayri Ürgüplü** coalition government, while still not a member of Parliament. Following the JP's victory in the November 10, 1965, general elections, he became prime minister of the JP government. On March 12, 1971, his government resigned when the military issued a memorandum that contained certain policy demands and indicated they would intervene if those demands were not met.

In the October 14, 1973, general elections—the first elections following the reinstatement of party politics—the Justice Party came in second and a new period of coalition governments began in Turkish politics. During this period, Demirel headed three governments: the First Nationalist Front (coalition) government that was formed in March 1975 and comprised the Justice Party, **National Salvation Party**, **Nationalist Action Party**, and **Republican Reliance Party**; the Second Nationalist Front (coalition) government that was formed in August 1977 and comprised the Justice Party, National Salvation Party, and Nationalist Action Party; and finally the minority government of the Justice Party (supported by the National Salvation Party and Nationalist Action Party from outside) formed in November 1979.

On September 12, 1980, the military once again intervened—the third intervention in the Republican period—and removed the Demirel government from power for the second time. Along with other pre-1980 political leaders, Demirel was banned from active politics for 10 years. From behind the scenes, Demirel masterminded the formation of the **Grand Turkey Party**, which was not, however, allowed by the military to take part in the November 1983 general elections, and the **True Path Party** (TPP). On September 6, 1987, the ban against Demirel and other pre-1980 political leaders taking part in active politics was lifted at a national referendum. On September 24, 1987, Demirel became chairman of the TPP, which came in third in the November 1987 general elections. In the October 1991 general elections Demirel's TPP came in first; the True Path Party-**Social Democratic Populist Party** coalition was formed and Demirel headed that coalition government until May 16, 1993, when he became president of the Republic. After having displayed an activist and responsible presidency for the constitutionally specified seven-year term, Demirel stepped down from that office on May 16, 2000.

DEMOCRACY PARTY (DP)/DEMOKRASİ PARTİSİ (DEP). Formed on May 7, 1993, the party was a defender of Kurdish (*see* KURDS) views. It succeeded the **People's Labor Party**. Its leader, Hatip Dicle, made provocative statements against the Republic of Turkey. The DP was closed by the Constitutional Court on June 16, 1994. In Turkey, separatist Kurdish parties are not allowed. *See also* PEOPLE'S DEMOCRACY PARTY.

DEMOCRATIC CENTER PARTY (DCP)/DEMOKRAT MERKEZ PARTİSİ (DMR). Founded in May 1990, by **Bedrettin Dalan**, the former metropolitan mayor of **Istanbul** from the **Motherland Party**. The party did not have an impact on Turkish politics. It disbanded itself and joined the **True Path Party** in September 1991.

DEMOCRATIC LEFT PARTY (DLP)/DEMOKRATİK SOL PARTİ (DSP). The party was founded on November 14, 1985, by Rahşan Ecevit, wife of former and present Prime Minister **Bülent Ecevit**. At the time, B. Ecevit's political rights, which had been taken away from him (along with other pre-1980 politicians), had not yet been returned. B. Ecevit (henceforth Ecevit), who was still looked upon as the natural leader of the Turkish social democratic movement, was naturally closely associated with the DLP.

In the post-1980 period, Ecevit felt betrayed by his close associates in the then defunct **Republican People's Party** (RPP), as in his opinion these former associates did not support him in his struggle against the **military** authorities. The constant bickering on the part of the factions within the old RPP put him off. A related point is that Ecevit had also become disenchanted with the far left. Consequently, in the early 1980s, the Ecevits kept their distance from both the **Populist Party** (PP) and the **Social Democracy Party** (SDP), and remained reluctant to join forces with these left-of-center parties. They were also very choosy when the PP and SDP deputies wished to join their party.

The DLP was unable to achieve a substantial showing in the 1986 by-elections, despite Ecevit's (illegal) campaigning for the party. With the lifting of the political bans in a nationwide referendum in September 1987, Ecevit became the chairperson of the party and his wife, Rahşan, took on the job of deputy chairperson.

In the 1987 general elections, the DLP could not pass a 10 percent nationwide barrier for representation in Parliament. The Ecevits quit politics and Necdet Karababa was elected chairman with their backing. The polls showed a decline in public support for the DLP under Karababa's leadership. The Ecevits returned to the party and to their previous posts in the party at the beginning of 1989.

Ecevit continued to reject taking part in a merger in the left of the political spectrum. He thought that the **Social Democratic Populist Party** (SDPP) (the other major left-of-center party from the end of 1985 onward) had not cleansed itself of the far left. Ecevit came up with concrete policies while the SDPP hardly took such initiatives.

Ecevit continued to have charisma with the crowds. The opposition in the DLP led by Karababa, however, accused the Ecevits of ruling the party in an authoritarian manner and not allowing the party to flourish.

In the October 1991 general elections, the DLP received 10.8 percent of the votes nationwide and returned seven members to Parliament. Because the **True Path Party** and the SDPP formed the government, the DLP remained in opposition. Ecevit decided not to participate in the opening convention of the new Republican People's Party in September 1992, and rejected calls for the merger of his party with the reestablished RPP. The new party emerged as a new and threatening rival to the DLP. By October 1992, the DLP had lost one deputy to the new party, and many members, including Karababa, had resigned from the party.

In the December 1995 elections, the DSP's votes increased to 14.7 percent, and the party returned 76 members to Parliament. In June 1997, the DSP formed a coalition government with the **Motherland Party** (MP) and the **Democratic Turkey Party**; the government was led by **Mesut Yılmaz** of the MP. This was followed by a DSP minority government (January 1999). In the April 18, 1999, general elections, the DSP captured the plurality of votes (22.1 percent), and Ecevit formed a coalition government with **Devlet Bahçeli's Nationalist Action Party** and **Mesut Yılmaz's** MP, he himself becoming prime minister. This last coalition government turned out to be a harmoniously functioning coalition government that took courageous decisions to bring down inflation and articulate the Turkish economy to the global one. In 2001, it directed its efforts to achieve Turkey's accession to the **European Union** (EU) as a full member.

DEMOCRATIC TURKEY PARTY (DTP)/DEMOKRATİK TÜRKİYE PARTİSİ (DTP). Founded on November 6, 1991, by **Hüsamettin Cindoruk**. In June 1997, the party joined a coalition government by the **Motherland Party**

and **Democratic Left Party.** Following the fall of this coalition in January 1999, the DTP became a moribund party.

DEMOKRAT **PARTY (DP)/DEMOKRAT PARTİ (DP).** Following **World War II,** partly as a consequence of the Soviet Union's (*see* RUSSIA) expansionist policies, Turkey drew closer to the Anglo-American axis. At the same time, a new class of entrepreneurs began opposing the statist policies of the ruling **Republican People's Party** (RPP). Finally, some within the educated and **Westernized** elite began pressing for a more pluralistic political regime. As a consequence, in 1945, four deputies of the RPP—**Celal Bayar, Refik Koraltan, Fuat Köprülü,** and **Adnan Menderes**—resigned from their parties and formed the *Demokrat* Party. In 1950, the DP won a landslide victory, and put an end to the RPP hegemony over Turkish politics.

The DP, led by Adnan Menderes as prime minister, reversed the statist policies of the earlier decades and began to place more emphasis on market forces. At the same time, particularly when the economic boom years of the early 1950s came to an end and the party began to lose popularity among the people, the DP condoned occasional infringement of the Republic's main principles, especially that of **secularism.** These policies and their authoritarian posture in the late 1950s brought the Democrats into conflict with the bureaucratic elite. The DP government was toppled from power by a **military** intervention on May 27, 1960, and the DP was closed.

The National Unity Committee of the military junta arrested the DP deputies, including Bayar and Menderes. After dramatic trials, Menderes and his finance minister (**Hasan Polatkan**) and foreign minister (**Fatin Rüştü Zorlu**) were hanged. The death penalty was also given to 10 other prominent DP members, but these latter sentences were commuted to life terms. These Democrats, along with others who received relatively lighter sentences, later benefited from a political amnesty.

In summer 1992, the pre-1980 political parties were allowed to be reestablished. The DP was reopened in September 1992 by some of its and the **Justice Party**'s surviving members. At the time, the new DP seemed to have no chance of flourishing against the two main rightist parties—the **True Path Party** (TPP) and the **Motherland Party.** Indeed, the new DP soon dissolved itself and merged with the TPP.

DEMOKRATİK **PARTY (DP)/DEMOKRATİK PARTİ (DP).** A splinter party from the **Justice Party** (JP). **Ferruh Bozbeyli,** the JP's respected Parliament speaker, formed it in 1970. The party represented the local-rural interests against the urban-industrial interests. The party refused to enter into a coalition with the JP after the 1973 general elections. In 1975, half of its deputies switched to the JP. In the October 1977 general elections, the party won just one seat in Parliament. It was closed, along with other parties in existence at the time, by the 1980 **military** junta.

DERELİ, CEVAT (1900–1989). Painter. He was the leading member of the group that formed the Society of Independent Painters and Sculptors in 1928. Dereli painted folkloric scenes in which geometrical masses often seem to be blended with two-dimensional forms.

DERVİŞ, KEMAL (1949–). Economist and politician. Derviş obtained B.A. and master's degrees from the London School of Economics and a Ph.D. degree from Princeton University. He taught at the **Middle East Technical University** and Princeton University, and served as senior deputy director of the World Bank. When the economy faced a financial crisis in late February 2001 (*see* MONETARY AND FISCAL POLICY), he was asked to return to Turkey and take up the post of minister of state responsible for the economy. In this post, he tried to introduce into Turkey a new economic philosophy: the state does not set the parameters of the economy; the market sets those parameters; the state intervenes only when necessary.

DERVİŞ VAHDETİ (1869–1909). Ottoman journalist. In his journal *Volcano* [Volkan], which he started to publish in December 1908, he vehemently opposed the **Committee for Union and Progress.** In April 1909, he founded the Association for the Union of Mohammedans, and *Volcano* became the mouthpiece of this association. Through these activities, Derviş Vahdeti played an important role in the religiously colored rebellion in **Istanbul** on April 13, 1909. A special army had to be dispatched to Istanbul from Salonica to quell the uprising. Derviş Vahdeti was tried at a court-martial and hanged.

DEVŞİRME SYSTEM. Conscription of non-Muslim youths for conversion and service to the Ottoman **sultan.** Some of the youths in question reached the highest positions in the Empire. The system was in effect from the late 14th century to the early 17th century.

DIASPORA. Turks living abroad mostly reside in Europe, North America, the Middle East, and Australia. In 1997, the largest concentration of Turkish citizens was in **Germany** (2.1 million), followed by the Netherlands (284,902), **France** (274,747), Austria (142,231), Saudi Arabia (120,000), the **United States** (85,505), Switzerland (79,556), Belgium (78,532), **Great Britain** (61,300), Australia (49,724), and Sweden (35,831). The total number of Turks living abroad in 1997 was 3,455,402. Of these, 3,122,764 lived in Western Europe, 137,380 in the Middle East and North Africa, and 175,358 in other countries.

Turks living in the United States are overwhelmingly in the professions. They have virtually no integration problems with the host country. Until the mid-1970s, they were hardly organized. The U.S. government's weapons embargo against Turkey in 1975, in the wake of the Turkish invasion of **Cyprus** the previous year, gave rise to nationalistic feelings among Turks in the United States and convinced them of the need to pool their resources and defend Turkey's interests.

From 1975 to 1978, 39 Turkish-American associations were established. Twenty of them, based in New York, New Jersey, and Connecticut, formed an umbrella organization in New York City in 1978—the Federation of Turkish-American Associations. The establishment of the Assembly of Turkish-American Associations in 1976 in Washington, D.C., that brought under one roof all the Turkish-American Associations in the United States followed this. The assembly, federation, and individual associations work in close cooperation with the Institute of Turkish Studies, set up in 1982 in Washington, D.C. (with a grant from the Turkish government), and the Information Center of the Turkish Embassy. The latter engages in lobbying and similar activities on behalf of the mother country.

In countries other than the United States, workers make up a significant portion of the Turks in the diaspora. In 1997, there were 978,578 Turkish workers abroad. Of this number, 559,842 of them worked in Germany, 115,000 in Saudi Arabia, 65,798 in France, 46,181 in Austria, 36,280 in Great Britain, 33,088 in Switzerland, 33,000 in the Netherlands, and 16,950 in Australia. Particularly in Europe and Australia (that is, in countries more developed than Turkey), many of the Turkish workers are in the manufacturing and construction sectors.

Turkish workers who first went to Western European countries were more qualified than workers from other labor-exporting countries; the rate of skilled labor among the Turkish workers was 35 percent versus 21 percent among others. The Turkish population in Western Europe is quite young. Turkish children in Germany make up the largest group among all foreigners attending grade school, yet their numbers decrease at higher levels and, consequently, the transition from school to a career proves difficult.

As of 1991, the Turkish state **television** began broadcasting in Turkish to all the Western European countries. Today, several Turkish newspapers have daily European editions, printed in Europe. Some of these newspapers have nationalistic or religious overtones. Most of the Turks in Europe read exclusively Turkish dailies. Video recorders are widespread among Turks in Western Europe; Turks in Europe spend long hours watching Turkish video films, which often have nationalistic religious messages.

There are numerous Turkish cultural organizations, mosques, education centers, Islamic schools, shops, and stores in Europe. Consulting and translating offices run by professional translators and hired by employers were the first Turkish ventures in Europe; they were set up in the early 1960s. These were followed by similar organizations established by the workers themselves with students replacing the professional translators. Workers' organizations dealt particularly with working and housing conditions. The first Turkish umbrella organization in Europe was the Federation of Students' Associations founded in Germany in 1970.

Between 1971 and 1975, Turks established several left-leaning political organizations. Some of these organizations attracted many Marxist intellectuals and were not active at the grassroots level. Others worked in the social and cultural areas and, among other things, provided translation services, held language courses and home country evenings, and dealt with immigration problems. Also during the 1970s, several right-wing-inclined organizations were formed, some of them having direct links with or at least sympathies for different political parties in Turkey. The 1980 **military** intervention in Turkey gave rise to a new wave of Turkish political refugees and asylum-seekers in Europe. The members of the latter group further politicized the left-leaning organizations, and these organizations started to pay less attention to the individual migrant's problems. As of the 1960s, **Islamic** organizations also began to be formed by Turks in Europe. The initial impetus for such organizations came from the Turks' search for a place to worship. Several mosque associations followed. In the 1970s, a number of Islamic Culture Centers were established that provided courses in religion. Large numbers of Turkish students attended these courses. In 1977, the religiously oriented **National Salvation Party** in Turkey founded the European National View Organization in Cologne, Germany. This organization came to have a large membership (as early as 1992, about 27,000). In 1982, the Turkish government, through the state-controlled Turkish Piety Organization, established a Piety Foundation Turkish-Islamic Union in Berlin. A chapter of the foundation was opened in Cologne in 1985. The foundation follows the official **secularist** line of the Turkish state. By 1992, 60 percent (or a little over 1,000) mosque associations in Germany had become members of the foundation.

DIRANAS, AHMET MUHİP (1909–1980). Poet and playwright. Dıranas tried to create a fourth dimension with words. In his poetry, he combined a traditional lyricism with unusual metaphors. *Poems* [Şiirler] and *Broken Lute* [Kırık Saz] are two collections of his poems. In his plays—*Shadows* [Gölgeler], *He Would Not Have Had It Thus* [O Böyle İstemezdi], and *Blind Alley* [Çıkmaz Sokak]— Dıranas blended psychological insight with prose.

DİLİPAK, ABDURRAHMAN (1949–). Journalist and author. Dilipak is one of the leading **Islamic** thinkers. His books include *Islamist Fighters* [Islam Savaşçıları], *Where Is Turkey Heading?* [Türkiye Nereye Gidiyor?], *Woman from a Different Perspective* [Bir Başka Açıdan Kadın], *Yes Unity But How?* [Evet Vahdet Ama Nasıl?], *The Road to Republic* [Cumhuriyete Giden Yol], *Toward an Islamic Community* [Islam Cemaatine Doğru], *Laicism* [Laisizm], *Problems, Questions, and Answers* [Sorunlar, Sorular ve Cevaplar], and *Constitution and Democracy* [Anayasa ve Demokrasi].

DİNAMO, HASAN İZZETTİN (1909–1989). Novelist and poet. Dinamo was a leading member of the group called the "1940 Generation" (on this group, *see* LITERATURE). Love of nature, humanity, pacifism, the story of his several imprisonments (on grounds of "crimes against the state"), and the realities of the country are the predominant themes of Dinamo's poetry. *Sacred Peace* [Kutsal Barış]—Dinamo's seven-volume account of the **Turkish War**

of Independence—and the "Moses Cycle" [Moses the Orphan [Öksüz Musa], *The Prison of Moses* [Musa'nın Mahpushanesi], and *Moses' Hut* [Musa'nın Gecekondusu]] are his best-known novels.

DİNÇMEN, FİLİZ (1939–). Turkey's first female ambassador. Dinçmen served as Turkey's ambassador to the Netherlands, and as permanent representative at the Council of Europe.

DİSK. Turkish acronym for the Confederation of Revolutionary Workers' Unions [Devrimci İşçi Sendikaları Konfederasyonu]. *See* INTEREST GROUPS.

DİVAN. Collection of a classical Ottoman poet's works. Also means "council."

DİVİTÇİOĞLU, SENCER (1927–). Professor of economics. Divitçioğlu, who has a Ph.D. degree from Paris University, is best known for his view that the Ottomans had an Asian-style production system and that this has had a profound impact on politics and society, and also for his works and recent studies on the origins of the Turks. His books include *Ottoman Society and the Asian Style Production* [Osmanlı Toplumu ve Asya Üretim Tarzı], *Le Modèle Economique de la Société Ottomane*, and *The Original Turks* [Köktürkler].

DİYARBAKIR. The largest city of the southeastern region with a population of 1,284,359 (1997). The city walls, which are the longest city walls after the Great Wall of China, were first constructed by the Roman Emperor Constantine. The Grand Mosque, initially the Saint Thomas Church, is the oldest and the largest mosque in the city. The Church of the Virgin Mary was built in the third century.

DOĞRAMACI, İHSAN (1915–). Professor of medicine. He founded the Child Health Institute in **Ankara** (1963), Hacettepe University (1967), and **Bilkent University** (1986). He served as rector of **Ankara University** and Hacettepe University, and as chairperson of the board of trustees of the **Middle East Technical University** and Bilkent University, head of the **Council of Higher Education**, the executive board of the Union of European University Rectors, UNICEF, and the International Institute of Pediatrics. Doğramacı is a member of the London Royal Medicine College, French Academy of Medicine, German Leopoldina Academy of Science, Indian National Academy of Medicine, and honorary member of the national institutes of pediatrics in 15 countries, including those of **France, Germany, Great Britain**, and the **United States**.

DORMEN, AHMET HALDUN (1928–). Author and actor. Dormen has a master's degree in **Fine Arts** from Yale University. From 1957–1972, he acted as manager-actor in his own Dormen Theater. Dormen was given several national awards for his performances and has written several movie scripts and plays; the best known of the latter genre is *Street Girl İrma* [Sokak Kızı İrma].

DORSAY, ATİLLA (1939–). Movie critique and journalist. Dorsay received the Légion d'honneur Palmes Académiques decoration as well as several national awards. His books include *Myth and Scepticism* [Mitos ve Kuşku], *Movies and Our Era* [Sinema ve Çağımız], *Those Names, Those Faces* [O İsimler, O Yüzler], *Those Who Turned Movies into an Art Form* [Sinemayı Sanat Yapanlar], *Directors, Movies, and Countries* [Yönetmenler, Filmler ve Ülkeler], and *The Hopeful Years of Our Movie Industry* [Sinemamızın Umut Yılları].

DÖNME. Descendants of the Jewish followers of a self-proclaimed messiah, Sabbatai Sebi (or Zevi, 1626–1676), who was forced by the **sultan** to convert to **Islam** in 1666. *Dönme* in Turkish means "convert," but it carries overtones of "turncoat" as well.

DÜMBÜLLÜ, İSMAİL (1897–1973). Actor. Famous for his parts in improvisatorial folk theater, he was one of the last masters in the genre.

– E –

EARTHQUAKES. Turkey lies on the Northern Anatolian fault line and Eastern Anatolian fault line. Most earthquakes in Turkey take place on the Northern Anatolian fault line; 27 of the 48 earthquakes that were 7.0 or above at the Richter scale occurred on this line. The line extends from Varto in the east through Erzincan, Koyulhisar, Reşadiye, Niksar, Tosya, Çerleş, Mengen, Bolu, Adapazarı, to the shores of the **Aegean** in the west. The Eastern Anatolian fault line lies between the Amik Plain and Karlıova.

The first known earthquake in Anatolia was the one in Niksar in 330 B.C.E. The major earthquakes in the following centuries were those of Antakya (69 B.C.E., 17,000 dead [D]), Kilikya (334 C.E., 40,000 D), Erzincan (1168, 12,000 D), **Istanbul** (1509, 12,000 D), Erzincan (1584, 15,000 D), **İzmir** (1668, 15,000 D), Erzincan (1784, 5,000 D), Palu (1789, 51,000 D), Antakya (1822, 22,000 D), Marmara Island (1877, 1,312 D), Malazgirt (1903, 6,000 D), Şarköy (1912, 1,850 D), and Burdur-Isparta (1914, 2,500 D). The major earthquakes in the Republican period include those of Erzincan (1939, 8.0 on the Richter scale [RS], 32,962 D), Niksar (1942, 7.3 RS, 3,000 D), Ladik (1943, 7.6 RS, 2,864 D), Gerede (1944, 7.4 RS, 3.959 D), Varto (1966, 6.5 RS, 2,394 D), Gediz (1970, 7.1 RS, 1,086 D), Lice (1975, 6.7 RS, 2,385 D), Çaldıran (1976, 7.5 RS, 3,840 D), Erzurum-Kars (1983, 7.1 RS, 1,400 D), and Gölcük-Adapazarı (1999, 7.1, 20,000 D).

The August 1999 earthquake brought **Greece** and Turkey closer. Immediately after the earthquake, Greek rescue teams, among others, rushed to Turkey. The Turks reciprocated a month later when Greece faced a similar calamity.

EASTERN QUESTION. European diplomatic relations regarding the question of how to cope with the decline of the Ottoman Empire in the 19th and 20th centuries.

EBUSSUUD EFENDİ (1491–1574). A learned religious personage in the Ottoman Empire, who for long years served as *sheikhülislam*, or the highest religious functionary. Ebussuud Efendi, who is author of more than 20 books on **Islam**, is best known for his religious decrees against reactionary Islam.

ECEVİT, BÜLENT (1926–). Politician, poet, and journalist. Bülent Ecevit graduated from **Robert College** in **Istanbul**. In 1957, he was elected to Parliament. In 1960, Ecevit joined the **Constituent Assembly** that prepared the 1961 **constitution**. He served as minister of labor in three coalition governments headed by **İsmet İnönü** between 1961 and 1964. From 1965 onward, Ecevit was the major proponent of the "left-of-center" movement within the **Republican People's Party** (RPP). In October 1966, he became the secretary-general of the party, a post he resigned following the March 12, 1971, coup-by-memorandum because, in his opinion, the RPP cooperated with the junta by allowing its members to become ministers in the above-party government formed following the coup. At the RPP's Fifth Extraordinary Congress, on May 7, 1972, the Ecevit faction came out on top; İnönü, the party's long-time chairman, resigned, and Ecevit was elected chairman on May 14, 1972.

On February 6, 1974, Ecevit forged a Republican People's Party-**National Salvation Party** coalition government. He was prime minister when Turkey conducted the "Peace Operation" in **Cyprus**, as one of the guarantor states of the Republic of Cyprus. As the coalition members could not get along well, the government resigned on September 18, 1974. At the June 1974 By-Laws Congress of the RPP, Ecevit introduced the notion of "Democratic Left"—"an indigenous leftist movement which is based on actual conditions of the country; which is not dogmatic; and which does not emulate blindly systems elsewhere."

On June 5, 1975, Ecevit formed a minority government of the RPP that could not secure a vote of confidence, however. Then, on January 5, 1978, Ecevit headed a coalition government comprising the RPP, *Demokratik* Party, **Republican Reliance Party**, and independents. It lasted until October 16, 1979, when the RPP did very badly at the by-elections and the government resigned.

Following the 1980 **military** intervention, Ecevit, along with other pre-1980 political leaders, was banned from active politics for 10 years. In 1985, Mrs. Rahşan Ecevit had established the **Democratic Left Party** (DLP). In 1987, Ecevit's and other political leaders' political rights were restored at a national referendum on the issue and in September 1987, Bülent Ecevit became the chairman of the DLP.

At the general elections held in the same year, the DLP could not pass the 10 percent nationwide barrier for representation in Parliament. Ecevit left active politics, but he returned to become the DLP's chairman in early 1989. In the October 1991 general elections, the DLP received 10.8 percent of the votes and returned seven members to Parliament, including Ecevit. In September 1992, the Republican People's Party (RPP), along with other political parties that had been closed by the 1980 military intervenors, was reopened. Ecevit, however, rejected a merger between the DLP and the new RPP. He thought the RPP was too far left, and was indifferent to formulating concrete policies. In the December 1995 elections, the DSP's votes increased to 14.7 percent, and the party returned to Parliament 76 members. In June 1997, the DSP formed a coalition government with the **Motherland Party** (MP) and the **Democratic Turkey Party**, which was led by **Mesut Yılmaz** of the MP. This was followed by a DSP minority government (January 1999). In the April 18, 1999, general elections, the DSP captured the plurality of votes (22.1 percent), and Ecevit formed a coalition government with **Devlet Bahçeli's Nationalist Action Party** and Mesut Yılmaz's MP. This coalition government turned out to be the most harmoniously functioning and most successful coalition government Turkey ever had.

Ecevit had studied Bengali and Sanskrit and translated poems by Rabindranath Tagore into Turkish. In Ecevit's philosophy, life is multidimensional; if a politician does not wish to remain a one-dimensional, narrow person, he should enrich politics with art. His poems were published in *His Poems* [Şiirleri] and *I Carved the Light from Stone* [Işığı Taştan Oydum]. His political treatises include *Left of the Center* [Ortanın Solu], *This System Must Change* [Bu Düzen Değişmelidir], and *Atatürk and Revolution* [Atatürk ve Devrimcilik].

ECONOMIC AND SOCIAL HISTORY FOUNDATION OF TURKEY. A nongovernmental organization established in 1991. It promotes publication and research on the economic, social, and cultural heritage of the region. The foundation convenes scholarly meetings, and holds exhibits and festivals. It publishes five periodicals and books on Turkish history, politics, economics, and social and cultural life. The foundation has a library that carries specialized archives.

ECONOMIC COOPERATION ORGANIZATION (ECO). Intergovernmental regional organization founded by **Iran**, Pakistan, and Turkey in 1985 for the promotion of conditions for sustainable economic growth in the region. In 1992, Afghanistan, **Azerbaijan**, Kazakhstan, Pakistan, Tajikistan, Turkestan, and Uzbekistan joined the ECO.

One of the basic aims of the ECO is to develop a road and railway network in the region, which would foster trade among the member countries.

ECZACIBAŞI, BÜLENT (1949–). Chemical engineer and owner-manager of the Eczacıbaşı Holding Company. Eczacıbaşı has a master's degree from the Massachusetts Institute of Technology. He served as the head of the board of directors of **TÜSİAD** (Turkish Industrialists' and Businessmen's Association) and the Turkish Economic and Social Studies Foundation.

ECZACIBAŞI, NEJAT (1913–1993). Chemist, industrialist, and businessmen. He established Turkey's pharmacological industry (which, after his death, was taken over by his son, **Bülent Eczacıbaşı**) as well the Istanbul Foundation of Culture and Arts. This foundation has organized the annual Istanbul International Festival of Arts and Culture since 1972.

EDUCATION. In the early years of the Republic, the educational system was extremely inadequate in both quantity and quality. In 1923, there were 4,894 secular elementary schools and 10,238 teachers. Literacy was 17 percent for males and 5 percent for females. Schools were of poor quality and they were concentrated in the urban areas. One of the first priorities set during the 1920s was to develop secondary education. Consequently, between 1923 and 1930, while the number of grade-school students increased 43 percent, those in secondary-low and secondary-high schools [*lycées*] grew almost fourfold.

In 1923–1925, village teachers' schools were established to train teachers qualified in both academic and "practical" subjects. A spin-off from this project was a network of village institutes set up in rural areas to train students from the villages themselves and to make them both village teachers and multipurpose development agents. Another project was the training of recently discharged noncommissioned officers as teachers for villages. The adoption of the Latin alphabet in 1928 made it necessary to open "nation schools" for adults. Later, **"People's Houses"** were set up for the same purpose.

Turkey started to apply eight-year uninterrupted compulsory secular education as of the 1997–1998 educational year. Since then, primary education has included the education and training of the children in the 6–14 years age group. Primary education is compulsory for all boys and girls in that age group, and free of charge in the state schools.

Secondary education includes all of the general high schools and those high schools that provide vocational and technical education for at least three years after the eight-year primary education. Within the scope of the general high schools are the Anatolia High Schools, the Science High Schools, the Anatolia Fine Arts and Teachers Schools, the evening high schools, and private high schools. In Anatolia High Schools and private high schools, the medium of instruction is usually English, French, or German. In 1950–1951, the schooling rate in high schools was 5.2 percent; in 1970–1971, 20.2 percent; in 1990–1991, 38.5 percent; and in 1996/1997, 59.8 percent.

The higher education institutions include all the educational institutions after secondary education, which provide at least two, but normally four, years of higher education. At the inception of the Republic, the only full university was Darulfünun, opened in 1900, although the Turkish Republic inherited a few specialized higher education institutions, such as the School of Engineering and the School for Civil Servants. In 1933, Darulfünun was reformed so as to make it serve the purposes of the new regime's **Westernization** goals and renamed **Istanbul University**.

By early 1992, there were 29 universities. By 2000, that number had risen to 76. Eighteen of the 76 were private universities backed by foundations.

Three additional private universities are in the process of being formed. In six universities—**Boğaziçi University, Bilgi University, Koç University,** and **Sabancı University** all in **Istanbul** and **Bilkent University** and the **Middle East Technical University** both in **Ankara**—the medium of instruction is English, and in **Galatasaray University** in Istanbul it is French. At some other universities, but only in certain programs, the teaching language is other than Turkish.

During the 1997–1998 academic year, 1,315,809 students, including those in an Open University, received education in higher institutions of learning. During the same education year, the number of students who had state scholarships and who received college education abroad was 1,199. Some 1,133 of these students were at graduate schools. The schooling rate at the universities had been less than 13 percent in 1977.

Despite significant growth in educational institutions since the inception of the Republic, supply lags far behind demand. The ratio of budget expenditures to education in GNP has always been low in Turkey as compared to both developed and developing countries. For the period 1981–1995, the average was 2.7 percent, reaching 4 percent in only two years. The standard of education has dropped during the last three decades. The expenditure per university student in 1995 (in constant prices) was 23 percent less than in 1990, even 17 percent less than the amount in 1975. Few of the high school graduates can enroll at universities, and there are not an adequate number of vocational and technical schools.

All schools are underequipped and understaffed. In 1997, the average size of classes was more than 30 at the primary level, and between 50 and 60 at the secondary level. There is the handicap of "teacher deficit" for specific courses at the secondary level. In many cases, schools resort to "substitute teachers," professionals in other fields but not trained to serve as teachers. Educational standards are far lower in eastern and southeastern Anatolia. Rote learning rather than personal investigation is the norm in virtually all schools. *See also* COUNCIL OF HIGHER EDUCATION.

EFENDİ. A title that was given to a learned man, member of the scribal or learned (cultural or **religious**) institutions of the Ottoman Empire. Later it was used for Ottoman princes and lower-ranked **military** officers.

EGELİ, EKREM ŞERİF (1901–1980). Professor of medicine. Egeli worked in Vienna, Hamburg, and Paris. He served as rector of **Istanbul University** from 1965 to 1973. During his career, he introduced many new diagnostic methods in Turkey.

ELDEM, SEDAD HAKKI (1908–1988). Architect. Eldem contributed to the development of an indigenous Turkish architectural style. *See also* ARCHITECTURE.

ELİF NACİ (1898–1987). Painter, journalist, and writer. With five other painters, Elif Naci founded the D Group in painting in 1933. He produced both abstract and figurative paintings.

EMIGRATION AND IMMIGRATION. Until the 1960s, Turkey was essentially a country that experienced several waves of immigration; from the 1960s to the present, Turkey has witnessed emigration, particularly to Europe.

Turks themselves migrated in great numbers from Central Asia to Anatolia toward the end of the 11th century. Upon the foundation of the Ottoman Empire at the close of the 14th century and its later growth into an empire, new waves of Turks came to Turkey from southeastern Europe, Egypt, North Africa, and the **Aegean** islands. On the other hand, following the Ottoman conquests in Europe, the Middle East and North Africa, the Ottomans settled Turkic elements in these new lands.

Then, from the end of the 17th century, with the retreat of the Ottomans in Europe and elsewhere, several waves of Turks immigrated to Anatolia from the Crimea, northeastern Caucasus, **Azerbaijan**, **Greece**, **Bulgaria**, Romania, former Yugoslavia, and **Cyprus**.

From 1771 until the beginning of the 19th century, close to 500,000 Crimean Turks came to Anatolia. During the 19th century, an additional one million came from the Crimea. Faced with intermittent Russian attacks, from 1768 until 1917, around 900,000 northern Caucasions immigrated to Turkey; about two-thirds of them remained in Anatolia and the rest were sent to Amman, Damascus, Aleppo, and Cyprus. From 1812 until 1920, again under pressure from Russia, about 100,000 Azerbaijanis also came to Anatolia.

Immigration from Greece started in the early 1820s upon the outbreak of the Greek rebellion that led to an independent Greece in 1829. By the end of **World War I**, around 800,000 Turks had immigrated to Turkey from Greece. Then, in accordance with the 1923 **Treaty of Lausanne**, a population exchange took place between Turkey and Greece; from 1923 to 1933, approximately 850,000 Turkish-Greeks went to Greece and around 400,000 Greek-Turks came to Turkey.

The first wave of immigrants from Bulgaria arrived during the 1828 and 1829 Turkish-Russian wars; they numbered around 30,000. The second wave of about 750,000 immigrants left Bulgaria during the 1877–1878 war with **Russia**, but approximately one-fourth of them died on the way. A little over 200,000 of the rest remained in the present borders of Turkey; the others were sent to other parts of the Ottoman Empire. Since then, an additional one million Turks have come from Bulgaria as either immigrants or refugees.

Immigration from Romania dates back to the first decade of the 19th century when the Russian armies made advances in the region. During the Ottoman period, the greatest waves of immigration took place in 1826 (200,000) and 1878–1880 (90,000). In the Republican period, about 35,000 immigrants came from Romania.

Immigration from the former Yugoslavia also started in the first decade of the 19th century as a consequence of the Russian-supported Serb insurrections. Initially, immigration took place to the areas that were still under Ottoman suzerainty. Around 150,000 Turks immigrated to Anatolia in 1826 and, in 1867, a similar number of Turks immigrated to Anatolia again. Upon the proclamation of the Turkish Republic, another 350,000 came (between 1923 and 1930). An additional 160,000 immigrated to Turkey after the establishment of a communist regime in the former Yugoslavia (from 1946 until 1961). Since 1961, total immigrants from that country have amounted to 50,000 people.

The first wave of immigration from Cyprus occurred in 1878 when the Ottomans were obliged to lease the island to **Great Britain**; at that time, 15,000 people moved to Anatolia. When the Treaty of Lausanne gave the island to Great Britain, another 30,000 immigrants came to Turkey.

The emigration of Turks to Europe, which started in earnest in the 1960s, was the consequence of demographic, economic, and social factors. Post–**World War II** Europe, in particular **Germany**, had labor-deficient economies. Turkey had a fairly young and rapidly increasing population that had more than doubled during the past three decades, and Turkey could not provide employment or social welfare to its increasing population.

As of the 1960s, Turkey opted for **industrialization** and an import-substitution strategy. The weak export potential of this strategy could not generate the foreign exchange necessary for importing, among other things, technology, machinery, and **energy** for industrialization. Furthermore, the absence of a **social security system** in Turkey made life precarious for many. Dispatching workers abroad that would send home remittances appeared to the Turkish government as a solution to these demographic, economic, and social problems.

Turkey signed bilateral emigration agreements with Germany in 1961 and with Austria, the Netherlands, and Belgium in 1968. In the 1961–1968 period, Turkey sent a total of 247,246 workers to Germany, **France**, Austria, Switzerland, the Netherlands, Belgium, Great Britain, and Australia. In the 1969–1974 period, an additional 563,252 workers were sent to these countries; 80 percent of these workers went to Germany in 1967, 94 percent in 1969, 74 percent in 1971, and 76 percent in 1973. In 1973, there were 605,000 officially employed workers in Germany, 47,326 in the Netherlands, 38,000 in France, 29,764 in Austria, 23,158 in Switzerland, 21,029 in Belgium, and 15,165 in other European countries (Great Britain, Denmark, Norway, and Sweden).

In 1966–1967, Germany experienced a recession and 70,000 Turkish workers lost their jobs. Then, in November 1973, Germany imposed an immigration ban. After 1980, many countries, including Germany, imposed visa requirements on the citizens of non-European Community (EC) (*see* EUROPEAN UNION [EU]) countries. As a consequence, during recent decades, emigration to those countries was made either illegally or took the form of family unification, i.e., spouses and children joining workers in those countries. After 1980, return migration also took place as a consequence of monetary incentives offered for this purpose by the host countries, worsening employment opportunities and/or social pressure in Turkey. For example, in the 1984–1985 period, 256,715 workers returned from Germany. In 1995, Turkish migrant populations in selected European countries were as follows: 2,049,900 in Germany, 198,900 in France, 167,000 in the Netherlands, 147,000 in Austria, 79,500 in Belgium. In that year, a total of 2,882,300 Turkish migrants lived in Europe. The increasing difficulty of emigration to European countries to a large extent diverted Turkish workers' emigration toward countries in the Middle East and Libya. For instance, 99 percent of all legal emigration that took place in 1985 was to the Middle East and Libya. In that year, 74 percent of the emigration to the countries in question was to Saudi Arabia (35,067 workers) and 20 percent to Libya (9,680 workers). However, by the mid-1990s, partly due to the completion of large-scale infrastructural projects in the oil-exporting countries and partly due to unfavorable circumstances caused by the **Gulf War**, the number of Turkish workers in Arab countries began to go down. Although there were around 250,000 workers in those countries in the late 1980s, that number fell to 140,000 in the early 1990s and to 120,000 in the late 1990s.

The last phase of Turkish emigration was to the countries of the former Soviet Union (*see* RUSSIA) following its collapse. In 1992, there were 8,000 workers in these countries, 20,000 in 1993, and 40,000 in 1994. It declined to 26,000 in 1996. *See also* DIASPORA.

ENERGY. For energy consumption in Turkey, such primary energy sources as anthracite coal, lignite, petroleum, natural gas, hydroelectric, geothermal, wood, animal and plant residues, and solar energy are used. Electrical energy and coke are used as secondary sources. Since the 1960s, the primary energy consumption and electricity consumption increased by an annual average of 5.2 percent and 11 percent, respectively.

Turkey is not self-sufficient in primary energy resources. Furthermore, the ratio of domestic production to total primary energy demand has been falling over the years. In 1994, the ratio was 45 percent; in 1999, it dropped to 37 percent. In 1999, the domestic production in oil could meet only 10 percent of demand; this ratio in natural gas was below 5 percent.

Since the 1980s, Turkey has made investments to boost lignite and hydroelectric energy in order to meet its energy deficit. One-fourth of commercial production in 1997 was obtained from these two sources. In the same year, in electricity production, hydroelectric power plants had a share of 38.3 percent, lignite thermal power plants 30.4 percent, and natural gas power plants 19.8 percent. During recent years, Turkey has signed contracts with several countries to import natural gas. Turkey has great potential in such renewable energy sources as geothermal, wind, and solar energy, and is planning to make greater use of them in the future.

ENVER PASHA (1881–1922). Ottoman general and politician. In 1907, Enver joined the Association for Fatherland and Freedom in Salonica. He played a role in the merger of this association with the Paris branch of the Committee for Progress and Union. The new Committee was given the name of the **Committee for Union and Progress** (CUP). In 1908, the then-Major Enver and Captain Ahmed Niyazi Bey took to the mountains and made a declaration to the effect that their aim was to topple the authoritarian regime of **Abdülhamit II**. Major Enver invaded the town of Köprülü in Macedonia and, on July 10, 1908, proclaimed the establishment of the Second Constitutional Period in the Ottoman Empire. This move forced the **sultan** to again put into effect the 1876 **constitution** and reconvene the Parliament, which he had prorogued in 1878. Enver then worked to recruit members for the CUP from among the officers. On January 23, 1913, he engineered the Sublime Porte [Babıâli] Raid that brought to the vizierate **Mahmut Şevket Pasha**.

Thus began the period of "the rule of three pashas"—Enver Pasha, **Cemal Pasha**, and **Talat Pasha**. Enver was promoted to the rank of general in January 1914 and, in March, Enver Pasha became the minister of war. He developed close relations with **Germany**. Consequently, the Ottoman Empire entered **World War I** on the German side. In 1917, Enver Pasha, who always nurtured an expanded Ottoman Empire that would include the Turkic peoples in Asia, opened the Caucacus front; this attempt ended in complete failure. Following the war, Enver Pasha escaped to Berlin.

ENVIRONMENT. Traditionally, environmental problems have been exacerbated in Turkey because urbanization and industrialization have taken place in a haphazard manner; there has been a lack of technical knowledge about the problem; and, worst of all, one came across a general indifference. To make up for the lost years, in 1983, the Undersecretariat of Environment affiliated to the Prime Ministry was created. This was followed by the establishment of a High Board of councils of environment at the provinces. The board was to coordinate activities of the other bodies. Then in 1991, the Ministry of Environment was set up.

Nongovernmental organizations (NGOs) also concern themselves with environmental problems. The most important among these is the Environmental Problems Foundation of Turkey. In the early 1990s, those NGOs active in environmental problems were able to block the construction of a thermal power plant in Gökova.

EPHESUS. Medieval city about 80 kilometers south of İzmir. The original Hellenic settlement of Ephesus was established by Ionians in about 1000 B.C.E. The ruins of the Temple of Artemis are the most ancient of the extant monuments of Ephesus. The temple dates back to the eighth century B.C.E. Ephesus is also the site of the ruins of the enormous Gymnasium of Vedius (built in 150 C.E.), a stadium (constructed in 37–68 C.E.), the Church of Haghia Maria (dating back to the second century C.E.), the theater (originally built in the third century B.C.E.), the Library of Celsus (founded in 110 C.E.), the Baths of Scholastica (from about 200 C.E.), and the supposed House of the Blessed Virgin.

ERBAKAN, NECMETTİN (1926–). Professor of engineering and politician. Erbakan graduated from **Istanbul Technical University** and obtained a Ph.D. degree from Aachen Technische Hoschshüle in Germany. In January 1970, he founded the **National Order Party** and became its chairman. The party was closed the next year by the Constitutional Court on the grounds that its program was against **secularism**. Erbakan participated in the 1973 general elections as a candidate of the **National Salvation Party** (NSP), which also had a religious orientation and was founded by the former members of the National Order Party. In the elections, the NSP obtained 11.8 percent of the votes and gained 48 seats in Parliament, including that of Erbakan. Erbakan was elected chairman of the party. Under Erbakan, the NSP adopted a policy known as the "National View" [Milli Görüş] that emphasized Islamic conservatism and aimed at promoting small enterprises. Erbakan became deputy prime minister in the **Republican People's Party**-NSP coalition government (formed in February 1974). He also served as deputy prime minister and minister of state in the first Nationalist Front (coalition) government of the **Justice Party** (JP), NSP, **Nationalist Action Party** (NAP), and **Republican Reliance Party** (RRP) (formed in March 1975) and in the Second Nationalist Front (coalition) government of the JP, NSP, and NAP (formed in August 1977).

Following the 1980 **military** intervention, along with other political leaders, Erbakan was banned from active politics for 10 years. Again along with other political leaders, his political rights were restored in September 1987 after a national referendum. On October 11, 1987, Erbakan became chairman of the **Welfare Party** (WP), which had been founded in July 1983 as a successor party to the NSP. In the October 29, 1987, general elections, as in the November 6, 1983, general elections, the WP's votes remained below 10 percent and the party could not win seats in Parliament because of the nationwide election barrier of 10 percent. In the October 1991 general elections, the WP overcame the election barrier as the party joined forces with the **Nationalist Labor Party** and the **Reformist Democracy Party**. Erbakan made efforts to take part in a coalition government, but other political parties turned him down.

On June 27, 1996, Erbakan became prime minister when **True Path Party** leader **Tansu Çiller** opted for a coalition government with Erbakan's WP. Erbakan managed to stay as prime minister only about a year. Toward the end of 1996, the military, through the **National Security Council**, began to put pressure upon the WP-TPP coalition on the grounds that the government was not taking adequate measures against the threat of "reactionary **Islam**." When the secularist **civil societal** groups, too, started adopting a determined opposition against the coalition, Erbakan was obliged to resign (July 18, 1997). Then, in January 1998, the Constitutional Court closed the WP, and banned Erbakan from active politics for five years. This was followed by another verdict in July 2000 by the same Court that banned him from politics for the rest of his life.

ERDENTUĞ, NERMİN (1917–2000). Turkey's first ethnology professor. Erdentuğ founded the Social Welfare Academy affiliated to the Ministry of Health and Social Welfare and served as permanent Turkish representative in the Council of the International Union of Anthropology and Ethnology. Her books include *An Ethnological Study of the Village of Hal* [Hal Köyünün Etnolojik Tetkiki], *An Ethnological Study of the Village of Sün* [Sün Köyünün Etnolojik Tetkiki], *A Study on Social Structure of a Turkish Village, Social Customs and Traditions* [Sosyal Adetler ve Gelenekler], and *The Relations between Education and Culture in Turkish Modernization* [Türkiye'nin Çağşdaşlaşmasında Eğitim ve Kültür Münasebetleri].

ERDOĞAN, RECEP TAYYİP (1954–). Politician. After having graduated from a prayer leader and preacher school and the Economics and Trade Department of Marmara University in **Istanbul**, Erdoğan worked as manager in various private sector companies. After 19 years with the Istanbul organization of the **Welfare Party** (WP), he became Istanbul metropolitan mayor from that party's list in 1994. As a moderate Islamist, he was exceedingly successful as a mayor and quickly made a name for himself in the WP. However, a poem ("Minarets are our bayonets; Domes are our helmets; Mosques are our barracks; Believers are our soldiers") that he recited in a political speech in 1998 got him into prison for 10 months and he was banned from active politics for life. However, he was considered the moral leader of the liberal faction within the **Virtue Party** (VP)— successor party to the WP. Following the closure of the Virtue Party in 1999, Erdoğan became the leader of the Development and Justice Party, one of the two successor parties to the VP. (It was argued that a political amnesty ruling concerning another party leader rendered null and void the political ban on Erdoğan as well. At the time of writing, the Constitutional Court was reviewing this claim.)

EREN, AHMET NURİ (1919–). Ambassador and consultant on international political economy. Eren obtained a Ph.D. degree from Princeton University. He served as Turkish ambassador to the People's Republic of China and as Turkey's permanent representative at the United Nations. Eren is the author of *Turkey: An Experiment in Modernization.*

ERHAT, AZRA (1915–1982). Author and translator. Erhat was one of the leading representatives of the humanistic approach. He tried to show the link between the past Anatolian civilizations and the cultural values of the present inhabitants of Anatolia.

ERİM, NİHAT (1912–1980). Professor of international relations and politician. Erim graduated from **Istanbul University**'s School of Law and obtained a Ph.D. in law from Paris University's Faculty of Law. In 1943, he became legal advisor to the Turkish Foreign Ministry. During the late 1940s, Erim served as minister of public works and deputy prime minister in different **Republican People's Party** governments. From 1950 to 1956, he wrote critical articles about the ruling *Demokrat* **Party** (DP) in the dailies *Nation* [Ulus], *New Nation* [Yeni Ulus], and *Populist* [Halkçı]. From 1956 onward, he offered his services to the DP on the **Cyprus** issue and headed the Turkish delegation for preparation of the constitution of the State of Cyprus, in line with the 1959 **Zurich** and London Treaties between **Great Britain**, Turkey, and **Greece**. Erim later became a member of the **Constituent Assembly** that prepared the 1961 **Constitution**. During the 1961–1970 period, he led the Turkish Parliamentary group in the European Council. Following the March 12, 1971, **military** intervention, he was asked twice by the military to form "above-party" governments. The second Erim government resigned on April 17, 1972. Erim left active politics after having served one term as senator. He was assassinated on July 19, 1980, for political reasons.

ERKİN, ULVİ CEMAL (1906–1972). Composer. One of the leading musicians in the Republican era, Erkin produced pieces such as the *String Quartet Piano Concerto, Dance Rhapsody, First Symphony, and Violin Concerto.*

ERSEK, SİYAMİ (1920–). Professor of medicine. Ersek was one of the pioneers of open-heart surgery in Turkey.

ERSOY, MEHMET AKİF (1873–1936). Poet and nationalist. Ersoy wrote the text of the Turkish national anthem. A member of the First Grand National Assembly (1920–1923), he found the **secular** reforms of the Republican leaders contrary to the Islamic worldview to which he subscribed. He had attempted to promote the cause of Muslim unity in Arabia during **World War I**. Ersoy's great theme was the resistance of Turkdom and **Islam** to foreign imperialism. In his poems, he used lyric-epic and lyric-didactic styles. All of Ersoy's later poetry was published in *Pages* [Safahat] (in seven volumes).

ERTUĞ, BEDRİ CELAL (1913–). Professor of medicine. Ertuğ was a visiting professor at Columbia University and Duke University in the United States and Cardiff University in Wales. He served as minister of health and social welfare. He became chairman of the Association to Fight against Air Pollution and formed the **Greens Party**. The latter remained moribund. Ertuğ, who has written a number of books on heart and related diseases, is the author of a biography of **Nejat Eczacıbaşı**.

ERTUĞRUL, MUHSİN (1892–1979). Leader and apostle of the contemporary Turkish **theater** from the 1920s onward. Ertuğrul served as artistic director of the **Istanbul** Municipal Theater from 1927 on. He was instrumental in the opening of a children's theater in 1935 and the State Ballet School in 1945 (*see* OPERA AND BALLET). Ertuğrul served as general director of the State Theater and Opera in the years 1948–1951 and 1955–1958. During this time, he opened neighborhood theaters in **Istanbul** and **Ankara** and provincial theaters in other cities. Ertuğrul introduced classical masterpieces and critically acclaimed contemporary plays, both Turkish and foreign, to the Turkish public.

ERZURUM CONGRESS (July 23–August 7, 1919). Convened by **Atatürk** and his associates. It was decided that that the Ottoman nation should be kept intact, with Muslims and non-Muslims having equal rights, and that, as the Istanbul government was controlled by the Allies, the national movement in Anatolia had no option but to assume responsibility for protecting the nation's rights, in the name of the **sultan-caliph**.

ETHNIC GROUPS. See LINGUISTIC AND ETHNIC GROUPS.

EURO-MEDITERRANEAN PROCESS. The process was started by the Barcelona Declaration of November 1995; the **European Union** (EU) and the **Mediterranaen** countries, including Turkey, declared their aim of establishing a multilateral and lasting framework of relations for the purpose of developing human resources, creating an area of shared prosperity, and thus giving rise to a common area of peace and stability. Although a partner in the process, Turkey has perceived "the Mediterranean" as essentially eastern Mediterranean, because Turkey has been preoccupied with its problems with **Greece** and **Syria**, the **Cyprus problem**, and the spillover effects of the Arab-**Israeli** conflict for the region as a whole. Also, because Turkey is a full member of the **North Atlantic Treaty Organization** (NATO) and an associate member of the West European Union, has a **Customs Union** with the EU, and a candidate state for the EU, Turks think that they have a different kind of relationship with Europe, compared to other Mediterranean countries. On the other hand, Turkey supports the EU's goal of completing the establishment of a Mediterranean free-trade area by 2010. *See also* CUSTOMS UNION; EUROPEAN UNION; FOREIGN POLICY.

EUROPEAN COMMUNITY (EC)/EUROPEAN UNION (EU). **Westernization** has been a long-cherished goal among the Turks. As part of this overall goal, Turkey applied for inclusion into the then-named European Economic Community (EEC) in 1959, shortly after the establishment of the community. The **Ankara** Agreement, signed on September 12, 1963, made Turkey an associate member of the community and adopted full membership as an ultimate goal. This final aim was to be reached in three consecutive stages—a preparatory stage lasting five years (1964–1969), a second stage that would include transition to the **Customs Union**, and a final stage of closer coordination of economic, financial, and competition policies. An additional protocol of 1973 set a timetable for the gradual introduction of free circulation of persons, goods, and services between Turkey and the community.

After having reduced its customs tariffs, liberalized its foreign economic relations, abolished its quantitative import restrictions, and introduced liberal foreign investment legislation, Turkey applied for full membership in April 1987. In its December 18, 1990, decision, the European Community (EC) reaffirmed the eligibility of Turkey for full membership but stated that Turkey needed some more time to overcome its economic and social difficulties and, therefore, new accession negotiations could not be started before 1993. The EC, however, came up with a cooperation package that "would contribute to the success of Turkey's efforts toward increased interdependence and integration," which involved achievement of the Customs Union by the end of 1995, economic cooperation, and "technical and political dialogue." However, progress within the framework of this cooperation package proved difficult due to **Greece**'s objection to the release of the so-called Fourth Financial Protocol, which provided aid to Turkey.

This protocol was considered by the community an indivisible part of the cooperation package. From 1997 to 2000, the European Union (EU) kept Turkey out of its enlargement process. Repeatedly, the EU confirmed Turkey's eligibility for full membership but indicated that, among other things, Turkey needed to further liberalize its economy, on the one hand, and resolve its conflict with Greece and deepen its democracy, on the other. The breakthrough came at the EU's December 10–11, 1999, Helsinki summit where Turkey was designated a "candidate state destined to join the Union on the basis of the same criteria as applied to other candidate states." Turkey was now expected to fully comply with the Copenhagen economic and political criteria in order for accession negotiations between the EU and Turkey to begin. In its **National Program** (March 2001), devised to indicate the steps Turkey will undertake to conform its institutions and practices to the said criteria in question, it was stated that the Turkish government regards EU membership as a new step forward, a milestone confirming the founding philosophy of the Republic, and that Turkey is fully resolved to adopt and implement the EU requirements.

In 1998, the number of Turks employed in the EU amounted to 1.2 million, which was 0.75 percent of the total working population of the Union. Their estimated contribution to the GNP of the EU was €55.1 billion—2.5 times the GNP of Luxembourg and 51 percent of **Greece**'s contribution. In 1999, 73,200 Turks had their businesses in the EU, employing 366,000 persons. In 2000, the total number of Turks living in the EU countries was 3.4 million. *See also* DIASPORA; EMIGRATION AND IMMIGRATION; EURO-MEDITERRANEAN PROCESS; EUROPEAN SECURITY AND DEFENSE IDENTITY.

EUROPEAN SECURITY AND DEFENSE IDENTITY. The concept behind the 60,000-strong army of the **European Union** (EU) that should be operational in 2003. For this purpose, the EU plans to make use of the combat units of the **North Atlantic Treaty Organization (NATO)**, without including in the decision-making process those countries that are members of NATO but not full members of the EU. As it is one of the countries in the latter category, Turkey opposed this plan. Turkey let it be known that unless it was not included in the decision-making process, it would veto the plan as a NATO member. Finally, Turkey agreed to support the plan when the EU gave assurances to Turkey that the army would not be used in the conflicts among the NATO countries, that is, in Turkish-Greek conflicts, and that Turkey would be consulted if the army is planned to be used in the politically unstable areas around Turkey.

EUROPEAN UNION. *See* EUROPEAN COMMUNITY(EC)/EUROPEAN UNION(EU).

EVLİYA ÇELEBİ (1611–1682). A famous traveller who reported his firsthand observations in a lively, if exaggerated, manner. Evliya Çelebi also conveyed in his writings his own interpretations of and thoughts on what he had seen. His *Book of Travels* [Seyahatname] has attracted a great deal of attention.

EVREN, KENAN (1918–). General and Turkey's seventh president. Evren graduated from the Army College in 1938 and from the Military Staff College in 1939. He became a four-star general in 1974. He served as commander of the **Aegean Army** from 1976 to 1977 and of the Landed Forces from 1977 to 1978. He was promoted to chief of the general staff on March 6, 1978. On September 12, 1980, the **military** intervened in politics "within the chain of command and with command." The **National Security Council**, made up of Chief of General Staff Kenan Evren and the commanders of the army, navy, air force, and gendarmerie, was endowed with the powers of the legislative and executive.

On June 29, 1981, the National Security Council decided to form a **Consultative Assembly**. The assembly started functioning on November 24, 1981. It prepared a constitution, which was finalized by the National Security Council and endorsed on November 7, 1982, by a nationwide referendum. According to the provisional Article 1 of the 1982 **constitution**, General Evren, until then head of state, became the seventh president of Turkey. On July 1, 1983, Kenan Evren turned over the function of chief of the general staff to General Nurettin Ersin and was retired from the military. From then until his term as presidency came to an end in 1989, Evren remained in that post as a civilian.

EYÜBOĞLU, BEDRİ RAHMİ (1913–1975). Painter, poet, and writer. Eyüboğlu belonged to the avant-garde D Group of painters (on the D Group, *see* FINE ARTS). Eyüboğlu, the most versatile artist of the Republican era, later formed the "Group of Ten," whose members based their work on the traditional Anatolian decorative arts. He worked with stained glass, silk screening, engravings, ceramics, textiles, and glass. He used acrylic, sand, ink, and collage. Eyüboğlu had an unending quest for experimentation. In his verse as well as his painting, he drew his inspiration from folk sources. Eyüboğlu's poems were published in *Letters to the Creator* [Yaradana Mektuplar], *Salt* [Tuz], *Three at Once* [Üçü Birden], *Four at Once* [Dördü Birden], and *Fill the Copper Cup* [Dol Karabakır Dol]. *See also* ELİF NACİ.

– F –

FACULTY OF POLITICAL SCIENCES, ANKARA UNIVERSITY. It was originally opened as the Civil Service School [Mekteb-i Mülkiye] in 1859 in **Istanbul** and became the School of Political Sciences in 1935. It was moved to **Ankara** in 1936. In 1950, it was renamed Faculty of Political Sciences. Until recent decades, the school trained the bulk of the Turkish bureaucratic and political elite.

FATHERLAND FRONT [Vatan Cephesi]. A fictive front concocted by the *Demokrat* **Party** in 1958 against the "front of malice and hostility being created by the Republicans" and in order to restore national unity and counteract "subversive activities." Every evening, the state radio gave long lists of names of people purported to have joined the "front." Following the 1960 **military** intervention that ended the Demokratic Party era, it was discovered that some of the persons to whom names belonged had long been dead.

FELEK, BURHAN (1889–1982). Journalist. Felek was well known for the anecdotes through which he humorously depicted the problems people face daily. From 1954 until his death, he was head of the Turkish Journalists' Association. This association designated him as the doyen of Turkey's journalists in 1975. That same year, the International Press Union selected Felek as the most senior member of international journalism.

FESTIVALS. More than 100 festivals are organized in Turkey every year. International art festivals are held in such major cities as **Istanbul, Ankara, İzmir**, and **Antalya**. The Istanbul Culture and Art Foundation, which celebrated its 30th year in 2002, organizes the International Istanbul Film Festival every April, the International Istanbul Theater Festival every May, the International Istanbul Music Festival every June and July, the International Istanbul Jazz Festival every July, and the International Istanbul Biennial once every two years.

FETVA. Muslim legal opinion supplied by a *mufti*, or jurisconsult.

FEYZİOĞLU, TURHAN (1922–1988). Politician and professor of constitutional law. In May 1956, Feyzioğlu became dean of the **Faculty of Political Sciences** of **Ankara University**. In 1957, he was elected a member of Parliament on the **Republican People's Party** (RPP) ticket. Following the May 27, 1960, **military** intervention, he was appointed rector of the **Middle East Technical University** in **Ankara**. Somewhat later, he was designated head of the Constitutional Commission in the **Constituent Assembly** that prepared the 1961 **constitution**. On January 5, 1961, Feyzioğlu was appointed minister of education in the cabinet of General **Cemal Gürsel**, who headed the National Unity Committee of the 1960 military intervenors. Feyzioğlu served as minister of state and deputy prime minister from November 20, 1961, until December 2, 1963, in the first and second coalition governments of İsmet İnönü. In 1964–1966, he represented Turkey in the Council of Europe.

Opposed to the left-of-center policy that flourished in the RPP during the mid-1960s, Feyzioğlu resigned from that party and, in May 1967, founded the **Reliance Party** (RP), whose chairman he became. Following the March 12, 1971, military intervention, the RP merged with the **Republican Party** and adopted the name of **Republican Reliance Party** (RRP). In 1972, Feyzioğlu became chairman of this new party. He served as minister of state and deputy prime minister in the First Nationalist Front coalition government that was formed in March 1975, headed by **Süleyman Demirel**, and comprised the **Justice Party**, **National Salvation Party**, **Nationalist Action Party**, and Republican Reliance Party. Feyzioğlu quit active politics following the September 1980 military intervention.

FINDIKOĞLU, ZİYAEDDİN FAHRİ (1902–1974). Professor of sociology. Fındıkoğlu obtained a Ph.D. from Strasbourg University in France. He was influenced by Emile Durkheim and **Ziya Gökalp**. He developed a socioeconomic model that was based on the assumption of solidarity between different occupations, and aimed at reconciling private and public ownership.

FINE ARTS. Ottoman artists, for the most part trained at the Palace Academy [*Enderun*], developed Ottoman classicism in arts and architecture during the 16th and 17th centuries. During the 18th century, just as Ottoman artists were beginning to escape from classicism and tending toward a lighter, almost manneristic understanding of art, Ottoman rulers turned their gaze to the West. From the reign of **Mahmut II** (1812–1839) onward, students were sent to Europe to study fine arts. In 1883, the Academy of Fine Arts was founded. This was followed by the establishment of the Ottoman Society of Painters in 1914. At the time, the prevalent mood and technique among the painters was impressionism. Sculpture developed at the end of the 19th century. The tendency of the era was toward naturalism and plastic effect.

The Republican leaders also sent students to Europe to study fine arts. Upon their return from Europe, young artists founded the Union of Independent Painters and Sculptors in 1928. In 1933, a new art society, "D Group," was established. D Group members were opposed to academism and imitating nature blindly; they placed emphasis on personal interpretation. In 1937, the National Museum of Painting and Sculpture was opened. Since 1939, the state has been organizing annual exhibitions of national painting and sculpture.

In the post–**World War II** period, the so-called New Group, or "Painters of the Port," adopted social realism as their philosophy of art. They did not wish to transfer art movements and techniques to Turkey from the West as D Group had done but rather to work with social problems. The members of the New Group went their separate ways after the mid-1950s. There were also artists who did not participate in group movements. Later, their numbers increased. The trends and movements varied.

Although the dispute of national versus universal art continued unabated, an atmosphere of freedom has always existed. One came across a diversity of figurative tendencies in the 1960s and 1970s. Since 1980, conceptual art works are common along with the traditional paintings on canvas. Meanwhile, state and private galleries and art shops mushroomed. Pioneering and experimental works were supported by annual exhibitions. The numbers of appreciators and especially connoisseurs increased.

After World War II, figurative art dominated sculpture for a while. With the increased awareness of developments elsewhere, nonfigurative and abstract art spread. In the Academy of Fine Arts, the movement of "Liberal Education" represented the latter trend.

After 1950, many artists took part in international exhibitions. Turkish sculpture became open to all movements in the world. In sculpture, the argument for national versus universal art came to the surface only intermittently and not in an intense form.

In 1998, there were 99 museum directorates connected to the Ministry of Culture, 87 private **museums**, and 1,028 private collections. *See also* ARCHITECTURE.

FOLKLORE. Since the 1920s, Turkish folklorists have unearthed and classified a large number of folk tales, riddles, folk dances, shadow plays, folk plays, long romances, epic stories, and tales. Sumerian proverbs, ancient Greek riddles, Aesop's fables, seasonal rituals of Mesopotamian type, and Shamanist beliefs and dances of Central Asia have influenced Turkish folklore.

Paralleling the significant socioeconomic changes since the inception of the Republic in 1923, Turkish folklore has gone through both textual changes and changes in content. A new vocabulary developed in folk poetry, which derived from the **military** terminology and new political ideas and concepts. Folk poetry has become politicized. The vocabulary, pronunciation, sentence structure, popular expressions, and other devices of oral narrative have gone through drastic mutations. Only very small percentages of audiences are local dwellers, so the narrator is obliged to use a common language developed by the mass media and national education. Turning to changes in content, the new riddles are no longer drawn from local scene but from national life. From the 1940s onward, political and social protest has emerged as a prevalent theme in folk poetry, which, in the pre-1960 period, targeted individual officeholders; in the post-1960 period, it aimed its barbs at the socioeconomic structure of society. In anecdote tradition, there was a great increase in political themes. The feelings of social despair on the part of some members of the intelligentsia produced political jokes about prime ministers and presidents. Today's oral narrators are better educated than their predecessors, and, in their digressions, they comment on all issues—national or international. One now finds a higher degree of rationalization in the narrations.

FOREIGN AID. Turkey has a long history of receiving aid from the **United States**. The beginnings of that aid go back to Point Four and Marshall Plan aid in the aftermath of **World War II**, which contributed to Turkey's postwar economic recovery. During the 1950s, the United States was virtually the only donor country to Turkey. The U.S. contribution was intended to be project assistance and centered primarily on infrastructure and agricultural development. This aid helped to construct a national road network both for economic development and the **North Atlantic Treaty Organization** (NATO)-**military** purposes and regional as well as agricultural development.

To improve agriculture, the United Nations Food and Agriculture Organization (FAO) lent support to the development of the forestry sector, fertilizer use, and animal health and production programs while the World Bank contributed to soil and water conservation, irrigation development, and the development of the livestock industry. The United States also provided assistance to agricultural inputs (tractors and fertilizer), land and water development, agricultural education, research and extension, and wheat production campaigns. Nearly 40,000 tractors were imported during the Marshall Plan period (1948–1952) alone. The U.S. Agency for International Development (US/AID) worked with the Turkish government on fertilizer-related questions.

During the second part of the 1960s and the early 1970s, both US/AID and the World Bank funded the Seyhan Irrigation Project, a large hydroelectric, flood control, and irrigation undertaking that became operational in the early 1980s. In 1960, US/AID helped to establish a Department of Land and Water Resource Development and TOPRAKSU (modeled on the U.S. Bureau of Reclamation). Beginning in 1955, US/AID provided support, through a contract with the University of Nebraska, for an extension-training institute and an agricultural experiment station in Erzurum in eastern Turkey, which developed into Atatürk University in 1957. In 1968, US/AID and the Turkish government started an Integrated Agricultural Services Project on a pilot basis in Denizli province in southwestern Turkey, to move agricultural planning to the provincial and county levels.

In the late 1960s and early 1970s, US/AID shifted its development assistance to the direct support of specific agricultural production objectives, in particular to the demonstration of the dramatic possibilities of new high-yield wheat varieties. US/AID also supported educational planning, school design and construction, mass literacy programs, integrated family planning, rural health programs, and school feeding programs.

As of the late 1950s, U.S. funds were supplemented by assistance from several European donors; program and project support were provided. Between 1960 and 1978, total program and project aid to Turkey reached just under $5.6 billion, or an average of just under $295 million per year. As of 1963, an international consortium organized under the sponsorship of the Organization for Economic Cooperation and Development (OECD) in which the most important contributors were the United States, **Germany**, Italy, Japan, and **Great Britain**, was instrumental in channeling this aid. At that time, Turkey obtained on the average about three-quarters of its foreign aid from this source. Outside the consortium, the Soviet Union (*see* RUSSIA) extended a $200-million loan in 1967 and a credit of $160 million in 1970. In 1975, Turkey and the Soviet Union signed a frame agreement worth $700 million. A further Soviet loan of $400 million was announced in 1979.

From 1963 to 1973, the **European Community** (EC) extended unilateral aid to Turkey in the form of preferential tariffs and quotas for four of its most important agricultural exports, plus $175 million in financial aid, spread over five years (1964–1969). In 1973, the EC granted Turkey a preferential zero tariff rate on products representing about 37 percent of its agricultural exports to the EC and partial preference for products accounting for a further 33 percent of the total. In 1980, the EC came up with a new package of measures, which included some $864 million in grants and loans.

In the 1980s, official development assistance to Turkey gradually decreased. Although it was $952 million in 1980, it dropped to $179 million in 1985 and $122 million in 1989. During the decade, Turkey received more loans than grants. For instance, in 1980, loans made up 37 percent and grants 12 percent of the total financial flows. In 1982, 1984, and 1986, those figures were 25 and 23 percent, 23 and 9 percent, and 16 and 10 percent, respectively.

In the 1980s, the sources of aid changed. The U.S. share registered a consistent decrease, from 23 percent in 1980 to 6 percent in 1986, while Japan's share rose steadily from 2 percent to 6 percent. There was a significant drop in German aid in the early 1980s (from 27 percent in 1980 to 7 percent in 1984), but then it began to pick up; by 1986, Germany was the largest single bilateral donor (12 percent). In the early 1990s, Turkey received substantial grants due to the part it played in the **Gulf War**. Those grants came from Saudi Arabia ($939 million in 1991, $198 million in 1992, and $200 million in 1993), Kuwait ($600 million in 1991, $300 million in 1992), United States ($249 million in 1991), and Germany ($88 million in 1991). Although the total amount of grants Turkey received in 1990 was $74 million, comparable figures for 1991, 1992, and 1993 were $1.9 billion, $506 million, and $280 million, respectively.

During the 1990s, Turkey sought not foreign aid but trade outlets. During these years, grants to Turkey did not appear in the balance of payments accounts. Turkey continued to receive technical aid; however, relatively speaking, it was so insignificant that it was included within another item. During that same decade, Turkey had been able to extend credits to other countries thanks to its successful export performance during the previous two decades. The major recipients have been the new Turkic republics in Central Asia. As of April 1999, Turkey's extension of credit to five Turkic republics were as follows: **Azerbaijan**, allowance $91.8 million, used, $88.1 million; Kazakhstan, allowance $213.1 million, used $213.1 million; Kyrgyzstan, allowance $48.1 million, used $48.1 million; Turkmenistan, allowance $163.2 million, used $104.3 million; and Uzbekistan, allowance $333.6 million, used $322.9 million.

FOREIGN POLICY. A Western orientation has dominated Turkey's foreign policy since the inception of the Republic in 1923. During the two decades following the establishment of the Republic, Turkish political leaders tried to keep the Great Powers at arm's length, but this was basically a consequence of the psychological mark left on them by the role those powers had played in the gradual dismemberment of the Ottoman Empire and not of an inherent hostility toward the West.

The Ottoman Empire itself was a European state. For centuries, not only did it operate within the European state system but it also made alliances with one European country or the other. Despite being "defenders of **Islam**," Ottoman rulers were principled pragmatists with a **secular** outlook. During the 19th century, the Ottomans pursued a realistic foreign policy and played one great power against another.

Atatürk, the founder of the Republic, created a nation-state with the foreign policy motto of "Peace at home and peace abroad." Atatürk formulated Turkish nationalism not on the basis of ethnicity and/or **religion** but on the basis of common citizenship within a defined territory. This approach facilitated the establishment of close relations between Turkey and the West. Atatürk refrained from pursuing a romantic or adventurous foreign policy.

In line with this realistic policy, Atatürk declared eternal friendship with **Greece**, bolstered the already existing relations with the Balkan countries, and improved relations with Italy, which had begun to pose a threat for Turkey. Cordial relations were established with **Great Britain** as well, after Turkey withdrew its claim on the Mosul region. During the 1920s and 1930s, Turkey also entered into several bilateral and multilateral security arrangements—the Treaties of Friendship and Non-aggression with the Soviet Union (*see* RUSSIA) (1921–1925), Kellogg-Briand Pact (1928), Balkan Entente (1934), Saadabad Pact (1936), the Mediterranean Pact (1936), alliance with Britain and **France** (1939), **North Atlantic Treaty Organization** (1952), Balkan Pact (1954), **Baghdad Pact** (1955), and several bilateral security treaties with the **United States**.

Soviet territorial demands on Turkey after **World War II** and the increasing instability in the Middle East served to encourage Turkey's close ties with its Western allies. When Turkey felt isolated during the **Cyprus** crisis from the mid-1960s onward, however, it attempted to diversify its foreign relations. Furthermore, in the 1970s, the oil-rich Muslim Middle East started to figure in Turkey's foreign policy considerations. The collapse of the former Soviet Union coincided with the emergence of a more prosperous and self-confident Turkey, which for some years had not been asking the Western countries to extend *aid* but to diversify and deepen their *trade* with Turkey. Turkey continues to be a firm ally of the United States. After having become a candidate state, it now strives to become a full member of the **European Union**. On the other hand, Turkey also plays an active role in its relations with countries to its north, east, south, and lately in the Balkans. Turkey initiated the **Black Sea Economic Cooperation**

Region, took an active role during the **Gulf War** and the war against terror in Afghanistan, has plans to provide water for the region, and established close relations with the new Turkic republics in central Asia. The strategic role Turkey can play vis-à-vis the new Turkic republics in Central Asia, in particular its potential to prevent Islamic fundamentalism from engulfing these countries, and its ability to export its **secularism** to them, further enhance Turkey's strategic importance. Lately, Turkey has also adopted an active stance concerning the developments in the former Yugoslavia.

From the early 1980s onward, Turkey gradually developed from a marginal state to a regional power. Increasingly, Turkey left behind a foreign policy formulated solely with a view to **military** balance between countries and began to display a liberal engagement. It has established bilateral economic, social, and cultural relations, and **civil societal** entities have been taking an active part in those relations. Such relations began to develop between Turkey, on the one hand, and even such countries as **Bulgaria**, Greece, **Iran** (on a limited basis because of the political regime there), and **Syria** on the other. *See also* FOREIGN AID.

FOREIGN TRADE. For several decades following the establishment of the Republic in 1923, the economy had shown unmistakable signs of autarchy. This resulted partly from the Republican leaders' reaction to the near economic colonization of the country during the 19th century and partly from consequences of the country's natural endowments. Under normal circumstances, Turkey covers most of its own needs for industrial raw materials and can more than feed itself. In **industry**, it is to a great extent self-sufficient in most manufactured goods, thanks to the pre-1980 policy of import substitution. On the other hand, Turkey is not a major supplier of any important internationally traded commodity. With the adoption of the export-oriented policy in 1980, in the place of import substitution, the situation changed drastically. Although the value of exports fluctuated between $1.3 and $2.9 billion and that of imports between $2.0 and $7.9 billion in the years between 1973 and 1980, the corresponding figures for the 1983–1990 period were $5.7 and $12.9 billion for exports and $9.2 and $22.3 billion for imports, and for the 1993–1999 period, $15.3 and $26.5 billion for exports and $29.4 and 40.6 billion for imports. In 1970, the ratio of exports to imports was 62.1 percent; in 1980, 36.8 percent; in 1990, 58.1 percent; and in 1999, 65.2 percent. In the 1973–1980 period, the share of exports within gross national product (GNP) was 4 percent and in the 1983–1990 period, 14 percent. In 1998, it climbed to 24 percent.

However, exports, which had begun to expand as of the early 1980s, slackened after 1988. While the ratio to imports was 81 percent in 1988, it fell to 74 percent in 1989 and 58 percent in 1990. In both 1991 and 1992, that ratio went up to 64 percent, but in 1997 it receded to 59 percent. In 1988, the share of exports in GNP was 13 percent. In 1993, it dropped to 8 percent. In 1997, it rose to 16 percent. In 1990, exports were worth $12.9 billion and imports $22.3 billion. In 1997, exports amounted to $30 billion and imports $50 billion. The foreign trade volume was $79.5 million. The agricultural sector provided 11 percent of Turkey's exports, mining 2 percent, and industry 87 percent. Of the total, 47 percent of Turkey's exports went to **European Union** (EU) countries, 2 percent to members of the European Foreign Trade Association (EFTA), and 11 percent to other countries in the Organization for Economic Cooperation and Development (OECD) countries, 41 percent to non-OECD countries, 15 percent to the countries in the **Black Sea Economic Cooperation Region**, 5 percent to countries belonging to the **Economic Cooperation Organization**, 13 percent to the Commonwealth of Independent States, 3 percent to the Turkic republics, and 16 percent to the member countries of the Islamic Conference Organization.

In 1997, 11 percent of Turkey's imports consisted of investment goods, 32 percent intermediate goods, and 4 percent consumption goods. About 51 percent of Turkey's imports came from EU countries, 3 percent from EFTA countries, 18 percent from other OECD countries, 12 percent from non-OECD countries, 9 percent from countries in the Black Sea Economic Cooperation Region, 2 percent from the countries belonging to the Economic Cooperation Organization, 7 percent from the Commonwealth of Independent States, less than 1 percent from the Turkic republics, and 11 percent from the member countries of the Islamic Conference Organization.

FORUM/YENİ FORUM. Weekly publication, later fortnightly, published in 1954–1979 (*Forum*) and 1982–1993 (*Yeni Forum*) by Professor Aydın Yalçın and his wife, Nilüfer Yalçın. It acted in the mid-1950s as the organ of the liberals (mostly academics) who opposed the emerging authoritarian tendencies on the part of the Democrats (*see DEMOKRAT* PARTY). In the 1980s and early 1990s, it propagated moderate center-right views to institutionalize a serious state and achieve political stability in Turkey.

FOUNDATIONS. The heyday of foundations in Turkish history was experienced during the Ottoman period when their numbers stood at hundreds of thousands. They contributed significantly to the social, economic, and cultural life of society.

Following the proclamation of the Republic in 1923, the management of all the pious foundations [*evkaf*] was taken over by the newly established General Directorate of Foundations, which is affiliated with the prime ministry. In 1998, there were 5,700 pious foundations. The directorate is also responsible for the supervision of other foundations that in 1998 included 162 Community and Artisans' Foundations set up by Armenian, Greek, and Jewish minority citizens.

Until the recent decades, the number of nonpious foundations was low. Then in 1967, the foundations were granted tax exemptions, and provisions favorable to donations to the foundations were enacted into law. Thanks to these and other state supports, the numbers of foundations have increased. Whereas there were 70 nonpious foundations in 1967, in 1998 there were 4,230.

Traditionally, nonpious foundations in Turkey occupied themselves with social assistance, **education**, and **health**. In recent years, they began to concern themselves with such matters as science, technology, democracy, **human rights**, **environmental** protection, and the like. Noteworthy among those are the Turkish Democracy Foundation, Turkish Human Rights Foundation, Contemporary Women's and Youth Foundation, Turkish Foundation for the Struggle against Erosion, Afforestation, and Protection of Natural Assets, **Economic and Social History Foundation of Turkey**, and **Turkish Economic and Social Studies Foundation**.

FOURTEEN, THE. The radical members of the National Unity Committee of the May 27, 1961, **military** intervenors. The Fourteen wished the military to stay in power for a fairly long time "in order to realize the reforms the country needed." On November 13, 1961, they were purged from the committee and sent to sinecures at Turkish embassies around the world. Their dismissal from the committee insured a speedy return to democracy.

FRANCE. France was the first country during the **Turkish War of Independence** to sign an agreement with Turkey (October 20, 1921), which ended the state of war between the two countries. However, at the **Lausanne** Conference (1922–1923), the French made the strongest objections to the abrogation of the **capitulations**. On February 18, 1926, Turkey and France signed a Friendship and Good Neighbor Treaty providing that, should the two countries not resolve their differences through diplomatic means, they would resort to arbitration and that each country was to stay neutral if the other faced armed aggression. Turco-French relations became quite cordial following the resolution of the issue of Ottoman debts in 1933.

Then, from 1936 to 1939, the question of the **Alexandretta** (Hatay) region in **Syria** dominated Turco-French relations. The October 20, 1921, agreement between Turkey and France had left this region outside of the Turkish borders despite the fact that the Turkish population in the area constituted a majority. According to the 1921 agreement, however, a special administration was to be created in Alexandretta; Turkish would be the official language and persons of Turkish origin were to have every opportunity to maintain their cultural identity.

The 1920 San Remo Treaty had placed Syria under French mandate. When, in 1936, Syria and France concluded a treaty to lift the French mandate, the issue of Alexandretta again appeared on the agenda between Turkey and France. Turkey demanded that France reach a similar accord with a delegation from Alexandretta. The French did not think that was possible. The question was referred to the League of Nations, who decided that Alexandretta should have an autonomous status. On July 4, 1938, Turkey and France signed a Treaty of Friendship. In September 1938, Alexandretta became a sovereign state and on June 29, 1939, the parliament of the new state took the historic decision of merging with Turkey. This development led to friendly relations between Turkey and France.

In October 1939, France, **Great Britain**, and Turkey signed a tripartite treaty of alliance. During **World War II**, Turkey remained neutral despite pressure from both sides.

In the post–World War II period, Turkey and France again became allies within the framework of the **North Atlantic Treaty Organization** when Turkey joined that organization in 1952. During the 1960s, Turkey and France pursued similar foreign policies; both distanced themselves from the **United States** and both refrained from supporting **Israel** in the 1967 Arab-Israeli conflict. In the early 1970s, France opted for greater cooperation with Turkey; the former perceived the latter as the foremost element of stability in the region.

During later years, however, Turco-French relations soured. What seemed to Turkey as moral support to Armenian terrorism against Turkish diplomats by the French was one reason for the deterioration of relations between the two countries. Another reason was France's siding with the Greeks regarding **Cyprus** and that country's providing arms to Greek Cypriots. Then the French government opposed the military regime of 1980–1983 in Turkey. Relations between the two countries improved somewhat when, in July 1984, President François Mitterand dispatched his personal envoy, Etienne Manach, to **Ankara**. At this time, France pledged that it would not tolerate terrorist actions against Turkey on French soil.

Relations again became strained when, as of 1988, Danielle Mitterand, the French president's wife, took too close an interest, according to the Turks, in the living conditions of Iraqi refugees (from the **Iraq-Iran** War) in Turkey. She visited the area and spoke rather critically of the conditions in the camps set up by the Turkish government. Mrs. Mitterand had earlier expressed support for Kurdish nationalism. Similarly, the French were the first to put pressure on Turkey to allow hundreds of thousands of Iraqi **Kurds** massed on the Turkish borders with Iraq (following the **Gulf War**), to be settled in Turkey. After letting in the Iraqi Kurds, Turkey found France's financial and relief assistance to the Iraqi Kurds settled on Turkish soil to be less than adequate.

In the 1990s, the relations between Turkey and France once more became harmonious. France was among the countries that invested most in Turkey. From time to time, the lower house of French Parliament revived the Armenian issue; however, the higher house did not act upon the resolutions adopted by that house. For all practical purposes, France placed the Kurdish issue on the back burner. Instead, it actively supported the inclusion of Turkey in the **Customs Union** as well as Turkey's successful bid for being designated as a candidate state to the **European Union**. One sore point between Turkey and France in the 1990s was the latter's unwillingness to include Turkey as a member with full rights in the European Union and relations were again disrupted by the adoption of a resolution on the Armenian genocide by the French Parliament in 2001. *See* ARMENIA.

Turkish-French trade volume remained on an even keel in the 1980s and early 1990s, and it picked up in the mid-1990s. In 1980, it was $534 million; in 1985, $729 million; in 1990, $2.1 billion; in 1995, $3 billion; and in 1999, $4.7 billion.

FREE TRADE ZONES. These are tax-free zones in a number of coastal cities. In 1997, there were eight free trade zones in Turkey. Between 1987 and 1997, the volume of trade realized in these zones exceeded $15 billion.

FREEDOM AND SOLIDARITY PARTY (FSP)/ÖZGÜRLÜK VE DAYANIŞMA PARTİSİ (ÖDP). Formed in 1996, the party is led by Ufuk Uras. It is fervently antimilitaristic and seeks to promote "freedom," "a healthy humannature relationship," "asexual socialism," "the political power of work in place of the sovereignty of capital" and opposes "imperialism." In the April 18, 1999, general elections, the party obtained only 0.8 percent of the vote.

FREEDOM PARTY (FP)/HÜRRİYET PARTİSİ (HP). Formed on December 20, 1955, by those who were expelled or had resigned from the *Demokrat* **Party** (DP). For the most part, the party's members had been liberals and "intellectuals" of the DP. They formed the Freedom Party when, in their opinion, the DP veered away from the essential struggle for democracy and liberalism. The party was led by **Fevzi Lütfü Karaosmanoğlu.** In the 1956 general elections, the FP could return only four deputies to Parliament. In November 1958, the party merged with the **Republican People's Party.**

FUAT PASHA (1815–1869). Ottoman grand vizier. Fuat Pasha served as temporary ambassador in Madrid (1843) and Lisbon (1844). From 1852 until his death, he was appointed foreign minister five times and grand vizier two times. He is considered one of the three architects of the *Tanzimat* **(Reform) Period** (1839–1876). He believed that the Ottoman Empire could survive only by playing such countries as Austria, England, France, and Russia against each other.

FUNDAMENTALISM. On a theoretical plane, fundamentalism has a short history in Turkey. Today, fundamentalist ideas are espoused by a handful of **Islamic** thinkers. What the latter propose is a utopian new order; how that new order will be established is not elaborated.

Islamic detractors of the 19th-century **Westernization** reforms in Turkey did not reject the adoption of Western technology; they only insisted that indigenous "civilization" (read "culture") should be kept intact. As of the 1950s, Islamists argued that the Republican version of **secularism** had meant state control over religion rather than the separation of the two spheres. They did not oppose the secular state but rather the fact that that state granted complete freedom to non-Muslim groups to exercise their faith while denying it to the overwhelmingly Muslim population by exercising close control over instruction in religion, appointing personnel to religious institutions, and the like (*see* RELIGION). From the 1970s onward, Islamists, who found a niche for themselves first in the **National Salvation Party** and then in the **Motherland Party**, the **Welfare Party**, and the **Virtue Party**, revived the earlier debate and criticized Western civilization while urging the adoption of Western **industry**.

As of the early 1980s, a small group of Islamic intellectuals who came from different religio-political platforms (i.e., from the established religious orders to the radical fundamentalist organizations, and received a secular education) began to espouse ideas no longer formulated in terms of Islam versus the West but in terms of a conflict between the Islamic conception of society and the nature of the modern technocratic-industrial civilization.

These Islamists claim that science in the modern world serves as a new idol. Reason replaced faith as the source of all knowledge, yet the human mind is not capable of understanding and explaining all the mysteries of the world and of God's creation. Knowledge originates with the *vahy* [God's revelation], which is written down in the Koran and *Hadith*. A true Muslim takes science as a limited source of understanding, refuses to believe in the omnipotence of the human mind, and, most important, does not test Koranic knowledge on the basis of secular notions of rationality. These new Islamists are critical of both the Westernized intellectuals who have been alienated from the history, culture, and people of their own society and the earlier Islamists who have accepted history and tradition without question and have remained oblivious to change. The former failed to produce original works; the latter's acquiescent attitude has resulted in the poverty of Islamic thought.

In the writings of new Islamists in Turkey, the issue of political opposition to the existing system is not very clear. Political activity of Islamic parties within the existing system is regarded as co-optation. New Islamists want a radical transformation of society spearheaded by Muslim intellectuals. This radicalism aims at destroying modern science and its derivatives—technology and industry—and establishing a new world based on the principles of the Koran and *Hadith*. The gaining of an Islamic consciousness is seen as the first step toward any radical transformation of society. In between the lines, however, there is also talk of a political struggle for the establishment of an Islamic society. However, no blueprint for this transformation is offered. The quest for a return to a preindustrial and pretechnological age emerges as a utopian vision.

Other Islamists, including those who were members of the Virtue Party, are opposed to Turkey's links with the West, which would result in a loss of political and economic independence and Islamic consciousness. They want Turkey to establish closer relations with the Muslim Middle East.

There has been no important religious movement in Turkey that aimed at the establishment of an Islamic republic. On the other hand, as of the late 1980s, a number of leading secular thinkers were assassinated. Who committed these crimes has never become known. Militant Muslim activities are basically carried out by certain religious orders and often in a clandestine manner. One militant Muslim group led by the late Celalettin Kaplan (known as "*Kara Ses*" or "black voice") was most vocal, basically because it was based in **Germany** and escaped prosecution by Turkish authorities. Another militant Muslim group was the **Hizbullah** group.

Such religious groups as that of Kaplan were involved in Islamic education and propaganda, and were believed to be financed by Saudi Arabia and **Iran** to a great extent. They provided the services of employment agencies for their followers, such as finding jobs in urban centers in Turkey and sponsoring Turkish guest-workers to West Berlin and other European cities. The religious orders also try to place their followers in governmental agencies; here, they are helped by conservative and/or religiously oriented members of coalition governments. To what extent they have been able to penetrate governmental agencies is difficult to gauge. Their efforts to penetrate the military has been successfully thwarted; the military from time to time summarily dismisses those who have been attracted to the cause of the religious groups in question. The officers along with the bulk of the intelligentsia as well as people in Turkey remain staunchly secular. Secularism in Turkey is a widely and strongly shared value. Increased demands of a religious nature, a spin-off of the extensive socioeconomic dislocations Turkey has experienced during recent decades, and the prodding from some of the neighboring Muslim countries are on the whole successfully moderated and accommodated within Turkey's democratic regime.

Still, at the turn of the century, there is a debate in the country on the extent to which the religiously oriented parties pose a threat for the secular-democratic state. Another thorny issue is the ban on wearing the turban or veil at university campuses. There is no consensus whether this is essentially part of a political and religious movement or derives primarily from sincere piety.

FUZULİ (1480–1556). Lyric poet and one of the masters of **Divan** poetry. His poems were dominated by the theme of love. For Fuzuli, the poem is a means to display thoughts and feelings, to depict man, and to expose problems. His leading work is *Leyla and Mecnun* [Leyla ile Mecnun].

FÜRUZAN (1935–). Short story writer and novelist. Using poetic language, Füruzan gave account of hard truths surrounding the poor and fallen women. Considered to be one of Turkey's best short story writers in the early 1990s, she conveyed the plight of the oppressed and despised groups in society but refrained from suggesting reforms. Her short stories include *The Charity Pupil* [Parasız Yatılı], *Siege* [Kuşatma], *My Cinema Shows* [Benim Sinemalarım], and *The Other Face of Night* [Gecenin Öbür Yüzü]. Among her novels are *The 47'ers* [47'liler] and *The New Guests* [Yeni Konuklar].

– G –

GALATASARAY LYCÉE. The first and most famous of the secondary schools in the Ottoman Empire and then in the Republic. It opened in 1869 as the Imperial Lycée. The language of instruction has been almost entirely French and the **education** secular. The school's graduates provided leadership in Ottoman governmental and commercial life until the end of the empire and then well into the Republican period.

GALATASARAY UNIVERSITY. Based in **Istanbul**, it is one of the leading private universities; the medium of instruction is French.

GARİH, ÜZEYİR (1929–2001). Engineer and manager. Was co-owner and manager of the Alarko Holding Company. Garih graduated from **Istanbul Technical University** and then obtained a master's degree in management. He also held an honorary degree in engineering. Garih was awarded the Golden Mercury medal and Trophea International a la Qualidad, among others. He is the author of *My Experiences* [Deneyimlerim], in eight volumes.

GAZİ. Warrior of the Islamic faith. The term was often awarded as a title in recognition of valor in battle. It is sometimes spelled "ghazi" in English.

GAZİ OSMAN PASHA (1832–1897). He gained national fame with his defense of Plevna against the invading Russian army in 1876.

GAZİANTEP. The city has a population of 1,347,023 (1997) and is situated in the northeastern corner of the **Mediterranean** region. It is the most important industrial and cultural center of the **Southeastern Development Project** (GAP) area, besides its agricultural wealth. The Kendirli Church, a Catholic church constructed during the French occupation following **World War I**, is one of the most important religious sites. The Monument of Martyrs was erected for those who died in the resistance against the French during the occupation. The martyrs' said resistance earned the city the title of "Gazi"—war veteran.

GECEKONDU. Shanty-like dwelling built illegally on someone else's or public land. All big urban centers are surrounded by them. The term usually refers to squatter housing. *See also* HOUSING.

GENÇER, LEYLA (1923–). Dramatic soprano of international reputation. Gençer appeared as soloist at La Scala Opera in Milan and as guest artist at the Munich, Vienna, San Francisco, Rome, and Venice Operas. She also gave concerts at the Albert Hall in London and Carnegie Hall in New York. She is best known for her performances in operas by Donizetti, Bellini, and Verdi.

GENDARMERIE. The gendarmerie functions, which are carried out outside the municipal borders (an area covering 92 percent of Turkey), are performed by the Gendarmerie General Command (GGC). The GGC has 11 gendarmerie regional commands, 80 gendarmerie provincial commands, and 2,581 gendarmerie internal security stations. Other gendarmerie units include gendarmerie aviation units for air interventions, which provide services throughout Turkey; gendarmerie commando units formed with the function of intervention and support with sufficient forces against the events that exceed the capacity of regular gendarmerie forces; and temporary public order stations with vans, which are established to provide peace and security in regions where the population swells at certain times of the year.

In recent years, the gendarmerie began to use more advanced means of combating crime, such as fingerprinting and criminal record archives, and special units for more effective operations, such as the criminal and narcotic teams and bomb disposal teams.

GERMANY. Keeping open the land route across the Ottoman Empire that connects Europe to Asia became one of the foreign policy objectives of Germany during the 19th century. This led to the Berlin-Baghdad railway scheme pursued by the German government at the turn of the century. Germany came to the brink of establishing its unchallenged influence over the territory concerned when, during the first two decades of the 20th century, the Ottomans favored a close alignment with Germany. In fact, in **World War I**, the Ottomans allied themselves with the Central powers led by Germany. Germany's hopes, however, were dashed when the Allied powers won the war.

In the late 1930s, Germany turned its attention to the Turkish **straits**. Following the German attack on the Soviet Union (*see* RUSSIA) and the invasion of the Soviet shore of the **Black Sea** during **World War II**, the Germans pressured the Turks to allow their warships to pass freely through the straits. Turkey did not succumb to these demands and adhered strictly to the provisions of the 1936 Montreux Treaty, which imposed limitations on the size of the warships that could pass through the straits and on the number permitted to pass at any one time.

On June 18, 1941, Turkey and Germany signed a nonaggression pact. During World War II, Turkey remained neutral (despite the 1939 tripartite alliance between **Great Britain**, **France**, and Turkey) and thus, among other things, it blocked the shipment of German arms and ammunition to the Middle East. In the closing hours of World War II, Turkey declared war on Germany in order to be admitted to the United Nations. This did not adversely affect the future Turkish-German relations. The two countries became allies within the framework of the **North Atlantic Treaty Organization** when Turkey joined that organization in 1952. From 1964 on, Germany extended military aid to Turkey (*see* FOREIGN AID), as a substitute for decreased **United States** military aid (due to America's entanglement in Vietnam). As far as Turkey was concerned, this was a welcome development because it decreased Turkey's **military** dependence on one country alone.

During recent decades, Turkish guest workers in Germany, which were 1.6 million in the early part of 1992 and reached 2.0 million in the mid-1990s, created problems between the two countries. Split families and never-ending visa problems led to a lingering conflict between Germany and Turkey (*see* EMIGRATION AND IMMIGRATION). In April 1990, a diplomatic crisis developed; Bonn requested **Ankara** to withdraw 15 of its diplomats in Germany on the grounds that they were involved in "intelligence work." Turkey reciprocated by asking Germany to withdraw eight of its diplomats from posts in Turkey on charges that they were involved in activities "incompatible with their diplomatic duties." Through secret diplomacy, however, the two countries reached a compromise solution.

In the 1990s, Turkish-German relations were on a roller coaster. In 1991, Germany came forth with generous help when Turkey had to allow the Iraqi **Kurds** to settle on its soil after both the **Iran-Iraq** War and the **Gulf War**. Germany also made efforts to help resettle the Iraqi Kurds in northern Iran. The next year, Germany put an embargo on arms shipments to Turkey on the grounds that the weapons were being used in the southeast against the Kurds. In 1993, Germany was one of the countries that overruled **Greece**'s objections to Turkey's becoming a member of the **Customs Union**. When, at the December 1998 Luxembourg summit of the **European Union** (EU), Turkey was not included among the candidate states and Germany backed this decision, Turkey accused it of wishing to create for itself a *lebensraum* [zone of inluence]. With the replacement of the Christian Democratic government by that of Socialist-Green one in Germany, relations between the two countries once more began to warm. Germany backed Turkey's wish to become a candidate state for the EU, and that support was crucial for Turkey being designated as such in December 1999.

Through financial and technical cooperation, Germany contributed significantly to Turkey's economic development since the early 1960s. The annual average value of Germany's financial assistance to Turkey during the 1980s reached 170 million marks. Germany has also been Turkey's major trade partner in Europe. Turkey's trade volume with Germany was $2.5 billion in 1984, $4.2 billion in 1988, $6.6 billion in 1990, $10.6 billion in 1995, and $11.4 billion in 1999.

GOVERNMENT, LOCAL. The Ottoman-Turkish polity did not have a tradition of local government. In the Ottoman polity, the center dominated the periphery. In contrast to the situation in European feudalism, the local notables did not have political-territorial rights in the Ottoman bureaucratic centralism. The Ottomans also lacked free cities. During the modernization efforts that the center undertook in the 19th century, the center chose to deal with "local affairs" by deconcentration, that is by more systematically extending itself to the localities.

The Republican governmental system in 1923 was characterized by centralization. An elaborate tutelage system was established over local government, exercised primarily by the ministries of interior and of reconstruction and resettlement. As in Ottoman times, the center subscribed to the idea that the central and local governments *together* formed a "unified whole." The tutelage in question bordered on hierarchical supervision.

Following **World War II**, Turkey underwent a rapid urbanization, a fair degree of *industrialization*, and growth of the private sector. These developments led to such problems as the increasing density of population in urban areas, emergence of squatter settlements in massive proportions (*see* GECEKONDU;

HOUSING), diversification of the urban population, and inadequacy of facilities for marketing and distribution of goods. The existing local governments could not deal with these problems. Among other things, local governments lacked the necessary financial resources as well as adequate expertise.

The **Motherland Party**, which came to power in 1983, decided to bring about a combination of political and administrative decentralization. Its view was that devolving powers to the localities would both promote democracy and make delivery of more and better services possible. From 1984 onward, in a number of urban centers, two-tiered metropolitan municipalities were established. These municipalities were provided with significant powers and relatively ample financial resources. Metropolitan municipal governments consisted of a metropolitan municipality and a number of district municipalities.

The decentralization in question stopped at the level of the metropolitan municipality; it did not extend to the district municipalities. Only such functions as waste disposal, repairing secondary roads, and issuing "second- and third-class" building permits were left to the district municipalities. The division of responsibility between the two sets of municipalities was also left unclear; many tasks were "coordinated" by the office of the metropolitan mayor. The metropolitan municipality could decide to carry out itself a task that was left to the district municipality but was wholly financed by the metropolitan municipality. The metropolitan municipality was a superior body that oriented, guided, and reviewed the activities of the district municipalities and could even take over functions performed by the latter.

As for financial resources, the metropolitan municipality's main sources of revenues were the municipal shares from the national taxes; municipal taxes, fees, and charges, including participation charges (that is, amounts charged to the beneficiaries of investments in transportation, road construction, utilities and the like); income from municipal real estate; and various municipal enterprises. District municipalities received a certain percentage of these revenues as determined by law. Thus, at least on paper, resource allocation between metropolitan and district municipalities was effected according to clear-cut rules.

In practice, however, district municipalities came to face serious financial problems. The variation in the population characteristics, nature of business activities, and needs and resources of the district municipalities was substantial; applying the same rules for resource allocation to all districts created inequalities. In case of need, the metropolitan municipality could extend financial assistance to district municipalities. But, in practice, this was done in a haphazard and partisan manner and the additional resources provided remained far below actual needs.

From the beginning, the decentralization of local government did not reach district municipalities; toward the end of the 1980s, however, the decentralization at the level of the metropolitan municipality was also partly reversed. As municipal expenditures were perceived to have exacerbated **inflation** and as an increasing number of district mayors were engaged in corrupt behavior, resources at the disposal of the municipalities were somewhat curtailed and some tutelage powers were returned to the Ministries of Interior and of Reconstruction and Resettlement.

Another factor that made things difficult for local governments in Turkey was the increased political competition in the late 1980s between the central and local governments. Early in the 1980s, many mayors had belonged to the governing party. Particularly after the 1989 local elections, this situation changed, and the reluctance of the central government to extend additional financial resources to the municipalities headed by mayors from opposition parties left the municipalities in question in dire straits. The coming to power in the mid-1990s of mayors from the religiously oriented **Welfare Party** in such major urban centers as **Ankara** and **Istanbul** created additional difficulties. *See also* GOVERNMENT, NATIONAL.

GOVERNMENT, NATIONAL. Turkey has a parliamentary system of government. The Turkish Grand National Assembly is a 450-seat unicameral body. Its members are elected for a five-year term through universal suffrage. Besides its legislative powers, Parliament elects the president, and has the authority to declare war, proclaim martial law, and ratify international treaties. Parliament can also amend the **constitution** with a two-thirds majority. The president of the Republic is the head of the state. He is elected by a two-thirds majority of the plenary session of Parliament for a term of seven years. (For the president's powers, *see* CONSTITUTIONS.)

The prime minister is appointed by the president from among the members of Parliament. Once the cabinet is approved by the president, the government program is submitted to the Parliament and a vote of confidence is taken. Ministers may be from outside Parliament. A minister may be dismissed by the president upon the request of the prime minister.

The cabinet may issue decree-laws (governmental decrees with the force of law). Decree-laws need to be submitted to the approval of Parliament within a specified period. *See also* GOVERNMENT, LOCAL.

GÖKBERK, MACİT (1908–1993). Student of philosophy and linguist. Gökberk is best known for his study of the views of Immanuel Kant and Johann Gottfried Herder on the question of history, which he first took up in his *Kant's and Herder's Approaches to History* [Kant ile Herder'in Tarih Anlayışları]. He focused on the same theme in his *History of Philosophy* [Felsefe Tarihi] and *Felsefenin Evrimi* [The Evolution of Philosophy].

GÖKÇEN, SABİHA (1913–2001). Turkey's first female air force pilot, flying combat aircraft as early as 1936. She took an active part in the bombing of targets during the Kurdish insurrection (*see* KURDS) in 1937 in the Dersim (now Tunceli) area. Gökçen was one of the adopted children of **Atatürk**.

GÖLPINARLI, ABDÜLBAKİ (1900–1982). Historian of **literature** with significant works on **Islam**, Sufism (*see* ISLAM), religious orders, **Divan** literature, and Iranian literature. Gölpınarlı successfully combined his Muslim identity with his intellectual identity.

GRAND TURKEY PARTY (GTP)/BÜYÜK TÜRKİYE PARTİSİ (BTP). Set up on May 21, 1983, by former **Justice Party** (JP) members. The party had a life of only 11 days. On May 31, 1983, the **military** administration dissolved the party on charges that it was an explicit heir to the JP. On June 23, 1983, some of the former JP supporters founded a new party—the **True Path Party**.

GREAT BRITAIN. British interest in the Ottoman Empire and Turkey goes back to the first part of the 19th century when, in 1833, the Russians (*see* RUSSIA) came close to establishing their control over the Bosporus and Dardanelles **Straits** that connect, through the **Marmara Sea**, the **Black Sea** to the **Aegean** and the **Mediterranean**. Maintaining their country's safe passage to India across the Mediterranean constituted one of the fundamental tenets of British foreign policy. Great Britain managed by the 1841 London Convention to reverse the provisions of the 1833 Treaty of Hunkiar İskelesi that had established virtual Russian control of the straits. The 1841 convention forbade the entry of foreign warships to the straits. When, during **World War I**, the Ottomans allied themselves with the Central powers and closed the straits to Allied shipping (thus cutting the most direct line of supply between Russia and its Western allies), the British, leading an Allied naval force, tried to break through the Turkish blockade of the straits in 1915 but was not successful. When the Central powers lost the war, **Istanbul** came under an international regime dominated by Great Britain. The control of the straits was later returned to Turkey, partly by the 1924 Treaty of **Lausanne** and completely by the 1936 Montreux Treaty.

Great Britain was not unfriendly to Turkey in the interwar period once the Mosul region was given to **Iraq** in 1925 by the League of Nations (at the time, Iraq was under British mandate). On October 19, 1939, Great Britain, **France**, and Turkey signed a tripartite treaty of alliance. During **World War II**, Turkey could not act on the obligations deriving from this treaty but, by adhering to strict neutrality that prevented the shipment of German arms and ammunition across Turkey to the Middle East, Turkey inadvertently helped the British cause—"inadvertently" because throughout the war the British exerted pressure on Turkey to abandon its neutrality. When, in the aftermath of World War II, the Soviets made territorial demands on Turkey and pressured the latter to let them have a share in the defense of the straits, Great Britain, alongside the **United States**, backed Turkey. However, Turkey relied more on the United States than Great Britain in its confrontation with the Soviet Union. For its part, at least for a while, Great Britain was not enthusiastic to have close relations with Turkey. It was unwilling to admit Turkey to the **North Atlantic Treaty Organization** (NATO), and instead wished to see Turkey organize a Western alliance system in the Middle East and, among other things, contribute to the defense of the Suez Canal. Turkey became a member of NATO in 1952. London, however, still wished **Ankara** to play an active role in the defense of the Middle East. The upshot was the 1955 **Baghdad Pact**, which was also enthusiastically supported by Washington. Great Britain, Turkey, Iraq, **Iran**, and Pakistan were the pact's members.

From the mid-1960s onward, the **Cyprus problem** dominated Turco-British relations. Great Britain contributed to reaching an agreement in 1959 between Turkey, **Greece**, Turkish Cypriots, and Greek Cypriots. Great Britain, along with Turkey and Greece, was to serve as a guarantor of the independence and sovereignty of the newly created Republic of Cyprus. In 1974, when a coup was carried out in Cyprus against President Archbishop Makarios by a Greek pro-*enosis* group, Turkey turned to Great Britain to act jointly against the perpetrators of the coup. London, however, adopted a hands-off policy, and Turkey unilaterally intervened in Cyprus. Great Britain did not attempt to prevent Turkey from invading northern Cyprus. However, when Turkish Cypriots formed the Turkish Republic of Northern Cyprus, Britain did not recognize this new political entity and joined other countries to apply an economic and political embargo to the new republic. During more recent years, Great Britain has insisted on a solution to the lingering Cyprus problem, without, however, pressuring for a specific game plan.

Still, from the early 1970s to the late 1990s, Turkey and Great Britain maintained cordial relations. Great Britain did not openly condone **Armenian** terrorism against Turkish diplomats as France did, nor did Great Britain turn out to be an ardent opponent of Turkey's entry to the **European Community/Union** as, for example, **Germany** has been. One sore spot was Britain's imposition of visas for Turks, starting on June 23, 1989, in response to a sudden increase in Turkish immigration to Britain. Turkey reciprocated, though any Briton who paid a certain nominal fee at Turkish customs obtained his/her visa automatically.

In the wake of the **Gulf War**, which once more underscored Turkey's geostrategic importance, the relations between Great Britain and Turkey developed further. Great Britain helped Turkey cope with a massive accumulation of Iraqi **Kurds** on the latter's borders after the Gulf War, and later with their resettlement in northern Iraq. On Turkey's arduous road to become a candidate state for the European Union (EU) (1999), Great Britain played a positive role. Economic relations with Britain have a long tradition. Turkey's trade volume with Britain amounted to $421 million in 1980, $1 billion in 1985, $1.8 billion in 1990, $3.7 billion in 1996, and $4.1 billion in 1999.

GREECE. Turkey's neighbor to the west. Greece obtained its independence from the Ottoman Empire in 1829. The Turks fought mainly against the invading Greek forces in the **War of Independence** (1920–1922). Following the establishment of the Turkish Republic in 1923, Mustafa Kemal (**Atatürk**) of Turkey and Eleftherios Venizelos of Greece opened a new era of friendly relations between the two countries. They signed and implemented a population exchange agreement. During the early 1930s, high-level visits took place between Turkey and Greece. In the following years, several pacts and agreements were signed. In 1952, both Greece and Turkey became members of the **North Atlantic Treaty Organization** (NATO).

From 1954 on, relations between the two countries began to deteriorate. Tensions broke out in **Cyprus** as the Greek majority was determined to exert control over the Turkish minority. In 1959, the London and **Zurich** agreements between **Great Britain**, Turkey, Greece, the Greek Cypriot community, and the Turkish Cypriot community gave birth to the Republic of Cyprus and made the first three countries the guarantors of the consociational rule established by those treaties.

The establishment of the Republic of Cyprus did not put an end to the communal strife. Turkey, as one of the guarantors of the republic, several times came to the brink of intervening in the island and in fact did so in 1974 when Greece engineered a coup on Cyprus and showed an unmistakable intention (to the Turks) of merging the island with Greece. When no progress was made in the prolonged negotiations that followed, the Turkish Cypriot community established the Turkish Republic of Northern Cyprus with the help of Turkey. The republic has expressed its readiness to accept a bizonal federation solution on the island, which did not find a sympathetic ear on the Greek-Cypriot side. The Cyprus conflict has not yet been resolved.

Turkish-Greek relations have been strained not only because the Cyprus issue remained unresolved but also because of Greek claims in the **Aegean**. Greece argued that the Aegean islands (most of which belong to Greece) have their own territorial waters. This claim, which would turn the Aegean into a Greek sea and entitle Greece to the natural resources on the continental shelf, was unacceptable to Turkey. The Greek claim to territorial waters was followed by a Greek claim to the airspace over the Aegean. Greece armed the Aegean islands, which were to be kept demilitarized according to international agreements. The Greek lobby in Washington managed a seven-to-ten ratio in American aid to Greece and Turkey. The Greeks used the so-called "Turkish threat" as leverage for Greece's ties with the **United States**, NATO, and the **European Community/Union**.

In January 1988, Turkish Prime Minister **Turgut Özal** and Greek Prime Minister Andreas Papandreou met at the Swiss town of Davos to initiate what was referred to as "the Davos spirit" in relations between the two countries—an agreement to work together toward a "lasting and peaceful solution." Bilateral talks followed, but the traditional tension between the two countries continued.

Those tensions reached a new high in June 1989 when Athens accused **Ankara** of interfering in the Greek election campaign through radio broadcasts supporting ethnic Turkish candidates. Turkey rejected the claims. This was followed by several Greek measures to frustrate the efforts of Turco-Greeks to get elected to the Greek Parliament. Anti-Turkish riots took place in Greece. In Turkey, a Turk, undergoing mental treatment, set fire to a double-decker bus carrying Greek tourists, killing 35. In 1992, Turkey and Greece continued to have serious differences on such matters as the Aegean continental shelf, territorial waters, the status of the Aegean islands, the Greek government's policies toward the Turkish-Muslim minority in western Thrace, and the Cyprus issue.

In 1994, Greece tried to block Turkey's accession to the **Customs Union** with the European Union (EU), but this was not successful, thanks to British and French support for Turkey. That same year, Turkey and Greece simultaneously conducted naval exercises in the Aegean. Greece reiterated that it has the right to extend its territorial waters to 12 miles, adding that it had no intention of implementing this right. Turkey had tersely declared that if Greece extends its territorial waters to 12 miles from their current 6 miles it would consider it a *casus belli*. U.S. President Bill Clinton had to urge restraint on both countries. In the event, the naval exercises were completed without incident. In 1996, the two countries again threatened each other with war over two rocky islets in the Aegean Sea. Again, the United States had to tell the NATO allies to cool off. Relations suffered further when Greece repeatedly blocked financial assistance to Turkey by the EU. Meanwhile, nongovernmental organizations (NGOs) from both countries organized contacts and conferences concerning relations between the countries. Then, at its summit in Luxembourg, the EU made Turkey's accession conditional upon better relations between Turkey and Greece.

A devastating **earthquake** in Turkey in August 1999 and the rushing of a Greek team to save victims from under the rubble helped turn the situation around. On the occasion of an earthquake in Greece a few months later, the Turks reciprocated. These events were preceded by a rapprochement between Ankara and Athens, brought about essentially by the statesmanship of Greek Foreign Minister Yorgos Papandreou and Turkish Foreign Minister **İsmail Cem**. At the Helsinki Summit of the EU in 1999, Athens lifted its objection to the recognition of Turkey as a candidate state to the EU. The EU declared that before 2004—the date when the EU will consider whether to admit Turkey as a full member to the EU—Greece and Turkey should resolve their differences. Turkey made it clear that it would oppose the accession of the Republic of Cyprus to the EU before the Cyprus issue is resolved.

GREENS PARTY (GP)/YEŞİLLER PARTİSİ (YP). The party was founded on June 6, 1988, and is led by **Bedri Celal Ertuğ**. It has not yet participated in any of the elections.

"GRAY WOLVES." Paramilitary arm of the **Nationalist Action Party**'s youth movement in the 1970s.

GULF WAR (1990–1991). During the Gulf crisis that started with the occupation of Kuwait by **Iraq** in August 1990, Turkey was one of the first countries that implemented the economic embargo imposed on Iraq by the United Nations (UN). It closed down the oil pipeline that carried the Iraqi oil to its Yumurtalık Port on the **Mediterranean**. Turkey suffered a great economic loss due to the embargo.

Turkey allowed the allies to use the **United States'** air bases in Turkey for air operations in Iraq.

Following the war, Turkey was confronted with an immigration wave of close to one million refugees, composed mainly of people of Kurdish origin (*see* KURDS). After the allies declared the Iraqi territory to the north of the 36th parallel as a "Security Zone," the bulk of the refugees returned to Iraq.

GÜL, ABDULLAH (1950–). Economist and politician. By challenging the leadership of **Mehmet Recai Kutan** in the **Virtue Party** (April 2000), he became the first politician to announce his candidacy against a leader in a religiously oriented party in Turkey.

GÜLEK, KASIM (1905–1996). Politician. Gülek received a B.A. degree in political science from Paris University, a Ph.D. degree in economics from Columbia University, and another Ph.D. degree in law from Berlin University. He became a member of Parliament in 1939. From 1947 to 1949, he served in different **Republican People's Party** (RPP) governments as minister of public works, transportation, and of state. In June 1950, Gülek was elected secretary-general of the RPP and remained in that post until 1959. During this time, he introduced into Turkish politics American style handshaking with electors prior to election campaigns. He took part in the post-May 1960 **military** intervention **Constituent Assembly** that prepared the 1961 **constitution**. In March 1961, Gülek started to publish a daily newspaper, *Tanin*. Between 1969 and 1971, he was a senator. Gülek quit active politics in 1973.

GÜLEN, FETHULLAH (1941–). Leader of the Fethullah religious order, the members of which belong to the movement of "the proponents of Light" [Nurcular] (*see* SAİD-İ NURSİ). Gülen subscribes to the ecumenical movement; he visited the Pope to break the ice between Christianity and **Islam**. In Turkey, he strove for the moral development of the people and for a successful marriage between a modernized Islam, on the one hand, and the secular and democratic republic, on the other. He opened several schools abroad, many of them in the **Turkic republics** but also in such countries as **Russia** and the **United States**. The curricula at these schools are mostly secular. Suspected of being a supporter of political Islam, Gülen was repeatedly prosecuted but not convicted. Many of his books were translated into English. They include *Truth through Colors* [Renkler Kuşağında], *Questions-I* [Tereddütler-I], *The Infinite Light-I* [Sonsuz Nur-I], *The Infinite Light-II* [Sonsuz Nur-II], *Toward the Lost Paradise* [Yitirilmiş Cennete Doğru], and *Criteria or the Lights of the Way* [Ölçü veya Yoldaki Işıklar].

GÜMÜŞPALA, RAGIP (1897–1964). General and politician. Gümüşpala became a four-star general in 1960. He served briefly as chief of the general staff following the May 27, 1960, **military** intervention. Following his abrupt retirement from the latter post, he joined the efforts to bring together the supporters of the

Demokrat **Party** (DP) closed by the military. Gümüşpala was elected chairman of the newly established **Justice Party** (JP), the successor party to the DP. He was elected to Parliament in the October 15, 1961, general elections and led the JP until his death.

GÜN, AYDIN (1940–). **Opera** conductor and first tenor in Turkish opera. Gün studied music in Vienna. He worked with Carl Ebert. Gün staged operas in Australia, Germany, and Italy. He played lead roles in such operas as *Aida, Carmen, Don Carlos, Don Giovanni, Macbeth, Madame Butterfly, Marriage of Figaro, Il Travatore, La Tosca, Rigoletto, Salome,* and many others.

GÜNALTAY, ŞEMSETTİN (1883–1961). Professor of history and politician. Günaltay studied at Lausanne University. He became a member of the **Committee for Union and Progress** and served in the Ottoman Parliament from 1915 until 1920, when that Parliament was dissolved. During the Republican period, Günaltay served in Parliament from 1923 until 1954. He was prime minister between January 15, 1949, and May 14, 1950. He became a member of the **Constituent Assembly** that prepared the 1961 **Constitution**. He also acted as head of the Turkish Historical Institute from 1941 until his death. Günaltay was known for his efforts to modernize **Islam**.

GÜNEŞ, TURAN (1922–1982). Professor of administrative law and politician. Güneş obtained a Ph.D. degree from Paris University. In 1954, he became a member of Parliament on the *Demokrat* **Party** (DP) ticket. He was dismissed from the party when he became critical of the DP's gradual shift to an authoritarian posture. Güneş was one of the founders and also secretary-general of the **Freedom Party**. In 1959, he joined the **Republican People's Party** (RPP). He was a member of the Constitutional Commission of the **Constituent Assembly** that prepared the 1961 **constitution**. After 1965, he contributed to the development of the left-of-center policy within the RPP. Güneş served as minister of foreign affairs in the 1973–1974 RPP-**National Salvation Party** coalition government. He represented Turkey at the peace conference, which was held following Turkey's invasion of northern **Cyprus**. He became minister of state and deputy prime minister in the 1977 RPP minority government. Güneş was known for his colorful personality and folksy behavior.

GÜNEY, EFLATUN CEM (1891–1981). Folklorist and tale writer. Güney rewrote tales, which he painstakingly collected without distorting their distinctive structures. He turned folk stories, tales, and epics into literary pieces. Güney won the Andersen Honors Diploma (1956) and the World Children Literature Certificate (1960), both awarded by the Hans Christian Andersen Institute in Denmark.

GÜNEY, YILMAZ (1937–1984). A popular and acclaimed filmmaker with a Marxist worldview. His movies strongly reflected his politics. *Hope* [Umut], a stylistically very pure and lucid film about a poor horse-carriage driver from Adana, marked a turning point in Turkish **cinema**. *The Herd* [Sürü], depicting the drama of a peasant girl who bore only stillborn children for her husband, and *The Path* [Yol], a great epic about a country beset by social change, became international successes, with the latter receiving The Golden Palm award at the Cannes Film Festival in 1982.

GÜNTEKİN, REŞAT NURİ (1889–1956). Novelist, short story writer, and playwright. Güntekin made a significant contribution to the development of the early Republican novel. His novel *The Wren* [Çalıkuşu] (Eng. trans., *The Autobiography of a Turkish Girl*), which depicted the trials and tribulations of social change in small towns and villages of Anatolia, was for a long time one of the most popular works among both the intellectuals and common people. His other important novels are *Falling Leaves* [Yaprak Dökümü], *The Green Night* [Yeşil Gece], *From the Lips to the Heart* [Dudaktan Kalbe], and *The Evening Sun* [Akşam Güneşi] (Eng. trans., *The Afternoon Sun*).

GÜNVER, SEMİH (1917–2000). Ambassador, author, and columnist. Günver represented **Ankara** in Cairo, Algiers, and the Council of Europe. He received medals and decorations from Egypt, **Germany**, Italy, and Poland. He is the author of *The Unknown Profession* [Bilinmeyen Meslek], *Like Z. Zorro* [Z. Zorro Gibi], and *If I Could Be a Cherry Tree* [Bir Kiraz Ağacı Olsaydım].

GÜRKAN, AYDIN GÜVEN (1941–). Professor of economics. In June 1985, Gürkan became the chairman of the **Populist Party** (PP) and, from November 1985 until May 1986, he led the **Social Democratic Populist Party**.

GÜRKAN, KAZIM İSMAİL (1905–1972). Professor of medicine. Gürkan worked at various hospitals in Paris and served as rector of **Istanbul University** in 1951–1953. Gürkan played an important role in the development of contemporary methods of surgery in Turkey.

GÜRPINAR, HÜSEYİN RAHMİ (1864–1944). Novelist, short story writer, and humorist. Gürpınar was concerned with exposing universal human foibles and attempted to elevate his readers to a lofty philosophy through folk humor. His most popular novels are *The Governess* [Mürebbiye], *The Mistress* [Metres], *Puppy Love* [Şıpsevdi], *A Marriage under the Tailed Comet* (i.e., Halley's Comet) [Kuyruklu Yıldız Altında Bir İzdivaç], and *The Bogeyman* [Gülyabani].

GÜRSEL, CEMAL (1894–1966). General and fourth president of Turkey. Gürsel graduated from Army Staff College in 1929, was promoted to four-star general in 1957, and appointed as commander of the land forces in 1958. He wrote a critical letter to the minister of defense when the *Demokrat* **Party** government did not allow the opposition party leader **İsmet İnönü** to enter the mid-Anatolian city of Kayseri during the latter's electoral campaign. Gürsel then sent a farewell letter to the army and left for **İzmir** on May 3, 1960. When the **military** took power on May 27, 1960, Gürsel became the head of state, prime minister, and commander of the Turkish armed forces. During the military rule that followed, he contributed to the relatively rapid return to civilian politics. Following the reinstallation of civilian government, Gürsel was elected president on October 26, 1961. During his presidency, he managed to get the **Republican People's Party** and the **Justice Party** to form a coalition government and rule the country together. In mid-1960, he was partially paralyzed. His situation became worse and on March 28, 1966, a medical report indicated that he could no longer perform his functions as president. His presidency came to an end and he died soon after.

GÜRSEY, FEZA (1921–1992). Professor of physics with a Ph.D. from Cambridge University. From 1977 until he died, he was a Josiah Willard Gibbs Professor at Yale University. Gürsey, who worked on mathematical physics, high energy, and basic particles, received the Oppenheimer Award (1979), Einstein Medal (1979), Morrison Award (1981), and Wigner Medal (1991).

GÜVENÇ, BOZKURT (1926–). Professor of anthropology and honorary member of the **Turkish Academy of Sciences**. Güvenç graduated from Georgia Tech. University, and received his master of science and master of art degrees from Massachusetts Institute of Technology and Columbia University, respectively. He was awarded the Japanese Emperor's Golden Rays of Rising Sun decoration. His books include *Turkish Demography* [Türkiye Demografyası], *The Problem of Culture* [Kültür Sorunu], *The Japanese Culture* [Japon Kültürü], *Turkish Identity* [Türk Kimliği], and *Cultural Change* [Kültürel Değişme].

– H –

HACI BEKTAŞ VELİ (1210?–1271?). Famous mystic thinker who is thought to have provided an inspiration to the **Bektashi mystic order.**

HAKİMİYET-İ MİLLİYE [National Sovereignty]. Leading newspaper of the Turkish nationalist movement during the **Turkish War of Independence**. It continued publication from 1920 until 1934. Its successor was *Ulus* [Nation].

HALET EFENDİ (1761–1822). Ottoman civil servant. He served as ambassador to Napoleon's **France** in 1802. He had great influence during **Mahmut II**'s reign.

HALİKARNAS BALIKÇISI (1886–1973). Novelist, short story writer, "nature lover," and painter. Halikarnas lived in **Bodrum**, a popular resort town on the southwest coast of Turkey. He represented the rebellious dimension of the

Turkish ethos and was inspired by themes of Greek mythology. His work reflected realism. Halikarnas was the major Turkish exponent of the "sea tale." His stories included *Greetings Mediterranean* [Merhaba Akdeniz] and *The Bottom of the Aegean* [Ege'nin Dibi]. Among his novels are *Captain Uluç* [Uluç Kaptan] and *Captain Turgut* [Turgut Reis].

HALMAN, TALAT SAİT (1931–). Professor of literature and art. Halman received a master of arts degree from Columbia University and an honorary Ph.D. degree from **Boğaziçi University**. He taught at Columbia, New York, and Princeton Universities. He presently teaches at **Bilkent University** in **Ankara**. Halman, who served as Turkey's Cultural Ambassador to the **United States** from 1980 to 1982, received the Knight Grand Cross of the British Empire from Queen Elizabeth. His books include *A Lust Lullaby, Living Poets of Turkey, A Republic of Poetry: An Anthology of Modern Turkish Poetry, Süleyman the Magnificent, A Dot on the Map: Selected Stories of Sait Faik, Mevlana Celadettin Rumi and the Whirling Dervishes, Contemporary Turkish Literature, Rain One Step Away: Selected Poems of Melih Cevdet Anday, Yunus Emre and His Mystical Poetry, Shadows of Love, I Am Listening to Istanbul: Selected Poems of Orhan Veli Kanık, Wallace Stevens, Selected Poems of Fazıl Hüsnü Dağlarca,* and many others.

HANÇERLİOĞLU, ORHAN (1916–1991). Novelist and essayist. National questions predominate Hançerlioğlu's novels, which include *The Game* [Oyun], *Unsown Soil* [Ekilmemiş Topraklar], *Big Fishes* [Büyük Balıklar], and *Master Ali* [Ali]. He also wrote *The Idea of Happiness* [Mutluluk Düşüncesi], *The Idea of Liberty* [Özgürlük Düşüncesi], *The Dictionary of Economy* [Ekonomi Sözlüğü], *The Dictionary of Belief* [İnanç Sözlüğü], and *The Encyclopedia of Philosophy: Concepts and Trends* [Felsefe Ansiklopedisi: Kavramlar ve Akımlar].

HAYREDDİN PASHA (BARBAROS) (1473–1546). Ottoman admiral. Hayreddin Pasha first achieved fame as a corsair operating out of Tunisia. He became Sultan **Selim I**'s governor-general of Algiers. He imposed Ottoman naval dominance in the **Mediterranean** and, in September 1538, won a great naval battle in Preveze against a combined European fleet.

HEALTH. From the early years of the Republic, the state assumed the responsibility of providing all kinds of health services free of charge. It set up various types of health institutions. In 1923, there were 89 hospitals and 6,437 hospital beds. By 1998, there were over 1,000 hospitals (some of which were private), and an additional 4,000 health centers, altogether 160,000 beds. In 1950, the population per bed was 1,100; it dropped to 600 in 1960, 409 in 1970, 304 in 1980, increased to 412 in 1990, and decreased to 406 in 1996.

Also, from the inception of the Republic, the state set out to train health personnel. Consequently, the population per doctor steadily dropped. In 1950, the number was 3,308; in 1960, it was 2,825; in 1970, 2,572; in 1980, 1,652; in 1990,

1,121; and in 1996, 903. There were similar improvements concerning the numbers of other health personnel too. From 1989 to the end of 1997, the population per pharmacist decreased from 3,655 to 3,354 and the population per nurse from 1,281 to 857. From 1989 to 1995, the population per dentist dropped from 5,485 to 4,561, the population per health officer from 2,945 to 1,449, and the population per midwife from 1,988 to 1,446.

Not unexpectedly over the decades, there has been a successful fight against infectious diseases. In 1925, per 100,000 of population, 10 persons died from dysentery, 398 from measles, 7 from scarlet fever, and 538 from diphtheria; in 1990, these figures had dropped to 6, 11, 1, and 1, respectively. However, what Turkey spent per person for health always remained less than satisfactory. In 1988, the health expenditure per person was $579 in **Germany** and $611 in **France**; the health expenditure in Turkey in 1988 was less than $7. The situation has worsened over the years. There is still a general shortage of hospital beds, and medical services are rather unevenly distributed; the overwhelming majority of doctors and hospital beds are in major urban centers.

This uneven development of health could not be turned around despite the fact that the government started a program of "socialization" in health services in 1961. The program aimed at bringing together the facilities operated by different institutions and opening "health houses" under a midwife in villages, health units under a physician for groups of three villages, and group hospitals in provincial and subprovincial centers. The government started the scheme in the most neglected eastern provinces. This program, however, could only be partially implemented. By the early 1980s, just over 50 percent of the number of doctors needed could be employed under the scheme because of inadequate financial incentives. Toward the end of the 1970s, an attempt was even made to prevent doctors who worked in the public sector from going into private practice (and in return provide them with substitute compensation). This scheme also ended in failure. Here, too, compensation was less than satisfactory.

A fresh scheme formulated in 1996 envisages the adoption of general health insurance. In the medium term, it is planned to bring all public **social security** agencies under one roof. At the end of 1997, more than 6.5 million persons who were under any social security scheme received free health services within the framework of the newly established "Green Card" system, which forms the first step toward the planned system.

HİSAR, ABDÜLHAK ŞİNASİ (1883–1963). Novelist. Hisar depicted, through the eyes of aristocratic families, the life and people of the period of Ottoman decline. He interwove detailed plots with lyrical description. His work reflected nostalgia for the "good old days." His most popular novels are *Fehim Bey and Us* [Fehim Bey ve Biz] and *Brother-in Law in Çamlıca* [Çamlıca'daki Eniştemiz].

HİSARLIK. The site of ancient Homer's Troy in northwest Turkey. The site was first inhabited in the Early Bronze Age.

HITTITES. An imperial Hittite state arose in Anatolia after 1800 B.C.E. in the northwestern margins of the Mesopotamian civilization. An amalgamation between Hittite and Mesopotamian elements produced in due course a derivative yet stylistically distinct Hittite culture and civilization. The Hittite Empire, which rested on a chariot aristocracy recruited from among barbarian tribesmen, came to an end about 1200 B.C.E.

HİZBULLAH. Islamic Movement Community [İslami Hareket Cemaati] that aims at creating a pristine Islamic state, if necessary by killing the "unbelievers." In recent years, organized in southeastern Turkey, its militants clashed with the Kurdistan Worker's Party (PKK), and abducted and killed by torture several Muslim businessmen in the southeast and elsewhere who had refused to finance the community. Hizbullah, which did not have a large following, was largely neutralized by the state in 2000.

HOUSING. Until **World War II**, the urbanization rate was rather low and the vast majority of people built their own houses from locally available material—timber, brick, and stone in the coastal regions, stone and mud-brick in central and eastern Anatolia. The rapid urbanization since World War II greatly increased the demand for housing, and there occurred a desperate shortage of decent low-cost housing. For instance, according to estimates, there was a total demand for around 1.2 million housing units (apartments and houses) from 1973 to 1977, but less than 980,000 units were constructed in accordance with building regulations.

An aggravating factor is that, due to persistent **inflation**, building a dwelling takes a long time: in 1986, 138,155 building permits were issued and in 1989, 121,551 were issued; on the other hand, in 1987, only 80,520 occupancy permits were granted, and in 1989, only 83,714 were granted. In addition, during recent years, the number of residential construction **cooperatives** went down—2,810 in 1987 and 1,490 in 1990. This was inevitably reflected in the number of building permits for apartments to be built by residential construction cooperatives—9,195 in 1987 and 3,600 in 1990.

According to calculations made in the mid-1990s, it was necessary to build more than 400,000 houses every year. In order to partially contribute to the fulfillment of this need, the Mass Housing Administration (MHA), established in 1984, provided credit for the construction of more than one million dwellings. Between 1984 and 1997, close to 90 percent of these were completed. In addition, the Possessions Bank constructs dwellings under a program coordinated by the MHA and sells them to low- and middle-income families. Also, by utilizing small savings, dwellings are constructed by cooperatives that are supported by the MHA. In 1998, the ratio of people who rented houses was 30 percent in the cities and 10 percent in small towns and villages.

The gap that remained between housing supply and demand led to a mushrooming of shantytowns (*see* GECEKONDU) around the major cities. For example, the shantytowns are estimated to house 65 percent of the population of

Ankara and 45 percent of that of **Istanbul**. Until the late 1950s, the shantytowns were perceived as a blot on the urban landscape, suitable only for demolition. Later, those capable of improvement (estimated as two-thirds of the total) were offered title deeds and provided public services. Also, low-interest loans were made available to the settlers in the shantytowns for improving their houses. Those shantytowns beyond redemption were to be demolished provided that municipal housing could be provided for the inhabitants.

As there was always a shortage of municipal housing, few houses were demolished over the years and the bulk of them immediately after their construction. Under these circumstances, the shantytowns kept on growing. There was political pressure for title deeds and services, and these demands have greatly taxed the means at the disposal of municipalities.

There were other factors that aggravated the shortage in housing. There have been too many cases of houses simply collapsing, sometimes due to earthquakes, but also because of poor building practices. The latter was a consequence of improperly issued permits and lax supervision.

HUMAN RIGHTS. The 1982 **constitution**, drawn up in the wake of the 1960–1970 decades, which were characterized by political polarization leading to near civil war, stipulated that "No protection shall be afforded to thoughts or opinions contrary to Turkish national interests, the principle of the existence of Turkey as an indivisible entity with its state and territory, Turkish historical and spiritual values, or the nationalism, principles, reforms and modernism of **Atatürk**; and as required by the principle of **secularism**, there shall be no interference whatsoever of sacred religious feelings in state affairs and politics."

Since then, legislation emanating from such a constitutional framework has been amended in a more liberal and democratic direction. Several Constitutional Court and Court of Appeals rulings reinforced freedom of belief. Aside from certain limitations in the name of public order, the freedom of worship is also protected. With changes made in 1991, provisions in some laws specifying "crimes of thought" were repealed. Only the Anti-Terrorism Act, with a view to maintaining social cohesion, stipulates punishment for incitement of resentment and enmity among the people based on class, race, religion, sect, or regional difference. The improvements made concerning the freedom of associations included the following: the repeal of the prohibition of political activity by associations, or their cooperation with political parties; the relative democratization of the process of suspension of such activities; the development of the role and security of judges in this regard; and the expansion of rights of civil servants, including the reinstatement of the civil servants' right to unionize. The Turkish Republic is based on civic nationalism. The constitution defines citizenship as follows: "Every person who is connected to the Turkish state through the bond of citizenship is a Turk." As such, Turkish law does not allow ethnic discrimination.

Still, Turkish law has a number of provisions that do not conform to the Copenhagen criteria concerning human rights. Turkey's efforts to bring its legislation into line with the Copenhagen criteria have been intensified since December 1999 when Turkey was designated by the **European Union** (EU) as a candidate state. The **National Program** (March 2001), in which Turkey has indicated the reforms it will undertake for accession to the EU, states that Turkey will "review the Turkish Constitution and relevant provisions of other legislation, in the light of the criteria referred to in Article 10 of the European Convention on Human Rights and Fundamental Freedoms." The National Program also indicates that "[t]he abolition of the death penalty in Turkish criminal law . . . will be considered in the medium term."

In recent decades, during the armed clashes between the government forces and the **Kurdistan Workers' Party** (PKK), Turkey has come under criticisms by foreign governments and others concerning the "heavy-handed" policies it adopted against the PKK and some of the other people in the southeast. There were some unacceptable practices often perpetrated without the approval of the government in **Ankara**. The National Program notes that Turkey will "[e]xplore the availability of financial resources for training law enforcement personnel for the prevention of human rights violations" and "[introduce] legal provisions on the joint and several liability of perpetrators of torture."

HÜRREM SULTAN(A) (ROXALINA) (1504–1558). Roxalina was brought to the Ottoman court as a concubine during the reign of Sultan **Selim I** (1512–1520). She became a favorite of Sultan **Süleyman I (the Magnificent)** (1520–1566). She managed, for the first time, to increase the influence of the harem on state affairs and personally influenced some of Süleyman I's important decisions.

– I –

İMAM. It has several meanings. In general, imam means the leader of congregational prayers, without any implication of ordination or special spiritual powers beyond sufficient knowledge to carry out this function. By many **Sunni** Muslims, it is also used to refer to the leader of the Islamic community. Among the Shiite Muslims, when capitalized, the word indicates that particular descendant of the House of Ali who is believed to have been God's designated repository of the spiritual authority inherent in that line. *See also* ISLAM.

IMMIGRATION. *See* EMIGRATION AND IMMIGRATION.

IMPERIAL RESCRIPT [Hatt-ı Hümayun; Hatt-ı Şerif]. Decree written or signed by the Ottoman **sultan**.

IMPERIAL RESCRIPT OF GÜLHANE (November 3, 1839). The **sultan** agreed to the establishment of new institutions that would safeguard his subjects' security of life, honor, and property; set up a regular system to assess and levy taxes; and develop new methods to assure a fair system of conscripting, training, and maintaining the soldiers of his armed forces.

INDEPENDENT GROUP (Müstakil Group). Allowed, at the Fifth Great Congress (1939) of the Republicans, to play the role of a loyal opposition and critic of the government. With the onset of **World War II**, this limited opening in Turkish politics came to an end and the **Republican People's Party** continued its single-party rule with a heavy hand.

INDUSTRY. In the period of planning that started in 1963, high growth rates and structural change toward industrialization were taken as the main targets. The Economic Stability Program of January 24, 1980, and the economic policies subsequently adopted displayed a substantial difference from these earlier goals. The new strategy derived from an export orientation instead of import substitution. Industrialization became based on exports and thus directed to foreign markets rather than being structured on imports with a view to domestic markets.

This structural change in the industrial sector was to be achieved by increasing the intermediary and investment goods in manufacturing industry production. Within the investment goods, emphasis was to be placed on the production of motor vehicles, nonelectrical machines, and metal goods. Petroleum and iron-steel products were going to have the largest share in the production of intermediary goods. At the same time, the imports of intermediary and investment goods were facilitated. **Free trade zones** and international fairs were opened, which contributed to the integration of Turkish industry with the world markets. As a consequence of these policies, the share of industrial products in total exports increased from 36 percent to 75.3 percent between 1980 and 1997. Although the share of the industrial sector in the gross national product (GNP) was 19.3 percent in 1980, it increased to 28.7 percent in 1997. In 1997, the industry capacity-utilization ratio reached 79.4 percent.

The primary source of growth in the industrial sector has been the investments and dynamism of the private sector. The increase in the private sector manufacturing industries was mainly in the machinery, metal main industry, and food-beverage-tobacco subsectors.

From the mid-1990s onward, Turkey became even more closely integrated with the world markets. The most important development here was Turkey's accession to the **Customs Union** with the **European Union** (EU) in 1996. Business visits to different parts of the world gained pace. And from 1996 onward, a new set of laws and regulations went into effect with the aim of increasing the competitive power of industry and conforming to the economies of the EU countries. With the experience and knowledge acquired and with the increased contacts, Turkey began to undertake direct or joint investments in many countries, especially in the Islamic Middle Eastern countries, the **Turkic republics** in Central Asia, and in **Russia**.

INFLATION. Turkey was one of the few countries that were still struggling to keep inflation under control during the 1990s. The inflation rate as measured by annual change in consumer price index (CPI) rose as high as 70–80 percent in 1979, dipped below 40 percent mark in the mid-1980s, again climbed to 60–70 percent at the end of the 1980s and the beginning of 1990s, further went up to 86 percent in 1997 and 81 percent in 1998, and receded to 71 percent in 1999. Under the disinflation program of 2000, the inflation rate (CPI) decelerated to 39 percent. With the collapse of the disinflation program in the post-February 2001 period, the inflation rate rose once again to around 70. (*See* MONETARY AND FINANCIAL POLICY).

The major cause of inflation has been large public budget deficits. On the average, personnel and **social security** expenditures constituted 90 percent of all public expenditures. Packing the public bureaucracy, in particular the state economic enterprises (SEE), by political party supporters—a practice that gained a particular pace in the post-1961 coalition-government periods—has worsened the situation. To make things worse, it has not been possible to increase public revenues substantially. Here, the major problem has been the fact that the public budget did not have an elastic structure. For measures to fight inflation, *see* MONETARY AND FISCAL POLICY.

INTEREST GROUPS. The Ottoman political regime was based on bureaucratic centralism. The state dominated **civil society**; civil societal institutions with political efficacy could not develop. The Ottoman guild system was the handwork of the state rather than civil society and functioned as an administrative link between the two. The chief officers of the guilds were generally agents of the state rather than spokesmen for the guilds. The non-Muslims in the Ottoman Empire, who played a prominent role in the economy, were organized under their *millet* systems, which again functioned as a one-way transmission from the state to civil society. The religious heads of these communities worked closely with the Ottoman government as subordinate agents responsible for the administration of their respective ethno-religious communities.

From the mid-19th century onward, interest group associations (organized into various chambers) emerged as the modified versions of traditional guilds, that is, as emanations of the state. During the *Tanzimat* **(Reform) Period** (1839–1876), the chambers were supposed to work in close cooperation with the Ministry of Trade and to promote trade and industry. During the Republican period, particularly during the single-party years (1923–1945), the chambers were expected to play a similar role. The secretary-general of the chamber of trade and industry was a civil servant from the Ministry of Trade and Industry.

With the coming to power of the *Demokrat* **Party** in 1950, Turkish politics entered a period of relative liberalism. The governments' formal control over the chambers was somewhat relaxed. The tutelage of the Ministry of Economy and Commerce was abolished. Governments, however, resorted to informal controls; they rewarded the members of the chambers that supported them and harassed those chambers that opposed them. They paid no attention to their views when those views clashed with their own. The situation was not different in respect to voluntary interest group associations either. **TÜSİAD**, the Turkish Industrialists' and Businessmen's Association, the leading voluntary interest group association since 1971, had to resort in the late 1970s to public complaints and advertisement campaigns in the newspapers as the means of articulating its interests.

As late as the early 1990s, the state's condescending attitude toward interest groups continued unabated. The term "interest group" still had a pejorative connotation. It was not proper, businessmen felt, to speak about *group* interests; the only legitimate interest was *public* interest. It was still not considered appropriate to claim the Turkish version of "what is good for General Motors is good for the United States." Voluntary interest groups placed emphasis on reasoned arguments based on research findings in order to establish *objectively* what was best for the country and only *indirectly* and *implicitly* for themselves. With increased pressure for democratization of political life in the early 1990s and because of Turkey's wish to accede to the **European Union**, what used to be monist rather than neocorporatist or pluralist interest group politics in Turkey began to undergo a mutation in a pluralist direction. Still, the interest group associations began to play some role in the making and unmaking of governments. For instance, this was what happened in the resignation of the **Welfare Party-True Path Party** coalition in June 1977. On the other hand, interest groups associations still play a marginal role in the making of policies. When faced with unfavorable policies, the more influential holding companies try to soften the impact of those policies in the implementation stage, and they attempt to do this only through informal channels.

Interest groups themselves are organized in a pluralist pattern. Businessmen are represented by the Turkish Union of Chambers and Commodity Exchanges, Turkish Industrialists' and Businessmen's Association, Turkish Confederation of Employers' Unions, and Young Businessmen's Association. The first two are the major and competing employers' associations.

Labor is represented by the Turkish Confederation of Trade Unions (better known by the Turkish acronym **Türk-İş**), Confederation of Revolutionary Trade Unions (better known by the Turkish acronym **DİSK**), and Hak-Labor Union Confederation. Türk-İş is the largest and relatively most influential labor association; it always had a pragmatic and "above political parties" attitude. DİSK had a Marxist political view and was closed after the 1980 military takeover on charges of inducing subversive activities. The confederation was allowed to be reestablished in 1991. Its earlier ideological stance now seems to be much mellowed though it has not adopted a strictly pragmatic approach. The Hak-İş Labor Union Confederation is on the religious end of the trade union spectrum. In addition to the three major labor associations, there are numerous independent trade unions in Turkey.

Other economic interest group associations are the Turkish Union of Agricultural Chambers and the Turkish Tradesmen and Artisans Confederation. Journalists are represented by several associations: the Press Council, Istanbul Journalists' Association, and Union of Writers. Associations representing professions include the Union of Turkish Doctors, Union of Pharmacists, and Union of Bars of Turkey. **Women** have their Union of Turkish Women and Foundation for Advancement and Recognition of Turkish Women. There are two associations concerning the **environment**: the Environmental Protection Foundation and the Association for the Protection of Environment. Other associations include the **Human Rights'** Association, Economic Development Foundation (to promote relations between Turkey and the **European Union**), and the Foundation for the Promotion of Turkey (abroad). *See also* LABOR UNIONS.

IRAN. Turkey's neighbor to the east. The Ottoman Empire and Persia had been rivals for centuries and the power play between the two empires was made worse by the fact that the Ottomans subscribed to **Sunnite** and the Persians to **Shiite Islam**. Following the establishment of the Turkish Republic in 1923, there emerged an opportunity to heal the wounds of the past centuries. Mohammad Shah Pahlavi's father, Reza Shah Pahlavi, had a great respect for **Atatürk** and shared his view that **religion** was incompatible with progress. Also, Turkey and Iran became parties to two major alliances. The first one was the 1937 Saadabad Pact (other members were **Iraq** and Afghanistan). The second one was the 1955 **Baghdad Pact** (other members were Iraq, Pakistan, and **Great Britain**, with the **United States** in a position of *de facto* member).

Muhammad Shah Pahlavi also tried to emulate Turkey—a secular state closely tied to the United States. The relationship between post–**World War II** Turkey and Iran, however, has been less than cordial. The shah of Iran, aspiring to elevate Iran to a regional superpower status, appeared to have a rather condescending attitude toward Turkey. Things only worsened under Ayatollah Khomeini and his successors. Still, the two countries had active trade relations, which increased tremendously during the Iran-Iraq War of 1980–1988. During the latter period, Iran could carry out its trade primarily through Turkey. It also had a sympathetic approach to Turkey's border security, especially when the guerrilla activities of the Kurdistan Worker's Party (PKK) intensified after 1984. In November 1984, the two countries agreed to prevent any activity on their territories that threatened the security of the other. It was an accord that was generally enforced.

The relations between the two countries might have been more cordial if the Islamic Revolution of 1979 had not taken place in Iran. Revolutionary Iran openly expressed contempt for **secular** Turkey. Its subversive broadcasting continuously targeted **Westernized** Turkey. Iranian official sources even compared Turkish President **Kenan Evren** with Salman Rushdie, the author of *Satanic Verses*, which was considered by many Muslims as an exercise in blasphemy concerning Islam in general and its Prophet in particular. The fact that Turkey did not reciprocate in kind, and that earlier it had quickly recognized the new (Islamic) regime in Tehran, and the fact that Turkey did not go along with the U.S. attempt to impose economic sanctions on Iran, probably prevented the tense situation from escalating into more serious conflicts. This facilitated the maintenance of political and economic relations during the difficult decade of the 1980s. After 1989, closer relations developed between the two countries. Contributing factors included the death of the uncompromising Khomeini, the election of pragmatic Ali Akbar Hashemi Rafsanjani as president, and the removal from office of a number of Islamic radicals. In May 1991, President Rafsanjani even paid an official visit to Turkey. During this visit, the two countries agreed to increase their **trade** and improve the communication (*see* TRANSPORTATION AND COMMUNICATION) network between them. The visit was heralded as the beginning of a new approach on the part of the two countries so that differences between their political regimes should not mar their overall relations.

In 1994, Turkey reciprocated Rafsanjani's visit when Prime Minister **Süleyman Demirel** made an official visit to Iran. The two countries continued to coordinate their efforts against the PKK and resolved to prevent at all costs the establishment of an independent Kurdish (*see* KURDS) state. Also, both countries were worried about the increased influence of **Russia** in the region. Toward the end of the 1990s, the coming to power of moderate President Muhammad Hatemi contributed to the maintenance of close relations between the two countries. However, the 2000 discovery of a series of murders in Turkey by members of the Islamic terrorist organization **Hizbullah** and some evidence that the Hizbullah had connections to Iran strained the mutual relations. The Turkish government considered the Iranian connection to be the handiwork of the conservative Islamic group(s) in Iran and not necessarily that of the Hatemi group, which prevented relations between the two countries from deteriorating further.

A recent bone of contention between the two countries has to do with the gas pipelines from the **Turkic republics** to the **Mediterranean**. Both **Ankara** and Tehran want those pipelines to pass through their respective territories. Another sore point is the unfavorable reaction of Iran, along with the Arab countries, to the recently flourishing of relations between Turkey and **Israel**.

Iran has been one of Turkey's leading trade partners in the Middle East. The trade volume between the two countries was $887 million in 1980, $2.3 billion in 1985, $988 million in 1990, $1.5 billion in 1997, and $810 million in 1999.

IRAQ. Turkey's neighbor to the southeast. Turkey's relations with Iraq during the Republican period started with a territorial controversy over the oil-rich Mosul region of Iraq, where **Great Britain** held a mandate. When, at the end of **World War I**, the Mudros Agreement was concluded between Turkey and the Allies, Mosul came under Turkish control. Shortly thereafter, Great Britain, invoking Article 7 of the treaty, occupied the Mosul region and refused to withdraw. After a prolonged diplomatic and legal battle, the final decision was made in 1926 by the League of Nations, which decided that the Mosul region should remain in Iraq. Turkey respected the League's decision.

Subsequently, Turkey and Iraq gradually developed closer relations. On March 29, 1926, they signed the Turkish-Iraqi Friendship and Good Neighbor Treaty. In

July 1931, King Faisal of Iraq made a state visit to Turkey. In July 1937, Turkey and Iraq became parties to the Saadabad Pact (a nonaggression treaty), alongside **Iran** and Afghanistan, and, in February 1955, to the **Baghdad Pact**, an organization for defense that was later joined by **Iran**, Pakistan, and **Great Britain** while the **United States** maintained a position of de facto member. The Baghdad Pact became a dead letter between Turkey and Iraq when General Abdulkerim Kasım staged a coup in Baghdad in July 1958.

Turkish-Iraqi relations made significant progress from the mid-1970s until the end of the 1980s. In 1977 and 1986, pipelines were laid from Kirkuk in Iraq to Yumurtalık in Turkey. In the first half of the 1980s, Iraq rose to second place after **Germany** among Turkey's foreign trade partners. During the 1980–1988 Iran-Iraq War, Turkey remained neutral and sold consumer goods to Iraq. In 1984, Iraq granted Turkey the right of "hot pursuit" concerning the guerrillas of the Kurdistan Worker's Party (PKK) carrying out a separatist struggle in Turkey. Many of these guerrillas operated in Turkey and then fled to safe havens in Iraq.

Beginning in 1989, the relations between the two countries soured. Iraq failed to pay its $1.5-million debt to Turkey on time. A conflict emerged on the question of how much of the waters of the Euphrates River Turkey should allow to flow to Iraq. Iraq continued to be excessively armed.

Iraq's invasion of Kuwait on August 2, 1990, added a new dimension to the already strained relations between the two countries. Turkey complied with the United Nations' embargo against Iraq and allowed U.S. planes to make sorties to Iraqi targets. Following the **Gulf War**, the Baghdad regime turned with vehemence on its own Kurds in northern Iraq, which resulted in the exodus of close to 60,000 **Kurds** to Turkey. The Kurds in question were given refuge in Turkey, but not a refugee status. Soon they began to return to Iraq.

In the early 1990s, Turkey frequently resorted to "hot pursuit" in Iraq, chasing the PKK guerrillas. Baghdad, battered by the Gulf War, chose to overlook such incursions into its territory. In April 1991, Turkey gave permission to stationing an international Rapid Deployment Mobile Force alongside its frontier with Iraq to guarantee the safety of the Kurds across the border.

Ankara, on the other hand, supports the territorial integrity of Iraq because an independent Kurdish state in northern Iraq would complicate matters for Turkey, which itself faces separatist Kurdish activities in its southeastern region. In 1998, Ankara called two rival Kurdish leaders in Northern Iraq and obtained from both of them assurances that they would not jeopardize Turkey's security, would cooperate with Turkey against the PKK, and would not strive for an independent Kurdistan. Both Ankara and Baghdad wish to a see regular and full-capacity flow of oil through the pipeline from Iraq to Yumurtalık on the **Mediterranean** as well as continuing **trade** across their borders.

Iraq has been one of Turkey's leading trade partners in the Middle East. The trade volume between the two countries was $1.4 billion in 1980, $2.1 billion in 1985, $1.3 billion in 1990, and $213 million in 1992. In the following years, the trade between the two countries became problematic because of the post–Gulf

War embargo for Iraqi goods and services. For those years, no official figures on trade volume have been released.

IRMAK, SADİ (1904–1990). Professor and politician. In 1945, Irmak became Turkey's first minister of labor. He was appointed senator in 1974 from the president's quota. After being appointed prime minister on November 17, 1974, his government could not obtain a vote of confidence but, because a new government could not be formed, it remained in power until March 31, 1975. Irmak later served in the **Consultative Assembly** formed by the 1980–1983 military regime.

ISLAM. The Turks acquired Islam in the sixth century during their progress from Central Asia westwards across Arab lands. An extensive body of religious tenets and practices circumscribe Muslim life and govern its thinking, to the extent that **secularism** is not prevalent. The sacred book of Islam is the Koran, which was revealed to Muhammad the Prophet (570–632 C.E.). This sacred compendium of God's injunctions, together with the collections of *Hadith*, or traditions, that represent the Prophet's point of view on a wide variety of questions, formed the basis of *Sharia*, [Şeriat], the Holy Law of Islam. Drawing upon these religious sources, the *ulema* (religious leaders and lawyers) could, by precedent or analogy, or sometimes quite imaginative interpretations [*ijtihad*] and with a view to local customary law, find a ruling applicable to any legal or social problem. The body of law that resulted from such application of rational activity in different areas was called *Sunna* [the living tradition]. The three categories of the *Sunna*'s content—the *Sunna* of the Prophet, the living tradition of the earliest generation, and deductions from these—created a wealth of material, which conflicted in its details. This material was, in the next step, brought together under the concepts of "agreed practice" [*al-amal*] and consensus [*ijma*].

Four great schools of Islam, however, had different interpretations of the Islamic sources. The Hanafi school was most characterized by the exercise of free opinion. The Maliki school placed emphasis on the *Sunna* of Medina but was equally anxious to support or vindicate this tradition through *Hadith*. The Shafi school regarded the verbal tradition as the sole vehicle of the prophetic *Sunna*. The Hambali school insisted on the *Hadith* in law to its extremes. Most of Turkey's Turkish citizens subscribe to the Hanafi school and its Kurdish citizens to the Shafi school (*see* KURDS; LINGUISTIC AND ETHNIC GROUPS).

Two basic sects of Islam also differ in the emphasis they place on religious sources. The **Shi'a** have evolved a doctrine of Divine Right over the centuries that rejects the very spirit of consensus [*ijma*], regarded as an important source of Islamic law by the **Sunni**. In Shi'ism only the **Imam**, the head of the sect, is able to arrive at the correct interpretation of the Koran, where multiple interpretations are possible, and penetrate its "hidden" levels of meaning. The majority of Turks are Sunnites and the minority Shiites.

Islam is also divided into orthodox and popular versions. Various Sufi schools represented popular Islam. Sufism claimed to lead its followers to a direct communion with God. Sufism also offered its adherents, through its organized rituals, a pattern of social life. It was through such socioreligious activities that Sufi orders came to be connected with organized professional and later political groups. For instance, the **Bektashi** order in the Ottoman Empire was associated with the guilds and with the **Janissary Corps**.

The orders also played a political role. Sufism, in its organized form, emerged as a protest movement against political tyranny. In the Ottoman Empire, the Sufi movement had been associated with numerous rebellions against the state. In Republican Turkey, religious orders were banned but they continued to function underground and were instrumental in a number of riots. **Sheikh Said**, a Kurdish tribal chief of the **Nakshibandi** order, led the 1925 Kurdish revolt in southeastern Turkey against the state (*see* KURDS.) Said tried to use **religion** to attain the larger goal of obtaining rights for Kurds. That same year the followers of the same religious order, in protest against the wearing of Western-style hats and the alleged decision of the government to outlaw the veil, attempted an armed rebellion in the city of Rize in northeastern Turkey.

This was followed by demonstrations in several cities against the "Hat Law." Two months later, the Association for the Protection of Religion and the Association for Advancing Islam played major parts in the march of a large crowd "against secularism" in Erzurum in eastern Turkey. In 1930, the adherents of the Nakshibandi order staged a rebellion in Menemen in western Turkey, and involved the beheading of a young reserve officer. The Nakshibandis were also instrumental in the riot in Bursa in northwestern Turkey in 1933 against the recital of *ezan*, the call to prayer, in Turkish as well as the uprisings in 1935 and 1936 in the east. The government suppressed all such upheavals in a severe manner that even involved death sentences.

In the post-1945 multiparty period, the religious orders again became active. During the 1950s, the **Ticani** sect, the followers of which numbered several thousands, revived the demand for the reinstatement of the call-to-prayer in Arabic and smashed statues of **Atatürk**. Following the virtual disappearance of the Ticanis from political activity, the Nurcular, or "disciples of Light," led by Saidi Kürdi (also called Saidi Nursi) (*see* SAİD-İ NURSİ) came to the fore. The Nurcular claimed that they had developed a 20th-century interpretation of the Koran most suitable for our times. They called for the establishment of a theocratic state, which would be based on this new understanding of the Koran and would end the previous "period of irreligion in Turkey" identified with secularism. The formation of a theocratic state was also demanded by the Süleymancılar [Suleymanists], named after their founder Süleyman Seyfullah (1863–1946) and based in eastern Turkey. The Süleymancılar preached a type of popular Islam that was extremist in character.

The members of the post-1945 religious orders were from time to time prosecuted, yet they survive to this day. They were assisted by a number of extreme religious organizations in the Middle East. Center-right governments on the whole also tended to tolerate them. In return, the religious orders came to have close relations with and supported one or the other of the basically secular center-right political parties such as the *Demokrat* **Party, Justice Party, True Path Party,** and **Motherland Party** in general and such religiously oriented political parties as the **National Salvation Party, Welfare Party,** and **Virtue Party** in particular. *See also* FUNDAMENTALISM; RELIGION.

ISLAMISM AND PAN-ISLAMISM. This movement first emerged in the 1850s as a reaction to the secularizing reforms of the *Tanzimat* **(Reform) Period** of 1839–1876, the manner in which oppressed Muslims were being treated in the Balkans and Crimea, and to the Ottoman financial plight. The **Young Ottomans** of the 1860s stressed the advances made under great Islamic leaders in other parts of the world and the need to form a united front against the "Western oppressor." **Abdülhamit II** adopted these ideas. At home, Islamic **education** and culture were emphasized. The **sultan** played an active role as **caliph** of all Muslims. In that capacity, he appointed religious officials in other Muslim countries. He also protested acts of misrule by Western powers against Muslims whenever they occurred. The sultan successfully used **Islam** as an ideological weapon against Western encroachments on both the Ottoman and other Muslim lands and against the minority nationalist movements that threatened his empire. Islamism continued as a significant movement until the proclamation of the Republic.

ISRAEL. Following **World War II**, Israel was at war or on hostile terms with the Arab and Muslim nations. Despite this, **Ankara** and Tel Aviv perceived mutual interests in matters of politics and defense. In the second part of the 1950s, the two countries cooperated in containing Soviet (*see* RUSSIA) influence and militant Arab nationalism. However, from the 1960s onward and particularly in the 1970s, Turkey tended toward the Arab view on the Palestinian issue. This change of course stemmed from Turkey's efforts to diversify its international relations and seek support from different quarters for its lingering **Cyprus problem** as well as from its expectations of preferential treatment from the Arab countries during the years of worldwide oil crisis. Nonetheless, even during those years when it tried to improve its relations with the Arab countries, Turkey maintained its relations with Israel, even if at a minimum diplomatic level. The Arab countries did not come up with preferential treatment for Turkey. To make matters worse, there was, on the one hand, suspicion of the Palestine Liberation Organization providing support for terrorism in Turkey and, on the other, the adoption of a hostile attitude toward Turkey by **Iraq** and **Syria**. Consequently, during the Cold War years, Turkey adopted a measured policy toward both Israel and the Arab countries.

With the end of the Cold War and progress registered in the Arab-Israeli peace process and Israel's taking initiatives, Ankara and Tel Aviv began to come closer. Early in the game, Turkey placed emphasis on economic relations, and was reluctant to enter into political and military cooperation. Later, increased security concerns on Turkey's part led the political and **military** elite to seek a wider framework of cooperation between the countries. In the mid-1990s, Ankara came to the conclusion that the most critical threats to national unity and territorial integrity of the country were reactionary **Islam** and ethnic separatism, and that both were supported by certain Arab countries. For its part, Israel wanted to play the Turkey card against Syria and **Iran**. Similarly, Turkey saw in the Israel card an effective weapon against those two countries. Furthermore, faced with intermittent U.S. weapons embargos, Turkey perceived Israel as an alternative while Israel considered Turkey a potential purchaser for its armaments industry.

Consequently, a February 1996 agreement between the two countries prepared the way for mutual military visits and training, staff exchanges, joint navy and army exercises, and acquisition of military know-how. In August 1996, the munitions **industries** in Turkey and Israel signed another agreement. In addition, the two countries began intelligence cooperation. On the civilian side, Turkey and Israel began to have increased interactions in the fields of culture, **education**, science, and telecommunications as well as the protection of the **environment** and nature. The prevention of smuggling of drugs and narcotics, solving **health** and **agricultural** problems, encouragement and protection of financial investments and avoidance of dual **taxation**, and technical and economic cooperation constituted other areas of joint efforts.

Israeli-Turkish **trade** has steadily grown. Whereas the trade volume in 1987 and 1991 was $54 million and $100 million, respectively, in 1995 it was $750 million and in 1999, $900 million. In 1999, the total trade, investment, and **tourism** volume reached $1.3 billion.

ISTANBUL. Turkey's most important and largest city with a population of 9,198,809 (1997). Istanbul is situated on both sides of the Bosporus—the seaway linking the **Black Sea** and **Marmara Sea**. It is the business and cultural center of Turkey. One-fourth of Turkey's gross national product (GNP) is created in Istanbul and its surrounding areas. Manufacturing has an important place in its economy; 36 percent of GNP come from **industry** while **trade** and services each has a share of 30 percent. Toward the 1950s, Istanbul became the hub of national banking and during the 1980s it opened its doors to international banking. Istanbul is also a major tourist attraction.

There are 18 universities, of which 13 are private. Turkey's "Hollywood" is also in Istanbul and is known as *Yeşilçam*. In the rich cultural life of the city, the International Istanbul Film **Festival**, International Istanbul **Theater** Festival, International Istanbul **Music** Festival, International Istanbul Jazz Festival, and International Istanbul Biennial have prominent places (*see* FESTIVALS).

Historically, Istanbul was the capital of two empires—the Byzantine and Ottoman. It is believed that the origin of the city goes back to the seventh century B.C.E. when Byzas the Megarian founded the Greek colony of Byzantium. In the year 330 C.E., the city was made the Byzantine capital of the Roman Empire by Constantine the Great and called New Rome. Soon after, its name was changed to Constantinople, the City of Constantine. The Turks conquered the city in 1453, and it served as the capital of the Ottoman Empire until 1923, when the Turkish Republic was founded and **Ankara** became the capital. The historical landmarks of the city include Yeni Cami [New Mosque] completed in 1663; Mısır Çarşısı [Egyptian Market], popularly known as the Spice Bazaar, which among other things carries a great variety of spices and medicinal herbs; Cağaloğlu Hamamı, one of the best public baths, built in Turkish baroque style in 1741; Yerebatan Sarayı [Underground Palace], which used to be one of the main public squares of Constantinople, built in 532 by the Emperor Justinian the Great and known at the time as Basilica Cistern; the venerable Hagia Sophia, a church built in its present form by Justinian the Great in the sixth century; **Topkapı Sarayı**, the great palace of the Ottoman **sultans**; the Mosque of Sultan Ahmet I, better known to foreigners as the Blue Mosque, which was built between 1609 and 1616; the Cistern of a Thousand-and-One Columns, originally built during the reign of Constantine the Great; Kapalıçarşı [Covered Bazaar], originally established by Sultan **Mehmet II**; the Süleymaniye mosque and pious foundations of Sultan **Süleyman I (the Magnificent)**, the most splendid of the imperial mosque complexes in the city; Dolmabahçe Palace, built in 1852 for Sultan Abdülmecit; and **Beylerbeyi Sarayı**, a palace built for Sultan Abdülaziz in 1865.

ISTANBUL STOCK EXCHANGE (ISE). The ISE is the sole securities exchange in Turkey, providing a fair and transparent environment for the trading of stocks, depository receipts, government bonds, Treasury bills, revenue-sharing certificates, bonds issued by the Privatization Administration, and real estate certificates.

At the turn of the century, the ISE became one of the top 10 emerging markets of the world. In 1999, the ISE ranked as the fourth most-liquid market among those markets, surpassing such important markets as Singapore, Tel Aviv, and Warsaw. Turkish capital markets offer on-line, real-time data dissemination, including market-depth data, clearing and settlement in accordance with international standards, advanced research, investment consultancy, portfolio management, and intermediary services.

The stock market is comprised of the National Market, the New Companies Market, and regional markets. In 1999, 253 major companies traded on the National Market. The main indicator of the National Market is the ISE National-100 Index comprising 100 companies, which have high market capitalization and liquidity and are representative of their sectors.

The average daily trading volume in the ISE has shown a rapid increase from $37 million in 1992 to $274 million at the end of October 1999.

ISTANBUL TECHNICAL UNIVERSITY. Originally opened as the Civil Engineering School in 1844. It became the Engineering School in 1908 and **Istanbul Technical University** in 1944. *See also* EDUCATION.

ISTANBUL UNIVERSITY. Turkey's largest university. Originally named as the Ottoman Imperial University [*Dar-ul Fünun-u Osmani*], the university had tentative beginnings in 1846, 1869, 1870–1871, and 1874–1881. The definitive opening was in 1900. The Ottoman Imperial University was reorganized as **Istanbul** University in 1933. *See also* EDUCATION.

ITRİ (?–1711/1712). Ottoman composer and poet. Itri was one of the founders of classical Ottoman-Turkish music, which with him became less influenced by Middle and Near Eastern patterns. He made innovations in the religious music played by the followers of **Mevlana Celalettin Rumi**. Mysticism is a general characteristic of his 40 works that have survived to this day, although he is known to have been a very prolific composer.

– i –

İBRAHİM MÜTEFERRİKA (1670?–1745). Ottoman publisher. Müteferrika founded the first Ottoman publishing house. He produced books on linguistics, history, geography, sciences, and **military** art. He suggested reforms to modernize the Ottoman **government**, including the **military**, and argued that the state could not be powerful if progress were not made in such fields as physics and geography.

İKTA. Assignment of a revenue-producing unit to an agent of the **sultan** in the Ottoman Empire, to foster **agriculture** and **trade** and collect **taxes**. The possessor of *ikta* had the right to administer a source of wealth and to collect its revenue.

İLHAN, ATİLLA (1925–). Novelist, poet, and journalist. İlhan is against blind imitation of the West. He is a supporter of enlightened **Kemalism** combined with sincere nationalism. He freely mixes slang and popular speech with the language and terminology of high culture. His essays include *Which Is the Left?* [Hangi Sol], *Which Is the West?* [Hangi Batı], *Which Sex?* [Hangi Seks?], and *Which Is the Right?* [Hangi Sağ?]. *Fog Boulevard* [Sisler Bulvarı] (title poem) is one of the most popular of his many poems.

İLMİYE. Learned, cultural, religious institution of the Ottoman ruling class. This institution was responsible for espousing the faith of **Islam**, keeping the Muslim community together, administering religious law, teaching religious sciences in the mosques and schools, and training new learned men.

İLTİZAM [Tax Farms]. The assignment in the Ottoman Empire of *ikta*s [revenue producing units] to tax farmers [*mültezim*] who had to pay in return fixed annual sums to the treasury each year. Tax farmers kept the balance of their collections as personal profit. It was an unjust **taxation** system, because in each locality first the amount of tax to be collected was determined and then that sum was divided into the number of persons living in that area. Furthermore, it was an inelastic taxation system; the taxes were not levied in accordance with the actualized incomes.

İNALCIK, HALİL (1918–). Professor of history and an honorary member of the **Turkish Academy of Sciences.** İnalcık carried out pioneering studies on the economic and social structure of the Ottoman Empire. He taught at such universities as Columbia, Princeton, Pennsylvania, and Chicago and, from 1970 to 1974, was chairman of the International Southeastern European Research Association. He was made an honorary member of the Royal Asiatic Society in England in 1978 and a member of the American Academy of Arts and Sciences in 1983. Presently, İnalcık is at **Bilkent University** in **Ankara.**

İNÖNÜ, ERDAL (1926–). Professor of physics, honorary member of the **Turkish Academy of Sciences**, and politician. The son of Turkey's second president, **İsmet İnönü,** he has a Ph.D. in physics from the California Institute of Technology. He taught at Princeton and Columbia Universities. His joint work with Eugene Wigner, "On the Contraction of Groups and Their Representations," also known as the "İnönü-Wigner Group Contraction," has become well known in mathematical physics. On June 6, 1983, İnönü became the chairman of the **Social Democracy Party** (SODEP). The military barred this party from the polls at the November 1983 general elections on the grounds that the SODEP was a continuation of the **Republican People's Party**, which was inadmissible at the time. In 1984, the SODEP merged with the **Populist Party**. At the first political convention of the new party thus formed—the **Social Democratic Populist Party** (SDPP)—İnönü was elected chairman. İnönü entered Parliament in 1986, through parliamentary by-elections. He became deputy prime minister when his SDPP and **Süleyman Demirel's True Path Party** formed a coalition government following the October 1991 general elections, with Demirel as prime minister. Following Demirel's election as president in May 1993, İnönü first left government and then quit politics. İnönü is the author of *Memoirs and Thoughts*, three volumes [Anılar ve Düşünceler].

İNÖNÜ, İSMET (1884–1973). General and Turkey's second president. İnönü completed the Army Staff College in 1906. The next year he entered the then-secret **Committee for Union and Progress** (CUP). Following the inception of the Second Constitutional Period in 1908, he became an active member of the Committee's Edirne branch. At the CUP's Second Congress in 1909, İnönü sided with the group that included Mustafa Kemal (**Atatürk**), which argued for the extrication of the **military** from active politics. He cut his ties with the CUP following the congress. In 1917, he worked with Mustafa Kemal in the Seventh Army on the Syrian front. In October 1918, İnönü was appointed undersecretary of the War Ministry. In April 1920, he joined Mustafa Kemal's nationalist independence movement in **Ankara.**

İnönü entered the first Turkish Grand National Assembly that was convened on April 23, 1920, and became minister of war in the first Ankara government. On October 25, 1920, he was appointed commander of the Western Front in the **Turkish War of Independence**, while retaining his ministry. He won the First and Second İnönü battles against the Greek forces. Following the war, he represented Turkey at the Mudanya Armistice Conference and Lausanne Peace Conference (*see* LAUSANNE, TREATY OF).

Following the proclamation of the Turkish Republic on October 29, 1923, İnönü became the Republic's first prime minister, at which post he stayed until November 20, 1924. Meanwhile, on November 19, 1923, he assumed the chairmanship of the **Republican People's Party** (RPP). On March 3, 1925, he was again appointed prime minister; this time his ministry continued until October 25, 1937. He retired from the army on June 30, 1927, with the rank of four-star general. In 1934, Mustafa Kemal gave him the last name "İnönü," when Turks for the first time adopted family names.

The day after Atatürk's death on November 10, 1938, İnönü became president. He kept Turkey out of **World War II**. In 1945, he opened the way for multiparty politics in Turkey. When the Republicans lost in the May 14, 1950, general elections, İnönü gracefully handed over power to the victorious Democrats. During the *Demokrat* **Party** governments of the 1950s, he became a staunch defender of Republican principles, in particular **secularism**.

When the military took power on May 27, 1960, İnönü extended his support to the military; at the same time, he did everything he could to accelerate the return to civilian politics. Following the reinstallation of civilian government in 1961, he headed as prime minister the coalition governments of the RPP-**Justice Party** (November 20, 1961–June 1, 1962), RPP-**New Turkey Party-Republican Peasant's Nation Party** (June 25, 1962–December 2, 1963), and RPP-Independents (December 25, 1963–February 13, 1965). He played a critical role in the prevention of both the February 22, 1962, and May 21, 1962, coup attempts. When the **United States** opposed Turkey's intervention in **Cyprus** in 1964, İnönü started the process of diversifying Turkey's **foreign policy**.

During the mid-1960s, he supported the left-of-center policy formulated by **Bülent Ecevit** and the latter's supporters within the RPP. Following the March 1971 military coup-by-memorandum, he lent ministers from the RPP to the above-party government formed by **Nihat Erim** (also from the RPP) at the behest of the military.

At the May 2, 1972, Extraordinary Congress of the RPP, Bülent Ecevit, who had earlier resigned as secretary-general of the party in protest against İnönü's support of Nihat Erim's government, challenged İnönü and ran for secretary-general against İnönü's candidate. When the Ecevit faction came out on top, İnönü resigned from the RPP (November 4, 1972). Soon afterward (November 16, 1972), he also resigned from Parliament, and, as a former president, took his place in the Senate, a post he occupied until his death.

İPEKÇİ, ABDİ (1929–1979). Journalist. For 25 years, İpekçi wrote editorials for the **Istanbul** daily *Milliyet.* He received several journalism awards and was elected to the executive committee of the International Press Institute. He contributed to the modernization of journalism in Turkey. By his calm and balanced writings, İpekçi became an element of moderation in Turkish political life.

İSMAİL DEDE EFENDİ (HAMMAMİZADE) (1778–1846). Ottoman composer. The last and most important representative of Ottoman-Turkish classical music, Hammamizade combined religious with nonreligious music. He was a master at striking a balance between melodies belonging to both genres. His music introduced numerous novel modulations and skillful and natural transitions from one modulation to another. He enriched classical music with romantic music.

İŞ-BANK. The most important private bank in Turkey. Founded in 1924, it played a major role in developing Turkish railways, lumber, coal, sugar, textile, glass, cement, electric, and insurance companies.

İZMİR (Ancient Smyrna). İzmir is Turkey's third-largest city with a population of 3,114,589 (1997). Situated on the **Aegean** Coast, İzmir is an important center for Turkey's imports and particularly exports. Such commercially important **agricultural** products as grapes, cotton, figs, tobacco, and the like grown in its hinterland are marketed in İzmir. The annual İzmir International Fair enlivens the economy and enriches the social life of the city. There are two universities in İzmir. The city's history goes back to an Aeolian colony of about the 10th century B.C.E. on the site of an Anatolian settlement dating back to the first half of the third millennium. Among its historical monuments are the Baths of Diana, thought to be the pool referred to in the Homeric Hymn to Artemis, and the Roman Agora, originally constructed in the middle of the second century C.E.

İZNİK (Ancient Nicaea). Situated in northwest Turkey near the **Marmara Sea**. The city was founded in 316 B.C.E. by Antigonus the One-Eyed, one of Alexander the Great's generals. In the first century B.C.E., it became the capital of the Roman province of Bithynia and later a leading city of Byzantium. The city also served as the capital of the Sultanate of Rum and as "İznik" of the Ottomans. Among the historical monuments of the city are the ruins of the Church of Hagia Sophia, the principal Byzantine monument of İznik; Yeşil Cami [Green Mosque], built in the years 1378–1391; Zaviye or Dervish Hospice of Nilüfer Hatun, built in 1388; and the ancient theater dating back to 111–112 C.E.

– J –

JANISSARY [YENİÇERİ] CORPS. The most important part of the permanent standing central army of the **sultan** in the Ottoman Empire. It was based on the

Ottoman *devşirme* [conversion] **system**, the Islamic legal principle that the ruler was entitled to one-fifth of the captives taken in war. On the basis of this principle, selected Christian boys in the empire between the ages of 12 and 20 were recruited, converted to **Islam**, and some of them were given a military training after which they entered the Janissary Corps. The Janissaries remained the leading fighting forces in the empire until well into the 17th century. They were complemented by *sipahis* (a general term for locally based cavalry) and *sipahis' cebeli*s [mounted men]. When such principles as the corps' men not being allowed to marry and having to train regularly were violated, the Janissary Corps gradually lost its military effectiveness and became an obstacle to reform. There was first an unsuccessful attempt by **Selim III** to replace the corps by a new army called the **Nizam-I Cedit** [New Order]. The Janissary Corps was finally dissolved in 1826 by Sultan **Mahmut II** and replaced by a new army called the **Triumphant Soldiers of Muhammad** [Asakir-i Mansure-i Muhammadiye].

JUSTICE PARTY (JP). The closure of the *Demokrat* Party by the **military** junta following the May 27, 1960, intervention left a vacuum on the right of the political spectrum. The Justice Party (JP), the **New Turkey Party**, and the **Republican Peasant's Nation Party** competed for this place, and the JP became the major party on the right during the 1960s and 1970s. The JP's first chairman was General **Ragıp Gümüşpala**, who was brought to that post to placate the military. Upon his death, the chairmanship was assumed by **Süleyman Demirel**, who remained in that post until the party, along with other parties, was closed by the military following the September 12, 1980, intervention. The JP was a liberal-conservative mass party with a tolerant eye to religious aspirations. It catered to rural demands. At the same time, the party was a champion of free **trade** and enterprise, although during the period the JP governments were in power, the state continued to be the biggest investor in Turkey. In time, some influential religious elements left the party and joined the **National Salvation Party**; similarly the hardline right-wing extremists quit the party and supported the **Nationalist Action Party**. In 1970, there was a further breakup of the JP. Some conservative deputies led by Sadettin Bilgiç, who in 1964 had competed with Demirel for leadership of the JP and lost, accused Demirel of "procrastinating" concerning the issue of amnesty for the former Democrats. Added to this rift was the more significant struggle within the party between local-rural and urban-industrial interests. These issues eventually led **Ferruh Bozbeyli**, the JP's respected Parliament speaker during the late 1960s, and 26 JP deputies to leave the party and form the *Demokratik* **Party** in 1970.

During the late 1960s and early 1970s, political violence in Turkey turned into virtual anarchy. On March 12, 1971, the military staged a "coup-by-memorandum" and asked for a strong government. Demirel's government resigned. The JP, however, participated in all four "above-party" governments formed between 1971 and 1973. The JP did poorly in the 1973 general elections. In 1975, Demirel engineered a division within the ranks of the *Demokratik* Party; half of the latter's deputies switched to the JP. Demirel then formed the first of the so-called Nationalist Front coalition governments, in 1975, with the National Salvation Party, **Republican Reliance Party**, and Nationalist Action Party. This coalition government was followed by the Second Nationalist Front coalition government formed after the October 1977 general elections, which comprised, alongside the JP, the National Salvation Party and Nationalist Action Party. The Second Nationalist Front government lasted until the last day of 1977 when some JP deputies crossed over to the **Republican People's Party**, enabling the latter party to form a coalition government.

At the 1978 party convention, JP deputy Kâmran İnan became a candidate against Demirel. This was the first time Demirel's leadership was challenged in this fashion since he had become the chairman of the party in 1964. İnan lost, but the challenge led to an extensive overhaul of the party organization; many young men began to fill the cadres. In the October 1979 by-elections, the JP won all the seats. The coalition government led by **Bülent Ecevit** resigned. Demirel formed a minority government, with the Nationalist Action Party and the National Salvation Party supporting his government from outside.

By the end of the 1970s, ideological polarization, political fragmentation, and bickering between political parties reached an all-time high. In the first days of his government, Demirel, together with other party leaders, received a warning message from the army commanders asking for cooperation among the party leaders in coping with the problems of law and order and economic crisis. The leaders, none of whom considered the memorandum to be addressed to themselves, ignored this warning. On the other hand, Parliament could not have passed the necessary measures. The parties chose not to form a national coalition, and they could not agree among themselves on an early election. Meanwhile, the escalating wave of terrorism hit record highs. Moreover, antisecular movements were in motion without any checks.

The end came when the **armed forces** intervened on September 12, 1980. The military first banned all political activities and then closed the political parties, including the JP. The party was reopened on December 19, 1992. That same day, the party convention decided to close the party and hand over all its property and its original emblem to the **True Path Party**.

– **K** –

KABAKÇI MUSTAFA (?–1808). Ottoman soldier. Kabakçı Mustafa led the rebellion known by his name on May 27, 1807, against the establishment by Sultan **Selim III** of a new army by the name of New Order [**Nizam-ı Cedit**]. Selim III was forced to relinquish his throne and was soon after killed, in accordance with a religious decree given by the *Sheikhulislam*, the highest religious dignitary. His New Order was disbanded. Kabakçı Mustafa became commander of the castles along the Bosporus and began to exercise influence over the court. He was killed by a unit from the army of **Alemdar Mustafa Pasha** that came to **Istanbul** to restore order.

KADI. Muslim judge who enforced the Ottoman religious law [Şeriat] in the Ottoman law courts. In his judicial district [kaza], the *kadı* had an administrative function as well; he enforced both the Islamic religious law and the sultan's **kanuns.** The *kadı* was fairly autonomous in his verdicts and higher authorities rarely countermanded his decisions.

KADRO GROUP. Led by such writers and intellectuals as **Yakup Kadri Karaosmanoğlu, Vedat Nedim Tör,** and others, the group tried to inject substantive ideological content in the Turkish revolution. According to the group, Turkey lacked capital and therefore there was no class struggle. The state (read "qualified and competent leaders" or a "cadre") had to accumulate and utilize capital in the interests of the masses and thus prevent the emergence of a class struggle. The members of the group perceived the Turkish revolution as another effort at liberation from both capitalism and imperialism. The government politely suppressed the journal of the group (*Kadro*) and its editor, **Yakup Kadri Karaosmanoğlu,** was sent as an ambassador to Albania.

KAĞITÇIBAŞI, ÇİĞDEM (1940–). Professor of social and cultural psychology at **Koç University** in **Istanbul,** a founding member of the **Turkish Academy of Sciences,** and an honorary fellow of the International Association for Cross-Cultural Psychology. She received an award from the International Association of Applied Psychology for her contribution to the international advancement of applied psychology and another award from the American Psychological Association for distinguished contributions to the international advancement of psychology. She is the author of *Changing Value of Children in Turkey* and *Family and Human Development across Cultures: A View from the Other Side,* the editor of *Growth and Progress in Cross-Cultural Psychology* and *Handbook of Cross-Cultural Psychology,* and co-editor of *Sex-Roles, Family, and Community in Turkey* and *Individualism and Collectivism.*

KAHRAMANMARAŞ INCIDENT. The **Sunni** versus **Alevi (Shi'a)** clash in this town in southeast Turkey in December 1978 took the lives of more than 100 persons, mostly Alevis, and left large numbers wounded (*see* ISLAM). The far left supported the Alevis and the far right the Sunnis. The clash was the outcome of extreme political polarization in Turkey. The government then declared martial law in 13 of Turkey's then 67 provinces.

KAMHİ, JAK (1925–). Engineer, industrialist, owner-manager of Profilo Holding Company. Kamhi received the Légion d'honneur award. He is a member of the Chief Executives Organization of the World Business Council.

KAMU, KEMALETTİN (1901–1948). Patriotic poet of the early Republican years. Kamu belonged to the Five Syllabists group (on this group, *see* LITERATURE). He wrote such powerful poems as "On the Roads to İzmir" and "Homesick for İzmir."

KAN, SUNA (1936–). World famous violinist. After graduating from Paris Conservatory, Kan won several international awards. Best known for her interpretations of Beethoven and Brahms, she has the title of State Artist.

KANIK, ORHAN VELİ (1914–1950). The best-known member of the literary movement called *Garip* [Strange] (on this movement, *see* LITERATURE). Kanık depicted scenes from the world of the impoverished minor clerks, young girls from poor neighborhoods, and sewage workers. His hero was Süleyman Efendi who "suffered from nothing as much as his corns." Kanık felt that we "must free ourselves from poetic conceptions and from the effort to make the use of words beautiful." He published *Our Literary World* [Edebiyat Dünyamız]. His complete works are in *His Complete Poems* [Bütün Şiirleri] and *Orhan Veli: Complete Works* [Orhan Veli: Bütün Eserleri],

KANUN (pl. Kavanin). Secular law issued by the Ottoman ruler, based on his "sovereign prerogative," in matters not covered by the Şeriat, the Ottoman Islamic law code.

KAPIKULU (pl. kapıkulları) [Slaves of the Porte]. The permanent standing central army of the **sultan**. Earlier manned by Muslim and non-Muslim prisoners and mercenaries, its main body later consisted of youths recruited through the *devşirme* system. *See also* JANISSARY CORPS.

KARA KEMAL (1868–1926). Politician. Kara Kemal made important contributions to the development of the "national economy" policy during the period of the **Committee for Union and Progress**. He opposed the founders of the new Turkish Republic (established in 1923). Considered to have been in complicity with an assassination attempt on **Atatürk**, Kara Kemal was condemned to capital punishment in absentia. He committed suicide when he was about to be caught.

KARABEKİR, KAZIM (1882–1948). General and politician. While commander of the Fifteenth Army Corps in Erzurum, Karabekir played an important part in the convening of the **Erzurum Congress**, a major milestone in the preparatory stage of the Turks' struggle for independence in the wake of **World War I**. During the **Turkish War of Independence** (1920–1922), he was a member of Parliament from Edirne and the successful commander of the Eastern Front. He was elected chairman of the **Progressive Republican Party**, which was established on November 15, 1924, and which opposed

Mustafa Kemal (**Atatürk**) and his associates' sweeping reforms. The party was closed on June 3, 1925, as it was considered to have had a role in the Sheikh Said rebellion in eastern Turkey. Karabekir, along with others, was tried but then acquitted. He returned to active political life 12 years later when he was again elected to Parliament and became the speaker of that body. He died while at this post.

KARACAOĞLAN (17th century). Popular lyric poet. Karacaoğlan started a new epoch in Turkish folk poetry through the way he used language and expressed popular feelings. He dwelt extensively on the themes of nature and love, and wrote in colloquial Turkish.

KARAGÖZ AND HACİVAT. Two characters in the shadow **theater** dating back to the Ottoman times. Hacivat played the role of the educated, worldly wise, self-righteous opportunist; Karagöz was the ordinary, unpretentious man, always able to turn a difficult situation to his benefit.

KARAOSMANOĞLU, FEVZİ LÜTFÜ (1900–1978). Politician. In the 1920s, he supported the short-lived **Progressive Republican Party**. In 1946, Karaosmanoğlu joined the **Demokratik Party** (DP), and was elected to Parliament in 1950. Between 1950 and 1954, he served as minister of state and of interior. Following the 1954 general elections, he disagreed with his party's policy of denying the press right of proof concerning their allegations against the government; he resigned from the DP and became one of the founders of the **Freedom Party** (FP). Shortly thereafter, Karaosmanoğlu became the FP's leader. In the aftermath of the failure of his party in the 1957 general elections, he joined the **Republican People's Party** (RPP). Karaosmanoğlu served in the post-1960 military coup **Constituent Assembly**. In 1961, he was again elected to Parliament on the RPP ticket. Karaosmanoğlu quit politics in 1962.

KARAOSMANOĞLU, YAKUP KADRİ (1889–1974). Leader in the first generation of literary figures of the Republican period. Karaosmanoğlu was chief writer for the newspaper *İkdam* of occupied **Istanbul** during the last phase of **World War I**. He took up in his novels—*An Exile* [Bir Sürgün], *Mansion for Rent* [Kiralık Konak], *Night of Verdict* [Hüküm Gecesi], *Father Light* [Nur Baba], and *Sodom and Gomorrah* [Sodom ve Gomora]—the last decades of the Ottoman Empire as reflected in the political regime, intellectuals' morality, and cosmopolitan circles of Istanbul. His novel *Yaban* [Wilderness] depicted the realities of an Anatolian village and the intellectuals' estrangement from village people. His whole writing is in *Complete Works* [Bütün Eserleri]. *See also* KADRO GROUP.

KARAL, ENVER ZİYA (1906–1982). Historian. Karal graduated from Lyon University in France. He is best known for his work on the 19th century Ottoman Empire. He headed the Constitutional Committee in the post-1960 **military** intervention-**Constituent Assembly** that prepared the 1961 **constitution**. From 1973 until his death, Karal was director of the Turkish Historical Society.

KARAY, REFİK HALİT (1888–1965). Humorist, novelist, and memoirist. Karay wrote melodramatic novels. *The Female Spider* [Dişi Örümcek], *The Courtier of Today* [Bugünün Saraylısı], and *The Women's Monastery* [Kadınlar Tekkesi] are some of his popular novels.

KARLOWITZ, TREATY OF (1699). This treaty marked the Ottoman transition from the offensive to the defensive. The Ottomans lost many lands, including Hungary. **Russia** and Austria obtained the right to intervene in Ottoman affairs to their own advantage.

KARPAT, KEMAL H. (1927–). Distinguished professor of history at the University of Wisconsin-Madison. Karpat obtained a Ph.D. degree from New York University and was president of the Middle East Studies Association of North America. He is editor of the *International Journal of Turkish Studies* and founder and president of the Association of Central Asian Studies. Karpat wrote extensively on Turkey's international and domestic politics and social structure. His books include *Turkey's Politics: The Transition to a Multi-Party System, The Gecekondu: Rural Migration and Urbanization*, and *Ottoman Population in 1830–1914: Demographic and Social Characteristics*.

KÂTİP ÇELEBİ (1609–1657). Scholar and writer. He attempted to apply the principles of nationalism to medieval **Islamic** concepts. Kâtip Çelebi produced important works on history and geography and criticized his times. His most important book is *Map of the World* [Cihannüma].

KAYA, ŞÜKRÜ (1883–1959). Politician. Kaya graduated from the Law School of Paris University in 1912. He served as minister of **agriculture** (1924), minister of foreign affairs (1924–1925), and minister of interior (1927–1938). In 1936, he became secretary-general of the **Republican People's Party** and remained in that post until 1938.

KAYSERİ (ancient Caesare). Historic city in east-central Anatolia with a population of 1,023,535 (1997). In classical times, it was the capital of **Cappadocia** under the name of Mazarca. Its name was changed to Caesare during the reign of the last king of Cappadocia, Archelaus I (37 B.C.E.–17 C.E.). The city later became the capital of the Roman province of Cappadocia Prima and in Byzantine times it was made the seat of an important bishopric. **Selim I** in 1515 annexed the city to the Ottoman Empire. Among its significant monuments are the Selcukiad fortress, which served as the citadel of the medieval town Ulu Cami [Great Mosque] dating back to about 1140, the theological schools [*medreses*] of

Sahibiye (founded in 1268), Melek Gazi, and Hatuniye (last two founded in 1432), and two tombs, Döner Kümbet and Sırçalı Kümbet.

KAZANCIGİL, TEVFİK REMZİ (1894–1969). Professor of medicine. Kazancıgil worked at Geneva and Dresden Universities. He made significant contributions to gynecology in Turkey.

KEL HASAN (?–1929). One of the most famous masters of improvised plays in folk **theater**.

KEMAL TAHİR (1910–1973). Novelist. Kemal Tahir thought that the true Turkish novel would emerge from the reality of the Turkish workers' and peasants' lives. Many of his works are "Anatolian novels." Some of his popular novels are *The Valley of the Deaf* [Sağırdede], *The People of the Captive City* [Esir Şehrin İnsanları], *The Village Hunchback* [Köyün Kamburu], *The Weary Warrior* [Yorgun Savaşçı], *Mother State* [Devlet Ana], *The Law of the Wolves* [Kurtlar Kanunu], *The Fork in the Road* [Yol Ayrımı], and *The Women's Cell Block* [Karılar Koğuşu]. *People of the Lake* [Göl İnsanları] is his collection of short stories.

KEMALISM. *See* ATATÜRKİSM.

KERİME NADİR (1914–1984). Novelist. She wrote numerous novels in serial form for popular magazines and has become one of the most widely read contemporary Turkish authors. Examples of such tales of love and adventure are *The Sob* [Hıçkırık], *The Thief of Hearts* [Gönül Hırsızı], *The Milky Way* [Samanyolu], and *The Night of Decision* [Karar Gecesi].

KIRAY, MÜBECCEL BELİK (1923–). Professor of sociology and honorary member of the **Turkish Academy of Sciences**. Kıray, who received a Ph.D. degree from Northwestern University, has been a visiting professor at the London School of Economics and a Morris Ginsberg Fellow at the University of London. Kıray played an important role in the development of sociology in Turkey. Her books include *Social Stratification as an Obstacle to Development* and *Eğreli: A Coastal City before the Introduction of Heavy Industry* [Eğreli: Ağır Sanayiden Önce Bir Sahil Kasabası].

KIRCA, COŞKUN (1927–). Ambassador, politician, and columnist. Kırca served as ambassador in Canada and as permanent representative to the United Nations (UN) and the **North Atlantic Treaty Organization** (NATO). Kırca was a member of the **Freedom Party** and the **Constituent Assembly** and a **Republican People's Party** and a **True Path Party** parliamentarian. While in Parliament, Kırca made important contributions to the drawing up of some important legislation. As a columnist, he has made acid comments on Turkey's politics and international relations. Kırca is the author of *Overcoming Corruption in the State* [Devlet'te Yozlaşmayı Yenmek], two volumes.

KISAKÜREK, NECİP FAZIL (1905–1983). Poet, playwright, and journalist. Kısakürek was the leading exponent of mysticism and **Islamic** nationalism in contemporary Turkey. He applied the forms of 19th century French poetry to national themes. With a rare mastery of meter, he displayed deep psychological insights. His Islamic writings include *Martyrs for Religion in Recent Times* [Son Devrin Din Mazlumları], *Caliph Ali: The Gate to the Land of Wisdom* [İlim Beldesinin Kapısı: Hazret-i Ali], *From the Pilgrimage* [Haç'dan], *101 Sayings of the Prophet* [Binbir Hadis], and *The Divine Light That Descended on the Desert* [Çöle İnen Nur].

KOCA YUSUF (1856–1898). Wrestler. Koca Yusuf gained great fame by beating leading European and American wrestlers of his time. He died when the ship bringing him back from the **United States** sank in the Atlantic Ocean.

KOÇ, RAHMİ (1940–). Owner-manager of Turkey's biggest company, Koç Holding. Koç graduated in industrial engineering from Johns Hopkins University. He was given the German government's *Grosses Verdienst Kreuz* decoration. Koç is the head of the board of trustees of **Koç University.**

KOÇ, VEHBİ (1901–1996). Businessman. The first great tycoon of the Republican period, Koç started in 1917 as a shopkeeper. He expanded his business by engaging in trade and import business and became the Turkish representative of a number of leading Western companies. Following **World War II,** he established several manufacturing industries. In 1963, Koç established Turkey's first holding company, known by his name, and in 1974 bought the bulk of the shares of Turkey's first supermarket chain. Following Vehbi Koç's death, Koç Holding, the largest group in Turkey, has been run by his son **Rahmi Koç.** Koç Holding established **Koç University** in Istanbul.

KOÇ UNIVERSITY. Founded in 1993, Koç is one of Turkey's leading private universities where the medium of instruction is English. It is situated in **Istanbul.** *See also* EDUCATION.

KOÇİ BEY (17th century). Historian. Koçi Bey taught at the Palace School [*Enderun*]. He is best known for his treatises in which he delineated faults in government and the causes of the Ottoman decline. He proposed that the Ottoman land system be improved, bribery eliminated, and **education** reformed. His views influenced Sultan Murat IV (1623–1640). His treatises on the Ottoman government and social system constitute invaluable source material for historians of the period.

KOÇU, REŞAD EKREM (1905–1975). Historian and author. Koçu wrote historical novels and the *Encyclopedia of Istanbul* [Istanbul Ansiklopedisi], which he did not complete. He published in simpler Turkish many important works written during the earlier centuries.

KODALLI, NÜVİT (1924–). Composer. He studied composition with Arthur Honegger and conducting with Jean Fournet at the *Ecole Normale de Musique* in France. Kodallı received the title of "Chevalier" from the French government. He used three styles in his works. The first reflected the characteristic rhythm and melody of Turkish **music** in general; the second was the polyphonic technique that he used to familiarize the Turkish people to polyphony; and the third was one he himself created. His best-known works are *Atatürk Oratorio* and *String Quartet No. 1.*

KONYA (Roman Iconium). A mid-Anatolian city with a population of 1,958,939 (1997). During the Roman period, it was the capital of the province of Karamania. Later, it became the capital of the Selcukiad Sultanate of Rum. Konya was captured by the Ottoman Sultan **Mehmet II** in 1467. Among its historical monuments are Alâeddin Camii, which dates back to the 12th century and is the largest Selçuk mosque in Konya; the theological schools [*medreses*] of İnce Minare, founded in 1258; Büyük Karatay, opened in 1251; Sırçalı Köşk, established in 1242; the Sahip Ata complex of a mosque and oratory, founded in 1258; İplikçi Camii, a mosque originally founded in the 12th century and rebuilt in 1332; and the Mevlana Tekke (monastery), the most famous monument in Konya. The Tekke is both a museum and national monument and one of the most sacred **Islamic** shrines in the country. It is the tomb of **Mevlana Celalettin Rumi**, the founder of the **Mevlevi** order of dervishes. Every year in a special ceremony in Konya, the present-day members of the Mevlevi order perform their *sema*, the ethereal whirling dance that made the Mevlevis famous throughout Europe as the "Whirling Dervishes." This event attracts thousands of visitors and tourists to Konya every year.

KORALTAN, REFİK (1889–1974). Politician. Koraltan served as governor and member of Parliament. He became one of the founders of the *Demokrat* **Party** established on January 7, 1946. He was Speaker of Parliament from 1950 to 1960.

KORUTÜRK, FAHRİ (1903–1987). Admiral and sixth president of Turkey. In 1957, Korutürk became commander of the naval forces. He served as ambassador to Moscow (1960–1964) and Madrid (1964–1965). Korutürk became senator in 1968 and president on April 6, 1973. After his seven-year presidency, he served for a while as senator.

KOSOVA (KOSSOVO). The First Battle of Kosova (1389): the first Ottoman victory against a major allied European force, comprising a number of Balkan princes. The Ottoman success opened northern Serbia to Ottoman conquest. Hungary was left as the only important opponent to the Ottomans in southeastern Europe. The Second Battle of Kosova (1448): won against a crusader army; Ottoman rule south of the Danube river in Hungary was assured.

KÖPRÜLÜ, FUAT (1890–1966). Historian, professor, and politician. In 1924, Köprülü founded the Institute of Turkish Studies. In 1927, he was appointed director of the Turkish Historical Society. He received several honorary degrees abroad and acted as editor of several journals of high intellectual caliber. In 1935, Köprülü was elected to Parliament. In 1946, he became one of the four founders of the *Demokrat* **Party** (DP). In 1950, he was appointed foreign minister. In 1957, Köprülü resigned from the DP and worked for the **Freedom Party**. Then, in 1961, with four others, he founded the New *Demokrat* Party, which was closed by the public prosecutor's office because the name of the party resembled that of the defunct *Demokrat* Party, which was inadmissible by law. Köprülü was also one of the founders of the modern discipline of history in Turkey. He introduced into Turkish historiography the method of using original sources, making comparisons among them, and saving Turkish history from being a mere chronology of events. He adopted the interdisciplinary method and treated Ottoman history not only as part of the history of **Islamic** dynasties but as part of world history. His most important works in history are *The Foundation of the Ottoman Empire* [Les Origines de L'Empire Ottoman] and *The Influence of Byzantine Institutions on Ottoman Institutions* [Bizans Müesseselerinin Osmanlı Müesseselerine Tesiri]. His works on **literature** include *Today's Literature* [Bugünkü Edebiyat], *The First Precursors of the National Literary Current and the Simplified Turkish Poetry Collection* [Milli Edebiyat Cereyanının İlk Mübeşşirleri ve Divan-ı Türk-i Basit], *Anthology of Classical Turkish Poetry* [Divan Edebiyatı Antolojisi], and *Turkish Folk Bards* [Türk Saz Şairleri.]

KÖSEM SULTAN(A) (1589–1651). Kösem entered the Ottoman court as a concubine and eventually married Sultan Ahmet I (1603–1617). In 1623, her son Murat IV (1623–1640) became **sultan**. Because Murat IV was only a minor, Kösem Sultan ruled the country in her son's name. Her influence on her son continued in the latter's major years. When Murat IV died, his brother, semi-lunatic İbrahim (1640–1648), became the next sultan. During İbrahim's reign, Kösem Sultan came to have complete control over state affairs. When İbrahim was dethroned, with the approval of Kösem Sultan because of his state of mind, Kösem Sultan's grandson Mehmet IV (1648–1687) became sultan at the age of seven. Kösem Sultan continued to rule the country. Kösem Sultan was killed by a faction within the court loyal to Mehmet IV's mother, Turhan Sultana.

KUÇURADİ, IOANNA (1936–). Professor of philosophy. Kuçuradi, who received a Goethe medal and an honorary Ph.D., is the chairwoman of the Fédération Internationale des Sociétés de Philosophie. Kuçuradi's books include *Tragic in Max Scheler and Nietzsche* [Max Scheler ve Nietzsche'de Trajik], *Nietzsche and*

Mankind [Nietzsche ve İnsan], *Schopenhauer and Mankind* [Schopenhauer ve İnsan], *Mankind and Its Values* [İnsan ve Değerleri], and *Art from a Philosophic Perspective* [Sanata Felsefe ile Bakmak].

KUDRET, CEVDET (1907–1992). Poet, novelist, and literary historian. Kudret was one of the most powerful of the "Seven Torches" School, which stressed "vitality, sincerity, and novelty." *Suleiman's World* [Süleyman'ın Dünyası], *Classmates* [Sınıf Arkadaşları], and *Not a Cloud in the Sky* [Havada Bulut Yok] (a trilogy) are among his novels. Kudret's linguistic studies include *Anthology of Turkish Short Stories and Novels* [Türk Hikaye ve Roman Antolojisi], *The Short Story and Novel in Turkish Literature, 1859–1959* [Türk Edebiyatında Hikaye ve Roman], and *They Have Their Languages, but They Do Not Resemble Our Language* [Dilleri Var Bizim Dile Benzemez].

KURBAN BAYRAMI (Id al Adha). Feast of Sacrifice. Also a four-day national holiday.

KURDS. Settled mostly in southeastern Turkey, the Kurds are estimated to number 10 to 20 million. The Kurdish language belongs to the Indo-European family of languages and is a close relative of Iranian. Kurdish is not a unified tongue; Kurdi (subdivided into Gurani and Sulaymani), Kirmanji (with its Mil and Zil subdialects), and Zaza are the three primary Kurdish dialects. Most Kurds in Turkey converse in Zaza and in the subdialect of Kirmanji. Although the overwhelming majority of Kurds are **Sunnis** of the Shafii Rite (*see* ISLAM), Kurds are particularly drawn to various popular religious orders (especially the **Nakshibandis** and the Kadiris) and unorthodox Islamic sects (such as Nurcular in Turkey). Traditionally, Kurds belonged to different tribes. However, tribal organization has for quite some time been breaking down. The Kurdish core area in the region is divided between Turkey, **Iraq**, and **Iran**. Close to half of the Kurds in the region live in Turkey.

In the Ottoman Empire, the Muslim community constituted the core group and Kurds, being Muslims, were perceived as an integral part of the community. The same tradition continued in Republican Turkey. As Turkey adopted a civic-cultural rather than ethnic nationalism, the notion of "Turk" came to have a generic meaning and subsumed within it the Kurds.

Consequently, Kurds in Turkey were not treated differently from Turks. They have had the same educational and employment opportunities, access to positions of power and status, and such rights as freely choosing their walks of life, owning real estate, and/or living in places they chose to settle. It is true that southeastern Turkey remained one of the most underdeveloped regions, but this was not the outcome of discriminatory policies pursued by Ottoman and Turkish governments. The concentration of land in the hands of relatively few notables since the latter half of the 19th century prevented productive **agriculture** from flourishing. Europeans first became interested in importing goods from the western regions of

Turkey, and thus the first spate of infrastructure investments was made in the west. The German Berlin-Baghdad Railway and the American project of the Chester Railway to the Mosul were both dropped because of Great Power rivalries. In the early decades of the Republic, rulers were reluctant to make investments in border areas because "it would have been difficult to defend them." The post-1960 five-year plans placed an emphasis on industrialization that adversely affected economic development in the east and southeast that depended on agriculture and lacked the infrastructure for the development of **industry**. Last but not least, as the area lacked infrastructure, the private sector has preferred the west rather than the east and southeast. In the 1980s and 1990s, as separatist activities in the southeast carried out by the **Syrian**-based Kurdistan Worker's Party (PKK) increased, not only private but also public investments in the region came to a virtual standstill. Many Kurds migrated to the more developed west and northwest. In 1935, persons whose native tongue was Kurdish constituted 72 percent of the population of the city of Diyarbakır in the southeast; by 1965, that had dropped to 62 percent. A respectable number of the migrant Kurds became successful entrepreneurs, rose in the professions, and some of them became ministers and prime ministers. The possibilities of substantial benefits from the system have discouraged successful Kurds from risking their positions by fomenting Kurdish nationalism. No systematic assimilationist policies were adopted against the Kurds; rather, over a long period of time, many Kurds became acculturated to mainstream values and attitudes. Although a series of major Kurdish insurrections took place intermittently from 1925 (the **Sheikh Said** revolt) to 1937 (revolt in Tunceli), they were not separatist in nature; there was no call for the creation of a Kurdish national state. One exception was the revolt that erupted in the city of Kars, but it was instigated by Kurds from neighboring countries. In the final analysis, the revolts in question were against the centralizing and secularizing policies of the reformist Republican leaders that would deprive the religious sheikhs of their legitimation in religious terms and uproot the traditional local power structure in Turkey. From 1937 to 1984, there were no serious Kurdish issues in Turkey, although the Marxist Turkish Labor Party attempted to openly exploit Kurdish nationalist sentiment in the 1960s. Then, from 1984 until recently, a Kurdish separatist movement, organized as the Kurdistan Worker's Party (PKK) and led by the Kurdish leader **Abdullah Öcalan** developed and took, as of early 1999, around 30,000 lives, both Turks and Kurds. That conflict halted with the capture of Öcalan and a few other leaders of the PKK. Öcalan expressed repentance, and vowed to work in the future if given a chance for the harmonization of relations between Kurds and Turks. Meanwhile, the government recognized the "Kurdish identity." There was a shift from "Turk" as a generic concept to the notion of "cultural mosaic." Previous President **Süleyman Demirel** declared that both Kurds and Turks are "first-class citizens," that is, both are entitled to full **human rights** and equal treatment and both can live in accordance with their cultural traditions; both can talk, sing, and publish in their native tongues, study their cultural heritages, celebrate their particular **festivals**, and even teach their offspring their native tongue. On the other hand, there is the requirement that names given to children conform to the national culture; place names in Kurdish continue to be replaced by names in Turkish; **education** in public schools cannot be in Kurdish; and radio and **television** broadcasting in Kurdish are not allowed. The government's policy has been to tolerate a cultural mosaic but within the framework of a unitary state. The government has always had plans to develop the southeast socioeconomically, among other things by making substantial investments there and providing generous incentives to private sector investments. During the last two decades, the armed conflict perpetrated by the PKK hampered such efforts. During recent years, the **military** has extended a helping hand to the region by, for instance, sending medical teams to villages. Now that for all practical purposes the PKK has been suppressed, governments would be expected to more effectively implement their policies of developing the region both in social and economic terms. The **National Program**, prepared in March 2001 as part of Turkey's efforts to become a full member of **European Union** (EU) has noted that "[t]he official language and the formal education language of the Republic of Turkey is Turkish. This, however, does not prohibit the free usage of different languages, dialects [şive], and tongues [ağız] by Turkish citizens in their daily lives. This freedom may not be abused for the purposes of separatism and division."

KUTAN, MEHMET RECAİ (1930–). Engineer and politician. Kutan became the chairman of the **Virtue Party** (VP) on May 15, 1998. He earlier served as minister of reconstruction and settlement and minister of energy and natural resources. As chairman, Kutan tried to play a conciliatory role between the hawks and doves in the party. Upon the closure of the Virtue Party in 1999, Kutan became chairman of the Felicity Party (Saadet Partisi), one of the two successor parties to the VP.

KÜÇÜK ALİ (HAYALİ) (1886–1974). One of the last masters of Turkish shadow **theater**. Küçük Ali did not adopt the vulgar and indecent dialogue among the protagonists of the shadow theater that was in vogue in earlier times. Rather, he introduced less artificial and more natural exchanges among the characters.

KÜÇÜK KAYNARCA, TREATY OF (1774). The Russians obtained a firm foothold on the **Black Sea** and also the right to build and protect an orthodox church in **Istanbul**. This was later taken to mean Russian protection over all Orthodox Christians in the empire, and during the century that followed, **Russia** freely intervened in Ottoman internal affairs to its own advantage.

– L –

LABOR UNIONS. The establishment of unions in Turkey became possible in 1947. First to be formed were syndicates of labor unions in certain provinces and federation of labor unions in certain work branches. In 1952, the syndicates and federations founded the Confederation of Workers' Labor Unions of Turkey (Türk-İş). In 1967, the Confederation of Revolutionary Workers Labor' Unions (DİSK) was established by some unions that left Türk-İş. These two confederations were followed by the founding of the Confederation of True Workers' Labor Unions of Turkey (Hak-İş), which was set up in 1976. The 1961 **Constitution** considerably extended the scope of the basic rights and liberties, and introduced the rights of collective bargaining, strikes, and lockouts. Because of this, there has been a rapid increase in the number of unionized workers since the early 1960s. Although in 1960 the number of the unionized workers was 282,967, that number exceeded one million in 1967 and reached 2,856,330 in 1998. In 1998, 73.2 percent of the unionized workers were members of the Türk-İş, 12.2 percent of the DİSK, 12.1 percent of the Hak-İş, and the rest of independent unions. That same year, there were 110 workers unions in Turkey. *See also* INTEREST GROUPS.

LAND REFORM ACT. Enacted in 1945 to provide land for peasants with none or too little land and to make possible full and effective use of the arable lands. The reform led to serious internal dissension within the **Republican People's Party** that, coupled with other factors, eventually led **Celal Bayar**, **Adnan Menderes**, **Fuat Köprülü**, and **Refik Koraltan** to leave the party and form the *Demokrat* **Party**.

LANGUAGE. Turkish is the official language of the Republic of Turkey. Arabic, Greek, Kurdish, Ladino, and Armenian are among the 70 languages spoken in the country. The Turkish spoken in Turkey is the southwestern branch of the Turkish language community within the Ural-Altaic branch. The communities that speak these languages spread from Central Asia. Following the acceptance of **Islam** by the Turks, Arabic and Persian loan words and phrase structures became part of the language. In the process, the Turks also began to use the Arabic script. Parallel to the total **Westernization** process launched in the Republican era (from 1923 to the present), Arabic script was replaced by the Latin one (1928). This was followed by the purification of the language of Arabic and Persian loan words. In 1932, the ratio of Turkish words in the written language was 35–40 percent; by 1998, that ratio reached 57–80 percent.

At present, Turkish is the seventh most widespread language among the close to 4,000 languages spoken in the world today. More than 200 million people speak Turkish.

LAUSANNE, TREATY OF (July 24, 1923). Signed in the wake of the **Turkish War of Independence** (1920–1922), the treaty granted Turkey full sovereignty within its present boundaries, except **Alexandretta** (Hatay) province, which was added to Turkey in 1939.

LIBRARIES. Turkey has a library tradition of 900 years. Their foundation goes back to the times of the Anatolian Seljuks and the "Period of Principalities" that preceded the emergence of the Ottoman State at the end of the 13th century. During the early periods of the Ottoman Empire, libraries were associated with theological schools, mosques, and charities. They were funded through **foundations** [evkaf] established by leading state officials and religious leaders. One such major library in the Ottoman era was Köprülü Library set up by Köprülü Fazıl Ahmet Pasha in **Istanbul** in 1678. The *Kütüphane-i Osmaniye,* built in 1884, was the first library built by the state in the Ottoman period. Library activities developed rapidly during the Republican period. In 1946, the **National Library** was established. This library has one copy of every publication in Turkey. In 1998, there were 1,326 public libraries, including special ones for children and historical handwritten manuscripts and volumes. Apart from these, there were also 69 mobile libraries, libraries of temporary collections, and libraries open on special occasions.

LINGUISTIC AND ETHNIC GROUPS. Turks constitute 65 to 75 percent of the population. The three most important Turkish population groups are the Anatolian Turks, the Rumelian Turks (primarily immigrants from the formerly Ottoman Balkan territories or their descendants), and the Central Asian Turks (immigrants from Asia). Central Asian Turks include Crimean Tartars and Turkomans, who live in scattered communities in various parts of the country. Most Turks belong to the Hanafi rite of **Sunni Islam**. The **Kurds** in Turkey, estimated between 10 and 20 million, are mainly concentrated in the southeast. They are found in most urban centers as well. The Kurds in Turkey speak the Mil and Zil subdialects of Kirmanji dialect and the Arabic Zaza dialect. The majority of the Kurds in Turkey are Sunnis, albeit of the Shafii rite and not, like most Turks, of the Hanafi rite. The Arabs in Turkey are heavily concentrated along the Syrian border, especially in **Alexandretta** (Hatay) povince.

Three distinct ethnic groups have their origins in the Caucasus, the region between the **Black Sea** and Caspian Sea in western Asia: Circassians, Georgians, and Laz (all Muslims). The Circassians live mainly in **Adana** province in southern Turkey while the Georgians and Laz are concentrated in the northeastern provinces. Greeks constitute a major non-Muslim minority in Turkey. Most of them are Eastern or Greek Orthodox Christians and many live in **Istanbul**. The largest non-Muslim minority group is the Armenians who are concentrated in Istanbul. Armenians adhere to an autonomous Orthodox church or to a Catholic church in union with Rome. Jews constitute the smallest non-Muslim minority group. They, too, are concentrated in Istanbul. Most are Sephardic Jews. The *Dönme* are former Jews converted to Islam. Their beliefs include elements related to tenets of Judaism and Islam. As neither Jews nor Muslims fully accept them, the *Dönme* hide their identity to avoid discrimination. *See also* ETHNIC GROUPS; MINORITIES.

LITERATURE. Some characteristics of present-day Turkish and modes of expression in today's Turkish literature, such as realism and critical stance, go back to pre-Islamic Turkic epics (Oğuz Kağan, Ergenekon, and the like) found in inscriptions of eighth-century Central Asia. The Ottoman antecedents of the Republican literature comprised two categories—**Divan** literature of the palace and high society versus popular literature. In the former, expression was achieved through skillfully woven symbols. The latter resembled the old epic literature, but later the written form dominated the oral tradition. Also, Divan literature was basically written with loan words from Persian and Arabic, which made it virtually unintelligible to the masses.

During the 19th century, Ottoman intellectuals came under Western influence. In their struggle against the absolute authority of the **sultan**, the intellectuals of the *Tanzimat* **(Reform) Period** (1839–1876) developed a clear and simple **language** as a medium to express their political and social views and favored a realistic and rationalistic approach. In the process, they contributed to the development of a new Turkish literature in prose for the **theater**, the novel, and social commentary. Toward the end of the century, the *Servet-i Fünun* [Treasure of the Sciences] movement took up the problems of the individual, including justice and liberty, and strived to improve the form of Turkish poetry.

The New Literary Movement, which emerged at the turn of the century, utilized simple vocabulary that common people could understand, and depicted the life of ordinary people. The first generation of writers of the Republic (proclaimed in 1923) continued in the steps of the New Literary Movement. The transfer of the capital to **Ankara** (situated on the Anatolian plateau) brought these writers into closer contact with the masses. These writers dealt, among other things, with the moral decline during the last decades of the Ottoman Empire and the clash between old and new in Turkey. The poetry of this period was influenced by the Five Syllabists, whose verses resembled popular literature in rhyme and meter. Their work took up the themes of patriotism and love with a heavy dose of sentimentality.

Meanwhile, **Atatürk** and his associates stressed that literature as well as art (*see* FINE ARTS) should seek their inspiration from historical and national realities, and underlined the revolutionary, populist, and realistic qualities of literature. The journal *Kadro* of the 1930s proposed the development of a literature stressing social responsibility and bypassing individualism and abstract art. *Kadro*'s life was not long. However, other writers soon began to work with the theme of "exploiters and exploited."

Parallel to these developments, the **People's Houses** of the 1932–1950 period supported folk poets and intellectual poets; the latter took the former as models and published their work in the journal *Ülkü* [Ideal]. At about the same time, the literary movement called *Garip* [Strange] developed as a reaction to the stylized clichés of accustomed sentimentality in rhyme and meter. This movement rejected the use of literary conventions such as "resemblance," trope, and metaphor.

Writers belonging to this movement utilized the language of the man in the street and gave sketches from the daily life of the "little man." Then the so-called

1940 Generation produced poetry of social consciousness. Following **World War II**, the Second New Movement developed as a reaction to the *Garip* movement. Its poetry reflected involuted imagery in an artificial language. This movement lasted until the beginning of the Second Republic (1961). During the liberal atmosphere of the Second Republic, a number of literary group movements concerning the have-nots mushroomed. Some affixed socialist slogans to traditional models. Many were realist writers, dealing with conditions in different walks of life.

During recent decades, Turkish poetry has represented several literary schools; it is a lively, active reflection of society dealing with almost every aspect of social life. The contemporary Turkish novel and short story are characterized particularly by their realism and close attention to social conditions. In novels, "magical realism," postmodernist style, and the like enriched that particular genre of literature. *See also* FOLKLORE.

LİVANELİ, ÖMER ZÜLFÜ (1946–). Composer, musician, author, columnist, and ambassador. Livaneli, who has been Turkey's ambassador at the United Nations Educational, Scientific, and Cultural Organization (UNESCO), gave concerts in Belgium, Denmark, **Germany**, **Great Britain**, **Greece**, the Netherlands, Spain, Sweden, and the **United States**. He received several awards for his songs, recordings, film music, and movies in Turkey and elsewhere. Livaneli became a member of the executive committee of the World Art Foundation. With renowned Greek composer Mikis Theodorakis, he founded the Greek-Turkish Friendship Association. Livaneli, who contributed columns to such newspapers as *Cumhuriyet, Sabah,* and *Milliyet,* is the author of *If They Kill the Snake* [Yılanı Öldürseler], *Collect the Sun for Me* [Güneş Topla Benim İçin], *Difficult Years* [Zor Yıllar], and *Sky Belongs to Everybody* [Gökyüzü Herkesindir].

– M –

MAHMUT II (1784–1839). The Ottoman **sultan** (1809–1839) who paved the way for the *Tanzimat* **(Reform) Period** (1839–1876). Mahmut II came to the throne at a very turbulent period in Ottoman history. He invited the local notables to **Istanbul** and made them sign the **Deed of Alliance** [Sened-i İttifak] in 1808. The local notables indicated their grievances in the decree and at the same time promised support for the sultan. Later, when the local notables persisted in their rebellious behavior, they were subdued. In 1836, Mahmut II abolished the much-degenerated **Janissary Corps**. Meanwhile, in 1833, he began creating a new army—the **Triumphant Soldiers of Muhammad**—and brought military advisors from Prussia.

Mahmut II also introduced major reforms in other sectors during the same period. He started compulsory **education** at the grade school level and opened secondary and higher schools that offered a secular education. Meanwhile, students were sent to study in Europe. He established the **Translation Office** in the **civil bureaucracy** in order to translate basic Western books (particularly in sciences) into Turkish. Then he modernized the civil bureaucracy itself: advisory boards were established, ministries were set up, and membership in the civil service was turned into a career. Another act was to start publication of an official gazette (*Takvim-i Vekayi*). In 1831, the first census in the Ottoman Empire was taken. The first Ottoman postal service and fire brigades were also established during Mahmut II's reign. Mahmut II placed emphasis on the development of a textile **industry**. The 1838 Trade Agreement with **Great Britain**, however, exposed the Ottoman economy to European competition, when Ottoman industries were still in their infant stages.

MAHMUT ŞEVKET PASHA (1856–1913). Commander of the Action Army [Harekât Ordusu] that suppressed the April 1909 religiously oriented rebellion in Istanbul. Mahmut Şevket Pasha played a critical role in the removal of **Abdülhamit II** (1876–1909) from the throne. He became minister of war in January 1910 and grand vizier in January 1913. He was assassinated the same year.

MAKAL, MAHMUT (1930–). A leading novelist in village **literature**. Makal made powerful observations in his novel *Our Village* [Bizim Köy] (Eng. Trans., *A Village in Anatolia*) on the difficulties of life for the villagers and the latter's backwardness. He drew the attention of the intellectuals to the plight of the villagers. *The Masters of the Country* [Memleketin Sahipleri] is another important novel by Makal.

MARDİN, ŞERİF (1927–). Professor of history and political sociology. Mardin received a Ph.D. degree from Stanford University. He taught at American, Columbia, California (Los Angeles), and Oxford Universities. In 1956, Mardin joined the short-lived **Freedom Party**. He is presently at **Sabancı University** in **Istanbul**. Mardin is best known for his work on Ottoman intellectual life and **religion** in modern Turkey. Mardin's most important books are *The Genesis of Young Ottoman Thought: A Study in the Modernization of Turkish Political Ideas* and *Religion and Social Change in Modern Turkey: Bediüzzaman Said Nursi*.

MARMARA SEA. An inland sea in the northwest of Turkey, which is connected by the Bosporus Strait to the **Black Sea** and by Dardanelles Strait to the **Aegean**. Turkey's most important city, **Istanbul**, is situated along the Bosporus Strait and on the Marmara coastline.

MASS MEDIA. Broadcasting has a dual structure in Turkey—on the one hand, the Turkish Radio and **Television** Agency (TRT) was established as a semiautonomous agency in 1964 and, on the other, the private television channels and radio stations started to broadcast later. TRT serves a public function and has six channels. TRT 1 addresses the general public and presents diverse broadcasting.

TRT 2 specializes in broadcasts of art and culture. TRT 3 broadcasts different types of music and sports, and has live broadcasts from the Turkish Grand National Assembly during certain hours of the day. TRT 4 is an educational channel. TRT-INT broadcasts abroad. TRT GAP broadcasts in the provinces covered by the **Southeastern Anatolia Project**. An amendment made in the **constitution** in 1993 made possible the operation of private TV channels. ATV, Kanal D, Show TV, NTV, and TGRT are among the most popular of the private television channels. In 1997, 96 percent of homes had a TV set. In addition, the satellite system and cable TV networks have gradually expanded in the large cities in recent years. In 1994, the Supreme Council of Radio and Television was established. Among other things, the council supervises the broadcasting of television channels and radio stations in terms of the broadcasting principles and fundamentals stipulated in the relevant legislation, according to which they are obliged to include **education** and culture programs in their broadcasts and promote proper use of Turkish.

In the Ottoman Empire, the first newspaper appeared in French in 1794. The first newspaper in Turkish was *Takvim-i Vekayi* that continues its publication today as the *Official Gazette*. Turkish journalism proper started in 1860 with *Tercüman-ı Ahval*. In 1878, there were 113 newspapers in **Istanbul** alone. In the closing decades of the empire, *Basiret, İbret, Tercüman-i Hakikat, İkdam, Sabah, Saadet,* and *Tarik* were the leading newspapers. Important newspapers during the **Turkish War of Independence** were *İrade-i Milliye* and *Hakimiyet-i Milliye*. The latter continued to be published as the mouthpiece of the **Republican People's Party** with the name of *Ulus. Tanin, İkdam, Akşam,* and *Cumhuriyet* were among the leading newspapers of the single-party years. In the 1950s, the rival newspaper to *Ulus* was *Zafer,* which represented the views of the *Demokrat* **Party**. During recent decades, leading newspapers have been the centrist *Hürriyet, Sabah,* and *Milliyet,* with the first two always competing in terms of sales. The three have been followed by the nationalist *Türkiye* and religiously oriented *Zaman*. In 1998, the total daily circulation of the 27 national newspapers reached 4.7 million copies. That same year, the leading weekly newsmagazines were *Tempo, Aktüel, Aksiyon, and Nokta,* their net sales being in that order.

There are also several newspapers published wholly or partly in languages other than Turkish. They include *IHO* and *Apoyev Matini* (both in Greek), *Jamanak* and *Mor Marmara* (both in Armenian), *Şalom* (a weekly published in Turkish with one page in Judeo-Spanish), *Welad* (a weekly in Kurdish), *Rewşan* (a monthly in Kurdish), *Turkish Daily News,* and *Turkish News*. There are several news agencies in Turkey. The **Anadolu Ajansı** (AA), established in 1920, is Turkey's semiofficial news agency; it is autonomous but funded by the state. The AA, which has an English language service, has agreements with such leading international news agencies as Reuters, Associated Press, and Agence France Press. All other news agencies are privately owned. The **Ankara** News Agency (better known as ANKA), Turkish News Agency, *Hürriyet* News

Agency, *Milliyet* News Agency, and *İhlas* News Agency are among the most important private news agencies. Turkey is widely covered by resident foreign representatives. They work, among others, for Agence France Presse, Agenzia Nationale Stampa Associata, Associated Press, Athens News Agency, Badische Zeitung, BBC, *Daily Telegraph, The Economist, Financial Times, Le Monde, Los Angeles Times, New York Times,* Reuters, Swiss Radio, *Tages Anzeiger, Time,* United Press International, Voice of America, *Washington Post,* and Worldwide Television News.

MECELLE. Ottoman code of civil laws. Prepared by a commission chaired by **Cevdet Pasha,** the Mecelle was issued from 1869 to 1878. It was replaced by the Civil Code of the Turkish Republic in 1926.

MEDITERRANEAN. The sea that lies to the south of Turkey. Turkey's favorite resort towns, such as **Antalya, Bodrum,** Kalkan, Kaş, Kemer, Marmaris, and **Side.** are situated on the Mediterranean coastline. Important port cities are İskenderun and Mersin.

MEHMET II (THE CONQUEROR) (1432–1481). Ottoman **sultan** in 1444 and from 1451–1481. Mehmet II received a good **education.** He knew Latin and Greek in addition to traditional oriental sciences. He conquered **Istanbul** in 1453, thus his cognomen "Conqueror." Mehmet II expanded Ottoman lands appreciably both in Europe and Anatolia. Ottoman **literature** made great progress during his reign. Mehmet II himself was interested in poetry. He invited the Italian painter Gentile Bellini and had his portraits made. He also had close relations with artists in the Middle East. Mehmet II brought the mathematician **Ali Kuşçu** to Istanbul. He was interested in war technology, too. Many secular codes were enacted during his reign and several educational institutions were opened. He turned the Ottoman Empire into a state with considerable weight in European politics.

MEHMET VI (VAHİDEDDİN) (1861–1926). The last Ottoman **sultan** who reigned from 19181992.. Mehmet VI pursued a passive policy when **Istanbul** and parts of Anatolia were being invaded by the Allied powers following **World War I.** He tried to suppress the nationalist resistance efforts. His submissive posture did not change, despite the fact that through the August 10, 1920, **Treaty of Sèvres,** the bulk of the remaining Ottoman lands were divided up among the Allied powers. After the success of the Nationalists in the **Turkish War of Independence** (1920–1922), the latter dissolved the sultanate. Vahideddin escaped from the country on a British warship.

MEHMET ÇELEBİ (YİRMİSEKİZ) (?–1732). Ottoman bureaucrat. He is known for his *Embassy Notes* [Sefaretname], which reflected for the first time the thoughts of an Ottoman elite member, at the time resident as ambassador in Paris, on the Western way of life. The *Notes* constitute an account of

Çelebi's firsthand observations of the new things he encountered, his relations with the French King Louis XV, and his descriptions of important cultural, religious, military, and political institutions in Paris. The *Notes* prompted the first **Westernization** efforts in the Ottoman Empire, including the founding of the first printing house in 1728.

MEHMET MURAT (MİZANCI) (1854–1917). Ottoman journalist and politician. For a while, Mehmet Murat played an important role in the **Young Turk** movement. He started publication of the pro–Young Turk daily *Mizan* in Cairo on January 21, 1896, and later in Paris. When a conflict developed between him and other Young Turks in Paris, he decided to move the headquarters of the Young Turk movement to Geneva and continued to publish *Mizan* there. Lingering conflicts among the Young Turks made him pessimistic about the future of the movement. He therefore made peace with Sultan **Abdülhamit II** and, on August 14, 1897, returned to Istanbul. Mehmet Murat tried to present himself as a Unionist during the **Committee for Union and Progress** governments but was rebuffed. He devoted himself to historical studies in his later life.

MEHMET PASHA (SOKULLU) (1506–1579). Ottoman grand vizier. Sokullu remained in that post during the reigns of Sultan **Süleyman I (the Magnificent)** (1520–1566), Selim II (1566–1574), and Murat III (1574–1595). He played an effective role in government, particularly during the reign of Selim II and, to a lesser extent, while Murat III was on the throne. He contributed to stretching the golden years of the Ottoman state beyond the death of Süleyman the Magnificent.

MEHMET PASHA (KÖPRÜLÜ) (1578–1661). Ottoman grand vizier. Köprülü restored the state's powers and made important reforms in government. He was made grand vizier on September 15, 1656, in the midst of a grave crisis the state faced. He took stern measures against riotous pashas and local notables and obliged the empire's tributary states to again act in a subservient manner to **Istanbul**. Thus began the "Period of Köprülüs" in Ottoman history. After his death, his sons Fâzıl Ahmet Pasha and Fâzıl Mustafa Pasha maintained, again as grand viziers, the Köprülü tradition of honest and firm government, which delayed for some decades the decline and eventual demise of the empire.

MEHMET RAUF (1875–1931). Novelist, storywriter, and playwright. Rauf had a fluent, clear, and fresh style. His novel *September* [Eylül] is regarded as the first Turkish psychological novel of substance. His other novels include *Carnation and Jasmine* [Karanfil and Yasemin], *A Young Girl's Heart* [Genç Kız Kalbi], *Last Star* [Son Yıldız], *Drop of Blood* [Kan Damlası], and *Deliverance* [Halâs].

MELEN, FERİT (1906–1988). Bureaucrat and politician. Melen first became a member of Parliament in 1950. Between 1962 and 1977, he acted at different times twice as minister of finance and twice as minister of defense. He was prime minister from May 22, 1972, until April 10, 1973.

MENDERES, ADNAN (1899–1961). Politician. Menderes started his political career in the **Republican Free Party**. When this party was closed, he joined the **Republican People's Party** and became a member of Parliament in 1931. On December 7, 1945, along with **Celal Bayar, Fuat Köprülü,** and **Refik Koraltan,** he founded the *Demokrat* **Party**. When the party won the general elections on May 14, 1950, he became prime minister and remained in that post until the May 27, 1960, **military** intervention. Menderes governments placed emphasis on **agriculture, transportation,** and other infrastructure and worked hard to transform the bureaucratic state in a more democratic direction. From the mid-1950s on, economic difficulties increased and the Menderes governments were criticized for their "antisecularist" policies. In response, they resorted to heavy-handed measures. Menderes was tried by the High Court of Justice created by the May 27, 1960, military intervenors and was given the death penalty, which was carried out.

MESUT CEMİL (1902–1963). Musician. A masterful player of the lute, he introduced the classical chorus to Turkish traditional music.

MEVLANA CELALETTİN RUMİ (1227–1273). Mystic, poet, and humanist philosopher, who came to recognize that the secret of all existence is love. Mevlana, for whom love was greater than any religion, embarked on a mystical search for his true God. He espoused a doctrine of ecstatic universal love. This doctrine was best expressed in his often-quoted quatrain:

> *Come, come again, come! Infidel, fire-worshipper, pagan*
> *Whoever you are, however often you have sinned, Come*
> *Our gates are not the gates of hopelessness*
> *Whatever your condition, Come*

The Mesnevi is Mevlana's masterpiece of Islamic mystical literature. *See also* IS-LAM; MEVLEVİ DERVISHES.

MEVLEVİ DERVISHES [Whirling Dervishes]. The religious order that subscribes to the moral teaching of **Mevlana Celalettin Rumi.** The members of the order recognize the moral and aesthetic imperatives of faith and their expression in love, which is envisioned for the whole of humanity. The Mevlevi service [*sema*] is the expression of the soul's unending search for the unattainable—God. During the *sema,* bowing means the complete submission to God, and holding the right arm upward to God and the left arm downward to the earth illustrates the dervish transmitting to fellow humans all that he receives from God. The order was abolished in 1925, along with all other religious orders. The lodge of the Mevlevis and the tomb of Mevlana in the city of **Konya,** where Mevlana lived, were turned into a museum. Now the date of Mevlana's death, December 17, is remembered every year in Konya with a weeklong celebration of the *sema. See also* ISLAM.

MIDDLE EAST TECHNICAL UNIVERSITY (METU). One of Turkey's leading universities, METU was founded in **Ankara** in 1956. The medium of instruction at the university is English. *See also* EDUCATION.

MİDHAT PASHA (1822–1884). Ottoman grand vizier. Midhat Pasha was a skillful administrator. While serving in different provinces, he came to the conclusion that underdevelopment was the real reason behind ineffective government. He developed considerably the provinces he administered and created new bureaucratic offices that would contribute to the transformation in question, setting up, among other things, the Agricultural Bank and the first municipality in the Ottoman Empire. He was appointed the municipalities head of the Council of State (*see also* GOVERNMENT, LOCAL). Made grand vizier on July 31, 1872, Midhat Pasha was soon dismissed because of his novel ideas. Following the removal of Abdülaziz (1830–1876) from the throne in May 1876, along with some intellectuals, he started to prepare a **constitution**.

As the problems the empire faced became worse and Murat V (1840–1904) was removed from the throne, it was decided that a constitution should be put into effect and **Abdülhamit II** (1876–1909) was made sultan. Midhat Pasha was again named grand vizier and was asked to complete the constitution, which he did with the help of **Ziya Pasha** and **Namık Kemal**. To this constitution was added, at the behest of Abdülhamit II, a provision according to which the **sultan** could send into exile persons deemed dangerous for the state. Midhat Pasha was again removed from grand vizierate for his overly frank criticisms of the state of affairs. He was appointed first to the **Syrian** and then the **İzmir** governorship. On July 1881, he was exiled, and soon afterwards strangled on orders from **Istanbul**. In the 19th century, after **Mustafa Reşit Pasha**, Midhat Pasha was the most important representative of the efforts to open a window to the West in the Ottoman Empire.

MILITARY AND POLITICS. The military has had a special place in the Ottoman-Turkish polity. Military warlords founded the Ottoman state. For long centuries, the goal of the state had been that of expanding the frontiers of **Islam**. In the Ottoman Empire, as in the Turkish Republic, the state had a more elevated status than **civil society**, and the military remained the backbone of the state. From the 19th century onward, the military, along with the **civil bureaucracy**, has been both the object and subject of modernization. A large number of **Westernizing** leaders came from the military ranks. They helped depose Sultan **Abdülhamit II** (1876–1909) in 1909 in order to bring about a more consultative regime in the place of the **sultan**'s personal rule. **Atatürk**, the founder of the Republic, and his associates always had the military's support in their drive for total Westernization of the country, which, in their opinion also called for institutionalizing a rationalist democracy. While introducing multiparty politics in 1945, **İsmet İnönü**, then president of the Republic, asked the leaders of the opposition to promise him that they would not resort to populism to garner votes, that is, they would not use **religion** for political gain. The military, heavily influenced by the Enlightenment tradition, came to have a rationalist notion of democracy. They have taken democracy as a regime in which, through enlightened debate, people strive to find out what is best for the country rather than to reconcile sectional interests. In line with this idealistic notion of democracy, the military overtly intervened in politics three times—in 1960–1961, 1971–1973, and 1980–1983. In each case, they concluded that the political government had drifted away from responsible governance and, in the process, the Westernizing reforms faced grave threats. Prior to the 1960 intervention, they thought that the **Demokratik Party** governments had made undue concessions on **secularism**. In 1970, they perceived the extreme left as too serious a threat to the regime and, in 1980, a threat to the regime from both extreme left and right. Following each of these interventions, the military initiated new constitutional arrangements (the 1961 Constitution, extensive constitutional amendments in the 1971–1973 period, and the 1982 constitution) so as "to inject more rationality into politics and keep **Atatürkist** principles alive" (*see also* CONSTITUTIONS).

The Turkish military took democracy as an end rather than as a means: (rationalist) democracy was indispensable for intelligent decision making. Consequently, in the eyes of the military, when things went wrong, the guilty party was the political class rather than democracy itself. Thus, in Turkey, unlike their counterparts elsewhere, the military never thought of staying in power indefinitely; after each intervention, they returned to their barracks in a reasonable period of time.

By the early 1990s, the military's inclination to take power into their own hands to promote rationalist democracy was on the wane. They came to the realization that democracy could not be shaped from above. On the other hand, during the 1990s, the military considered itself responsible for the internal as well as the external security of the country. During that decade, in their opinion, "reactionary **Islam**" and "separatist ethnic nationalism" (*see* KURDS) continued to pose grave threats to the national unity and territorial integrity of Turkey. When they concluded that civilian governments proved inadequate to deal with those threats, they intervened behind the scenes without removing civilian governments from power. In the case of "separatist ethnic nationalism," for some of the critical operations conducted against the separatist Kurdistan Worker's Party (PKK) (*see* KURDS), they did not seek prior political approval. (Some prime ministers like **Tansu Çiller** were only too happy to delegate on this issue all power and, therefore responsibility, to the military.) In the case of "reactionary Islam," the military chose to pressure governments through the **National Security Council** while at the same time briefing other state institutions, **civil societal** organizations, and the **mass media** about the gravity of the situation and trying to obtain their moral support. The military managed to bring about the resignation of the **Welfare Party-True Path Party** coalition in this manner in June 1997.

MİLLET. A community defined by **religion** in the Ottoman Empire. It was a system of autonomous self-government under religious leaders. **Armenians,**

Greeks, Jews, and other major non-Muslim **minorities** in the Ottoman Empire lived under this system. *See also* MINORITIES.

MİMAROĞLU, İLHAN (1926-). Composer who lives in the **United States**. In 1955–1956, he studied with Paul Henry Lang and Douglas Moore at Columbia University. He also worked with Edgar Varèse and Stefan Wolpe; Vladimir Ussachevsky was his mentor when he composed several electronic works at the Columbia-Princeton Electronic Music Center. Mimaroğlu taught electronic music at the Teachers College of Columbia University. He regarded atonality as best suited for his freely expressive style. He selected his materials from all kinds of sounds, not just electronic sounds. Mimaroğlu's works in chamber music include *String Quartets 4, Songs of Darkness,* and *Music for Four Bassoons and One Violoncello.* Among his piano pieces are *Three Pieces, Sonata, Valses Ignobles et Sentencieuses, From the Other Diary, Closely Farfetched Refrains. Le Tombeau d'Edgar Poe, Intermezzo, Anacolutha, La Ruche, Wings of the Delirious Demon, Hyperboles,* and *Provocations* are some of his electronic works. Mimaroğlu is the author of *The Sounds of America* [Amerika Sesleri], *The Art of Jazz* [Caz Sanatı], *A History of Music* [Müzik Tarihi], *Eleven Contemporary Composers* [Onbir Çağdaş Besteci], *Diary without Datelines* [Günsüz Günce], *Electronic Music* [Elektronik Müzik], *The Diary After* [Ertesi Günce], *The Corner Across* [Karşı Köşe], and *Project Utopia* [Yokistan Tasarısı].

MINORITIES. People belonged to various **religions** during the Ottoman Empire. In 1454, minority status was granted to members of religions other than **Islam**. Each minority group, known as a *millet* (literally "nation"), was permitted to maintain its traditions, determine the rules and regulations under which it would live, and levy taxes in its own community. These *millet*s were granted legal corporate personality. As of the beginning of the 17th century, through various bilateral treaties, the Ottomans recognized the right of various European states to act as protectors of the non-Muslims in the empire. According to the Paris Treaty of 1856, concluded after the **Crimean War**, the Ottoman state became accountable to all the signatories of the treaty for fair treatment of the minorities within its borders. In the Ottoman Empire, non-Muslims received **education** in their own tongue and in accordance with curricula that they themselves designed. The numbers of **Armenian**, Greek, and Jewish schools increased dramatically when the 1876 Ottoman **Constitution** granted liberty of education to all the subjects of the empire. A law enacted in 1915, however, obliged minority schools to teach Turkish and Turkish culture. The Treaty of **Lausanne** (1924) also defined minorities in Turkey as the non-Muslims in the Republic (i.e., Armenians, Bulgarians, Greeks, and Jews). According to this treaty, the minorities in Turkey had such basic rights and liberties as conscience, moving from one place to another, emigration, civil and political equality, use of the minority **language** in courts, establishing minority schools, using the minority language and conducting religious ceremonies in these schools, state aid so that minorities could have education in their native tongues, living according to their own traditions and customs, and maintaining their own places of worship.

The Treaty of Lausanne, on the other hand, brought minority schools under close state control. They were not permitted to make religious and political propaganda. Turkish, history, geography, and civics were to be taught by Muslim ("Turkish") citizens. Minorities could have only grade, secondary, and high schools of their own. Except for certain courses, the curriculum in the minority schools had to resemble the curriculum in other schools. As of 1965, the minorities were not allowed to open new schools and erect new school buildings. In the 1996–1997 academic year, the minorities had 36 preschool schools, 34 grade schools, 13 secondary schools, and 13 high schools. That same academic year, a total of 4,983 pupils attended these schools. The minority population in Turkey has gradually declined. In the early 1990s, the Orthodox Armenian population was estimated to stand at 60,000, that of Jews at 20,000, and that of Greek Orthodox at 5,000. Almost all minorities in Turkey live in **Istanbul**. *See also* LINGUISTIC AND ETHNIC GROUPS.

MOHACS, BATTLE OF (1526). Won against the Hungarians. The Ottomans then invaded most of that country.

MONETARY AND FISCAL POLICY. In the 1980–1987 period, the economy became increasingly export-oriented. It was marked by commodity **trade** liberalization and support of exports that were accompanied by efforts to reduce the role of the state in the economy. In 1988–1989, there was a slowdown in the economy. The 1989 capital account liberalization paved the way for the injection of liquidity into the economy in terms of short-term capital that, in turn, made possible the financing of the accelerated public expenditures and cheapened costs of imports. Then, erratic movements in the current account, a rising trade deficit, and the deterioration of fiscal balances led to a financial crisis in 1994. The disequilibrium could only be accommodated by the increased real rates offered on the government's debt instruments and considerable decrease in the remunerations of wage-labor. In the process, there has arisen a vicious circle of "debt-servicing with further accumulation of debt." In December 1999, a disinflation program was adopted. The main elements of the program are the use of the exchange rate as a nominal anchor, the restriction of the monetary expansion to net increases in the foreign assets of the Central Bank, and a policy of no-sterilization to ensure rapid declines in the interest rate. The program succeeded in reducing the rate of price inflation at the cost of increased fragility of the banking system and increased external vulnerability of the economy. In the first 14 months of the implementation of the program, the inflation rate was brought down to 40, from its peak of 72 percent in January 1999; the growth rate of the gross national product (GNP) has accelerated to an average of 6.5 percent over 2000; and the fiscal position of the government improved significantly. On the other hand, the Turkish lira appreciated, which led to an expansion of the current account deficit to above 5 percent of the GNP; furthermore, the bank's (*see* BANKING) continued reliance on short-term borrowing in the foreign markets led to a rapid rise of the stock of short-term foreign debt. Although the ratio of short-term foreign debt to international reserves of the Central Bank was 101 percent at the inception of the program, it jumped to 152 percent in December 2000. Under the circumstances, the direction of short-term capital flows became negative and the economy suffered two financial crises—one in November 2000 and another in February 2001. The economy faced an acute liquidity crisis and the disinflation program collapsed. The lira was forced to be taken off the fixed anchor and it started to free-float on February 22, 2001. The lira depreciated by 47.7 percent against the U.S. dollar in six weeks. The economy began to suffer from a severe recession as crisis conditions spread to the real economy.

On April 14, 2001, "Turkey's Program for the Transition to Strong Economy" was announced. The new program aimed at fighting inflation within the framework of a fluctuating exchange rate, revamping the banking system as a whole so that the public sector banks will not be used as a source of political patronage, bringing lasting solutions to the problem of public deficits, and rendering the economy bureaucracy more rational and accountable. Tax revenues have always remained low in Turkey. Wage earners are heavily taxed whereas self-employed workers, corporate professionals, and farmers escape lightly. The yield of corporate tax is not high since many private businesses are still unincorporated; those that are subject to corporate tax benefit from tax rebates on investments and exports. The rates of direct taxation on inheritance and capital transfers are also low. Tax evasion is widespread. Persistently high rates of inflation along with balance-of-payment considerations led governments to adopt a cautious approach to economic growth. In accordance with the economic **stabilization program** initiated in 1980, in 1986 public sector borrowing dropped from around 10 percent of GNP to less than 5 percent. However, this restrictive stance could not be maintained in more recent years; the central and municipal governments gradually embarked on more expansionist expenditure programs, which led to a rise in the public sector borrowing requirement over 14 percent in 1990 and 22 percent in 1998. In 1990, reserve money expanded at a rate of around 42 percent; in 1998, the increase was only 17 percent. At the end of 1997, foreign reserves were $18 billion; by July 1998, they had increased to $25 billion. Currency in circulation in 1992 was 30.6 trillion liras; in 1994, 102.4 trillion liras; in 1996, 400.6 trillion liras; and in 1998, 1.1 quadrillion liras. In 1992, Central Bank credits stood at 51.3 trillion liras; in 1994, 160.5 trillion liras; and in 1996, 361.9 trillion liras. In 1998 and 1999, the credits extended by the Central Bank were drastically reduced; although in 1997 they were 346.4 trillion liras, in 1998 and 1999 they dropped to 8.7 and 9.8 trillion liras, respectively. The privately run exchange bureaus filled the vacuum, their credits up from the rising 1997 figure of 6.4 billion liras to 10.4 billion liras in 1998 and to 15.6 billion liras in 1999. In 2000, Turkey had a foreign debt of $116.1 billion and domestic debt of 36,414,000 billion liras. The 2000 budget expenditure (appropriations) was 46.7 quadrillion liras.

Current expenditures were 13.7 quadrillion liras (personnel, 9.9 quadrillion liras; other current, 3.8 trillion liras); investment expenditures were 2.4 quadrillion liras; and transfer expenditures were 30.6 quadrillion liras. Expected budget revenues stood at 32.6 quadrillion liras, 24 quadrillion liras being tax revenues, 5.6 quadrillion liras nontax revenues, 2.8 quadrillion liras special revenues and funds, and 125 trillion liras annexed budget. While at the end of 1999, $1 was worth 590,098 liras, at the end of 2001, it became 1,450,000 liras. (Foreign exchange rates for 1990–1999 in the Appendix.)

MOTHERLAND PARTY (MP)/ ANAVATAN PARTİSİ (ANAP). Founded on May 20, 1983, by **Turgut Özal** and his associates. There were rumors that the **military** did not favor the Motherland Party (MP) participating in the elections. In fact, before the polls, President **Kenan Evren**, who had led the 1980 military takeover, made a television speech in which he urged the voters in a roundabout way not to support the MP. The Motherland Party, however, won a landslide victory in the November 6, 1983, general elections. Özal became prime minister and he and Evren buried their past differences.

The MP's objective was to act as a melting pot for the four political tendencies of the pre-1980 period—social democracy (of the **Republican People's Party**), center-right approach (of the **Justice Party**), nationalism (of the **Nationalist Action Party**), and religious stance (of the **National Salvation Party**). Early on, with his forceful personality, Özal indeed kept factionalism at bay. The MP under Özal quickly initiated an ambitious and revolutionary program to liberalize the economy, privatize state economic enterprises, decentralize government (by transferring authority and resources to local government), and overcome Turkey's sluggish bureaucracy and red tape. The MP was quite successful in liberalizing the economy; it registered limited success in decentralizing and debureaucratizing government. Little progress was made in the **privatization** of state economic enterprises (*see* PRIVATIZATION).

The MP also had the task of furthering the transition to democracy. Its performance in this regard was relatively satisfactory; the party played a significant role in the civilian government coming to have the upper hand vis-à-vis the military. The MP was successful again in the March 25, 1984, local elections. As of the mid-1980s, however, the MP's popularity began to wane. This was accompanied by a joining of forces of the nationalistic and religious elements in the party against the "liberals." At the party's general convention in 1988, the nationalistic-religious "Holy Alliance" captured the majority of the seats on the party's executive board. Meanwhile, the party was subjected to heavy criticism by the press. It was hurt by continuous price hikes and charges of corruption in high places. In the March 1989 local elections, the MP managed to carry only two out of the country's 67 provincial municipalities.

From 1990 onward, Özal faced serious opposition within his party. In February 1990, Foreign Minister **Mesut Yılmaz** resigned. Then Hasan Celal Güzel, then deputy from **Gaziantep**, launched an opposition movement within the party.

On October 31, 1991, Özal was elected president by Parliament. His candidacy had stirred extended controversy. The opposition and much of the press regarded the MP majority in Parliament as hollow because "the MP had lost popular support." Özal appointed as prime minister the MP's Speaker of Parliament **Yıldırım Akbulut,** bypassing the party's more prominent members. Speaker Akbulut received harsh criticism both within and outside the MP as the "guided" party chief of Özal. In March 1991, Mrs. Semra Özal was elected the Istanbul chairwoman of the party. This led to another serious conflict within the party as Mrs. Özal was supported by the "liberals" and opposed by members of the "Holy Alliance." In the June 1991 party convention, Mesut Yılmaz was elected chairman of the party. Both President Özal's support for Yılmaz and polls indicating that with Yılmaz the MP would gain credibility seemed to have played a role here. Yılmaz became prime minister. His government lasted until the October 1991 general elections in which the **True Path Party** (TPP) won a plurality of votes and the MP came in second. The TPP formed a coalition government with the **Social Democratic Populist Party** and the MP became the main opposition party under Yılmaz. In opposition, Yılmaz was determined to behave in a responsible and constructive manner. For a while, he even refrained from criticizing the new government. Such a stance on his part brought him into conflict with Özal, who urged him publicly to act more assertively. When Özal also attempted to dictate policy lines to Yılmaz, their relationship was very badly damaged. Yılmaz, who had for long acted in a circumspect manner toward Özal, at one point told the latter in public "to mind his own business." Özal in return asked his sympathizers within the MP to hold an extraordinary convention of the party and remove Yılmaz from his position of chairman. To make things worse for Yılmaz, at the November 1, 1992, local elections, the Motherland Party did poorly and lost four district municipalities to the religiously oriented **Welfare Party.** An extraordinary convention was convened on November 30, 1992, but the Özalists led by Mehmet Keçeciler lost. This was followed by the resignation from the party of Keçeciler and 14 other pro-Özal deputies. Özal declared that he was withdrawing all his material and moral support from the MP. At the end of 1992, there was talk that the Özalists would form a new party and Özal would eventually join and lead that party. In the Motherland Party itself, Yılmaz had sought to consolidate his power base by trying to attract to the party some leading personalities. One such person was Sevgi Gönül, the daughter of business tycoon **Vehbi Koç,** who joined the party on December 28, 1992. On April 17, 1993, Özal passed away. Some Özalists such as Akbulut returned to the MP. At the December 24, 1995, general elections, the MP obtained 19.8 percent of the votes and came in second behind the Welfare Party. In March 1996, Yılmaz formed a coalition government with **Tansu Çiller**'s True Path Party and became prime minister. From the beginning, this was a conflict-ridden coalition. Instead of cooperating with each other, Yılmaz and Çiller used every occasion to bolster their own position and become the undisputed leader of the center-right. Among other things, when Çiller was accused of financial wrongdoing, Yılmaz joined the bandwagon. As a consequence, the coalition collapsed in June 1996. Yılmaz's opportunity to return to power came when the Welfare Party-True Path Party coalition, which was formed in the wake of the collapse of the MP-True Path party coalition, ended in June 1997. On June 30, 1997, Yılmaz's MP joined a coalition government with **Bülent Ecevit**'s **Democratic Left Party** and **Hüsamettin Cindoruk**'s **Democratic Turkey Party**. The coalition was supported from outside by the (new) **Republican People's Party**. Initially, this coalition tended toward holding early elections. Later, it changed course and initiated successful policies in several areas. However, the effective performance of the coalition received a setback due to the charges of corruption brought against Yılmaz. The Republican People's Party withdrew its support and the coalition ended when it failed to obtain a vote of confidence. At the April 18, 1999, general elections, the MP did poorly, and came in fourth. However, the party was taken on board in the new coalition government with the Democratic Left Party and the **Nationalist Action Party**. Yılmaz was determined to clear himself of charges brought against him and, therefore, he decided not to take a ministerial portfolio. Later, he was cleared of charges, and he joined the cabinet as deputy prime minister. This coalition displayed more harmony than had ever existed among the members of coalition governments in Turkey and adopted much-needed policies on several fronts (*see* the Introduction).

MOUNT ARARAT [Ağrı Dağı]. Turkey's highest mountain peak, about 5,166 meters high. It is situated near the tripod where the boundaries of Turkey, **Iran**, and **Armenia** meet. The mountain is where Noah's Ark is believed to have come to a rest.

MUALLİM NACİ (1850–1893). Ottoman poet and writer. Naci was a leading literary figure of the *Tanzimat* **(Reform) Period** (1839–1876). He published the literary *Teacher's Journal* [Mecmua-ı Muallim] for a while and emphasized the simplification of the language. Collections of his poems include *Morsel of Fire* [Ateşpâre], *Luminous* [Füruzan], and *Spark* [Şerare].

MUFTI [Jurisconsult]. Gave legal opinions in the Ottoman Empire, based on **Islamic** law and precedent. He was appointed by the **Şeyhülislam**.

MURAT PASHA (KUYUCU) (? –1611). Ottoman grand vizier. Between 1606 and 1609, Murat Pasha suppressed the **Celali revolts** and reestablished Ottoman suzerainty in many parts of Anatolia. In the process, he killed between 70,000 and 90,000 people. His sobriquet "well-sinker" comes from the fact that he had many of those who were killed buried in wells.

MUSAHİPZADE CELAL (1870–1959). Playwright. Stylistically and chronologically, Celal linked the Ottoman to the Republican literary world. Many of his plays, mostly romantic comedies portraying a background of the Ottoman era,

142 • MUSEUMS

were produced both in the pre- and post-Republican period. Among those plays
are *The Judge of Mount Athos* [Aynaroz Kadısı], *A Turban Has Been Overturned*
[Bir Kavuk Devrildi], *The Dervishes' Orgy* [Mum Söndü], and *The Istanbul Gentleman* [Istanbul Efendisi].

MUSEUMS. When the Turkish Republic was proclaimed in 1923, there were only
the **Istanbul** Archaeological Museum (called the *Asar-ı Atika Müzesi*), the Military Museum in St. Irene Church in Istanbul, the *Evkaf-ı Islamiye* Museum **(Islamic)** in the Süleymaniye Mosque Complex, again in Istanbul, and the branches
of the Müze-i Humayun in the few large cities of Anatolia. The Türk Asar-ı
Atikası [Turkish Archaeological Museum], which was opened in the early years
of the Republic, was instrumental in the restoration of several ancient churches,
mosques, and caravanserais in various provinces of Anatolia and in the opening
of new museums. The *Topkapı Sarayı*, where the **sultans** had resided until the
19th century, was turned into a museum and opened to the public in 1927. That
same year, the Evkaf-ı İslamiye Museum was reorganized as the Museum of
Turkish and Islamic Works of Art and the **Mevlana** Dergahı (seminary) in **Konya**
was also turned into a museum. In 1930, the Ankara Ethnographic Museum was
opened. This was followed by the opening of new museums in the cities of
Adana, Afyon, **Antalya**, **Bergama** (Pergamum), **Bursa**, Edirne, **İzmir**, **Kayseri**, and Manisa. In **Ankara**, the **Hittite** Museum was restored and opened as the
Museum of Anatolian Civilizations. It exhibits works of arts and relics belonging
to the **Hittite**, Ionian, Lydian, Hellenic, Roman, Byzantine, and Islamic civilizations. Anatolia has been settled since the Paleolithic age and has been a cradle of
civilizations. In 1998, there were 99 major public museums, 87 private museums,
and 1,028 private collections.

Another group of museums in Turkey are Museum Houses and Heritage Museums. They include the Çakırağa Mansion in Birgi, Hazeranlar Mansion in
Amasya, **Ziya Gökalp** House in **Diyarbakır**, and **Tevfik Fikret** Aşiyan House
in Istanbul. The transformation of some historic buildings into museums started
in 1930. The Dolmabahçe Palace, where sultans lived from the 19th century onward, the Kariye, Fethiye and İmrahor Mosques, the Hagia Sophia [St. Sophia]
in Istanbul, the Yeşil Türbe [the Green Tomb], and the Muradiye Külliyesi in
Bursa are the most important examples of these. Meanwhile, the ruins of many
ancient cities and settlements such as Aphrodisias, **Aspendos**, Bergama,
Boğazköy, **Ephesus**, Göreme, Karatepe, and Perge have been organized as openair museums.

MUSIC. At the beginning of the 20th century, three traditions of music existed side
by side in Turkey—folk music, traditional art music, and Occidental music. Folk
music comprised seven or eight regional and several more local types and
evinced a great variety in scales, meters, forms, types of composition, use of instruments, performing practices as well as in style of composition and performance. All types, however, had common characteristics, such as a general tendency

to make use of symmetrical meters of ascending melodies. Traditional art music was a purely melodic music; the Western traditions of polyphony and instrumentation were alien to it. Traditionally, it included such branches as the open-air Ottoman music [*mehter musikisi*], the sacred music of the **dervish orders**, the religious music of the mosque, indoor art music [*incesaz* or *fasıl*], recreational or "light" music, and urban popular music. Western music was adopted during the first part of the 18th century. It included classical and romantic masterpieces as well as **military, operatic**, dance, and light music. Following the proclamation of the Republic (in 1923), Turkey's rulers regarded the traditional art music as "inane" and an "opium left over from the past." They encouraged the creation of a new Turkish music from the music of peasants and by using Western techniques such as polyphonization. This was followed by the collection of folk songs and their transcription. From the 1940s onward, folk music was itself considered as an art to be transmitted in its original form. Soon, urban "composers" of folk songs appeared, and some "folk singers," along with a number of bards from the countryside, attained great fame. Suppressed for a while, traditional art music began to receive a new emphasis. However, out of the six former branches of the traditional art music, only entertainment music has flourished. During the past 30 years, arabesque songs, drawing on orchestral effects and cheap dramatic turns and using grief-stricken and fatalistic themes, have also become popular. During the Republican period, Western music also benefited from state encouragement and support. In 1923, the Municipal Conservatory of **Istanbul** was opened, with a department on Western music. The next year, the Presidential Music Ensemble was created, later renamed the first Presidential Philharmonic Orchestra, and yet later the Presidential Symphony Orchestra. As of the mid-1920s, the government sent promising young musicians to a number of Western countries to study musical composition. Renowned foreign composers and artists were brought to Turkey. In time, Turkish composers and their works became equally successful at home and abroad and some sopranos, pianists, violinists, and other such artists have achieved international reputations. By the 1960s, people in Turkey started to follow every kind of musical movement in the West. Rock and roll music, "beat," and rapid rhythms became favorites with the youth. The first examples of Turkish pop music were only rearrangements—merely writing Turkish lyrics to foreign melodies—but soon led to authentic compositions that united elements of Western pop music with Turkish folk music. Recently, there have been efforts to create original works, using traditional instruments in a hybrid genre. Compositions giving importance to the artistic interpretation, creation, and quality of music gained popularity.

MUSTAFA REŞİT PASHA (1800–1858). Ottoman grand vizier. Mustafa Reşit Pasha served as ambassador in Paris and London in 1835 and 1836, respectively. He also occupied these posts later, whenever **Istanbul** wanted to get rid of him. In 1837, he became foreign minister and played a pivotal role in the August 1838 signing of a trade treaty with **Great Britain** that eliminated monopolies and granted that country broad trade privileges in Ottoman lands. He was also involved with the proclamation of the **Imperial Rescript of Gülhane** in 1839 that started the *Tanzimat* **(Reform) Period** and granted equal rights and freedoms to all Ottoman subjects. He opened trade courts and secular secondary schools and initiated some administrative reforms. Mustafa Reşit Pasha pursued a successful **foreign policy**, attempted to integrate the Ottoman economy in the European economy, and sought to reform the Ottoman government in line with the European model. He was the leading representative of the **Westernization** policy in the 19th-century Ottoman Empire.

MUSTAFA SUPHİ (1883–1921). Politician. Mustafa Suphi, who studied in Paris, opposed the **Committee for Union and Progress** and left Turkey for **Russia**. He became a member of the Third International and founded the **Turkish Communist Party** in September 1920 in Baku, **Azerbaijan**. He returned to Turkey in December of that year. He died when his boat sank off **Trabzon** for unknown reasons.

MÜEZZİN. Man who calls believers to prayer five times a day.

MÜRİT. Teacher or master in a **tarikat**.

– N –

NABİ (1642–1712). Ottoman lyric poet. Nabi wrote didactic poems that often contained maxims. He criticized what he considered the ills of his age.

NAİMA (1655–1716). Ottoman historian. Although an official chronicler, Naima came to have a distinctive interpretation of history. His *History of Naima* [Naima Tarihi] is an indispensable source for students of 17th-century Ottoman society and Ottoman worldview. Naima thought that history should help people learn lessons from the past.

NAKSHIBANDI (NAKŞİBENDİ) ORDER. One of the most influential religious orders (*tarikat*) in the Ottoman Empire and Republican Turkey. For instance, Şeyhülislam Musa Kazım Efendi was a Nakshibandi. The order had members in the first Turkish Grand National Assembly. Its members have been close to orthodoxy and at times displayed aggressive fanaticism. Along with other religious orders, the Nakshibandi order was prosecuted during later decades, yet the order kept its vitality and came to form links with such **political parties** as the **Motherland Party** during the multiparty period (from 1945 to the present). *See also* ISLAM.

NAMIK KEMAL (1840–1888). A prominent literary figure. In the second part of the 19th century, Namık Kemal helped develop a new Turkish **literature** in prose for the **theater**, novel, and social commentary that had not existed in traditional Ottoman literature. In his writing, he emphasized patriotism and freedom. His important works include the play *Fatherland or Silistre* [Vatan Yahut Silistre], the novel *Awakening* [İntibah], and the critique *Defense Concerning Renan* [Renan Müdafaanamesi].

NASREDDİN HOCA (1208–1284). Folk philosopher. Although Nasreddin Hoca lived in the pre-Ottoman period, funny but thoughtful anecdotes attributed to him that reflect Anatolian people's daily life have been told and retold to this day.

NATION PARTY (NP)/ MİLLET PARTİSİ (MP). Some pro-Islamic right-wingers in the **Demokrat Party** (DP) left this party in 1948 and formed the Nation Party. The party had the blessings of **Turkish War of Independence** hero Field Marshal **Fevzi Çakmak**. Though led by the colorful **Osman Bölükbaşı**, the party did not flourish. The NP was closed in 1953 for its stance against **secularism**. It reemerged the following year with a new name—the Republican Nation Party (RNP). On the eve of the 1957 general elections, the RNP merged with the Peasant's Party (formed in 1952 by another group of dissatisfied right-wingers in the DP) and took the name of **Republican Peasant's Nation Party** (RPNP). In 1962, Bölükbaşı left the RPNP and formed the new Nation Party, but the latter remained moribund.

NATIONAL ACCOUNTS. Turkey's gross national product (GNP) stood at 953 million liras at the time of the establishment of the Republic in 1923; it had risen to 55 quadrillion liras by 1999. The 1923 state budget of 94 million liras shot up to 32.6 quadrillion liras in 1999. From 1923 to 1998, **agriculture**'s share of GNP decreased from 42 percent to 15 percent, **industry**'s share increased from 11 percent to 23 percent, and the services' share rose from 47 percent to 62 percent. The share of industry in GNP surpassed that of agriculture (at constant prices) for the first time in 1973, and since then the difference between the two has continued increasing. In 1928, GNP per capita was $56; it rose $6,486 (PPP, purchasing power parity) in 1998.

NATIONAL LIBRARY. Established in 1946, presently occupies a space of 39,000 square meters. It is possible to add new modules. According to law, one copy of all works published in Turkey must be sent to the library. By January 2001, the collection included 993,904 books and 581,763 volumes of periodicals containing newspapers, magazines, annuals, bulletins, and the like, as well as 100,344 other material like posters, maps, musical scores, sound recordings (disc or cassette), and paintings. The library also holds more than 55,000 Turkish books printed in the Arabic alphabet and 25,366 manuscripts and rare books. *See also* LIBRARIES.

NATIONAL ORDER PARTY (NOP)/ MİLLİ NİZAM PARTİSİ (MNP). Formed in January 1970 by **Necmettin Erbakan** and 17 colleagues. The party had a religious orientation. It was closed the next year by the Constitutional Court on the grounds that its program violated the constitutional norm that the Turkish state is a secular state. *See also* NATIONAL SALVATION PARTY; VIRTUE PARTY; WELFARE PARTY.

NATIONAL PACT [Misak-ı Milli]. Issued on February 17, 1920, by the last Ottoman chamber of deputies meeting secretly in **Istanbul**, at that time occupied by the Allied powers. The pact expressed the will of the Turkish people to regain full national integrity and independence. This was in effect an acceptance of the declaration made at the **Sivas Congress** of September 4–11, 1919, which had been convened by the nationalists and presided by Mustafa Kemal **Atatürk**.

NATIONAL PROGRAM. Adopted on March 19, 2001, the program comprises general principles and strategy governing the reforms Turkey will make for accession to the **European Union** as a full member. (For some of the other reforms envisaged, *see* CIVIL SOCIETY; HUMAN RIGHTS; NATIONAL SECURITY COUNCIL; WOMEN).

NATIONAL SALVATION PARTY (NSP)/ MİLLİ SELAMET PARTİSİ (MSP). The party was a successor to the **National Order Party**, which was established by **Necmettin Erbakan** in 1970 and was dissolved by court order in 1971 on grounds of anti-**secularism**. The National Salvation Party was formed by the caretaker Süleyman Arif Emre in 1972; Emre turned over the leadership to Erbakan after a short time. The NSP favored a strengthening of moral and national values and promoted heavy **industry**. It advocated free enterprise, though opposed to capitalism and foreign investments as well as to communism. The party stood against close ties with the West; instead, it wished to improve political and economic relations with Muslim countries. The NSP presented these views under the label of "National View." At times, the party made no secret of its hostility to **Atatürk** and his reforms. The party's members were for the most part technocrats and religious local elements. The NSP was supported by local notables, some landowners, and small to medium-large business enterprises with a local color and afraid of big capital. Its votes have mostly come from illiterate Muslim puritans in the economically backward areas. The NSP formed a coalition government with the **Republican People's Party** after the 1973 general elections and took part in the first and second Nationalist Front governments, in 1975 and 1977, respectively. The party's unorthodox views created problems for the smooth conduct of government in all the coalitions in which it participated. Along with others, the NSP was closed following the September 12, 1980, **military** intervention. *See also* ISLAM; VIRTUE PARTY; WELFARE PARTY.

NATIONAL SECURITY COUNCIL (NSC). (1) Formed by the 1961 **constitution**. This council comprised the president, prime minister, ministers of defense, foreign affairs, and interior, chief of the general staff, and commanders of the army, navy, air force, and the general commander of the gendarmerie. According to the 1982 constitution, the council of ministers has to give priority to policy recommendations made by the NSC. In 2001, as part of the constitutional amendments that were made to facilitate Turkey's accession to the **European Union**, the composition and role the NSC plays in Turkish politics were changed in a more liberal direction. The number of its civilian members has been increased; deputy prime ministers and the minister of justice are now members of the NSC; and the NSC does not now recommend measures but conveys its view while the council of ministers does not give priority to but assesses the views passed on to it. (2) This council was formed after the September 12, 1980, **military** intervention. It comprised the makers of the intervention—the chief of general staff and commanders of the army, navy, air force and the general commander of the **gendarmerie**. It exercised legislative powers. The NSC appointed the members of the **Consultative Assembly**, which prepared the 1982 constitution, and gave final shape to that constitution, which was then approved in a national referendum. *See also* MILITARY AND POLITICS.

"NATIONAL WILL (MİLLİ İRADE)." Repeatedly emphasized by the Democrats of the 1950s and their successors in the **Justice Party** and **True Path Party** to underline their claim that their power derived from vote and, therefore, the intellectual-bureaucratic elite should not think that "because they represent the state" they are in a superordinate position vis-à-vis the politicians.

NATIONALIST ACTION PARTY (NAP) / MİLLİYETÇİ HAREKET PARTİSİ (MHP). This party came into being with a change of name in the **Republican Peasant's Nation Party** (RPNP) after the RPNP was taken over by **Alparslan Türkeş**. The Nationalist Action Party subscribed to **Turkism/Pan-Turkism** and nationalism. The party's ideology was expressed as "Nine Lights" (read, "Principles")—nationalism, idealism, moralism, corporatism, scientism, populism, progressivism, technologism, and the defense of freedom and peasantry. The NAP advocated a strong state bringing about solidarity among all social strata, with the public and the private sectors cooperating in a "corporatist" spirit. The party catered mostly to youth groups with strong ties to a rural lifestyle, small merchants and craftsmen, local and noncompetitive enterprises, and a number of civil servants. The NAP played a significant part in the right-wing political violence of the 1970s. The **military** intervenors of September 12, 1980, closed the NAP, along with other **political parties** existing at the time. The nationalist left was not represented in Parliament in any meaningful way until after the April 18, 1999, general elections (*see* NATIONALIST LABOR PARTY). In the 1999 elections, the NAP came second after the **Democratic Left Party** (DLP), and joined the coalition government with the DLP and the **Motherland Party**. The party's new leader **Devlet Bahçeli** became deputy prime minister. Since the 1999 elections, the NAP has subscribed to cultural rather than ethnic nationalism, displayed a tendency toward consensual politics, and favored a prudent and clean government. The transformation of the party along these lines had started from the early 1980s onward while Türkeş (again) led the party.

NATIONALIST DEMOCRACY PARTY (NDP)/MİLLİYETÇİ DEMOKRASİ PARTİSİ (MDP). First party to be established (on May 16, 1983) after the **military** intervention of September 12, 1980. The party was founded by retired General **Turgut Sunalp** and his close associates. The NDP was thought to have the implicit support of the military. In the November 6, 1983, general elections, however, the party came in third behind the **Motherland Party** and **Populist Party**. In the March 25, 1984, local elections, the parties that were not allowed by the military to participate in the November 6, 1983, general elections (the **True Path Party**, **Social Democracy Party**, and **Welfare Party**) also competed. In both these elections, the NDP could not even obtain the percentage of votes required countrywide in a general election to win seats in Parliament (10 percent). The party's chairman General Sunalp was removed from office. Ülkü Söylemezoğlu became the new chairman. This change did not help revive the party. The NDP dissolved itself on May 4, 1986.

NATIONALIST LABOR PARTY (NLP)/MİLLİYETÇİ ÇALIŞMA PARTİSİ (MÇP). Founded on July 7, 1983. The party's leader was **Alparslan Türkeş**, for a long time the veteran leader of the Turkish nationalist right. In the 1980s, the NLP did poorly in the elections. In the October 21, 1991, general elections, some of the party's candidates for Parliament were elected on the **Welfare Party**'s lists. Thus the party had representation in the post-October 21, 1991, Parliament. Yet, unlike its predecessor, the **Nationalist Action Party**, the NLP has had little impact on Turkish politics.

NAZIM HİKMET (1901–1963). The best-known socialist and realist poet of Turkey. One of the founders of free verse in Turkey, Nazım Hikmet drew his inspiration from both the **Divan** tradition and folk poetry. His style became the model for poetry dealing with social questions. His masterpiece title poem, *Human Panoramas from My Country* [Memleketimden İnsan Manzaraları], described the social realities of Turkey from 1908 to **World War II**. He spent long years as a political prisoner because of his Marxist views and late in his life escaped to the then Soviet Union (*see* RUSSIA) where he subsequently died. Other well-known books of poems by Nazım Hikmet are *The Legend of Sheikh Bedreddin: Son of the Judge of Simnavna* [Simnavna Kadısı Oğlu Şeyh Bedreddin Destanı] and *The Legend of the War of Independence* [Kurtuluş Savaşı Destanı].

NEF-İ (?–1635). Ottoman lyric poet. He was well known for his masterfully designed satires, some of which bordered on outright curses on people.

NESİN, AZİZ (1915–1995). Turkey's leading satirist as well as short story writer, playwright, and philanthropist. For his stories and plays, Nesin received several awards in various countries. Nesin continuously made fun of inefficiency, corruption, and nepotism in government. Among his short stories are *Hamdi the Elephant* [Fil Hamdi], *There Is a Madman on the Roof* [Damda Deli Var], *The Ceremony of the Cauldron* [Kazan Töreni], *The Monster of the Toros Mountains* [Toros Canavarı], *The Madmen Broke Loose* [Deliler Boşandı], *We'll Never Amount to Anything* [Biz Adam Olmayız], and *How We Made the Revolution* [İhtilâli Nasıl Yaptık]; among his novels are *Zübük* and *The Children Are Prodigies Nowadays* [Şimdiki Çocuklar Harika], and among his memoirs *It Has Always Happened This Way in the Past But It Won't in the Future* [Böyle Gelmiş Böyle Gitmez] are particularly popular.

NEW DEMOCRACY MOVEMENT [Yeni Demokrasi Hareketi]. Founded and led by textile tycoon **Cem Boyner**. Not unlike other **Mediterranean** business tycoons such as France's Bernard Tapie and Italy's Silvio Berlusconi, Boyner went into politics and pursued an unconventional, informal style. He challenged some of Turkey's long-held taboos, advocating full religious freedoms and a political solution to the Kurdish problem (*see* KURDS). The movement was supported by those in big business who wished to see the thorny issues resolved and thus have stability in politics. On the eve of the 1995 general elections, the movement changed into the New Democracy Party, which had a very poor showing in the 1995 general elections and, consequently, gradually petered out.

NEW TURKEY PARTY (NTP)/YENİ TÜRKİYE PARTİSİ (YTP). One of the three parties (the other two parties being the **Justice Party** and **Republican Peasant's Nation Party**), which competed for a place on the right of the political spectrum after the closure of the *Demokrat* **Party** by the **military** following the May 27, 1960, military intervention. The NTP, formed in 1961 and led by **Ekrem Alican**, was backed by several influential eastern Anatolian landlords. The party took part in the second coalition formed after the reinstallation of multiparty politics, with the **Republican People's Party**, Republican Peasant's Nation Party, and some independents as other partners. In the 1965 general elections, the NTP lost its votes to the Justice Party (JP). In 1973, It merged with the JP.

NEWS AGENCIES. *See* MASS MEDIA.

NEWSPAPERS. *See* MASS MEDIA.

NEYZEN TEVFİK (1879–1953). Poet and musician. Neyzen Tevfik extemporized satirical poetry while playing the *ney*, the reed flute. He made fun of any and every social institution or "lofty" sentiment. Many of his satires, being very critical socially and politically, were never published. Some of the others are in *Nothing* [Hiç] and *Sacred Suffering* [Azab-ı Mukaddes].

NİZAM-I CEDİT [New Order]. The reformed army of Selim III. It was established as of 1794 and organized, trained, and dressed in the European manner by experts brought from various European countries. Modern weapons were introduced and European instructors engaged. For the most part, Muslim peasant boys from Anatolia manned the new army, which was stationed in Anatolia and the Balkans as well as in Istanbul. The Nizam-ı Cedit Army was resisted by the Janissary Corps, religious leaders, and courtiers who did not want to see the old order changed. It was disbanded by Selim III in an effort to bring to an end to the Kabakçı Mustafa riot in Istanbul in 1807 that was encouraged and supported by the dissidents.

NORTH ATLANTIC TREATY ORGANIZATION (NATO). Turkey became a member of the North Atlantic Treaty Organization in 1952. From the Cold War years of the 1950s until the collapse of the Soviet Union (see RUSSIA), Turkey's significance as a NATO member derived from the fact that it is situated in an area of crucial geostrategic political and economic importance. This significance continues in the post-Soviet period, since it borders unstable and important regions of southwest Asia and the Middle East. Turkey's importance to its Western allies was underlined by the cooperative role it played during the Gulf War and in Afghanistan. Turkey has welcomed NATO's project of enlargement in recent years.

– O –

OKTAY RIFAT (1914–1988). Poet and playwright. He was one of the leading members of the literary movement called Garip [Strange] (on this movement, see LITERATURE). Forceful love themes as well as new forms and contents dominate Oktay Rıfat's poetry; he ascribed secondary importance to aesthetic considerations. Examples of his poetry are Ode [Güzelleme], The Street of Tassels [Perçemli Sokak], Freedom Has Hand [Elleri Var Özgürlüğün], and Shepherd's Poems [Çobanın Şiirleri].

OKYAR, FETHİ (1880–1943). Officer and politician. Okyar served as military attaché in Paris and was later appointed ambassador to Bulgaria. He became a member of the Ottoman Parliament in 1912 and was made minister of interior in 1918. Okyar joined the Turkish Grand National Assembly in 1921 and served as minister of interior between October 10, 1921, and July 9, 1922; prime minister between August 23, 1923, and October 27, 1924, and again between November 22, 1924, and March 2, 1925; and ambassador to Paris between March 26, 1925, and August 9, 1930. With Atatürk's encouragement, he formed the Republican Free Party in August 1930 and became its chairman. The party dissolved itself in November 1930 because those against the Republican reforms rushed to the party and this was not approved by Atatürk. Okyar was appointed ambassador to

Great Britain in 1934. He was again elected member of Parliament in 1939 and served as minister of justice between April 3, 1939, and March 12, 1941. He quit active politics in 1942.

OPERA AND BALLET. Opera was introduced to the Turks during the Ottoman period by the renowned Italian composer Gaetano Donizetti who was invited to the Ottoman Palace as the general instructor of the Ottoman State Bands. In the course of the 19th century, the growing interest led to the building of numerous opera houses, particularly in **Istanbul.** Following the founding of the Republic in 1923, **Atatürk** started a cultural revolution in Turkey. Opera was viewed as the highest form of music. In 1934, Verdi's *La Traviata* was staged by the Grand Opera Assembly. In 1936, Ankara State Conservatory was opened. In 1940, *Bastien and Bastienne* by Mozart and the second act of *Madame Butterfly* by Giacomo Puccini were staged; these were followed in 1941 by Puccini's *Tosca,* the complete *Madame Butterfly,* and Beethoven's *Fidelio.* The first state-sponsored ballet school was opened in Istanbul in 1948. Dame Ninette de Valois, the founder of the British Royal Ballet, made important contributions to the development of ballet in Turkey. Her students staged the first ballet performance in 1950. During recent years, the State Opera and Ballet, a corporate body affiliated to the Ministry of Culture, stages 24–30 performances per month in Istanbul and **Ankara,** and several others in other major cities. The **Aspendos** Opera and Ballet **Festival** held every year in the third and fourth weeks of June attracts 80,000 to 100,000 people.

ORBAY, RAUF (1881–1964). Officer and politician. Orbay attained fame in the navy during the 1912 **Balkan War**. He became minister of war in October 1918. That same month, Orbay headed the Ottoman delegation at the Mudros Armistice conference. Orbay cooperated with Mustafa Kemal **Atatürk** during the early months of the Turkish national independence movement. He joined the Turkish Grand National Assembly on November 11, 1921, and served as minister of public works between November 17, 1921, and January 4, 1923. Later, he became a member of the opposition group in Parliament. With this group, he founded the **Progressive Republican Party** on November 17, 1924, and became its acting chairman. The party was closed on June 3, 1925, on the grounds that it encouraged bigotry by emphasizing **religion**. Orbay was tried along with other party leaders who were thought to have been involved in the assassination attempt on President Mustafa Kemal. Orbay, who was in Europe at the time, was sentenced to 10 years. He returned to Turkey following an amnesty and his name was cleared in a High Military Court decision. Orbay became a member of Parliament in 1932. He served as ambassador in London between 1942–1944. Orbay spent the rest of his life away from politics.

ORGANIZATION FOR SECURITY AND COOPERATION IN EUROPE (OSCE). Founded in 1975, the OSCE is an organization including both members of the Western alliance and former Eastern communist states. It did much to reduce tensions and eventually end the Cold War. Since then, it has sought to enhance security and stability by normalizing relations between countries and promoting cooperation among them. From the very beginning, Turkey has been actively involved in the OSCE. The last summit meeting of the organization was held in **Istanbul** on November 18–19, 1999. *See also* EUROPEAN SECURITY AND DEFENSE IDENTITY; NORTH ATLANTIC TREATY ORGANIZATION.

ORGANIZATION OF THE ISLAMIC CONFERENCE (OIC). Founded in 1970, the OIC aims at strengthening solidarity and cooperation among Islamic states in the political, economic, cultural, scientific, and social fields. Although the bulk of Turkey's population believes in **Islam**, the state does not regard itself as Islamic. Turkey therefore endeavors to promote solidarity and close cooperation in nonpolitical fields in general and in the economy in particular.

ORHAN KEMAL (1914–1970). Author of short novels and short stories. Kemal wrote in a realistic genre. He dwelt on the agricultural and factory workers of Turkey's Çukurova region in the south in general and in the city of **Adana**. Later in life, he turned his attention to the plight of migrant workers of **Istanbul** living in poor neighborhoods. *Barrack No. 72* [72'nci Koğuş] and *Murtaza the Night Watchman* [Bekçi Murtaza] are among his most popular stories. Among his popular novels are *Ms. Cemile* [Cemile] and *On Fertile Soil* [Bereketli Topraklar Üzerinde].

ORTAOYUNU PLAY. The traditional improvisational arena play in which originally certain types represented different ethnic groups living in **Istanbul**. The types in question were later conventionalized and became theatrical figures. Types seem to be thrown together by accident, yet their relationships bring forth an organic whole in the aesthetic sense. The plot is usually episodic. The chain of events is of secondary importance; the emphasis is on the typical reaction of each class or group to changing circumstances. Narration is a significant part of the play; the time and place of the action is described as well as represented on the stage.

OSMAN I (1258–1326). Founder of the Ottoman Empire who ruled 1299 to 1324. In 1288, the Selcukiad **sultan** made Osman's clan in Söğüt near **Bursa** a frontier principality of his empire and Osman the chief of that principality. Osman I gradually expanded his principality's territory at the expense of other principalities and the Byzantine Empire. Osman I lived modestly and treated his subjects with justice and equity.

OSMAN II (GENÇ) (1604–1622). Ottoman **sultan** (1618–1622) who tried to reform the **Janissary Corps** and government. Afraid that their corps would be dissolved and encouraged by a court faction led by **Kösem Sultan(a)**, the Janissaries removed Osman II from the throne and killed him.

OSMAN BEY (TAMBURİ, BÜYÜK) (1816–1885). Ottoman composer. Osman Bey was known for his novel overtures in traditional Turkish **music**. He masterfully played the lute—thus his cognomen Tamburi (literally, player of the lute). His other cognomen, Büyük ("older"), distinguished him from a contemporary (and younger) lute player and composer.

OSMAN HAMDİ BEY (1842–1910). Ottoman painter and archaeologist. Osman Hamdi Bey was the first painter in Turkey to draw figures, and the founder of the first school of painting and first archaeology museum in Turkey. He became an honorary member of the Archaeology Institute of Athens (1895) and correspondent member of the Royal Academy of Arts in London (1909). He received honorary Ph.D. degrees from Leipzig University (1906), Aberdeen University (1907), and Oxford University (1909), and was given decorations by the Prussian Kingdom (1872, 1903), Wurtemberg Kingdom (1892), French government (1892, 1904), Duchy of Baden (1892), and Duchy of Saxony (1908).

OTTOMANISM. Doctrine developed in the wake of the **Reform Decree** of 1856. It aimed at holding Muslim and non-Muslim elements of the Ottoman Empire together. For this purpose, the doctrine provided that all subjects of the empire were equal before the law. Non-Muslims began to be conscripted into the **military** and admitted to secular schools and were no longer required to pay the *cizye* [head tax]. Ottomanism could not stem the separatist movements in the empire.

OYAK. The Army Mutual Assistance Association [*Ordu Yardımlaşma Kurumu*]. The association runs one of the largest conglomerates in the country.

– Ö –

ÖCALAN, ABDULLAH (1949–). Kurdish separatist. Öcalan for a while attended **Istanbul University**'s Law School and **Ankara University**'s School of Political Sciences. In 1978, he initiated the establishment of the Kurdistan Worker's Party (PKK) and started small-scale armed opeations in the southeast "for the Kurdish cause." Following the **military** intervention in 1980, he escaped to Syria. Then, from the Bekaa Valley in Lebanon, he directed the armed attacks of the PKK in Turkey against both the security forces and civilians of both Turkish and Kurdish origin. Öcalan was captured in February 1999, tried, and was given the death sentence. The case is now before the European Human Rights Court. *See also* KURDS.

ÖKE, MİM KEMAL (1884–1955). Surgeon. Öke is best known for his contributions to abdominal surgery. A particular gastroenterostomy operation to relieve the stomach of unwanted fluid is known in the medical literature as the "Mim Kemal method."

ÖMER SEYFETTİN (1884–1920). Short story writer. Ömer Seyfettin was a prominent representative of the National Literary Movement (on this movement, *see* LITERATURE). He led the trend toward writing in simple Turkish, and contributed to the emergence of a new literary genre. Ömer Seyfettin provided successful works of this sort. *Bomb* [Bomba], *White Tulip* [Beyaz Lale], *High Heels* [Yüksek Ökçeler], and *Secret Temple* [Gizli Mabet] are the best-known collections of his short stories.

ÖRF. The "sovereign prerogative" of the Ottoman **sultan** to take the initiative and issue secular regulations (*kanun*; pl. *kavanin*).

ÖYMEN, ALTAN (1932–). Journalist and politician. Öymen wrote in such newspapers as *Yeni Ulus, Tercüman, Yeni Gün,* and *Cumhuriyet* and worked as chief editor of the **Istanbul** daily *Milliyet.* He served as a member of the **Constituent Assembly** (1961) and as minister of **tourism** (1977–1978), and was chairman of the (new) **Republican People's Party** from May 1999 to September 2000.

ÖZAL, TURGUT (1927–1993). Turkey's eighth president. Özal graduated from **Istanbul Technical University** in 1950. He studied economics and engineering in the **United States**. Upon his return to Turkey, he became deputy director of the Electrical Studies and Research Administration. He headed the State Planning Organization from 1967 to 1971. For a while, Özal taught at the **Middle East Technical University** in **Ankara**. Between 1972 and 1973, he worked as a special projects advisor at the World Bank. When he returned to Turkey, he joined the **Sabancı** Holding Company. On March 31, 1975, Özal was appointed undersecretary of the prime ministry and acting head of the State Planning Organization. Özal became a candidate for Parliament from the religiously oriented **National Salvation Party** in the 1977 general elections but was not elected. Then he distanced himself from the traditional Muslim image; for instance, he publicly held hands with his wife. In late 1979, as Prime Minister **Süleyman Demirel**'s chief aide, he prepared the January 24, 1980, austerity program. During the 1980–1983 **military** regime, Özal served for a while as deputy premier in charge of economic affairs. In 1983, he formed the **Motherland Party** (MP) and became its chairman. The MP won a landslide victory at the 1983 general elections and Özal became prime minister and remained in that post until October 31, 1989, when he was elected president. While prime minister, Özal brought about Turkey's transition from an import-substitution economy to an export-oriented economy. Özal died of a heart attack on April 17, 1993, while still president.

ÖZBUDUN, ERGUN (1937–). Professor of constitutional law and politics and a member of the **Turkish Academy of Sciences**. He is best known for his work on the problems of the consolidation of democracy in Turkey. Özbudun is the author of *Social Change and Political Participation in Turkey* and *Contemporary Turk-*

ish Politics: Challenges to Democratic Consolidation, and co-editor of *Electoral Politics in the Middle East* and *Competitive Elections in Developing Countries.*

ÖZGÜÇ, TAHSİN (1916–). Professor of archaeology. Özgüç served as rector of **Ankara University.** He was designated member of the German Archaeology Institute, English Archaeology Academy, and **Turkish Academy of Sciences** and honorary member of the American Archaeology Institute. He was awarded the German president's High Merit Award. Özgüç is best known for his digs that shed light on the transition of Anatolia from the prehistorical to historical periods.

ÖZTÜRK, YAŞAR NURİ (1945–). Professor of theology and columnist. Öztürk, who served as a visiting professor at the Theological Seminary of Barrytown, New York, is best known for his efforts to cleanse **Islam** of the superstitions that have accumulated over centuries. Öztürk's books include *The Spirit of Sufism and the Tariqats in Turkey, The Bektashi Order, The Sufi Thought* [Tasavvufi Düşünce], *Existence and Mankind* [Varlık ve İnsan], *Sufism According to the Koran and Hadith* [Ku'ran ve Sünnete Göre Tasavvuf], *The Last Prophet* [Son Peygamber], *The Spirit of Sufism and the Religious Orders* [Tasavvufun Ruhu ve Tarikatlar], *The Primary Tenets of the Koran* [Kur'an'ın Temel Kavramları], *Great Sins* [Büyük Günahlar], and *Toward an Understanding of the Koran* [Kur'an'ı Anlamaya Doğru].

– P –

PAMUKKALE [Cotton Castle]. One of the most extraordinary sights in southwest Turkey—a plateau more than a hundred meters high rising out of the plain with its cliff face displaying a dazzling chalk-white array of fantastically shaped stalactites. Vaporous water flows down the face through a widening succession of scallop-shell basins and petal-like elfin pools surfaced in glistening limestone.

PAMUK, ORHAN (1952–). The most popular postmodernist novelist of Turkey, who uses a different literary genre in each of his novels. His first novel that achieved recognition was *Cevdet Esquire and His Sons* [Cevdet Bey ve Oğulları]. He gained national as well as international fame by his novel *Black Book* [Kara Kitap]. His other novels include *Quiet House* [Sessiz Ev], *White Castle* [Beyaz Kale], *New Life* [Yeni Hayat], *Red Book* [Kırmızı Kitap] and *Snow* (Kar). Pamuk received several awards, including the French Prix de la Découverte Européenne.

PAMUK, ŞEVKET (1950–). Professor of economics and a member of the **Turkish Academy of Sciences.** Pamuk, who has a B.A. degree from Yale University and M.A. and Ph.D. degrees from the University of California, Berkeley, is best known for his studies on the monetary history of the Ottoman Empire. Pamuk is the author of *The Ottoman Empire and European Capitalism,*

1820–1913: Trade, Investment, and Production and *A Monetary History of the Ottoman Empire,* co-author of *A History of the Middle East Economies in the Twentieth Century,* and co-editor of *Long Run Economic Change in the Mediterranean Basin, 1850–1950* and *La Monnaie et les Monnaies dans l'Empire Ottomane.*

PAN-TURKISM. *See* TURKISM/PAN-TURKISM.

PAN-ISLAMISM. *See* ISLAMISM/PAN-ISLAMISM.

PASHA (Paşa). The title given to the leading statesmen early in Ottoman history—the governor of the governors (*beylerbeys* of Anatolia and Rumelia) and viziers of the capital. It was later extended to a larger group of higher bureaucrats. After 1839, however, the title of "pasha" was primarily given to the first four (out of nine) grades of the civil and **military** hierarchy. The Turkish Republic retained the title for generals and admirals until 1934 when it was abolished. The word is still used to refer informally to generals and admirals.

PASSAROWITZ, TREATY OF (1718). This treaty came in the wake of the capture of Temesvar and Belgrade by the Austrians and Dalmatia by the Venetians. The Austrians and Venetians held the lands they captured. The Ottomans finally realized that they were no match for the technologically superior European armies and became much more cautious about new involvement in wars with the Europeans.

PATRONA HALİL (?–1730). A vagabond all his life. Patrona was one of the leaders of the riot, which later came to be known by his name, that opposed all that the **Tulip Era** stood for and that removed Sultan Ahmet III (1703–1730) from his throne and brought Mahmut I (1730–1754) to power. For two months, Patrona exercised considerable (de facto) power; he was killed at a meeting at the court, to which he was skillfully lured by his opponents.

PEKER, RECEP (1889–1950). Officer and politician. Peker entered Parliament in 1923. He wrote editorials for the daily *National Sovereignty* [**Hakimiyet-i Milliye**], the organ of the ruling single party—the **Republican People's Party** (RPP). He served as minister of finance between March 6 and November 22, 1924, minister of interior and acting minister of exchange [of populations], and reconstruction and resettlement between November 22, 1924, and March 3, 1925. Then he was appointed acting minister of defense; Peker resigned from this ministry in 1927 because he felt that the measures the **İsmet İnönü** government had taken against the **Sheikh Said** rebellion were not stern enough. Between 1927 and 1930, he acted as minister of public works. Peker also became secretary-general of the RPP at different times from 1923 to 1936; in 1936, he was relieved of this post because of his authoritarian tendencies. In 1942, and again in 1943, he was appointed minister of interior. On August 7, 1946, he was appointed prime minister, following the transition to multiparty politics in 1945, which he had vehemently opposed. Once prime minister, Peker resorted to authoritarian rules, which polarized politics and led to resignations from the RPP. He was obliged to resign as prime minister on September 9, 1947. In the 1948 RPP Congress, Peker challenged İnönü for the chairmanship and quit active politics when he lost.

PEOPLE'S DEMOCRACY PARTY (PDP)/HALKIN DEMOKRASİ PARTİSİ (HADEP). Formed on May 11, 1994, the PDP represents Turkish citizens of Kurdish origin. The predecessors of the PDP—the **Democracy Party** (DP) [Demokrasi Partisi-DEP] and the **People's Labor Party** (PLP) [Halkın Emek Partisi-HEP] were banned by the Constitutional Court. Separatist ethnic parties are not allowed in Turkey. In the 1995 general elections, the PDP obtained 4.17 percent of the votes, and in the 1999 elections 4.75 percent of the votes. Most of the party's support comes from the southeast where Turkish citizens of Kurdish origin are concentrated. The present chairman of the PDP is Ahmet Turan Demir. *See also* KURDS.

PEOPLE'S HOUSES [Halk Evleri]. Organs of adult **education** founded in cities and larger towns on February 19, 1932. The People's Houses propagated the Republic's ideals as well as principles advocated by the **Republican People's Party**. They were closed on August 8, 1953, by the *Demokrat* **Party** government.

PEOPLE'S LABOR PARTY (PLP)/HALKIN EMEK PARTİSİ (HEP). Formed on June 7, 1990. The PLP's first chairman was Fehmi Işıklar. The founding members of the party were for the most part deputies who had resigned from the **Social Democratic Populist Party** (SDPP) and deputies who were dismissed from the SDPP on grounds that they had acted against party discipline by attending an international conference in Paris on the rights of the **Kurds**. The PLP, which was later led by Ahmet Türk, sought to bring solutions to Turkey's southeastern issue as well as to the problems of workers in Turkey. The party continued to be represented in Parliament following the October 21, 1991, general elections; its deputies were elected on the SDPP lists and later resigned from that party. By October 1992, the public prosecutor started proceedings against the PLP on grounds that the party had defended views that clashed with the unitary character of the Turkish state. The Constitutional Court closed the party on July 14, 1993. *See also* DEMOCRACY PARTY; PEOPLE'S DEMOCRACY PARTY.

PEOPLE'S ROOMS [Halk Odaları]. Established in 1940 in villages and smaller towns. The People's Rooms functioned along the same lines as the **People's Houses**. They were closed on August 8, 1953, along with the People's Houses.

PERA. Beyoğlu (European) section of **Istanbul** during Ottoman times. This was the most cosmopolitan district of the city, mainly inhabited by non-Muslims.

PERİDE CELAL (1915–). Novelist. Peride wrote mostly novels of love and adventure and later in her life also produced psychosociological novels. She often reflected Turkish middle-class attitudes in her work. Examples of her novels are *From the Diary of a Married Woman* [Evli Bir Kadının Günlüğünden] and *Three Twenty-Four Hours* [Üç Yirmi Dört Saat].

PERİNÇEK, DOĞU (1942–). Politician and journalist. Perinçek served as chairman of such minor and leftist parties as the Labor and Peasant Party of Turkey, **Socialist Party**, and Labor Party. His books include *The State and Society from the Ottomans to Today* [Osmanlı'dan Bugüne Devlet ve Toplum], *Constitution and Political Party System* [Anayasa ve Partiler Rejimi], *Kemalist Revolution* [Kemalist Devrim], *The Sources of Anarchy and Revolutionary Politics* [Anarşinin Kaynağı ve Devrimci Siyaset], *The Path of Revolution in Turkey* [Türkiye Devriminin Yolu], *Political Party and Art* [Parti ve Sanat], *The Turkish Problem* [Türk Sorunu], *The Writings of Lenin, Stalin, and Mao on Turkey* [Lenin, Stalin ve Mao'nun Türkiye Yazıları], *The Enlightened and Culture* [Aydın ve Kültür], and *Turkey in the Documents of the Communist International* [Komünist Enternasyonel Belgelerinde Türkiye] (five volumes).

PEYAMİ SAFA (1899–1961). Novelist and journalist. He was known for his psychological novels as well as his columns in dailies. Earlier in his life, he had sympathies for the left; however, he defended the National Socialists during **World War II**. In his last years, Peyami was interested in metaphysics. His best-known works are his novel *Ninth External Diseases Ward* [Dokuzuncu Hariciye Koğuşu] and his essay "Notes on Turkish Revolution" [Türk İnkılâbına Bakışlar].

PİR SULTAN ABDAL (16th century). Ottoman poet and mystic. Pir Sultan Abdal helped disseminate **Shi'a** beliefs in Anatolia. He contributed to the development of a genre of poems in which most delicate feelings were expressed by means of folk expressions.

PİRİ REİS (?–1554). Ottoman sailor. He is well known for his world maps as well as his books on naval subjects. In his maps, Piri Reis also provided historical and geographical accounts based on the firsthand observations he had made during his trips to distant lands.

POLATKAN, HASAN (1915–1961). Politician. Polatkan was minister of labor from May 22, 1950, until March 8, 1951, and minister of finance from the latter date until May 27, 1960. He was tried, along with **Adnan Menderes** and **Fatin Rüştü Zorlu**, by the High Court of Justice set up by the May 27, 1960, **military** intervenors and was given the death penalty, which was carried out.

POLICE. The first police organization in Turkey was founded in 1845. Today, police functions are the responsibility of the General Directorate of Security (GDS), which is affiliated with the Ministry of Interior. The police are responsible for the areas within the borders of municipalities; outside of these areas, police functions are carried out by the **gendarmerie**. In recent years, further efforts have been made to inculcate in the police a respect for **human rights**. The Central Criminal Laboratory established in **Ankara** in 1993 aids the police.

POLITICAL PARTIES. Political parties have a long history in Turkey. The New Ottoman Society, formed in 1865, is the lineal ancestor, among others, of the **Republican People's Party** (RPP), established in 1923, and the **Social Democratic Populist Party** (SDPP), founded in 1963. At times, however, party activity was completely halted—under Sultan **Abdülhamit II**'s absolute rule (1876–1909), the military dictatorship of the **Committee for Union and Progress** (1913–1918), and under the **military** intervention of 1980–1983. Genuine party life with lively, and at times bitter, competition in Turkey began at the beginning of **Young Turk** period of 1908–1918, but it lasted only until 1913. From 1923 to 1945, Turkey had a single-party regime under RPP governments. The RPP took upon itself the mission of **Westernizing** the country. During this period, two experiments with an opposition party—the **Progressive Republican Party** formed in 1924 and the **Free Republican Party** (encouraged by the Republican leaders-to-be) established in 1930—"failed" because the opponents of the Republican reforms tended to mobilize public opinion against them, and both parties were summarily closed. Following a further experiment with an **Independent Group** within Parliament, a multiparty regime was inaugurated in 1945. In 1950, the *Demokrat* **Party** (DP) toppled the RPP from power. With the onset of the multiparty regime, only some minor reversals were registered concerning the Westernizing reforms, such as limited concessions in response to popular religious sentiments, but on the whole, the clock was not turned back, as some had feared. Yet, due to lingering political tensions between the opposition and government parties that did not lessen even during crisis situations, the regime drifted toward authoritarianism in the late 1950s and witnessed widespread violence between the left and right during the 1960s and 1970s. These political tensions engendered the three **military** interventions of 1960–1961, 1971–1973, and 1980–1983 and the temporary shelving of political party life. The ongoing conflict between the parties derived from two different notions of democracy. The RPP espoused rationalist democracy, namely finding what is best for the country rather than reconciling sectional interests (for further elaboration, *see* INTEREST GROUPS), while the DP of the 1950s and the **Justice Party** (JP) of the 1960s and 1970s adhered to populist policies. The military interventions undertaken to institutionalize rationalist democracy in Turkey further heightened these tensions. The interventions led to the urge for vengeance sought by the Justice Party (seeking "justice") and the **True Path Party** (TPP) of the 1980s (seeking to replace the "mistaken notion of democracy") and to personal animosity between political

leaders. The domination of the parties by these leaders exacerbated the legitimation crisis. Consequently, during political crises, the relatively moderate elements
within the parties could not find an attentive ear. These tensions also created an
intense antimilitarism among the bulk of the intelligentsia and the members of
SDPP and TPP, which regarded themselves as "democrats." They overlooked the
facts that, although the military for a long time favored rationalist democracy, the
military was not against democracy, and that during the course of the 1980s, even
the military gradually abandoned the notion of rationalist democracy. Consequently, the **Motherland Party** (MP), which won the general elections of 1983
and 1987 and ruled the country until 1991, was perceived as the "creature" and
even the "emanation" of the military. This was because the Social Democratic
Populist Party—the successor to the RPP—and the True Path Party—-the successor to the JP—were not allowed by the military to participate in the 1983 elections. In fact, at the time, the MP was the most antimilitary party. It played an important role in the civilianization (replacement of military personnel by civilian
ones at some key agencies) and demilitarization (lessening the influence of the
military in public decision making) of the regime. This particular stance created
another round of legitimation crises during the 1980s. One glaring example was
the election of **Turgut Özal** (MP prime minister from 1983 to 1991) as president.
He was not attributed legitimacy for a long time "because the MP majority in the
Parliament that elected him did not have popular support." Following the October 1991 general elections, Turkey was ruled by a TPP-SDPP coalition, that is,
by the successor parties to the DP-JP and RPP, respectively. Despite their inter-
minable feuds in the past there was a basic harmony within that coalition government. Furthermore, the MP in the opposition acted responsibly. This turn of
events was due to the good will and prudence of the leaders at the helms of those
parties—**Süleyman Demirel** at the TPP, **Erdal İnönü** at the SDPP, and **Mesut
Yılmaz** at the MP.

With the death of Özal in 1993, the presidency of Demirel, and İnönü's resignation from the government, coalition politics reverted to its usual overly conflict-ridden pattern. Both the left and the right were fragmented, and there was an
intense competition among the leaders to unify their side of the political spectrum under their own leadership. Because leaders dominate political parties in
Turkey, adversarial politics turn out to be no more than personal feuds between
the leaders. This state of affairs led to extreme political instability with a rapid
turnover of weak coalition governments. A related development was the increased success of the religiously oriented parties both at the local and general
elections and the willingness of some secularly oriented parties to enter into
coalitions with those parties in order to prevent other secularly oriented parties
from holding office. The latter development made the military extremely nerv-
ous and, through the **National Security Council** (NSC), that institution began
to play a more prominent role in state affairs. Through indirect pressure that it
exerted via the NSC, the military caused the resignation of the **Welfare Party**-
TPP coalition in June 1997. Viewed from this perspective, the April 18, 1999,

general elections opened a new chapter in political party life in Turkey. In these elections, the **Democratic Left Party** led by **Bülent Ecevit** and the **Nationalist Action Party** under **Devlet Bahçeli** came in first and second, respectively. These two parties and the Motherland Party formed a coalition government; Ecevit became prime minister and Bahçeli deputy prime minister. Yılmaz later joined the government as deputy prime minister. These leaders displayed a mature leadership, and Turkey began to enjoy not only political stability but also a responsible and effective government.

This state of affairs continued until late 2000 and early 2001 when Turkey faced two financial crises. In the wake of these crises, the trust in political parties and party leaders plummeted. The public began to have greater faith in President **Ahmet Necdet Sezer** who came from outside the Parliament, and in **Kemal Derviş**, minister of state responsible for the economy, who was recruited from the World Bank to save the country from the financial abyss it found itself in by February 2001.

PONTUS MOUNTAINS. A chain of folded highlands that generally parallels the **Black Sea** coast. Elevations rise in an easterly direction to heights greater than 3,000 meters south of Rize.

POPULIST PARTY (PP)/HALKÇI PARTİ (HP). Formed on May 19, 1983, by **Necdet Calp**. The left-of-center Populist Party was rumored to have the approval of the **military**. In the November 6, 1983, general elections, the PP came in second behind the **Motherland Party**. In the March 25, 1984, local elections, the parties that were not allowed to take part in the November 1983 general elections (the **True Path Party**, **Social Democracy Party**, and **Welfare Party**), were allowed to compete. In these local elections, the PP could not even obtain the percentage of votes required countrywide in a general election to win seats (10 percent). Party Chairman Calp was ousted from office and was replaced by Professor **Aydın Güven Gürkan**. Soon after his election, Gürkan aimed at merging his party with the **Social Democracy Party**. On November 2, 1985, the PP changed its name to **Social Democratic Populist Party** (SDPP). The next day, the Social Democracy Party decided to join the SDPP.

PRESS, THE. See MASS MEDIA.

PREVEZE, NAVAL BATTLE OF (1538). Won against a Holy League fleet, including the Genoese and Venetians, by the Ottoman navy under the command of **Hayreddin Pasha** (Barbaros). The Ottomans began to control the Ionian and Aegean Seas.

PRIVATIZATION. The privatization program was initiated in 1984 as an integral part of the liberal economic policies of the 1980s. It was decided that the role of government in the economy should be confined to areas the private sector could not and would not enter due to considerations of profitability, scale, or the nature of the activity, such as **defense, health, education**, and infrastructure. Within this framework, state economic enterprises (SEEs), their subsidiaries, and equity participations were to be privatized by opening them to domestic and foreign capital. Initially, the Public Participation Administration and then the Privatization Administration were vested with the authority to conduct the privatization program. Capital requirements of firms under the privatization program and other privatization expenditures have been financed with funds that come from a share of the fuel consumption tax, toll revenues generated by bridges and highways, revenues from the generation of electricity from certain dams, drinking water facilities, and **free trade zones**, revenue-sharing notes issued and foreign credit obtained by the privatization agencies, as well as from funds generated by privatization. Between 1985–1998, 30 plants of animal feed production, 38 plants of milk and dairy products, public shares in 30 cement plants, Sümerbank, Etibank, Denizbank, Anadolu Bank, 12.3 percent of the state shares in **İş-Bank**, and 50 percent of the state shares in companies operating in **tourism**, textile, meat processing, and forestry products sectors were privatized. In addition, public shares in Netaş and Tofaş were issued to foreign investors through offerings to international markets and public shares in several other companies were issued to the public. Furthermore, a start was made for the institutionalization of stocks. The distribution of capital was achieved when such stocks were quoted on the **Istanbul Stock Exchange**. In the 1985–1998 period, the total income from privatization reached $6 billion.

The privatization program for 1999–2000 involved new strategies. They included easing the negative effects of unemployment due to privatization through employment guarantees, enhancing public participation in the implementation of privatization, protecting the free market from anticompetitive mechanisms, preventing the negative effects of possible monopolization by privatizing natural resources only through the transfer of management rights, expanding the property ownership base while attracting shareholders who can assume professional management, and safeguarding public interest through "golden shares" in strategic enterprises. The government's plan was to withdraw completely from the wood products, iron and steel, fertilizer, textile, and maritime sectors by the end of 2000. The privatization plans for 1999–2000 included Turkish Cargo Lines, Tüpraş Petroleum Refinery, Turkish Airlines, Turkish Telekom, and the Global Systems for Mobile Communications (GSM) licenses.

PROGRESSIVE REPUBLICAN PARTY (PRR)/TERAKKİPERVER CUMHURİYET FIRKASI (TCF). Formed in 1924 by a conservative group that objected to some of the radical Kemalist reforms in the making. The party was soon considered to be closely linked to antisecular and even antirepublican elements. In 1925, when it was also thought to be associated with the Kurdish (*see* KURDS) separatist movement in southeastern Turkey, the party was closed by the government.

– R –

RAMADAN (Ramazan). Month of fasting. The fast—not eating, drinking, smoking, or having sexual intercourse during daylight hours—is widely observed in rural areas, but relatively less so in metropolitan areas. Şeker Bayramı [Sugar Feast] ends the month of Ramadan.

RECAİZADE MAHMUT EKREM (1847–1914). A well-known literary figure of the late 19th century. Ekrem belonged to the Servet-i Fünun [Treasure of the Sciences] movement (on this movement, *see* LITERATURE). His most important work is the only novel he wrote—*Obsession with a Carriage* [Araba Sevdası], in which he satirically treats the urbanites who imitate Western lifestyles without having internalized the parallel culture patterns.

REFORM DECREE, THE (1856). The sultan promised provincial reform and gave legal guarantees to non-Muslims. The decree was drawn up to stem the non-Muslims' aspiration for autonomy or independence and prevent the European powers from interfering in the internal affairs of the empire on the latter's behalf.

REFORMIST DEMOCRACY PARTY (RDP)/ISLAHATÇI DEMOKRASİ PARTİSİ (IDP). Formed on March 21, 1984, by Aykut Edibali. The party has an ethnic-right line. It has remained moribund.

RELIANCE PARTY (RP)/GÜVEN PARTİSİ (GP). Came into existence as a consequence of the conflict in the **Republican People's Party** (RPP) over the left-of-center policy adopted in the mid-1960s. When the RPP lost to the **Justice Party** in the 1965 general elections, centrists led by Professor **Turhan Feyzioğlu** tried to reverse the left-of-center stance of the RPP. When they could not succeed in this endeavor against the left-of-centrists led by **Bülent Ecevit**, Feyzioğlu founded the Reliance Party in 1967. In 1973, the Reliance Party merged with the **Republican Party** and took the name of **Republican Reliance Party**.

RELIGION. Turkey is a predominantly Muslim country. The non-Muslim citizens of Turkey constitute less than one percent of the population (*see* MINORITIES). Yet Turkey is a secular state with a religion that has been to a great extent privatized. Even in the formative centuries of the Ottoman state, the **sultans** could issue laws and regulations that would do away with Islamic precedents. In fact, the "Muslim institution" was a prop for and subservient to the state. Unlike their **Shi'a** (*see* ISLAM) counterparts, the Ottoman religious dignitaries did not equate temporal power with injustice. The religious orders did not pose a serious threat to the Ottoman state. In the early part of the 19th century, the Ottoman modernizers adopted the "cast-iron theory of Islam" (i.e., that Islam has fallen out of life and cannot be adapted to modern circumstances). The proponents of

Ottomanism posed in the 1860s the concepts of fatherland and patriotism against the concept of *umma*, or religious community. At the end of the century, **Abdülhamit II's** policy of **Pan-Islamism** was, unlike Pan-Arabism, an international rather than a supranational ideology. At the turn of the century, **Ziya Gökalp** emerged as an influential proponent of the separation of religion and state. The **Young Turks**, drawing upon Gökalp's ideas, introduced the notion that the nation is the source of all authority. **Atatürk** and his associates' target was the hold of religion on the polity and society. They took nationalism as a substitute for Islam and adopted civic-cultural rather than religious nationalism. An intensive socialization was started to increase the awareness of one's identity as a Turk and patriot. This socialization was carried out through the **mass media**, schools, **People's Houses**, flag saluting, national anthem singing, state parades, and non-religious holidays and national anniversaries. At the level of the individual, the aim was a *reformation* rather than a *renaissance* of Islam, namely gradual crystallization of a Turkish concept of Islam resembling the Protestant tradition that placed emphasis on the absolute privacy of individual conscience. In an attempt to suppress folk Islam, religious orders [*tarikat*] were banned. Measures were taken to improve the quality of religious personnel, all of whom were now members of the **civil bureaucracy**. The Koran and the *Hadith* (the Traditions of the Prophet) were translated into Turkish. All public displays of religious observance were discouraged. People had been touched by other secularizing experiences, too, even before being affected by a market economy. These included adoption of Western dress and headgear, taking a surname, submitting to a system of **education** couched in the scientific terms of the West, learning to write in an alphabet of Latin rather than Arabic origin, having the days of the week and calendar year changed, and allowing **women** to vote. The modernization of religion in a Protestant direction was not relaxed in the post-1945 multiparty period. The "concessions" granted during the multiparty period consisted of a reintroduction of the call to prayer in Arabic for a while and somewhat expanded religious instruction in grade and junior secondary schools. However, the courses on religion were offered by lay teachers and the textbooks were duly approved by the Ministry of Education. Effective legal procedures were initiated against the leaders of a number of religious orders that tended to play an active role after 1950 (*see* ISLAM). The state has supervised even the selection of prayer leaders at the village and neighborhood level. All in all, growing interest in religion in the multiparty period was not the product of profound soul searching or a spiritual crisis but chiefly of utilitarian and political considerations—the quest for a secure foundation of common morality, the need for a united front against the left and, above all, the competition for electoral votes. In Turkey, the role that religion has played in politics was limited. The political parties that emphasized religion in their programs but were unsuccessful in service delivery could obtain little support. In the 1990s, the religiously oriented **Welfare Party** could not obtain the votes of one-fifth of the electorate; two-thirds of that one-fifth cast their votes not because the party was religiously oriented but primarily because it was responsive to their nonreligious needs and demands. As democracy became the only game in town, politics emerged as a functional alternative to religion for people to air their frustration and satisfy their needs. The Republican reforms and policies concerning religion had a strong impact on society. A great majority of people in Turkey regard themselves as Turks rather than as Muslims, value secular education, do not see a relationship between power and being pious, and do not view urban areas "as a conglomerate of humanity profaned by infidels." In Turkey, practicing one's religion is weakly associated with believing that religion should not be separated from politics and thinking that there should be a return to Islamic law. Although formal religion in Turkish villages is booming, villagers know much more about alternative facts.

To the extent that one came across an Islamic resurgence in Turkey during recent decades, excepting a small group of Islamic intellectuals (*see* FUNDA-MENTALISM), it did not aim at the establishment of an Islamic republic; nor did it take Islam as a focus of identity. The Islamic resurgence in Turkey took different forms: a more pronounced observance of Islamic tenets among people (particularly among the new urbanites going through a cultural dislocation and among those Turks in the **diaspora** who find it difficult to integrate into the host country), people articulating their religious demands more clearly and forcefully and governments to a certain extent complying, and governments attempting to turn religion into a "civil religion," that is, (again) trying to make religion serve as a bond of social unity. Given the fact that as of the 1930s an entire generation was educated thinking religion to be some evil and irrational force of mere orthodoxy and blind tradition, the recent "resurgence of Islam" in Turkey was in fact a correction of the balance in society between the secular and the sacred. *See also* SECULARISM.

REPUBLICAN FREE PARTY (RFP)/CUMHURİYETÇİ SERBEST FIRKA (CSF). Founded in August 1930 by **Atatürk**'s close friend and former prime minister **Fethi Okyar**. Atatürk had wanted such a party to be formed in order to foster political debate in Parliament. The party stood for politico-economic liberalism as opposed to the statist policies of the ruling **Republican People's Party**. When the party was seen as an instrument for antirepublican religious tendencies, Atatürk told Okyar that he could no longer give his blessings to the party and, consequently, Okyar closed the party.

REPUBLICAN PARTY (RP)/CUMHURİYETÇİ PARTİ (CP). Came into being as a consequence of the clash between **Bülent Ecevit** and **İsmet İnönü** and the ideas they represented within the **Republican People's Party** (RPP) of the early 1970s. At the time, İnönü, the party's leader, parted company with his secretary-general, Bülent Ecevit, when the latter openly opposed the March 12, 1971, "coup-by-memorandum." At the May 1972 extraordinary convention of the RPP, İnönü's nominee for secretary-general, **Kemal Satır**, lost against Ecevit. İnönü resigned from the party and Satır left the party and formed the Republican Party with right-wing RPP members. In 1973, the Republican Party merged with the **Reliance Party** and took the name of **Republican Reliance Party**.

REPUBLICAN PEASANT'S NATION PARTY (RPNP)/CUMHURİYETÇİ KÖYLÜ MİLLET PARTİSİ (CKMP). One of the three parties (the other two being the **Justice Party** and **New Turkey Party**) that competed for a place on the right of the political spectrum after the closure of the *Demokrat* Party by the **military** following the May 27, 1960, military intervention. The Republican Peasant's Nation Party was formed in 1958 by the merger of the Peasant's Party (established in 1952) and the Republican Nation Party (founded in 1954 as a successor to the Nation Party, which in turn was founded in 1948 and dissolved in 1953). The RPNP and its predecessors adopted a conservative political stance and were quite responsive to religious interests. In time, the RPNP was taken over by **Alparslan Türkeş**, a leading member of the junta that carried out the May 27, 1960, **military** intervention (from which he was later excluded for his authoritarian tendencies). The party then began to form paramilitary youth bands "determined to fight communism." The youth bands in question soon started to clash with their leftist counterparts. In 1969, the party's name was changed to **Nationalist Action Party**.

REPUBLICAN PEOPLE'S PARTY (RPP)/CUMHURİYET HALK PARTİSİ (CHP). Formed on September 9, 1923, by Mustafa Kemal (**Atatürk**), as the political expression of the **Turkish War of Independence** and national unity and integrity. The RPP ruled Turkey under a single-party regime until the end of **World War II**. Each of the "six arrows," the symbol of the RPP and referred to as **Kemalism**, represented the ideals the party was to realize—republicanism, nationalism, populism, **secularism**, statism, and reformism-revolutionism. The RPP set out to obliterate Turkey's Ottoman heritage and create a **Westernized** state and society. In order to carry out this ambitious task, it opted for a tutelary authoritarian regime. Then it introduced a number of reforms, extending from law to **education** and even forms of dress. As a result of these efforts, between the two **world wars**, Turkey's urban (if not the rural) scene changed considerably in a Westernizing direction. The RPP also perceived itself as the guardian of the Kemalist state and republic. The RPP spent the decade of the 1950s in opposition, after having lost in the May 14, 1950 general elections to the *Demokrat* Party (DP). During that decade, the party stood against the slide toward laissez-faire capitalism and the violation of the principle of secularism. Later in the decade, when the ruling DP resorted to authoritarian measures, **İsmet İnönü** (leader of the party from 1938 to 1972) and his RPP became the champions of basic rights and liberties. Following the May 27, 1960, **military** intervention, the DP was toppled from power, a new **constitution** (1961) was enacted and, on October 6, 1961, general elections were held. From 1961 on, İnönü and the RPP again came to power, although in coalitions. In the first three of the four coalition governments that were formed in the 1961–1965 period, İnönü acted as prime minister; in this capacity, he placed emphasis on the consolidation of democracy by performing a juggling act between intellectual-bureaucratic-military elites on the one hand, and their political opponents on the other. Toward the mid-1960s, the RPP adopted a left-of-center political stance—a rather watered-down version of social democracy—in the hope of stealing the appeal of the more radical political milieu provided by the 1961 Constitution. The guiding spirit behind this new policy was **Bülent Ecevit,** who at the time was minister of labor. The 1965 general elections, however, were a big disappointment for the RPP, as the **Justice Party** (JP) obtained a majority in Parliament. Some in the party attributed this defeat to the left-of-center policy; others, led by Ecevit, claimed that what was needed was a more radical transformation of the party in the leftist direction. In the power game that ensued, the left-of-centrists came out on top and Ecevit became secretary-general of the party. The RPP under Ecevit placed emphasis on the land and agrarian reform issues and established close relations with both the moderate and radical **trade union** confederations. Ecevit's slogan was "land to the one who sows it, water to the one who uses it." İnönü, however, acted as a check against the party's further slide to the left. In the 1969 general elections, the RPP vote went up, though the Justice Party again won a clear majority. Following the March 12, 1971, coup-by-memorandum, the generals wished a civilian and above-party (national) coalition to be formed. Ecevit, the only leading politician who openly stood against the coup, claimed that the coup was a movement against the left-of-center approach of the RPP and resigned his post of secretary-general. İnönü cooperated with the generals; he thought that such an approach would facilitate a speedy return to democracy. These developments led to a rivalry between Ecevit and İnönü. At the extraordinary convention of the party in May 1972, İnönü declared war against Ecevit by saying, "Either me or him!" When the convention chose Ecevit as the party's secretary-general against İnönü's candidate for the same post (**Kemal Satır**), İnönü resigned from the party. Ecevit became the third chairman of the RPP, and remained in that post until he resigned following the September 12, 1980, military intervention. In the 1973 elections, the RPP under Ecevit garnered a plurality of the votes and formed a coalition government, under Ecevit's premiership, with the **National Salvation Party** (NSP), led by **Necmettin Erbakan**. This coalition government between the traditionally secular and now also leftist-oriented RPP and the religiously oriented NSP turned out to be a friction-ridden government. The RPP was not comfortable with the NSP's efforts to shape public policy in accordance with religious considerations; the NSP was uneasy concerning the RPP's leniency toward the militant left. Following Turkey's invasion of northern **Cyprus** in July 1974, Ecevit pressed for an early election to which the NSP and other **political parties** objected, and Ecevit's government resigned. During the First Nationalist Front government of the Justice Party, National Salvation Party, **Nationalist Action Party**, and **Republican Reliance Party**, from March 1975 to June 1977, the RPP remained in opposition. In the 1977 general elections, the RPP again obtained a plurality of votes. Ecevit formed a minority government that, however, was denied a vote of confidence by Parliament. This was followed by the coming to power of the Second Nationalist Front government—a coalition government of the Justice Party, National Salvation Party, and Nationalist Action Party. The Second Nationalist Front government faced serious economic problems and had to grapple with increased street violence between the left and the right. On January 17, 1978, Ecevit was again able to form a government that included the single parliamentarian of the *Demokratik* Party (Faruk Sükan), **Turhan Feyzioğlu** and his second deputy of the Republican Reliance Party, some independents, and 11 Justice Party dissidents who had resigned from their party. This government stayed in power for 22 months. The government registered no tangible success concerning anarchy and economic woes, and the party became divided into four leading factions—the Ecevit group, the **Deniz Baykal** group, the Orhan Eyüboğlu-Ali Topuz group, and radical leftists. At the October 1979 by-elections, the Justice Party swept the votes. The Ecevit government resigned and the JP formed a minority government and the RPP took its place in the opposition. The September 12, 1980, military intervention first banned all political party activities and then closed the political parties, including the RPP. The legislation enacted by the military government of the 1980–1983 period did not allow the revival of the pre-1980 parties following the restoration of political party activity in 1982. Not until autumn 1992 was this legislation amended. The RPP was reopened in September of that year with Deniz Baykal elected chairman of the party. Those who initiated the reestablishment of the RPP had hoped that the former Republicans operating since 1985 primarily within the ranks of the **Democratic Left Party** of Bülent Ecevit and the **Social Democratic Populist Party** (SDPP) of **Erdal İnönü** would come under one roof in their old party. By the end of 1992, some parliamentarians of the latter two parties became RPP members, and the RPP took its place in Parliament alongside the DLP and the SDPP. Deniz Baykal was elected chairman. The SDPP merged with the (new) RPP. The RPP replaced the SDPP as the coalition partner of the True Path Party. The party dropped the discourse of "social democracy"; it emphasized democracy and secularism. In the December 24, 1995, general elections, the party barely cleared the nationwide election threshold with a vote of 10.7 percent and came in fifth. In the post-1995 election period, the party has not joined any government. Baykal, who was accused of promoting factionalism within the party, dominated the party. The party supported the Democratic Left Party-**Motherland Party** (MP)-**Democratic Turkey Party** coalition from outside. More often than not, that "support" turned out to be blackmail. Baykal joined the opposition in accusing the MP leader **Mesut Yılmaz** of corruption. In the April 18, 1999, general elections, with only 8.7 percent of the votes, the party could not clear the nationwide threshold and remained outside of Parliament for the first time in its history. Baykal resigned and **Altan Öymen** became chairman. In September 2000, Baykal again became the chairman of the party.

REPUBLICAN RELIANCE PARTY (RRP)/CUMHURİYETÇİ GÜVEN PARTİSİ (CGP). The party was formed in 1973 with the merger of the **Reliance Party** and the **Republican Party**, both splinter parties from the **Republican People's Party**. The Republican Reliance Party, led by **Turhan Feyzioğlu**, participated in the first of the two Nationalist Front governments, formed in March

31, 1975. The party, however, was virtually lost in the 1977 general elections. Still, Feyzioğlu and his second deputy became members of the **Bülent Ecevit** government, formed after the elections and which lasted until the October 14, 1979, by-elections. Along with other political parties, the RRP was closed following the September 12, 1980, **military** intervention.

RESMİ GAZETE. Official Gazette, abbreviated "RG." First established as *Ceride-i Resmiye* (1920–1927), then for a while published as *Resmi Ceride* (1927–1930), and published since 1930 as *Resmi Gazete.*

RESURRECTION PARTY (RP)/YENİDEN DOĞUŞ PARTİSİ (YDP). Founded on November 23, 1992, by Hasan Celal Güzel, a former minister of education and member of the **Motherland Party**. The party has made no headway since its foundation.

REŞİT GALİP (1893–1934). Professor of medicine and politician. He joined the nationalist movement and was elected to the Parliament in 1923. As minister of education in 1932–1933, he recruited German refugee academics to the reformed **Istanbul University.**

REY, CEMAL REŞİT (1904–1985). One of the leading composers of the Republican era. His works include *Instantanés, Concerto Chromatique, String Quartet, L'Appel,* and *Pièces Concertantes.*

"RIGHT OF PROOF" [İspat Hakkı]. The issue of giving journalists the right to prove their assertions in court about which the dissidents in the *Demokrat* **Party** closed their ranks in 1955. The proposal to amend the Press Act was rejected by the Justice Commission of the party and nine of the dissidents were expelled from the party.

RIZA NUR (1878–1942). Doctor of medicine. He opposed the **Committee for Union and Progress** (after having served briefly in the Committee). He joined the nationalists and served as minister of health and of education. Rıza Nur then became a fierce critic of **Atatürk** and moved to Paris.

ROBERT COLLEGE. Founded in 1863 and originally an American educational institution in **Istanbul**. A large number of Turkey's elite, particularly in the private sector, arts, and professions, graduated from Robert College. The college became a Turkish institution in 1971 and took the name of **Boğaziçi University**. *See* EDUCATION.

RUSSIA (TSARIST RUSSIA, SOVIET UNION, RUSSIAN FEDERATION). Turkey's neighbor to the north. The sea route connecting the **Black Sea** with the **Aegean** and **Mediterranean** via the narrow **straits** of the Bosporus, the

Marmara Sea, and the Dardanelles has made the Ottoman Empire and Republican Turkey strategically very important to its northern neighbor. The control of **Istanbul** and the straits continued to be a major policy goal of tsarist Russia. The Russians came close to achieving this goal in 1833 when they obliged the Ottomans to sign the Treaty of Hunkiar Iskelesi (in return for their coming to the aid of the Ottomans against the army of Muhammad Ali of Egypt), which brought about virtual Russian control of the straits. The provisions of this treaty were reversed by the 1841 London Convention because of the British effort, as the British perceived the 1833 treaty as a grave threat to their free passage to India. The 1841 convention forbade the entry of foreign warships to the straits. During the **Turkish War of Independence** (1920–1922), the Soviet Union provided financial aid to the Nationalist forces in the hope of turning the emerging regime in **Ankara** into a Bolshevik one. In 1921, the two countries signed a Friendship Treaty, which safeguarded Turkey's eastern flank. **Atatürk** and his associates accepted the Soviet support without showing their true colors. Even a Turco-Soviet Neutrality and Non-aggression Treaty was signed in 1925, which was followed by a trade agreement in 1927. In 1939, however, the Soviets again revived the issue of the straits. They asked Turkey not to allow passage of non–Black Sea warships through the straits. Turkey did not accept this demand. During **World War II**, Stalin put pressure on Turkey to enter the war on the side of the Allies; Turkey, however, again did not oblige. In the aftermath of World War II, the Soviets came up with even more critical demands and in a more forceful manner: the Soviets denounced the 1921 Turco-Soviet Friendship Treaty; they asked Turkey to share the responsibility for **military** defense of the straits; and they also made territorial demands in the Caucasus border region. With the backing of the **United States** and **Great Britain**, Turkey rejected these claims. The Soviet pressure on Turkey pushed Turkey further toward the West, one consequence of which was that Turkey joined the **North Atlantic Treaty Organization** in 1952, to complete the southern flank of the defense system against the Soviet Union. This was followed by Turkey's taking its place in the 1955 **Baghdad Pact** along with **Iraq, Iran**, Pakistan, and Great Britain, with the United States as a de facto member. The pact was conceived as a shield against possible Soviet incursions in the Middle East. The conclusion of the pact further escalated the confrontation between the Soviet Union and Turkey.

The July 1958 coup that swept away the pro-Western Iraqi government and weakened the Baghdad Pact was seen by the Turkish government as the handiwork of international communism and the Soviet Union. The government readily acquiesced to the sending of American marines to Lebanon (to help the Lebanese government in the civil war in that country) via the İncirlik air base near **Adana** in southern Turkey. This was followed by a series of bilateral agreements between **Ankara** and Washington against the Soviet threat. Soon, American intermediate ballistic missiles targeted on the Soviet Union were stationed in Turkey. Later, they were replaced by U.S. aircraft armed with nuclear weapons. The Soviets started to make moves to seek reconciliation with Turkey only after Stalin's death in 1953 but these moves were slow in coming. By the late 1950s, Turkey was firmly in the Western alliance system. In the mid-1960s, however, the strained relations between Turkey and the Soviet Union began to mend. As Turkey felt itself rather isolated concerning the conflict over **Cyprus**, it began to make overtures to several countries, including the Soviet Union. Moscow readily responded. Reciprocal high-level visits took place. In the following decade, Turco-Soviet relations became even closer. The West's unwillingness to support Turkey on the Cyprus issue, the U.S. arms embargo on Turkey following the Turkish intervention in Cyprus in 1974, and the lack of European enthusiasm to grant Turkey full membership in the **European Community** induced Turkey to become more self-reliant and diversify its economic and foreign relations. One consequence was a significant rapprochement with the Soviet Union (as well as the Warsaw Pact countries). In February 1991, Turkey and the Russian Federation signed the Agreement on Economic and Commercial Cooperation and the **Agricultural** Reform and Rural Development Protocol. **Trade** and commerce increased between the two countries. Economic relations flourished further after the Soviet Union was succeeded by the Russian Federation. By 1997, the Russian Federation had become Turkey's largest export market after **Germany**. Turkish firms came to have a 50 percent share in all the construction in the federation realized by foreigners. Turkey began to satisfy the bulk of its natural gas needs from the federation and an agreement was made to increase Turkey's natural gas imports from that country in 2000. In 1996, the federation and Turkey signed the Blue Stream Project—the construction of a natural gas pipeline from Russia to Turkey underneath the Black Sea starting in 2001. On the other hand, Turkey opposed the transportation of petroleum by Russian tankers through the Turkish straits because of the danger a possible accident posed to lives, property, and environment, and both countries wanted the pipelines carrying natural gas and petroleum from the **Turkic republics** in Central Asia to the West to be laid in their own territories. Furthermore, both Ankara and Moscow tried to induce the Turkic republics to sell them natural gas. On the last issue, with the coming to power of Vladimir Putin in Russia, that country began to have the upper hand; in early 2000, the Russian Federation made a natural gas agreement with Turkmenistan. In the late 1990s, the two countries did not see eye-to-eye concerning some political issues. The Russian willingness to sell S-300 missiles to the Greek Cypriot government strained the relations between Ankara and Moscow. Even more seriously, Russian endeavors to set up military bases in the Caucasus and to again turn the Turkic republics into its sphere of influence have caused great discomfort in Turkey. Despite these problems, economic relations continued to flourish between the two countries. Russian and Turkish firms set up partnerships, particularly in construction and manufacturing. In 1992, Turkey's trade volume with the Russian Federation was $1.5 billion; it became $2.4 billion in 1996, $4.2 billion in 1998, and $4.7 billion in 1999.

– S –

SABA, OSMAN ZİYA (1910–1957). Short story writer and poet. An introverted writer, Saba's poetry reflected a preoccupation with submission to fate, the longing for death, and death. *Passing Time* [Geçen Zaman] and *To Breathe* [Nefes Almak] are two popular collections of his poems.

SABAHADDİN (PRENS) (1878–1948). Ottoman intellectual and politician. Sabahaddin thought that the Ottomans could break the shackles of underdevelopment by placing emphasis on private property and entrepreneurship and by having a social structure based on individualism. In his opinion, there was a need in the Ottoman polity for the development of intermediary social and political structures that would stand against the centralized authority.

SABANCI, HACI ÖMER (1906–1966). Businessman. Sabancı was the founder of one of Turkey's largest holding companies known by his name. The company is presently run by his son, **Sakıp Sabancı**.

SABANCI, SAKIP (1933–). Manager-owner of the Sabancı Holding, one of the largest holding companies in Turkey. Sabancı, who has folksy manners and a colorful personality, is the most outspoken representative of big business in Turkey (*see* TÜSİAD). Sabancı has received several honorary Ph.D. degrees in Turkey and abroad as well as the Belgian king's decoration, the Japanese government's decoration of Sacred Treasury Gold and Silver Star, the European Economics Institute's European Crystal World Award, and Turkish president's Superior Service Award. Sabancı has written a number of books, including *This Is My Life, Turkey: Changing and Developing, Money Is the Award of Success* [Para Başarının Mükafatıdır], *From My Heart's Gallery* [Gönül Galerimden], *My Travels and Observations: From Russia to the United States* [Rusya'dan Amerika'ya Gezdiklerim Gördüklerim], and *More Work More Food* [Daha Fazla İş Daha Fazla Aş].

SABANCI UNIVERSITY. Founded in 1999, Sabanci is already one of Turkey's leading private universities, where the medium of instruction is English. It is situated in **Istanbul**. *See also* EDUCATION.

SADR-I AZAM (SADRAZAM, VEZİR-İ AZAM). Grand vizier and the first minister who became the chief executive officer of state beginning about 1360.

SAĞLAM, TEVFİK (1882–1963). Professor of medicine. Sağlam made a significant contribution to the first campaign against tuberculosis in Turkey.

SAİD-İ NURSİ (1873–1960). Religious thinker. He is also known as "Said-i Kürdi" and "Bediüzzaman" and is the founder of the movement of "the proponents of light" (Nurcular). Said-i Nursi played a role in the establishment of the Association for the

Union of Muslims [İttihad-ı Muhammedi Cemiyeti] and wrote in several dailies and periodicals following the proclamation of the Second Constitutional Period in 1908. He brought a new interpretation to **Islam**. More specifically, Said-i Nursi developed a paradigm that, in his opinion, would enable individual Muslims to draw meaning from the Koran, Islam's holy book. He attempted to enrich Islam to make it fit the requirements of a modern society. Nurculuk, as the movement was called, had a strong and lingering impact during the Republican period. At the turn of the century, its most prominent representative in Turkey has been **Fethullah Gülen**.

SAİT HALİM PASHA (1863–1921). Ottoman grand vizier. Sait Halim Pasha served as senator, head of the Council of State, secretary-general of the **Committee for Union and Progress,** and foreign minister before he was made grand vizier on June 12, 1913. He remained grand vizier until February 3, 1917. One of the significant figures of **Islamism** that, along with **Turkism** and **Westernism**, flourished in the Ottoman polity at the turn of the century, he was critical of the efforts to emulate the West blindly. In his opinion, the salvation of the empire was dependent upon a contemporary reinterpretation of the Islamic premises on which the Ottoman polity and society had rested in the past.

SAİT PASHA (KÜÇÜK) (1838–1914). Ottoman grand vizier. Sait Pasha came to that post nine times during the reign of **Abdülhamit II** and following the Second Constitutional Period that started in 1908. He played an important part during the 1880s in streamlining the bureaucracy and opening several new Western-type secondary schools and high schools.

SAKA, HASAN (1886–1960). Politician. Saka graduated from the *Ecole Libre des Sciences Politiques* in Paris. He was a member of the last Ottoman Parliament. Between 1921 and 1947, at different times, he served as minister of finance, economy, trade, and foreign affairs. He was a professor of economics at the School of Political Science of **Ankara University** between 1936 and 1941. From September 10, 1947, to June 10, 1948, Saka served as prime minister. He contributed to the democratization process, which had started with the installation of the multiparty politics in 1945. In the two cabinets he formed, he included proponents of a liberal economy. He quit active politics when he lost in the 1954 general elections.

SAMİPAŞAZADE SEZAİ (1860–1936). Novelist and playwright. Sezai joined the **Young Turks** in 1901. He served as ambassador to Spain from 1909 to 1914. His novels, the best known being *Adventure* [Sergüzeşt], reflected a shift in the Ottoman-Turkish **literature** from romanticism to realism.

SARACOĞLU, ŞÜKRÜ (1887–1953). Politician. Saracoğlu graduated from the Political Science Faculty of the University of Geneva (1918). He entered the Turkish Grand National Assembly in 1923. He headed the Turkish delegations in the Turco-**Greece** population exchange negotiations in 1926 and during the 1932 discussions in Paris concerning the payment of Ottoman debts. Saracoğlu served as minister of **education** (November 24, 1924–March 3, 1925), finance (November 2, 1927–December 22, 1930), justice (May 4, 1933–November 11, 1938), and foreign affairs (November 11, 1938–January 25, 1939 and January 25–April 3, 1939). He became prime minister twice, from July 9, 1942, to March 8, 1943, and from March 15, 1943, to August 5, 1946. Saracoğlu left active politics after serving as speaker of the Grand National Assembly from November 1, 1948 until May 22, 1950.

SARICA, AYŞEGÜL (1935–). Pianist. Sarıca graduated from the Paris Conservatory in 1951. She attained fame in particular through her interpretations of the German Romantic Period composers. She was given several awards abroad, including the Chevalier de l'Ordre des arts et lettres conferred on her by the French government (1974). The Turkish government named her a State Artist in 1971.

SARISÖZEN, MUZAFFER (1899–1963). Promoter of folk **music**. Sarısözen published the first textbook on folk music in the Republican period, *Selected Village Folk Songs* [Seçme Köy Türküleri]. He started the program "Voices from the Country" [Yurttan Sesler] at Radio **Ankara** and published a book by the same name, in addition to *Rhythms in Turkish Folk Music* [Türk Halk Musikisi Usulleri].

SATIR, KEMAL (1911–1991). Doctor of medicine and politician. Satır became secretary-general of the **Republican People's Party** (RPP) on December 1962. He served as deputy prime minister between December 25, 1963, and February 20, 1965, and deputy prime minister and minister of state between April 7, 1973, and January 25, 1974. During the second part of the 1960s, he was one of the prominent members of the group within the RPP that opposed the left-of-center policy promoted by the party's secretary-general **Bülent Ecevit**. In May 1972, at the RPP's Fifth Extraordinary Congress, Satır ran against Ecevit for the post of secretary-general and lost. He then left the RPP, formed the **Republican Party** (RP), and became its chairman. The RP merged with the **Reliance Party** to become the **Republican Reliance Party** the next year and Satır quietly phased himself out of active politics.

SAY, FAZIL (1970–). Composer and pianist. He attended the master class of David Levine at the Robert Schumann Institute of Music in Düsseldorf, **Germany**. Say's *Black Hymns* written at the age of 16 was performed during Berlin's 750th Jubilee Year celebration. In his works, the rhythmical elements supersede the melody and the original structure of Turkish rhythms combines with the percussive character of contemporary music. *Five Debussy Preludes* and a Liszt sonata are two of his orchestral compositions. Among his concertos are *Reflections, Concertante Symphonia, Silk Road, Two Romantic Ballades,* and *Concerto for Guitar and Chamber Orchestra.* Examples of his chamber music are *Preludes, Black Hymns, Sonata,* and *Three Legends.* His pieces for piano include *Sonata, Phrigian, Preludes, Suit, Mystical Voice, Paganini Variations, Reflections,* and *Fantasy Pieces.* Say won the first prize in the European Young Concert Artists audition and the Young Concert Artists International Award in New York. Sholomo Mintz, Yuri Bashmet, Maxim Vengerov, Lawrence Foster, Leon Fleisher, and Kurt Masur are some of the artists he performs with.

SAYDAM, REFİK (1881–1942). Military doctor of medicine and politician. Saydam developed a vaccine against typhus that is mentioned in the medical literature. He entered the Turkish Grand Assembly in 1920. At various times, he served as minister of **health** (May 19, 1921–July 9, 1922, October 30, 1923–November 22, 1924, and March 4, 1925–October 25, 1937) and interior (November 1, 1938–January 25, 1939). As minister of health, he organized health services against contagious diseases. He was appointed prime minister on January 25, 1939, and died three months later, while still in that post.

SAYGUN, AHMET ADNAN (1907–1991). Pioneer of Turkish national **opera**. Among his creations are the oratorio "Yunus Emre," "First String Quartet," "Second String Quartet," and "Piano Concerto."

SEBER, SÜREYYA CEMAL (1931–). Poet of the post–**World War II** Second New Movement (on this movement, *see* LITERATURE). Seber presents humanity in the abstract. He values self-expression and individualism. *Nomad* [Göçebe] and *Kiss and Then Cut Me Up* [Beni Öp Sonra Doğra] are examples of his collections of poems.

SECOND GROUP. Faction in the Turkish Grand National Assembly (1922) that opposed **Atatürk** and his associates' First Group. It included Unionists (those who wished to see the perpetuation of the policies of the **Committee for Union and Progress**), Westernists, supporters of the **caliphate**, and others who opposed Atatürk for personal reasons.

SECULARISM. This is one of the most important principles on which the Turkish Republic is based. In the view of **Atatürk** and his associates, the basic reason for the Ottoman Empire's decline was that **Islam** was a retrogressive religion. Consequently, the founders of the Republic aimed at substituting reason for religious tenets. Influenced by the Enlightenment tradition, Atatürk and his associates tried to create a new kind of Turk who would think and act "logically" (i.e., Turk's decisional premises would not be religious norms). New generations of Turks indeed became steeped in a secular outlook on life. For instance, during the 1950s, the intellectual-bureaucratic elites indicated their dissatisfaction in rather strong terms with "the concessions made by the *Demokrat* **Party** to religious demands." The average Turk, too, began to think in secular rather than religious categories, although many Turks continued to practice their **religion**; for many, Islam continued to be salient as an ethical system and as a bond of social solidarity. The 1960 and 1971 **military** interventions were made primarily to maintain the position of secularism in the Turkish polity. Secularism was also cherished by the

1980 military intervenors, but this time the military elite, perhaps because secularism by now had become a widely shared value, had a more balanced approach vis-à-vis this significant principle of the Republic. The 1980 intervenors recognized the significance of religion as an ethical system and as a bond of social solidarity. They thought that religion could act as an effective antidote against polarization in social and political life. They also attempted to use religious arguments in their attempts to further modernize Turkey. In his public speeches, President **Kenan Evren** freely quoted verses from the Koran. Governments have had a sympathetic attitude to religious demands while conforming to the requirement of separating politics from religion (i.e., not basing political decisions on religious premises and not using religion for political ends). *See also* FUNDAMENTALISM.

SELİM I (THE TOUGH) (1466–1520). The Ottoman **sultan** who was on the throne from 1512 until 1520. Selim I extended Ottoman suzerainty to eastern Anatolia, **Syria**, and Egypt and brought the Mamluk state to an end. Thus he prevented **Shi'ism** (*see* ISLAM) from becoming widespread in the Ottoman realms. Selim I wrote poems on such themes as love and passion; his poetry was influenced by the Persian literary tradition.

SELİM III (1761–1807). Ottoman **sultan**. Selim III came to the Ottoman throne on April 7, 1789. In 1793, he started to implement his New Order [**Nizam-ı Cedit**] program. Priority was placed on the development of the nucleus of a new army known by the name of the program. Experts in different fields were brought from Europe, but Selim III faced stiff resistance to his reform efforts from different quarters, including the **Janissary Corps**, traditionally the backbone of the Ottoman army. Eventually, a riot broke out and the rebels obtained a religious decree from the **Şeyhülislam**, the highest religious dignitary in the Ottoman Empire. This decree gave religious backing to the removal of the sultan from the throne. Selim III abdicated on May 29, 1807. On July of the same year, he was killed on the orders of the new sultan. Selim III was an enlightened sultan bent on reforming the traditional Ottoman institutions, but he could not carry out his projects. He initiated the balance of power policy in foreign affairs. Aside from this, Selim III was interested in **literature**, **music**, and history. He played the flute and *tanbura*; about 70 pieces he composed reached our day. He was also a mystic.

SERTEL, SABİHA (1895–1968). Journalist. Sabiha Sertel studied sociology at Columbia University. With her husband, **Zekeriya Sertel**, she published several magazines and dailies. She gradually came under pressure from the government due to her leftist tendencies. In 1945, the Sertels' Tan publishing house was set on fire and destroyed. She and her husband left the country in 1950 and only returned to Turkey for a brief period. She spent her last years in Baku, **Azerbaijan**.

SERTEL, ZEKERİYA (1890–1980). Journalist. Zekeriya Sertel graduated from Sorbonne University (Paris) and Columbia University. He began publishing various magazines and dailies in 1912. He was prosecuted several times in the 1920s and 1940s for his leftist tendencies. His and his wife **Sabiha Sertel**'s Tan publishing house was set on fire and destroyed in 1945. In 1950, he and his wife left the country. He later returned to Turkey, wrote for a while in several dailies, and then left the country again. He spent his last years in Paris.

SEZER, AHMET NECDET (1941–). Turkey's current president. He graduated from **Ankara University**'s Law School in 1962. After having served as judge in the townships of Dicle and Yerköy, Sezer was appointed to the Controls Board of the High Court of Appeals. In 1978, he obtained a master's degree in civil law. Sezer was elected member of the High Court of Appeals in 1983. In 1988, he became chairman of the Constitutional Court. The Turkish Grand National Assembly elected Sezer as Turkey's tenth president, and he took over that post from **Süleyman Demirel** on May 15, 2000.

SÉVRES, TREATY OF (August 10, 1920). Signed between the Allies and the Ottoman government at the end of **World War I**. Under this treaty, the Ottomans lost the Arab provinces, virtually all of Eastern Thrace, the Aegean Islands, and the Dodecanese. The territory called Kurdistan east of the Euphrates gained autonomy; if the **Kurds** wished, Kurdistan could within a year proclaim independence. **Armenia** was recognized as an independent state. International control was set up on the **straits**; the adjacent territory was to be demilitarized. The **capitulations** were restored. The Ottoman army could be no more than 50,000-strong. The Turkish nationalists led by **Atatürk** rejected the treaty and resorted to armed struggle (**Turkish War of Independence**), which ended in victory for them. Turkey obtained its independence and sovereignty, and came to have its present borders, minus the **Alexandretta** (Hatay) region, by the **Treaty of Lausanne** of July 24, 1923.

SHEIKH SAID (1865–1925). Kurdish-Turkish man of religion. Sheikh Said started a major Kurdish (*see* KURDS) rebellion against the state in February 1925, which spread rapidly. His forces took a number of cities in southeastern Turkey. The rebellion could only be suppressed in April of the same year. Sheikh Said was tried at the Eastern Independence Court and sentenced to death, a judgment that was carried out.

SHI'A. From *Shiat Ali*, the Party of Ali. A member of the smaller of the two great sects of **Islam**. The Shi'a (Shiite) believe in the claims of Ali and his line to presumptive right to the **caliphate** and leadership of the Muslim community, and on this issue they differ from the **Sunni**. The Alevi community of Turkey is usually considered a Shi'a sect, but Shi'a theologians of **Iran** and **Iraq**, each of which has a large Shi'a population, reject the **Alevis** as heretical.

SIDE. A historic town in southern Turkey near **Antalya**. It was established in the seventh century B.C.E. as a colony of the Aeolion city of Cyme. It is famous for the ruins of the Roman agora of the second century B.C.E., a Roman theater of the same century, and the Roman baths.

SIVAS. The ancient Sebasteia of **Cappadocia** in east-central Anatolia. First established in 65 B.C.E., Sivas was one of the principal cities of the Sultanate of Rum, occasionally serving as its capital. Among its historical monuments are the theological schools [*medreses*] of Muzaffer Bürücirde, Çifte Minare, and Gökali (founded in 1271), Darüşşifa of Keykâvus I (opened in 1218, the largest and most elaborate medical institution ever constructed by the Selcukiads), and Ulucami [Great Mosque], built in 1197. In 1997, the population of the city was 735,619.

SIVAS CONGRESS (September 4–11, 1919). This congress came in the wake of the **Erzurum Congress** of July 23–August 7, 1919. At the Sivas Congress, resolutions made at the Erzurum Congress were reaffirmed. The Sivas Congress was attended by delegates from all parts of Turkey. The name of the Society for the Defense of the Rights of Eastern Anatolia was changed to Society to Defend the Rights and Interests of the Provinces of Anatolia and Rumelia.

SIYAVUŞGIL, SABRI ESAT (1907–1968). Professor of psychology, poet, author, and translator. Siyavuşgil studied philosophy in **France**. He was a member of the "Seven Torches" [Yedi Meşaleciler] group in poetry and is well known for his translation of *Cyrano de Bergerac* (by Edmond Rostand) into Turkish.

SOCIAL DEMOCRACY PARTY (SDP)/SOSYAL DEMOKRASI PARTISI (SODEP). Formed on May 29, 1983, by **Erdal İnönü**, the son of former President **İsmet İnönü**. The Social Democracy Party could not take part in the November 6, 1983, general elections because the **military** repeatedly vetoed the party's founding members, disqualifying them through the use of a special clause that was operative during the military rule of 1980–1983. The SDP was allowed to compete in the March 25, 1984, local elections. In these elections, the SDP came in second behind the ruling **Motherland Party**. On November 2, 1985, the **Populist Party** changed its name to **Social Democratic Populist Party** (SDPP). The next day, the SDP joined the SDPP.

SOCIAL DEMOCRATIC POPULIST PARTY (SDPP)/SOSYAL DEMOKRAT HALKÇI PARTI (SHP). Formed on November 3, 1985, through the merger of the **Social Democracy Party** (SDP) and the **Populist Party** (PP). The Social Democratic Populist Party was led from November 1985 until May 1986 by **Aydın Güven Gürkan** and from the latter date to September 1993 by **Erdal İnönü**. From the very beginning, the SDPP suffered from uncompromising factional politics within its ranks. The members from the PP were more statist than those from the SDPP. Also, the party's deputies elected in the

1987 general elections had all been nominated in primaries and consequently had significantly different approaches to Turkey's problems and how to go about implementing social democratic principles. One of the factions was a pro-**Kurdish** group. The inner strife brought party Chairman İnönü, on February 28, 1988, to the brink of resigning from his post as chairman as well as from Parliament. It took party stalwarts two days to change İnönü's mind. In the summer of 1988, **Deniz Baykal** became secretary-general of the SDPP. The new party administration under Baykal made an effort to purge the party organization of its far left elements and give the party a unified and truly social democratic image. Some provincial chairmen and administrators were sacked, which caused an uproar within the party. Following the party's success in the March 1989 local elections (the SDPP captured a majority of the provincial municipalities including the metropolitan mayoralties of **Istanbul, Ankara**, and **İzmir**), Baykal and his associates continued the cleansing in an even more determined manner. As a consequence, many left-wing deputies, including Gürkan, left the party in protest. The Baykal group was next opposed by "the renovative social democrats." This latter group criticized Baykal for following too closely the **Republican People's Party** line "when in fact the party needed change." During the last years of the 1980s, the SDPP placed particular emphasis on the issue of "democratization." It frequently applied to the Constitutional Court to get "anti-democratic" law-decrees passed by the government annulled. In most cases, it succeeded. This campaign, however, did not bring votes to the party. The August 19, 1990, local by-election was a major setback. This defeat brought into the open the long concealed conflict between Chairman İnönü and Secretary-General Baykal. In Baykal's opinion, İnönü was not successful as the leader of the party; Baykal was looking for an opportunity to replace him. İnönü called for an extraordinary convention in which Baykal and his supporters lost, and Hikmet Çetin became secretary-general. Baykal did not give up. He ran against İnönü in the party's Third Grand Convention of July 1991 and again lost, although he managed to receive 451 votes against İnönü's 534. Party members continued to prefer İnönü, who stood for unity and harmony within the party but who did not *lead* the party, to Baykal, who showed glimmers of leadership but who they feared could divide the party by giving short shrift to party members who did not belong to his faction.

The October 1991 general elections turned out to be another defeat for the SDPP; the party trailed behind both the **True Path Party** (TPP), which came in first, and the **Motherland Party** (MP), which came in second. When the TPP leader **Süleyman Demirel** bypassed the MP and chose to form a coalition with the SDPP, however, the party found itself in the government. Demirel dominated the TPP-SDPP coalition government. İnönü's SDPP played the role of an obedient coalition partner. In September 1993, Murat Karayalçın replaced İnönü as party chairman. In the March 1994 local elections, the party could obtain only 14 percent of the votes. In November 1994, the party leadership decided to close the party and merge it with the new Republican People's Party.

SOCIALIST PARTY (SP)/SOSYALİST PARTİ (SP). Founded on February 1, 1988, by **Doğu Perinçek**. The Socialist Party's views had been colored by orthodox Marxism. The Constitutional Court closed the party on July 8, 1992, on grounds that the party expressed views contrary to the unitary nature of the Republic.

SOCIAL SECURITY SYSTEM. There are three public social security agencies in Turkey: the Social Security Administration (SSA) for wage earners in the public bureaucracy and private sector, the Retirement Fund (RT) for salaried personnel working for the government, and Bağ-Kur for others. In 1998, the SSA had 32,752,000 members, Bağ-Kur 12,680,000, and the RT 7,942,000. That same year, 315,000 persons had insurance policies issued by private companies. At the beginning of 1998, the ratio of the population included in the social security programs was 85 percent.

SPORTS. The state of Turkey took an active part in encouraging and supporting sports. It built large sports facilities and made other major investments in sports. In recent decades, private initiatives have also started to play a significant role. As of 1998, 555 of the 1,670 sports facilities had been built by private initiative. The highest sports organization of the state is the General Directorate of Youth and Sports (GDYS), which is affiliated with the prime ministry. Within the GDYS, there are federations for archery, automobile sports, badminton, basketball, bicycling, body building, boxing, chess, fencing, gymnastics, golf, handball, the handicapped, horseback riding, ice sports, judo, karate, marksmanship and hunting, mountaineering, sailing, scouting, skiing, soccer, sports for everyone, swimming, tae kwon-do, table tennis, tennis, track and field, traditional sports branches, underwater and water skiing, the universities, wrestling, and volleyball.

The perception of mass sports and widespread sports are accepted as the most important component of sports activities in Turkey. In 1998, those who took part in performance sports participated in the sports activities of 5,988 sports clubs. Beşiktaş, Eczacıbaşı, Efes Pilsen, Fenerbahçe, Galatasaray, Ülker, and Vakıfbank are among the major sports clubs. Soccer is the most popular sport in Turkey. Basketball, volleyball, and wrestling are also popular, but not as much. Turkey obtained its first Olympic championship in 1936 in wrestling. In 2000, the Galatasaray soccer team won the European UEFA Cup.

SOUTHEASTERN ANATOLIA PROJECT/GÜNEYDOĞU ANADOLU PROJESİ (GAP). The GAP aims at the socioeconomic development of southeastern Turkey with the objective of removing inequalities between this and the other regions. This project of integrated and sustainable development involves the construction of dams, hydroelectric power plants, and irrigation facilities on and around the Euphrates and Tigris Rivers, investments in urban and rural infrastructure, **agriculture**, **education**, **health**, **housing**, **industry**, **tourism**, **transportation**, and other sectors. The project is administered by the GAP Regional Development Agency, which was established in 1969. The project envisages the construction of 22 dams, 19 hydroelectric power plants, and irrigation canals to provide irrigation for 1.7 million hectares of land. The area to be irrigated is equal to 20 percent of the country's economically irrigable lands; planned annual electric production is equivalent to 22 percent of Turkey's hydroelectric energy potential. When the project is completed, an area equal in size to the lands already irrigated by the state will be opened for such agriculture. According to present estimates, the rate of production increase in agriculture will be 90 percent for wheat, 43 percent for barley, 600 percent for cotton, 700 percent for tomatoes, 250 percent for lentils, and 167 percent for vegetables. The construction of 13 organized industrial sites and 21 small industrial sites is part of the project. With the completion of the GAP, the region will be an export center for agricultural and agromanufacturing industry. The total investment cost of the project is $32 billion. Up until the end of 1997, $12 billion had been spent; the bulk of the money came from the country's own resources. The rest came from the contributions of the **United States**, Canada, **Israel**, **France**, some other European countries, the World Bank, and some foreign funds and credit institutions. As of the beginning of 1998, the completed hydroelectric power plants provided 48.7 percent of Turkey's total hydroelectric energy production. In early 1998, the total lands opened for irrigation in the region reached 183,080 hectares.

SOVIET UNION. *See* RUSSIA.

STABILIZATION PROGRAM. During the 1980s, a profound shift in philosophy took place concerning the role of the state in the economy. The new economic strategy initiated in 1980 aimed at making prices flexible, removing controls not only on prices but also on quantities, reducing direct government participation in the economy, and avoiding the destabilization of the economy through fiscal deficits, **inflation**, and external debt accumulation. The new approach represented a fundamental break with the import-substitution strategy of the earlier decades.

The export performance of the stabilization program has been a success story, notably in the first half of the 1980s. However, exports were realized by newly created foreign **trade** companies to which governments provided extensive incentives. In addition, public investment continued to be the dominant form of capital accumulation in the economy. This was paralleled by an extension of governmental power primarily based on extrabudgetary funds created and placed at the government's disposal. These were in contradiction with the alleged aim of creating a liberal economy. Over the years, the government has increasingly relaxed fiscal discipline and followed an expansionary strategy. The results were fiscal deficits as well as volatile and high loan rates of interest. In early 1988, austerity measures were introduced to reinstitute fiscal discipline. The immediate outcome was a reduction in the rate of growth although inflation remained at very high levels. In the 1990s, under popular pressure, political rationality played a greater role than market rationality more often than not; governments found it increasingly difficult to implement the long-term program of economic liberalization and structural adjustment. The situation again changed following the April 1999 general elections. Under the able leadership of Prime Minister **Bülent Ecevit** and Deputy Prime Minister **Devlet Bahçeli**, the **Democratic Left Party-Nationalist Action Party-Motherland Party** coalition government has taken courageous steps to restore fiscal discipline and boost the economy. However, in November 2000 and February 2001, the economy faced financial crises. In February 2001, a change of course was decided upon: the market rather than the state was to set the parameters of the economy; the state will interfere in the economy only when absolutely necessary. *See also* FOREIGN TRADE; MONETARY AND FISCAL POLICY; PRIVATIZATION.

STRAITS. The straits of Istanbul (Bosporous, 31 kilometers) and Çanakkale (Dardanelles, 70 kms) that connect the **Black Sea** with the **Marmara Sea** and the Marmara Sea with the **Aegean**, respectively, have repeatedly given rise to conflict in European diplomacy. When **Russia** captured the northern shores of the Black Sea in the 18th century, the Ottoman Empire granted to that country free passage for its commercial vessels. Furthermore, by the 1774 and 1798 treaties between the two countries, the Ottoman Empire closed the straits to the warships of other countries. During the Ottoman-Russian war of 1807, the Ottomans declared these agreements null and void. In 1809, the Ottoman Empire signed a treaty with **Great Britain** and closed the straits to the warships of all countries. In 1829, the Ottomans opened the straits to all commercial vessels. In 1833, the Ottoman Empire once again closed the straits to the warships of all countries except Russia. This particular status of the straits was abrogated by the 1841 London Treaty.

During the **Crimean War** of 1853–1855, the Ottoman Empire, which was now an ally of Great Britain and **France**, allowed those two countries to send their warships to the Black Sea. The **Lausanne** Straits Agreement once again opened the straits to the warships of all countries. In 1936, the Montreux Agreement gave Turkey the exclusive right to militarize the straits and bring limits to the free passage of warships. During **World War II**, the Soviets demanded that Turkey unilaterally amend the provisions of the Montreux Agreement to the sole advantage of that country. Turkey responded by noting that the Montreux Agreement could be reconsidered only through an international conference. Since then, no new developments concerning the straits have taken place; the Montreux Agreement is still in force.

The straits are hazardous, crowded, and difficult to navigate. Their narrow and winding shapes are more akin to that of a river. Currents can reach seven to eight knots at some sharp turns. Approximately 45,000 vessels transit the straits each year. The number of daily local crossings by intracity ferries and other shuttle boats is approximately 1,000. Everyday, 1.5 million people are on the move at sea. The risks and dangers associated with tanker navigation, maritime accidents, and **environmental** catastrophe are further aggravated by the constant increase in the density of traffic, tanker size and cargo capacity, as well as the nature of cargoes, which include oil, LNG/LPG chemicals, and other explosive material. It is for these reasons that Turkey is apprehensive about the shipment of the Caucasus oil from the straits.

SUFISM. *See* ISLAM.

SULTAN/SULTANATE. The sultan was the principal bond of the Ottoman system. The members of the ruling class were his "slaves" and his Muslim subjects were his "protected flock." He was "emperor" [*Hünkâr* or *hüdâvendigâr*] of his non-Muslim subjects. The sultan alone had the right to legislate through decrees. As compared to other Islamic states, it was in the Ottoman Empire that the sultans had the greatest authority to make secular rules. The Turkish Republic abolished the sultanate on November 1, 1922.

SUMELA MONASTERY. An enormous white monastery perched some 300 meters (on the **Pontus** Mountains) above the rushing stream in a valley 30 kilometers south of **Trabzon** (ancient Trebizond). This was the largest and most important monastic establishment in Asia Minor of Byzantine times. It is believed that the original monastery was founded in 385 by two monks from Greece. In 1349, Alexius III Comnenus chose it as the most suitable site for his coronation as emperor of Trebizond.

SUN-LANGUAGE THEORY [Güneş-Dil Teorisi]. Nationalist theory of **language** and history of the late 1920s. The claim was that the first language on Earth was Turkish and other languages were derived from it, that Turks had made significant contributions to the flourishing of civilization, and that there was a continuous thread of Turkish history in Anatolia dating back to the Sumerians and **Hittites**. The theory was part of an effort to return pride and self-confidence to the Turks, who had been badly shaken during several centuries of decline and the eventual collapse of the Ottoman Empire.

SUNALP, TURGUT (1917–1999). General and politician. Sunalp studied at General Staff College in Kansas (1949–1950). He served as military attaché in Moscow (1955–1957), operations officer in NATO headquarters in Paris (1957–1958), and commander of the Aegean Army with the rank of four-star general. Sunalp became Turkey's ambassador to Canada and remained in that post from 1980–1982. In 1983, he formed the short-lived **Nationalist Democracy Party** and became its chairman.

SUNAY, CEVDET (1899–1982). General and Turkey's fifth president. Sunay became a four-star general in 1958, commander of the landed forces in May 1960, and the chief of general staff in August of the same year. He was elected president on March 28, 1966, and stayed in that post until March 28, 1973. He was not an activist president and, as such, did not leave an indelible mark on Turkish politics. Between March 28, 1973, and September 12, 1980, he took his place in the Senate as a former president.

SUNNI. From *Sunna*, legally binding precedent established by the early Muslim community. A member of the larger of the two great sects of **Islam**, who believes in the traditional (consensual) method of election to the **caliphate** and accepts the Umayyad line. On this issue, the Sunni differ from the **Shi'a**.

SÜLEYMAN I (KANUNİ; THE MAGNIFICENT) (1495–1566). Ottoman sultan. Süleyman I came to the throne on September 30, 1520. During his reign, the Ottoman state became the largest and strongest empire of its time. **Iraq** in the east and Hungary and parts of Austria in the west were added to the Ottoman territories. Incomparable advances took place in the sciences, arts, administration, and military. The military was reorganized. Several new laws were enacted that regulated security and governmental matters and the economy—thus his cognomen Kanuni, the Lawmaker. Süleyman I knew Arabic and Persian, read literature in those languages, and wrote poems under the pseudonym of Mutibbî. His Western contemporaries referred to him as Suleiman the Magnificent.

SÜLEYMAN ÇELEBİ (1351–1422). Ottoman poet. He wrote the first Turkish version of the *mevlid*, an account in poetic form of the significant events in the life of Prophet Mohammed, which is chanted in particular at the religious celebrations held on the evening of the Prophet's birth.

SÜLEYMAN NAZİF (1870–1927). Ottoman poet and author. Süleyman Nazif used sophisticated and ornamented Ottoman language. He opposed syllabic meter and espoused prosodic meter. He published some of his work under the pseudonyms of İbrahim Cehdi and Abdüllahrar Tâhir. His collected poems appear in *Secret Cries* [Gizli Figânlar].

SYRIA. Turkey's neighbor to the south. Turkey's relations with Syria were initially marred by the **Alexandretta** (Hatay) question. At the end of **World War I**, that region, with an absolute majority of Turkish inhabitants, was in the hands of the Turkish forces. After the war, **France** occupied southeastern Turkey, including Alexandretta. Following the **Turkish War of Independence**, **Ankara** and Paris made an agreement under which the French withdrew from southeastern Turkey, except Alexandretta. Later, when the French prepared to recognize the independence of Syria, Turkey put pressure on France to recognize the independence of the Alexandretta region in its own name. On May 29, 1937, by a resolution of the League of Nations, Alexandretta became in law a "distinct entity." On June 23, 1939, France recognized the right of the inhabitants of Alexandretta to choose their nationality. On June 29, 1939, the Parliament of Hatay voted for the union of the region with

Turkey. Consequently, after it gained its independence in 1946, Syria was unwilling to establish cordial relations with Turkey. For some time, official Syrian maps showed Alexandretta within the boundaries of Syria. Turkey's efforts to contain the Soviet threat while overlooking the "**Israeli** threat" to Arab, including Syrian, interests did not ameliorate the strained relations between Turkey and Syria.

In 1965, the Baath Party came to power in Syria. The Baathists maintained close relations with the Soviets (*see* RUSSIA), which had started in 1956 when the Soviets had begun to provide arms to Syria. Damascus's flirtations with the Soviets further cooled the relations between Syria and Turkey, which has been a member of the **North Atlantic Treaty Organization** (NATO) since 1952.

Following the coming to power in 1971 of Hafez al Assad in Syria, Turco-Syrian relations experienced several ups and downs. In order to lessen the isolation of his country, Assad tried to avoid further tensions with Turkey at times. On other occasions, particularly during recent years, Syria provided training grounds and safe havens to different militant groups that tried to destabilize Turkey. Conflicts have also erupted between the countries about the way Turkey regulated the flow of the waters of the Euphrates into Syria. Following numerous visits by statesmen of both countries and protracted discussions, the two countries signed a protocol for "Cooperation on Security Problems" in 1987. This protocol envisaged the prevention and surveillance of the illegal smuggling of goods and people across the common border. The protocol also specified measures to be taken to prevent the activities of groups and individuals who sought to harm the security and stability of the two countries. This protocol, however, did not contribute to a mending of relations between the two countries because Turkey had concluded that Syria did not comply with the protocol. In the wake of the collapse of the Soviet Union, Damascus once again seemed eager to improve relations with Ankara. However, no concrete steps were taken in that direction. In the 1990s, the relations between Turkey and Syria continued to be rather tense. For one thing, despite repeated promises, Syria kept providing a safe haven to the separatists of the Kurdistan Worker's Party (PKK) and hosted its leader, **Abdullah Öcalan**. Secondly, the conflict on the **water issue** between Ankara and Damascus showed no signs of peaceful resolution. Being the source country and controlling the head waters of the cross-border Euphrates River, Turkey was willing to allow Syria to have its fair share of water. Syria, however, insisted on its claims of equal rights on the Euphrates and rejected Turkish aid for more efficient use of the water on its side of the border.

For a while, Ankara tried to ease tension with Damascus; starting in late 1996, however, President **Süleyman Demirel** repeatedly asked Syrian leaders to put an end to their support of "terrorist" activities in Turkey. These warnings culminated in 1998 when Turkey threatened Syria with war unless Syria sent away Öcalan and closed the PKK bases in Syria and the Bekaa Valley, which Syria controlled. Syria summarily sent Öcalan to **Russia**.

In June 2000, in an attempt to turn a new page in the relations between the two countries, the new Turkish President **Ahmet Necdet Sezer** attended the funeral ceremony of Hafez al Assad. In any case, Turkish and Syrian officials have been working on various joint projects to develop economic relations for some years now. Turkey is interested in buying petroleum and natural gas from Syria and boosting Turkish firms' construction work in Syria.

– Ş –

ŞANLIURFA. A southeastern city with a population of 1,258,855 (1997). Its history dates back 9,000 years. Şanlıurfa is where the Prophet Abraham was born and where the Prophet Job lived. Jesus blessed it as the most sacred city. The cave where the Prophet Abraham was born is located in the courtyard of the Mevlid Halil Mosque. The Şanlıurfa Citadel is located to the south of this sacred area.

ŞATIROĞLU, AŞIK VEYSEL (1894–1973). One of the last representatives of the traditional folk **literature** in the Republican era. Blind since the age of seven, Aşık Veysel combined lyricism and feeling in his poems with simple local realities. He made use of local terms. Nature, love, mysticism, and social issues constituted the themes of his poems. Aşık Veysel also used themes familiar to the modern era such as national feelings, love of country, and social protest. His folk poetry was published in *Folk Poems* [Deyişler] and *Voices from My Folk Lyre* [Sazımdan Sesler]. His posthumous memoirs were published as *May My Friends Remember Me* [Dostlar Beni Hatırlasın], the title of the book being his last words.

ŞEFİK HÜSNÜ (1887–1958). Doctor of medicine and politician. He studied medicine in Paris where he was influenced by socialist ideas. Upon his return to Turkey, he founded the Turkish Workers and Peasants Party [Türkiye İşçi ve Köylü Partisi], and tried to spread socialism. Şefik Hüsnü participated in the sixth and seventh Komintern congresses. In 1946, he founded the Turkish Socialist Workers and Peasants Party [Türkiye Sosyalist İşçi ve Köylü Partisi]. Şefik Hüsnü was convicted in 1925, 1926, and 1952 on the grounds that he was trying to spread communism in Turkey.

ŞEKER BAYRAMI (Id al Fitr). Literally Sugar Feast. The three-day holiday and feast that ends the holy month of **Ramadan** (Ramazan).

ŞEMSEDDİN SAMİ (1850–1904). Ottoman author and linguist. Şemseddin Sami wrote the first Turkish novel—*Love between Talat and Fitnat* [Taaşşuk-ı Talat ve Fitnat]. He was a proponent of writing in simple Turkish. He also wrote encyclopedias and dictionaries.

ŞERİAT (SHARIA). Ottoman religious law. Derived from the Koran, Islam's holy book, and early Muslim tradition. It is highly specific in the fields of personal be-

TALU, ERCÜMENT EKREM (1888–1956) • 187

havior and community life, but rather general for most matters of public law, particularly in respect to state organization and administration.

ŞEVKİ BEY (1860–1891). Ottoman composer. He was one of the pioneers of the new genre of songs that developed during the second part of the 19th century. A prolific musician, Şevki Bey's popularity continues to this day.

ŞEYH. Sheikh or chief. Often used as an honorific title for the master of a *tarikat*.

ŞEYHÜLİSLAM. The grand mufti (jurisconsult) of the empire and mufti of Istanbul.

ŞİNASİ (1826–1871). Poet and journalist. Şinasi contributed in the second part of the 19th century to the development of a new Turkish **literature** in prose for the **theater**, the novel, and social commentary forms that did not exist before. He was a proponent of **Westernization**. *The Wedding of the Poet* [Şair Evlenmesi] is his best-known play.

– T –

TAKVİM-İ VEKAYİ [Calendar of Events]. Official Ottoman government newspaper, published from 1831 until 1923.

TALAT PASHA (1874–1921). Ottoman politician. Talat Pasha founded the Ottoman Freedom Association and then merged it with the **Committee for Union and Progress**. He entered the first Ottoman Parliament following the proclamation of the Second Constitutional Period in 1908 and became its acting speaker. He served as minister of interior (August 8, 1909–February 18, 1910; June 12, 1913–July 4, 1918), communications (February 4, 1911–July 22, 1912), and finance (February 4, 1917–October 14, 1918). In 1915, he planned the forced deportations of **Armenians** in eastern Anatolia on the grounds that some Armenian organizations had started militant action against the state. The organizations in question declared Talat Pasha the foremost enemy of Armenians. He was made grand vizier on February 4, 1917. He also took charge of the ministries of interior and finance; the first ministry he kept until July 4, 1918. He resigned from the grand vizierate on October 14, 1918. Talat Pasha quit politics and left the country on November 1, 1918. An Armenian militant assassinated Talat Pasha in Berlin on March 15, 1921.

TALU, ERCÜMENT EKREM (1888–1956). Novelist. Talu's work reflected life in old **Istanbul** and provided colorful depictions of its common people. His most popular novel is *The Pilgrim from Mashhad Hunts Lions* [Meşhedi Aslan Peşinde].

TALU, NAİM (1919–). Financier and politician. Naim Talu served as head of the Central Bank and minister of finance (December 11, 1971–April 17, 1972 and May 22, 1972–April 10, 1973). He was prime minister from April 15, 1973 to October 14, 1973.

TANER, GÜNEŞ (1949–1998). Banker and politician. Taner obtained an M.S. degree from the Polytechnic Institute of New York. He served as manager and deputy director at Citibank (New York) and chairman of the board of directors of TURAMCO, before becoming one of the founders of the **Motherland Party**. In the 1980s, as minister of state responsible for the economy, along with **Turgut Özal**, he played a critical role in initiating the **privatization** of state economic policies and maintaining a high growth rate while keeping **inflation** at reasonable rates.

TANER, HALDUN (1916–1986). Playwright. Taner criticized the evolving cultural patterns in the Republican period. He provided a deft treatment of contradictions and hypocrisies in human and social relations. Among his popular plays are *The Legend of Ali of Keshan* [Keşanlı Ali Destanı] and *I Close My Eyes and Diligently Do My Duty* [Gözlerimi Kaparım Vazifemi Yaparım]. His most popular cabaret theater play is *The Clever Wife of the Stupid Husband* [Sersem Kocanın Kurnaz Karısı].

TANİN. Principal newspaper of the **Committee for Union and Progress**, published from 1908 until 1925.

TANPINAR, AHMET HAMDİ (1901–1962). Novelist. Tanpınar had a keen interest in traditions and **Westernization** during the second part of the 19th and the first part of the 20th centuries. His short story *Abdullah Efendi's Dreams* [Abdullah Efendinin Rüyaları] and his novel *The Watches Setting Institute* [Saatleri Ayarlama Enstitüsü] attracted much attention.

TANRIÖVER, HAMDULLAH SUPHİ (1886–1966). Professor of fine arts, ambassador, and politician. From 1913 until 1933, he was the driving force behind the nationalist **Turkish Hearth** movement. He served as ambassador in Bucharest, Romania, and as minister of education. *Mountain Road* [Dağ Yolu] is a collection of his speeches, and *Facing Days* [Günebakiş] is a collection of his articles.

TANTAN, SADETTİN (1941–). Bureaucrat and politician. He studied economics and has a master's degree in business administration. Tantan served as **police** chief in the provinces of Giresun and Tekirdağ and mayor in the Fatih district municipality in **Istanbul**. He served as minister of interior between 28 May 1999 and 5 June 2001. Under his ministry, the police have been able to uncover several past and present criminal cases.

TANZİMAT (REFORM) PERIOD/TANZİMAT-I HAYRİYE [BENEFICENT REORDERING] (1839–1876). Proclaimed with the **Imperial Rescript of Gül-**

hane of 1839. The Rescript introduced the revolutionary (from the Ottoman perspective) principle of equality of the Muslim and non-Muslim subjects of the state and created new rules and new institutions. The provincial administration was centralized. Departments along Western lines were introduced. New penal (1840) and commercial (1850) codes were promulgated. The Ottoman Bank was established and paper money was issued. Semisecular schools were opened alongside the religious ones. The reforms gained a new impetus with the **Reform Decree** of 1856. More codes were enacted. Additional governmental bodies, including the Council of State, were set up. The **Galatasaray Lycée**, the first serious attempt by a Muslim government to provide modern **education** at secondary level in a Western language (French), was established. A new civil code—**Mecelle**—was promulgated.

The greatest achievement of the *Tanzimat* was in education; a new educated elite with a modern worldview began to evolve. None of the reforms, however, could be completely implemented because of the religious resistance encountered. The outcome was a duality of the religious and the secular existing side by side, which lingered until the establishment of the Republic (1923).

TARANCI, CAHİT SITKI (1910–1956). Poet. Tarancı dealt with themes of lost love and invincible death. *Thirty-Five Years Old* [Otuz Beş Yaş], containing his title poem, brought him national fame.

TARCAN, BÜLENT (1914–1991). Doctor of medicine and composer. He took violin lessons from Karl Berger. In his preliminary work, Tarcan employed Turkish folk songs and certain rhythms of folk dances. Later on, he developed his own folk tunes, employing a neomodal structure. *His Tales* (symphonic poem), *Sonata for Violin and Piano* (chamber music), and *Third Suite* (for orchestra) reflect variations in his compositions.

TARİK. Path of instruction of spiritual perfection undertaken by a **Sufi** devotee, usually in a *tarikat*.

TARİKAT. Popular religious orders. To reach a mystic union with God, the *tarikat* required all members to follow a certain pattern of behavior, as specified by the founders and leaders of each order. These religious orders were widespread in Anatolian society in Ottoman times. They provided refuge, protection, and religious fulfillment for the individual in a society that otherwise was organized to fulfill the purposes of the ruling groups. The orders were banned in Republican Turkey. *See also* ISLAM; TEKKE.

TASVİR-İ EFKAR. Leading newspaper of the *Tanzimat* **(Reform) Period** of 1839–1876. It was published from 1861 until 1870.

TAURUS MOUNTAINS. Extend parallel to Turkey's southern shore. They are quite rugged and rarely dissected by rivers.

TAXATION. *See* MONETARY AND FISCAL POLICY.

TECER, AHMET KUTSİ (1901–1967). Poet and playwright. A sensitive poet, inspired by folk culture, Tecer dwelt on the beauties of the country and nature. During the years 1941–1945, he edited the journal *Ülkü,* published by the **People's Houses.** *Poems* [Şiirler] is a collection of Tecer's poetry. *On the Corner* [Köşebaşı] and *One Sunday* [Bir Pazar Günü] are examples of his novels.

TEKKE. Residential convent attached to a *tarikat.*

TELEVISION. *See* MASS MEDIA.

TENGİRŞENK, Y. KEMAL (1878–1969). Lawyer and politician. Tengirşenk entered the Ottoman Parliament in 1908. He obtained a doctorate in law and political science from Paris Law School in 1913. He also served in the last Ottoman Parliament. When the Allies invaded **Istanbul,** Tengirşenk joined the nationalist movement in Anatolia and became a member of the Turkish Grand National Assembly. He acted as minister of economics (May 3, 1920–January 24, 1921), foreign minister (January 24, 1921–July 9, 1922, and July 12–October 26, 1922) and minister of justice (September 27, 1930–May 25, 1933). He headed Turkish delegations in negotiating the Moscow Treaty with the Soviet Union (*see* RUSSIA) (signed on March 21, 1921) and the Ankara Treaty with **France** (signed on October 20, 1921). His years in Parliament ended in 1950. Tengirşenk also served in the post-1960 **military** intervention **Constituent Assembly,** which prepared the 1961 **constitution.**

TERCÜMAN-I AHVAL. Young Ottoman newspaper. It was published from 1861 until 1866.

TEVFİK FİKRET (1887–1915). Prominent bard and poet. Tevfik Fikret belonged to the late-19th-century *Servet-i Fünun* [Treasure of the Sciences] literary movement (on this movement, *see* LITERATURE). He played a leading role in perfecting the forms in Turkish poetry. His poems encouraged the fight against injustice and struggle for freedom, and emphasized the need for an awareness of the great issues of his time. Tevfik Fikret's best-known collections of poems are *Broken Harps* [Rübab-ı Şikeste] and *Haluk's Notebook* [Haluk'un Defteri].

TİCANİ ORDER. A Berber offshoot of the Halvetiyya order. It spread to Turkey during the Republican period. It staged demonstrations when a leader of the order, Kemal Pilavoğlu, was arrested and brought to trial in 1950 in **Ankara.** Members of the order expressed their protest of the secular Republic by destroying statues and busts of **Atatürk.** They have not been active during recent decades. *See* TARİKAT.

TİMAR. Fief held in return for **military** or other service to the state. It was a substitute for a salary given to members of the military who kept themselves and their retainers ready to join military campaigns, or bring arms, supplies, and food to support those campaigns. The system was gradually terminated at the end of the 17th and beginning of the 18th centuries.

THEATER. Folk theater, popular theater, court theater, and Western theater make up the four main theatrical traditions in Turkey. Although different in many respects, folk theater and popular theater have similar genres—puppetry, acted-out storytelling, dramatic dancing, and rudimentary play by an all-male cast for (all) male audiences and an all-female cast for (all) female audiences. In the folk theater, the actors are nonprofessionals while in the popular theater they are professionals. Turkey had no distinctive court theater tradition; for the most part, court theater imitated popular theater. The development of Turkey's Western theater traditions is fairly recent; it dates back to the early part of the 19th century.

During the Republic, theater was considered an ideal instrument for inculcating in the masses the Republic's cultural nationalism and populism. Many actors and playwrights started their careers as amateurs in the activities of the **People's Houses** founded by the government with the objective of cultural indoctrination. Drama became an essential instrument in the **Westernization** of Turkey. In 1936, a State Conservatory was established in **Ankara**, which still operates. Once the program at the Conservatory is completed, the student becomes a member of the State Theater and draws a fairly good salary. A general director appointed by the Ministry of Culture runs the State Theater. In 1998, the State Theater staged more than 125 plays in the 32 theaters it operates, 9 of which are in Ankara and 4 each in **Istanbul, İzmir**, and **Bursa**. The 12 provincial chapters of the State Theater (in Istanbul, **Adana**, Ankara, **Antalya**, Bursa, Diyarbakır, Erzurum, İzmir, **Konya, Sivas, Trabzon**, and Van) organizes such tours as Great Anatolian Tours and Children's Plays Festivals every year and performs in all provincial centers and several subprovincial towns. There are also the "city theaters" run by the municipalities in many provinces. In 1998, the latter staged 20 different plays in five theaters in various districts of Istanbul. That same year, the Open Air Theater in Istanbul attracted large audiences during the summer months.

During the 1960s, many private theaters were opened in Istanbul and Ankara. The plays they staged addressed current political and social problems. In the 1970s, private theaters faced critical problems. Street violence and the frequent imposition of martial law kept many people at home. During the same decade, **television** became quite popular. In the 1970s and the following decade, numerous theaters were converted to other purposes such as shops and warehouses. Consequently, some successful private theaters closed down, leaving others struggling for survival. As of 1982, the state began subsidizing private theaters. The number of private theaters went up, the artistic level improved, and new and original works of distinction have been staged.

Until the 1960s, plays reflected few of the changes that had overtaken the country. Dramatists' characters worked out their fate in an almost society-less vacuum. Plays on the inevitability of faith, plays involving dreams and psychoanalytic themes, plays on the eternal triangle and the vicissitudes of married life, sentimental plays on themes of love, altruism, and self-sacrifice, and the like were prevalent. Following the adoption of the 1961 **Constitution**, which enlarged the scope of basic rights and liberties, the theater became an outspoken medium of contemporary problems. Many plays dealt with issues and problems such as contemporary man's sense of isolation, alienation and loss of identity, generational conflicts, sexual mores and problems, individuals caught up in cultural conflict, problems arising from mass migration to the cities, families fighting against disintegration, **women's** issues, village life, political and social ideals, social structure, and contemporary mores. In recent years, Turkish dramatists no longer see Western culture as an ideal model but as a contrasting tradition. They have also come to the conclusion that recent theatrical trends in the West have their counterparts in Turkish traditional theater characterized by a sense of anti-illusionistic rapport between the actors and the audience, an open or flexible form, the attempt to give the impression of improvisation, and total theater in performance and the use of **music**, dance, and songs as adjuncts to drama. Some playwrights have developed contemporary "Western" styles in their plays based on their own all-but-forgotten heritage.

THIRTY FIVE, THE. The faction within the **Republican People's Party** (RPP) that was led by **Nihat Erim** (Nihat Erim, in turn, was supported by President **İsmet İnönü**). The group refused to give a vote of confidence to the RPP's authoritarian **Recep Peker** government. The government had to resign, and this development constituted the defeat of the "single-party mentality" in the RPP.

TİSK (CONFEDERATION OF EMPLOYERS' UNIONS OF TURKEY). Established in 1962, TİSK is the main organization of 18 employers' unions in industrial and service sectors. It sees its function as the maintenance of work harmony so as to contribute to increases in production and productivity, price stability, the development of exports, and creation of additional employment opportunities. *See also* INTEREST GROUPS; TÜSIAD.

TOGAN, ZEKİ VELİDİ (1890–1970). Professor of history. Togan obtained a Ph.D. from Vienna University. He is best known for his work on the origins of Turkic clans in **Russia** and Central Asia. In the early 1940s, he was tried for his "ethnic nationalism" but was acquitted.

TOKAT. A historic city in central Anatolia dating back to Byzantine times. The Ottoman Empire in the latter part of the 15th century annexed it. The Pasha Hamamı (baths) founded in 1425, the Ali Pasha Mosque built in 1573, the Voyvoda Hanı (market building) constructed in 1631, the Gök Theological School [**medrese**] built in about 1270, the Hatuniye Mosque, and the Theological School are the most important historical monuments in Tokat. In 1997, the population of the city was 750,717.

TONGUÇ, İSMAİL HAKKI (1897–1960). Educator. Tonguç played a critical role in planning and structuring the village institutes in Turkey. Pilot institutes were opened in 1936. Tonguç became director general of grade school **education** on January 31, 1940. In August of that year, his directorate was given the responsibility of administering 21 village institutes. Students who completed a five-year grade school in a village were admitted to five-year village institutes where they were trained as teachers to serve in the villages. Curricula at the institutes emphasized applied sciences and technical skills. Each institute was located on a plot of land to be cultivated. The program came under criticism. Some thought that the education at these institutes deviated from its original purpose of developing villages; others argued that the institutes had become a means of propagating leftist views. Tonguç was relieved of the responsibility of administering the village institutes program on September 21, 1946.

TOPKAPI SARAYI. Ottoman imperial court built during the reign of **Mehmet II** (1444, 1451–1481) and used as such until the 19th century. The residence contained, among other things, the **sultan**'s privy chambers, harem, imperial council chambers, inner treasury, as well as holy relics of the Prophet. Today it is a **museum**.

TOURISM. There are many historical sites in Turkey as it has been home to numerous civilizations during the past 7,000 years, including **Hittite**, Greco-Roman, Hellenistic, Seljuk, and Ottoman. Three major religions—Judaism, Christianity, and **Islam**—all matured in Anatolia. **Şanlıurfa** is the birthplace of the Prophet Abraham, the genetic grandfather of Judaism, Christianity, and Islam. It was from Antakya that the apostles took to the road to spread Christianity in the south. The **Cappadocia** is the region where the early Christians carved underground cities, churches, and monasteries out of rocks.

The two most important councils that gave a direction to the history of Christianity were convened in **İznik** in 325 C.E. and 385 C.E. Tarsus is the birthplace of St. Paul. Ephesus is the place where the Virgin Mary is believed to have spent her final days and died. In 1995, "Religious Belief Tourism" was started.

Extending from the eastern corner of the Black Sea through the **Marmara Sea** and the **Aegean** to the eastern end of the **Mediterranean**, Turkey has over 8,000 kilometers of natural coastline. The holiday towns such as Alanya, **Antalya, Bodrum**, Fethiye, Kaş, Kuşadası, and Marmaris are among the places where summer tourism is most concentrated. In 1997, there were 1,936 licensed tourist facilities and 311,920 beds in Turkey. Besides these, such modern facilities as thermal springs, apartment hotels, roadside rest stop facilities, and auto-caravan tourism complexes provide services for Turkish tourism. The government provides incentives for investments by foreign companies to develop new hotels and motels, resort villages, thermal resorts, golf courses, ski resorts, marinas, and entertainment centers.

In 1993, Turkey's revenue from tourism was $4 billion; in 1998 it stood at $7.2 billion. In 1997, more than 15 million people made tourist trips in Turkey. That same year more than 4.5 million Turks travelled abroad.

TÖR, VEDAT NEDİM (1897–1985). Playwright, essayist, and novelist. Tör was one of the founders of the periodical *Kadro*. He used the conventional theatrical style in his plays. *Among the Three People* [Üç Kişi Arasında], *All and Nothing* [Hep ve Hiç], and *Black and White* [Siyah ve Beyaz] are his plays. He also wrote the essay "The Drama of Kemalism" [Kemalizmin Dramı] and the novel *The Painting Teacher* [Resim Öğretmeni].

TRABZON (Ancient Trebizond). The historic city on the Black Sea in northeastern Turkey with a population of 782,406 (1997). It was founded in the eighth century. In 1204, Alexius III Comneus founded what would become the Byzantine Empire of Trebizond. Trabzon's most renowned monument is the magnificent Church of Hagia Sophia with its priceless works of art. The Gülbahar Hatun Mosque built in 1514 and Yeni Cuma [New Friday] Mosque, the former church of St. Eugenios, are two other renowned historic monuments in Trabzon. The famous **Sumela Monastery** is 30 kilometers south of Trabzon.

TRANSLATION OFFICE. Created within the Foreign Ministry in 1833. It constituted an important opening to the West. Some members of future Ottoman elites with a Western orientation received their first training in this office.

TRANSPORTATION AND COMMUNICATIONS. Following the establishment of the Republic in 1923, one primary goal has been to cover the whole country with railroads. The rationale behind this policy was **defense** considerations. The Democrats (*see DEMOKRATİK* PARTY), who came to power in 1950, instead gave preference to road transport at the expense of railroads as well as coastal shipping. In 1923, the length of railways was 3,756 kilometers; by 1950, it had gone up to 7,671 kms (a 204 percent increase) but in 1990, the length of railways was 8,429 kms (only an 11 percent increase from 1950 to 1990). During the next seven years, the increase in the length of railways was only 2,071 kms. In 1997, the length of railways with electrification was 2,065 kms, which was 20 percent of the total main lines. The share of railways in the domestic cargo transportation is 5.6 percent.

In 1997, the total length of the highways was around 62,000 kms and the length of the other roads 350,000 kms. In the second part of the 1990s, the freeway network expanded rapidly. In 1997, the total length of the network of freeways was 1,596 kms. Improvements in road transport integrated isolated regions with the rest of the country and provided fast and flexible intercity services.

There have been significant developments in international cargo transportation since 1990. The number of companies serving the sector increased almost 50 percent and reached 360 and the number of vehicles reached the level of 22,000 between 1990 and 1996. The number of refrigerated trucks exceeded 2,500. Between 1986 and 1996, the amount of foreign currency carried by this subsector increased 100 percent and went from $500 million to $1 billion. The highways lead the domestic cargo transportation with a share of 87.3 percent.

Maritime transportation has the second place after highways in the international cargo transportation. The total length of shores in Turkey is 8,333 kms. In 1997, there were a total of 140 ports of different capacity, 14 marinas with **tourism** certificates, and 7 marinas with tourism investment certificates. In 1997, the total tonnage of the Turkish maritime fleet reached 10 million DWT, excluding the ships that were leased. The number of ships over 3000 gross tons was 950. The share of seaways in the domestic cargo transportation is 5.2 percent.

The Turkish Airlines (TA) fleet is among the youngest fleets in the world with an average age of 8.9 years. In 1997, TA reached a capacity of 10,038 seats with 63 passenger planes and 3 cargo planes. That same year, it had scheduled flights to 87 points in the world. In 1997, there were nine private airlines in Turkey with 62 planes and a seating capacity of 12,272.

The communications technologies of the most developed countries were brought to Turkey especially after 1980. In 1998, more than 80 percent of telephone lines were digitized. Close to 100 percent of all transmissions in Turkey are digitized. At the end of 1997, the automatic switchboard capacity stood at 17,584,26 lines; there were 15,744,020 automatic telephone subscribers, 126,659 vehicle telephone subscribers, and 1,483,149 cellular telephone subcribers. That same year, Turkey had 5,021 TV transmitters and 511,706 cable TV subscribers. Turkey's Türksat 2A communications satellite is the most powerful satellite of its kind; it has 32 channels and high power levels in the coverage areas.

Global Systems for Mobile Communications (GSM) services were introduced in Turkey in 1994. In 1994–1999, this sector reached a penetration rate of 12 percent, making Turkey one of the fastest growing markets. The Internet became available in Turkey in 1993. By the end of 1999, there were 750,000 Internet dial-ups in the country. The three companies with the largest market share are Superonline, Vestelnet, and Turk.net. With those in the universities, public bureaucracy and business offices, and Internet cafes, the figure rises to close to one million Internet users.

TRIUMPHANT SOLDIERS OF MUHAMMAD [Asakir-i Mansure-i Muhammadiye]. Formed 1826 by **Mahmut II** to replace the **Janissary Corps**. Its organization was based on the post-1789 French model. Eight musket companies made up a battalion and two or three battalions a regiment. Some elements of the old Janissary Corps were retained and incorporated into the new army. The new forces were dressed in European-style uniforms. Western-style marches and bands were also introduced.

In 1833, an officers' training college was opened. In 1835, a small team of Prussian officers were recruited as advisors. In 1842, the forces were structured as six armies. In the second part of the 1860s, there were separate **military** grade schools [*rüşdiye*], military secondary schools [*idadi*], and the military high school [*Harbiye*]. The system was capped by the Staff College [*Erkan-ı Harbiye Mektebi*]. The separate school system inculcated in officers a different worldview, which could easily be maintained because of a corporate social homogeneity among officers. These particular characteristics of the officer corps turned them into agents of change. They played an important role in removing **Abdülhamit II** from the throne; impinging upon governments, albeit from behind the scenes, during the **Committee for Union and Progress** period; and spearheading modernization and later safeguarding it in the Republican era.

TRUE PATH PARTY (TPP)/DOĞRU YOL PARTİSİ (DYP). The party was founded on June 23, 1983, as a successor to the center-right **Justice Party** (JP). The True Path Party could not participate in the November 6, 1983, general elections. The party met the requirement of having formed provincial organizations in at least 34 provinces by the August 25 deadline, one of the two conditions that had to be satisfied in order to be eligible to run in the 1983 elections. However, it could not satisfy the second condition of having its 30 founding members endorsed by the ruling military **National Security Council** (NSC). Between the date the TPP was founded and the deadline in question, the council vetoed some members in each of the four different lists submitted by it. The NSC did not want the post-1980 political parties to be reincarnations of the pre-1980 political parties. In the **military**'s view, political parties were responsible for the pre-1980 political crisis that Turkey faced. The TPP had not concealed the fact that it was a continuation of the JP.

The TPP's first leader was Ahmet Nusret Tuna; **Süleyman Demirel**, the leader of the defunct Justice Party, was at the time barred from politics by a decree passed by the ruling NSC. Tuna's founding membership was vetoed on July 7, 1983. On July 11, 1983, Yıldırım Avcı, a former member of the **Consultative Assembly** founded by the military, was elected as the party's new chairman. Avcı later appeared in various martial law court trials for his criticism of the regime.

The TPP was allowed to participate in the March 25, 1984, local elections. The party won 14 percent of the votes and came in third behind the **Motherland Party** (MP) and the **Social Democracy Party**. At the time, of these three parties, only the MP was represented in Parliament. The **National Democracy Party**, which was founded with the covert encouragement of the military to represent the right and was at the time represented in Parliament, received only 7 percent of the votes. In autumn 1984, the public prosecutor started trial proceedings against the TPP on charges that the party was a continuation of the Justice Party. The Constitutional Court ruled against the prosecutor's demand that the party be closed.

On May 14, 1985, **Hüsamettin Cindoruk**, the TPP's provincial head in **Istanbul**, became chairman of the party. Cindoruk was deputy chairman of the **Grand Turkey Party**, which was the first successor party to the JP and which was closed by the military. With Cindoruk, the TPP pressed for more democratization, including the lifting of the bans on former politicians. In May 1986, the National Democracy Party was dissolved. Some of that party's deputies (and a number of independents and one Motherland Party member) joined the TPP. Later, more deputies became TPP members. The party was now represented in Parliament. It could have its voice heard on radio and television as now it had a parliamentary group. In the September 1986 by-elections, the party obtained 4 of the 11 seats contested. Finally, in a nationwide referendum held on September 6, 1987, the ban on former political leaders was lifted. Cindoruk stepped down and Demirel was elected chairman of the TPP.

In the November 1987 general elections, the TPP came in third, behind the Motherland Party and the **Social Democratic Populist Party**. Demirel began arguing that the representation in Parliament was undemocratic because the election law was advantageous to the party with more votes. Later, when the ruling Motherland Party wished to hold early local elections, the TPP opposed it and presented the referendum held on the issue as a "yes" or "no" vote for Prime Minister **Turgut Özal**. On September 25, 1988, people voted against early local elections, and Demirel started calling on Özal to resign. The local elections, which were held on time (March 26, 1989), brought victory for the TPP. The party now emerged as the second party in the country. Demirel called for early general elections by arguing that a party (the MP) with only 22 percent popular support (that it received in the local elections) could not continue to rule the country. At the time, bringing Özal down from the presidency and coming to power had been the main focus of the TPP. On the eve of the October 21, 1991, general elections, Demirel defended a more democratic platform and promised to raise the living standards of the have-nots. In the elections, the TPP won a plurality of the votes. Demirel chose to form a coalition government with the Social Democratic Populist Party of **Erdal İnönü**. Since İnönü acted in a conciliatory manner toward Demirel, the coalition turned out to be virtually a TPP government. This government faced three major problems—**inflation**, further democratization of the polity, and Kurdish (*see* KURDS) separatism in southeastern Turkey. By the end of 1992, inflation was still high although the economy had not drifted into a crisis situation, as pundits had earlier predicted. Moreover, inflation seemed to have been brought under control. The TPP was under attack from the bulk of the intelligentsia for not having brought about significant democratization, even though the coalition had managed to enact a new and relatively liberal Criminal Trials Procedure Act. The Kurdish issue remained at an impasse although there was less bloodshed. Then, in early 1993, the Kurdish separatists unilaterally declared a cease-fire and the hostilities came to an end only to be resumed a few months later. The government had earlier "recognized the Kurdish reality" and decided to further develop the southeast. The TPP survived the reopening of its predecessor parties in autumn 1992 with virtually no scars. On September 10, 1992, the **Demokrat Party** (DP), banned after the 1980 military takeover, was reopened. This was followed by the reopening on November 30, 1992, of the

Justice Party, closed after the 1980 military intervention. The JP's reincarnation caused greater tremors than that of the DP because from the beginning the DP remained moribund while the JP was the party that Demirel had led.

Demirel urged the JP to disband and hand over its assets to the TPP. Demirel's former and present rivals, however, wanted all the center-right parties, including the TPP, to reunite under the JP. In the end, Demirel won. The JP closed itself and turned over its assets to the TPP. In May 1993, Demirel was elected president.

Since June 1993, the TPP has been led by **Tansu Çiller**, who, in the last Demirel government, was minister of state responsible for the economy. In November 1994, the TPP-Social Democratic Populist Party coalition was replaced by the TPP-(new) **Republican People's Party** (RPP) coalition. However, Çiller and the RPP leader **Deniz Baykal** could not get along well. The coalition came to an end in September 1995. Following the December 25, 1995, general elections, the TPP formed a coalition government with the Motherland Party (MP) of **Mesut Yılmaz**. Yılmaz and Çiller could not leave behind their intense competition for the leadership of the center-right. Yılmaz joined the opposition in levelling corruption charges against Çiller, which brought the collapse of the TPP-MP coalition. On June 27, 1996, Çiller agreed to form a coalition government with the religiously oriented **Welfare Party** (WP) of **Necmettin Erbakan.** Earlier Çiller had accused the WP of being a party that was trying to take Turkey back to the Dark Ages. The WP saved Çiller from being tried at the High Court of Justice. The TPP-WP coalition came under pressure from the military as well as the other public and private institutions of the secular establishment in Turkey. On June 17, 1997, the coalition came to an end.

In the April 18, 1999, general elections, the TPP obtained only 12.0 percent of the votes. Since then, there has been a clear tendency on the part of the other secular political parties to prevent the TPP led by Çiller from again being a partner in government.

TULIP PERIOD [Lale Devri] (1718–1730). An Ottoman period of extravagance as well as intellectual awakening. A new pleasure palace inspired by Fontainebleau in Paris, and named appropriately *Sa'dabat* [Place of Happiness], was built for the **sultan**. Similar palaces, pavilions, gardens, and fountains were privately built throughout **Istanbul**. Tulips were planted everywhere, thus the name of the period. Garden parties and **festivals** followed each other. For the first time, there was a great deal of emulation of European customs and manners. Poets were promoted and subsidized. Secular interests and pleasures were emphasized, which prepared the ground for the adoption of new ways and ideas. Emissaries were sent to Europe and reported on European ways to the Ottoman rulers and those around them. The first Ottoman press was started by İbrahim Müteferrika.

TUNAYA, TARIK ZAFER (1916–1991). Professor of constitutional law. Tunaya was the first scholar in Turkey who formed a link between constitutional law and political science. He was a member of the Constitutional Committee of the **Constituent Assembly** that prepared the 1961 **constitution**. His opus magnum is *Political Parties in Turkey* [Türkiye'de Siyasi Partiler] (1952).

TURANİ, ADNAN (1925–). Painter. Turani used the abstract mode, with calligraphic tracings and sketchy figurations.

TURGUT REİS (?–1565). Ottoman corsair who from time to time worked in the service of the Ottoman government. Turgut Reis played a significant part in the establishment of Ottoman naval sovereignty in the **Mediterranean**.

TURKIC REPUBLICS. Following the collapse of the Soviet Union (*see* RUSSIA) in 1991, five of the newly independent republics—**Azerbaijan**, Kazakhstan, Kyrgyzstan, Uzbekistan, and Turkmenistan—where the majority of the population is Muslim, were regarded as Turkic republics. Turkish governments as well as the people assume a shared history and culture (both in linguistic and religious terms) between Turkey, on the one hand, and the Turkic republics, on the other. Turkey, therefore, has aspired to develop and maintain special ties with these republics. Since Turkish nationalism is a civic-cultural and not an ethnic nationalism and since Turkey rejects irredentism, Turkey has been careful to promote that relationship on cultural and economic, not political, premises.

Turkey has provided a significant scholarship program to students from the republics. In the 2000–2001 academic year, around 7,000 students were attending schools in Turkey. Turkey has also supplied equipment, training material, and teachers to vocational schools in the republics. Around 2,500 Turkish companies have business there. By 1999, their investments had reached $8.4 billion. In 1999, the **trade** volume between Turkey and these countries was $5.6 billion.

TURKISH ACADEMY OF SCIENCES. Established in September 1993 and became active in January 1994. The academy endeavors to elevate the level of scholarship in Turkey. In 2000, it had 110 members, divided into honorary, regular, and associate categories.

TURKISH COMMUNIST PARTY (TCP)/TÜRKIYE KOMÜNIST PARTISI (TKP). Formed on October 18, 1920, with the permission of Mustafa Kemal **Atatürk**. Led by some of Atatürk's close associates, the party was a means both to placate the Soviet Union (*see* RUSSIA), from whom Turkey received aid during the **Turkish War of Independence** (1920–1922), and to confuse the communists and their supporters in Turkey. When real communists attempted to steer the party in a Bolshevik direction, the party was suppressed and the communist members brought to trial.

TURKISH ECONOMIC AND SOCIAL STUDIES FOUNDATION (TESEV). Based in **Istanbul**, TESEV is a private, independent, and nonprofit organization that conducts and supports policy-oriented research. Its roots go back to 1961. It was restructured as a **foundation** in 1994. The research conducted under the auspices of TESEV fall into five broad categories: human resources, social and cultural institutions and structure, economic structure and work, political, legal, and administrative structure, and **foreign policy** and international relations.

TURKISH HEARTH ORGANIZATION. Founded in **Istanbul** on March 22, 1912. The organization was closed and reopened several times between that date and May 10, 1949, when it was definitively closed. Its branches were established in every city, school, and major public body. The organization promoted Turkish nationalism as developed by **Ziya Gökalp**; its target was to destroy **Ottomanism** and **Islamism** and replace them with **Turkism**. It also made contacts with Turks outside the empire. The organization urged the government to increase the use of Turkish in official business.

TURKISH LABOR PARTY (TLP)/TÜRKIYE İŞÇİ PARTİSİ (TİP). Formed in 1961 by 12 **labor union** leaders belonging to the biggest (moderate left-wing) labor confederation **Türk-İş**. Later, left-wing intellectuals joined the party. In the 1965 general elections, the TLP, under the leadership of **Mehmet Ali Aybar**, a former university professor, won 3 percent of the votes and became the first leftist party in Turkey to return members to Parliament. In July 1971, the TLP was dissolved by the Constitutional Court on charges of carrying out communist propaganda and encouraging activities designed to divide the country.

TURKISH WAR OF INDEPENDENCE (1920–1922). Resorted to by the Turkish nationalists when the Treaty of **Sévres** attempted to reduce the Ottoman realms to a virtual nonentity. It was fought against **Greece**, who had tried to conquer Anatolia with the implicit approval of the European powers. Initially, the Greeks made considerable advances. It took three defensive battles—the first and second battles around the township of İnönü, (January 1921 and March–April 1921, respectively) and the third battle along the Sakarya River (August–September 1921)—and one offensive battle—the Great Offensive (August 26–September 18, 1922)—for the Turks to drive the Greeks out of Anatolia. The war came to an end with the Armistice of Mudanya, signed on October 11, 1922. With the **Lausanne Treaty** of July 24, 1923, Turkey gained its full sovereignty and its present boundaries except the **Alexandretta** region (which was added to Turkey in 1939).

TURKISM/PAN-TURKISM. During the 17th century, a number of European and later Ottoman Turcologists began to discover the pre-Ottoman Turkish past. Ottoman intellectuals were also influenced by the emerging nationalism in Europe and among the religious minority groups in the Ottoman Empire. The non-Ottoman Turkish refugees flowing into the empire following the **Crimean War** (1853–1856) and giving accounts of persecution and repression in non-Ottoman lands also played a role. An additional factor was that several Central Asian intellectuals came to Turkey to teach the history and languages of their (Turkic) peoples. There was considerable Turkish intellectual ferment, mainly in Crimea and **Azerbaijan**. They published newspapers in which they promoted the idea of Turkism. Some came to Turkey and continued their intellectual activities in **Istanbul**. Among them were **Ahmet Ağaoğlu** and **Yusuf Akçura**. **Abdülhamit II** suppressed Turkish nationalist writings because of his preference for **Islamism**.

Gradually, however, the words "Turk" and "Turkish" began to be used more frequently. History books started Turkish history with pre-Ottoman times; there were now references to the ancient Turkish nomads of Central Asia. **Ahmet Midhat** and **Mehmed Murat (Mizancı)** were the earliest representatives of this new genre of historiography in Turkey. The popular press began to pay attention to Turks in Crimea, China, and Samarkand. When Abdülhamit II tried to stifle this new interest in "outer Turks" for fear of a **Russian** reprisal, the attention was largely focused on Anatolian nationalism, taking Anatolia as the real homeland of the Turks. The Anatolian peasant and his language were glorified. There were efforts to use words of Turkic/Turkish rather than Arabic and Persian origins. When the Turkish Republic was established in 1923, **Westernism** was emphasized and Turkism was relegated to a secondary place. Its nature also changed. The founders of the new Republic adopted a civic-cultural rather than ethnic nationalism, and they rejected Pan-Turkism.

TURSUN BEG (15th century). Ottoman historian and chronicler. He was well known for his important work on the period (1451–1481) during which **Mehmet II (The Conqueror)** served as **sultan**.

TÜBİTAK (SCIENTIFIC AND TECHNICAL RESEARCH INSTITUTE OF TURKEY). Founded in 1963, TÜBİTAK organizes, supports, and coordinates research and development activities in basic and life sciences. It also provides consultancy to government on science and technology.

TÜRK, HİKMET SAMİ (1935–). Professor of law and politician. After having graduated from **Istanbul University**'s Law School, he obtained a Ph.D. degree in law from Cologne University in Germany. Türk, who served as minister of state and of defense, is presently minister of justice. He is looked upon as one of the politicians who may succeed **Bülent Ecevit** in the **Democratic Left Party**.

TÜRKEŞ, ALPARSLAN (1917–1997). Colonel and politician. Türkeş was tried in 1944 for his "racist-Turanist" views, convicted, and then acquitted in 1945. He graduated from the American War Academy and Infantry School (1948). An important member of the junta that carried out the 1961 **military** intervention, he served as undersecretary of the prime ministry during the ensuing National Unity Committee (NUC) rule. Türkeş was a member of the Group of **Fourteen** in the NUC that opposed handing over power to the civilian governments, and consequently he was retired on September 22, 1960, and unceremoniously sent to the Turkish legation in India. He returned to Turkey on February 23, 1963, entered the **Republican Peasant's Nation Party** on March 31, 1965, and became the party's chairman in August 1965. Türkeş developed his doctrine of "Nine Lights," which emphasized nationalism. In February 1969, the party's name was changed to **Nationalist Action Party** (NAP). Türkeş served as minister of state and deputy prime minister in the First and Second Nationalist Front governments (March 31, 1975–June 13, 1977 and August 1–December 31, 1977). He was tried following the 1980 military intervention on the grounds that the NAP youth organizations were involved in right-wing political violence in the 1970s. He formed the **Nationalist Labor Party** on July 7, 1983, and became its chairman. He entered Parliament on October 21, 1991.

Young Türkeş for a while toyed with the idea of ethnic nationalism. In the 1970s he took communism as the most serious threat to Turkey, and to deal with it he was not averse to resorting to militancy. He also thought some degree of authoritarianism was necessary in order to modernize the country. From the 1980s onward, Türkeş left behind ethnic nationalism, his tendency toward militancy, and authoritarianism.

TÜRK-İŞ. Turkish acronym for the Confederation of Turkish Unions. *See* INTEREST GROUPS.

TÜRKLER, KEMAL (1926–1980). Unionist. He rose to prominence in the metal workers union in **Istanbul**. In 1967, he was one of the founders of the left-wing trade unions confederation **DİSK**. Later, he became president of that confederation. Rightist militants assassinated him in 1980.

TÜSİAD (TURKISH INDUSTRIALISTS' AND BUSINESSMEN'S ASSOCIATION). Set up in 1971, TÜSİAD is a voluntary **interest group** association that represents the largest, most modern, and politically most influential holding companies, the bulk of which are based in **Istanbul**. It has always been a proponent of limiting the role of the state in the economy, reforming the economic bureaucracy, and creating an efficient and competitive market economy in Turkey. In recent years, TÜSİAD has become critical of the role the **military** plays in Turkey (through the **National Security Council**) and called for further democratization of politics.

TÜZÜN, FERİT (1929–1977). Composer. Tüzün worked with Fritz Lehmann, Adolf Mennerich, and Gothold Lessing at the Munich Staatliche Hochschule für Musik. He was director of the **Ankara** State **Opera and Ballet**. In those works of his in which one comes across Turkish folk motifs, he developed his themes in a personal style, using colors and rhythms of folk songs. At the same time, his works reflected the influence of such contemporary composers as Stravinsky and Bartók. For him, the content of a musical piece was more important than its form.

Tüzün's best-known work is from the ballet *Çeşmebaşı.* His other works include *The Ears of Midas* (opera), *Lullaby, Symphony, Anatolia, Turkish Cappriccio* (orchestra), *Trio/Violin, Piano and Violoncello, Duo/Violin and Piano* (chamber music), and *Pieces for Piano, Thèmes et Variations,* and *Canzonetta and Gavotta* (piano).

"TWELFTH OF JULY DECLARATION." Made on July 12, 1947, by President **İsmet İnönü.** İnönü defended the opposition *Demokrat* **Party** (DP), accused by authoritarian Prime Minister **Recep Peker** of trying to come to power through revolutionary means. İnönü pointed out that the DP was acting within a legal framework and must be allowed to carry out its activities under the same conditions as the government party—the **Republican People's Party**. The declaration accelerated the transition to democracy in Turkey.

– U –

ULEMA. High-ranking members of the religious institution; the members of the Ottoman *İlmiyye* [professorial] class. *See also* ISLAM.

ULUS [Nation]. The **Republican People's Party** newspaper in the 1950s. It succeeded *Hakimiyet-i Milliye.*

ULUSU, BÜLEND (1923–). Admiral and politician. Ulusu served as commander of the naval forces between August 9, 1977, and August 30, 1980. He was appointed prime minister by the 1980–1983 **military** regime. On November 6, 1983, he entered Parliament on the **Nationalist Democracy Party's** ticket, but as an independent. His active political life ended in 1987.

UNITED STATES. Turkish-U.S. relations reach back in time. The first high point in those relations was the American support of Turkey in March 1947 in the form of the Truman Doctrine, which started a period of close relations between the two countries. Until the 1960s, they had rather harmonious and warm relations. Starting in 1952, Turkey and the United States worked as staunch allies within the framework of the **North Atlantic Treaty Organization** (NATO). During the 1950s, the United States also extended economic aid to Turkey (*see* FOREIGN AID). The only sore point during the 1950s was that while the United States wanted Turkey to use its economic aid for bolstering the Turkish economy, the *Demokrat* governments of the time tended to use that aid for political purposes as well. During the 1960s, relations between the two countries became problematic. Leftist groups in Turkey, which flourished because of the liberal provisions of the 1961 **constitution**, systematically pursued a policy of anti-Americanism. In 1964, U.S. President Lyndon Johnson sent a letter to Turkish Prime Minister **İsmet İnönü**, in which he warned that if Turkey intervened in **Cyprus** and the

Soviet Union (*see* RUSSIA) used arms to stop Turkey, NATO would not consider Soviet action as directed against a NATO member and would not come to Turkey's aid. This brought the relations between the two countries almost to the breaking point. İnönü expressed Turkish sentiment by saying, "A new world order would be established and Turkey would take its proper place in that new order." The next critical development was the U.S. arms embargo of Turkey on the grounds that during its 1974 intervention in Cyprus, Turkey had used weapons that could be utilized only in NATO operations. The embargo was lifted only in 1978. A lingering sore point in Turkish-American relations is the ratio the United States maintains in its aid to Turkey and **Greece**: for every dollar allocated to Turkey as military assistance, Greece receives 70 cents of aid. Turks consider this ratio unfair because they think that Turkey has made a far greater contribution to NATO than Greece. Despite such setbacks and friction-prone policies and action, since Turkey has essentially been devoted to democracy and the free market economy and has been a strategically important country for the United States, Washington considered its ties with **Ankara** significant. The legal basis of the relations between the two countries during the last two decades is the Defense and Economic Agreement (DECA) signed in 1980. According to the DECA, Turkey authorizes the United States to participate in joint defense measures at specified Turkish Armed Forces installations. The United States provides security assistance to Turkey in the form of contributions to the modernization of the Turkish army. In the first part of the 1990s, the annual security assistance in question was around $500 million.

Turkish-American relations reached a new high point during the Gulf crisis that erupted in August 1990 and the ensuing **Gulf War**. Turkey was one of the first countries to enforce an economic embargo on **Iraq**. During the war, Turkey allowed American planes to make sorties to Iraq from bases in Turkey. Throughout the armed clashes, U.S. President George H. W. Bush and Turkish President **Turgut Özal** continuously consulted each other over the phone. In March 1991, President Bush and his wife hosted the Özals at Camp David. In July 1991, President Bush visited Turkey, this being the first visit by a U.S. president in 32 years. At both encounters, the two presidents reaffirmed their countries' determination to develop close cooperation in every field. In the post-Bush and Özal era, too, relations between the two countries have remained close and amicable. The United States supported Turkey's accession to the **European Union** (EU) and the **Baku-Ceyhan pipeline**. The United States views with satisfaction the increased Turkey-**Israel** rapprochement. In return, Turkey readily took part in America's war against terrorism. On the other hand, the two countries' views on certain issues differ. The United States wishes to maintain a nonflying zone in northern Iraq, to extend aid to the **Kurds** there, and see Saddam Hussein removed from power, while Turkey is disturbed by the de facto autonomy of the Kurds in northern Iraq lest it be a stepping stone toward a sovereign Kurdish state in the region. Turkey wishes to improve its economic relations with Iraq, including the reopening of the pipeline from Iraq to the port city of Yumurtalık in southern

Turkey. Similarly, while the United States wishes to see a rapid resolution to the Cyprus problem, Turkey is reluctant to agree to an "unjust" solution for the sake of agreement. Finally, the United States joins the EU in urging Turkey to improve its **human rights** record. On this issue, Turkey has no reservations and continues its endeavors concerning that problem. In 2000, the U.S. government began seeking ways and means of facilitating investments by American firms in southeastern Turkey. The United States has been one of Turkey's leading **trade** partners. The trade volume between the two countries was $570 million in 1980, $1.7 billion in 1985, $3.3 billion in 1990, and $5.5 billion in 1999.

USMAN, MAZHAR OSMAN (1884–1961). Doctor and professor. Usman attended Munich and Berlin Universities. He was a pioneer in the modern treatment of psychological and psychiatric disorders in Turkey. He was elected honorary member of neurological associations in **Germany**, **France**, and the **United States**.

USMANBAŞ, İLHAN (1921–). Composer. He studied with David Zirkin. Usmanbaş received the Fromm Music Award for his *String Quartet '47* (**United States**, 1955) and the Koussevitzky Award for his *Music with a Poem* (United States, 1958). He won first prizes in the Wieniawsky Competition with his composition entitled *A Jump into Space* (Poland, 1966) and a ballet music contest with his *Music for Ballet* (Switzerland, 1969). In the 1945–1952 period, having been influenced by Stravinsky and Hindemith, Usmanbaş placed emphasis on modal and tonal structure. In the years 1952 to 1960, he moved toward serialism. In the 1960–1970 decade, Usmanbaş used mobile forms and made aleatory (chance) compositions. In later years, he experimented with minimal music. His work other than the ones noted above includes *Where Do the Clouds Go?* (ballet), *Eine Kleine Nacht Musik, Symphony No. 1, Symphony No. 2, Symphony No. 3, Perpetium Mobile, Shadows, Bursting Sinfonietta* (orchestra), *Sonata for Violin and Piano, Three Paintings by Dali, Three Sonatinas, Octet Winds, Great Rotation, Trio di tré soli* (chamber music), *Six Preludes, They Were Immortal Sea Stones,* and *Questionnaire* (piano).

UŞAKLIGİL, HALİT ZİYA (1866–1945). Novelist. Uşaklıgil was fond of using artificial Turkish and a complicated story line. His most popular novels are *The Blue and the Black* [Mai ve Siyah] and *Forbidden Love* [Aşk-ı Memnu].

UŞAKLIGİL, ÖMER BEDRETTİN (1904–1946). Poet. Uşaklıgil belonged to the Five Syllabists group (on this group, *see* LITERATURE). He concentrated on the themes of nature and romantic interpretations of human sentiments, longing, and unrequited love. *The Drunkards of the Sea* [Deniz Sarhoşları] and *The Marbles of the Blond Maiden* [Sarıkız Mermerleri] are examples of his poetry.

UZUNÇARŞILI, İSMAİL HAKKI (1888–1977). Historian and member of the Turkish Historical Society since 1931. Uzunçarşılı wrote his well-known history of the Ottoman Empire from its inception until the end of the 18th century. He also produced invaluable works on the structure of the Ottoman government. Among his books are *Introduction to the Ottoman Government Organization* [Osmanlı Devleti Teşkilâtına Medhal], *Court Organization in the Ottoman State* [Osmanlı Devletinin Saray Teşkilâtı], *Ottoman History* [Osmanlı Tarihi] (four volumes), *Central and Naval Organization in the Ottoman Empire* [Osmanlı Devletinin Merkez ve Bahriye Teşkilâtı], and *Religious Institution in the Ottoman Empire* [Osmanlı Devletinin İlmiyye Teşkilâtı].

– Ü –

ÜLGENER, SABRİ (1911–1983). Ülgener introduced Keynesian economics to economic studies in Turkey, and for the first time examined the Ottoman-Turkish society in the light of Max Weber's notion of Protestant ethic. His most important work is *The Moral and Cultural Problems in the History of Our Economic Decline* [İktisadi İnhitat Tarihimizin Ahlâk ve Zihniyet Meseleri] (1951).

ÜLKEN, HİLMİ ZİYA (1901–1974). Professor of sociology and philosophy. Ülken strived to base his work on philosophical premises; he therefore looked at issues from a broad perspective. He had a didactic style. His best-known book is *The History of Contemporary Thought in Turkey* [Türkiye'de Çağdaş Düşünce Tarihi].

ÜLKÜ. Journal of the **People's Houses** movement.

ÜMMET. A community of people who believe in a prophet; often used to refer to Muslims, in the meaning of the community of the faithful.

ÜNVER, SÜHEYL (1898–). Professor of medicine and art researcher, best known for his contributions to Turkish miniature, gilding, and ornamentation.

ÜREN, EŞREF (1897–1984). Painter. In the late 1920s, Üren worked in André Lhote's art studio in Paris. He became a member of the D Group in Turkey (on this group, *see* FINE ARTS). Üren was given the title of the State Artist in 1981. He is best known for landscapes, in which he perceived nature from a panoramic perspective.

ÜRGÜPLÜ, SUAT HAYRİ (1903–1981). Politician. Ürgüplü served as member of Parliament between 1936 and 1946 and acted as minister of customs and monopolies (March 15, 1943–February 19, 1946). Following this ministry, he was tried at the High Court of Justice on the grounds that he was involved in some irregularities, but was acquitted. He was elected to Parliament in 1950 on the *Demokrat* **Party**

ticket, but as an independent. Appointed ambassador to Bonn (1952), London (1955), Washington (1957), and Madrid (1960), he then became senator in 1961 and served as speaker of the Senate between October 28, 1961, and November 6, 1963. Ürgüplü headed the February 20–October 22, 1965, coalition government as prime minister. He quit active politics when his term in the Senate ended in 1972.

– V –

VÂLÂ NUREDDİN (1901–1967). Journalist. Vâlâ Nureddin studied at the Vienna Trade Academy and graduated from Moscow East University. He is best known for his masterfully written columns in newspapers. He was a prolific writer with wide interests.

VILLAGE INSTITUTES. *See* TONGUÇ, İSMAİL HAKKI.

VIRTUE PARTY (VP)/FAZİLET PARTİSİ (FP). Set up on November 17, 1997, it is the successor party to the **Welfare Party** (WP). The former members of the WP, which had been closed on January 17, 1998, by the Constitutional Court, joined the VP on February 24,1998. On May 15, 1998, **Recai Kutan** became the chairman of the party, taking over that position from the caretaker leader, İsmail Alptekin. As compared to its predecessor parties—the **National Order Party**, **National Salvation Party**, and WP—there has been a greater tendency to turn it into a mass party. Furthermore, a liberal group within the party has sought to democratize the internal functioning of the party. They were not successful; **Necmettin Erbakan**, who was chairman of the predecessor parties and who has been banned from active politics by the Constitutional Court, continued to rule the party from behind the scenes. On May 7, 1999, the chief prosecutor asked the Constitutional Court to ban the VP, claiming that the party attempted to form a state based on **Islam**. The court closed the party.

– W –

WATER ISSUE. It is predicted that the rapid population growth in the Middle East will soon lead to a disastrous water shortage in the area. In the Middle East, water is now regarded as a more critical resource than oil. The problem has become aggravated by severe droughts in recent decades. That transboundary watercourses are the main sources of water in the Middle East adds a particular twist to the problem.

The Euphrates and Tigris Rivers that originate in Turkey are two such transboundary watercourses. For a decade now, Turkey has started building a number of facilities that would make greater use of the waters of these two rivers for irrigation and hydropower generation. The aim has been the economic and social development of one of the most underdeveloped regions of the country—the southeast (*see* SOUTHEASTERN ANATOLIAN PROJECT). Turkey is not a water-rich country. In 1993, water quantities per capita were 10,000 cubic meters per year in the water-rich countries; in Turkey, it was 1,830 cubic meters per year. That same year, those figures for **Iraq** were 2,110 and for **Syria** 1,420, indicating that Iraq is in a better position than Turkey and that Syria is not terribly worse off. Still, Turkey unilaterally pledged to maintain the flow of water from the Euphrates-Tigris at the Syrian border of 500 cubic meters per second. Syria and Iraq, however, continued to object to Turkey's making greater use of the waters of the two rivers.

The three countries could not come to an agreement because they have not even been able to agree on the very definition of the river system. For Turkey, the Euphrates and Tigris together form a "transboundary water system"; for Syria and Iraq, they constitute "international waters." Turkey claims sovereignty over the rivers because it is an upstream country; Syria and Iraq argue that the three countries should have equal rights. What constitutes an "equitable" and "reasonable" distribution of water is at the heart of the problem. While Turkey sees it as a water management problem, that is, as optimal use of water by identifying the water needs of all three countries, the other two riparian countries feel the issue is one of "rights." Turkey has also considered providing water to the Middle East from its other rivers. One such project was the "Peace Pipeline" proposed by Turkey in 1986; it involved Turkey's construction of two pipelines to carry water from the Seyhan and Ceyhan Rivers in southern Turkey to Syria, Jordan, Saudi Arabia, Kuwait, Oman, United Arab Emirates, Qatar, and Bahrain. The project required a very simple technology and it was estimated that the project was more economical than the alternative water supply process of desalination. It was thought that the project would be attractive to international finance circles. The only concern was the possibility of sabotage because the area is politically unstable. This project was never realized.

Another project was the "Manavgat Project," under which water would be transported to the Middle East in "plastic balloons" towed behind ships. The project could not be pursued when the Arab countries thought that **Israel** would also buy water from Turkey and that Turkey would use the project to further upgrade its relations with Israel. At the turn of the century, Turkey was still not exporting water to the Arab countries. On the other hand, in recent years Turkish-Israeli relations became quite close. At the same time, the probability of Israel no longer availing itself of the water resources in the Golan Heights and the West Bank should the Arab-Israeli peace process progress smoothly led Israel to be very much interested in importing water from Turkey. In early 2000, the two countries started having talks on the issue. At the end of 2001, they still had not agreed upon a project.

WELFARE PARTY (WP)/REFAH PARTİSİ (RP). Founded on July 19, 1983, as a successor party to the **National Salvation Party** (NSP). The WP had links with the Muslim **fundamentalists** who had supported the NSP. The Welfare

Party could not participate in the November 1983 elections because the **military** continuously vetoed the party's founding members, disqualifying them through the use of a special clause that remained in force during the military rule of 1980–1983. The party's votes remained below 10 percent in the elections it took part in during the 1980s. In the October 1991 general elections, the WP joined forces with the **Nationalist Labor Party** and **Reformist Democracy Party** and could thus overcome the nationwide election barrier (10 percent) and return deputies to Parliament. In the 1994 local elections, the party did quite well and captured the metropolitan mayoralities of several urban centers, including **Istanbul** and **İzmir**. The WP made good use of its control of municipalities, and garnered the plurality of votes in the 1995 general elections. This was followed by the formation of WP-**True Path Party** coalition in June 1996 and the party's leader **Necmettin Erbakan** becoming prime minister. The coalition lasted only one year; in the face of pressure from the military as well as the leading **interest group** associations, Erbakan had to resign in June 1997. On January 16, 1998, the Constitutional Court closed the party on the grounds that it had acted against the secular premises of the Republic.

WESTERNIZATION. Intellectual current developed during the 1910s. There were partial and total Westernization versions. The proponents of partial Westernization made a distinction between technical and "real" civilization (read "culture"). "Real" civilization could not be transferred from one country to another and, in any case, "Islamic civilization was far superior to the Western one." A leading spokesman of this view was Celal Nuri. Total Westernization was summed up by **Abdullah Cevdet** as follows: "There is no second civilization; civilization means European civilization, and it must be imported with both its roses and thorns." The founders of the Republic adopted the second version of Westernization.

WOMEN. Atatürk and his associates were interested in nothing less than a complete modernization of social life in Turkey. Their notion of civilization, which was contrasted to "culture," implied among other things a "contemporary lifestyle." Atatürk thus insisted on the active participation of women in all walks of life on a par with men. This was regarded as part of the efforts to elevate people to a higher cultural level. **Ziya Gökalp's** earlier claim that "feminism is an integral part of Turkish values" had prepared the ground for assuming (within the framework of the Turkish Historical Thesis of the 1930s) that Turks had in the past contributed to the development of that high culture referred to as civilization and that that culture perceived women as men's equal. In Republican Turkey, the promotion of women's rights had been a very important aspect of the Atatürkist cultural revolution of substituting reason for "retrogressive **Islamic** tenets." **Secularism** was the gist of this cultural revolution. An important dimension of this principle was the emphasis placed on women's rights in a Muslim country. Furthermore, the goal was to improve first and foremost the status of the "Anatolian women" who "had always constituted the backbone of the community." In addition to granting women political rights (women in Turkey obtained the right to vote and be elected in municipal elections in 1930 and in the general elections in 1934), perhaps more importantly, women were no longer expected to live behind shuttered windows. It was now regarded as civilized for husband and wife to visit with others and participate in entertainment "*en famille*." Women quickly began to emulate their European counterparts in fashion. Such behavior patterns led to a nationalistic-patriotic reaction. According to the detractors, women were to be civilized not for personally leading a Western lifestyle but in order to participate in public life as teachers and nurses and thus become useful to their country. The Atatürkist woman was to be a symbol of nationalistic civilization. The Republican woman had to have both a modern appearance and social responsibility. In 1926, the Swiss Civil Law was adopted almost intact in Turkey. Women were thus liberated from the constraining provisions of Islamic law in such matters as family relations, inheritance, and the like. However, in some areas, like equality between wife and husband, the law still had conservative provisions, such as the inability of the wife to use her maiden name or work without the husband's permission. Still, the new civil law had a revolutionary impact; on the whole, it brought about near equality between men and women in a Muslim country. In the late 1990s, further progress was made on this issue. Married women were enabled to use their maiden names; the joint representation of men and women in marital unity was accepted; the wife and husband could now together determine the place of their home; and they would have equal ownership of assets acquired during the marriage. In 2001, the Civil Law was further amended. Among other things, a husband is no longer the "master of the household," and thus wife and husband have equal rights and responsibilities. Over the decades, women—particularly in urban Turkey—have made considerable progress in attaining literacy, obtaining an **education**, and having a profession. In 1935, female literacy was 10 percent; in 1990, it stood at 69.3. In 1994–1995, 88.6 percent of females of grade school age attended school. That same year, the corresponding figures for secondary low and secondary high schools were 52.5 percent and 39.5 percent, and the percentage of female students at the college level was 13.8 percent. In 1995, women constituted 30 percent of the labor force. That same year, the share of women in higher education was the same. In 1999, 16.5 percent of the membership of the **Turkish Academy of Sciences** was female—the highest percentage among the academies in the world. As a consequence of the Atatürkist revolution, women in Turkey were socially liberated, but, until recently, this was not accompanied by sexual liberation. The price that women paid for their liberation was suppression of their gender (and their individualism). Women were expected to maintain their modesty. Men continued to address them as their "sisters" or "sisters-in-law." As of the early 1980s, this "state feminism," later reinforced by "revolutionary left" and Islamic traditional ideologies, was challenged by the proponents of "autonomous feminism." Novels and movies began to emphasize female individualism and gender. Women were encouraged to discover their sexuality. Consequently, from the early 1990s onward, the question of women once again tended to occupy the center stage, this time in the debate between Atatürkists, revolutionary leftists, and Islamists on the one hand and "autonomous feminists" on the other.

WORLD WAR I. In November 1914, the Ottoman Empire joined the war on the side of the Central powers (**Germany** and Austria) against the Allied powers (**France**, **Great Britain**, and **Russia**). The Turks fought on several fronts—the Romanian and Galician fronts in Europe, the Dardanelles **Strait** in the west, the Caucacus on the east, **Iraq**, **Syria**, Palestine, and Arabia in the Middle East. It was on the Dardanelles that Colonel Mustafa Kemal (future **Atatürk**) made a name for himself. However, along with the Central powers, the Turks lost the war. The Allied victors forced the Ottoman Empire to sign the Treaty of **Sèvres**. If it had been implemented, Turkey would have had no more territory than an enclave in Anatolia. The Turks resorted to a **War of Independence** and, as a consequence, Turkey came to have its present borders minus the province of **Alexandretta**, which became part of Turkey in 1939.

WORLD WAR II. Turkey stayed out of this war by playing a balancing act between the Allied powers and the Central powers. In June 1941, Turkey signed a nonaggression pact with Germany. In 1943 and 1944, the Allies, led by British Prime Minister Winston Churchill, pressured Turkey to join the war on their side. For this purpose, in December 1943, U.S. President Franklin D. Roosevelt and Churchill met Turkey's then President **İsmet İnönü** in Cairo. Turkey did not refuse to take part in the war against the Central powers; yet Turkey asked for military aid, and kept insisting that what was offered was less than adequate. Turkey declared war against **Germany** only at the closing hours of the war (February 23, 1944), and thus was invited to become a founding member of the United Nations.

– Y –

YALÇIN, HÜSEYİN CAHİT (1874–1957). Novelist and critic journalist. Yalçın is best known for his often liberal but sometimes dogmatic polemics. During the 1930s, he edited the important periodical *Fikir Hareketleri* [Intellectual Trends]. His two books—*Literary Memoirs* [Edebi Hatıralar] and *Political Memoirs* [Siyasal Anılar]—are particularly important.

YALMAN, AHMET EMİN (1885–1972). Journalist. Yalman graduated from Columbia University. From 1918 on, he published several magazines and dailies. His strongly expressed liberal views often displeased the authorities. Consequently, Yalman was frequently prosecuted and once convicted. Yalman was a proponent of "Western democracy." His journalism, based on firsthand observations, created a new genre in the Turkish press. He published *Turkey in My Time* and *What I Have Seen and Experienced in Recent History* [Yakın Tarihte Gördüklerim ve Geçirdiklerim], two volumes.

YAŞAR KEMAL (1922–). Novelist, journalist, and short story writer. Yaşar Kemal was a realist who in his work depicted poetically the natural beauty of the Çukurova (plain) in southern Turkey and life in the countryside. He based his work on epics, songs, and popular **literature**. His well-known novel *Thin Memet* [İnce Memed] in two volumes (Eng., first volume, *Memed My Hawk*; second volume, *They Burn the Thistles*), the tale of a heroic bandit in the **Taurus Mountains**, made him internationally famous. The novel was translated into 26 languages and reprinted. Yaşar Kemal produced several other important novels—*The Main Stay* [Orta Direk] (Eng., *The Wind from the Plain*), *Iron Earth and Copper Sky* [Yer Demir, Gök Bakır] (Eng., *Iron Earth, Copper Sky*), *Immortal Grass* [Ölmez Otu] (Eng., *The Undying Grass*), *The Murder in the Iron Market* [Demirciler Çarşısı Cinayeti], and *Yusufcuk Yusuf,* and epic novels, *Three Anatolian Myths* [Üç Anadolu Efsanesi] (Eng., *Anatolian Tales*), *The Myth of Ararat* [Ağrıdağı Efsanesi] (Eng., *The Legend of Ararat*), and *The Legend of a Thousand Bulls* [Binboğalar Efsanesi] (Eng., *Legend of a Thousand Bulls*).

YAŞARGİL, M. GAZİ (1925–). Professor of medicine and honorary member of the **Turkish Academy of Sciences**. Yaşargil completed his medical education at Friedrick von Schiller University in Germany and Basel University in Switzerland. He worked at Zurich University in Switzerland, Vermont University, and the Arkansas University of Medical Sciences. He was given several medals for his innovative work in neurosurgery, including one by the World Federation of Neurosurgery Association, as well as several awards, one of them being the Robert Bing Award of the Swiss Academy of Medical Sciences. The November 1999 issue of *Neurosurgery*—the official publication of the U.S. Neurological Association—selected Yaşargil as Man of the Century in neurology.

YEKTA, RAUF (1871–1935). Started musicology in the modern sense in Turkey. He devised an accurate system of notation for the traditional art music (on traditional art music, *see* MUSIC) and published a series of musical scores.

YENİ FORUM. *See* FORUM/YENİ FORUM.

YESARİ, MAHMUT (1895–1945). Novelist and playwright. Yesari focused on the problems of people from different cross-sections of society during the early years of the Republic. Poverty, the importance of money in life, conformity to traditions, and love were the basic themes of his novels, which included *Shepherd Star* [Çoban Yıldızı], *Woodcock* [Çulluk], *Young Girl with a Grey Hair* [Aksaçlı Genç Kız], *Swallows* [Kırlangıçlar], and *Water Flies* [Su Sinekleri].

YILMAZ, MESUT (1947–). Politician. Yılmaz did graduate work at Cologne University, Germany. He worked in the private sector before entering Parliament in 1983. He served as minister of state, culture and tourism, and foreign affairs between 1983 and 1991, and as prime minister in July 5, 1991–November 20, 1991, March 1996–June 1996, and July 1997–November 1998. Presently, Yılmaz is chairman of the **Motherland Party** (MP) and deputy prime minister in the **Democratic Left Party-Nationalist Action Party**-MP coalition government. As deputy prime minister, he is responsible for coordinating efforts toward Turkey's accession to the **European Union** (EU) as a full member. Yılmaz is a liberal who tries to combine it with conservatism.

YOUNG OTTOMANS. Formed in 1865 as a secret association that called for freedom and justice. The members of the association, including **Şinasi**, **Namık Kemal**, **Ziya Pasha**, and Ali Suavi, thought that the salvation of the Ottoman Empire depended on the enactment of a constitution and convening of an assembly, the elected members of which would assume the country's administration. The Young Ottomans were organized in the Young Ottoman Society and expressed their views in, among other organs, the daily *Tasvir-i Efkâr*.

YOUNG TURKS. In 1878, **Abdülhamit II** prorogued the Parliament and started to rule the country in an authoritarian fashion. Gradually, a reaction developed against him among intellectuals. In 1889, five students at the Imperial Medical School—İshak Sükûti, Mehmet Reşit, **Abdullah Cevdet**, İbrahim Temo, and Hüseyinzade Ali (Turan)—formed a secret organization—the Association for the Union of Ottomans. The association called for freedom and justice and aimed at removing Abdülhamit II from power. In 1895, the association took the name of **Committee for Union and Progress**. As the Committee came under pressure from the authorities, branches were opened abroad. **Ahmet Rıza** began publishing the journal *Consultation* [Meşveret] in 1895 out of Paris and İshak Sükûti, **Mehmed Murat (Mizancı)**, and Abdullah Cevdet started the journal *Ottoman* [Osmanlı] in 1897 in Geneva. Members of the Young Turk group in Europe gradually fell into conflict among themselves. In 1899, Abdülhamit II managed to lure some of them back to **Istanbul**. However, that same year, Abdülhamit II's brother-in-law Damad Mahmut Pasha and the latter's sons **Prince Sabahaddin** and Prince Lütfullah gave a new impetus to the Young Turk movement, although the falling-out among the Young Turks continued during the following years. In 1902, at the initiative of Prince Sabahaddin, the First Congress of Ottoman Liberals was convened in Paris. In 1907, the Ottoman Freedom Association in Salonica merged with the Paris branch of the Committee for Union and Progress. The Second Congress of Ottoman Liberals, convened toward the end of the same year, made a resolution to remove Abdülhamit II from power, if necessary by force. The Young Turks saw their aims realized when Abdülhamit II felt obliged to start the Second Constitutional Period in 1908. The **sultan** was forced to step down the next year. In the post-1909 period, some members of the Young Turk group took on governmental jobs, some remained in the opposition against the new regime (which increasingly adopted an authoritarian posture), some among the latter continued their struggle against the new regime abroad, and some continued their activities on an intellectual plane.

YOUTH. Turkey has a rather young population, with approximately one-fourth of the total populaton under 24 years of age. The state provides various services to youth, coordinates such activities as scouting, youth camps, chess, and other social and cultural activities, and helps to solve the financial and housing problems of college students. In 1998, there were 82 Youth Centers in Turkey. They organized activities to increase the knowledge and capabilities of youth in art, science, **sports**, cartoon drawing, handicrafts, and the like. Young people are encouraged to participate in international activities organized for the youth, and they are provided support for this purpose. Among other things, the state organizes an international Folk Dance **Festival** with the objective of strengthening cross-cultural friendship and fraternity.

YÖN. Weekly, founded in 1961. The organ of the non-Marxist, left-wing radicals led by **Doğan Avcıoğlu**, who flirted with the interventionist radicals within the **military**.

YUNUS EMRE (1238?–1320). The great humanist. Yunus Emre helped to develop *tasavvuf* [mysticism]—the heterodox method of explaining **Islam**. His most prominent works are *Collection of Poems* [Divan] and *A Pamphlet of Advice* [Risaletü'n-Mushiye].

YURDAKUL, MEHMET EMİN (1869–1914). Poet, patriot, and politician. Yurdakul was a prominent representative of the National Literary Movement (on this movement, *see* LITERATURE). In his work, he glorified the Turkish revolution and its leader **Atatürk**. Yurdakul also produced realistic poetry, oriented toward social reform. His poetry included *Oh Turk, Awake* [Ey, Türk Uyan], *The Legend of My Army* [Ordumun Destanı], and *Toward Turan* [Turan'a Doğru].

YÜCEL, HASAN-ÂLİ (1897–1961). Educator, poet, and politician. As minister of **education**, Yücel established the **village institutes** in 1941. Another significant project of his was the World Classics Series, under which more than 500 foreign masterpieces were translated into Turkish and published. Yücel wrote the literary criticisms *A Collected View of Turkish Literature* [Türk Edebiyatına Toplu Bir Bakış] and *Goethe: The Story of a Genius* [Goethe, Bir Deha'nın Romanı].

– Z –

ZİYA GÖKALP (1876–1924). Sociologist, educator, and patriot. A pioneer in Turkish sociology, Ziya Gökalp adopted a positivist approach to social problems. He acted as an ideologue for the **Committee for Union and Progress**. He defended the view that Turks should abandon **Ottomanism** and **Islamism/Pan-Islamism** and adopt **Turkism** instead. He felt that Turks should subscribe to Western civilization but retain their culture. He first toyed with ethnic nationalism, then he adopted cultural nationalism. Ziya Gökalp provided the Turkist movement with the most coherent ideology. His best-known collection of poems is *Red Apple* (the goal of Turkdom) [Kızıl Elma]. He wrote two books: *To Become Turkish, Muslim, and Modern* [Türkleşmek, Islamlaşmak, Muasırlaşmak] (published in English as *Turkish Nationalism and Western Civilization*) and *The Principles of Turkism* [Türkçülüğün Esasları].

ZİYA PASHA (1825–1880). Poet and playwright. Ziya Pasha had a positive impact during the second part of the 19th century on the development of a new Turkish **literature** in prose for the **theater**, novel, and social commentary that was absent in the traditional Ottoman literature. His best-known works are *Ode to Glory* [Zafername], *Ruins* [Harabat], and *Stanzaic Verses* [Terci-i Bend ve Terkib-î Bend].

ZORLU, FATİN RÜŞTÜ (1910–1961). Diplomat and politician. Zorlu graduated from Paris Political Science Faculty and Geneva Law School. He was Turkey's ambassador to the **North Atlantic Treaty Organization**. In 1954, he entered Parliament and served as acting foreign minister and deputy premier (May 17, 1954–November 30, 1955), minister of state (July 28–November 1, 1957), and foreign minister (November 25, 1957–May 27, 1960). He was tried by the High Court of Justice following the May 27, 1960, **military** intervention and was given a death sentence, along with **Adnan Menderes** and **Hasan Polatkan**, that was carried out.

ZURICH TREATY. Signed between **Great Britain**, Turkey, and **Greece** in 1959 to guarantee the independence of the Republic of Cyprus (*see* CYPRUS PROBLEM).

Appendix

TURKEY ID CARD

Geography and Resources

Total Area: 779,452 square kilometers; Thrace (Europe): 23,764 km^2; Anatolia (Asia): 755,688 km^2; maximum length: 1,565 km; average width: 550 km.

Coastline: total 8,333 km; the Aegean: 2,805 km; the Mediterranean: 1,577 km; the Black Sea: 1,695 km; the Marmara Sea: 927 km.

Frontiers: total 2,753 km; Syria: 877 km; the Russian Federation countries of Georgia, Armenia, and the Nakhichevan Autonomous Region, 610 km; Iran: 454 km; Greece: 212 km.

Land: 30 percent arable, 4 percent permanent crops, 12 percent meadows and pastures, 26 percent forest and woodland, 28 percent other.

Lakes: 8,933 km^2. In the order of size: Van, Tuz, Beyşehir, Eğridir, Akşehir, İznik, Burdur, Manyas, Acıgöl, Ulubat.

Mountains: Highest peak: Ağrı (Mt. Ararat), 5,165 meters; Kaçkar, 3,932 m; Erciyes 3,917 m; B. Hasan, 3,268 m; Nemrut, 2,828 m; Uludağ (Mt. Olympus), 2,543 m.

Population: 62,865,574 (November 1997 census).

Rivers: Kızılırmak, 1,355 km; Fırat (Euphrates), 971 km in Turkey; Sakarya, 824 km; Büyük Menderes, 584 km; Seyhan, 564 km, Aras, 548 km in Turkey; Dicle (Tigris), 523 km in Turkey; Yeşilırmak, 519 km; Ceyhan, 509 km; Porsuk, 488 km; Çoruh, 442 km; Gediz, 401 km.

Islands: Avşa Isles, Büyükada, Heybeliada, Kınalı, Burgaz, Sedef (Marmara Sea); Gökçeada, Bozcaada, Uzunada, Alibey (the Aegean); Karaada, Salih, Kekova (the Mediterranean).

Straits: Bosphorus, 29.9 km (links the Black Sea to the Marmara Sea); Dardanelles, 62 km (links the Marmara Sea to the Aegean).

Regions: Marmara, Aegean, Mediterranean, Black Sea, Central Anatolian, Eastern, Southeastern.

Climate: Three climatic zones: the Mediterranean (hot and dry summers, mild and wet winters), inland (hot and dry summers, cold and harsh winters), the Black Sea (temperate and wet all year long).

Major Hydroelectric Generators: Atatürk, Karakaya, Keban, Oymapınar, Gökçekaya, Hirfanlı, Hasan Uğurlu, Altınkaya, Kılıçkaya, Köklüce, Mezelet, Sarıyar, Gezende, Adıgüzel, Kesikköprü, Demirköprü, Kadıncık 1 and 2, Doğankent 1 and 2, Seyhan 1 and 2, Seyhan 1 and 2, Sır, Karacaören 1 and 2.

Major Thermoelectric Generators: Ambarlı, Hamitabat, Çatalağzı, Tunçbilek, Soma, Seyitömer, Kemerköy, Orhaneli, Yeniköy, Yatağan, Kangal, Çayırhan.

Agricultural Products: Barley, corn, cotton, figs, grapes, hazelnuts, oranges, mandarins, soy beans, sugar beets, sunflower seeds, tea, tobacco, wheat.

Natural Resources: Antimony, borate, borax, coal, copper, chromium, iron ore, lead, lignite, mangenese, oil, mangenese, meerschaum, mercury, phosphate, sulphur, zinc.

Administration

Official Language: Turkish. **Government type:** Parliamentary democracy. **Administrative Divisions:** 80 provinces. **Capital:** Ankara. **Currency:** Turkish lira. **Proclamation of Republic:** October 29, 1923. **Constitution:** Adopted in 1982; amendments in 1987, 1995, and 2001. **Legislature:** Unicameral, Grand National Assembly with 550 members (general elections every five years, last general elections on April 18, 1999; voting age 18). **Executive:** President with one seven-year term; Council of Ministers headed by prime minister. **Judiciary:** Independent, with Constitutional Court supervising conformity of statutes to the constitution. Major law codes based on French (administrative), German (commercial), Italian (penal), and Swiss (civil) law codes. **Religion:** Muslim 98 percent; Gregorian, Jewish, Catholic, Protestant, and other Christian denominations, 2.0 percent. Greek Orthodox and Armenian Patriarchates located in Istanbul.

International Organizations and Banks

Major International Organizations: United Nations (UN), European Parliament, European Union (EU) (European Union candidate member/member of Customs Union with EU), North Atlantic Treaty Organization (NATO), Organization for Economic Cooperation and Development (OECD), Organization of Security and Cooperation in Europe (OSCE), General Agreement on Tariffs and Trade (GATT), International Labor Organization (ILO), International Monetary Fund (IMF), United Nations Educational, Scientific, and Cultural Organization (UNESCO), Food and Agriculture Organization (FAO), International Development Bank (IDB), International Criminal Police Organization (INTERPOL).

Foreign Banks (with branch offices in Turkey): ABN Amnro Bank, Banca di Roma, Bank Mellat, Chase Manhatan, Citibank, Crédit Lyonnais, Crédit Suisse, Habib Bank, ING Bank, Islamic Development Bank, Rabobank Nederland, Société Générale, Westdeutsche Landesbank Girozentrale; **(with representative offices** in Turkey): American Express Bank, Banca Commerciale Italiana, Bank for Trade of Russian Federation, Bank für Handel und Effekten, Bank Kreiss, Bank of New York, Bank of Tokyo-Mitsibushi, Bankers Trust Company, Banque de Commerce et de Placements, Banque Indosuez, Banque Internationale de Commerce, Banque Nationale de Paris, CBI-TDB Union Bancaire Privée, Commerz Bank, Deutsche Bank, Dresdner Bank, Generale de Bank, Instituto Bancario San Paulo di Torino, Paribas, Sovran Bank, Sumitomo Bank, Taib Bank.

OTTOMAN SULTANS AND TURKISH PRESIDENTS AND PRIME MINISTERS

Ottoman Sultans

Sultans	Dates on Throne
Osman I*	1299–1324
Orhan	1334–1359
Murat I	1359–1389
Bayezit I (Thunderbolt)	1389–1402
The Interregnum	1402–1413
Mehmet I	1413–1421
Murat II	1421–1451
Mehmet II (the Conqueror)	1444, 1451–1481
Bayezit II	1481–1512
Selim I (the Tough)	1512–1520
Süleyman I (the Magnificent)	1520–1566
Selim II	1566–1574
Murat III	1574–1595
Mehmet III	1595–1603
Ahmet I	1603–1617
Mustafa I	1617–1618, 1622–1623
Osman II	1618–1622
Murat IV	1623–1640
İbrahim	1640–1648
Mehmet IV	1648–1687
Süleyman II	1687–1691
Ahmet II	1691–1695
Mustafa II	1695–1703
Ahmet III	1703–1730
Mahmut I	1730–1754
Osman III	1754–1757
Mustafa III	1757–1774
Abdülhamit I	1774–1789
Selim III	1789–1807
Mustafa IV	1807–1808
Mahmut II	1808–1839
Abdülmecit	1839–1861

Ottoman Sultans (continued)

Sultans	Dates on Throne
Abdülaziz	1861–1876
Abdülhamit II	1876–1909
Mehmet Reşat	1909–1918
Mehmet VI (Vahideddin)	1918–1922

*Names in bold indicates entry in Dictionary.

Presidents of Turkish Republic

Presidents	Dates in Office
Mustafa Kemal (Atatürk)*	October 1923–November 1938
İsmet (İnönü)	November 1938–May 1950
Celal Bayar	May 1950–May 1960
Cemal Gürsel Head of State (also Prime Minister)	May 1960–October 1961
Cemal Gürsel (also Prime Minister)	October 1961–March 1966
Cevdet Sunay	March 1966–March 1973
Fahri Korutürk	April 1973–April 1980
İhsan Sabri Çağlayangil (Acting)	April 1980–September 1980
Kenan Evren (Head of State)	September 1980–November 1982
Kenan Evren	November 1982–October 1989
Turgut Özal	October 1989–April 1993
Süleyman Demirel	April 1993–May 2000
Ahmet Necdet Sezer	May 2000–

*Here and below, the names in parentheses are family names adopted following the passage of the relevant act on June 21, 1934, effective January 1, 1935. There are entries in the Dictionary for all presidents.

Prime Ministers of Turkish Republic

Prime Minister	Dates in Office	Prime Minister's Party
İsmet (İnönü)	October 1923–March 1924	Republican People's Party
İsmet (İnönü)	March 1924–November 1924	Republican People's Party
Ali Fethi (Okyar)	November 1924–March 1925	Republican People's Party
İsmet (İnönü)	March 1925–November 1927	Republican People's Party
İsmet (İnönü)	November 1927–September 1930	Republican People's Party
İsmet (İnönü)	September 1930–May 1931	Republican People's Party
İsmet (İnönü)	May 1931–March 1935	Republican People's Party
İsmet (İnönü)	March 1935–November 1937	Republican People's Party
Celal Bayar	November 1937–November 1938	Republican People's Party
Celal Bayar	November 1938–January 1939	Republican People's Party
Refik Saydam	January 1939–April 1939	Republican People's Party
Refik Saydam	April 1939–July 1942	Republican People's Party
Şükrü Saraçoğlu	July 1942–March 1943	Republican People's Party

Prime Minister	Dates in Office	Prime Minister's Party
Şükrü Saraçoğlu	March 1943–August 1946	Republican People's Party
Recep Peker	August 1946–September 1947	Republican People's Party
Hasan Saka	September 1947–June 1948	Republican People's Party
Hasan Saka	June 1948–January 1949	Republican People's Party
Şemsettin Günaltay	January 1949–May 1950	Republican People's Party
Adnan Menderes	May 1950–March 1951	Demokratik Party
Adnan Menderes	March 1951–May 1954	Demokratik Party
Adnan Menderes	May 1954–November 1955	Demokratik Party
Adnan Menderes	December 1955–November 1957	Demokratik Party
Adnan Menderes	November 1957–May 1960	Demokratik Party
Cemal Gürsel	May 1960–January 1961	Interregnum
(also Head of State)		
Cemal Gürsel	January 1961–October 1961	Interregnum
(also Head of State)		
İsmet (İnönü)	November 1961–June 1962	Republican People's Party
İsmet (İnönü)	June 1962–December 1963	Republican People's Party
İsmet (İnönü)	December 1963–February 1965	Republican People's Party
Suat Hayri Ürgüplü	February 1965–October 1965	Independent
Süleyman Demirel	October 1965–October 1969	Justice Party
Süleyman Demirel	November 1969–February 1970	Justice Party
Süleyman Demirel	March 1970–March 1971	Justice Party
Nihat Erim	March 1971–December 1971	Interregnum
Nihat Erim	December 1971–April 1972	Interregnum
Ferit Melen	May 1972–April 1973	Independent
Naim Talu	April 1973–December 1973	Independent
Bülent Ecevit	January 1974–September 1974	Republican People's Party
Sadi Irmak	November 1974–March 1975	Independent
Süleyman Demirel	March 1975–June 1977	Justice Party
Bülent Ecevit	June 1977–July 1977	Republican People's Party
Süleyman Demirel	July 1977–December 1977	Justice Party
Bülent Ecevit	January 1978–October 1979	Republican People's Party
Süleyman Demirel	November 1979–September 1980	Justice Party
Bülend Ulusu	September 1980–November 1983	Interregnum
Turgut Özal	December 1983–December 1987	Motherland Party
Turgut Özal	December 1987–October 1989	Motherland Party
Yıldırım Akbulut	October 1989–June 1991	Motherland Party
Mesut Yılmaz	June 1991–November 1991	Motherland Party
Süleyman Demirel	November 1991–May 1993	True Path Party
Tansu Çiller	July 1993–September 1995	True Path Party
Tansu Çiller	October 1995–October 1995	True Path Party
Tansu Çiller	November 1995–February 1996	True Path Party
Mesut Yılmaz	March 1996–June 1996	Motherland Party
Necmettin Erbakan	July 1996–June 1997	Welfare Party
Mesut Yılmaz	July 1997–November 1998	Motherland Party
Bülend Ecevit	January 1999–April 1999	Democratic Left Party
Bülent Ecevit	April 1999–	Democratic Left Party

There are entries in the Dictionary for all prime ministers.

GENERAL ELECTIONS IN THE
REPUBLICAN PERIOD (1923 TO THE PRESENT)

First Turkish Republic, 1923–1960

July 21, 1946, Elections
Electoral system: Plurality system with multimember constituencies

Political Parties	Votes (%)*	Seats
Republican People's Party		396
Demokrat Party		62
Independents		7

*The distribution of votes in the 1946 elections was not officially announced. Only at these general elections in Turkey, voting was open, counting of votes secret.

May 14, 1950, Elections
Electoral system: as in 1946

Political Parties	Votes (%)	Seats
Demokrat Party	53.3	403
Republican People's Party	39.9	69
Nation Party	3.1	1
Independents	4.8	9

May 2, 1954, Elections
Electoral system: as in 1950

Political Parties	Votes (%)	Seats
Demokrat Party	56.6	490
Republican People's Party	34.8	30
Republican Nation Party	4.8	5
Independents	1.5	10

October 27, 1957, Elections
Electoral system: as in 1950

Political Parties	Votes (%)	Seats
Demokrat Party	47.3	419
Republican People's Party	40.6	173
Republican Peasants Nation Party	7.0	4
Freedom Party	3.8	4
Independents	0.1	2

Second Turkish Republic, 1960–1980

October 15, 1961, Elections
Electoral system: proportional representation, d'Hondt
system with electoral quotient (barrier)

Political Parties	Votes (%)	Seats
Republican People's Party	36.7	173
Justice Party	34.8	158
New Turkey Party	13.7	65
Republican Peasants Nation Party	4.0	54
Independents	0.8	—

October 15, 1965, Elections
Electoral system: proportional representation with
national remainder

Political Parties	Votes (%)	Seats
Justice Party	52.9	240
Republican People's Party	28.7	134
Nation Party	6.3	31
New Turkey Party	3.7	19
Turkish Labor Party	3.0	15
Nationalist Action Party	2.2	11
Independents	3.2	—

October 12, 1969, Elections
Electoral system: proportional representation, d'Hondt
system without electoral quotient (barrier)

Political Parties	Votes (%)	Seats
Justice Party	46.5	256
Republican People's Party	27.4	143
Reliance Party	6.6	15
Nation Party	3.2	6
Nationalist Action Party	3.0	1
Turkish Union Party	2.8	8
Turkish Labor Party	2.7	2
New Turkey Party	2.2	6
Independents	5.6	13

October 14, 1973, Elections
Electoral system: as in 1969

Political Parties	Votes	Seats
Republican People's Party	33.3	185
Justice Party	29.8	149
Demokratik Party	11.9	45
National Salvation Party	11.8	48
Republican Reliance Party	5.3	13
Nationalist Action Party	3.4	3
Turkish Labor Party	1.1	1
Independents	2.8	6

June 5, 1977, Elections
Electoral system: as in 1969

Political Parties	Votes (%)	Seats
Republican People's Party	41.4	213
Justice Party	36.9	189
National Salvation Party	8.6	24
Nationalist Action Party	6.4	16
Republican Reliance Party	1.9	3
Demokratik Party	1.9	1
Independents	2.5	4

Third Turkish Republic, 1980 to Present

November 6, 1983, Elections
Electoral system: proportional representation, d'Hondt system with national and provincial electoral quotient (barrier)

Political Parties	Votes (%)	Seats
Motherland Party	45.2	211
Populist Party	30.5	117
National Democracy Party	23.3	71
Independents	1.1	—

November 29, 1987, Elections
Electoral system: as in 1983

Political Parties	Votes (%)	Seats
Motherland Party	36.3	292
Social Democratic Populist Party	24.9	99
True Path Party	19.1	59
Democratic Left Party	8.5	—
Reformist Democracy Party	0.8	—
Nationalist Work Party	2.9	—
Welfare Party	7.2	—
Independents	0.4	—

October 20, 1991, Elections
Electoral system: as in 1987

Political Parties	Votes (%)	Seats
True Path Party	27.0	178
Motherland Party	24.0	115
Social Democratic Populist Party	20.8	88
Welfare Party	16.8	62
Democratic Left Party	10.8	7
Socialist Party	0.5	—
Independents	0.2	—

December 24, 1995, Elections
Electoral system: proportional representation, d'Hondt system with national quotient (barrier)

Political Parties	Votes (%)	Seats
Welfare Party	21.4	158
Motherland Party	19.7	132
True Path Party	19.2	135
Democratic Left Party	14.6	76
Republican People's Party	10.7	49
Nationalist Action Party	8.0	—
People's Democracy Party	4.2	—
New Democracy Party	0.5	—
Nation Party	0.5	—
Resurrection Party	0.3	—
Labor Party	0.2	—
New Party	0.1	—
Independents	0.5	—

April 18, 1999, Elections
Electoral system: as in 1995 elections

Political Parties	Votes (%)	Seats
Democratic Left Party	22.1	136
Nationalist Action Party	17.9	129
Virtue Party	15.4	111
Motherland Party	13.2	86
True Path Party	12.0	85
Republican People's Party	8.7	—
People's Democracy Party	4.7	—
Grand Union Party	1.4	—
Freedom and Solidarity Party	0.8	—
Democratic Turkey Party	0.5	—
Liberal Democratic Party	0.4	—
Democratic Party	0.3	—
Harmony Party	0.2	—
Nation Party	0.2	—
Labor Party	0.1	—
Party of Toilers	0.1	—
New Resurrection Party	0.1	—
Party of Changing Turkey	0.1	—
Socialist Party	0.1	—
Democracy and Harmony Party	0.8	—
Independents	0.8	—

BASIC ECONOMIC INDICATORS

GDP Per Capita, Exports, Imports and Exchange Rates

Years	GDP Per Capita ($)(PPP)	Exports (millions$)	Imports (millions$)	Exchange Rates TL/US$ (End of Year)
1970	936	588	947	15.0
1980	1,019	2,910	7,513	89.2
1985	3,354	8,255	11,230	574.0
1990	4,699	13,026	22,581	2,927.1
1995	5,691	21,975	35,187	45,705.4
1996	6,114	32,446	43,028	107,505.0
1997	6,413	32,647	48,005	205,110.0
1998	6,486	31,220	45,440	313,707.0
1999	—	29,326	39,773	540,098.0

Tourism Revenues and Expenditures (Millions US$)

	1980	1985	1990	1995	1996	1997	1998	1999
Revenues	326	1,094	3,225	4,955	5,650	7,002	7,177	5,203
Expenditures	104	324	520	991	1,265	1,716	1,754	1,471

Foreign Direct Investments (Millions US$)

	1970	1980	1985	1990	1995	1996	1997	1998	1999
Permits	88	97	103	1,861	2,938	3,837	1,678	1,645	1,690
Realizations	58	18	99	700	772	267	1,032	976	817

Balance of Payments (Millions US$)

	1993	1994	1995	1996	1997	1998	1999
Trade Balance	−14,160	−4,216	−13,212	−10,582	−15,358	−14,220	−10,447
Total Goods/Services Balance	−10,201	−461	−6,835	−6,884	−7,504	−3,743	−6,539
Private Unrequited Transfers	3,035	2,709	3,425	3,892	4,552	5,685	4,813
Official Unrequited Transfers	733	383	1,071	555	314	159	362
Current Account Balance	−6,433	2,631	−2,339	−2,437	−2,638	−1,984	−1,364
Overall Balance	308	202	4,658	4,545	3,344	447	5,206

Inflation (End of the year, percentage change)

	1990	1992	1994	1995	1996	1997	1998	1999*
Consumer Prices	60.4	66.0	125.5	78.9	79.7	99.1	69.7	64.6
Wholesale Prices	48.6	61.4	149.6	64.9	84.9	91.0	54.3	56.3
Agriculture	47.9	49.3	134.0	91.1	89.6	96.5	71.9	31.5
Mining	61.3	57.0	144.2	68.8	93.7	72.6	34.0	77.9
Manufacturing	48.5	63.4	159.1	58.9	80.6	91.2	47.1	66.2
Energy	45.1	94.6	100.9	35.7	129.6	64.1	69.9	69.3

*As of September 1999, 12-month percentage change.

BASIC SOCIAL INDICATORS

Population

Total, Urban, and Rural (Millions)

	1950	1960	1970	1980	1985	1990	1993	1995	1997
Total	20.9	27.7	36.6	44.7	50.6	56.4	60.0	62.1	62.8
Urban	3.0	6.2	11.5	18.8	23.9	30.5	34.6	37.8	40.9
Rural	17.9	21.5	24.1	25.9	26.7	25.9	25.4	24.3	21.9

Urbanization Rate (percentages)

	1965–1970	1970–1975	1975–1980	1980–1985	1985–1990	1990–1995
Urbanization Rate	6.03	5.62	4.40	4.91	4.99	4.4

Demographic Rates

	1965–1970	1970–1975	1975–1980	1980–1985	1985–1990	1990–1995	1995–2000
Population Growth (%)	2.52	2.50	2.06	2.49	2.17	1.85	1.62
Total Fertility Rate	5.31	4.46	4.33	4.05	3.76	2.80	2.45
Crude Birth Rate (per thousand)	30.0	34.5	32.2	30.8	29.9	23.5	21.4
Crude Death Rate (per thousand)	13.5	11.6	10.0	9.0	7.8	6.7	6.5
Life Expectancy at Birth (years)	54.9	57.8	61.2	63.0	66.8	67.2	69.0
Infant Mortality (per thousand)	158.0	140.4	110.7	82.9	65.2	50.6	39.0

Education

Rate of Schooling (percentages)

	1950–1951	1960–1961	1970–1971	1980–1981	1990–1991	1992–1993	1994–1995	1996–1997
Grade	69.1	81.1	99.7	97.7	101.9	99.7	104.4	100.0
Middle	4.8	15.8	30.7	40.6	60.3	63.4	65.6	64.3
High	5.2	13.2	20.1	28.4	38.5	44.9	53.0	54.7
College	1.3	3.1	5.7	6.4	15.7	18.1	22.1	23.4

Note: Addition of the percentage of adults receiving education at grade-school levels to that of pupils at the age of grade-school levels makes the grade-school enrollment more than 100 percent in some years.

Literacy Rate (%)

	1950	1960	1970	1980	1985	1990	1996
Literacy Rate	33.6	39.5	56.2	67.5	77.4	80.5	87.0

Health Services

	1950	1960	1970	1980	1990	1995	1996	1997
Number of Hospital Beds (thousands)	18.8	45.8	87.1	114.2	137.6	151.9	155.8	159.2
Population (per bed)	1,100	600	409	394	412	409	406	402
Population (per physician)	3,038	2,825	2,572	1,652	1,121	925	903	876
Number of Health Clinics	?	?	851	1,827	3,454	4,927	5,055	5,185
Number of Small Clinics	?	?	2,231	6,594	11,075	11,888	11,90	12,151

Bibliography

The present volume covers a history of more than 700 years, thus the long bibliographical section that follows. Those interested in the Ottoman period should first consult two books by Halil İnalcık, *The Ottoman Empire: The Classical Age, 1300–1600* and *Ottoman Empire: Conquest, Organization and Economy.* Also useful are Stanford J. Shaw, *History of the Ottoman Empire and Modern Turkey, vol. I: The Rise and Decline of Ottoman Empire, 1208–1808,* and Stanford J. Shaw and Ezel Shaw, *History of the Ottoman Empire and Modern Turkey, vol. II: Reform, Revolution, and the Republic, 1808–1975.* One can deepen one's grasp of the Ottoman period by turning to Feroz Ahmad, *The Young Turks: The Committee of Union and Progress in Turkish Politics, 1908–1914;* Selim Deringil, *Well-Rooted Domains: Ideology and Legitimation of Power in the Ottoman Empire;* Suraiya Faroqhi, *Towns and Townsmen of the Ottoman Anatolia: Trade, Crafts, and Food Production in an Urban Setting, 1520–1650;* Carter Findley, *Bureaucratic Reform in the Ottoman Empire: The Sublime Porte, 1789–1922* and *Ottoman Civil Officialdom: A Social History;* Cornell Fleischer, *Bureaucrat and Intellectual in the Ottoman Empire: The Historian Mustafa Arif;* Huri İslamoğlu-İnan, *The Ottoman Empire in World Economy;* Cemal Kafadar, *Between Two Worlds: The Construction of the Ottoman Empire;* Şevket Pamuk, *A Monetary History of the Ottoman Empire;* and Donald Quataert, *Ottoman Manufacturing in the Age of Industrial Revolution.* Of particular interest is a general reference work by Selçuk Akşin Somel, *Historical Dictionary of the Ottoman Empire.*

Those who wish to study the Westernization process in Turkey should start with Bernard Lewis, *The Emergence of Modern Turkey.* Şerif Mardin's, *The Genesis of the Young Ottoman Thought: A Study in the Modernization of Turkish Political Ideas* would serve the same purpose for political ideas in Turkey.

Those who wish to familiarize themselves with the basic developments in Republican Turkey should read Erik Zürcher's *Turkey: A Modern History.* One can come to grips with Turkish foreign policy by perusing George Harris, *Troubled Alliance: Turkish-American Problems in Historical Perspective;* Dankwart A. Rustow, *Turkey: America's Forgotten Ally;* Heinz Kramer, *A Changing Turkey: Challenges to Europe and the United States,* and William Hale, *Turkish Foreign Policy, 1774–1999.* C. H. Dodd, *The Crisis of Turkish Democracy;* Frederick W. Frey, *The Turkish Political Elite;* Metin Heper, *The State Tradition in Turkey;* Frank Tachau, *Turkey: The Politics of Authority, Democracy, and Development;* Kemal H. Karpat,

Turkey's Politics: The Transition to Multi-Party Politics; William Hale, *Turkish Politics and the Military;* Andrew Mango, *Turkey: The Challenge of a New Role;* Ergun Özbudun, *Social Change and Political Participation in Turkey* and *Contemporary Turkish Politics: Challenges to Democratic Consolidation* are useful to obtain a basic idea on various aspects Turkish polity and society.

This bibliography contains works in English only. It covers the period from the establishment of the Ottoman Empire to the present. The bibliography starts with reference works and is followed by general studies and works on geography and travel. Works listed as general studies have either a broad scope or do not fit in the other sections of the bibliography. The section on general studies has three subsections: Ottoman Empire, Ottoman Empire and Turkish Republic, and Turkish Republic. The bibliography then assumes a chronological form. The sections on the rise of the Ottoman Empire (ca.1280–1566); decline and traditional reform (ca. 1566–1808); the era of modern Ottoman reform (1808–1909); the Young Turk period (1909–1918); and defeat, disintegration, and revival (1918–1922) contain works on a variety of topics. The works about the Republican period (1923 to the present) is divided into four sections: government and politics, international relations and foreign policy, the economy, and sociocultural life. The section on sociocultural life has several subsections: general studies; art and literature; attitudes, values, and culture; demography; education and health; language; mass media; religion; urbanization, urbanism, and housing; and women and the family. This last section contains works both on the Ottoman Empire and Republican Turkey.

Each title has been listed under only one section or subsection. Several kinds of works have been excluded from the bibliography. These include theses and dissertations, anonymously written articles, working papers, documents, and reports. Individual chapters in collected volumes have not been listed if the collected volume itself has been cited. Works that are general in nature but have section(s) on Turkey have also not been included.

REFERENCE WORKS

Akarlı, Engin. "Ottoman Documents Concerning the Governorate of Mount Lebanon (1861–1918)." *Studies on Turkish-Arab Relations* (Istanbul) 1 (1986): 13–19.

Aksan, Virginia. "Ottoman Sources of Information on Europe in the Eighteenth Century." *Archivum Ottomanicum* 11 (1986): 5–16.

———. "Recent Works on Ottoman Foreign Relations." *Turkish Studies Association Bulletin* 16 (1992): 97–102.

———. "Ottoman Political Writing, 1768–1808." *International Journal of Middle East Studies* 25 (1993): 53–69.

Altan, M., J. Mottenry, and R. Jennings. "Archival Materials and Research Facilities in the Cyprus Turkish Federated State: Ottoman Empire, British Empire, Cyprus Republic." *International Journal of Middle East Studies* 8 (1977): 29–42.

And, Metin. "Bibliography: Theater in Turkey." *Turkish Studies Association Bulletin* 7 (1983): 20–31.

Ataöv, Türkkaya. "Selective Turkish Bibliography on International Relations." *Turkish Yearbook of International Relations* (Ankara) 6 (1965): 272–98.

Balım-Harding, Çiğdem, ed. *Turkey.* Rev. ed. Vol. 27 of *World Bibliographical Series.* Santa Barbara, Calif.: Clio Press, 1999.

Baltacı, Cahit. "The Importance of Kadı Registers for the Islamic World." *Studies on Turkish-Arab Relations* (Istanbul) 2 (1987): 165–69.

Beeley, Brian W., ed. *Rural Turkey: A Bibliographic Introduction.* Ankara: Hacettepe University, Institute of Population Studies, 1969.

Behar, C. "Sources of the Demographic History of the Ottoman Empire: The Tahrirs [censuses] of 1885 and 1907." *Population* 53, nos. 1–2 (1998): 161–77.

Bibliography of Social Science Periodicals and Monograph Series: Turkey. Washington, D.C.: Library of Congress, 1964.

Bibliography of Turkey, Turks, and Turkish Language. Ankara: Prime Ministry, Directorate General of Press and Information, 1986.

Blair, William. "Three Catalogues of Ottoman and Early Turkish Republic Journals and Newspapers." *Turkish Studies Association Bulletin* 15 (1991): 371–78.

Bodurgil, A. *Atatürk and Turkey: A Bibliography, 1919–1938.* Washington, D.C.: Library of Congress, 1974.

———. *Turkey: Politics and Government, A Bibliography, 1938–1975.* Washington, D.C.: Library of Congress, 1978.

Brummett, Palmira. "The Jacopo Castelvetro Collection: A Renaissance Man with Documents on Istanbul." *Turkish Studies Association Bulletin* 11 (1987): 1–8.

Clark, J. "Computer Mapping of the *Maliyeden Müdevver Register* 7075." *Turkish Studies Association Bulletin* 13 (1989): 79–90.

Coins of the Ottoman Empire and the Turkish Republic: A Detailed Catalogue of the Jem Sultan Collection. 2 vols. Thousand Oaks, Calif.: B & R, 1977.

Cooper, D. W. "Turkey's Research Libraries and the Turkic Republics." *Eurasian Studies* 2, no. 3 (1995): 105–12.

Cvetkova, Bistra A. "Early Ottoman Tahrir Defters as a Source for Studies of the History of Bulgaria and Balkans." *Archivum Ottomanicum* 8 (1983): 133–213.

Darling, Linda. "Ottoman Salary Registers as a Source for Economic and Social History." *Turkish Studies Association Bulletin* 14 (1990): 13–33.

Davison, Roderic H. "Archives in the Near East with Special Reference to Ottoman History." *News from the Center* (Library of Congress, Washington, D.C.), no. 4 (1968): 1–11.

———. "Ottoman Documents in the National Archives in Washington." *Turkish Studies Association Bulletin,* no. 4 (1978): 1–2.

Deringil, Selim, ed. *The Ottoman Almanacs of the Arab Provinces, 1888–1902.* London: Archive Editions, 1999.

Dumont, Paul. "Turkey at the Beginning of the Twentieth Century as Seen through the 'Autochrones' and the Films of the Albert Kahn Collection." *Turkish Studies Association Bulletin* 3 (1979): 16–23.

———. "Turkey in the Military Archives of the Chateau de Vincennes." *International Journal of Turkish Studies* 2 (1981): 64–88.

Eleazar, Birnbaum. "Turkish Manuscripts: Cataloguing since 1960 and Manuscripts Still Uncatalogued. Part I: The Berlin Catalogue." *Journal of the American Oriental Society* 103 (1983): 413–20.

Epstein, M. "Comments on Capsali as a Source for Ottoman History, 1450–1523." *Turkish Studies Association Bulletin* 3 (1979): 4–8.

Erdemli, Özgül. "Researching Turkey on the Internet: A Guide." *Turkish Studies* (London) 1, no. 1 (2000): 190–205.

Erünsal, İ. "Medieval Ottoman Libraries." *Erdem* (Ankara), no. 3 (1985): 745–54.

———. "Abdurrahman el-Askeri's *Mir'atül'Isk:* A New Source for the Melami Movement in the Ottoman Empire during the 15th and 16th Centuries." *Wiener Z. für die Kunde des Morgenlandes* 84 (1994): 204–17.

Faroqhi, Suraiya. *Approaching Ottoman History: An Introduction to the Sources.* Cambridge: Cambridge University Press, 1999.

Finefrock, Michael M. "Atatürk's Legacy: A Select Bibliography." *Journal of the American Institute for the Study of Middle Eastern Civilization* 1 (1980): 33–38.

Fisher, Alan. "Sources and Perspectives for the Study of Ottoman-Russian Relations in the Black Sea Area." *International Journal of Turkish Studies* 1 (1980): 77–84.

Foder, P. "Ahmedi's Dasitan as a Source of Early Ottoman History." *Acta Orientalia* (Budapest) 38 (1985): 41–54.

Gökman, Muzaffer. *Bibliography of the History of Atatürk and His Reforms.* Istanbul: Milli Eğitim Basımevi, 1968.

Greening, Anna. "The Women's Library in Istanbul: The International Context." *Gender and History* 12, no. 2 (2000): 467–71.

Griswold, W. "The National Archives in Turkey." *Muslim World* 64 (1974): 40–44.

Güçlü, Meral. *Turkey.* Vol. 27 of *World Bibliographical Series.* Santa Barbara, Calif.: Clio Press, 1981.

Halén, H. "Bibliography of Current Finnish Turcological Studies." *Turcica: Revue d'Etudes Turques* (Paris) 12 (1980): 187–91.

Hanioğlu, Şükrü. *Turkish Nationalist Writings.* Cambridge: Cambridge University Press, 1998.

Harvard University Library Catalogue of Arabic, Persian and Turkish Books. 5 vols. Cambridge, Mass.: Harvard University Press, 1968.

Hathaway, J. "Library and Archival Research in Turkey and Egypt." *Middle East and South Asia Folklore Bulletin* 13, no. 2 (1996): 12–16.

Hattox, R. "Some Ottoman Tapu Defters for Tripoli in the Sixteenth Century." *al-Abhath* (Beirut) 29 (1981): 65–90.

———. "Mehmed II, Qo'itbay, and the Karamanids: Notes on TKS [Topkapı Sarayı Museum Archives] E. 5848, E. 8363 and E. 10740." *Turkish Studies Association Bulletin* 15 (1991): 253–72.

Heyd, Uriel. *Ottoman Documents in Palestine, 1552–1615.* London: Oxford University Press, 1960.

Horniker, A. L. "Ottoman-Turkish Diplomatics: A Guide to the Literature." *Balkan Studies* 7 (1966): 135–54.

Howard, D. "The BBA Ruznamce Tasnifi: A New Resource for the Study of the Ottoman Timar System." *Turkish Studies Association Bulletin* 10 (1986): 11–19.

İlhan, M. "Studies in the Medieval History of Diyarbakır Province: Some Notes on the Sources and Literature." *Belleten* (Ankara) 53 (1989): 199–231.

İnalcık, Halil. "Fermans of Fatih Sultan Mehmed in the Bursa Şer'iye Sicilleri." *Belleten* (Ankara) 11 (1947): 693–708.

———. "The Ruznamce Registers of the Kadıasker of Rumeli as Preserved in the Istanbul Müftülük Archives." *Turcica* (Paris) 20 (1988): 251–75.

———. *Sources and Studies on the Ottoman Black Sea.* Vol. 1: *Customs Registers of Caffa, 1487–90.* Cambridge, Mass.: Harvard University Ukranian Research Institute, 1997.

Jeffs, Joseph E. *The George C. McGhee Library: A Catalogue of Books on Asia Minor and the Turkish Ottoman Empire.* Washington, D.C.: Georgetown University Library, 1984.

Karayan, S. "Bibliography: Histories of Armenian Communities in Turkey." *Armenian Review* 33 (1980): 89–96.

Koç, Yıldırım. "Sources on the Laborers in Turkey in Foreign Languages." *METU Studies in Development* (Ankara) 9 (1982): 99–128.

Köhbach, Markus. "Friedrich Kraelitz Edler von Greifenhorst (1876–1932) [Bibliography at the] University of Vienna." *Turkish Studies Association Bulletin* 3 (1979): 14–16.

Kut, Günay. "Union Catalogue of Manuscripts on Turkey." *Middle East Studies Association Bulletin* 25 (1991): 38–39.

Kut, Günay, and Michael Daly. *Catalogue of Turkish Manuscripts in the Bodleian Library* [Oxford University, U.K.]. Oxford: Oxford University Press, 1996.

Landau, Jacob. "Recent Soviet Books on Turkey." *Middle Eastern Studies* 6 (1970): 212–14.

———. "Recent Russian Works on the Republic of Turkey." *Middle Eastern Studies* 22 (1986): 435–41.

Lewis, Bernard. "Studies in the Ottoman Archives, Part 1." *Bulletin of the School of Oriental and African Studies* 16 (1954): 469–501.

Library Catalogs of the Hoover Institution, Stanford: Catalogs of the Turkish and Persian Collections. Boston, Mass.: G. K. Hall, 1969.

Little, D., and A. Turgay. "Documents from the Ottoman Period in the Khâlidi Library in Jerusalem." *Die Welt des Islams* 20 (1980): 44–72.

Lowry, Heath W. "The Reorganization of the Ottoman Archives." *Turkish Studies Association Bulletin* 13 (1989): 107–12.

Mandaville, J. "The Ottoman Court Records of Syria and Jordan." *Journal of American Oriental Society*, no. 3 (1966): 311–18.

McCarthy, Justin. "Ottoman Imperial and Provincial Salnames." *Middle East Studies Association Bulletin* 13 (1979): 10–20.

———. *The Arab World, Turkey, and the Balkans, 1878–1914: A Handbook of Historical Statistics.* Boston, Mass.: G. K. Hall, 1982.

———. "The Defters of the Late Ottoman Period." *Turkish Studies Association Bulletin* 8 (1984): 5–15.

Menage, V. "On the Constituent Elements of Certain Sixteenth-Century Ottoman Documents." *Bulletin of the School of Oriental and African Studies* 48 (1985): 283–304.

Minkov, Anton. "Ottoman Tapu Title Deeds in the Eighteen and Nineteenth Centuries: Origin, Typology, and Diplomatics." *Islamic Law and Society* 7, no. 1 (2000): 65–101.

Mitler, Louis. *Contemporary Turkish Writers: A Critical Bio-Bibliography of Leading Writers of the Turkish Republican Period up to 1980.* Bloomington: Indiana University, Research Institute for Inner Asian Studies, 1988.

———. *Ottoman Turkish Writers: A Bibliographical Dictionary of Significant Figures in Pre-Republican Turkish Literature.* New York: Lang, 1988.

Moran, Berna. *A Bibliography of the Publications in English Concerning the Turks, Fifteenth to Eighteenth Centuries.* Istanbul: Istanbul Matbaası, 1964.

Nagata, Yuzo. "Some Documents on the Big Farms [Çiftliks] of the Notables in Western Anatolia." *Studia Culturae Islamicae* 4 (1976): 37–67.

Ortaylı, İlber. "The Archives of Russia and Ottoman History." Trans. from Turkish Douglas A. Howard. *Turkish Studies Association Bulletin* 23, no. 2 (1999): 12–15.

Os, Nicole A. N. M. van. "Ottoman Women's Organizations: Sources of the Past, Sources for the Future." *Islam and Christian-Muslim Relations* 11, no. 3 (2000): 369–83.

Ökçün, Gündüz. *A Guide to Turkish Treaties (1920–1964)*. Ankara: Ankara Üniversitesi Basımevi, 1966.

Özbaran, S. "A Review of Portuguese and Turkish Sources for the Ottomans in Arabia and the Indian Ocean in the Sixteenth Century." *Belleten* (Ankara) 49 (1985): 65–78.

Partington, David H. "Turkish Collections in the U.S.: The Harvard College Library." *Turkish Studies Association Bulletin* 5 (1981): 20–1.

Peachy, W. "Register of Copies or Collection of Drafts? The Case of Four *Mühimme* Defters from the Archives of the Prime Ministry in Istanbul." *Turkish Studies Association Bulletin* 10 (1986): 79–86.

Quataert, Donald, and Nadir Özbek. "The Eğreli-Zonguldak Coal Mines: A Catalog of Archival Documents." *Turkish Studies Association Bulletin* 23, no. 1 (1999): 55–67.

Rogan, Eugene L. *Frontiers of the State in the Late Ottoman Empire: Transjordan, 1850–1921*. Cambridge: Cambridge University Press, 1999.

Rogozhin, Nikolai Mikhailovich, and Hans-Heinrich Nolte. "The Ottoman Empire in the Sixteenth and Seventeenth Centuries in Documents of the *Pasol'skii Prikaz*." *Turcica* 30 (1998): 373–81.

Romer, Claudia. "A Firman of Süleyman the Magnificent to the King of France Preserved in an Exercise Book of the 'K. K. Academie Orientalischer Sprachen' in Vienne, 1831 "*Turcica* 31 (1999): 461–70.

Selected Annotated Bibliography of Basic Books and Selected Monographs in English on Modern Turkey. Ankara: Türk-Amerikan Eğitim Derneği, 1959.

Seng, Yvonne. "The Şeriye Sicilleri of the Istanbul Müftülüğü as a Source for the Study of Everyday Life." *Turkish Studies Association Bulletin* 15 (1991): 293–306.

Shaw, Stanford J. "Archival Sources for Ottoman History: The Archives of Turkey." *Journal of the American Oriental Society* 80 (1960): 1–12.

———. "Yıldız Palace Archives." *Archivum Ottomanicum* 3 (1971): 214–16, 224.

———. "Ottoman Archival Materials for the Nineteenth and Early Twentieth Centuries: The Archives of Istanbul." *International Journal of Middle East Studies* 6 (1975): 94–114.

———. "The Archives of Turkey: An Evaluation." *Wiener Zietschrift für die Kunde des Morgenlandes* 49 (1977): 91–98.

———. "Recent Catalogs and Inventories of the Coins of the Ottoman Empire and the Turkish Republic." *International Journal of Turkish Studies* 1 (1979–1980): 114–19.

Singer, Ami. "Tapu Tahrir Defterleri and Kadı Sicilleri: A Happy Marriage of Sources." *Tarih* (Istanbul) 1 (1990): 95–125.

Skilliter, S. A. "List of Works towards a Bibliography of Current British Turcological Studies." *Turcica: Revue d'Etudes Turques* (Paris) 9 (1977): 252–63.

Somel, Selçuk Akşin. *Historical Dictionary of the Ottoman Empire*. Lanham, Md.: Scarecrow Press, 2003.

Soysal, Ö. "A Historical Glance at the Development of the Current Turkish National Bibliography and Other Major Bibliographical Sources in Turkey." *Middle East Studies Association Bulletin* 11 (1977): 1–30.

Stewart-Robinson, James. "The Ottoman Biographies of Poets." *Journal of Near Eastern Studies* 14 (1965): 57–74.

Sturm, Albert L., and Cemal Mıhçıoğlu. *Bibliography on Public Administration in Turkey, 1923–1957*. Ankara: Ankara University Publication, 1959.

Suzuki, Peter T. *Social Change in Turkey since 1950: A Bibliography of 866 Publications*. Heidelberg, Germany: High Speed Press Center, 1969.

Şakiroğlu, Mahmut. "The Importance of the Venetian Archives in Turkish-Arab Studies." *Studies on Turkish-Arab Relations* (Istanbul) 2 (1987): 91–94.

Şeşen, Ramazan, Cemil Akpınar, and Cevad İzgi. *Catalogue of Islamic Manuscripts (in Arabic, Turkish, and Persian) in the Libraries of Turkey.* Ed. Ekmeleddin İhsanoğlu. Istanbul: Research Center for Islamic History, Art, and Culture, 1984.

———. *Catalogue of the Manuscripts in the Köprülü Library.* Istanbul: Research Center for Islamic History, Art, and Culture, 1986.

Şimşir, Bilal N., ed. *British Documents on Ottoman Armenians, 1856–1880.* Vol. 1. Ankara: Türk Tarih Kurumu Basımevi, 1982.

Tamkoç, Metin. *A Bibliography on the Foreign Relations of the Republic of Turkey, 1919–1967, and Brief Biographies of Turkish Statesmen.* Ankara: Middle East Technical University, 1968.

Tsardanidis, Charlambos. *Bibliography for Turkey: 1923–1990.* Athens: Foundation for Mediterranean Studies, 1990. In Greek and English.

Turkey: A Bibliography of Literature Published in Pakistan and India. Comp. Hamdard Library. Karachi: Hamdard University Press, 1987.

Türkmen, E. "Khusrau's MS at Istanbul." *Islam and Modern Age* 13 (1982): 153–61.

Uluç, Lale. "Ottoman Book Collectors and Illustrated Sixteenth-Century Shiraz Manuscripts." *Revue des mondes Musulmans et de la Mediterranée* 87/88 (1999): 85–110.

Walker, Warren S. "Turkish Oral Narrative in Texas: The Archive of Turkish Oral Negative." *Oral Tradition* 1, no. 1 (1992): 171–75.

Walker, Warren S., Michael D. Felker, and Elizabeth K. Brandt, comps. *The Archive of Turkish Oral Narrative—Preliminary Catalogue III: The First 1,500 Tales.* Lubbock, Tex.: Archive of Turkish Oral Negative, 1994.

———. *The Archive of Turkish Oral Narrative—Preliminary Catalogue IV: The First 2,000 Tales.* Lubbock, Tex.: Archive of Turkish Oral Narrative, 1998.

Walsh, John R. "Turkey: Bibliographical Spectrum." *Review of National Literatures* 4 (1973): 115–32.

GENERAL STUDIES

Ottoman Empire

Acun, Fatma. "Ottoman Administrative Priorities: Two Case Studies of Karahisar-ı Şarki (Şebinkarahisar) and Giresun." *Archivum Ottomanicum* 17 (1999): 213–32.

Akbayrak, H. "The Ottoman Historical Society." *Journal of the Middle East Studies* 2 (1988): 87–109.

Aksan, Virginia. "Locating the Ottomans among Early Modern Empires." *Journal of Early Modern History* 3 (1999): 21–39.

———. *The Ottoman Wars, 1700–1870.* London: Longman, 2000.

Alderson, A. D. *The Structure of the Ottoman Dynasty.* New York: Oxford University Press, 1956.

Anderson, M. S. *The Eastern Question, 1774–1923: A Study in International Relations.* London: Macmillan, 1966.

Arnakis, George G. "Futuwwa Traditions in the Ottoman Empire." *Journal of Near Eastern Studies* 12 (1953): 232–47.

———. *The Near East in Modern Times.* Vol. 1 of *The Ottoman Empire and the Balkan States to 1900.* Austin, Tex.: Pemberton Press, 1969.

Ayalon, David. *Eunuchs, Caliphs, and Sultans: A Study of Power Relationships.* Jerusalem: Magnes Press, 1999.

Baer, Gabriel. "Monopolies and Restrictive Practices of Turkish Guilds." *Journal of the Economic and Social History of the Orient* 13 (1970): 145–65.

———. "The Administrative, Economic, and Social Functions of Turkish Guilds." *International Journal of Middle East Studies* 1 (1970): 28–50.

Barkey, Karen, and Mark von Hagen, eds. *After Empire. Multiethnic Societies and Nation Building: The Soviet Union, and Russian, Ottoman, and Habsburg Empires.* Boulder, Colo.: Westview, 1997.

Barsoumian, H. "Economic Role of the Armenian Amira Class in the Ottoman Empire." *Armenian Review* 31 (1979): 310–16.

Black, Cyril E. "A Comparative Approach to the Preconditions of Ottoman Modernization." *International Journal of Turkish Studies* 1 (1980): 25–37.

Braude, Benjamin, and Bernard Lewis, eds. *Christians and Jews in the Ottoman Empire: The Functioning of a Plural Society.* Vol. 1: *The Central Lands*; Vol. 2: *The Arabic Speaking Lands.* New York: Holmes & Meier, 1982.

Breebaart, D. "The Fütüvvet Nâme-i Kebir: A Manual on Turkish Guilds." *Journal of the Economic and Social History of the Orient* 15 (1972): 203–15.

Brookes, D. "Of Swords and Tombs: Symbolism in the Ottoman Accessional Ritual." *Turkish Studies Association Bulletin* 17, no. 2 (1993): 1–2.

Brown, L. Carl, ed. *Imperial Legacy: The Ottoman Imprint on the Balkans and the Middle East.* New York: Columbia University Press, 1996.

Cantemir, Dimitrius. *The History of the Growth and Decay of the Ottoman Empire.* Trans. from Latin N. Tindal. London: James John and Paul Knapton, 1734–35.

Cooke, W. S. *The Ottoman Empire and Its Tributary States (Excepting Egypt): With a Sketch of Greece.* Amsterdam: B. R. Grüner, 1968.

Creasy, E. S. *History of the Ottoman Turks: From the Beginning of Their Empire to the Present Time.* London: Richard Bentley, Bradbury & Evans, 1854 (vol. 1), 1856 (vol. 2).

Davison, Roderic H. *Essays in Ottoman and Turkish History, 1774–1923: The Impact of the West.* Austin: University of Texas Press, 1990.

Deringil, S. "The Ottoman Empire and the Russian Muslims: Brothers or Rivals." *Central Asian Survey* 13, no. 3 (1994): 409–16.

Eliot, Charles. *Turkey in Europe.* 1900. 2nd ed. 1908. Reprint, London: Edward Arnold, 1966.

Farah, Ceasar. "Great Britain, Germany, and the Ottoman Caliphate." *Der Islam* 46 (1989): 264–88.

Faroqhi, Suraiya. *Pilgrims and Sultans: The Hajj under the Ottomans.* London: I. B. Tauris, 1993.

———. "Consumption and Elite Status in the Eighteenth and Nineteenth Centuries: Exploring the Ottoman Case." In *Studies in Ottoman Social and Economic Life*, ed. Raou Motika, Cristoph Herzog, and Michael Ursinus. Heidelberg: Heidelberg Orientverlag, 1999.

Fleet, Kate. *European and Islamic Trade in the Early Ottoman State: The Merchants of Genoa and Turkey.* Cambridge: Cambridge University Press, 1999.

Fodor, Pal. *In Quest of the Golden Apple: Imperial Ideology, Politics, and Military Administration in the Ottoman Empire.* Istanbul: ISIS Press, 2000.

Friedman, Isaiah. *Germany, Turkey, and Zionism, 1897–1918.* Fairlawn, N.J.: Oxford University Press, 1978.

Gerber, Haim. "Jews and Money-Lending in the Ottoman Empire." *Jewish Quarterly Review* 52 (1981): 100–18.

Ghazarian, Vatche. *Armenians in the Ottoman Empire: An Anthology of Transformation, 13th–19th Centuries*. Waltham, Mass.: Mayreni Publishing, 1997.

Goodwin, Godfrey. *Ottoman Turkey*. London: Scorpion Publication, 1977.

Goodwin, Jason. *Lords of the Horizon: A History of the Ottoman Empire*. New York: Henry Holt, 1999.

Gould, A. "Lords or Bandits? The Derebeys of Cilicia." *International Journal of Middle East Studies* 7 (1976): 485–506.

Griswold, William J. "An Approach to Ottoman History through Islamic Civilization." *Turkish Studies Association Bulletin* 1 (1976): 14–16.

Hathaway, Jane. "Grand Vizier and the False Messiah: The Sabbatai Sevi Controversy and Ottoman Reform in Egypt." *Journal of the American Oriental Society* 117, no. 4 (1997): 665–71.

———. *Politics of Households in Ottoman Egypt: The Rise of Qazdağlıs*. New York: Cambridge University Press, 1997.

Heper, Metin. "Center and Periphery in the Ottoman Empire with Special Reference to the Nineteenth Century." *International Political Science Review* 1 (1980): 81–105.

Heyd, Uriel. "The Ottoman Ulema and Westernization in the Time of Selim III and Mahmud II." *Scripta Hierosolymitana* 9 (1961): 63–96.

———. *Kanun and Shari'a in Old Ottoman Criminal Justice*. Jerusalem: Israel Academy of Sciences and Humanities, 1967.

———. *Studies in Old Ottoman Criminal Law*. Ed. V. L. Ménage. Oxford: Clarendon Press, 1973.

Heywood, C. "The Evolution of the Ottoman Provincial Law-Code (*Sancak Kanunname*): The Kanun-name-i Liva-i Semendire, Part 1." *Turkish Studies Association Bulletin* 15 (1991): 223–51.

Hurewitz, J. C. "The Ottoman Diplomacy and the European State System." *Middle East Journal* 15 (1961): 141–52.

İnalcık, Halil. "Bursa and the Commerce of the Levant." *Journal of the Economic and Social History of the Levant* 3 (1960): 131–47.

———. "The Place of the Ottoman-Turkish Empire in History." *Cultura Turcica* (Ankara) 1 (1964): 57–64.

———. "Capital Formation in the Ottoman Empire." *Journal of Economic History* 29 (1969): 97–140.

———. "The Heyday and Decline of the Ottoman Empire." *Cambridge History of Islam* 1 (1970): 324–53.

———. "The Ottoman Economic Mind and Aspects of the Ottoman Economy." In *Studies in the Economic History of the Orient*, ed. M. A. Cook. London: Oxford University Press, 1970.

———. *The Ottoman Empire: Conquest, Organisation, and Economy*. London: Variorum, 1978.

———. "Yük (Himl) in Ottoman Silk Trade, Mining, and Agriculture." *Turcica* (Paris) 16 (1984): 131–56.

———. "Tax Collection, Embezzlement, and Bribery in Ottoman Finances." *Turkish Studies Association Bulletin* 15 (1991): 327–46.

———. "The Status of the Greek Orthodox Patriarch under the Ottomans." *Turcica* (Paris) 21–23 (1991): 407–36.

———. "Islamization of Ottoman Laws on Land and Land Tax." In *Festgabe an Joseph Matuz: Osmanistik-Turkologie-Diplomatik*, ed. Christa von Fragner and Klaus Schwarz. Berlin: Klaus Schwarz Verlag, 1992.

——. *Essays in Ottoman History*. Istanbul: Eren Yayınevi, 1998.

İnalcık, Halil, and Donald Quataert. *The Ottoman Empire: Its Economy and Society, 1300–1914*. Cambridge: Cambridge University Press, 1994.

——. eds. *An Economic and Social History of the Ottoman Empire*. Cambridge: Cambridge University Press, 1994.

İslamoğlu, Huri, and Çağlar Keyder. "Agenda for Ottoman History." *Review* 1 (1987): 31–55.

——. *The Ottoman Empire and the World Economy*. Cambridge: Cambridge University Press, 1987.

Itzkowitz, Norman. *Ottoman Empire and Islamic Tradition*. New York: Knopf, 1972.

Kafadar, Cemal. "On the Purity and Corruption of the Janissaries." *Turkish Studies Association Bulletin* 15 (1991): 273–80.

——. "The Ottomans and Europe." In *Handbook of European History, 1400–1600*. Vol.1: *Late Middle Ages, Renaissance, and Reformation*, ed. Thomas A. Brady, Heiko A. Oberman, and James D. Tracy. Leiden: E. J. Brill, 1994.

Kaiser, Hilmar. *Imperialism, Racism, and Development Theories: The Construction of a Dominant Paradigm on Ottoman Armenians*. Princeton, N.J.: Gomidas Institute, 1998.

Karpat, Kemal H., ed. *The Ottoman State and Its Place in the World History*. Leiden: E. J. Brill, 1974.

Kent, Marian. "Great Britain and the End of the Ottoman Empire, 1900–1923." In *The Great Powers and the End of the Ottoman Empire*, ed. Marian Kent. London: Allen & Unwin, 1984.

Khoury, Dina Rızk. *State and Provincial Society in the Ottoman Empire: Mosul, 1540–1834*. Cambridge: Cambridge University Press, 1997.

Kinross, Lord. *The Ottoman Centuries: The Rise and Fall of the Ottoman Empire*. London: Jonathan Cape, 1977.

Knolles, Richard. *The Turkish History from the Origins of that Nation to the Growth of the Ottoman Empire: With the Lives and Conquests of Their Princes and Emperors (with a Continuation to This Present Year 1687 Where unto Added the Present State of the Ottoman Empire, by Sir Paul Rycaut)*. 2 vols. London: J. D. Anno, 1687.

Köprülü, Mehmed Fuad. *Some Observations on the Influence of Byzantine Institutions on Ottoman Institutes*. Ankara: Türk Tarih Kurumu, 1999.

Le Gall, M. "The Ottoman Government and the Sanusiyya: A Reappraisal." *International Journal of Middle East Studies* 21 (1989): 91–106.

Levy, Avigdor. *The Sephardim in the Ottoman Empire*. Princeton, N.J.: Darwin Press, 1992.

Lewis, Bernard. "Ottoman Land Tenure and Taxation in Syria." *Studia Islamica* 50 (1979): 21–35.

Mandaville, J. "Usurious Piety: The Cash-Waqf Controversy in the Ottoman Empire." *International Journal of Middle East Studies* 10 (1979): 289–308.

Mansurnoor, I. "Religious Scholars and State: Patterns of Recruitment among the Ottoman Ulama." *Islamic Studies* 31 (1992): 35–51.

Mardin, Şerif. "Power, Civil Society, and Culture in the Ottoman Empire." *Comparative Studies in Society and History* 11 (1969): 258–81.

McCarthy, Justin. *The Ottoman Turks: An Introductory History to 1923*. New York: Longman, 1997.

——. *The Ottoman Peoples and the End of the Empire*. London: Arnold, 2001.

Meyer, M. "Economic Thought in the Ottoman Empire in the 14th to Early 19th Century." *Archiv Orientalni* (Prague) 57 (1989): 305–18.

Mihailovic, Konstantin. *Memoirs of a Janissary*. Trans. Benjamin Stolz; historical commentary by Svat Soucek. Ann Arbor: University of Michigan Press, 1975.

Miller, Barnette. *Beyond the Sublime Porte: The Grand Seraglio of Istanbul.* 1931. New York: AMS Press, 1970.

Moore, Andrew. *A Compendious History of the Turks.* London: J. Streater, 1663.

Motika, Raoul, Christoph Herzog, and Michael Ursinus. *Studies in Ottoman Social and Economic Life.* Heidelberg, Germany: Heidelberger Orientverlag, 1999.

Murphey, Rhoads. *Regional Structure in the Ottoman Empire.* Wiesbaden, Germany: Otto Harrassowitz, 1987.

———. *Ottoman Warfare, 1500–1700.* New Brunswick, N.J.: Rutgers University Press, 1999.

Nezan, Kendal. "The Kurds under the Ottoman Empire." In *People without a Country: The Kurds and Kurdistan,* ed. Gerard Chaliand. London: Zed, 1986.

Olson, Robert. "Jews in the Ottoman Empire and Their Role in Light of New Documents: Addenda and Revisions to Gibb and Bowen." *Tarih Enstitüsü Dergisi* (Ankara), nos. 7–8 (1976–1977): 119–44.

Ongley, F. *The Ottoman Land Code.* London: William Clowes and Sons, 1892.

Os, Nicole A. N. M. van. "The Ottoman State as a Breadgiver: *Muinsiz Aile Maaşı.*" In *Arming the State: Military Conscription in the Middle East and Central Asia,* ed. Erik Zürcher. London: I. B. Tauris, 1999.

Palmer, Alan. *The Decline and Fall of the Ottoman Empire.* London: John Murray, 1992.

Pamaite, Viorel. *The Ottoman Law of War and Peace: The Ottoman Empire and Tribute Payers.* Boulder, Colo.: East European Monographs, 2000.

Pamuk, Şevket. "The Decline and Resistance of Ottoman Cotton Textiles, 1820–1913." *Explorations in Economic History* 23 (1986): 205–25.

———. "The Ottoman Empire in Comparative Perspective." *Review* 11 (1988): 127–49.

———. *A Monetary History of the Ottoman Empire.* Cambridge: Cambridge University Press, 2000.

Parry, V. J., H. İnalcık, A. N. Kurat, and J. S. Bromley. *A History of the Ottoman Empire to 1730: Chapters from the Cambridge History of Islam and the New Cambridge Modern History.* Ed. M. A. Cook. New York: Cambridge University Press, 1976.

Quataert, Donald. "The Commercialization of Agriculture in Ottoman Turkey." *International Journal of Turkish Studies* 1 (1980): 38–55.

———. "Some Preliminary Observations on Silk and Carpet Workers in the Ottoman Empire, 1750–1914." *Turkish Studies Association Bulletin* 8 (1984): 1–5.

———. *A History of the Ottoman Empire, 1700–1922.* Cambridge: Cambridge University Press, 2000.

———. ed. *Consumption Studies and the History of the Ottoman Empire, 1550–1922.* Albany: SUNY Press, 2000.

Reilly, I. "Rural Vaqfs of Ottoman Damascus: Rights of Ownership, Possession, and Tenancy." *Acta Orientalni* (Prague) 51 (1990): 343–46.

Repps, Richard C. "Some Observations on the Development of the Ottoman Learned Hierarchy." In *Scholars, Saints, and Sufis: Muslim Institutions in the Middle East since 1500,* ed. Nikkie R. Keddie. Berkeley: University of California Press, 1972.

———. *The Mufti of Istanbul: A Study in the Development of the Ottoman Learned Hierarchy.* London: Ithaca Press, 1986.

Shaw, Stanford J. *History of the Ottoman Empire and Modern Turkey.* Vol.1 of *The Rise and Decline of the Ottoman Empire, 1280–1808.* New York: Cambridge University Press, 1976.

Singer, Amy, and Amon Cohen, eds. *Aspects of Ottoman History.* Jerusalem: Magnes Press, 1994.

Stoianovich, Traian. "Balkan Peasants and Landlords and the Ottoman State: Familial Economy, Market Economy, and Modernization." In *La révolution industrielle dans le sud-est européen*, ed. Nikolay Todorov. Sofia: N.p., 1954.

Sugar, Peter F. *Southeastern Europe under Ottoman Rule, 1354–1804*. Seattle: University of Washington Press, 1977.

Swanson, G. "The Ottoman Police." *Contemporary History* 7 (1972): 243–60.

Toledona, Ehud R. *Slavery and Abolition in the Ottoman Middle East*. Seattle: University of Washington Press, 1998.

Toynbee, Arnold. *The Ottoman Empire's Place in World History 1350–1700*. London: Chatham House, 1971.

Wallerstein, Immanuel. "The Ottoman Empire and the Capitalist World Economy: Some Questions for Research." *Review* 2 (1979): 389–98.

Wallerstein, Immanuel, and Reşat Kasaba. "Incorporation into the World Economy: Change in the Structure of the Ottoman Empire, 1750–1839." *METU Studies in Development* (Ankara) 8 (1981): 537–70.

Weiker, Walter F. "Ottoman Bureaucracy: Modernization and Reform." *Administrative Science Quarterly* 8 (1968): 451–70.

Wheatcroft, Andrew. *The Ottomans: Dissolving Images*. London: Penguin, 1993.

William, S. "Ottoman Land Policy and Social Change: The Syrian Provinces." *Acta Orient* (Hungary) 35 (1981): 89–120.

Winter, Michael. *Egyptian Society under Ottoman Rule, 1517–1798*. London: Routledge, 1992.

Ottoman Empire and Turkish Republic

Bentwich, Norman. "The Turkish Constitutions, 1876–1942." *Contemporary Review* 162 (1942): 213–18.

Berkes, Niyazi. "Ziya Gökalp: His Contribution to Turkish Nationalism." *Middle East Journal* 8 (1954): 375–90.

Castle, Wilfred T. F. *Grand Turk: An Historical Outline of Life and Events, of Culture and Politics, of Trade and Travel during the Last Years of the Ottoman Empire and the First Years of the Turkish Republic*. London: Hutchinson, 1943.

Davison, Roderic. *Turkey: A Short History*. 3rd ed. Huntingdon, U.K.: Eothen Press, 1998.

Deringil, Selim. "Aspects of Continuity in Turkish Foreign Policy: Abdülhamit II and İsmet İnönü." *International Journal of Turkish Studies* 4 (1987): 39–54.

———. *The Ottomans, the Turks, and World Power Politics*. Istanbul: ISIS Press, 2000.

Dodd, C. H. "Revolution in the Ottoman Empire and Modern Turkey." In *Revolutionary Theory and Political Reality*, ed. N. K. Sullivan. Brighton, U.K.: Harvester, 1983.

———. "Political Succession in the Ottoman Empire and Modern Turkey." In *Political Succession*, ed. P. Calvert. London: Macmillan, 1987.

Eleazor, Birnbaum. "Turkey: From Cosmopolitan Empire to Nation State." In *Introduction to Islamic Civilization*, ed. R. M. Savory. Cambridge: Cambridge University Press, 1976.

Göçek, Müge. *Rise of the Bourgeoisie, Demise of Empire: Ottoman Westernization and Social Change*. New York and Oxford: Oxford University Press, 1996.

Gökalp, Ziya. *Turkish Nationalism and Western Civilization*. Trans. and ed. Niyazi Berkes. New York: Columbia University Press, 1959.

———. *The Principles of Turkism*. Trans. and ed. Robert Devereux. Leiden: E. J. Brill, 1968.

Haddad, William W., and William Ochsenwold. *Nationalism in a Non-National State: The Dissolution of the Ottoman Empire.* Columbus: Ohio State University Press, 1977.

Heper, Metin. "Patrimonialism in the Ottoman-Turkish Public Bureaucracy." *Asian and African Studies* 13 (1979): 3–21.

———. "The Ottoman Legacy and Turkish Politics." *Journal of International Affairs* 54, no. 1 (2000): 63–86.

Heywood, C. *The Turks.* Oxford: Blackwell. 1998.

İnalcık, Halil. "Land Reforms in Turkish History." *Muslim World* 45 (1955): 221–28.

Jackh, Ernest. *The Rising Crescent: Turkey Yesterday, Today, and Tomorrow.* New York: Farrar and Rinehart, 1944.

Karpat, Kemal H., ed. *Ottoman Past and Today's Turkey.* Leiden: E. J. Brill, 2000.

Landau, Jacob. *Pan-Turkism in Turkey: A Study in Irredentism.* London: C. Hurst, 1981.

Lapidot-Firilla, Anat. "The Memoirs of Halide Edip (1884–1964): The Public Persona and the Personal Narrative." *New Perspectives on Turkey*, no. 21 (1999): 61–77.

Lewis, Bernard. "The Impact of the French Revolution on Turkey." *Journal of World History* 1 (1953): 105–25.

———. *The Emergence of Modern Turkey.* London: Oxford University Press, 1961.

———. "The Ottoman Empire and Its Aftermath." *Journal of Contemporary History* 15 (1980): 27–36.

Luke, Harry. *The Old Turkey and the New: From Byzantium to Ankara.* Rev. ed. London: Geoffrey Bles, 1955.

Mango, Andrew. *Atatürk: The Biography of the Founder of Modern Turkey.* London: John Murray, 1999.

Mardin, Şerif. "The Mind of the Turkish Reformer." *Western Humanities Review* 15 (1960): 413–36.

Olson, Robert. *Imperial Meanderings and Republican By-Ways: Essays on Eighteenth-Century Ottoman and Twentieth-Century History of Turkey.* Istanbul: ISIS Press, 1996.

Parla, Taha. *The Social and Political Thought of Ziya Gökalp.* Leiden: E. J. Brill, 1985.

Quataert, Donald, ed. *Manufacturing in the Ottoman Empire and Turkey.* New York: SUNY Press, 1994.

Quataert, Donald, and Erik Zürcher, eds. *Workers and the Working Class in the Ottoman Empire and the Turkish Republic, 1839–1950.* New York and London: I. B. Tauris, 1995.

Shaw, Stanford J. *The Jews of the Ottoman Empire and the Turkish Republic.* New York: New York University Press, 1991.

———. *A Life with the Ottomans: The Ottoman Empire and Turkey in History.* Istanbul: ISIS, 2000.

Shaw, Stanford J., and Ezel Kural Shaw. *History of the Ottoman Empire and Modern Turkey.* Vol. 2 of *Reform, Revolution, and Republic—The Rise of Modern Turkey, 1808–1975.* New York: Cambridge University Press, 1977.

Toynbee, Arnold. *Turkey: A Past and Future.* New York: George H. Doran, 1917.

Toynbee, Arnold, and Kenneth P. Kirkwood. *Turkey.* New York: Scribner's Sons, 1927.

Ward, Robert E., and Dankwart A. Rustow, eds. *Political Modernization in Japan and Turkey.* Princeton, N.J.: Princeton University Press, 1964.

Waugh, Telford. *Turkey: Yesterday, Today, and Tomorrow.* London: Chapman and Hall, 1930.

Weiker, Walter F. *Ottomans, Turks and the Jewish Polity: A History of the Jews of Turkey.* Lanham, Md.: University Press of America, 1992.

Turkish Republic

Ahmad, Feroz. *The Making of Modern Turkey.* London: Routledge, 1993.

Barchard, David. *Turkey and the West.* London: Routledge & Kegan Paul, 1985.

Benedict, Peter, Erol Tümertekin, and Fatma Mansur, eds. *Turkey: Geographic and Social Perspectives.* Leiden: E. J. Brill, 1974.

Bisbee, Eleanor. *The New Turks: Pioneers of the Republic, 1920–1950.* Philadelphia: University of Pennsylvania Press, 1951.

Bozdoğan, Sibel, and Reşat Kasaba, ed. *Rethinking Modernity and National Identity in Turkey.* Seattle: University of Washington Press, 1997.

Brown, J. M. "Tansu Çiller and the Question of Turkish Identity." *World Policy Journal* 11, no. 3 (1994): 55–60.

Cizre-Sakallıoğlu, Ümit, and Erinç Yeldan. "Politics, Society, and Financial Liberalization: Turkey in the 1990s." *Development and Change* 31, no. 2 (2000): 525–44.

Cohn, Edwin J. *Turkish Economic, Social, and Political Change: The Development of a More Prosperous and Open Society.* New York: Praeger, 1970.

Cornell, E. *Turkey in the 21st Century: Opportunities, Challenges, Threats.* Richmond, U.K.: Curzon, 1999.

Eralp, Atilla, Muharrem Tünay, and Birol A. Yeşilada, eds. *The Political and Socioeconomic Transformation of Turkey.* Westport, Conn.: Praeger, 1993.

Eren, Nuri. *Turkey Today and Tomorrow: An Experiment in Westernization.* New York: Praeger, 1963.

Finkel, Andrew, and Nükhet Sirman. *Turkish State, Turkish Society.* London: Routledge, 1990.

Grothusen, Klaus-Detlev, ed. *Türkei: Südost-Europa-Handbuch* [Turkey: Handbook on Southeastern Europe]. Göttingen, Germany: Vandenhoeck and Ruprecht, 1985.

Hale, William, ed. *Aspects of Modern Turkey.* London: Bowker, 1976.

———. *The Political and Economic Development of Modern Turkey.* New York: St. Martins, 1981.

———. "Turkey." In *Middle East Contemporary Survey 1988*, ed. Ami Ayalan and Haim Shaked. Boulder, Colo.: Westview, 1990.

Karpat, Kemal H. "Society, Economics, and Politics in Contemporary Turkey." *World Politics* 17 (1964): 50–74.

Kedourie, Sylvia, ed. *Turkey before and after Atatürk: Internal and External Affairs.* London: Frank Cass, 1999.

Landau, Jacob M. "Politics, Economics and Religion: Turkey and the European Common Market." *Oriento Moderno* (Rome) 60 (1980): 163–71.

———. ed. *Atatürk and the Modernization of Turkey.* Boulder, Colo.: Westview, 1984.

Lewis, Bernard. *Turkey Today.* London: Hutchinson, 1940.

Lewis, Geoffrey. *Modern Turkey.* New York: Praeger, 1974.

Magnarella, P. *Anatolia's Loom: Studies in Turkish Culture, Society, Politics, and Law.* Istanbul: ISIS, 1998.

Mango, Andrew. "The Turkish Model." *Middle Eastern Studies* 29, no. 4 (1993): 726–57.

———. *Turkey: The Challenge of a New Role.* London: Praeger, 1994.

Mears, E. G., ed. *Modern Turkey.* New York: Macmillan, 1924.

Orga, Irfan. *Phoenix Ascendant.* London: Robert Hale, 1958.

Ostrorog, Leon. *The Angora Reform.* London: University of London Press, 1927.

Öncü, Ayşe, Çağlar Keyder, and Saad Eddin İbrahim, eds. *Developmentalism and Beyond: Society and Politics in Egypt and Turkey.* Cairo: American University in Cairo Press, 1994.

Rittenberg, Libby. *The Political Economy of Turkey in the Post-Soviet Era: Going West and Looking East.* Westport, Conn.: Praeger, 1998.

Robinson, Richard D. *The First Turkish Republic: A Case Study in National Development.* Cambridge, Mass.: Harvard University Press, 1963.

Rustow, Dankwart A. "Mehmed Akif's Independence Hymn: Religion and Nationalism in Atatürk's Movement of Liberation." *Journal of the American Institute for the Study of Middle East Civilizations* 1 (1980–1981): 112–17.

———. *Turkey: America's Forgotten Ally.* New York: Council on Foreign Relations, 1987.

Shaw, Stanford J. *Turkey and the Holocaust: Turkey's Role in Rescuing Turkish and European Jewry from Nazi Persecution, 1933–1945.* New York: New York University Press, 1993.

Shick, Irvin Cemil, and Ertuğrul Ahmet Tonak, eds. *Turkey in Transition: New Perspectives.* New York: Oxford University Press, 1987.

Thomas, Lewis V., and Richard N. Frye. *The United States and Turkey and Iran.* Hamden, Conn.: Archon, 1971.

Turkey and Europe in a Cultural Context. Cambridge: Centre of Middle Eastern Studies, University of Cambridge, 1988.

Turkish Political Science Association. *Turkey in the Year 2000.* Ankara: Sevinç Matbaası, 1989.

Ward, Barbara: *Turkey.* London: Oxford University Press, 1942.

Weiker, Walter F. *The Modernization of Turkey: From Atatürk to the Present Day.* New York: Holmes and Meier, 1981.

Yalman, Ahmet Emin. *Turkey in My Time.* Norman: University of Oklahoma Press, 1956.

Geography and Travel

Albaum, M., and C. Davies. "The Spatial Structure of Socio-Economic Attributes of Turkish Provinces." *International Journal of Middle East Studies* 4 (1973): 288–310.

Aksoy, A., and K. Robins. "Istanbul between Civilization and Discontent." *New Perspectives in Turkey,* no. 10 (1994): 57–74.

Akurgal, Ekrem. *Ancient Civilizations and Ruins of Turkey.* Istanbul: Haşet, 1985.

Bean, George E. *Aegean Turkey: An Archaeological Guide.* London: Ernest Benn, 1966.

———. *Turkey's Southern Shore: An Archaeological Guide.* London: Ernest Benn, 1968.

———. *Turkey beyond the Meander: An Archaeological Guide.* London: Ernest Benn, 1971.

———. *Lycian Turkey: An Archaeological Guide.* London: Ernest Benn, 1978.

Bean, George E., and Terence B. Milford. *Journeys in Rough Cilicia, 1964–1968.* Cologne, Germany: Böhlau, 1970.

Beeley, Brian. "The Greek-Turkish Boundary: Conflict at the Interface." *Institute of British Geography Transactions* 3 (1977): 351–66.

Blake, Everett C., and Anna G. Edmonds. *Biblical Sites in Turkey.* Istanbul: Redhouse Press, 1977.

Blohm, Kurt W. *Gateway Guide to Turkey.* London: Methuen, 1968.

Childs, W. J. *Across Asia Minor on Foot.* New York: Dodd, 1971.

Darke, Diana. *Guide to Eastern Turkey and the Black Sea Coast.* London: Michael Haag, 1987.

———. *Guide to Aegean and Mediterranean Turkey.* London: Michael Haag, 1989.

Davis, Peter A. *Flora of Turkey and East Aegean Islands.* Edinburgh: Edinburgh University Press, 1970.

Denham, H. M. *Southern Turkey, The Levant, and Cyprus: A Sea-Guide to the Coasts and Islands.* London: John Murray, 1973.

Dewdney, J. C. *Turkey: An Introductory Geography.* New York: Praeger, 1971.

Edmonds, Anna G. *Turkey's Religious Sites (Biblical Sites, Churches, Mosques, Synagogues, Temples).* Istanbul: Damko, 1997.

Ellis, W., and W. Parks. "City Astride Two Continents: Istanbul." *National Geography* 159 (1973): 501–34.

Fellows, Charles. *Travels and Researches in Asia Minor, More Particularly in the Province of Lycia.* Hildesheim, Germany: Georg Olms Verlag, 1973.

Gardner, G. Peabody. *Turkish Delight: A Cruise along the Southern Coast of Turkey.* Salem, Mass.: Peabody Museum, 1964.

Gough, Mary. *Travel into Yesterday: An Account of Archaeological Journeying through the Plain and Rough Places of the Roman Province of Cilicia, in Southern Turkey.* Garden City, N.Y.: Doubleday, 1954.

Güçlü, Y. "Turkey and Faith Tourism." *Perceptions* (Ankara) 3, no. 2 (1998): 135–41.

Hamblin, Dora Jane. *Buried Cities and Ancient Treasures.* New York: Simon & Schuster, 1973.

Harrell, Betsy. *Mini Tours Near Istanbul, Book II.* Istanbul: Redhouse Press, 1978.

Harrell, Betsy, and Evelyn Kalças. *Mini Tours Near Istanbul, Book I.* Istanbul: Redhouse Press, 1975

Haynes, Sybille. *Land of Chimaera: An Archaeological Excursion in the South-West of Turkey.* London: Chatto and Windus, 1974.

Hills, Denis C. *My Travels in Turkey.* London: Allen and Unwin, 1964.

Jackson, Monica. *Turkish Time Machine.* London: Hodder and Stoughton, 1966.

Johnson, Stower. *Turkish Panorama.* London: Robert Hale, 1968.

Kalças, Evelyn Lyle. *Breakfast in Asia and Lunch in Europe: Life on the Bosphorus.* Bornova, Turkey: Bilgehan Matbaası, 1977.

———. *Food from the Fields: Edible Wild Plants of Aegean Turkey.* Bornova, Turkey: Birlik Matbaası, 1980.

Kinross, John Patrick Douglas Balfour. *Within the Taurus: A Journey in Asiatic Turkey.* London: John Murray, 1954.

———. *Europa Minor: Journeys in Coastal Turkey.* London: John Murray, 1956.

Kolars, John F., and William A. Mitchell. *The Euphrates River and the Southeast Anatolia Development Project.* Carbondale: South Illinois University Project, 1991.

Leake, William Martin. *Journal of a Tour of Asia Minor, with Comparative Remarks on the Ancient and Modern Geography of that Country.* Hildesheim, Germany: Georg Olms Verlag, 1976.

Lister, R. P. *Turkey Observed.* London: Eyre and Spottiswoode, 1967.

Lowe, W. "The Dardanelles: Time's Turkish Sea Lane." *Middle East* 6 (1966): 23–31.

Mango, Andrew. *Discovering Turkey.* London: Batsford, 1971.

Mansel, Philip. *Constantinople: City of the World's Desire.* New York: St. Martin's, 1996.

Marriner, John. *Trebizond and Beyond.* London: Rupert Hart-Davis, 1969.

———. *Journey into the Sunrise.* London: William Kimber, 1970.

Neave, Dorina Lockhart (Clifton). *Twenty-Six Years on the Bosphorus.* London: Grayson and Grayson, 1933.

Pardoe, Julia. *The Beauties of the Bosphorus.* London: Virtue and Co., 1855.

———. *City of the Sultan.* 2 vols. London: H. Colburn, 1837.

Patterson, Harriet-Louise H. *Travelling through Turkey: An Excursion into History and Religion.* Valley Forge, Pa.: Hudson Press, 1969.

Pereira, Michael. *Mountains and a Shore: A Journey through Southern Turkey.* London: Geoffrey Bles, 1966.
———. *Istanbul: Aspects of a City.* London: Geoffrey Bles, 1968.
Phelan, Nancy. *Welcome to the Wayfarer: A Traveller in Modern Turkey.* New York: Macmillan, 1965.
Pillement, Georges. *Unknown Turkey.* London: Johnson, 1973–1974.
Piri Reis-Kitab-ı Bahriye. Vol. 2. Istanbul: Historical Research Foundation, 1988 [16th-century text in Turkish and English].
Pitcher, Donald Edgar. *An Historical Geography of the Ottoman Empire from Earliest Times to the End of the Sixteenth Century.* Leiden: E. J. Brill, 1972.
Ramsay, W. M. *The Historical Geography of Asia Minor.* Amsterdam: Adolph M. Hakkert, 1972.
Reed, Fred. A. *Anatolian Junction: A Journey into Hidden Turkey.* Burnaby: Talon Books, 1999.
Schneider, Dux. *Turkey.* London: Jonathan Cape, 1975.
Settle, Mary Lee. *Turkish Reflections: A Biography of a Place.* London: Grafton Books, 1991.
Stark, Freya. *Ionia: A Quest.* London: John Murray, 1954.
———. *The Lycian Shore.* London: John Murray, 1956.
———. *Gateways and Caravans: A Portrait of Turkey.* New York: Macmillan, 1971.
Sykes, John. *A Summer in Turkey.* London: Hutchinson, 1970.
Taylor, Jane. *Imperial Istanbul: A Traveller's Guide.* New York: I. B. Tauris, 1998.
Warne, Osmund H. *Your Guide to Turkey.* New York: Funk & Wagnalls, 1968.
Waslander, Christine, ed. *Turkey: Hoş Geldiniz* [Welcome]. London: Kegan Paul, 1992.
Williams, Gwyn. *Turkey: A Traveller's Guide and History.* London: Faber & Faber, 1967.
———. *Eastern Turkey: A Guide and History.* London: Faber & Faber, 1972.

CHRONOLOGICAL BIBLIOGRAPHY

The Rise of the Ottoman Empire, circa 1280–1566

Babinger, Franz. *Mehmed the Conqueror and His Time.* Ed. William C. Hickman, trans. Ralph Manheim. Princeton, N.J.: Princeton University Press, 1978.
———. "Mehmed the Conqueror and His Time." *American Historical Review* 86 (1979): 500–501.
Brummett, Palmira. "Foreign Policy, Naval Strategy, and the Defense of the Ottoman Empire in the Early Sixteenth Century." *International History Review* 11 (1989): 613–27.
Faroqhi, Suraiya. "Sixteenth-Century Periodic Markets in Various Anatolian *Sancaks.*" *Journal of the Economic and Social History of the Orient* 22 (1979): 38–80.
Fisher, Sidney N. "Civil Strife in the Ottoman Empire, 1481–1503." *Journal of Modern History* 13 (1941): 448–66.
———. *The Foreign Relations of Turkey: 1481–1512.* Urbana: University of Illinois Press, 1948.
Fleischer, Cornell. "Royal Authority, Dynastic Cyclicism, and 'Ibn Khaldunism' in Sixteenth-Century Ottoman Letters." *Journal of Asian and African Studies* 18 (1983): 198–220.
Forster, Edward Seymour. *The Turkish Letters of Ogier Ghiselin de Busbecq: Imperial Ambassador at Constantinople, 1554–1562.* London: Oxford University Press, 1968.
Hattox, Ralph S. "Mehmed the Conqueror, the Patriarch of Jerusalem, and the Mamluk Authority." *Studia Islamica* 90, no. 1 (2000): 105–24.

Hess, A. "The Evaluation of the Ottoman Seaborn Empire in the Age of the Oceanic Discoveries, 1453–1525." *American Historical Review* 75 (1970): 1892–919.

———. "The Ottoman Conquest of Egypt (1517) and the Beginnings of the Sixteenth-Century World War." *International Journal of Middle East Studies* 4 (1973): 55–76.

İnalcık, Halil. "Ottoman Methods of Conquest." *Studia Islamica* 2 (1954): 104–29.

———. "Mehmed the Conqueror (1432–1481) and His Time." *Speculum* 35 (1960): 408–27.

———. "Bursa and the Commerce of the Levant." *Journal of the Economic and Social History of the Orient* 3 (1960): 131–47.

———. "Süleyman the Lawgiver and Ottoman Law." *Archivum Ottomanicum* 1 (1969): 105–38.

———. "The Policy of Mehmed II toward the Greek Population of Istanbul and the Byzantine Buildings of the City." *Dumbarton Oak Papers*, no. 23 (1970): 213–49.

———. "The Conquest of Edirne." *Archivum Ottomanicum* 3 (1971): 185–210.

———. *The Ottoman Empire: The Classical Age, 1300–1600*. Trans. Norman Itzkowitz and Colin Imber. New York: Praeger, 1973.

———. "Tursun Beg, Historian of Mehmed the Conqueror's Time." *Wiener Zietschrift für die Kunde des Morgenlandes* (Vienna) 69 (1977): 55–71.

———. "A Case Study in Renaissance Diplomacy: The Agreement between Innocent VIII and Bayezid II on Djem Sultan." *Journal of Turkish Studies* 3 (1979–1980): 209–30.

———. "The Question of the Emergence of the Ottoman State." *International Journal of Turkish Studies* 2 (1981–1982): 71–79.

———. "The Appointment Procedure of a Guild Warden (Kethuda)." In *Festschrift Andreas Tietze*, ed. Arne A. Ambros and Anton C. Schaendlinger. Vienna: Im Selbstverlag des Institut für Orientalistik, 1986.

———. "The Ottoman Turks and the Crusades, 1329–1451." In *A History of the Crusades*. Vol. 6 of *The Impact of the Crusades on Europe*, ed. K. M. Setton. Madison: University of Wisconsin Press, 1989.

———. "Comments on 'Sultanism': Max Weber's Typification of the Ottoman Polity." *Princeton Papers in Near Eastern Studies* 1 (1992): 49–72.

Jennings, Ronald C. "Some Thoughts on the Gazi-Thesis." *Wiener Zeitschrift für die Kunde des Morgenlandes* 76 (1986): 151–61.

Kafadar, Cemal. *Between Two Worlds: The Construction of the Ottoman State*. Los Angeles: University of California Press, 1995.

Kaldy-Nagy, Gyula. "The Holy War (Jihad) in the First Centuries of the Ottoman Empire." *Harvard Ukranian Studies* 3, no. 4 (1979–80): 467–73.

Köprülü, M. Fuad. *The Origins of the Ottoman Empire*. Trans. and ed. by Gary Leiser. Albany: SUNY Press, 1992.

Kurat, A. N. "The Ottoman Empire under Mehmed IV." *New Cambridge Modern History* 5 (1968): 500–18.

Labib, S. "The Era of Süleyman the Magnificent: Crisis of Orientation." *International Journal of Middle East Studies* 10 (1979): 435–51.

Langer, William L., and Robert P. Black. "The Rise of the Ottoman Turks and Its Historical Background." *American Historical Review* 37 (1932): 468–505.

Lindner, Rudi Paul. *Nomads and Ottomans in Medieval Anatolia*. Bloomington: Indiana University, Research Institute for Inner Asian Studies, 1983.

———. "Stimulus and Justification in Early Ottoman History." *Greek Orthodox Theological Review* 27 (1982): 207–24.

Lybyer, Albert Howe. *The Government of the Ottoman Empire in the Time of Suleiman the Magnificent*. Cambridge, Mass.: Harvard University Press, 1913.

Ménage, V. L. "Some Notes on Devshirme." *Bulletin of the School of Oriental and African Studies* 30 (1967): 64–78.

Miller, Barnette. *The Palace School of Muhammad the Conqueror.* Cambridge, Mass.: Harvard University Press, 1941.

Mitler, L. "The Genoese in Galata: 1453–1682." *International Journal of Middle East Studies* 10 (1979): 71–91.

Özel, Oktay. "Limits of the Almighty: Mehmed II's 'Land Reform' Reunited." *Journal of the Economic and Social History of the Orient* 42, no. 2 (1999): 226–46.

Parry, V. J. "The Ottoman Empire (1481–1520)." *New Cambridge Modern History* 1 (1957): 395–410.

———. "The Ottoman Empire (1520–1566)." *New Cambridge Modern History* 11 (1958): 510–33.

Pixley, M. "The Development and Role of the Şeyhülislam in Early Ottoman History." *Journal of American Oriental Society* 96 (1976): 89–96.

Riggs, Charles T. *History of Mehmed the Conqueror.* Princeton, N.J.: Princeton University Press, 1969.

Runciman, Steven. *The Fall of Constantinople, 1453.* Cambridge: Cambridge University Press, 1969.

Shaw, Stanford J. "The Land Law of Ottoman Egypt (960–1553): A Contribution to the Study of Landholding in the Early Years of Ottoman Rule in Egypt." *Der Islam* 38 (1962): 106–37.

Shinder, J. "Early Ottoman Administration in the Wilderness: Some Limits on Comparison." *International Journal of Middle East Studies* 9 (1978): 89–106.

Stierlin, Henri. *Turkey: From the Selçuks to the Ottoman.* New York: Taschen, 1998.

Turan, Osman. "Ideal of World Domination among the Medieval Turks." *Studia Islamica* 4 (1955): 77–90.

Tursun Beg. *The History of Mehmed the Conqueror.* Trans. Halil İnalcık and Rhoads Murphey. Minneapolis, Minn.: Bibliotheca Islamica, 1978.

Wittek, Paul. *The Rise of the Ottoman Empire.* London: Royal Asiatic Society, 1938.

Woodhead, C. "From Scribe to Litterateur: The Career of a 16th-Century Ottoman Katib." *British Society for Middle Eastern Studies Bulletin* 9 (1982): 55–74.

Decline and Traditional Reform in the Ottoman Empire, circa 1566–1808

Abou El-Haj, Rıfa'at A. "Ottoman Diplomacy at Karlowitz." *Journal of the American Oriental Society* 87 (1967): 498–512.

———. "The Formal Closure of the Ottoman Frontier in Europe: 1679–1703." *Journal of the American Oriental Society* 89 (1969): 467–75.

———. "Ottoman Attitudes toward Peace Making: The Karlowitz Case." *Der Islam* 51 (1974): 131–37.

———. "The Ottoman Vezir and Paşa Households, 1683–1703: A Preliminary Report." *Journal of the American Oriental Society* 94 (1974): 438–47.

———. *The 1703 Rebellion and the Structure of Ottoman Politics.* Leiden: E. J. Brill, 1984.

———. *Formation of the Modern State: The Ottoman Empire, Sixteenth to Eighteenth Centuries.* Albany: SUNY Press, 1992.

Aksan, Virginia. "Ottoman-French Relations, 1739–1768." In *Studies on Ottoman Diplomatic History,* ed. Sinan Kuneralp. Istanbul: ISIS Press, 1987.

———. "The One-Eyed Fighting the Blind: Mobilization, Supply, and Command in the Russo-Turkish War of 1765–1774." *International History Review* 15 (1993): 221–38.

————. *An Ottoman Statesman in War and Peace: Ahmed Resmi Efendi, 1700–1783*. Leiden: E. J. Brill, 1995.

————. "Feeding the Ottoman Troops on the Danube, 1765–1774." *War and Society* 13 (1995): 1–14.

————. "Whatever Happened to the Janissaries? Mobilization for the 1765–1774 Russo-Ottoman War." *War in History* 5 (1998): 23–36.

————. "Mutiny and the Eighteenth-Century Ottoman Army." *Turkish Studies Association Bulletin* 22 (1998): 116–25.

Anderson, M. S. "Great Britain and the Russo-Turkish War of 1768–1774." *English Historical Review* 64 (1954): 39–58.

Barkan, Ömer, and Justin McCarthy. "The Price Revolution of the Sixteenth Century: A Turning Point in the Economic History of the Near East." *International Journal of Middle East Studies* 6 (1975): 3–28.

Barkey, Karen. "Rebellious Alliances: The State and Peasant Unrest in Early 17th-Century France and the Ottoman Empire." *American Sociological Review* 56 (1991): 699–715.

————. *Bandits and Bureaucrats: The Ottoman Route to State Centralization*. Ithaca: Cornell University Press, 1994.

————. "In Different Times: Scheduling and Social Control in the Ottoman Empire, 1550–1650." *Comparative Studies in Society and History* 38, no. 3 (1996): 460–83.

Barkey, Karen, and R. van Rossem. "Networks of Contention: Villages and Regional Structure in the Seventeenth-Century Ottoman Empire." *American Journal of Sociology* 102, no. 5 (1997): 1345–82.

Bayerle, Gustav. *Ottoman Diplomacy in Hungary: Letters from the Pashas of Buda*. Bloomington: Indiana University Press, 1972.

Bon, Ottaviano. *A Description of the Grand Signor's Seraglio, or Turkish Emperour's Court*. London: J. Martin and J. Ridley, 1650.

Brummetts, Palmira. *Ottoman Seapower and Levantine Diplomacy in the Age of Discovery*. Albany: SUNY Press, 1994.

Cassels, Lavender. *The Struggle for the Ottoman Empire, 1717–1740*. London: John Murray, 1967.

Chapman, Maybelle Rebecca. *Great Britain and the Baghdad Railway, 1888–1914*. Northampton, Mass.: Smith College, 1948.

Cohen, Ammon. "The Ottoman Approach to Christians and Christianity in the Sixteenth Century." *Islam and Christian-Muslim Relations* 7, no. 2 (1996): 205–12

Çizakça, M. "Price History and the Bursa Silk Industry: A Study in Ottoman Industrial Decline, 1550–1650." *Journal of Economic History* 40 (1980): 533–50.

Dankoff, Robert, and Robert Elsie. *Euliya Çelebi in Albania and Adjacent Regions (Kosovo, Montenegro, Chri): The Relevant Sections of the Seyahutname*. Leiden: E. J. Brill, 2000.

Darling, Linda T. *Revenue-Raising and Legitimacy: Tax Collection and Finance Administration in the Ottoman Empire, 1560–1660*. Leiden: E. J. Brill, 1996.

Davison, Roderic. "Russian Skill and Turkish Imbecility: The Treaty of Kuckuk Kainardji Reconsidered." *Slavic Review* 35 (1976): 463–83.

De Groot, A. "A Seventeenth-Century Ottoman Statesman 'Kayseriyeli' Khalil Pasha (1565–1629) and His Policy towards European Powers." *Die Welt des Islam* 54 (1977): 305–8.

Eldem, Ethem. *French Trade in Istanbul in the Eighteenth Century: The Ottoman Empire and Its Heritage. Politics, Society, and Economy*. Leiden: E. J. Brill, 1999.

Embassy to Constantinople: The Travels of Lady Mary Wortley Montagu. Ed. Christopher Pick. New York: New Amsterdam, 1988.

Eton, William. *A Survey of the Turkish Empire*. 1798. Reprint, New York: Arno Press, 1973.
Evliya Çelebi in Bitlis: The Relevant Section of the Seyahatname. Ed. Robert Dankoff. Leiden: E. J. Brill, 1990.
Faroqhi, Suraiya. "Social Mobility among the Ottoman Ulema in the Late Sixteenth Century." *International Journal of Middle East Studies* 4 (1973): 204–18.
———. "*Vakf* Administration in Sixteenth-Century Konya: The *Zaviye* of Sadredin-i Konevi." *Journal of the Economic and Social History of the Orient* 17 (1974): 145–72.
———. "The *Tekke* of Hacı Bektaş: Social Position and Economic Activites." *International Journal of Middle East Studies* 7 (1976): 183–208.
———. "Rural Society in Anatolia and the Balkans during the Sixteenth Century." *Turcica* (Ankara), part one: 9 (1977): 161–95; part two: 11 (1979): 103–53.
———. "Taxation and Urban Activities in the Sixteenth-Century Anatolia." *International Journal of Turkish Studies* 1 (1979–1980): 19–53.
———. "Textile Production in Rumeli and the Arab Provinces: Geographical Distribution and Internal Trade (1560–1650)." *Osmanlı Araştırmaları* (Istanbul) 1 (1980): 61–83.
———. "Camels, Wagons, and the Ottoman State in the Sixteenth and Seventeenth Centuries." *International Journal of Middle East Studies* 14 (1982): 523–39.
———. *Towns and Townsmen of Ottoman Anatolia: Trade, Crafts, and Food Production in an Urban Setting, 1520–1650*. New York: Cambridge University Press, 1984.
———. "Town Officials, Tımar-Holders, and Taxation: The Late Sixteenth-Century Crisis as Seen from Çorum." *Turcica* (Ankara) 18 (1986): 53–92.
———. "Towns, Agriculture, and the State in Sixteenth-Century Ottoman Anatolia." *Journal of the Economic and Social History of the Orient* 32 (1990): 125–56.
———. "Red Sea Trade and Communications as Observed by Evliya Çelebi, 1671–1672." *New Perspectives on Turkey*, nos. 5–6 (1991): 87–105.
———. "Traders and Customs Officials in 1660s Erzurum." *New Perspectives on Turkey*, nos. 5–6 (1991): 151–65.
———. "Counterfeiting in Ankara." *Turkish Studies Association Bulletin* 15 (1991): 281–92.
———. "Political Activity among Ottoman Taxpayers and the Problem of Sultanic Legitimation, 1570–1650." *Journal of the Economic and Social History of the Orient* 35 (1992): 1–39.
———. *Pilgrims and Sultans: The Hajj under the Ottomans*. London: I. B. Tauris, 1996.
———. "Migration into Eighteenth-Century 'Greater Istanbul' as Reflected in the Kadi Registers of Eyüp." *Turcica* 30 (1998): 163–84.
———. "A Builder as Slave Owner and Rural Moneylender: Hacı Abdullah of Bursa." In *Mélanges Prof. Machiel Kiel*, ed. Abaljelil Temimi. Zaghouan: Fondation Temimi, 1999.
———. *Subjects of the Sultan: Culture and Daily Life in the Ottoman Empire*. New York: I. B. Tauris, 2000.
Finkel, Caroline. *The Administration of Warfare: The Ottoman Military Campaigns in Hungary*. Vienna: VWGO, 1988.
Fisher, Sydney Nettleton. "The Foreign Relations of Turkey, 1481–1512." *Electronic Journal of Oriental Studies* 3, no. 3 (2000): 1–111.
Fleischer, Cornell. "Royal Authority, Dynastic Cyclism, and 'Ibn Khaldunism' in Sixteenth-Century Ottoman Letters." In *Ibn Khaldun and Islamic Ideology*, ed. B. B. Lawrence. Leiden: E. J. Brill, 1984.
———. *Bureaucrat and Intellectual in the Ottoman Empire: The Historian Mustafa Ali, 1541–1600*. Princeton, N.J.: Princeton University Press, 1986.
Fodor, P. "State and Society, Crisis and Reform, in a 15th–17th Century Ottoman Mirror for Princes." *Acta Orientalni* (Prague) 40 (1986): 217–40.

Frangakis-Syrett, Elena "Trade between Ottoman Empire and Western Europe: The Case of İzmir in the 18th Century." *New Perspectives on Turkey* 2 (1988): 1–18.

———. *The Commerce of Smyrna in the Eighteenth Century, 1700–1820.* Athens: Centre for Asia Minor Studies, 1992.

Fraser, Charles. *Annals of the Ottoman Empire from 1591 to 1659 of the Christian Era.* London: J. L. Cox & Sons, 1832.

Gerber, Haim. "Guilds in the Seventeenth-Century Bursa." *Asian and African Studies* 11 (1976): 59–86.

———. *Economy and Society in an Ottoman City: Bursa, 1600–1700.* Jerusalem: Hebrew University of Jerusalem, 1988.

Gibb, H. A. R., and Harold Bowen. *Islamic Society and the West.* Vol. 1 of *Islamic Society in the Eighteenth Century.* London: Oxford University Press, part 1, 1950; part 2, 1957.

Ginio, Eyal. "The Administration of Criminal Justice in Ottoman Selânik (Salonica) during the Eighteenth Century." *Turcica* 30 (1998): 185–210.

Goffman, Daniel. *İzmir and the Levantine World, 1550–1650.* Seattle: University of Washington Press, 1990.

———. "Ottoman *Millets* in the Seventeenth Century." *New Perspectives on Turkey,* no. 11 (1994): 135–58.

———. *Britons in the Ottoman Empire, 1642–1660.* Seattle: University of Washington Press, 1998.

Göçek, Müge. *East Encounters West: France and the Ottoman Empire in the Eighteenth Century.* New York: Oxford University Press, 1987.

Grant, Jonathan. "Rethinking the Ottoman 'Decline': Military Technology Diffusion in the Ottoman Empire, Fifteenth to Eighteenth Centuries." *Journal of World History* 10, no. 1 (1999): 179–201.

Griswold, William. *The Great Anatolian Rebellion, 1000–1020/1591–1611.* Berlin: Klaus Schwarz, 1983.

Hess, Andrew C. "Catastrophe or Continuity: Two Viewpoints on the Sixteenth-Century Ottoman Crisis." *Turkish Studies Association Bulletin,* no. 3 (1977): 1–2.

Hill, Aaron. *A Full and Just Account of the Present State of the Ottoman Empire in All Its Branches.* London: G. Parker, 1733.

Hurewitz, J. C. "The Europeanization of Ottoman Diplomacy: The Conversion from Unilateralism to Reciprocity in the 19th Century." *Belleten* (Ankara) 25 (1961): 455–66.

———. "Russia and the Turkish Straits: A Reevaluation of the Origins of the Problem." *World Politics* 14 (1962): 606–32.

———. "The Background of Russia's Claims to the Turkish Straits: A Reassessment." *Belleten* (Ankara) 28 (1964): 459–503.

Imber, C. "The Persecution of the Ottoman Shi'ites According to the Mühimme Defterleri, 1565–1585." *Der Islam* 56 (1979): 245–73.

Intimate Life of an Ottoman Statesman, Melek Ahmed Pasha (1588–1662) as Portrayed in Evliya Çelebi's Book of Travels (Seyahat-name). Trans. Robert Dankoff, with historical introduction by Rhoads Murphey. Albany: SUNY Press, 1992.

Itzkowitz, N. "Eighteenth-Century Ottoman Realities." *Studia Islamica* 16 (1962): 73–94.

İnalcık, Halil. "The Ottoman Decline and Its Effects on the Reaya." *IIe congrès international des etudes du sud-est européenne* 3 (1978): 73–90.

———. "Military and Fiscal Transformation in the Ottoman Empire, 1600–1700." *Archivum Ottomanicum* 6 (1980): 283–337.

İslamoğlu, Huri, and Suraiya Faroqhi. "Crop Patterns and Agricultural Production: Trends in Sixteenth-Century Anatolia." *Review* 2 (1979): 401–36.

İslamoğlu-İnan, H. *State and Peasant in the Ottoman Empire: Agrarian Power Relations and Regional Economic Development during the Sixteenth Century.* Leiden: E. J. Brill, 1994.

İsvan, Nurhan. "Illegal Local Trade in the Ottoman Empire and the Guilds of Istanbul, 1725–1726: Suggested New Hypotheses." *International Journal of Turkish Studies* 5 (1990–1991): 1–26.

Jennings, Ronald C. "Loans and Credit in Early 17th-Century Ottoman Judicial Records: The Sharia Court of Kayseri." *Journal of the Economic and Social History of the Orient* 16 (1973): 168–216.

———. "The Office of Vekil (Wakil) in the 17th-Century Ottoman Sharia Courts." *Studia Islamica* 45 (1975): 147–69.

———. "Limitations of the Judicial Powers of the Kadı in 17th-C. Ottoman Kayseri." *Studia Islamica* 50 (1979): 151–84.

———. "Firearms, Bandits, and Gun Control: Some Evidence on Ottoman Policy towards Firearms in the Possesian of Reaya, from Judicial Records of Kayseri, 1600–1627." *Archivum Ottamanicum* 6 (1980): 339–58.

Kafadar, Cemal. "A Death in Venice (1575): Anatolian Muslim Merchants Trading in the Serenissima." *Journal of Turkish Studies* 10 (1986): 191–218.

———. "The Question of Ottoman Decline." *Harvard Middle Eastern and Islamic Review* 4, nos. 1–2 (1997–1998): 30–75.

Kaiser, T. "The Evil Empire? The Debate on Turkish Despotism in Eighteenth-Century French Political Culture." *Journal of Modern History* 72, no. 1 (2000): 6–34.

Katip Çelebi. *The Balance of Truth.* Trans. G. L. Lewis. London: Allen & Unwin, 1957. First printed in 1656.

Kortepeter, C. Max. *Ottoman Imperialism during the Reformation: Europe and the Caucasus.* New York: New York University Press, 1972.

Kunt, Metin. "Ethnic-Regional (*Cins*) Solidarity in the Seventeenth-Century Ottoman Establishment." *International Journal of Middle East Studies* 5 (1974): 233–39.

———. *The Sultan's Servants: The Transformation of Ottoman Provincial Government, 1550–1650.* New York: Columbia University Press, 1983.

Kurat, Akdes Nimet. "The Retreat of the Turks, 1683–1730." *New Cambridge Modern History* 6 (1970): 608–47.

Lewis, Bernard. "Some Reflections on the Decline of the Ottoman Empire." *Studia Islamica* 9 (1958): 111–27.

———. "Ottoman Observers of Ottoman Decline." *Islamic Studies* 50 (1962): 71–87.

Matar, Nabil I. *Turks, Moors, and Englishmen in the Age of Discovery.* New York: Columbia University Press, 1998.

McGowan, Bruce. "The Study of Land and Agriculture in the Ottoman Provinces within the Context of an Expanding World Economy in the 17th and 18th Centuries." *International Journal of Turkish Studies* 2 (1981): 57–63.

———. *Economic Life in Ottoman Europe: Taxation, Trade, and the Struggle for the Land, 1600–1800.* New York: Cambridge University Press, 1982.

Montagu, Mary Wortley. *Letters from the Levant during the Embassy to Constantinople.* 3 vols. Ed. Robert Halsband. Oxford: Clarendon Press, 1965–1966.

Murphey, Rhoads. *Regional Structure in the Ottoman Economy: A Sultanic Memorandum of 1636 A.D. Concerning the Sources and Uses of the Tax-Farm Revenues of Anatolia and the Coastal and Northern Portions of Syria.* Wiesbaden, Germany: Otto Harrassowitz, 1987.

Naff, Thomas. "Reform and the Conduct of Ottoman Diplomacy in the Reign of Selim III, 1789–1807." *Journal of the American Oriental Society* 83 (1963): 295–315.

Naima, Mustafa. *Annals of the Turkish Empire from 1591 to 1659 of the Christian Era.* London, 1832. Reprint, New York: Arno Press, 1976.

Olson, Robert W. *The Siege of Mosul and Ottoman-Persian Relations, 1718–1743: A Study of Rebellion in the Capital and War in the Province of the Ottoman Empire.* Bloomington: Indiana University Press, 1975.

———. "The Ottoman Empire in the Middle of the Eighteenth Century and the Fragmentation of Tradition: Relations of the Nationalities (Millets), Guilds (Esnaf), and the Sultan, 1740–1768." *Die Welt des Islams* 17 (1976–1977): 72–77.

———. "Jews, Janissaries, Esnaf, and the Revolt of 1740 in Istanbul: Social Upheaval and Political Realignment in the Ottoman Empire." *Journal of Economic and Social History of the Orient,* no. 20 (1977): 185–207.

Ortaylı, İlber. "The Problem of Nationalities in the Ottoman Empire Following the Second Siege of Vienna." In *Das Osmaniche Reich und Europa 1683 bis 1789: Konflikt, Entspannung und Austausch,* ed. Gernot Heiss and Grete Klingenstein. München: R. Oldenbourg Verlag, 1983.

Özoğlu, H. "State-Tribe Relations: Kurdish Tribalism in the 16th- and 17th-Century Ottoman Empire." *British Journal of Middle East Studies* 23, no. 1 (1996): 5–27.

Quataert, Donald. *Ottoman Manufacturing in the Age of the Industrial Revolution.* Cambridge: Cambridge University Press, 1993.

Rycaut, Paul. *The Present State of the Ottoman Empire.* London: J. Starkey and H. Broome, 1668.

Sarı Mehmed Pasha. *Ottoman Statecraft. The Book of Counsel for Vezirs and Governors.* Trans. Walter Livingston Jr. Princeton, N.J.: Princeton University Press, 1935.

Shaw, Stanford J. *The Financial Administration and Organization of Ottoman Egypt, 1517–1798.* Princeton, N.J.: Princeton University Press, 1961.

———. "The Established Ottoman Army Corps under Sultan Selim III (1789–1807)." *Der Islam* 40 (1965): 142–84.

———. "The Origins of Ottoman Military Reform: The Nizam-ı Cedit Army of Sultan Selim III." *Journal of Modern History* 37 (1965): 291–306.

———. *The Budget of Ottoman Egypt, 1005–1006/1596–1597.* The Hague: Mouton, 1968.

———. "Selim III and the Ottoman Navy." *Turcica* (Paris) 1 (1969): 212–41.

———. *Between the Old and New: The Ottoman Empire under Sultan Selim III, 1789–1807.* Cambridge, Mass.: Harvard University Press, 1971.

Shinder, Joel. "Career Line Formation in the Ottoman Bureaucracy, 1648–1750." *Journal of the Economic and Social History of the Orient* 16 (1973): 217–37.

Skilliter, S. A. *William Harborne and the Trade with Turkey, 1578–1582: A Documentary Study of the First Anglo-Ottoman Relations.* London: Oxford University Press, 1977.

Skiotis, Dennis. "From Bandit to Pasha: First Steps in the Rise to Power of Ali of Tepedelen." *International Journal of Middle East Studies* 2 (1971): 219–44.

Sutton, Robert. *Despatches of Sir Robert Sutton: Ambassador in Constantinople, 1710–1714.* Ed. Akdes Nimet Kurat. London: Offices of the Royal Historical Society, 1953.

Şaşmazer, Lynne M. "Policing Bread Price and Production in Ottoman Istanbul, 1793–1807." *Turkish Studies Association Bulletin* 24, no. 1 (Spring 2000): 21–40.

Thomas, Lewis V. *A Study of Naima.* Ed. Norman Itzkowitz. New York: New York University Press, 1972.

Tietze, Andreas, ed. *Mustafa Ali's Counsel for the Sultan of 1581.* Vienna: Verlag der Österreichischen Akademie der Wissenschaften, 1973.

Zilfi, Madeline. "Elite Circulation in the Ottoman Empire: Great Mollas of the Eighteenth Century." *Journal of the Economic and Social History of the Orient* 26 (1983): 318–64.

———. *The Politics of Piety: The Ottoman Ulema in the Post-Classical Age, 1600–1800.* Minneapolis, Minn.: Bibliotheca Islamica, 1988.

The Era of Modern Ottoman Reform, circa 1808–1909

Abu-Jaber, K. S. "The Millet System in the Nineteenth-Century Ottoman Empire." *Muslim World* 57 (1967): 212–23.

Abu-Manneh, Butrus. "Sultan Abdülhamid II and the Sharifs of Mecca (1880–1900)." *Asian and African Studies* 9 (1973): 1–21.

———. "The Islamic Roots of the Gülhane Rescript." *Die Welt des Islams* 34, no. 2 (1994): 173–203.

———. "The Sultan and the Bureaucracy: The Anti-Tanzimat Concepts of Grand Vizier Mahmud Nedim Paşa." *International Journal of Middle East Studies* 21 (1990): 257–74.

Ahmad, Feroz. "Ottoman Perceptions of Capitulations, 1800–1914." *Journal of Islamic Studies* 11, no. 1 (2000): 1–20.

Akarlı, Engin. *The Long Peace: Ottoman Lebanon 1861–1920.* Berkeley: University of California Press, 1993.

Arai, Masami. "An Imagined Nation: The Idea of the Ottoman Nation as a Key to Modern Ottoman History." *Orient* 27 (1991): 1–20.

Bailey, Frank E. *British Policy and the Turkish Reform Movement: A Study in the Anglo-Turkish Relations, 1826–1853.* 1942. Reprint, New York: Fertig, 1970.

Blaisdell, Donald C. *European Financial Control in the Ottoman Empire.* New York: Columbia University Press, 1929.

Blind, Karl. "The Prorogued Parliament." *North American Review*, no. 175 (1902): 42–52.

Bryne, Leo Gerald. *The Great Ambassador: A Study of the Diplomatic Career of Rt. Hon. Stratford Canning.* Columbus: Ohio State University Press, 1965.

Burke, Edmund. "Rural Unrest in the Ottoman Empire, 1830–1914." In *Peasants and Politics in the Modern Middle East*, ed. Farhad Kazemi and John Waterbury. Miami: Florida International University Press, 1991.

Chambers, Richard L. "The Education of a Nineteenth-Century Ottoman Alim: Ahmed Cevdet Paşa." *International Journal of Middle East Studies* 3 (1973): 440–64.

Clark, E. "The Ottoman Industrial Revolution." *International Journal of Middle East Studies* 5 (1974): 65–76.

Clay, Christopher. *Gold for the Sultan: Western Bankers and Ottoman Finances, 1856–1881.* London: I. B. Tauris, 2000.

Davison, Roderic H. "Turkish Attitudes Concerning Christian-Muslim Equality in the Nineteenth Century." *American Historical Review* 49 (1954): 844–64.

———. *Reform in the Ottoman Empire, 1856–1876.* Princeton, N.J.: Princeton University Press, 1963.

———. "The Question of Ali Paşa's Political Testament." *International Journal of Middle East Studies* 11 (1980): 209–25.

———. "Halil Şerif Paşa: Ottoman Diplomat and Statesman." *Osmanlı Araştırmaları* [The Journal of Ottoman Studies] (Istanbul) 2 (1981): 203–21.

———. "Midhat Paşa and Ottoman Foreign Relations." *Osmanlı Araştırmaları* [The Journal of Ottoman Studies] (Istanbul) 6 (1986): 161–73.

——. "Britain, the International Spectrum, and the Eastern Question, 1827–1841." *New Perspectives on Turkey*, no. 7 (1992): 15–36.

Deringil, Selim. "The Ottoman Response to the Egyptian Crisis of 1881–1882." *Middle Eastern Studies* 24 (1988): 17–30.

——. "Legitimacy Structures in the Ottoman Empire: Abdülhamid II, 1876–1909." *International Journal of Middle East Studies* 23 (1991): 345–59.

——. "The Invention of Tradition as Public Image in the Late Ottoman Empire, 1808 to 1908." *Comparative Studies in Society and History* 35 (1993): 1–27.

——. "The Ottoman Origins of Kemalist Nationalism: Namık Kemal to Mustafa Kemal." *European History Quarterly* 23 (1993): 165–93.

——. *The Well-Protected Domains: Ideology and Legitimation of Power in the Ottoman Empire 1876–1909.* London: I. B. Tauris, 1999.

Devereux, Robert. *The First Ottoman Constitutional Period: A Study of the Midhat Constitution and Parliament.* Baltimore, Md.: Johns Hopkins University Press, 1963.

Duguid, Stephen. "The Politics of Unity: Hamidian Policy in Eastern Anatolia." *Middle Eastern Studies* 9 (1973): 139–56.

Earle, Edward Mead. *Turkey, the Great Powers, and the Baghdad Railway: A Study in Imperialism.* 1923. Reprint, New York: Russell and Russell, 1966.

Ergene, Boğaç. "Wages in the Nineteenth-Century Anatolia: A Comparison of Urban and Agricultural Trends." *New Perspectives on Turkey*, no. 19 (1998): 125–40.

Elliott, Henry. "The Death of Abdül Aziz and of Turkish Reform." *Nineteenth Century* 23 (1888): 276–96.

Findley, Carter V. "The Legacy of Tradition to Reform: Origins of the Ottoman Foreign Ministry." *International Journal of Middle East Studies* 1 (1970): 334–57.

——. "The Foundations of the Ottoman Foreign Ministry: The Beginnings of Bureaucratic Reform under Selim III and Mahmud II." *International Journal of Middle East Studies* 3 (1972): 388–416.

——. "Sir James W. Redhouse (1811–1892): The Making of a Perfect Orientalist?" *Journal of the American Oriental Society* 99 (1979): 573–600.

——. *Bureaucratic Reform in the Ottoman Empire: The Sublime Porte, 1789–1922.* Princeton, N.J.: Princeton University Press, 1980.

——. "The Advent of Ideology in the Islamic Middle East." Part 1 *Studia Islamica* 55 (1982): 143–69; part 2 *Studia Islamica* 56 (1983): 147–80.

——. "Economic Bases of Revolution and Repression in the Late Ottoman Empire." *Comparative Studies in Society and History* 28 (1986): 81–106.

——. "A Vision of a Brilliant Career." *Wiener Zeitschrift für die Kunde des Morgenlandes* 76 (1986): 95–101.

——. "Factional Rivalry in Ottoman Istanbul: The Fall of Pertev Paşa, 1837." *Journal of Turkish Studies* 10 (1986): 127–34.

——. *Ottoman Civil Officialdom: A Social History.* Princeton, N.J.: Princeton University Press, 1989.

——. "Social Dimensions of the Dervish Life, as Seen in the Memoirs of Aşçı Dede İbrahim Halil." In *The Dervish Lodge in the Ottoman Empire*, ed. Raymond Lifchez. Berkeley: University of California Press, 1992.

——. "The Ottoman Administrative Legacy and the Modern Middle East." In *The Ottoman Imprint on the Balkans and the Middle East*, ed. L. Carl Brown. New York: Columbia University Press, 1996.

——. "An Ottoman Occidentalist in Europe, 1889: Ahmed Mithat Meets Madame Gülnar, 1889." *American Historical Review* 103, no. 1 (1998): 15–49.

Frangakis-Syrett, Elena. "Implementation of the 1838 Anglo-Turkish Convention on İzmir Trade: European and Minority Merchants." *New Perspective on Turkey*, no. 7 (1992): 91–112.

Gawrych, G. "Tolerant Dimensions of Cultural Pluralism in the Ottoman Empire: The Albanian Community, 1800–1912." *International Journal of Middle East Studies* 15 (1983): 519–36.

Gibb, H. A. R. "Lütfi Paşa on the Ottoman Caliphate." *Oriens* 15 (1962): 287–95.

Grigorian, M. G. *Armenians in the Service of the Ottoman Empire, 1860–1908*. London: Routledge & Kegan Paul, 1978.

Güran, T. "The State's Role in the Grain Supply of Istanbul, 1723–1839." *International Journal of Turkish Studies* 3 (1985): 27–42.

Hurewitz, Jay C. "Ottoman Diplomacy and the European State System." *Middle East Journal* 15 (1961): 141–52.

Issawi, Charles. *The Economic History of Turkey, 1800–1914*. Chicago: University of Chicago Press, 1980.

Itzkowitz, Norman. "'Kimsiniz Bey Efendi' or a Look at *Tanzimat* through Namier-Colored Glasses." *Near Eastern Round Table* 1 (1967–1968): 41–52.

Itzkowitz, Norman, and Joel Shinder. "The Office of Şeyh ül-Islam and the Tanzimat: A Prosopographic Enquiry." *Middle Eastern Studies* 8 (1972): 93–102.

İnalcık, Halil. "Application of the Tanzimat and Its Social Effects." *Archivum Ottomanicum* 5 (1973): 97–127.

Jelavich, Barbara. *The Ottoman Empire, the Great Powers, and the Straits Question, 1870–1887*. Bloomington: Indiana University Press, 1973.

Karpat, Kemal H. "The Ottoman Parliament of 1877 and Its Social Significance." *Association Internationale d'Etudes du sud-est Européen* 5 (1969): 247–57.

———. "The Transformation of the Ottoman State, 1789–1908." *International Journal of Middle East Studies* 3 (1972): 243–81.

Kasaba, Reşat. "Was There a Comprador Bourgeoisie in Mid-19th-Century Western Anatolia?" *Review* 11 (1988): 215–28.

———. *The Ottoman Empire and the World Economy: The Nineteenth Century*. Albany: SUNY Press, 1988.

———. "Open Door Treaties: China and the Ottoman Empire Compared." *New Perspectives on Turkey*, no. 7 (1992): 71–90.

———. "Economic Foundations of a Civil Society: Greeks in the Trade of Western Anatolia, 1840–1876." In *Ottoman Greeks in the Age of Nationalism*, ed. C. Issawi and D. Gondicas. Princeton, N.J.: Darwin Press, 1999.

Kayalı, Hasan. "Elections and the Electoral Process in the Ottoman Empire, 1876–1919." *International Journal of Middle East Studies* 27, no. 2 (1995): 141–56.

Kellner-Heinkele, Barbara, and Kerem Dayı. "A Season in Crete: Hăfiz Nüri's Dïvăn as a Source for Life in the Periphery during the Tanzimat Period." *Archivum Ottomanicum* 17 (1999): 5–76.

Kent, Marian, ed. *The Great Powers and the End of the Ottoman Empire*. London: Frank Cass, 1996.

Keyder, Çağlar, ed. "Ottoman Empire: Nineteenth-Century Transformations." *Review* 11, no. 2 (special issue, 1988): 119–286.

Kortepeter, C. M. "Another Look at the Tanzimat." *Muslim World* 54 (1964): 49–55.

Kuran, Ercümend. "Küçük Said Paşa (1840–1914) as a Turkish Modernist." *International Journal of Middle East Studies* 1 (1970): 124–32.

Kushner, David. *The Rise of Turkish Nationalism, 1876–1908*. London: Frank Cass, 1977.

Landau, Jacob M. *The Hejaz Railway and the Muslim Pilgrimage: A Case of Ottoman Political Propaganda.* Detroit, Mich.: Wayne State University Press, 1971.

Lee, D. E. "The Origins of Pan-Islamism." *American Historical Review* 38 (1942): 278–87.

Levy, Avigdor. "The Military Policy of Sultan Mahmud II, 1808–1839." *International Journal of Middle East Studies* 2 (1971): 21–39.

———. "The Ottoman Ulema and the Military Reforms of Sultan Mahmud II." *Asian and African Studies* 7 (1971): 13–39.

Lewis, Bernard. "The Ottoman Empire in the Mid-Nineteenth Century: A Review." *Middle Eastern Studies* 1 (1965): 283–95.

———. "Ali Pasha on Nationalism." *Middle Eastern Studies* 10 (1974): 77–79.

Mardin, Şerif. "Some Explanatory Notes on the Origins of 'Mecelle' (Medjelle)." *Muslim World* 51 (1961): 189–96, 274–79.

———. "Some Notes on an Early Phase in the Modernization of Communications in Turkey." *Comparative Studies in Society and History* 3 (1961): 250–71.

———. "Libertarian Movements in the Ottoman Empire." *Middle East Journal* 16 (1962): 169–82.

———. *The Genesis of the Young Ottoman Thought: A Study in the Modernization of Turkish Political Ideas.* Princeton, N.J.: Princeton University Press, 1962.

McCarthy, Justin. *Death and Exile: The Ethnic Cleansing of Ottoman Muslims, 1821–1922.* Princeton, N.J.: Darwin Press, 1996.

Miller, William. *The Ottoman Empire and Its Successors, 1801–1927.* London: Frank Cass, 1966.

Mithat, Ali Haydar. *The Life of Mithat Pasha.* London: John Murray, 1983.

Owen, Roger. "The 1838 Anglo-Turkish Convention: An Overview." *New Perspectives on Turkey*, no. 7 (1992): 7–14.

Öke, Mim Kemal. "The Ottoman Empire, Zionism, and the Question of Palestine (1880–1908)." *International Journal of Middle East Studies* 14 (1982): 329–41.

Pamuk, Şevket. "The Ottoman Empire in the 'Great Depression' of 1873–1896." *Journal of Economic History* 44 (1984): 107–18.

———. "The Decline and Resistance of Ottoman Cotton Textiles, 1820–1913." *Explorations in Economic History* 23 (1986): 205–25.

———. *The Ottoman Empire and European Capitalism, 1820–1913: Trade, Investment, and Production.* New York: Cambridge University Press, 1987.

———. "The Disintegration of the Ottoman Monetary System during the Seventeenth Century." In *Metals and Monies in an Emerging Global Economy*, ed. Dennis O. Flynn and Arturo Giraldez. Aldershot, U.K.: Variorum, 1997.

———. "In the Absence of Domestic Currency: Debased European Coinage in the Seventeenth-Century Ottoman Empire." *Journal of Economic History* 57 (1997): 345–66.

———. "Ottoman Interventionism in Economic and Monetary Affairs." *Revue d'Histoire Maghrebine* 25 (1998): 361–7.

Patrick, Mary Mills. *Under Five Sultans.* New York: Century, 1929.

Pears, Edwin. *Life of Abdülhamid.* New York: Appleton, 1917.

Polk, William R., and Richard L. Chambers, eds. *Beginnings of Modernization in the Middle East: The Nineteenth Century.* Chicago: University of Chicago Press, 1968.

Quataert, Donald. "Dilemma of Development: The Agricultural Bank and Agricultural Reform in Ottoman Turkey, 1888–1908." *International Journal of Middle East Studies* 6 (1975): 210–27.

———. "Limited Revolution: The Impact of the Anatolian Railway on Turkish Transportation and the Provisioning of Istanbul, 1890–1908." *Business History Review* 51 (1977): 139–60.

———. "The Economic Climate of the 'Young Turk Revolution' in 1908." *Journal of Modern History* 51 (1979): 1147–61.

———. "The 1908 Young Turk Revolution: Old and New Approaches." *Middle East Studies Association Bulletin* 13 (1979): 22–29.

———. "The Commercialization of Agriculture in Ottoman Turkey, 1800–1914." *International Journal of Turkish Studies* 1 (1980): 38–55.

———. "Agricultural Trends and Government Policy in Ottoman Anatolia, 1800–1914." *Asian and African Studies* 15 (1981): 69–84.

———. *Social Disintegration and Popular Resistance in the Ottoman Empire, 1881–1908: Reactions to European Economic Penetration*. New York: New York University Press, 1983.

———. "Machine Breaking and the Changing Carpet Industry of Western Anatolia, 1860–1908." *Journal of Social History* 19 (1985–1986): 473–89.

———. "Ottoman Handicrafts and Industry in the Age of European Industrial Hegemony, 1800–1914." *Review* 11 (1988): 169–78.

———. "Labor and Working-Class History during the Late Ottoman Period, ca. 1800–1914." *Turkish Studies Association Bulletin* 15 (1991): 357–69.

Rahme, Joseph G. "Namık Kemal's Constitutional Ottomanism and Non-Muslims." *Islam and Christian-Muslim Relations* 10, no. 1 (1999): 23–40.

Rogan, E. L. "*Aşiret Mektebi*: Abdülhamid II's Schools for Tribes (1892–1907)." *International Journal of Middle East Studies* 28, no. 1 (1996): 83–107.

Salt, Jeremy. "A Precarious Symbiosis: Ottoman Christians and Foreign Missionaries in the Nineteenth Century." *International Journal of Turkish Studies* 3 (1985–1986): 53–67.

———. "Britain, the Armenian Question, and the Cause of the Ottoman Reform, 1894–1896." *Middle Eastern Studies* 26 (1990): 308–28.

———. *Imperialism, Evangelism, and the Ottoman Armenians, 1878–1896*. London: Frank Cass, 1993.

Shaw, Stanford J. "The Origins of Representative Government in the Ottoman Empire: An Introduction to the Provincial Councils, 1830–1876." *Near Eastern Round Table* 1 (1967–1968): 53–142.

———. "Ottoman History (past–1789)." *Middle East Studies Association Bulletin* 4 (1970): 1–14.

———. "The Central Legislative Councils in the Nineteenth-Century Ottoman Reform Movement before 1876." *International Journal of Middle East Studies* 1 (1970): 51–84.

———. "A Promise of Reform: Two Complimentary Documents." *International Journal of Middle East Studies* 4 (1973): 359–65.

———. "The Nineteenth-Century Ottoman Tax Reforms and Revenue System." *International Journal of Middle East Studies* 6 (1975): 421–59.

Somel, A. "Sırat-ı Müstakim: Islamic Modernist Thought in the Ottoman Empire." *Journal of Middle East Studies Society at Columbia University* 1 (1987): 55–80.

———. "Ottoman Islamic Education in the Balkans in the Nineteenth Century." *Islamic Studies* 36, no. 23 (1997): 439–64.

Toledano, Ehud R. "The Legislative Process in the Ottoman Empire in the Early Tanzimat Period: A Footnote." *International Journal of Turkish Studies* 1 (1980): 99–106.

———. *The Ottoman Slave Trade and Its Suppression, 1840–1890*. Princeton, N.J.: Princeton University Press, 1982.

———. "Reflections on Themes in Late Ottoman History." *Asian and African Studies* 20 (1984): 357–73.

Toprak, Zafer. "Modernization and Commercialization in the Tanzimat Period, 1838–1876." *New Perspective on Turkey*, no. 7 (1992): 57–70.

Ubicini, Jean Henri. *Letters on Turkey: An Account of the Religious, Political, Social, and Commercial Condition of the Ottoman Empire.* 1856. Trans. from French by Lady Easthope. Reprint, New York: Arno Press, 1976.

Vambery, Arminus. "Personal Recollections of Abdul Hamid and His Court." *Nineteenth Century* 65 (1909): 980–83; 66 (1909): 69–88.

The Young Turk Period, 1908–1918

Ahmad, Feroz. "Great Britain's Relations with the Young Turks, 1908–1914." *Middle Eastern Studies* 2 (1966): 302–29.

———. "The Young Turk Revolution." *Journal of Contemporary History* 3 (1968): 19–36.

———. *The Young Turks: The Committee of Union and Progress in Turkish Politics, 1904–1914*, Oxford: Clarendon Press, 1969.

———. "War and Society under the Young Turks." *Review* 11 (1988): 256–86.

Arai, M. *Turkish Nationalism in the Young Turk Era.* Leiden: E. J. Brill, 1991.

Bilinski, A. Rüstem Bey de. "The Turkish Revolution." *Contemporary Review* 93 (1908): 253–72.

Buxton, Noel. "The Young Turks." *Nineteenth Century* 65 (1909): 16–24.

———. *Turkey in Revolution.* London: T. Fisher Unwin, 1909.

———. "Young Turks after Two Years." *Nineteenth Century* 69 (1911): 417–32.

Danışman, H. "The Last Ottomans." *Asian Affairs* 27 (1986): 161–76.

Davison, Roderic H. "The Armenian Crisis, 1912–1914." *American Historical Review* 43 (1948): 481–505.

Devereux, R. "Süleyman Pasha's 'The Feeling of the Revolution.'" *Middle Eastern Studies* 15 (1979): 3–35.

Dillon, E. J. "The Unforeseen Happens as Usual." *Contemporary Review* 95 (1908): 364–84.

———. "A Clue to the Turkish Tangle." *Contemporary Review* 96 (1909): 743–56.

Djemal, Pasha. *Memories of a Turkish Statesman, 1913–1919.* New York: George H. Doran, 1922.

Erickson, Edward J. *Ordered to Die: A History of the Ottoman Army in the First World War.* Westport, Conn.: Greenwood, 2000.

Farhi, David. "The Şeriat as a Political Slogan—or the 'Incident of the 31st March.'" *Middle Eastern Studies* 7 (1971): 275–316.

Friedman, Isaiah. "The Young Turks and Zionism: International Implications." *CEMOTI* (Paris) 28 (1999): 31–40.

Hagen, Gottfried. "The Prophet Muhammed as an Exemplar in War: Ottoman Views on the Eve of World War I." *New Perspectives on Turkey* 22 (2000): 145–72.

Haley, C. D. "The Desperate Ottoman: Enver Paşa and the Germany Empire." *Middle Eastern Studies* 30, no. 1 (1994): 1–51; 30, no. 2 (1994): 224–51.

Halil Halid (Bey). "The Origins of the Revolt in Turkey." *Nineteenth Century* 65 (1909): 755–60.

Hamilton, Angus. "Turkey: The Old Regime and the New." *Fortnightly Review* 84 (1908): 369–82.

Hanioğlu, M. Şükrü. "Genesis of the Young Turk Revolution of 1908." *Osmanlı Araştırmaları* [The Journal of Ottoman Studies] (Istanbul) 3 (1982): 277–300.

———. *Young Turks in Opposition.* New York: Oxford University Press, 1995.

———. *Preparation for a Revolution: The Young Turks, 1902–1908*. New York: Oxford University Press, 2001.

Herbert, Captain von. "Kiamil Pasha and the Succession in Turkey." *Fortnightly Review* 84 (1908): 419–29.

Kansu, Aykut. *The Revolution of 1908 in Turkey*. Leiden: E. J. Brill, 1997.

———. *Politics in Post-Revolutionary Turkey, 1908–1913*. Leiden: E. J. Brill, 2000.

Katz, Yossef. "Paths of Zionist Political Action in Turkey, 1882–1914: The Plan for Jewish Settlement in Turkey in the Young Turk Era." *International Journal of Turkish Studies* 4 (1987): 115–35.

Kayalı, Hasan. *Arabs and Young Turks: Ottomanism, Arabism, and Islamism in the Ottoman Empire, 1908–1918*. Berkeley: University of California Press, 1997.

Kedourie, Elie. *England and the Middle East: The Destruction of the Ottoman Empire, 1914–1921*. Totowa, N.J.: Rowman & Littlefield, 1977.

Lowry, Heath. *The Story behind Ambassador Morgenthau's Story*. Istanbul: ISIS Press, 1990.

Macfie, A. L. *The End of the Ottoman Empire, 1908–1923*. London: Longman, 1998.

Mardin, Şerif. *Continuity and Change in the Ideas of Young Turks*. Istanbul: Robert College, 1969.

Margoliouth, D. C. "Constantinople at the Declaration of the Constitution." *Fortnightly Review* 84 (1908): 563–70.

McCullagh, Francis. "The Constantinople Mutiny of April 13th." *Fortnightly Review* 86 (1909): 58–69.

Morgenthau, Henry. *Secrets of the Bosphorus: Constantinople, 1913–1916*. London: Hutchinson, n.d. [1919].

Ostrorog, Léon. *The Turkish Problem*. London: Chatto and Windus, 1919.

Öke, Mim Kemal. "Young Turks, Freemasons, Jews, and the Question of Zionism in the Ottoman Empire, 1908–1913." *Studies in Zionism* 7 (1986): 199–218.

Pears, Edwin. "Turkey, Islam, and Turanism." *Contemporary Review* 114 (1918): 371–79.

Pinon, René. "The Young Turk Policy in Asia." *Current History* 11 (1919): 331–36.

Quataert, Donald. "The 1908 Young Turk Revolution: Old and New Approaches." *Middle East Studies Association Bulletin* 13 (1979): 22–29.

Ramsaur, Ernest E., Jr. *The Young Turks: Prelude to the Revolution of 1908*. Princeton, N.J.: Princeton University Press, 1957.

Ramsay, W. M. *The Revolution in Constantinople and Turkey*. London: Hodder and Stoughton, 1909.

Rustow, Dankwart A. "Enver Pasha." Vol. 2 of *Encyclopedia of Islam* (Leiden). 2nd ed. (1965): 698–702.

Sadıq, M. "Ziya Gökalp: The Making of an Ideology." *Cultura Turcica* (Ankara) 5–6 (1968–1970): 5–18.

Sanders, Liman von. *Five Years in Turkey*. Annapolis, Md.: Williams & Wilkins, 1928.

Sonyel, Salahi. *The Great War and the Tragedy of Anatolia: Turks and Armenians in the Maelstrom of Major Powers*. Ankara: Türk Tarih Kurumu, 2000.

Stoddard, T. L. "Pan-Turanism." *American Political Science Review* 11 (1917): 12–23.

Talaat. "Posthumous Memoirs of Talaat Pasha." *Current History* 15 (1921): 287–95.

Trumpener, Ulrich. "Turkey's Entry into World War I: An Assessment of Responsibilities." *Journal of Modern History* 34 (1962): 369–80.

———. *Germany and the Ottoman Empire, 1914–1918*. Princeton, N.J.: Princeton University Press, 1968.

Turfan, M. N. *Rise of the Young Turks: Politics, Military, and the Ottoman Collapse*. London: I. B. Tauris, 1998.

Ünal, H. "Ottoman Policy during the Bulgarian Independence Crisis: The Ottoman Empire and Bulgaria at the Outset of the Young Turk Revolution." *Middle Eastern Studies* 34, no. 4 (1998): 135–76.

Weber, Frank G. *Eagles on the Crescent: Germany, Austria, and the Diplomacy of the Turkish Alliance, 1914–1918*. Ithaca, N.Y.: Cornell University Press, 1970.

Yale, William. "Ambassador Morganthau's Special Mission of 1917." *World Politics* 1 (1949): 308–20.

Defeat, Disintegration, and Revival, 1918–1922

Brown, Philip M. "The Lausanne Conference." *American Journal of International Law* 17 (1923): 290–96.

———. "From Sèvres to Lausanne." *American Journal of International Law* 18 (1924): 113–16.

Criss, Nur Bilge. *Istanbul under Allied Occupation, 1918–1923*. Leiden: E. J. Brill, 1999.

Cruickshank, A. A. "The Young Turk Challenge in Postwar Turkey." *Middle East Journal* 22 (1968): 17–28.

Davison, Roderic. "Turkish Diplomacy from Mudros to Lausanne." In *The Diplomats*, ed. Gordon Craig and Felix Gilbert. Princeton, N.J.: Princeton University Press, 1953.

Dumont, Paul. "French Freemasonry and the Turkish Struggle for Independence (1919–1923)." *International Journal of Turkish Studies* 3 (1985–1986): 1–15.

Ellison, G. *An English Woman in Ankara*. London: Hutchinson, 1923.

Finefrock, M. "The Second Group in the First Turkish National Assembly." *Journal of South Asian and Middle Eastern Studies* 3 (1979): 3–20.

Gaillard, Gaston. *The Turks and Europe*. London: Thomas Murby, 1921.

Gökay, Bülent. *A Clash of Empires: Turkey between Russian Bolshevism and British Imperialism, 1918–1923*. London: I. B. Tauris, 1997.

Helmreich, Paul C. *From Paris to Sèvres: The Partition of the Ottoman Empire at the Peace Conference of 1919–1920*. Columbus: Ohio State University Press, 1974.

Howard, Harry N. *The Partition of Turkey: A Diplomatic History, 1913–1923*. Norman: University of Oklahoma Press, 1931.

———. *The King-Crane Commission: An American Inquiry in the Middle East*. Beirut: Khayats, 1963.

Maurice, Frederick. "The Crisis as Seen in Constantinople." *Contemporary Review*, no. 683 (1922): 556–61.

Sadıq, M. "Intellectual Origins of the Turkish National Liberation Movement." *International Studies* 15 (1976): 509–30.

Shaw, Stanford J. "Life in Ankara during the Turkish War of National Liberation." In *Suna Kili'ye Armağan*. Istanbul: Boğaziçi University, 1998.

———. *From Empire to Republic: The Turkish War of National Liberation*. 7 vols. Ankara: Türk Tarih Kurumu, 2001.

Shutleworth, D. I. "Turkey: From the Armistice to the Peace." *Journal of the Central Asian Society* 11 (1924): 61–62.

Smith, Elaine Diana. *Turkey: The Origins of the Kemalist Movement and the Government of the Grand National Assembly*. Washington, D.C.: private publication, 1959.

Sonyel, S. R. *Turkish Diplomacy, 1918–1923: Mustafa Kemal and the Turkish National Movement*. Beverly Hills, Calif.: Sage, 1975.

———. "Mustafa Kemal and Enver in Conflict, 1919–1922." *Middle Eastern Studies* 25 (1989): 506–15.

Zürcher, Erik Jan. "Atatürk and the Start of the National Resistance Movement." *Anatolia* (Istanbul) 8 (1981): 99–113.

———. *The Unionist Factor: The Role of the Committee of Union and Progress in the Turkish National Movement, 1905–1926*. Leiden: E. J. Brill, 1984.

Government and Politics in the Republican Period, 1923–2001

Abadan, Nermin. "Values and Political Behavior of Turkish Youth." *Turkish Yearbook of International Relations* (Ankara) 4 (1963): 81–102.

———. "The Politics of Students and Young Workers in Turkey." *Ankara Üniversitesi Siyasal Bilgiler Fakültesi Dergisi* (Ankara) 26 (1971): 89–111.

Abadan-Unat, Nermin. "Patterns of Political Modernization and Turkish Democracy." *Turkish Yearbook of International Relations* 18 (1979): 1–16.

Adıvar, Halide Edip. *Memoirs of Halide Edip*. New York: Century, 1926.

———. "Dictatorship and Reforms in Turkey." *Yale Review* 29 (1929): 27–44.

Adnan, Abdülhak (Adıvar). "Ten Years of Republic in Turkey." *Political Quarterly* 6 (1935): 240–52.

Ahgrist, M. P. "The Expression of Political Dissent in the Middle East: Turkish Democratization and Authoritarian Continuity in Tunisia." *Comparative Studies in Society and History* 41, no. 4 (1999): 730–57.

Ahmad, Feroz. *The Turkish Experiment in Democracy, 1950–1975*. London: C. Hurst, 1975.

Akarlı, Engin D., with Gabriel Ben-Dor, ed. *Political Participation in Turkey: Historical Background and Present Problems*. Istanbul: Boğaziçi University, 1975.

Akıncı, Uğur. "The Municipal Radicalism of Political Islam in Turkey." *Middle East Journal* 53, no. 1 (1999): 3–17.

Aksüm, Birol. "Aspects of Party System Development in Turkey." *Turkish Politics* 2, no. 1 (2001): 71–92.

Aleskerow, Fuad, Hasan Ersel, and Yavuz Sabuncu. "Power and Coalitional Stability in the Turkish Parliament (1991–1999)." *Turkish Studies* 1, no. 2 (2000): 21–38.

Alkan, Türker. "Turkey: Rise and Decline of Legitimacy in a Revolutionary Regime." *Journal of South Asian and Middle Eastern Studies* 4 (1980): 37–48.

Aral, B. "Turkey's Insecure Identity from the Perspective of Nationalism." *Mediterranean Quarterly* 8, no. 1 (1997): 77–91.

———. "Dispensing with Tradition? Turkish Politics and International Society during the Özal Decade, 1983–1993." *Middle Eastern Studies* 37, no. 1 (2001): 72–88.

Arıkan, E. Burak. "The Programme of the Nationalist Action Party: An Iron Hand in a Velvet Glove?" *Middle Eastern Studies* 34, no. 4 (1998): 120–34.

Armstrong, Harold C. *Grey Wolf Mustafa Kemal: An Intimate Study of a Dictator*. London: Arthur Barker, 1932.

Arnakis, George G. "Turanism: An Aspect of Turkish Nationalism." *Balkan Studies* (Salonica) 1 (1960): 19–32.

Atabaki, T., and E. Zürcher. *Men of Order: Authoritarian Modernization in Turkey and Iran*. London: I. B. Tauris, 2000.

Atiyas, Nimet. "The Kurdish Conflict in Turkey: Issues, Parties, and Prospects." *Security Dialogue* 28, no. 4 (1997): 439–52.

August, Ritter von Kral. *Kamal Atatürk's Land: The Evolution of Modern Turkey*. London: P. S. King and Son, 1938.

Ayata, Ayşe. "The Emergence of Identity Politics in Turkey." *New Perspectives on Turkey*, no. 17 (1997): 59–73.

Ayberk, Ural, and Emre Boduroğlu. "Turkish Interest Groups Facing the European Community." *Yapı Kredi Economic Review* (Istanbul), no. 3 (1989): 125–58.

Baer, Gabriel. "The Transition from Traditional to Western Criminal Law in Turkey and Egypt." *Studia Islamica*, no. 45 (1977): 139–58.

Baran, Zeyno. "Corruption: The Turkish Challenge." *Journal of International Affairs* 54, no. 1 (Fall 2000): 128–46.

Barkey, Henri J. "The People's Democracy Party (HADEP): The Travails of a Legal Kurdish Party in Turkey." *Journal of Muslim Minority Affairs* 18, no. 1 (1998): 129–38.

———. "The Struggles of a 'Strong' State." *Journal of International Affairs* 54, no. 1 (Fall 2000): 87–105.

Barkey, Henri J., and Graham Fuller, "Turkey's Kurdish Question: Critical Turning Points and Missed Opportunities." *Middle East Journal* 51, no. 1 (1997): 59–79.

———. *Turkeys Kurdish Question*. Lanham, Md.: Rowman & Littlefield, 1998.

Belge, Murat. "The Kurdish Question in Turkey Today: A Personal Assessment." *Zeitschrift für Türkeistudien* (Bonn) 2 (1992): 259–66.

Bent, Frederick T. "The Turkish Bureaucracy as an Agent of Change." *Journal of Comparative Administration* 1 (1969): 47–64

Berberoğlu, Berch. *Turkey in Crisis: From State Capitalism to Neo-Colonialism*. Westport, Conn.: Lawrence Hill, 1982.

Berkes, Niyazi. "The Two Facets of the Kemalist Revolution." *Muslim World* 64 (1974): 292–306.

Bianchi, Robert. *Interest Groups and Political Development in Turkey*. Princeton, N.J.: Princeton University Press, 1984.

Birand, Mehmet Ali. *The General's Coup in Turkey: An Inside Story of 12 September 1980*. Trans. M. A. Dikerdem. London: Brassey's Defence Publishers, 1987.

Bosworth, C. E. "Language Reform and Nationalism in Modern Turkey: A Brief Conspectus." *Muslim World* 55 (1965): 58–65, 164–67.

Bozdağhağlu, Yürel. "Identity Crisis and the Struggle for Recognition in Turkey." *Journal of South Asian and Middle Eastern Studies* 23, no. 2 (2000): 18–36.

Bozdoğan, S. "Architecture, Modernism, and Nation-Building in Modern Turkey." *New Perspectives on Turkey*, no. 10 (1994): 37–55.

Brockeyy, G. D. "Collective Action and Turkish Revolution: Towards a Framework for the Social History of the Atatürk Era." *Middle Eastern Studies* 34, no. 4 (1998): 24–41.

Brown, James. "The Military and Society: The Turkish Case." *Middle Eastern Studies* 25 (1989): 387–404.

Buğra, Ayşe. *State and Business in Turkey: A Comparative Study*. Albany: SUNY Press, 1994.

———. "Class, Culture, and State: An Analysis of Interest Representation by Two Turkish Business Associations." *International Journal of Middle East Studies* 30, no. 4 (1998): 521–39.

Cizre-Sakallıoğlu, Ümit. "Labour and State in Turkey: 1960–1980." *Middle Eastern Studies* 28 (1992): 712–28.

———. "The Ideology and Politics of the Nationalist Action Party of Turkey." *CEMOTİ* (Paris) 13 (1992): 141–64.

———. "Liberalism, Democracy, and the Turkish Centre-Right: The Identity Crisis of the True Path Party." *Middle Eastern Studies* 32 (April 1996): 142–61.

———. "Historicizing the Present and Problematizing the Future Kurdish Problem: A Critique of the TOBB Report on the Eastern Question." *New Perspectives on Turkey*, no. 14 (1996): 1–22.

———. "Kurdish Nationalism from an Islamist Perspective: The Discourses of Turkish Islamist Writers." *Journal of Muslim Minority Affairs* 18, no. 1 (1998): 73–89.

———. "Rethinking the Connections between Turkey's 'Western' Identity versus Islam." *Critique*, no. 12 (1998): 3–18.

Cizre-Sakallıoğlu, Ümit, and Erinç Yeldan. "Politics, Society, and Financial Liberalization: Turkey in the 1990s." *Development and Change* 31, no. 2 (2000): 481–508.

"[1961] Constitution of the Turkish Republic." *Middle East Journal* 16 (1962): 215–38.

Cornell, Svante. "The Kurdish Question in Turkish Politics." *Orbis* 45, no. 1 (2001): 31–46.

Cousins, Jane. *Turkey: Torture and Political Persecution.* London: Pluto Press, 1973.

Criss, Nur Bilge. "Development in Managing Terrorism in Turkey." *Perceptions* 1, no. 4 (December–February 1996/1997): 76–86.

Çandar, Cengiz. "Redefining Turkey's Political Center." *Journal of Politics* 10, no. 4 (October 1999): 129–41.

Çarkoğlu, Ali. "Macro Economic Determinants of Electoral Support for Incumbents in Turkey, 1950–1995." *New Perspectives on Turkey*, no. 17 (1997): 75–96.

———. "The Turkish Party System in Transition: Party Performance and Agenda Change." *Political Studies* 46 (1998): 544–71.

———. "The Geography of the April 1999 Turkish Elections." *Turkish Studies* 1, no. 1 (2000): 149–71.

Çarkoğlu, Ali, and Emre Erdoğan. "Fairness in the Apportionment of Seats in the Turkish Legislature: Is There Room for Improvement?" *New Perspectives on Turkey*, no. 19 (1998): 97–124.

Çetinsaya, G. "Rethinking Nationalism and Islam: Some Preliminary Notes on the Roots of 'Turkish-Islamic Synthesis' in Modern Turkish Political Thought." *Muslim World* 89, nos. 3–4 (July–October 1999): 377–88.

Development and Consolidation of Democracy in Turkey. Ankara: Turkish Democracy Foundation, 1989.

Die Türkische Krise [The Turkish Crisis]. Bonn: Friedrich-Ebert-Stiftung, 1981. [Several chapters in English.]

Dodd, C. H. "The Social and Educational Backgrounds of Turkish Officials." *Middle Eastern Studies* 2 (1965): 268–76.

———. *Politics and Government in Turkey.* Berkeley: University of California Press, 1969.

———. *Democracy and Development in Turkey.* Northgate, U.K.: Eothen Press, 1979.

———. *The Crisis of Turkish Democracy.* Walkington, U.K: Eothen Press, 1983.

———. "Aspects of the Turkish State: Political Culture, Organized Interests, and Village Communities." *British Society for Middle Eastern Studies Bulletin* 15 (1988): 78–86.

———. "The Development of Turkish Democracy." *British Journal of Middle Eastern Studies* 19 (1992): 16–30.

———. "The Revival of Turkish Democracy." *Asian Affairs* 23 (1992): 305–14.

Dunér, Bertil, and Liv Hammargren. "Turkey: Politicization of Torture Care." *Turkish Studies* 2, no. 2 (2001): 41–62.

Ellis, Ellen Deborah. "Turkish Nationalism in the Postwar World." *Current History* 36 (1959): 86–91.

Ellison, Grace. *Turkey Today.* London: Hutchinson, 1928.

Emrence, Cem. "Politics of Discontent in the Midst of the Great Depression: The Free Republican Party (1930)." *New Perspectives on Turkey*, no. 23 (Fall 2000): 31–52.

Eren, Nuri. "Turkey: Problems, Politics, Parties." *Foreign Affairs* 40 (1962): 95–104.

———. "Turkey: Prospects for Democratic Development." *Journal of International Affairs* 19 (1965): 170–80.

Ergil, Doğu. "Class Relations and the Turkish Transformation in Historical Perspective." *Studia Islamica*, no. 39 (1974): 77–94.

———. "Class Conflict and Turkish Transformation (1950–1973)." *Studia Islamica*, no. 40 (1975): 137–61.

———. "The Kurdish Question in Turkey." *Journal of Democracy* 11, no. 3 (2000): 122–35.

———. "Identity Crises and Political Instability in Turkey." *Journal of International Affairs* 54, no. 1 (Fall 2000): 43–62

Ergüder, Üstün. "Changing Patterns of Electoral Behavior in Turkey." *Boğaziçi University Journal* (Social Science Series), nos. 8–9 (1980–1981): 45–61.

Ergüder, Üstün, and Richard Hofferbert. "Restoration of Democracy in Turkey?" In *Elections in the Middle East: Implications of Recent Trends*, ed. Linda L. Layne. Boulder, Colo.: Westview, 1987.

Erman, Tahire, and Emrah Göker. "Alevi Politics in Contemporary Turkey." *Middle Eastern Studies* 36, no. 4 (2000): 99–118.

Finefrock, Michael. "Laissez-Faire, the 1923 İzmir Economic Congress, and Early Turkish Development Policy in Political Perspective." *Middle Eastern Studies* 17 (1981): 375–92.

Fisher, Sydney N. "The Role of the Military in Society and Government in Turkey." In *The Military in the Middle East: Problems in Society and Government*, ed. Sydney N. Fisher. Columbus: Ohio State University Press, 1963.

Fox, Clifton C. "Turkish Army's Role in Nation Building." *Military Review* 47 (1967): 68–74.

Frey, Frederick W. "Arms and the Man in Turkish Politics." *Land Reborn* 11 (1960): 3–14.

———. *The Turkish Political Elite*. Cambridge, Mass.: MIT Press, 1965.

———. "Political Development, Power and Communications in Turkey." In *Communications and Political Development*, ed. Lucien W. Pye. Princeton, N.J.: Princeton University Press, 1967.

———. "Socialization to National Identification among Turkish Peasants." *Journal of Politics* 30 (1968): 934–65.

———. "Patterns of Elite Politics in Turkey." In *Political Elites in the Middle East*, ed. George Lenczowski. Washington, D.C.: American Enterprise Institute for Public Policy Research, 1975.

Gençkaya, Ömer Faruk. "Revival of the Periphery: Need for Consensus or Threat to National Integrity in Turkey." *Journal of Behavioral and Social Sciences* 1 (1997): 75–90.

Gilead, Baruch. "Political Parties in Turkey." *Middle Eastern Affairs* 9 (1958): 101–17.

Giritli, İsmet. "Some Aspects of the New Turkish Constitution." *Middle East Journal* 11 (1962): 1–17.

———. *Fifty Years of Turkish Political Development, 1919–1969*. Istanbul: Istanbul University, 1969.

Göymen, Korel. "Stages of Etatist Development in Turkey: The Interaction of Single-Party Politics and Economic Policy in the 'Etatist Decade.'" *METU Studies in Development* (Ankara), no. 10 (1976): 89–114.

Gunter, Michael M. *The Kurds in Turkey: A Political Dilemma*. Boulder, Colo.: Westview, 1990.

———. *The Kurds and the Future of Turkey*. New York: St. Martin's, 1997.

———. "Susurluk: The Connection between Turkey's Intelligence Community and Organized Crime." *International Journal of Intelligence and Counter Intelligence* 11 (1998): 119–41.

———. "The Silent Coup: The Secularist-Islamist Struggle in Turkey." *Journal of South Asian and Middle Eastern Studies* 21 (1998): 1–12.

———. "The Continuing Kurdish Problem in Turkey after Ocalan's Capture." *Third World Quarterly* 21, no. 5 (2000): 849–69.

Gülalp, H. "Nationalism, Statism, and the Turkish Revolution: An Early 'Dependency' Theory." *Review of Middle East Studies* 4 (1988): 69–85.

Gülek, Kasım. *Development of Democracy in Turkey*. Ankara: Ulus Basımevi, 1953.

Hale, William. "Turkish Democracy in Travail: The Case of the State Security Courts." *World Today* 33 (1977): 186–94.

———. "The Role of the Electoral System in Turkish Politics." *International Journal of Middle East Studies* 11 (1980): 401–17.

———. *Turkish Politics and the Military*. London: Routledge, 1993.

———. "Turkey's Domestic Landscape: A Glance at the Past and the Future." *The International Spectator* 34, no. 1 (1999): 27–46

Harris, George S. "The Role of the Military in Turkish Politics." *Middle East Journal* 19 (1965): 54–66, 169–76.

———. *The Origins of Communism in Turkey*. Stanford, Calif.: Hoover Institution, 1967.

———. "The Causes of the 1960 Revolution in Turkey." *Middle East Journal* 24 (1970): 438–54.

———. "The Left in Turkey." *Problems of Communism* 29 (1980): 26–41.

———. "Bureaucratic Reform: Atatürk and the Turkish Foreign Office." *Journal of the American Institute for the Study of Middle Eastern Civilization* 1 (1980–1981): 39–51.

———. *Turkey: Coping with Crisis*. Boulder, Colo.: Westview, 1985.

Henderson, Alexander. "The Pan-Turanian Myth in Turkey Today." *Asiatic Review* 41 (1945): 88–92.

Heper, Metin. "Political Modernization as Reflected in Bureaucratic Change: The Turkish Bureaucracy and a 'Historical Bureaucratic Empire' Tradition." *International Journal of Middle East Studies* 7 (1976): 501–21.

———. "The Recalcitrance of the Turkish Public Bureaucracy to 'Bourgeois Politics': A Multi-Factor Political Stratification Analysis." *Middle East Journal* 30 (1976): 485–500.

———. "Negative Bureaucratic Politics in a Modernizing Context: The Turkish Case." *Journal of South Asian and Middle Eastern Studies* 1 (1977): 65–84.

———. "Recent Instability in Turkish Politics: End of a Monocentrist Polity?" *International Journal of Turkish Studies* 1 (1979–1980): 102–13.

———. "Transformation of Charisma into a Political Paradigm: Atatürkism in Turkey." *Journal of American Institute for the Study of Middle Eastern Civilization* 1 (1980–1981): 65–82.

———. "A Methodological Note on Bureaucratic Modernization: Prevalent Attitudes of the Turkish Civil Servants." *International Review of Modern Sociology* 12 (1982): 75–103.

———. "A Weltanschauung-Turned-Partial Ideology and Normative Ethics: 'Atatürkism' in Turkey." *Orient* (Hamburg) 25 (1984): 83–94.

———. *The State Tradition in Turkey*. Walkington, U.K.: Eothen Press, 1985.

———. ed. *Dilemmas of Decentralization: Municipal Government in Turkey*. Bonn: Friedrich-Ebert-Stiftung, 1986.

———. "State, Democracy, and Bureaucracy in Turkey." In *The State and Public Bureaucracies: A Comparative Perspective*, ed. Metin Heper. New York: Greenwood Press, 1987.

———. "The State, the Military, and Democracy in Turkey." *Jerusalem Journal of International Relations* 9 (1987): 52–64.

———. ed. *Democracy and Local Government in Turkey: Istanbul in the 1980s*. Walkington, U.K.: Eothen Press, 1987.

———. "The Motherland Party Governments and Bureaucracy in Turkey: 1983–1988." *Governance* 2 (1989): 457–68.

———. ed. *Local Government in Turkey: Governing Greater Istanbul*. London: Routledge, 1989.

———. "The State, Political Party, and Society in Post-1983 Turkey." *Government and Opposition* 25 (1990): 321–33.

———. "The State and Bureaucracy: The Turkish Case in Historical and Comparative Perspective." In *Handbook of Comparative and Development Public Administration*, ed. A. Farazmand. New York: Marcel Dekker, 1990. Second Edition. Revised and Expanded, 2001.

———. "Executive in the Third Turkish Republic, 1982–1989." *Governance* 3 (1990): 299–319.

———. "Turkey." In *Public Administration in the Third World: An International Handbook*, ed. V. Subramaniam. New York: Greenwood, 1990.

———. "The State and Debureaucratization: The Turkish Case." *International Social Science Journal*, no. 126 (1990): 605–15.

———. "Mayors and Party Elites in Post-1983 Turkey: Dynamics of Intergovernmental Relations." In *Perspectives in the Center-Local Relations: Political Dynamics in the Middle East*, ed. Takeji Ino. Tokyo: Institute of Developing Economies, 1991.

———. ed. *Strong State and Economic Interest Groups: The Post-1980 Turkish Experience*. Berlin and New York: Walter de Gruyter, 1991.

———. "Local Government in Turkey with Special Reference to Metropolitan Municipalities." In *Local Government and Urban Affairs in International Perspective*, ed. Joachim Jens Hesse. Baden-Baden, Germany: Nomos, 1991.

———. "Turkish Democracy Reconsidered: Illusion Breeding Disillusion?" In *Institutional Aspects of the Economic Integration of Turkey into the European Community*, ed. Heiko Körner and Rasul Shams. Hamburg: HWWA, 1991.

———. "Consolidating Turkish Democracy." *Journal of Democracy* 3 (1992): 105–17.

———. "Extremely 'Strong State' and Democracy: Turkey in Comparative and Historical Perspective." In *Democracy and Modernity*, ed. S. N. Eisenstadt. Leiden: E. J. Brill, 1992.

———. "Strong State as a Problem for the Consolidation of Democracy: Turkey and Germany Compared." *Comparative Political Studies* 25 (1992): 169–94.

———. "Bureaucracy in the Ottoman-Turkish State." In *Handbook of Bureaucracy*, ed. A. Farazmand. New York: Marcel Dekker. 1994.

———. "Islam and Democracy in Turkey: Toward a Reconciliation?" *Middle East Journal* 51 (1997): 32–45.

———. "Urbanization and Metropolitan Municipal Politics in Turkey." In *Population, Poverty, and Politics: Middle East Cities in Crisis*, ed. Michael Bonine. Miami, Fla.: University Press of Miami, 1997.

———. *İsmet İnönü: The Making of a Turkish Statesman*. Leiden: E. J. Brill, 1998.

———. "Strong State and Bureaucrat-Politician Relationship: The Turkish Case." *European Studies Journal* 17, no. 1 (2000): 67–96.

———. "The Ottoman Legacy and Turkish Politics." *Journal of International Affairs* 54, no. 1 (Fall 2000): 63–82.

Heper, Metin, and Filiz Başkan. "The Politics of Coalition Government in Turkey, 1961–1999: Toward a Paradigmatic Change?" *International Journal of Turkish Studies* 7 (Summer 2001): 68–89.

Heper, Metin, and Menderes Çınar. "Dilemmas of Parliamentarism with a Strong Presidency: The Post-1989 Turkish Experience." *Political Science Quarterly* 111, no. 3 (1996): 483–503.

Heper, Metin, and Ahmet Evin, eds. *State, Democracy, and the Military: Turkey in the 1980s*. New York: Walter de Gruyter, 1988.

———. eds. *Politics in the Third Turkish Republic*. Boulder, Colo.: Westview, 1994.

Heper, Metin, and Aylin Güney. "The Military in the Third Turkish Republic." *Armed Forces and Society* 22, no. 4 (1996): 619–42.

———. "Military and the Consolidation of Democracy: The Turkish Case." *Armed Forces and Society* 26, no. 4 (2000): 625–47.

Heper, Metin, and Ersin Kalaycıoğlu. "Organizational Socialization as Reality-Testing: The Case of the Turkish Higher Civil Servants." *International Journal of Political Education* 6 (1983): 175–98.

Heper, Metin, and Fuat Keyman. "Double-Faced State: Political Patronage and the Consolidation of Democracy in Turkey." *Middle Eastern Studies* 34, no. 4 (1998): 259–77.

Heper, Metin, Chong Lim Kim, and Seang-Tong Pai. "The Role of Bureaucracy and Regime Types: A Comparative Study of Turkish and South Korean Higher Civil Servants." *Administration and Society* 12 (1980): 137–57.

Heper, Metin, and Jacob Landau, eds. *Political Parties and Democracy in Turkey*. London: I. B. Tauris, 1991.

Heper, Metin, and Selçuk Sancar. "Is Legal-Rational Bureaucracy a Prerequisite for Rational-Productive Bureaucracy? The Case of Turkey." *Administration and Society* 30, no. 2 (1998): 143–65.

Heper, Metin, and Sabri Sayarı, eds. *Political Leaders and Democracy in Turkey*. Lanham, Md.: Lexington Books, 2002.

Heyd, Uriel. *Foundations of Turkish Nationalism: The Life and Teachings of Ziya Gökalp*. London: Harvell Press, 1949.

Hopper, Jerry R., and Richard I. Levin, eds. *The Turkish Administrator: A Cultural Survey*. Ankara: USAID, 1967.

Hurni, F. "Democracy and the Turkish Military." *Swiss Review of World Affairs* 21 (1971): 13–14.

İbrahim, Ferhad, and Gülistan Gürbey, eds. *The Kurdish Conflict in Turkey: Obstacles and Chances for Peace and Democracy*. New York: St. Martin's Press, 2000.

İyduygu, Ahmet, David Romano, and İbrahim Sirkeci. "The Ethnic Question in an Environment of Insecurity: The Kurds in Turkey." *Ethnic and Racial Studies* 22, no. 6 (1999): 991–1011.

Kalaycıoğlu, Ersin. "Why Legislatures Persist in Developing Countries: The Case of Turkey." *Legislative Studies Quarterly* 5 (1980): 123–40.

———. "The Turkish Political System in Transition: Multi-Party Politics in the 1980s." *Current Turkish Thought* (Istanbul), no. 56 (1985): 2–38.

———. "Elite Political Culture and Regime Stability: The Case of Turkey." *Journal of Economic and Administrative Studies* (Istanbul) 2 (1988): 149–79.

———. "Cyclical Breakdown, Redesign, and Nascent Institutionalization: The Turkish Grand National Assembly." In *Parliaments and Democratic Consolidation in Southern Europe: Greece, Italy, Portugal, Spain, and Turkey*, ed. Ulrike Liebert and Maurizio Cotta. London: Pinter, 1990.

———. "Elections and Party Preferences in Turkey: Changes and Continuities." *Comparative Political Studies* 27, no. 3 (1994): 402–24.

———. "Unconventional Political Participation in Turkey: Comparative Perspectives." *Il Politico* 41, no. 3 (1994).

———. "The Turkish Political Culture in Comparative Perspective." In *Society and Politics in South-East Europe*, ed. Nikolai Genov. Sofia: National and Global Development, 1996.

———. "Constitutional Viability and Political Institutions in Turkish Democracy." In *Designs for Democratic Stability: Studies in Viable Constitutionalism*, ed. Abdo I. Baaklini and Helen Desfosses. London: M. E. Sharpe, 1997.

———. "The Shaping of Party Preferences in Turkey: Coping with the Post–Cold War Era." *New Perspectives on Turkey*, no. 20 (1999): 47–76.

———. Turkish Democracy: Patronage versus Governance." *Turkish Politics* 2, no. 1 (2001): 54–57.

Kapani, Münci. "Outlines of the New [1961] Turkish Constitution." *Parliamentary Affairs* 15 (1961–1962): 94–110.

Karabelias, Gerassimas. "The Evolution of Civil-Military Relations in Postwar Turkey, 1980–1995." *Middle Eastern Studies* 35, no. 4 (1999): 130–51.

Karaömerlioğlu, M. A. "The People's Houses and the Cult of the Peasant in Turkey." *Middle Eastern Studies* 34, no. 4 (1998): 67–91.

Karpat, Kemal H. *Turkey's Politics: The Transition to a Multi-Party Politics*. Princeton, N.J.: Princeton University Press, 1959.

———. "The People's Houses in Turkey: Establishment and Growth." *Middle East Journal* 17 (1963): 55–67.

———. "Ideology in Turkey after the Revolution of 1960: Nationalism and Socialism." *Turkish Yearbook of International Relations* (Ankara) 6 (1965): 68–118

———. "The Turkish Left." *Journal of Contemporary History* 1 (1966): 169–86.

———. "Socialism and Labor Party of Turkey." *Middle East Journal* 21 (1967): 157–72.

———. "The Military and Politics in Turkey, 1960–1964: A Socio-Cultural Analysis of a Revolution." *American Historical Review* 75 (1970): 1654–83.

———. "Political Developments in Turkey: 1950–1970." *Middle Eastern Studies* 8 (1972): 349–75.

———. ed. *Social Change and Politics in Turkey: A Structural-Historical Analysis*. Leiden: E. J. Brill, 1973.

———. "The Impact of the 'People's Houses' on the Development of Communications in Turkey: 1931–1951." *Die Welt des Islams,* no. 15 (1974): 69–84.

———. "Turkish Democracy at Impasse: Ideology, Party Politics, and the Third Military Intervention." *International Journal of Turkish Studies* 2 (1981): 1–43.

Kasaba, Reşat. "Populism and Democracy in Turkey." In *Rules and Rights in the Middle East: Democracy, Law, and Society*, ed. E. Goldberg, R. Kasaba, and J. Migdal. Seattle: University of Washington Press, 1993.

Kazancıgil, Ali, and Ergun Özbudun, eds. *Atatürk: Founder of a Modern State*. Hamden, Conn.: Archon Books, 1981.

Kedourie, Sylvia, ed. *Turkey: Identity, Democracy, Politics*. London: Frank Cass, 1996.

———. *Seventy-Five Years of the Turkish Republic*. London: Frank Cass, 2000.

Key, Kerim Kami. "[The 1961] Constitution of the Turkish Republic." *Middle East Journal* 16 (1962): 215–38.

Keyder, Çağlar. *State and Class in Turkey: A Study in Capitalist Development*. London: Verso, 1987.

Kılıç, H. Ayla. "Democratization, Human Rights, and Ethnic Policies in Turkey." *Journal of Muslim Minority Affairs* 18, no. 1 (1998): 91–110.

Kınıklıoğlu, Suat. "Bülent Ecevit: The Transformation of a Politician." *Turkish Studies* 1, no. 2 (2000): 1–20.

Kili, Suna. *Kemalism*. Istanbul: Robert College, 1969.

———. *Turkish Constitutional Developments and Assembly Debates on the Constitutions of 1924 and 1961*. Istanbul: Boğaziçi University, 1971

Kim, Chang Lim, J. D. Barkan, Malcolm Jewell, and İlter Turan. *The Legislative Connection: The Politics of Representation in Kenya, Korea, and Turkey*. Durham, N.C.: Duke University Press, 1984.

Kinross, Lord. *Atatürk: A Bibliography of Mustafa Kemal, Father of Modern Turkey*. New York: William Murrow, 1978. [First published in London in 1964.]

Kirişçi, Kemal, and Gareth Winrow. *The Kurdish Question and Turkey: An Example of a Trans-State Ethnic Conflict*. London: Frank Cass, 1997.

Koelle, Peter Brampton. "The Inevitability of the 1971 Turkish Military Intervention." *Journal of South Asian and Middle Eastern Studies* 24, no. 1 (2000): 38–56.

Kortepeter, C. Max. "Kemal Atatürk and the Ottoman Tradition of Leadership and Reform." *Journal of the American Institute for the Study of Middle Eastern Civilization* 1 (1980–1981): 83–98.

Köker, Levent. "Local Politics and Democracy in Turkey: An Appraisal." *Annals of the American Academy of Political and Social Science*, no. 540 (1995): 51–62.

Köksal, Duygu. "Fine-Tuning Nationalism: Critical Perspectives from Republican Literature in Turkey." *Turkish Studies* 2, no. 2 (2001): 63–84.

Köprülü, Fuat. *On the Way to Democracy*. Ed. Tibot Halasi-Kun. The Hague: Mouton, 1964.

Kuran, Ercüment. "Atatürk and Ziya Gökalp." *Cultura Turcica* (Ankara) 2 (1965): 137–40.

Landau, Jacob M. *Radical Politics in Modern Turkey*. Leiden: E. J. Brill, 1974.

———. *Pan-Turkism in Turkey: A Study in Irredentism*. Hamden, Conn.: Archon Books, 1981.

———. "The Nationalist Action Party in Turkey." *Journal of Contemporary History* 17 (1982): 587–606.

———. *Tekinalp: Turkish Patriot, 1883–1961*. Leiden: Nederlands Instituut voor het Nabije Oosten, 1984.

———. *Atatürk and the Modernization of Turkey*. Boulder, Colo.: Westview, 1984.

Landau, Jacob M., Ergun Özbudun, and Frank Tachau, eds. *Electoral Politics in the Middle East: Issues, Voters, and Elites*. London: Croom Helm, 1980. [Several chapters on Turkey.]

Leder, Arnold. *Catalysts of Change: Marxist versus Muslim in a Turkish Community*. Vol. 1 of Middle East Monographs. Austin: University of Texas at Austin, 1976.

———. "Party Competition in Rural Turkey: Agent of Change or Defender of Traditional Rule?" *Middle Eastern Studies* 15 (1979): 82–105.

Lerner, Daniel, and Richard D. Robinson. "Swords and Ploughshares: The Turkish Army as a Modernizing Force." *World Politics* 13 (1960): 19–44.

Lewis, Bernard. "Democracy in Turkey." *Middle Eastern Affairs* 4 (1953): 55–72.

———. "History-Writing and National Revival in Turkey." *Middle Eastern Affairs* 4 (1953): 218–86.

Lewis, Geoffrey L. "Turkey: The End of the First Republic." *World Today* 16 (1960): 370–86.

———. "Turkey: The Thorny Road to Democracy." *World Today* 18 (1962): 182–91.

———. *Atatürk and His Republic*. Princeton, N.J.: Princeton University Press, 1982.

———. "The Present State of the Turkish Republic." *Asian Affairs* 19 (1988): 261–71.

Lipovsky, Igor P. *The Socialist Movement in Turkey, 1960–1980*. Leiden: E. J. Brill, 1992.

Mackenzie, Kenneth. *Turkey under the Generals*. London: Institute for the Study of Conflict, 1981.

Magnarella, Paul J. "Regional Voting in Turkey." *Muslim World* 57 (1967): 224–34.

———. "Turkey's Experience with Political Democracy." *Studies in Third World Sociology*, no. 27 (1984): 43–60.

Mango, Andrew. "Purpose in Turkish Politics and Its Outcome." *Middle Eastern Studies* 3 (1967): 301-8.

————. *Turkey*. London: Thames & Hudson, 1968.

————. "The State of Turkey." *Middle Eastern Studies* 13 (1977): 261–73.

————. "Turkey: Democracy under Military Tutelage." *World Today* 39 (1983): 429–35.

————. "The Third Turkish Republic." *World Today* 39 (1983): 30–38.

————. "A Speaking Turkey." *Middle Eastern Studies* 33, no. 1 (1997): 152–70.

————. "Atatürk and the Kurds." *Middle Eastern Studies* 35, no. 4 (1999): 1–25.

————. "Progress and Disorder: 75 Years of the Turkish Republic." *Middle Eastern Studies* 35, no. 3 (1999): 156–77.

————. "Atatürk and the Future of Turkey." *Turkish Studies* 1, no. 2 (2000): 113–24.

Mardin, Şerif. "Opposition and Control in Turkey." *Government and Opposition* 1 (1966): 375–88.

————. "Ideology and Religion in the Turkish Revolution." *International Journal of Middle East Studies* 2 (1971): 197–211.

————. "Center-Periphery Relations: A Key to Turkish Politics?" *Daedalus* 102 (1973): 169–90.

McCally, Sarah P. "Party Government in Turkey: Development of Political Parties." *Journal of Politics* 18 (1956): 297–323.

McFadden, John H. "Civil-Military Relations in the Third Turkish Republic." *Middle East Journal* 39 (1985): 69–85.

Meeker, Michael E. "The Great Family Aghas of Turkey: A Study of Changing Political Culture." In *Rural Politics and Social Change in the Middle East*, ed. R. Antoin and I. Harik. Bloomington: Indiana University Press, 1972.

Narlı, Nilüfer. "Civil-Military Relations in Turkey." *Turkish Studies* 1, no. 1 (2000): 107–27.

Nye, R. "Civil-Military Confrontation in Turkey: The 1973 Presidential Election." *International Journal of Middle East Studies* 8 (1977): 209–28.

Olson, Robert. "Al-Fatah in Turkey: Its Influnce on the March 12 Coup." *Middle Eastern Studies* 9 (1973): 197–206.

————. *The Emergence of Kurdish Nationalism and the Sheikh Said Rebellion, 1880–1925*. Austin: University of Texas Press, 1989.

————. "Kurds and Turks: Two Documents Concerning Kurdish Autonomy in 1922 and 1923." *Journal of South Asian and Middle Eastern Studies* 15 (1991): 20–31.

————. "The Kurdish Question: Four Years on the Policies of Turkey, Syria, Iran, and Iraq." *Middle East Policy* 3, no. 3 (1994): 136–44.

————. "The Kurdish Rebellions of Sheikh Said (1925), Mt. Ararat (1930), and Dersim (1937–1938): Their Impact on the Development of the Turkish Air Force and on Kurdish and Turkish Nationalism." *Die Welt des Islams* 40, no. 1 (2000): 67–94.

Olson, Robert, and W. Tucker. "The Sheikh Sait Rebellion in Turkey (1925)." *Die Welt des Islams* 18 (1978): 195–211.

Onulduran, Ersin. *Political Development and Political Parties in Turkey*. Ankara: Ankara University School of Political Sciences, 1974.

Orga, Irfan, and Margaret Orga. *Atatürk*. London: Michael Joseph, 1962.

Öniş, Ziya. *State and Market: The Political Economy of Turkey in Comparative Perspective*. Istanbul: Boğaziçi University Press, 1998.

————. "Turkey, Europe, and the Paradoxes of Identity: Perspectives on the International Context of Democraticization." *Mediterranean Quarterly* 10, no. 3 (1999): 107–26.

————. "Neoliberal Globalization and the Democracy Paradox: Interpreting the Turkish General Elections of 1999." *Journal of International Affairs* 54, no. 1 (Fall 2000): 283–306.

Öniş, Ziya, and Umut Türem. "Business, Globalization, and Democracy: A Comparative Analysis of Turkish Business Associations." *Turkish Studies* 2, no. 2 (2001): 94–120.

Öniş, Ziya, and Steven B. Webb. "Turkey: Democratization and the Adjustment from Above." In *Voting for Reform: The Politics of Adjustment in New Democracies*, ed. Stephan Haggard and Steven B. Webb. New York: Oxford University Press, 1994.

Özbudun, Ergun. *The Role of the Military in Recent Turkish Politics*. Cambridge, Mass.: Harvard University, Center for International Affairs, 1966.

———. "Established Revolution versus Unfinished Revolution: Contrasting Patterns of Democratization in Mexico and Turkey." In *Authoritarian Politics in Modern Society: The Dynamics of Established One-Party Systems,* ed. Samuel P. Huntington and Clement H. Moore. New York: Basic, 1970.

———. *Social Change and Political Participation in Turkey*. Princeton, N.J.: Princeton University Press, 1976.

———. "Turkey: The Politics of Political Clientelism." In *Political Clientelism, Patronage, and Development,* ed. S. N. Eisenstadt and René Lemarchand. Beverly Hills, Calif.: Sage, 1981.

———. "The Turkish Party System: Institutionalization, Polarization, and Fragmentation." *Middle Eastern Studies* 17 (1981): 228–40.

———. "Turkey [Postauthoritarian Democracies]." In *Comparative Elections in Developing Countries*, ed. Myron Weiner and Ergun Özbudun. Durham, N.C.: Duke University Press, 1987.

———. ed. *Perspectives on Democracy in Turkey*. Ankara: Turkish Political Science Association, 1988.

———. "Turkey: Crises, Interruptions and Reequilibrations." In *Politics in Developing Countries: Comparing Experiences with Democracy*, ed. Larry Diamond, Juan J. Linz, and Seymour Martin Lipset. Boulder, Colo.: Lynne Riener, 1990.

———. "State Elites and Democratic Political Culture in Turkey." In *Political Culture and Democracy in Developing Countries*, ed. Larry Diamond. Boulder, Colo.: Lynne Reiner, 1993.

———. "Democratization in Turkey: How Far from Consolidation?" *Journal of Democracy* 7, no. 3 (1996): 123–38.

———. *Contemporary Turkish Politics: Challenges to Democratic Consolidation*. Boulder, Colo.: Lynne Riener, 2000.

Özbudun, Ergun, and Frank Tachau. "Social Change and Electoral Behavior toward a 'Critical Realignment'?" *International Journal of Middle East Studies* 6 (1975): 460–80.

Özbudun, Ergun, and Aydın Ulusan, eds. *The Political Economy of Income Distribution in Turkey*. New York: Holmes & Meier, 1980.

Özcan, Yusuf. "Determinants of Political Behavior in Istanbul, Turkey." *Party Politics* 6, no. 4 (2000): 505–19.

Özler, S. Ilgu. "Politics of the Gecekondu in Turkey: The Political Choices of Urban Squatters in National Elections." *Turkish Studies* 1, no. 2 (2000): 39–58.

Özman, Aylin. "The Politics of Privatization in Turkey during the 1980s." *Journal of South Asian and Middle Eastern Studies* 23, no. 4 (2000): 21–35.

Pamuk, Şevket. "War, State Economic Policies, and Resistance by Agricultural Producers in Turkey, 1939–1945." In *Peasants and Politics in the Modern Middle East*, ed. Farhad Kazemi and John Waterbury. Miami: Florida International University Press, 1991.

Parla, Taha. "Mercantile Militarism in Turkey." *New Perspectives on Turkey*, no. 19 (1998): 29–52.

Polatoğlu, Aykut. "Turkish Local Government: The Need for Reform." *Middle Eastern Studies* 36 (2000): 156–57.

Poulton, Hugh. *Top Hat, Grey Wolf, and Crescent: Turkish Nationalism and the Turkish Republic*. London: Hurst, 1997.

Radu, Michael. "The Rise and Fall of the PKK." *Orbis* 45, no. 1 (2001): 47–64.

Ramazanoğlu, Hüseyin, ed. *Turkey in the World Capitalist System: A Study of Industrialization, Power and Class*. Brookfield, Vt.: Gower, 1985.

Roos, Leslie L., Jr., and Noralou P. Roos. *Managers of Modernization: Organizations and Elites in Turkey (1950–1969)*. Cambridge, Mass.: Harvard University Press, 1971.

Roos, Leslie L., Jr., Noralou P. Roos, and G. R. Field. "Students and Politics in Turkey." *Daedalus* 97 (1968): 184–203.

Rosenthal, S. T. *The Politics of Dependency: Urban Reform in Turkey*. Westport, Conn.: Greenwood Press, 1980.

Rouleau, Eric. "Turkey's Dream of Democracy." *Foreign Affairs* 79, no. 6 (2000): 100–14.

Rubin, Barry, and Metin Heper, eds. *Political Parties in Turkey*. London: Frank Cass, 2002.

Rustow, Dankwart A. "The Army and the Founding of the Turkish Republic." *World Politics* 11 (1959): 513–52.

———. "Turkey's Second Try at Democracy." *Yale Review* 52 (1963): 518–38.

———. "The Development of Parties in Turkey." In *Political Parties and Political Development*, ed. Joseph LaPalombara and Myron Weiner. Princeton, N.J.: Princeton University Press, 1966.

———. "Turkey: The Modernity of Tradition." In *Political Culture and Political Development*, ed. Lucien W. Pye and Sidney Verba. Princeton, N.J.: Princeton University Press, 1965.

———. "Atatürk's Political Leadership." *Near Eastern Round Table* 1 (1967–1968): 143–55.

———. "Atatürk as Founder of a State." *Daedalus* 98 (1968): 793–828.

———. "Turkey's Travails." *Foreign Affairs* 58 (1979): 82–102.

———. "Turkey: The Roses and Thorns." *Spettatore Internazionale* (Rome) 16 (1981): 337–65.

———. "Turkey's Liberal Revolution." *Middle East Review* 12 (1985): 5–11.

Salt, Jeremy. "Some Reflections on Arab and Turkish Nationalism." *Studies on Turkish-Arab Relations* (Istanbul) 4 (1989): 97–105.

Sayarı, Sabri. "Aspects of Party Organization in Turkey." *Middle East Journal* 30 (1976): 187–199.

———. "Political Patronage in Turkey." In *Patrons and Clients in Mediterranean Societies*, ed. Ernest Gellner and John Waterbury. London: Duckworth, 1977.

———. "Turkish Party System in Transition." *Government and Opposition* 13 (1978): 39–57.

———. *The Changing Domestic and Regional Environment of Turkish Foreign Policy*. Ebenhausen, Germany: Stiftung Wissenschaft und Politik, 1980.

———. "The Development of Political Terrorism in Turkey: An Analysis of Generational Changes in Terrorist Groups." *Journal of Economics and Administrative Studies* (Istanbul) 1 (1987): 171–84.

———. "Turgut Özal." In *Political Leaders of the Contemporary Middle East and North Africa*, ed. Bernard Riech. Westport, Conn.: Greenwood, 1990.

———. "Political Parties, Party Systems, and Economic Reforms: The Turkish Case." *Studies in Comparative International Development* 31, no. 4 (1997): 29–45.

Saybaşılı, Kemali. "Chambers of Commerce and Industry, Political Parties, and Governments: A Comparative Analysis of the British and Turkish Cases." *METU Studies in Development* (Ankara) 11 (1976): 104–26.

Sherill, Charles H. *A Year's Embassy to Mustafa Kemal*. New York: C. Scribner's Sons, 1934.

Sherman, A. V. "Turkey: A Case Study in Constructive Nationalism." *Commentary* 30 (1960): 93–101.

Sherwood, W. B. "The Rise of the Justice Party in Turkey." *World Politics* 20 (1967): 54–65.

Shmuelevitz, Aryeh. "Süleyman Demirel." In *Political Leaders of the Contemporary Middle East and North Africa*, ed. Bernard Reich. New York: Greenwood, 1990.

———. "Adnan Menderes." In *Political Leaders of the Contemporary Middle East and North Africa*, ed. Bernard Reich. New York: Greenwood, 1990.

Smith, Edward. "Debates on the Turkish Constitution of 1924." *Ankara Üniversitesi Siyasal Bilgiler Fakültesi Dergisi* (Ankara) 13 (1958): 82–105.

Speech Delivered by Ghazi Mustafa Kemal, President of the Turkish Republic. Leipzig: K. F. Koehler, 1929.

Steinbach, Udo. "Turkey's Third Republic." *Aussen Politik* 3 (1988): 237–56.

Sunar, İlkay. *State and Society in the Politics of Turkey's Development.* Ankara: Ankara University Faculty of Political Sciences, 1974.

———. "Transition to Democracy in Turkey." *Current Turkish Thought* (Istanbul), nos. 52–53 (1982): 9–17.

Sunar, İlkay, and Sabri Sayarı. "Democracy in Turkey: Problems and Prospects." In *Transitions from Authoritarian Rule: Southern Europe*, ed. Guillermo O'Donnell, Philippe C. Schmitter, and L. Whitehead. Baltimore, Md.: Johns Hopkins University Press, 1986.

Szyliowicz, Joseph S. "The Political Dynamics of Rural Turkey." *Middle East Journal* 16 (1962): 430–42.

———. "The 1961 Turkish Constitution." *Islamic Studies* (Karachi) 2 (1963): 363–81.

———. *Political Change in Turkey: Erdemli.* The Hague: Mouton, 1966.

———. "Political Participation and Modernization in Turkey." *Western Political Quarterly* 19 (1966): 266–84.

———. "Education and Political Development in Turkey, Egypt, and Iran." *Comparative Education Review* 12 (1968): 150–66.

———. "Students and Politics in Turkey." *Middle Eastern Studies* 6 (1970): 7–10.

———. "Elite Recruitment in Turkey: The Role of the Mülkiye." *World Politics* 23 (1971): 371–98.

———. *A Political Analysis of Student Activism: The Turkish Case.* Beverly Hills, Calif.: Sage, 1972.

———. "Elites and Modernization in Turkey." In *Political Elites and Political Development in the Middle East*, ed. Frank Tachau. New York: Wiley, 1975.

Tachau, Frank. "The Face of Turkish Nationalism as Reflected in the Cyprus Dispute." *Middle East Journal* 13 (1959): 262–72.

———. "The Search for National Identity among the Turks." *Die Welt des Islams* 8 (1963): 165–76.

———. "Language and Politics: Turkish Language Reform." *Review of Politics* 26 (1964): 191–204,

———. "Local Politicians in Turkey." In *Regional Planning, Local Government, and Community Development in Turkey.* Ankara: Sevinç Matbaası, 1966.

———. "Republic of Turkey." In *The Middle East: Its Governments and Politics*, ed. Abid A. Marayat. Belmont, Calif.: Duxbury Press, 1972.

———. "The Anatomy of Political and Social Change: Turkish Parties, Parliaments, and Elections." *Comparative Politics* 5 (1973): 551–74.

———. "Social Backgrounds of Turkish Parliamentarians." In *Commoners, Climbers, and Notables: A Sampler of Social Ranking in the Middle East*, ed. C. A. O. van Niewenhuijze. Leiden: E. J. Brill, 1977.

———. *Turkey: The Politics of Authority, Democracy, and Development.* New York: Praeger, 1984.

———. *Kemal Atatürk.* New York: Chelsea House, 1987.

———. "Turkish Political Parties and Elections: Half a Century of Multi-Party Democracy." *Turkish Studies* 1, no. 1 (2000): 128–48.

Tachau, Frank, and Metin Heper. "The State, Politics, and the Military in Turkey." *Comparative Politics* 16 (1983): 17–33.

Tamkoç, Metin. "Stable Instability of the Turkish Polity." *Middle East Journal* 27 (1973): 319–41.

———. *The Warrior Diplomats: Guardians of the National Security and Modernization of Turkey*. Salt Lake City: University of Utah Press, 1976.

———. *Inconsistency between the Form and Essence of the Turkish Political System*. Salt Lake City: Middle East Center, University of Utah, 1985.

———. "The Essence of the Turkish State." *Turkish Studies Association Bulletin* 11 (1987): 71–81.

Tekeli, İlhan. "Democracy in Local Administrations and the Development of Municipalities." *Turkish Public Administration Annual* 9–10 (1982–1983): 22–52.

Tepe, Sultan. "Kemalism, Islamism, and the Nationalist Action Party in Turkey." *Turkish Studies* 1, no. 2 (2000): 59–71.

Thomas, David. "Yusuf Akçura and the Intellectual Origins of 'Üç Tarz-ı Siyaset.'" *Journal of Turkish Studies* 2 (1978): 127–40.

Thus Spoke Atatürk: His Sayings, Thoughts, and Memoirs, Compiled from His Speeches, Addresses, Declarations, and Interviews. Ed. and trans. Herbert Melzig. Istanbul: Kenan Printing House, 1943.

Toynbee, Arnold J. "Mustafa Kemal." In *Men of Turmoil: Biographies by Leading Authorities of the Dominating Personalities of Our Day*. Freeport, N.Y.: Books for Libraries, 1969.

Trask, Roger R. "Unnamed Christianity in Turkey during the Atatürk Era." *Muslim World* 55 (1965): 66–76; 101–11.

Trimberger, Ellen Kay. *Revolution from Above: Military Bureaucrats in Japan, Turkey, Egypt, and Peru*. New Brunswick, N.J.: Transaction, 1977.

Turan, İlter. "Political Perspectives [in Turkey]." *Current Turkish Thought* (Istanbul), no. 33 (1977): 1–21.

———. "Attitudinal Correlates of Political Democracy: The Case of Korea and Turkey." *Orient* (Hamburg) 21 (1980): 77–88.

———. "Changing Horses in Midstream: Party Changers in the Turkish National Assembly." *Legislative Studies Quarterly* 10 (1985): 21–34.

———. "The Recruitment of Cabinet Members as a Political Process: Turkey, 1946–1979." *International Journal of Middle East Studies* 18 (1986): 455–72.

Turfan, M. N. "'Looking After and Protecting the Republic': The Legitimation of the Military's Authority in Turkey." *CEMOTI* (Paris), no. 5 (1988): 53–71.

Turk, H. S. "Human Rights in Turkey." *Perceptions* (Ankara) 3, no. 4 (1999): 5–25.

Turkey in the Year 2000. Ankara: Turkish Political Science Association, 1989.

Turner, Michael. "Changing Patterns of Turkish Politics: A Developmental Perspective." *Turkish Studies Association Bulletin*, no. 1 (1976): 6–13.

———. "Politics and the Future of Turkish Democracy." *Turkish Studies Association Bulletin* 5 (1981): 1–4.

Türkeş, Alparslan. *Turkey and the World*. Ankara: Ayyıldız Matbaası, 1979.

Türkeş, M. "The Ideology of the Kadro (Cadre) Movement: A Patriotic Leftist Movement in Turkey." *Middle Eastern Studies* 34, no. 4 (1998): 92–119.

Ülman, A. Haluk, and Frank Tachau. "Dilemmas of Turkish Politics." *Turkish Yearbook of International Relations* (Ankara) 2 (1962): 1–34.

———. "Turkish Politics: The Attempt to Reconcile Rapid Modernization with Democracy." *Middle East Journal* 19 (1965): 153–68.

Versan, Vakur. "Evolution of the Rule of Law and the New Constitution in Turkey." *Pakistan Horizon* 17 (1964): 122–29.

———. "Local Government in Turkey." *Journal of Administration Overseas* 5 (1966): 251–57.

———. "The 1982 Constitution of the Republic of Turkey." *Current Turkish Thought* (Istanbul), nos. 52–53 (1982): 1–9.

Volkan, Namık D., and Norman Itzkowitz. *The Immortal Atatürk: A Psychobiography*. Chicago: University of Chicago Press, 1984.

Van Bruinnessen, M. "Shifting National and Ethnic Identities: The Kurds in Turkey and the European Diaspora." *Journal of Muslim Minority Affairs* 18, no. 1 (1998): 39–52.

Waterbury, John. "Export-Led Growth and the Center-Right Coalition in Turkey." *Comparative Politics* 25 (1992): 127–45.

Watt, D. C. "The Experience of Opposition Parties in Turkey." *Quarterly Review* 296 (1961): 56–63.

Watts, Nicole F. "Allies and Enemies: Pro-Kurdish Parties in Turkish Politics." *International Journal of Middle East Studies* 31, no. 4 (November 1999): 631–56.

———. "Relocating Dersim: Turkish State-Building and Kurdish Resistance, 1931–1938." *New Perceptions on Turkey*, no. 23 (Fall 2000): 5–30.

Waugh, A. Telford. "Nine Years of Republic in Turkey." *Journal of the Royal Central Asian Society* 20 (1933): 52–69.

Webster, Donald E. "State Control of Social Change in Republican Turkey." *American Sociological Review* 4 (1939): 247–56.

Weiker, Walter F. "The Aydemir Case and Turkey's Political Dilemma." *Middle Eastern Affairs* 14 (1963): 258–71.

———. *The Turkish Revolution, 1960–1961: Aspects of Military Politics*. Washington, D.C.: Brookings, 1963.

———. *Political Tutelage and Democracy in Turkey: The Free Party and Its Aftermath*. Leiden: E. J. Brill, 1973.

———. "Atatürk as a National Symbol." *Turkish Studies Association Bulletin* 6 (1982): 1–6.

Weise, Jurgen. "Turkey and Her Armed Forces." *Military Review* 43 (1963): 80–86.

White, P. J. "Economic Marginalization of Turkey's Kurds: The Failed Promise of Modernization and Reform." *Journal of Muslim Minority Affairs* 18, no. 1 (1998): 139–58.

———. *Primitive Rebels or Revolutionary Modernizers? The Kurdish National Movement in Turkey*. London: Zed Books, 2000.

Wortham, H. E. *Mustafa Kemal of Turkey*. Boston: Little, Brown, 1931.

Yalçın, Aydın. "Turkey: Emerging Democracy." *Foreign Affairs* 45 (1967): 706–14.

———. "New Trends in European Communism: The Case of Turkey." *Foreign Policy* (Ankara) 7 (1978): 28–50.

Yalman, Ahmet Emin. "The Struggle for Multi-Party Government in Turkey." *Middle East Journal* 1 (1947): 46–58.

———. *Turkey in My Time*. Norman: University of Oklahoma Press, 1956.

Yalman, Nur. "Intervention and Extrication: The Officer Corps in the Turkish Crisis." In *The Military Intervenes: Case Studies in Political Development*, ed. Henry Bienen. New York: Russell Sage Foundation, 1969.

———. "On Land Disputes in Eastern Turkey." In *Islam and Its Cultural Dimensions: Studies in Honour of G. E. von Grunebaum*, ed. G. Tikku. Urbana: University of Illinois Press, 1971.

Yashin, Yael-Navaro. "Uses and Abuses of 'State and Civil Society' in Contemporary Turkey." *New Perspectives on Turkey*, no 18 (1998): 1–22.

Yavuz, M. Hakan. "A Preamble to the Kurdish Question: The Politics of Kurdish Identity." *Journal of Muslim Minority Affairs* 18, no. 1 (1998): 9–18.

Yayla, A. "Turkey's Leaders: Erbakan's Goals." *Middle East Quarterly* 4, no. 3 (1997): 150–67.

Yeğen, Mesut. "The Kurdish Question in Turkish State Discourse." *Journal of Contemporary History* 34, no. 4 (October 1999): 555–68.

Yeşilada, Birol A. "Problems of Political Development in the Third Turkish Republic." *Polity* 21 (1988): 345–72.

Yılmaz, Hakan. "Democratization from Above in Response to the International Context: Turkey, 1945–1950." *New Perspectives on Turkey*, no. 17 (1997): 1–37.

Zürcher, Erik Jan. *Political Opposition in the Early Turkish Republic: The Progressive Republican Party, 1924–1925.* Leiden: E. J. Brill, 1991.

———. *Turkey: A Modern History.* 2nd ed. London: I. B. Tauris, 1997.

International Relations and Foreign Policy in the Republican Period, 1923–2001

Açıkalın, Cevat. "Turkey's International Relations." *International Affairs* 23 (1947): 477–91.

Adams, T. W., and Alvin J. Cottrell. "The Cyprus Conflict." *Orbis* 8 (1964): 66–83.

Adamson, Fiona B. "Democratization and the Domestic Source of Foreign Policy: Turkey in the 1974 Cyprus Crisis." *Political Science Quarterly* 116, no. 2 (2001).

Aegean Issues: Problems and Prospects. Ankara: Foreign Policy Institute, 1989.

Akgönenç, Oya. "EU Policies and Turkey's Security Concerns in the Eastern Mediterranean." *Foreign Policy* (Ankara) 22, nos. 1–2 (1998): 33–44.

Alford, Jonathan, ed. *Greece and Turkey: Adversity in Alliance.* New York: St. Martin's, 1984.

Ali, O. "The Kurds and Lausanne Peace Negotiations." *Middle Eastern Studies* 33, no. 3 (1997): 521–34.

Altuğ, Yılmaz. "Minorities in Turkey." *Annales de la Faculté de Droit d'Istanbul*, no. 7 (1957): 98–114.

———. "Early Foreign Relations of the Turks." *Turkish Yearbook of International Relations* (Ankara) 2 (1961): 143–52.

———. "The Cyprus Conflict." *Foreign Policy* (Ankara) 6 (1977): 118–47.

———. "Atatürk's Foreign Policy." *Turkish Review* (Ankara) 4 (1990): 21–28.

Andrew, J. A. "Turkey and the Middle East." In *The Middle East in Transition: Studies in Contemporary History*, ed. Walter Z. Laquer. Freeport, N.Y.: Books for Libraries, 1971.

Aras, Bülent. "Turkey's Policy in the Former Soviet South: Assets and Options." *Turkish Studies* 1, no. 1 (2000): 36–58.

———. *The New Geopolitics of Eurasia and Turkey's Position.* London: Frank Cass, 2000.

———. "Turkish-Israeli-Iranian Relations in the Nineties: Impact on the Middle East." *Middle East Policy* 7, no. 3 (2000): 151–60.

Asopa, Sheek K. *The Foreign Policy of Modern Turkey, 1923–1968.* Aligarch, India: Centre of West Asian Studies, Aligarch Muslim University, 1971.

Aşiroğlu, V. "Cultural Ties between Turkey and Islamic Countries." *Foreign Policy* (Ankara) 5 (1976): 54–59.

Ataöv, Türkkaya. "Turkish Foreign Policy, 1923–1938." *Turkish Yearbook of International Relations* (Ankara) 2 1961: 103–42.

———. *Turkish Foreign Policy, 1939–1945.* Ankara: Ankara University Faculty of Political Sciences, 1965.

———. *NATO and Turkey.* Ankara: Sevinç Matbaası, 1970.

Athanassopoulou, Ekavi. "Ankara's Foreign Policy Objectives after the End of the Cold War." *Orient* 36, no. 2 (1995): 269–85.

———. *Turkey: Anglo-American Security Interests, 1945–1952: The First Enlargement of NATO.* London: Frank Cass, 1999.

———. "American-Turkish Relations." *Middle East Policy* 8 (September 2001): 144–64.

Attaman, Muhittin. "The Kurdish Question and Its Impact on Turkey's Foreign Policy, 1923–2000." *Journal of South Asian and Middle Eastern Studies* 24, no. 2 (2001): 33–49.

Ayata, Sencer, and Ayşe Güneş-Ayata. "Religious Communities, Secularism, and Security in Turkey." In *New Frontiers in the Middle East Security*, ed. Lenore G. Martin. New York: St. Martin's, 1999.

Aybars, E., and K. Arı. "The Past and Present of Western Thrace." *Turkish Review* (Ankara), no. 20 (1990): 102–11.

Aybet, Gülnur. "Turkey and European Institutions." *International Spectator* 34, no. 1 (1999): 103–10.

Aydın, Mustafa. "Turkey and Central Asia: Challenges of Change." *Central Asian Survey* 20, nos. 1–2 (1996): 3–22.

———. "Cacophony in the Aegean: Contemporary Turkish-Greek Relations." *Turkish Yearbook of International Relations* (Ankara) 27 (1997): 109–40.

———. *Turkish Foreign Policy during the Gulf War of 1990–91.* Cairo: American University in Cairo Press, 1999.

———. "Determinants of Turkish Foreign Policy: Historical Frameworks and Traditional Inputs." *Middle Eastern Studies* 35, no. 4 (1999): 152–86.

———. "Determinants of Turkish Foreign Policy: Changing Patterns and Conjectures during the Cold War." *Middle Eastern Studies* 36, no. 1 (2000): 103–39.

Aykan, Mahmut Bali. "The Palestinian Question in Turkish Foreign Policy from the 1950s to the 1990s." *International Journal of Middle East Studies* 25 (1993): 91–110.

———. "Turkish Perspectves on Turkish-US Relations Concerning Persian Gulf Security in the Post–Cold War Era." *Middle East Journal* 50, no. 3 (1996): 344–58.

———. "The Turkey-US-Israel Triangle: Continuity, Change, and Implications for Turkey's Post–Cold War Middle East Policy." *Journal of South Asian and Middle Eastern Studies* 22, no. 4 (1999): 1–31.

Bacık, Gökhan. "The Blue Stream Project: Energy Cooperation and Conflicting Interests." *Turkish Studies* 2, no. 2 (2001): 85–93.

Bal, İdris. *Turkey's Relations with the West and the Turkic Republics.* Aldershot, U.K.: Ashgate, 2000.

———. "Rise of Turkey as a Model in International Relations in Post-Cold War Era and American Ratification." *Eurasian Studies* (Ankara) 18 (2000): 127–36.

Bahçeli, Tözün. *Greek-Turkish Relations since 1955.* Boulder, Colo.: Westview, 1990.

———. "1974 and After: New Realities for Cyprus, Greece, and Turkey." *Turkish Review* (Ankara), no. 28 (1992): 17–43.

———. "Searching for a Cyprus Settlement: Considering Options for Creating a Federation, a Confederation, or Two Independent States." *Publius: The Journal of Federalism* 30, nos. 1–2 (2000): 203–16.

Balkır, Canan, and Allan M. Williams, eds. *Turkey and Europe.* London: Pinter, 1993.

Barkey, Henri J. *Reluctant Neighbor: Turkey's Role in the Middle East.* Washington, D.C.: United States Institute of Peace, 1996.

Barlas, Dilek. *Etatism and Diplomacy in Turkey: Economic and Foreign Policy Strategies in an Uncertain World*. Leiden: E. J. Brill, 1998.

Batu, Hamit. "Turkish Foreign Policy in a Changing World." *Studies on Turkish-Arab Relations* (Istanbul) 6 (1991): 85–93.

Baytok, Taner. "Changing Europe and Turkey's Role." *Foreign Policy* (Ankara) 16 (1990): 51–57.

Bayülken, Ümit Halûk. "Turkish Minorities in Greece." *Turkish Yearbook of International Relations* (Ankara) 4 (1963): 145–64.

———. "Turkey and the United Nations." *Foreign Policy* (Ankara) 1 (1971): 95–108.

Beckingham, Charles F. "Turkey: Political Institutions and Foreign Policy." *University of Toronto Quarterly* 21 (1960): 207–24.

Bekar, O. "NATO's Enlargement: Russia and Turkey." *Eurasian Studies* (Ankara) 3, no. 1 (1996): 65–79.

Bilge, Suat. "The Situation in the Aegean Sea." *Foreign Policy* (Ankara) 14 (1988): 5–20.

———. "Commonwealth of Independent Sates and Turkey." *Eurasian Studies* (Ankara) 1, no. 4 (1995): 63–100.

Bilman, L. "The Regional Cooperation Initiatives in Southeast Europe and Turkish Foreign Policy." *Perceptions* (Ankara) 3, no. 3 (1998): 58–81.

Bingöl, Y. "Turkey's Policy towards Post-Soviet Central Asia: Opportunities and Challenges." *Eurasian Studies* (Ankara), no. 14 (1998): 2–19.

Birge, John K. *Turkey between Two World Wars*. New York: Foreign Policy Association, 1944.

Bishku, Michael M. "Turkey, Greece, and the Cyprus Conflict." *Journal of Third World Studies* 8, no. 1 (1991): 165–79.

———. "Turkey and Its Middle Eastern Neighbors since 1945." *Journal of South Asian and Middle Eastern Studies* 15 (1992): 51–71.

———. "Turkey and Iran during the Cold War." *Journal of Third World Studies* 16, no. 1 (1999): 13–28.

Blank, Stephen J., Stephen C. Pelletiere, and William T. Johnsen, eds. *Turkey's Strategic Position at the Crossroads of World Affairs*. Carlisle Barracks, Pa.: Strategic Studies Institute, 1993.

Bleda, Tanşu. "Black Sea Economic Cooperation Region." *Foreign Policy* (Ankara) 16 (1990): 58–62.

Brey, H. "Turkey and the Cyprus Question." *International Spectator* 34, no. 1 (1999): 111–21.

Boll, M. "Turkey between East and West: The Regional Alternative." *World Today* 35 (1979): 360–76.

Borovalı, Ali. "Kurdish Insurgencies, the Gulf War, and Turkey's Changing Role." *Conflict Quarterly* 7 (1987): 29–45.

———. "Turkey and the Persian Gulf: A Regional Power in Strategic Perspective." *Iranian Journal of International Affairs* 2 (1990): 49–58.

———. "Turkish Foreign Policy in a Changing World." *Mediterranean Quarterly* 1 (1990): 15–25.

———. "The Caucasus within a Historical-Strategic Matrix: Russia, Iran, and Turkey." *Foreign Policy* (Ankara)18 (1994): 22–47.

———. "Turkish American Relations in Recent Conjuncture." *Foreign Policy* (Ankara) 20, nos. 1–2 (1996): 69–74.

Bölükbaşı, Süha. *The Superpowers and the Third World: Turkish-American Relations and Cyprus*. Lanham, Md.: University Press of America, 1988.

———. "Turkey Copes with Revolutionary Iran." *Journal of South Asian and Middle Eastern Studies* 13 (1989): 94–109.

———. "The Evolution of a Close Relationship: Turkish-American Relations between 1917–1960." *Foreign Policy* (Ankara) 14 (1990): 80–104.

———. "Ankara, Damascus, Baghdad, and the Regionalization of Turkey's Kurdish Secessionism." *Journal of South Asian and Middle Eastern Studies* 14 (1991): 15–36.

———. "Turkey Challenges Iraq and Syria: The Euphrates Dispute." *Journal of South Asian and Middle Eastern Studies* 16, no. 4 (1993): 9–32.

———. "Ankara's Bakü-Centered Transcaucasia Policy: Has It Failed?" *Middle East Journal* 51, no. 1 (1997): 80–94.

———. "The Cyprus Dispute and the United Nations: Peaceful Non-Settlement between 1954 and 1996." *International Journal of Middle East Studies* 30, no. 3 (1998): 411–34.

Brown, James. "Turkey's Foreign Policy in Flux." *Current History* 81 (1981): 26–30.

———. "Turkey and the Persian Gulf Crisis." *Mediterranean Quarterly* 2 (1991): 46–54.

Burr, Malcolm. "A Note on the History of the Turkish-Caucasian Border." *Asiatic Review* 43 (1947): 351–55.

Burrows, Bernard. "Turkey in Europe?" *World Today* 36 (1980): 226–71.

Buzan, B., and T. Diez. "The European Union and Turkey." *Survival* 41, no. 1 (1999): 41–57.

Calı, S. "Turkey in the International System of Western States." *Pakistan Horizon* 50, no. 3 (1997): 75–100.

Campany, Richard C. *Turkey and the United States: The Arms Embargo Period.* New York: Praeger, 1986.

Carley, Patricia M. "Turkey and Central Asia: Reality Comes Calling." In *Regional Power Rivalries in the New Eurasia: Russia, Turkey, and Iran,* ed. Alvin Z. Rubinstein and Oles M. Smolansky. Armonk, N.Y.: M. E. Sharpe, 1995.

Cem, İsmail. "Setting Sail to the 21st Century." *Perceptions* (Ankara) 2, no. 3 (1997): 5–12.

Cornell, S. E. "Turkey and the Conflict in Nagorno-Karabakh: A Delicate Balance." *Middle Eastern Studies* 34, no. 1 (1998): 51–72.

———. *Turkey in the 21st Century: Opportunities, Challenges, Threats.* Richmond, U.K.: Curzon Press, 2000.

Coufoudakis, V. "Greek-Turkish Relations in the Post–Cold War Era: Implications of the American Response." *Cyprus Review* 9, no. 1 (1997): 7–21.

Couloumbis, Theodore A. *The United States, Greece, and Turkey: The Troubled Triangle.* New York: Praeger, 1983.

Criss, Nur Bilge, and Yavuz Turan Çetiner. "Terrorism and the Issue of International Cooperation." *The Journal of Conflict Studies* 20, no. 1 (Spring 2000): 127–39.

Cyr, A. "Turkey and the West." *Perceptions* (Ankara) 1, no. 3 (1996): 108–19.

Çelik, Yasemin. *Contemporary Turkish Foreign Policy.* New York: Praeger, 1999.

Dağı, İ. "Turkey in the 1990s: Foreign Policy, Human Rights, and the Search for a New Identity." *Mediterranean Quarterly* 4, no. 4 (1993): 60–77.

Davison, Roderic C. "Middle East Nationalism: Lausanne Thirty Years After." *Middle East Journal* 7 (1953): 324–48.

De Luca, Anthony R. *Great Power Rivalry at the Turkish Straits: The Montreux Conference and the Convention of 1936.* New York: Columbia University Press, 1981.

Demirel, S. "Turkey and NATO at the Threshold of New Century." *Perceptions* (Ankara) 4, no. 1 (1999): 5–13.

Deringil, Selim. *Turkish Foreign Policy during the Second World War: An "Active" Neutrality.* Cambridge: Cambridge University Press, 1989.

Dini, L. "Italy, Turkey, and the European Union." *International Spectator* 34, no. 1 (1999): 7–9.

Dodd, C. H., ed. *Turkish Foreign Policy: New Prospects*. Huntingdon, U.K.: Eothen Press, 1992.

———. *The Cyprus Imbroglio*. Huntingdon, U.K.: Eothen Press, 1998.

Dunér, Bertil, and Edward Deverell. "Country Cousin: Turkey, the European Union, and Human Rights." *Turkish Studies* 2, no. 1 (2001): 1–24.

Earle, Edward Mead. *Turkey, Great Powers, and the Baghdad Railway*. New York: Macmillan, 1923.

Edmonds, C. J. *Kurds, Turks and Arabs*. New York: Oxford University Press, 1957.

Endruweit, G. "Turkey and the European Union: A Question of Cultural Difference?" *Perceptions* (Ankara) 3, no. 2 (1998): 54–72.

Eralp, A. "Turkey and the European Community: Forging New Identities along Old Lines." *New Perspectives on Turkey* 8, no. 1 (1992): 1–14.

Eren, Nuri. *Turkey, NATO and Europe: A Deteriorating Relationship?* Paris: Atlantic Institute for International Affairs, 1977.

———. "Can Turkey Meet Its New Obligations as the New Superpower of the Region?" *Turkish Review* (Ankara), no. 33 (1993): 340–65.

Ergüvenç, Feridun. "Turkey: Strategic Partner of the European Union." *Foreign Policy* (Ankara) 20, nos. 1–2 (1996): 1–10.

Ergüvenç, Ş. "Turkey in the European Security Context: Turkey's Role and Expectations in the Transatlantic Partnership." *Foreign Policy* (Ankara) 21, nos. 1–2 (1997): 22–33.

———. "Turkey's Security Perceptions." *Perceptions* (Ankara) 3, no. 2 (1998): 32–42.

Erim, Nihat. "The Development of the Anglo-Turkish Alliance." *Asiatic Review* 42 (1946): 347–51.

Esmer, Ahmed Şükrü. "The Straits: Crux of World Politics." *Foreign Affairs* 25 (1947): 290–302.

———. "Cyprus: Past and Present." *Turkish Yearbook of International Relations* (Ankara) 3 (1962): 35–46.

Evert, M. "Turkey's Strategic Goals: Possibilities and Weaknesses." *Mediterranean Quarterly* 4, no. 4 (1993): 30–37.

Evin, A. Ö., and G. Denton, eds. *Turkey and the European Community*. Opladen, Germany: Luske & Budrich, 1990.

———. "Turkey-EU Relations on the Eve of IGC: The Social and Cultural Dimension." *Foreign Policy* (Ankara) 20, no. 1–2 (1996): 35–54.

Fisher, Alan. *A Precarious Balance: Conflict, Trade and Diplomacy on the Turkish-Russian Frontier*. Istanbul: ISIS Press, 1999.

Fisher, Sydney N. "Two Centuries of American Interests in Turkey." *Festchrift for Frederick B. Artz*. Durham, N.C.: Duke University Press, 1964.

Fuller, Graham. "Turkey in the New International Security Environment." *Foreign Policy* (Ankara) 16 (1992): 29–44.

Fuller, Graham, and Ian O. Lesser, eds. *Turkey's New Geopolitics: From the Balkans to Western China*. Boulder, Colo.: Westview, 1993.

Gebert, Boleslaw. "Five Hundred Fifty Years of Diplomatic Relations between Turkey and Poland." *Turkish Yearbook of International Relations* (Ankara) 4 (1963): 103–9.

Gençkaya, Ömer Faruk. "The Black Sea Economic Cooperation Project: A Regional Challenge to European Integration." *International Social Science Journal* 45, no. 4 (1993): 549–57.

Glasgow, George. "Turkey and the Straits." *Contemporary Review* 157 (1940): 491–96.

Gökay, B. "Caspian Uncertainties: Regional Rivalries and Pipelines." *Perceptions* (Ankara) 3, no. 1 (1998): 49–66.

Gözen, R. "The Turkish-Iraqi Relations: From Cooperation to Uncertainty." *Foreign Policy* (Ankara) 19, nos. 3–4 (1995): 49–98.

———. "Two Processes in Turkish Foreign Policy: Integration and Isolation." *Foreign Policy* (Ankara) 21, nos. 1–2 (1997): 106–28.

Graves, Philip Perceval. *Briton and Turks*. London: Hutchinson, 1941.

Gresh, Alain. "Turkish-Israeli-Syrian Relations and Their Impact on the Middle East." *Middle East Journal* 52, no. 2 (1998): 188–203.

Gruen, George E. "Turkey's Emerging Regional Role." *American Foreign Policy Interests* 17, no. 2 (April 1995): 13–24.

———. "Dynamic Progress in Turkish-Israeli Relations." *Israel Affairs* 1, no. 4 (Summer 1995): 40–70.

———. "Turkish Waters: Source of Regional Conflict or Catalyst for Peace?" *Water, Air, and Soil Pollution* 123, nos. 1 4 (2000): 565 79.

Gunter, Michael M. "United States Foreign Policy toward the Kurds." *Orient* 40 (1999): 427–37.

———. "The Legal Regulation of Passage through the Turkish Straits." *Mediterranean Quarterly* 11, no. 3 (2000): 87–99.

———. "Life and Career of a Turkish Statesman: Cevat Açıkalın." *Atatürk Araştırma Merkezi Dergisi* (Ankara) 16 (2000): 205–24.

Güçlü, Yener. "Turkish-German Relations on the Eve of World War Two." *Turkish Studies* 1, no. 2 (Autumn 2000): 73–94.

———. *The Question of the Sancak of Alexandretta (1936–1939): A Study in Turkish-French-Syrian Relations*. Ankara: Türk Tarih Kurumu, 2001.

Güneş-Ayata, Ayşe, and Sencer Ayata. "Ethnicity and Security Problems in Turkey." In *New Frontiers in the Middle East Security*, ed. Lenore G. Martin. New York: St. Martin's, 1999.

Gürkan, İhsan. "The Western European Integration and Turkey." *Foreign Policy* (Ankara) 14 (1988): 89–102.

Haktanır, Korkmaz. "New Horizons in Turkish Foreign Policy." *Foreign Policy* (Ankara) 22, nos. 3–4 (1998): 1–9.

Hale, William, and Ali İhsan Barış. *Four Centuries of Turco-British Relations*. Walkington, U.K.: Eothen Press, 1984.

———. "Turkey, the Middle East, and the Gulf Crisis." *International Affairs* 68 (1992): 679–92.

———. "Turkey's Regional Policy." In *Turkey and the European Community*, ed. Mary Strang and Arlene Bedmond. Brussels, Belgium: Forum Europe, 1992.

———. *Turkish Foreign Policy, 1774–1999*. London: Frank Cass, 2000.

Harris, George S. *The Troubled Alliance, The United States, and Turkey: Their Problems in Historical Perspective, 1945–1971*. Washington, D.C.: Hoover Institution-American Enterprise Institute for Public Policy Research, 1971.

———. "Cross-Alliance Politics: Turkey and the Soviet Union." *Turkish Yearbook of International Relations* (Ankara) 12 (1972): 1–32.

———. "The Soviet Union and Turkey." In *The Soviet Union and the Middle East*, ed. Ivo J. Lederer and Wayne S. Vucinich. Stanford, Calif.: Hoover Institution, 1974.

———. ed. *The Middle East in Turkish-American Relations*. Washington, D.C.: Heritage Foundation, 1985.

Henze, Paul B. *Turkey, the Alliance, and the Middle East: Problems and Opportunities in Historical Perspective*. Washington, D.C.: Woodrow Wilson Center, 1981.

———. "Why Turkey Is Not a Friendly Tyrant." In *Friendly Tyrants: An American Dilemma*, ed. Daniel Pipes and Adam Garfinkle. New York: St. Martin's, 1991.

———. *Turkey and Georgia: Expanding Relations*. Washington, D.C.: RAND Corporation, 1991.

———. "Turkey and Armenia: Past Problems and Future Prospects." *Eurasian Studies* (Ankara) 3, no. 1 (1996): 44–53.

Hitchens, Christopher. *Cyprus*. New York: Quartet Books, 1984.

Howard, Harry N., ed. *The Problem of the Turkish Straits: Principal Treaties and Conventions*. Washington, D.C.: U.S. Department of State, 1947.

———. *Turkey, the Straits, and U.S. Policy*. Baltimore, Md.: Johns Hopkins University Press, 1975.

Hucul, Walter C. "Soviet Russia and the Turkish Straits: An Historical Sketch." *World Affairs Quarterly* 27 (1956): 236–68.

Hudson, Geoffrey F. *Turkey, Greece, and the Eastern Mediterranean*. Oxford: Clarendon Press, 1939.

Hunter, S. "Bridge or Frontier: Turkey's Post–Cold War Geopolitical Posture." *International Spectator* 34, no. 1 (1999): 63–78.

İnalcık, Halil. "The Main Problems Concerning the History of Cyprus." *Cultura Turcica* (Ankara) 1 (1964): 44–51.

———. "Turkey between Europe and the Middle East." *Foreign Policy* (Ankara) 8 (1980): 7–31.

İnan, Kâmran. "The Southeastern Anatolia Project and Its Contribution to Regional Cooperation in the Middle East." *Studies in Turkish-Arab Relations* (Istanbul) 4 (1989): 47–54.

Ireland, Philip W. "Turkish Foreign Policy after Munich." *Political Quarterly* 10 (1939): 185–201.

Israeli, Raphael. "The Turkish-Israeli Odd Couple." *Orbis* 45, no. 1 (2001): 65–80.

Joseph, S. Joseph. *Cyprus: Ethnic Conflict and International Concern*. New York: Lang, 1985.

Jung, D., and W. Piccoli. "The Turkish-Israeli Alignment: Paranoia Pragmatism." *Security Dialogue* 31, no. 1 (2000): 91–104.

Kahraman, Sevilay Ergün. "Rethinking Turkey-European Relations." *Turkish Studies* 1, no. 1 (2000): 1–20.

Kaleağası, Bahadır. "New Challenges in the Relations between the European Union and Turkey." *Turkish Area Studies* (London), no. 50 (Spring 2000): 9–16.

Kamel, Ayhan. "Turkish-Russian Relations during the Republican Era." *Foreign Policy* (Ankara) 22, nos. 1–2 (1998): 45–57.

Kandemir, Nüzhet. "Turkey: Secure Bridge over Troubled Waters." *Mediterranean Quarterly* 8, no. 4 (1997): 1–12.

Karaosmanoğlu, Ali L. "Cyprus: What Kind of a Solution?" *Journal of South Asian and Middle Eastern Studies* 3 (1980): 33–46.

———. "Turkey's Security and the Middle East." *Foreign Affairs* 62 (1983): 157–75.

———. "NATO's Southeastern Region: Between Central Europe and the Middle East." *International Defence Review* 10 (1985): 1569–76.

———. "Turkey's Policy in the Middle East." *Studies on Turkish-Arab Relations* (Istanbul) 1 (1986): 159–75.

———. "Remarks on Soviet Strategy and Turkey's Conventional Deterrence." *Foreign Policy* (Ankara) 13 (1987): 87–93.

———. "Turkey and the Southern Flank? Domestic and External Contexts." In *NATO's Southern Allies: Internal and External Challenges*, ed. J. Chipman. London: Routledge, 1988.

———. "Turkey's Security Policy: Continuity and Change." In *Politics and Security in the Southern Region of the Atlantic Alliance*, ed. D. T. Stuart. New York: Macmillan, 1988.

———. "Turkey and the Southern Flank? Domestic and External Contexts." In *NATO's Southern Allies: Internal and External Challenges*, ed. John Chipman. London: Routledge, 1988.

———. "The International Context of Democratic Transition in Turkey." In *Encouraging Democracy: The International Context of Regime Transition in Southern Europe*, ed. G. Pridham. Leicester, U.K.: Leicester University Press, 1991.

———. "Turkey's Defense Policy: Problems and Prospects." In *European Security Policy after the Revolutions of 1989*, ed. Jeffrey Simon. Washington, D.C.: National Defense University Press, 1991.

———. "The Southeast European Countries and the CSCE-CFE Negotiations." In *European Security in the 1990s: Problems of South-East Europe*. New York: United Nations, 1992.

———. "Maritime Security and Arms Control in the Mediterranean and Black Seas: A Turkish View." *International Spectator* 28, no. 4 (1993): 79–84.

———. "Turkey between the Middle East and Western Europe." *International Journal of Turkish Studies* 6, nos. 1–2 (1992–1994): 11–23.

———. "A Turkish Perspective on Arms Control." In *Arms Control and Security in the Middle East*, ed. Richard Eisendorf. Washington, D.C.: Initiative for Peace and Cooperation in the Middle East, 1995.

———. "Turkey and New Geo-Economics in the Black Sea Region." In *Parameters of Partnership: the US-Turkey-Europe*, ed. H. Bağcı, J. Jones, Z. Jones, and Z. Kühnhardt. Baden-Baden: Nomos Verlagsgesellschaft, 1999.

———. "NATO Enlargement and the South: A Turkish Perspective." *Security Dialogue* 30, no. 2 (1999): 213–24.

———. "The Evolution of the National Security Culture and the Military in Turkey." *Journal of International Affairs* 54, no. 1 (Fall 2000): 199–216.

Karpat, Kemal H., ed. *Turkey's Foreign Policy in Transition, 1950–1974*. Leiden: E. J. Brill, 1975.

Kent, Marian. "British Policy, International Diplomacy, and the Turkish Revolution." *International Journal of Turkish Studies* 3 (1985–1986): 33–51.

Kesiç, O. "American-Turkish Relations at Crossroads." *Mediterranean Quarterly* 6, no. 1 (1995): 97–108.

Ker-Lindsay, J. "The 1990–91 Gulf Crisis and Turkish Foreign Policy Decision-Making: A Window of Opportunity for Cyprus." *Cyprus Review* 7, no. 1 (1995): 77–102.

Kızılyürek, N. "Turkey and Greece in the Realm of Western Politics towards the Near East, 1945–1985." *Cyprus Review* 6, no. 2 (1994): 52–68.

Kirişçi, Kemal. "Turkey and the Kurdish Safe Haven in Northern Iraq." *Journal of South Asian and Middle Eastern Studies* 19, no. 3 (1996): 21–39.

Kolars, John. "Defining the Political/Ideological Threshold for the Euphrates and Tigris Rivers." *Arab Studies Quarterly* 22, no. 2 (2000): 101–12.

Kramer, Heinz. *A Changing Turkey: Challenges to Europe and the United States*. Washington. D.C.: Brookings, 1999.

Krüger, Karl. *Kemalist Turkey and the Middle East*. London: Allen & Unwin, 1932.

Kubalı-Camoğlu, İ. "Turkey in the Eye of the Storm: The Indecisiveness of the West and Demise of NATO." *Journal of Muslim Minority Affairs* 16, no. 2 (1996): 305–7.

Kuniholm, Bruce. *The Origins of the Cold War in the Middle East: Great Power Conflict and Diplomacy in Iran, Turkey, and Greece*. Princeton, N.J.: Princeton University Press, 1980.

———. "Turkey and NATO: Past, Present, and Future." *Orbis* 27 (1983): 421–25.

————. "Greece and Turkey in NATO." *SAIS Review* 6 (1986): 137–58.

————. "Turkey and the West." *Foreign Affairs* 70 (1991): 34–48.

————. *The United States and Turkey*. New York: Scribner, 1998.

————. "Turkey's Accession to the European Union: Differences in European and U.S. Attitudes, and Challenges for Turkey." *Turkish Studies* 2, no. 1 (2001): 25–53.

Kürkçüoğlu, Ömer E. "An Analysis of Turkish-Arab Relations." *Ankara Üniversitesi Siyasal Bilgiler Fakültesi Dergisi* 27 (1972): 117–34.

————. "British Policy during the 1974 Cyprus Crisis." *Foreign Policy* (Ankara) 4 (1974): 184–88.

————. "Turkey's Attitude towards the Middle East Conflict." *Foreign Policy* (Ankara) 5 (1976): 23–33.

————. "Arab and Turkish Public Opinion Attitudes towards the Questions of the Two Nations." *Foreign Policy* (Ankara) 12 (1985): 22–43.

Ladas, Stephan. *The Exchange of Minorities—Bulgaria, Greece, and Turkey*. New York: Macmillan, 1932.

Landau, Jacob. *Pan-Turkism: From Irredentism to Cooperation*. Bloomington: Indiana University Press, 1995.

Leighton, Marian Kirsch. *Greco-Turkish Friction: Changing Balance in the Eastern Mediterranean*, London: Institute for the Study of Conflict, 1979.

Lesser, Ian O. "Turkey and the West after the Gulf War." *International Spectator* 27 (1992): 33–46.

————. "Turkey's Strategic Options." *International Spectator* 34, no. 1 (1999): 79–88.

————. "Turkey in a Changing Security Environment." *Journal of International Affairs* 54, no. 1 (Fall 2000): 183–98.

Lewin, Anat. "Turkey and Israel: Reciprocal and Mutual Imagery in the Media." *Journal of International Affairs* 54, no. 1 (Fall 2000): 239–61.

Liel, Alon. *Turkey in the Middle East: Oil, Islam, and Politics*. Boulder, Colo.: Lynne Reiner, 2001.

Lochery, Neill. "Israel and Turkey: Deepening Ties and Strategic Implications, 1995–1998." *Israeli Affairs* 5, no.1 (1998): 45–62.

Lorc, A. V. "Turkey: The Door to Central Asia." *Eurasian Studies* (Ankara) 2, no. 3 (1995): 62–68.

Lütem, Ömer E. "The Past and Present State of Turkish-Bulgarian Relations." *Foreign Policy* (Ankara) 23, nos. 1–4 (1999): 101–23.

Macfie, A. "The Straits Question: The Conference of Lausanne (November 1922–July 1923)." *Middle Eastern Studies* 15 (1979): 211–38.

Mackenzie, Kenneth. *Turkey in Transition: The West's Neglected Ally*. London: Institute for European Defence and Strategic Studies, 1984.

Makovsky, Alan. "The New Activism in Turkish Foreign Policy." *SAIS Review* 19, no. 1 (1999): 92–113.

Makovsky, Alan, and Sabri Sayarı, eds. *Turkey's New World: Changing Dynamics in Turkish Foreign Policy*. Washington, D.C.: Washington Institute for Near East Policy, 2000.

Mango, Andrew. *Turkey: A Delicately Poised Ally*. Beverly Hills, Calif.: Sage, 1975.

————. "Greece and Turkey: Unfriendly Allies." *World Today* 43 (1987): 144–48.

————. "European Dimensions." *Middle Eastern Studies* 28 (1992): 397–439.

————. "Turkey and the Enlargement of European Mind." *Middle Eastern Studies* 34, no. 2 (1998): 171–92.

Manisalı, Erol, ed. *Turkey's Place in the Middle East*. Istanbul: Middle East Business and Banking, 1989.

——. *Turkey's Relations with the Soviet Union and East Europe*. Girne, Cyprus: Middle East Business and Banking, 1991.

——. "Turkey's Relations with the Caucuses and Asian Turkish Republics." *Foreign Policy* (Ankara) 21, nos. 1–2 (1997): 65–75.

Martin, Lenore. "Turkey's National Security in the Middle East." *Turkish Studies* 1, no. 1 (2000): 83–106.

Mastny, Vojtech, and R. Craig Nation, eds. *Turkey between East and West: New Challenges for a Rising Regional Power*. Boulder, Colo.: Westview, 1996.

McGhee, George C. *The US-Turkish-NATO Middle East Connection: How the Truman Doctrine Contained the Soviets in the Middle East*. New York: St. Martin's, 1990.

McLaren, Lauren M. "Turkey's Eventual Membership of the EU: Turkish Elite Perspectives on the Issue." *Journal of Common Market Studies* 38, no. 1 (2000): 117–29.

Mhitaryan, N. "Turkish-Ukranian Relations." *Eurasian Studies* (Ankara) 3, no. 2 (1996): 2–13.

Millman, Brock. *The Ill-made Alliance: Anglo-Turkish Relations, 1934–1940*. Montreal: McGill-Queens University Press, 1999.

Mufti, M. "Daring and Caution in Turkish Foreign Policy." *Middle East Journal* 52, no. 1 (1998): 32–50.

Müftüler, Meltem. "Turkey and the European Community: An Uneasy Relationship." *Turkish Review* (Ankara), no. 33 (1993): 31–41.

——. "Turkish Economic Liberalization and European Integration." *Middle Eastern Studies* 31, no. 1 (1995): 85–98.

——. "Turkey: A New Player in Middle Eastern Politics." *Mediterranean Quarterly* 6, no. 4 (1995): 110–20.

Müftüler-Baç, Meltem. "Turkey's Predicament in the Post–Cold War Era." *Futures* 28, no. 3 (1996): 255–68.

——. *Turkey's Relations with a Changing Europe*. Manchester, U.K.: Manchester University Press, 1997.

——. "The Never Ending Story: Turkey and the European Union." *Middle Eastern Studies* 34, no. 4 (1998): 240–58.

——. "Turkey and Israel? An Axis of Tension and Security." *Security Dialogue* 29, no. 1 (1998): 121–23.

——. "Turkey's New Vocation." *Journal of South Asian and Middle Eastern Studies* 22, no. 3 (1999): 1–15.

——. "Through the Looking Glass: Turkey in Europe." *Turkish Studies* 1, no. 1 (2000): 21–35.

——. "The Impact of the European Union on Turkish Politics." *East European Quarterly* 34, no. 2 (2000): 159–79.

Müftüler-Baç, Meltem, and Müberra Yüksel. "Turkey: Middle Power in the New Order." In *Niche Diplomacy: Middle Powers after the Cold War*, ed. Andrew Power. London: Macmillan, 1997.

"New Horizons of Turkish Foreign Policy in the Year 2000 and Beyond." *Foreign Policy* (Ankara) 25, nos. 1–2 (2000): 1–133; 25, nos. 3–4 (2000): 1–177. Special issues.

Okyar, Osman. "A Survey of Arab-Turkish Relations." *Middle East Forum* 42 (1966): 43–54.

Olcay, H. B. "The Euphrates-Tigris Watercourse Controversy and the 1997 Convention on the Law of the Non-Navigational Uses of International Watercourses." *Foreign Policy* (Ankara) 21, nos. 3–4 (1998): 48–81.

Olson, Robert. "The Creation of a Kurdish State in the 1990s." *Journal of South Asian and Middle Eastern Studies* 15 (1992): 1–25.

——. "The Kurdish Question and Chechenya: Turkish and Russian Foreign Policies since the Gulf War." *Middle East Policy* 4, no. 3 (1996): 106–18.

——. *The Kurdish Question and Turkish-Iranian Relations: From World War I to 1998.* Costa Mesa, Calif.: Mazda Publishers, 1998.

——. "Turkish and Russian Foreign Policies, 1991–1997: The Kurdish and Chechnya Questions." *Journal of Muslim Minority Affairs* 18, no. 2 (1998): 209–27.

——. "Turkey-Iran Relations, 1997 to 2000: The Kurdish and Islamist Questions." *Third World Quarterly* 21, no. 5 (2000): 871–90.

——. *Turkey's Relations with Iran, Syria, Israel, and Russia, 1991–2000: The Kurdish and Islamist Questions.* Costa Mesa, Calif.: Muzda Publishers, 2001.

O'Malley, B., and G. Craig. *The Cyprus Conspiracy: America, Espionage, and the Turkish Invasion.* London: I. B. Tauris, 1999.

Oral, N., and G. Aybay, "Turkey's Authority to Regulate the Passage of Vessels through the Turkish Straits." *Perceptions* (Ankara) 3, no. 2 (1998): 84–108.

Orhun, O. "Turkey, Norway, and the US in the New European Security Context." *Foreign Policy* (Ankara) 21, nos. 1–2 (1997): 5–12.

Öğütçü, O. "Religious 'Bias' in the West against Islam: Turkey as a Bridge in Between?" *Foreign Policy* (Ankara) 18 (1994): 87–119.

Öğütçü, M. "Turkey and China." *Perceptions* (Ankara) 1, no. 3 (1996): 155–79.

Öniş, Ziya. "Turkey in the Post–Cold War Era." *Middle East Journal* 49, no. 1 (1995): 48–68.

——. "Luxembourg, Helsinki, and Beyond: Turkey-EU Relations." *Government and Opposition* 34, no. 4 (Autumn 2000): 463–83.

——. "An Awkward Partnership: Turkey's Relations with the European Union in Comparative-Historical Perspective." *Journal of European Integration History* 7, no. 1 (2001): 105–19.

Özen, C. "Neo-Functionalism and the Change in the Dynamics of Turkey-EU Relations." *Perceptions* (Ankara) 3, no. 3 (1998): 34–57.

Özer, E. "The Black Sea Economic Cooperation and the Regional Security." *Perceptions* (Ankara) 2, no. 3 (1997): 76–106.

Papacosma, S. "The Eastern Question Revisited: Greek-Turkish Relations in the Historical Context of Great Power Policy Making." *Cyprus Review* 10, no. 1 (1998): 77–92.

Pesmazoglou, Stephanos. "Turkey and Europe, Reflections and Refractions: Towards a Contrapuntal Approach." *New Perspectives on Turkey*, no. 13 (1995): 1–23.

Psomiades, Harry J. *The Eastern Question—The Last Phase: A Study in Greek-Turkish Relations.* Thessaloniki, Greece: Institute for Balkan Studies, 1968.

Ramazani, Rouhollah K. The *Northern Tier: Afghanistan, Iran, and Turkey.* Princeton, N.J.: D. Van Nostrand, 1966.

Robins, Philip. *Turkey and the Middle East.* London: Pinter, 1991.

——. "Between Sentiment and Self-Interest: Turkey's Policy toward Azerbaijan and the Central Asian States." *Middle East Journal* 47, no. 4 (1993): 593–610.

——. "'Silent Competition': Iran and Turkey in the New Muslim Republics." *Japanese Institute of Middle Eastern Economies Review*, no. 21 (1993): 37–51.

Romeril, P. E. A. *War Diplomacy and the Turkish Republic: A Study in Neutrality.* Leiden: E. J. Brill, 1970.

Ronzitti, N. "The Aegean Demilitarization, Greek-Turkish Relations, and Mediterranean Security." *Foreign Policy* (Ankara) 14 (1988): 60–76.

Roper, J. "The West and Turkey: Varying Roles, Common Interests." *International Spectator* 34, no.1 (1999): 89–102.

Rumford, Chris. "Turkey and European Enlargement: Cross-Border Projects and the Pre-Accession Strategy for Non-Members." *New Perspectives on Turkey*, no. 19 (1998): 71–96.

Ruseckas, Laurent. "Turkey and Eurasia: Opportunities and Risks in the Caspian Pipeline Derby." *Journal of International Affairs* 54, no. 1 (Fall 2000): 217–36.

Rustow, Dankwart A. "Foreign Policy of the Turkish Republic, 1923–1939." In *Foreign Policy in World Politics*, ed. Roy Macridis. Englewood Cliffs, N.J.: Prentice Hall, 1962.

Sander, Oral. "Turkish-Bulgarian Relations." *Foreign Policy* (Ankara) 12 (1986): 7–19.

———. "The Aftermath of the Gulf War and Turkey." *Studies on Turkish-Arab Relations* (Istanbul) 6 (1991): 109–17.

———. "Turkish Foreign Policy: Forces of Continuity and Change." *Turkish Review* 7, no. 34 (1993): 31–46.

———. "Turkey and the Turkic World." *Central Asian Survey* 13, no. 1 (1994): 37–44.

Satterthwaite, J. "The Truman Doctrine: Turkey." *Annals: American Academy of Political and Social Sciences*, no. 401 (1972): 74–84.

Sayarı, Sabri. "Turkey: The Changing European Security Environment and the Gulf Crisis." *Middle East Journal* 46 (1992): 9–21.

———. "Turkey, Caucasus, and Central Asia." In *The New Geopolitics of Central Asia and Its Borderlands*, ed. Ali Banuazizi and Myron Weiner. Bloomington: Indiana University Press, 1994.

———. "Turkey and the Middle East in the 1990s." *Journal of Palestine Studies* 26, no. 3 (1997): 44–55.

———. "Turkish Foreign Policy in the Post–Cold War Era: The Challenges of Multi-Regionalism." *Journal of International Affairs* 54, no. 1 (Fall 2000): 169–82.

Sencer, Ayata. "Turkey's Security Problems." In *Security in the Middle East*, ed. Richard A. Norton. Boulder: Lynne Reiner, 1998.

Sever, Ayşegül. "Compliant Ally? Turkey and the West in the Middle East, 1954–1958." *Middle Eastern Studies* 34, no. 2 (1998): 73–90.

———. "The Evolution of Turkish-American Relations in the Middle East, 1945–1958." *Turkish Review of Middle East Studies* (Istanbul) 10 (1998–1999): 143–169.

Sezer, Duygu Bazoğlu. *Turkey's Security Policies*. London: International Institute for Strategic Studies, 1981.

———. "Turkey's Grand Strategy Facing a Dilemma." *International Spectator* 27 (1992): 17–32.

———. "Turkish-Russian Relations: The Challenges of Reconciling Geopolitical Competiton with Economic Partnership. *Turkish Studies* 1, no. 1 (2000): 59–82.

Sharabi, Hisham Bashir. "Turkey's Foreign Policy." In *Governments and Politics of the Middle East in the Twentieth Century*. Princeton, N.J.: Van Nostrand, 1962.

Shaw, Stanford J. *Turkey and the Holocaust: Turkey's Role in Rescuing Turkish and European Jews from Nazi Persecution, 1933–1945*. New York: New York University Press, 1992.

Shotwell, J. T., and F. Deak. *The Problem of the Turkish Straits*. New York: Macmillan, 1940.

Silier, Oya. "The Place of Anglo-Turkish Relations in the Foreign Policy of the Turkish Republic, 1923–1929." *Turkish Yearbook of International Relations* (Ankara) 11 (1971): 86–101.

Sokolnichi, Michel. *The Turkish Straits*. Beirut: American Press, 1950.

Sonyel, Salahi R. *Cyprus. The Destruction of a Republic. British Documents, 1960–1965*. Huntingdon, U.K.: The Eothen Press, 1997.

———. "Disinformation—The Negative Factor in Turco-Greek Relations." *Perceptions* (Ankara) 3, no. 1 (1998): 39–48.

———. "The European Union and the Cyprus Imbroglio." *Perceptions* (Ankara) 3, no. 2 (1998): 73–83.

Souter, D. "The Cyprus Conundrum: The Challenge of the Intercommunal Talks." *Third World Quarterly* 11 (1989): 76–91.

Soysal, İsmail. "Turkish-Arab Diplomatic Relations after the Second World War." *Studies on Turkish-Arab Relations* (Istanbul) 1 (1986): 249–66.

———. "1937 Sadabad Pact." *Studies on Turkish-Arab Relations* (Istanbul) 3 (1988): 131–53.

———. "Political Relations between Turkey and Egypt in the Last Six Decades." *Turkish Review* (Ankara), no. 20 (1990): 13–20.

———. "Seventy Years of Turkish-Soviet Relations." *Turkish Review* (Ankara), no. 24 (1991): 15–24.

———. "70 Years of Turkish-Arab Relations and an Analysis on Turkish-Iraqi Relations." *Studies on Turkish-Arab Relations* (Istanbul) 6 (1991): 23–84.

Soysal, Mümtaz, and Münir Ertegün. "Federal Solution for Cyprus." *Foreign Policy* (Ankara) 14 (1988): 15–29.

Söylemez, Yüksel. *Foreign Policy of Turkey at the United Nations between the Years 1966–1972: Public Interventions, Selected Documents, and Official Communications.* Ankara: Ministry of Foreign Affairs, 1973.

Spain, James W. "The United States, Turkey, and the Poppy." *Middle East Journal* 29 (1975): 295–309.

———. *American Diplomacy in Turkey: Memoirs of an Ambassador Extraordinary and Plenipotentiary.* New York: Praeger, 1984.

Stearns, M. "The Greek-American-Turkish Triangle: What Shape after the Cold War?" *Mediterranean Quarterly* 4, no. 4 (1993): 16–29.

Suyetina, L. "Turkey: 'Atlantic' and National Interests." *International Affairs* (Moscow) 7 (1980): 116–33.

Şimşir, Bilâl. "The Fate of the Turkish Minority in the People's Republic of Bulgaria." *Foreign Policy* (Ankara) 12 (1986): 20–66.

———. "Migrations from Bulgaria to Turkey: 1950–1951 Exodus." *Foreign Policy* (Ankara) 12 (1986): 67–101.

———. "The Legal Status of the Turkish Minority in Bulgaria under Bilateral and Multilateral Treaties." *Foreign Policy* (Ankara) 12 (1986): 102–44.

———. "The Latest Bulgarian Coup: Forced Changing of Turkish Names." *Foreign Policy* (Ankara) 12 (1986): 145–61.

Tachau, Frank. "Turkish Foreign Policy: Between East and West." *Middle East Review* 17 (1985): 21–7.

Tamkoç, Metin. *The Warrior Diplomats: Guardians of the National Security and Modernization of Turkey.* Salt Lake City: University of Utah Press, 1976.

Taşhan, Seyfi. "Turkish-U.S. Relations and Cyprus." *Foreign Policy* (Ankara) 4 (1974): 164–77.

———. "Contemporary Turkish Policies in the Middle East: Prospects and Constraints." *Middle East Review* 17 (1985): 5–11.

———. "Turkey between Europe and the Arab World." *Studies on Turkish-Arab Relations* (Istanbul) 2 (1987): 57–62.

———. "Turkey's Alternatives and EC." *Foreign Policy* (Ankara) 14 (1988): 103–10.

———. "Turkish Foreign Policy in the Balkans." *Turkish Review* (Ankara), no. 20 (1990): 5–11.

———. "Turkey: From Marginality to Centrality." *Foreign Policy* (Ankara) 16 (1992): 1–12.

———. "MENA Regions: A Perspective from Ankara." *Foreign Policy* (Ankara) 19, nos. 3–4 (1995): 39–47.

———. "A Review of Turkish Foreign Policy in the Beginning of 1998." *Foreign Policy* (Ankara) 22, nos. 1–2 (1998): 1–32.

Tayfur, M. Fatih. "Turkish Foreign Policy towards the Euro-Mediterranean Partnership and the Black Sea Economic Cooperation: A Comparative Analysis." *Foreign Policy* (Ankara) 23, nos. 1–4 (1999): 75–100.

Tevetoğlu, F. "Atatürk's Soviet Policy." *Cultura Turcica* (Ankara) 2 (1965): 3–12.

Theophylactou, D. "American Foreign Policy vis-à-vis Turkey, Greece, and Cyprus: A Historical Perspective." *Cyprus Review* 5, no. 1 (1993): 28–45.

Thomas, Lewis V. "Turkey: Guardian of the Straits." *Current History* 48 (1951): 8–11.

———. "The National and International Relations of Turkey." In *Near Eastern Culture and Society: A Symposium on the Meeting of East and West*, ed. T. Cuyler Young. Princeton, N.J.: Princeton University Press, 1951.

Thomas, Lewis V., and Richard N. Frye. *The United States and Turkey and Iran*. Cambridge, Mass.: Harvard University Press, 1951.

Tomanbey, Mehmet. "Turkey's Approach to the Utilization of the Euphrates and Tigris Rivers." *Arab Studies Quarterly* 22, no. 2 (2000): 79–100.

Torumtay, Necip. "Turkey's Military Doctrine." *Foreign Policy* (Ankara) 15 (1989): 18–27.

Trask, Roger R. *The United States Response to Turkish Nationalism and Reform, 1914–1939*. Minneapolis: University of Minnesota Press, 1971.

Tsakonas, Pamayotis J. "Turkey's Post-Helsinki Turbulence: Implications for Greece and the Cyprus Issue." *Turkish Studies* 2, no. 2 (2001): 1–40.

Turan, İlter. "Whither Turkish Foreign Policy?" *Conflict* 2 (1980): 17–30.

———. "Mediterranean Security in the Light of Turkish Concerns." *Perceptions* (Ankara) 3, no. 2 (1998): 16–31.

Turkey and the United Nations. Prepared under the auspices of the Institute of International Relations of the Faculty of Political Sciences, University of Ankara, for the Carnegie Endowment for International Peace. New York: Manhattan Publishing, 1961.

Turlington, Edgar. "The Settlement of Lausanne." *American Journal of International Relations* 18 (1924): 696–706.

Tütsch, Hans E. *From Ankara to Marrakesh: Turks and Arabs in a Changing World*. London: Allen & Unwin, 1964.

Uğur, Mehmet. *The European Union and Turkey*. Aldershot, U.K.: Ashgate, 1999.

Ülman, A. Haluk, and Ruhollah H. Dekmejian, "Changing Patterns in Turkish Foreign Policy, 1959–1967." *Orbis* 11 (1967): 772–85.

Váli, Ferenc A. *Bridge across the Bosphorus: The Foreign Policy of Turkey*. Baltimore, Md.: Johns Hopkins University Press, 1970.

———. *The Turkish Straits and NATO*. Stanford, Calif.: Hoover Institution, 1971.

Vere-Hodge, Edward Reginald. *Turkish Foreign Policy, 1918–1948*. Ambilly-Annemasse, Switzerland: Imprimerie Franco Suisse, 1949.

Villaverde, J. A. N. "Turkey and the EU: An Endless Hurdle-Race." *Perceptions* (Ankara) 3, no. 3 (1998): 15–33.

Vucinich, Wayne. "Growing Unity in Yugoslavia, Greece, and Turkey." *Current History* 24 (1953): 103–8.

Weber, Frank G. *The Evasive Neutral: Germany, Britain, and the Quest for a Turkish Alliance in the Second World War*. Columbia: University of Missouri Press, 1979.

Weisband, Edward. "The Sancak of Alexandretta, 1920–1939: A Case Study." *Near Eastern Round Table* 1 (1967–1968): 156–224.

———. *Turkish Foreign Policy, 1943–1945: Small State Diplomacy and Great Power Politics.* Princeton, N.J.: Princeton University Press, 1973.

Wilson, A. *The Aegean Dispute.* London: International Institute for Strategic Studies, 1979.

Winrow, Gareth M. "Turkey and Former Central Asia: National and Ethnic Identity." *Central Asian Survey* (London) 11, no. 3 (1992): 101–11.

———. *Where East Meets West: Turkey and the Balkans.* London: Institute for European Defence and Strategic Studies, European Security Studies Series, no. 18, 1993.

———. "Turkish Relations with the Newly Independent Republics of the Caucasus." *Oxford International Review* 5, no. 1 (1993): 45–48.

———. *Turkey in Post-Soviet Central Asia.* London: Royal Institute of International Affairs, Former Soviet South Series, no. 1, 1995.

———. "Turkey and Former Soviet Central Asia: A Turkic Culture Area in the Making?" In *Central Asia: Emerging New Order*, ed. K. Warikoo. New Delhi: Har-Anand Publishers, 1995.

———. "Turkey's Relations with the Transcaucacus and the Central Asian Republics." *Perceptions* (Ankara) 1, no. 1 (1996): 128–45.

———. "A Threat from the South? NATO and the Mediterranean." *Mediterranean Politics* 1, no. 1 (1996): 43–59.

———. "Turkish Policy in the Central Asia." In *Security Politics in the Commonwealth of Independent States: The Southern Belt*, ed. Mehdi Mozaffari. London: Macmillan, 1997.

———. "Turkey and ECO." *Himalayan and Central Asian Studies* (New Delhi) 2, no. 2 (1998): 3–29.

Woodhouse, C. M. "The Problems of Cyprus." *Indiana Social Studies Quarterly* 32 (1979): 111–12.

Xydis, Stephen George. "The 1945 Crisis over the Turkish Straits." *Balkan Studies* (Athens) 1 (1960): 65–90.

———. "Toward 'Toil and Moil' in Cyprus." *Middle East Journal* 20 (1966): 1–19.

———. *Cyprus: Reluctant Republic.* The Hague: Mouton, 1973.

Yavuz, M. Hakan. "Turkish Identity and Foreign Policy in Flux: The Rise of Neo-Ottomanism." *Critique*, no. 2 (1998): 19–42.

Yılmaz, Bahri. "Turkey's New Role in International Politics." *Aussenpolitik* (Vienna) 45, no. 1 (1994): 90–98.

Yılmaz, Mesut. "Turkish Foreign Policy." *Foreign Policy* (Ankara) 14 (1988): 9–14.

Yu'lin, Shao. *Those Who Try to Damage the Sino-Turkish Friendship.* Ankara: Turkish Daily News, 1963.

Yüksel, Mevhibe. "Turkey and the Organisation of Islamic Conference (OIC)." *Foreign Policy* (Ankara) 15 (1989): 67–71.

Yüksel, Süreyya. "NATO-Turkey-Middle East." *Studies on Turkish-Arab Relations* (Istanbul) 6 (1991): 119–29.

Zeine, Zeine N. *Arab-Turkish Relations and the Emergence of Arab Nationalism.* Beirut: Khayat's, 1958.

———. *The Emergence of Arab Nationalism: With a Background Study of Arab-Turkish Relations in the Near East.* Delmar, N.Y.: Caravan Books, 1973.

Zhivkova, Ludmila. *Anglo-Turkish Relations, 1933–1939.* London: Secker & Warburg, 1976.

Zimová, N. "Kemalist Turkey's Concept of Foreign Relations and Its Value in the Contemporary Context: Turkey and the Balkans in the Early 1930s." *Archiv Orientalni* (Prague) 56 (1988): 201–15.

Zuzul, M. "Croatia and Turkey: Toward a Durable Peace in Southeastern Europe." *Perceptions* (Ankara) 3, no. 3 (1998): 82–88.

The Economy in the Republican Period, 1923–2001

Ahmad, F. "The Development of Capitalism in Turkey." *Journal of Third World Studies* 15 (1998): 137–44.

Akat, Asaf Savaş. "The Political Economy of Turkish Inflation." *Journal of International Affairs* 54, no. 1 (Fall 2000): 265–82.

Akçetin, Elif. "Anatolian Peasants in the Great Depression." *New Perspectives on Turkey*, no. 23 (Fall 2000): 79–102.

Akder, Halis. "Reflections on Turkish Agriculture and Common Agricultural Policy." *METU Studies in Development* (Ankara) 12 (1985): 343–51.

———. "Turkey's Export Expansion in the Middle East, 1980–1985." *Middle East Journal* 41 (1987): 553–67.

Aktan, C. C. "The Privatization of State Economic Enterprises in Turkey." *Boğaziçi Journal* (Istanbul) 7, nos. 1–2 (1993): 39–52.

Aktan, O. "An Estimate of Changes in Trade Flows between Turkey and the EEC, 1960–1970." *Hacettepe Bulletin of Social Sciences and Humanities* (Ankara) 6 (1973): 19–80.

Aktan, Reşat. "The Common Market and the Turkish Economy." *Cultura Turcica* (Ankara) 1 (1964): 156–63.

———. "Agricultural Problems of Turkey." *Mediterranea* (1966): 266–76.

———. "Problems of Land Reform in Turkey." *Middle East Journal* 20 (1966): 317–34.

Akyüz, Y. *Money and Inflation in Turkey, 1950–1968*. Ankara: Ankara Üniversitesi Siyasal Bilgiler Fakültesi, 1973.

Alexander, Alec P. "Turkish Economic Development." In *Economic Development*, ed. Irma Adelman and Adam Pepelassis. New York: Harper, 1960.

———. "Industrial Entrepreneurship in Turkey: Origins and Growth." *Economic Development and Cultural Change* 8 (1960): 349–65.

———. "Turkey." In *Economic Development: Analysis and Case Studies*, ed. Adamantis Pepelasis, Leon Mears, and Irma Adelman. New York: Harper & Row, 1961.

Algan, Ümit R., and Mahir Fisunoğlu. "Elasticities of Import Demand: The Turkish Experience." *Journal of Economics and Administrative Studies* (Istanbul) 4 (1990): 105–13.

Alkin, Erdoğan. *Turkey's International Economic Relations*. Istanbul: Istanbul University Publications, 1982.

Altuğ, Yılmaz. "Turkish Aspects of Migration for Employment to Europe." *Annales de la Faculté de Droit d'Istanbul* 16 (1966): 1–17.

Andıç, Fuat M. "Development of Labor Legislation in Turkey." *Middle Eastern Affairs* 8 (1957): 366–72.

Aresvik, Oddvar. *The Agricultural Development of Turkey*. New York: Praeger, 1975.

Arıcanlı, Tosun, and Dani Rodrik. *The Political Economy of Turkey: Debt, Adjustment, and Sustainability*. London: Macmillan, 1990.

Ayarslan, Solmaz D. "The Convertible Turkish Lira Accounts and Their Impact on the Turkish Economy." *Turkish Studies Association Bulletin* 3 (1979): 9–11.

Aydın, T. "Turkey's Rising Economic Capacity." *Perceptions* (Ankara) 1, no. 3 (1996): 137–54.

Aydın, Zülküf. *Underdevelopment and Rural Structures in Southeastern Turkey: The Household Economy in Gisgis and Kalhana*. London: Ithaca Press, 1986.

Bahmani-Oskooee, M., and İ. Domaç. "Export Growth and Economic Growth in Turkey: Evidence from Cointegration Analysis." *METU Studies in Development* (Ankara) 22, no. 1 (1995): 67–77.

Balasa, Bela. "Outward Orientation and Exchange Rate Policy in Developing Countries: The Turkish Experience." *Middle East Journal* 37 (1983): 429–47.

Balkan, Erol, and Erinç Yeldan. "Financial Liberalization in Developing Countries: The Turkish Experience." In *Financial Liberalization in Developing Countries*, ed. R. Medhora and J. Fanelli. London: Macmillan, 1998.

Baran, Tuncer. "The Impact of Foreign Trade Investments on the Turkish Economy." *Turkish Yearbook of International Relations* (Ankara) 13 (1973): 85–101.

Barkey, Henri J. *The State and Industrialization Crisis in Turkey*. Boulder, Colo.: Westview, 1990.

Başak, Zafer Z. "AID, Indebtedness, and Foreign Trade: The Turkish Case 1960–1972." *Turkish Yearbook of International Relations* (Ankara) 12 (1972): 78–88.

Bayar, A. H. "The Developmental State and Economic Policy in Turkey." *Third World Quarterly* 17, no. 4 (1996): 773–86.

Bayrı, T., and W. Furtan. "An Economic Analysis of Technological Change in the Spring-Wheat Region of Turkey." *METU Studies in Development* (Ankara) 14 (1987): 291–313.

Baysan, Tercan, and Charles Blitzer. "Turkey." In *Liberalizing Foreign Trade*, vol. 6, ed. D. Papageorgiou, M. Michaely, and A. M. Choksi. Cambridge: Basil Blackwell, 1991.

Berk, Niyazi. *The Harmonization Requirements of the Turkish Banking System from the Standpoint of Full Membership in the European Community*. Istanbul: Friedrich-Ebert-Stiftung, 1988.

Blitzer, Charles R. "A Dynamic Five-Sector Model for Turkey, 1967–1982." *American Economic Review* 60 (1970): 70–75.

Boratav, Korkut. *Turkey: Stabilization and Adjustment Policies and Programmes*. Helsinki, Finland: WIDER, 1988.

———. "State and Class in Turkey: A Study in Capitalist Development." *Review of Radical Political Economics* 25, no. 1 (1993): 129–47.

———. "Distributional Dynamics in Turkey under 'Structural Adjustment' of the 1980s." *New Perspectives on Turkey*, no. 11 (1994): 43–69.

Boratav, Korkut, and Oktar Türel. "Turkey." In *The Rocky Road to Reform*, ed. L. Taylor. Cambridge, Mass.: MIT Press, 1993.

Boratav, Korkut, Oktar Türel, and Erinç Yeldan. "Distributional Dynamics in Turkey under 'Structural Adjustment of the 1980s.'" *New Perspectives on Turkey*, no. 11 (1994): 43–69.

———. "The Turkish Economy in 1982–92: A Balance Sheet, Problems, and Prospects." *METU Studies in Development* (Ankara) 22, no.1 (1995): 1–36.

———. "Dilemmas of Structural Adjustment and Environmental Policies under Instability: Post–1980 Turkey." *World Development* 24, no. 2 (1996): 373–93.

Buğra, Ayşe. "Non-Market Mechanisms of Market Formation: The Development of the Consumer Durables Industry in Turkey." *New Perspectives on Turkey*, no. 19 (1998): 1–28.

Bulutay, Tuncer. "An Overview of the External Financing Mechanism of the Turkish Economy." *Turkish Yearbook of International Relations* (Ankara) 8 (1967): 85–147.

Bulutay, Tuncer, and Hasan Ersel. "The Distribution of Income in Certain Turkish Cities." *Turkish Yearbook of International Relations* (Ankara) 8 (1967): 29–84.

Can, Tevfik. "Economic Relations of Turkey with the Common Market, 1955–1965." *Turkish Economic Review* (Ankara) 7 (1966): 35–37.

Carey, Jane P. C., and Andrew G. Carey. "Turkish Industry and Five-Year Plans." *Middle East Journal* 25 (1971): 337–54.

———. "Turkish Agriculture and Five-Year Development Plans." *International Journal of Middle East Studies* 3 (1972): 45–58.

Celasun, Merih. *Perspectives on Economic Growth in Turkey*. Ankara: Middle East Technical University, 1975.

———. "Real and Monetary Aspects in the Turkish Economic Planning." *METU Studies in Development* (Ankara) 6 (1980): 1–36.

———. "Income Distribution and Domestic Terms of Trade in Turkey, 1978–1983." *METU Studies in Development* (Ankara) 13 (1986): 193–216.

———. "A General Equilibrium Model of the Turkish Economy: SIMLOG 1." *METU Studies in Development* (Ankara) 13 (1986): 29–94.

———. "Income Distribution and Employment Aspects of Turkey's Post-1980 Adjustment." *METU Studies in Development* (Ankara) 16 (1989): 1–31.

———. "Income Distribution and Employment Aspects of Turkey's Post-1980 Adjustment." In *Institutional Aspects of Economic Integration of Turkey into the European Community*, ed. Heiko Körner and Rasul Shams. Hamburg: Verlag Weltarchiv, 1990.

———. "Trade and Industrialization in Turkey: Initial Conditions, Policy, and Performance in the 1980s." In *Trade Policy and Industrialization in Turbulent Times*, ed. Gerald K. Helleiner. London and New York: Routledge, 1994.

Celasun, Merih, and I. Arslan. "Sustainability of Industrial Exporting in a Liberalizing Economy: The Turkish Experience." In *Manufacturing for Export in the Developing World: Problems and Possibilities*, ed. Gerald K. Helleiner. London and New York: Routledge, 1995.

Celasun, Merih, and Dani Rodrik. *Debt, Adjustment, and Growth: Turkey*. New York: National Bureau of Economic Research, 1987.

Ceyhun, Fikret. "Turkey's Debt Crisis in Historical Perspectives: A Critical Analysis." *METU Studies in Development* (Ankara) 19 (1992): 9–49.

Cenani, Rasim. *Foreign Capital Investments in Turkey*. London: Simpkin Marshall, 1954.

Chakraverti, A. "Some Aspects of the Structural Characteristics of the Turkish Economy." *Artha Vijnana, J. Gokhale Institute of Politics and Economics* (Poona, India) 11 (1969): 236–55.

Cizre-Sakallıoğlu, Ümit, and Erinç Yeldan. "Politics, Society, and Financial Liberalization." *Development and Change* 31, no. 2 (March 2000): 481–508.

Conway, P. *Economic Shocks and Structural Adjustments: Turkey after 1973*. Amsterdam: Elsevier, 1987.

Cornelisse, Peter A., and Bahadır Akın. "An Economic Appraisal of the Association Agreement between the European Community and Turkey." *METU Studies in Development* (Ankara) 13 (1986): 259–73.

Crabbe, Geoffrey. "Turkey: A Record of Industrial and Commercial Progress in the Last Quarter of a Century." *Royal Central Asian Society Journal* 31 (1941).

Çakman, M. Kemal. "The Public Finance Problem of Turkey." *Turkish Studies Association Bulletin* 14 (1990): 1–12.

Çeçen, A. Aydın, A. Suut Doğruel, and Fatma Doğruel. "Economic Growth and Structural Change in Turkey, 1960–1988." *International Journal of Middle East Studies* 26, no. 1 (1994): 37–56.

Çınar, E., and B. Uyar. "Deficits and Long-Term Interest Rates in an Open Developing Country: Testing the Ricardian Equivalence Hypothesis for Turkey." *Boğaziçi Journal* (Istanbul) 9, no. 1 (1995): 77–92.

Çınar, E., Mehmet Kaytaz, and Güner Evcimen. "A Case Study on the Growth Potential of Small-Scale Manufacturing Enterprises in Bursa, Turkey." *METU Studies in Development* (Ankara) 14 (1987): 123–46.

Çiller, Tansu. "The Economics of Exporting Labour to the EEC: A Turkish Perspective." *Middle Eastern Studies* 12 (1976): 173–86.

Demirgil, Demir. *Labor-Management Relations in Turkey.* Istanbul: Economic Research Foundation, 1969.

Dereli, Toker. "The Economic and Social Effects of Trade Unionism and Collective Bargaining in Turkey." *Istanbul Üniversitesi İşletme Fakültesi Dergisi*, no. 1 (1978): 93–120.

Dereli, Toker, and İsmail Zeytinoğlu. "Public Sector Industrial Relations on the Eve of Mass Privatization in Turkey." *International Labor Review* 132, nos. 5–6 (1993): 689–702.

Derviş, Kemal, and Sherman Robinson. *The Foreign Exchange Gap, Growth, and Industrial Strategy in Turkey.* Washington, D.C.: World Bank, 1978.

Devereux, Robert. "Turkish Economic Doctrine and Organization: Old and New." *Social Science* 37 (1962): 99–107.

Duggal, O. P. "A Review of the State Economic Enterprises in Turkey." *Annals of Public and Co-operative Economics* 40 (1969): 469–79.

Durdağ, Mete. "Inflation in a Development Economy: The Case of Turkey, 1950–1961." *Economia Internazionali* (Genoa) n.v. (1967): 493–500.

———. *Some Problems of Development Financing: A Case Study of the Turkish Five-Year Plan, 1963–1967.* Dordrecht, the Netherlands: Reidel, 1973.

Ebiri, Kutlay. "Turkish Apertura." *METU Studies in Development* (Ankara) 7 (1980): 209–53.

———. "Impact of Labor Migration on the Turkish Economy." In *Guests Who Come to Stay: The Effects of Labor Migration on Sending and Receiving Countries*, ed. Rosemarie Rogers. Boulder, Colo.: Westview, 1985.

Ekin, Nusret. "Strikes and Lockouts in Turkey." *Istanbul Üniversitesi İktisat Fakültesi Dergisi* 36 (1966): 131–54.

Ekinci, Nazım Kadri. "Macroeconomic Developments in Turkey: 1980–1988." *METU Studies in Development* (Ankara) 17 (1990): 73–114.

Ekmekçioğlu, Çuna, and Haluk Kasnakoğlu. "Supply Response in Turkish Agriculture." *METU Studies in Development* (Ankara) 6 (1979): 113–41.

Eldridge, Robert Huyck. "Emigration and the Turkish Balance of Payments." *Middle East Journal* 20 (1966): 296–316.

Ercan, Metin R., and Ziya Öniş. "Turkish Privatization: Institutions and Dilemmas." *Turkish Studies* 2, no. 1 (2001): 109–34.

Erden, Deniz. "Export Performance of Foreign Direct Investment Firms in Developing Countries: The Case of Turkey." *Boğaziçi Journal* (Istanbul) 9, no. 1 (1995): 93–112.

Erdilek, Asım. *Direct Foreign Investment in Turkish Manufacturing.* Tübingen, Germany: Mohr, 1984.

———. "Turkey's New Open-Door Policy of Direct Foreign Investment: A Critical Analysis of Problems and Prospects." *METU Studies in Development* (Ankara) 13 (1986): 171–92.

Eren, Nuri. "Financial Aspects of Turkish Planning." *Middle East Journal* 20 (1966): 187–95.

Erginbilgiç, F. S., and B. Özer. "The Effects of Inflation on Compositions of Revenues and Deposits, and Profitability of Commercial Banks in Turkey." *Boğaziçi Journal* (Istanbul) 7, nos. 1–2 (1993): 167–87.

Erol, Turan. "Short-Term Macroeconomic Adjustment Process in a Developing Economy: The Turkish Case, 1960–1980 and 1981–1988." *METU Studies in Development* (Ankara) 19 (1992): 51–65.

Ersel, Hasan. "The Timing of Capital Account Liberalization: The Turkish Experience." *New Perspectives on Turkey*, no. 15 (1996): 45–64.

Ersu, Ahmet. "Oil Industry in Turkey." *Studies on Turkish-Arab Relations* (Istanbul) 3 (1988): 31–40.

Filiztekin, Alpay, and İnsan Tunalı. "Anatolian Tigers: Are They for Real?" *New Perspectives on Turkey*, no. 20 (1999): 77–106.

Fry, Maxwell J. *Finance and Development Planning in Turkey.* Leiden: E. J. Brill, 1972.

———. "Alternative Stabilization Strategies from a Model of Short-Run Price and Output Fluctuations in Turkey." *METU Studies in Development* (Ankara), no. 18 (1978): 21–35.

———. "The Money Supply Mechanism in Turkey." *METU Studies in Development* (Ankara) 4 (1978): 49–59.

———. "Turkey's Great Inflation." *METU Studies in Development* (Ankara) 13 (1986): 95–116.

Gazioğlu, Şaziye. "Consumption and Wealth Effect in Turkey." *METU Studies in Development* (Ankara) 10 (1983): 131–53.

———. "Government Deficits, Consumption and Inflation in Turkey." *METU Studies in Development* (Ankara) 13 (1986): 117–34.

Gitmez, Ali. "Developmental Outcomes of External Migration: The Turkish Experience." *METU Studies in Development* (Ankara) 15 (1988): 1–21.

Gsönger, Hans. *Turkey-European Community: National Development Policy and the Process of Rapprochement.* Berlin: German Development Institute, 1979.

Gürkan, A. "The Regional Structure of Agricultural Production in Turkey: A Multivariate Perspective." *METU Studies in Development* (Ankara) 12 (1985): 27–47.

Hale, William. "Ideology and Economic Development in Turkey, 1930–1945." *British Society for Middle Eastern Studies Bulletin* 7 (1980): 100–17.

———. "Turkey and the EC: Options and Prospects." In *Widening the Community Circle*, ed. Clive Church. London: University Association for Contemporary European Studies, 1990.

Hansen, B. *Egypt and Turkey: The Political Economy of Poverty, Equity, and Growth.* Oxford: Oxford University Press, 1991.

Hatiboğlu, Zeyyat. "Economic Aspects of the Upsurge in Turkey after Atatürk." *Journal of the American Institute for the Study of Middle Eastern Civilization* 1 (1980–1981): 52–64.

Hershlag, Zvi Y. "Turkey: Achievements and Failures in the Policy of Economic Development during the Inter-War Period, 1919–1939." *Kyklos* 7 (1954): 323–50.

———. *Turkey: An Economy in Transition.* The Hague: Mouton, 1958.

———. *Turkey: The Challenge of Growth.* Leiden: E. J. Brill, 1968.

———. *The Contemporary Turkish Economy.* London: Routledge, 1988.

———. "Growth, Development, Equity: A Case Study of Turkey." *Journal of Economics and Administrative Studies* (Istanbul) 4 (1990): 25–34.

Hiç, Mükerrem. "The Question of Foreign Private Capital in Turkey." *Orient* (Hamburg) 21 (1980): 371–84.

———. "Economic Policies Pursued by Turkey: Their Effects on the Performance of the Economy and on Her International Relations." *Orient* (Hamburg) 22 (1982): 220–42.

———. "Market Economy and Democracy: Turkey as a Case Study for Developing Countries and Eastern Europe." *Orient* (Hamburg) 33 (1992): 205–26.

Hirsch, Abraham, and Eva Hirsch. "Changes in the Trade of Farmers and Their Effect on Real Farm Income per Capita of Rural Population in Turkey, 1927–1960." *Economic Development and Cultural Change* 14 (1966): 440–57.

Hirsch, Eva. "Tax Reform and the Burden of Direct Taxation in Turkey." *Public Finance*, no. 3 (1966): 337–71.

———. *Poverty and Plenty on the Turkish Farm: A Study of Income Distribution in Turkish Agriculture*. New York: Columbia University Press, 1970.

Işıklılar, G. A. "Privatization in Turkey." *Journal of Economic Cooperation among Islamic Countries* 18, no. 1 (1997): 121–47.

İlkin, Selim, and E. İnanç, eds. *Planning in Turkey: Selected Papers*. Ankara: Middle East Technical University, 1967.

Jackson, D. "The Political Economy of Collective Bargaining: The Case of Turkey." *British Journal of Industrial Relations* 9 (1971): 69–81.

Karataş, Cevat. "Public Economic Enterprises in Turkey: Reform Proposals, Pricing, and Investment Policies." *METU Studies in Development* (Ankara) 13 (1986): 135–70.

———. "Public Debt, Taxation System, Government Spending Changes in Turkey, 1980–1992." *Journal of Economic and Administrative Studies* (Istanbul) 6, nos. 1–2 (1992): 41–82.

———. "Privatization and Its Future Prospects in Turkey." *Journal of Economic Cooperation among Islamic Countries* 1, nos. 3–4 (1993): 111–27.

Kasnakoğlu, Z. "Estimation of Price Elasticities for Turkish Exports Using Cross-Section Data." *METU Studies in Development* (Ankara) 15 (1988): 1–18.

Kaytaz, Mehmet. "The Role of Small and Medium Industries in Development: A Case Study of Selected Sectors in Turkey." *Journal of Economics and Administrative Studies* (Istanbul) 4 (1990): 53–68.

Kaytaz, Mehmet, Günar Evcimen, and E. Mine Çınar. "A Case Study of Some Economic Characteristics of Small Scale Manufacturing Enterprises." *Journal of Economic and Administrative Studies* (Istanbul) 3 (1989): 1–20.

Kazgan, Gülten. *Income Distribution in Turkey: Yesterday and Today*. Istanbul: Friedrich-Ebert-Stiftung, 1991.

Keddie, N. "Development in the Middle East: A Comparison between Iran, Turkey, and Egypt." *Communications and Development Review* 1 (1977): 6–9.

Keyder, Çağlar. *The Definition of a Peripheral Economy: Turkey, 1923–1929*. New York: Cambridge University Press, 1981.

———. "Social Structure and the Labor Market in Turkish Agriculture." *International Labor Review* 128 (1989): 731–44.

Keyder, Çağlar, and Ayhan Aksu-Koç. *External Labor Migration from Turkey and Its Impact: An Evaluation of the Literature*. Ottowa: International Development Research Centre, 1988.

Keyder, Çağlar, and Faruk Tabak, eds. *Landholding and Commercial Agriculture in the Middle East*. Albany, N.Y.: SUNY Press, 1991.

Keyder, Nur. "The Money Stock Determination in Turkey." *METU Studies in Development* (Ankara) 12 (1985): 1–26.

———. "Velocity and Monetary Targeting in Turkey." *METU Studies in Development* (Ankara) 16 (1989): 31–66.

Kirkpatrick, Colin, and Ziya Öniş. "Turkey." In *Aid and Power: The World Bank and Policy Based Lending*, vol. 2, ed. Paul Mosley, Jean Harrigan, and John Toye. London: Routledge, 1991.

Kolars, John. "The Hydro-Imperative of Turkey's Search for Energy." *Middle East Journal* 40 (1986): 53–67.

Köse, Ahmet Haşim, and Erinç Yeldan. "Turkish Economy in the 1990s: An Assessment of Fiscal Policies, Labor Markets, and Foreign Trade." *New Perspectives on Turkey*, no. 18 (1998): 51–78.

Krane, R. E. *Manpower Mobility across Cultural Boundaries: Social, Economic, and Legal Aspects: The Case of Turkey and Germany.* Leiden: E. J. Brill, 1975.

Krueger, Anne O. *Foreign Trade Regimes and Economic Development: Turkey.* New York: National Bureau of Economic Research, 1974.

Krueger, Anne O., and Okan H. Aktan. *Turkey: Trade Reforms in the 1980s.* San Francisco, Calif.: ICS Press, 1992.

Krueger, Anne O., and Baran Tuncer. *Microeconomic Aspects of Productivity under Import Substitution: Turkey.* New York: National Bureau of Economic Research, 1980.

Kurnow, Ernest. *The Turkish Budgetary Process.* Ankara: Yeni Matbaa, 1956.

Lavy, V., and H. Rapoport. "External Debt and Structural Adjustment: Recent Experience in Turkey." *Middle Eastern Studies* 28 (1992): 313–38.

"Learning to Live with Volatile Capital Movements and Contagion: An Emergent Market Perspective in Turkey." *Boğaziçi Journal-Review of Social, Economic and Administrative Issues* (Istanbul) 14, no. 1 (special issue, 2000): 1–117.

Lingeman, E. R. *Economic and Commercial Conditions in Turkey.* London: H.M.S. Stationary Office, 1948.

Malik, A. "Inflation in a Developing Economy: The Case of Turkey." *Economia Internazionali* (Genoa) 19 (1966): 88–112.

Manisalı, Erol. "The Economic Complementariness between Turkey and Arab Countries." *Studies on Turkish-Arab Relations* (Istanbul) 2 (1987): 97–101.

Metin-Özcan, Kıvılcım. "The Relationship between Inflation and the Budget Deficit in Turkey." *Journal of Business Economic Statistics* 16 (1998): 412–22.

Meyer, A. J. "Turkish Land Reform: An Experiment in Moderation." In A. J. Meyer, ed. *Middle Eastern Capitalism: Nine Essays.* Cambridge, Mass.: Harvard University Press, 1959.

Milor, Vedat. "The Genesis of Planning in Turkey." *New Perspectives on Turkey*, no. 4 (1990): 1–30.

Moore, Clement Henry. "Islamic Banks and Competitive Politics in the Arab World and Turkey." *Middle East Journal* 44 (1990): 234–55.

Morris, James. "Recent Problems of Economic Development in Turkey." *Middle East Journal* 14 (1960): 1–14.

Mutlu, Servet. "Regional Inequalities in Turkey." *Journal of Economics and Administrative Sciences* (Istanbul) 3 (1989): 107–41.

———. "Price Scissors in Turkish Agriculture." *METU Studies in Development* (Ankara) 17 (1990): 163–212.

Nadaroğlu, Halil. "The European Economic Community and Turkey." *Turkish Economic Review* (Ankara) 5 (1964): 33–38.

Nas, Tevfik F., and Mehmet Odekon, eds. *The Liberalization of the Turkish Economy.* Westport, Conn.: Greenwood, 1988.

———. eds. *Economics and Politics of Turkish Liberalization.* London: Associated University Press, 1992.

———. "Effects of Post-1980 Macroeconomic Policies on Turkish Manufacturing." *Journal of Developing Areas* 30, no 2 (1996).

Noel, Emile. "Turkey's Relations with the EEC." *Turkish Economic Review* (Ankara) 10 (1969): 22–8.

Oğuzman, Kemal. "The Collective Agreement, Strike, Lockout, and Arbitration System in Turkey." *Annales de la Faculté de Droit d'Istanbul* 22 (1972): 147–69.

Okyar, Osman. "Industrialization in Turkey." *Middle Eastern Affairs* 4 (1953): 209–17.

———. "Economic Framework for Industrialization: Turkish Experiences in Retrospect." *Middle Eastern Affairs* 9 (1958): 261–67.

———. "The Turkish Stabilization Experiment: Before and After." *Middle Eastern Affairs* 11 (1960): 238–46.

———. "Turkey." *World Survey*, no. 14 (1970): 1–19.

———. "Development Background of the Turkish Economy, 1923–1973." *International Journal of Middle East Studies* 10 (1979): 325–44.

———. "Turkey and the IMF: A Review of Relations." In *IMF Conditionality*, ed. John Williamson. Washington, D.C.: Institute for International Economics, 1983.

———. "Development Background of the Turkish Economy, 1923–1973." *Turkish Review* (Ankara) 7, no. 34 (1993): 11–30.

Okyar, Osman, and Okan H. Aktan, eds. *Economic Relations between Turkey and the EEC*. Ankara: Hacettepe University, 1976.

Olgun, Hasan. "The Structure of Protection in Turkish Manufacturing Industries." *METU Studies in Development* (Ankara), no. 6 (1975): 129–63.

Osman, A. "The Politics of Privatization in Turkey during the 1980s." *Journal of South Asian and Middle Eastern Studies* 23, no. 4 (2000): 21–36.

Ökte, Faik. *The Tragedy of the Turkish Capital Tax*. Trans. Geoffrey Cox. London: Croom Helm, 1987.

Öncü, Ahmet. "The Extent of Financial Repression in the Turkish Economy during 1971–1985." *METU Studies in Development* (Ankara) 15 (1988): 73–84.

Öniş, Ziya. "Stabilisation and Growth in a Semi-Industrial Economy: An Evaluation of the Recent Turkish Experience." *METU Studies in Development* (Ankara) 13 (1986): 7–28.

———. "Inflation and Import-Substituting Industrialization: An Interpretation of the Turkish Case." *Journal of Economics and Administrative Studies* (Istanbul) 1 (1987): 1–23.

———. "The Evolution of Privatization in Turkey: The Institutional Context of Public-Enterprise System." *International Journal of Middle East Studies* 23 (1991): 163–76.

———. "Globalization and Financial Blow-ups in the Semi-Periphery: Perspectives on Turkey's Financial Crisis of 1994." *New Perspectives on Turkey*, no 15 (1996): 1–23.

Öniş, Z., and A. F. Aysan. "Neoliberal Globalization, the Nation-State, and Financial Crises in the Semi-periphery: A Comparative Analysis." *Third World Quarterly* 21, no. 1 (2000): 113–39.

Özatay, Fatih. "The 1994 Currency Crisis in Turkey." *Policy Reform* 1, no. 1 (1999): 1–26.

Özçiçek, Ömer, and Hasan Kirmanoğlu. "The Effect of Short-Term Capital Flows on the Turkish Economy." *Yapı Kredi Economic Review* (Ankara) 10 (1999): 27–34.

Özel, Işık. "An Evaluation of the Economic Performance of Turkey in the 1930s Based on Late-Ottoman Economy." *New Perspectives on Turkey*, no. 23 (Fall 2000): 125–46.

Özer, Bengi, and Sibel Yamak. "Effects of the Gulf Crisis on Risk-Return Relationship and Volatility of Stocks in Istanbul Stock Exchange." *METU Studies in Development* (Ankara) 19 (1992): 209–23.

Özler, Ş. "Sources of Debt Rescheduling: Turkey in the 1970s." *JÜSUR: UCLA Journal of Middle Eastern Studies* 5 (1989): 45–55.

Özmucur, Süleyman. "Productivity and Profitability in the 500 Largest Firms of Turkey, 1980–1992." *Boğaziçi Journal* (Istanbul) 7, nos. 1–2 (1993): 63–71.

Özmucur, Süleyman, and Cevat Karataş. "Total Factor Productivity in Turkish Manufacturing, 1973–1988." *Journal of Economics and Administrative Studies* (Istanbul) 4 (1990): 289–322.

Paine, Suzanne. *Exporting Workers: The Turkish Case*. Cambridge: Cambridge University Press, 1974.

Pamuk, Şevket. "Intervention in Response to the Great Depression: Another Look at the Turkish Case, 1929–1939." In *Globalization and Economic Response in the Mediterranean Basin before 1950*, ed. Şevket Pamuk and Jeffry Williamson. London: Routledge, 2000.

Parvin, M., and M. Hiç. "Land Reform versus Agricultural Reform: Turkish Miracle or Catastrophe Delayed?" *International Journal of Middle East Studies* 16 (1984): 207–32.

Penninx, R., and L. Van Velzen. *The Export of Manpower from a Rural District in Central Turkey*. The Hague: Institute for Social Science Research in Developing Countries, 1977.

Porokhovsky, A. "A Comparative Study of Indicative Planning in Turkey and Planning in Socialist Countries." *METU Studies in Development* (Ankara) (special issue 1981): 133–43.

Poroy, Ibrahim. "Planning without a Large Public Sector: Turkey (1963–1967)." *International Journal of Middle East Studies* 3 (1972): 348–60.

———. "Expansion of Opium Production in Turkey and the State Monopoly." *International Journal of Middle East Studies* 13 (1981) 191–211.

Republic of Turkey. "Implications of the Uruguay Round on the Turkish Foreign Trade." *Journal of Economic Cooperation among Islamic Countries* 16, nos. 3–4 (1995): 59–69.

———. "Industrial Property Protection in Turkey." *Journal of Economic Cooperation among Islamic Countries* 16, nos. 3–4 (1995): 71–82.

Rivkin, Malcolm D. *Area Development for National Growth: The Turkish Precedent*. New York: Praeger, 1965.

Robbins, G. "Initial Reasons for Accelerated Migration in Turkey, 1945–1955: The Farmer's Viewpoint." *Turkish Studies Association Bulletin* 7 (1983): 6–16.

Robinson, Richard D. *High-Level Manpower in Economic Development: The Turkish Case*. Cambridge, Mass.: Harvard University Press, 1967.

Rosen, S. "Turkey." In *Labor in Developing Countries*, ed. Walter Galenson. Berkeley: University of California Press, 1962.

Roy, D. "Labour and Trade Unionism in Turkey: The Ereğli Coalminers." *Middle Eastern Studies* 12 (1976): 125–72.

Sağbaş, İsa. "Central-Local Fiscal Relations in Turkey: A Technical Analysis of Fiscal Equalization." *Turkish Studies* 2, no. 2 (2001): 121–42.

Sarç, Ömer Celal. "Economic Policy of the New Turkey." *Middle East Journal* 2 (1948): 430–46.

Schachter, Gustov. "Economic Conditions in Turkey." *Turkish Studies Association Bulletin*, no. 2 (1977): 1–10.

Selçuk, Faruk. "Currency Substitution in Turkey." *Applied Economics* 26, no. 3 (1994): 509–18.

———. "Consumption Smoothing and Current Account: Turkish Experience." *METU Studies in Development* (Ankara) 24, no. 4 (1997): 519–29.

Shaker, Sallama. *State, Society, and Privatization in Turkey, 1979–1990*. Baltimore, Md.: Johns Hopkins University Press, 1995.

Shorter, F. C., J. F. Kolars, D. A. Rustow, and O. Yenal. *Four Studies on the Economic Development of Turkey*. London: Frank Cass, 1967.

Simpson, Dwight. "Development as a Process: The Menderes Phase in Turkey." *Middle East Journal* 19 (1965): 141–52.

Singer, Morris. *Economic Development in the Context of Short-Term Public Policies: The Economic Advance of Turkey, 1938–1960.* Ankara: Türkiye Ekonomi Kurumu, 1978.

Snyder, W. W. "Turkish Economic Development: The First Five-Year Plan." *Journal of Development Studies* 6 (1969): 58–71.

Sugur, Nadir. "Small Firm Flexibility in Turkey:" *New Perspectives on Turkey*, no. 16 (1997): 87–104.

Szyliowicz, Joseph S. *Politics, Technology, and Development: Decision-Making in the Turkish Iron and Steel Industry.* New York: St. Martin's, 1991.

Şener, Orhan. *The Effects of Capital Markets on Industrialization in Turkey.* Istanbul: Friedrich-Ebert-Stiftung, 1989.

Şenses, Fikret. "The Nature and Main Characteristics of Recent Turkish Growth in Export of Manufactures." *Developing Economies* 27 (1989): 19–33.

———. *Recent Industrialization Experience of Turkey in a Global Context.* Westport, Conn.: Greenwood, 1994.

———. ed. *Industrialization Experience of Turkey in the 1980s.* New York: Greenwood, 1994.

Şenses, F., and T. Yamada. *Stabilization and Structural Adjustment Program in Turkey.* Tokyo: Institute of Developing Economies, 1990.

Tansel, A. "An Engel Curve Analysis of Household Expenditure in Turkey, 1978–1979." *METU Studies in Development* (Ankara) 13 (1986): 239–57.

Taşkıran, M. "Turkey and the Arab World: Seeking New Markets." *Middle East* 115 (1984): 73–8.

Thornburg, Max Weston, Graham Spry, and George Soule. *Turkey: An Economic Appraisal.* 1949. Reprint, New York: Greenwood, 1968.

Togan, Sübidey, and V. N. Balasubramanyam. *The Economy of Turkey since Liberalisation.* London: Macmillan, 1996.

———. eds. *Turkey, East European Countries, and European Union.* London: Macmillan, 2000.

Togan, Sübidey, Hasan Olgun, and Halis Akder. *External Economic Relations of Turkey.* Istanbul and Ankara: Turktrade, 1987.

Tunalı, İnsan. "Choice of Contracts in Turkish Agriculture." *Economic Development and Cultural Change* 42, no. 1 (1993): 67–86.

Tuncer, Baran. "An Overview of the External Financing Mechanism of the Turkish Economy." *Turkish Yearbook of International Relations* (Ankara) 8 (1967): 1–14.

Turkey-EEC Relations 1963–1977. Ankara: Office of the Commission of the European Communities, 1977.

Tümertekin, Erol. "The Structure of Agriculture in Turkey." *Review of the Geographical Institute* (Istanbul), no. 5 (1959): 77–93.

———. "Turkey's Industrialization." *Review of the Geographical Institute* (Istanbul), no. 6 (1960): 22–31.

Tünay, Muharrem. "Establishment of Centralized Control over Labour in Turkey, 1950–1960." *METU Studies in Development* (Ankara) 6 (1979): 31–50.

Uca, Mehmet Nezir. *Worker's Participation and Self-Management in Turkey: An Evaluation of Attempts and Experiences.* The Hague: Institute of Social Studies, 1983.

Uğurlu, Mine. "Capital Structure Determinants: Evidence for Turkish Manufacturing Firms at Istanbul Stock Exchange." *METU Studies in Development* (Ankara) 19 (1992): 225–47.

Uyar, B. "Public Finances in Turkey in the 1980s." *Journal of Economic and Administrative Studies* (Istanbul) 6, nos. 1–2 (1992): 1–40.

Üstünel, Besim. "Problems of Development Financing: The Turkish Case." *Journal of Development Studies* 3 (1967): 130–54.

Walstedt, Bertil. *State Manufacturing Enterprise in a Mixed Economy: The Turkish Case.* Baltimore, Md.: Johns Hopkins University Press, 1980.

Wolff, Peter. *Stabilization Policy and Structural Adjustment in Turkey, 1980–1985.* Berlin: German Development Institute, 1987.

Wölker, G. "Turkish Labour Migration to Germany: Impact on Both Economies." *Middle Eastern Studies* 12 (1976): 42–76.

Wyatt, Stomley C. "Turkey: The Economic Situation and the Five-Year-Plan." *International Affairs* 13 (1934): 826–44.

Yağcı, Fahrettin. "Macro Planning in Turkey: A Critical Evaluation." *METU Studies in Development* (Ankara) n.v. (special issue, 1981): 407–25.

———. "Turkish Manufacturing Industry. A General Evaluation." *Boğaziçi University Journal* (Social Sciences Series, Istanbul) 10 (1983): 13–29.

Yeldan, A. Erinç. "Structural Adjustment and Trade in Turkey: Investigating the Alternatives beyond 'Export-Led Growth.'" *Journal of Policy Modeling* 11 (1989): 273–97.

———. "A General Equilibrium Investigation of the Optimum Benefits of Turkish Structural Adjustment, 1979–1983." *METU Studies in Development* (Ankara) 17 (1990): 25–72.

———. "Surplus Creation and Extraction under Structural Adjustment: Turkey, 1980–1992." *Review of Radical Political Economics* 27, no. 2 (1995): 38–72.

———. "On Structural Sources of the 1994 Turkish Crisis: A CGE Modeling Analysis." *International Review of Applied Economics* 12, no. 3 (1998): 397–414.

Yıldırım, E. "Total Factor Productivity Growth in Turkish Manufacturing Industry, 1963–1983: An Analysis." *METU Studies in Development* (Ankara) 16 (1989): 65–96.

SOCIOCULTURAL LIFE IN THE
OTTOMAN EMPIRE AND REPUBLICAN TURKEY

General Studies

Abadan-Unat, Nermin, ed. *Turkish Workers in Europe, 1960–1975: A Socio-Economic Appraisal.* Leiden: E. J. Brill, 1976.

———. "Turkish Migration to Europe and the Middle East: Its Impact on Social Structure and Social Legislation." In *Social Legislation in the Contemporary Middle East,* ed. Laurence O. Michelak and Jeswold W. Salacuse. Berkeley: University of California Institute of International Studies, 1986.

———. "The Socio-Economic Aspects of Return Migration in Turkey." *Revue Européenne des Migrations Internationales* (Poitiers), no. 3 (1988): 29–59.

Abadan-Unat, Nermin, R. Keleş, R. Penninx, H. V. Resnelorar, L. V. Velzen, and L. Yenisey. *Migration and Development: A Study of the Effects of International Labour Migration in Boğazlıyan District.* Ankara: Ajans-Türk, 1976.

Allen, Henry Elisha. *The Turkish Transformation: A Study in Social and Religious Development.* Chicago: University of Chicago Press, 1935.

And, Metin. *Istanbul in the 16th Century: The City, the Palace, Daily Life.* Istanbul: Akbank, 1994.

Arı, Oğuz, and Cavit Orhan Tütengil. "Some Indications of Labour Commitment and Adjustment to Social Millieu: A Turkish Case Study." In *Social Stratification and Development in the Mediterranean Basin,* ed. Mübeccel B. Kıray. The Hague: Mouton, 1973.

Aswad, B. "Visiting Patterns among Women of the Elite in a Small Turkish City." *Anthropological Quarterly* 47 (1974): 9–27.

Ataman, J., and S. Epir. "Age, Socioeconomic Status, and Classificatory Behavior among Turkish Children." In *Mental Tests and Cultural Adaptation*, ed. L. J. Crenbach and P. J. D. Renth. The Hague: Mouton, 1972.

Başgöz, İlhan, and Norman Furniss. *Turkish Workers in Europe.* Bloomington: Indiana University Press, 1986.

Bates, Daniel G. "Differential Access to Pasture in a Nomadic Society: The Yörük of Southeastern Turkey." In *Perspectives on Nomadism*, ed. W. Irons and N. Dyson-Hudson. Leiden: E. J. Brill, 1972.

———. "Normative and Alternative Systems of Marriage among the Yörük of Southeastern Turkey." *Anthropological Quarterly* 47 (1974): 270–87.

———. "Yörük Settlement in Southeastern Turkey." In *When Nomads Settle: Processes of Sedentarization as Adaptation and Response*, ed. Philip Carl Saldman. New York: Praeger, 1980.

Beeley, Brian. "The Turkish Village Coffee-House as a Social Institution." *Geographical Review* 60 (1970): 475–93.

Benedict, Peter. "The Kabul Günü: Structured Visiting in an Anatolian Provincial Town." *Anthropological Quarterly* 47 (1974): 28–47.

———. *Ula: An Anatolian Town.* Leiden: E. J. Brill, 1974.

Blunt, Fanny Janet (Sandison). *My Reminiscences.* London: John Murray, 1918.

Bradburn, Norman. "Interpersonal Relations within Formal Organizations in Turkey." *Journal of Social Issues* 19 (1963): 61–67.

Buğra, Ayşe. "The Late-Coming Tycoons of Turkey." *Journal of Economics and Administrative Studies* (Istanbul) 1 (1987): 143–55.

———. "The Turkish Holding Company as a Social Institution." *Journal of Economics and Administrative Studies* (Istanbul) 4 (1990): 35–51.

Busbecq, Ogier Ghislian de. *The Turkish Letters of Ogier Ghislian de Busbecq, Imperial Ambassador at Constantinople, 1554–1562.* Oxford: Clarendon Press, 1968. First published in Latin in 1633.

Canson, Ronald W., and Banu Özertuğ. "Semantic Structure and Social Structure in a Central Anatolian Village." *Anthropological Quarterly* 47 (1974): 347–73.

Dubetsky, Alan R. "Kinship, Primordial Ties, and Factory Organization in Turkey: An Anthropological View." *International Journal of Middle East Studies* 7 (1976): 433–45.

———. "Class and Community in Urban Turkey." In *Commoners, Climbers, and Notables: A Sampler of Studies on Social Ranking in the Middle East*, ed. C. A. O. van Niewenhuijze. Leiden: E. J. Brill, 1977.

Eberhard, Wolfram. "Nomads and Farmers in Southeastern Turkey." *Oriens* 6 (1953): 32–49.

———. "Change in Leading Families in Southern Turkey." *Anthropos* 49 (1954): 992–1003.

Erdentuğ, Nermin. *A Study on the Social Structure of a Turkish Village.* Ankara: Ankara Üniversitesi Dil, Tarih ve Coğrafya Fakültesi, 1959.

Eubank, Earle E. "Social Reconstruction in Turkey." *Journal of Applied Sociology* 9 (1925): 450–56.

Faroqhi, Suraiya. *Subjects of the Sultan: Culture and Daily Life in the Ottoman Empire.* London: I. B. Tauris, 1998.

Frey, Frederick W., and Leslie L. Roos. *Social Structure and Community Development in Rural Turkey: Village and Elite Leadership Relations.* Cambridge, Mass.: MIT Press, 1967.

Gallagher, C. F. "Language Reform and Social Modernization in Turkey." In *Can Language Be Planned?* ed. J. Rubin and B. H. Jernudd. Honolulu: University of Hawaii Press, 1971.

Garnett, Lucy Mary Jane. *The Turkish People, Their Social Life, Religious Beliefs and Institutions, and Domestic Life*. London: Methuen, 1909.

Gerber, Haim. *Economy and Society in an Ottoman City, Bursa 1600–1700*. Jerusalem: Hebrew University Institute of Asian and African Studies, 1988.

Gitmez, Ali. "Geographical and Occupational Reintegration of Returning Turkish Workers." In *The Politics of Return*, ed. D. Kubat. New York: Center for Migration Studies, 1984.

Glazer, Mark. "The Dowry as Capital Accumulation among the Sephardic Jews of Istanbul, Turkey." *International Journal of Middle East Studies* 9 (1978): 297–305.

Helling, Barbara, and George Helling. *Rural Turkey: A New Socio-Statistical Appraisal*. Istanbul: Fakülteler Matbaası, 1958.

Hinderink, Jan, and Mübeccel Kıray. *Social Stratification as an Obstacle to Development: A Study of Four Turkish Villages*. New York: Praeger, 1970.

Hotham, David. *Turkey: The Land and Its People*. London: Macdonald, 1975.

Hottinger, A. "Turkey's Search for Identity: Kemal Atatürk's Heritage." *Encounter* 48 (1977): 75–81.

Jameson, Samuel H. "Social Mutation in Turkey." *Social Forces* 14 (1936): 482–96.

Jennings, R. "Sakaltutan Four Centuries Ago." *International Journal of Middle East Studies* 9 (1978): 89–98.

Johnson, Clarence Richard. *Constantinople Today—Or, the Pathfinder Survey of Constantinople: A Study in Oriental Social Life*. New York: Macmillan, 1922.

Kağıtçıbaşı, Çiğdem, ed. *Sex Roles, Family, and Community in Turkey: Current Perspectives*. Bloomington: Indiana University Turkish Studies Series, no. 3, 1982.

Kandiyoti, Deniz. "Some Social-Psychological Dimensions of Social Change in a Turkish Village." *British Journal of Sociology* 25 (1974): 47–62.

Karpat, Kemal H. "Social Effects of Farm Mechanization in Turkish Villages." *Social Research* 27 (1960).

Kasaba, Reşat. "A Time and a Place for a Non-State: Social Change in the Ottoman Empire during the 'Long Nineteenth Century.'" In *State Power and Social Forces*, ed. J. Migdal and Atul Kohli, 207–30. Cambridge: Cambridge University Press, 1994.

Kıray, Mübeccel, ed. *Structural Change in Turkish Society*. Bloomington: Indiana University Press, 1991.

Kolars, John F. *Tradition, Season, and Change in a Turkish Village*. Chicago: University of Chicago, Department of Geography, 1963.

Kortepeter, C. Max. "The Islamic-Ottoman Social Structure: The Quest for a Model of Ottoman History." *Near Eastern Round Table* 1 (1967–1968): 1–40.

Kudat, Ayşe. "Institutional Rigidity and Individual Initiative in Marriages of Turkish Peasants." *Anthropological Quarterly* 47 (1974): 288–303.

Lewis, Bernard. *Istanbul and the Civilization of the Ottoman Empire*. Norman: University of Oklahoma Press, 1963.

Lewis, Raphaela. *Everday Life in Ottoman Turkey*. London: Batsford, 1971.

Linke, Lilo. "Social Changes in Turkey." *International Affairs* 16 (1937): 540–63.

Magnarella, Paul J. *Tradition and Change in a Turkish Town*. New York: Wiley, 1974.

———. *The Peasant Venture: Tradition, Migration, and Change among Georgian Peasants in Turkey*. Boston, Mass.: Schenkman, 1979.

———. *Anatolia's Loom: Studies in Turkish Culture, Society, Politics, and Law.* Istanbul: ISIS Press, 1998.

Mair, Craig. *A Time in Turkey.* London: John Murray, 1973.

Makal, Mahmut. *A Village in Anatolia.* Ed. Paul Sterling, trans. W. Deeds. London: Vallentine Mitchell, 1953.

Mansur, Fatma. *Bodrum: A Town in the Aegean.* Leiden: E. J. Brill, 1972.

Mardin, Şerif. "Historical Determinants of Social Stratification: Social Class and Class Consciousness in Turkey." *Ankara Üniversitesi Siyasal Bilgiler Fakültesi Dergisi* 22 (1968): 111–42.

———. "Youth and Violence in Turkey." *European Journal of Sociology* 19 (1978): 229–54.

McCarthy, Justin. "Foundations of the Turkish Republic: Social and Economic Change." *Middle Eastern Studies* 19 (1983): 139–51.

Merani, Shambhu T. *The Turks of Istanbul.* New York: Macmillan, 1980.

Micklewright, Nancy. "Late Nineteeth-Century Ottoman Wedding Costumes as Indicators of Social Change." *Moqarnas* (Leiden) 6 (1989): 162–73.

Mitchell, William A. "Turkish Villages in Interior Anatolia and von Thünen's 'Isolated State': A Comparative Analysis." *Middle East Journal* 25 (1971): 355–69.

Morel, Mme. *From an Eastern Embassy.* Philadelphia: Lippincott, 1920.

Olson, Emelie A. "They Work Harder Now: Postponed Retirement in Village Turkey." *New Perspectives on Turkey,* no. 13 (1995): 121–50.

Ozankaya, Özer. "Social Life in Four Anatolian Villages." *Ankara Üniversitesi Siyasal Bilgiler Fakültesi Dergisi* 3 (1973): 613–33.

Öncü, Ayşe. "Inter-Organizational Networks and Social Structures: Turkish Chambers of Industry." *International Social Science Journal* 21 (1979): 646–60.

Özcan, Yusuf Ziya. "Occupational Structure and Social Mobility in Turkey, 1968." *METU Studies in Development* (Ankara) 15 (1988): 151–82.

Pears, Edwin. *Turkey and Its People.* London: Methuen, 1911.

Pierce, J. E. *Life in a Turkish Village.* New York: Holt, Rinehart, and Winston, 1965.

Porter, David. *Constantinople and Its Environs: A Series of Letters, Exhibiting the Actual State of Manners, Customs, and Habits of the Turks, Jews, and Greeks, as Modified by the Policy of Sultan Mahmoud by an American Long Resident at Constantinople.* 2 vols. New York: Harper and Brothers, 1835.

Salamone, S. D. "The Dialectics of Turkish National Identity: Ethnic Boundary Maintenance and State Ideology." *East European Quarterly* 23 (1989): 33–61, 225–48.

Sertel, Ayşe. "Kidnapping and Elopement in Rural Turkey." *Hacettepe Bulletin of Social Sciences and Humanities* (Ankara) 1 (1969): 99–104.

———. "A Study of Power Conceptions in a Turkish Village." *Hacettepe Bulletin of Social Sciences and Humanities* (Ankara) 2 (1970): 49–83.

Spencer, Robert F. "Aspects of Turkish Kinship and Social Structure." *Anthropological Quarterly* 33 (1960): 40–50.

Starr, June. *Dispute and Settlement in Rural Turkey: An Ethnography of Law.* Leiden: E. J. Brill, 1978.

Stirling, Paul. *The Turkish Village.* London: Weidenfeld and Nicolson, 1965.

———. ed. *Culture and the Economy: Changes in Turkish Villages.* Huntingdon, U.K.: Eothen Press, 1993.

Suzuki, Peter, ed. and trans. *Aspects of Modern Turkish Society: Six Papers.* Wiesbaden, Germany: WDS-Schnelldruck, 1971.

Tinto, V. "Perceptions of Occupational Structure and Career Aspirations among the Turkish Elite." *International Journal of Middle East Studies* 8 (1977): 329–38.

Tomlin, Eric. Walter F. *Life in Modern Turkey.* New York: T. Nelson, 1946.

Webster, Donald Everett. *The Turkey of Atatürk: Social Process in the Turkish Reformation.* Philadelphia, Pa.: American Academy of Political and Social Sciences, 1939.

Yasa, İbrahim. *Hasanoğlan: Socio-Economic Structure of a Turkish Village.* Ankara: Yeni Matbaa, 1957.

Art and Literature

Akurgal, Ekrem, ed. *The Art and Architecture of Turkey.* New York: Rizzoli, 1980.

Al'Kaeva, L. "İnce Memed." *Edebiyat* (Philadelphia) 5 (1980): 69–82.

Altan, Ö. "Modern Turkish Painting." *Turkish Treasures* (Istanbul) 1 (1978): 72–77.

And, Metin. "Dances of Anatolian Turkey." *Dance Perspectives* 3 (1959): 1–76.

———. *A History of Theatre and Popular Entertainment in Turkey.* Ankara: Forum Yayınları, 1963–1964.

———. "Shakespeare in Turkey." *Theatre Research/Recherches Théatrales* 62 (1964): 75–84. Illustrations.

———. "Turkey." In *The Oxford Companion to the Theatre*, ed. Phyllis Hartnoll. London: Oxford University Press, 1967.

———. *Turkish Miniature Painting.* Ankara: Dost Yayınları, 1974.

———. *Karagöz: Turkish Shadow Theatre.* Ankara: Dost Yayınları, 1975.

———. *A Pictorial History of Turkish Dancing from Folk Dancing to Whirling Dervishes, Belly Dancing to Ballet.* Ankara: Dost Yayınları, 1976.

———. "The Mevlana Ceremony." *Drama Review* 3 (1977): 83–94.

———. *Culture, Performance, and Communication in Turkey.* Tokyo: Institute for the Study of Languages and Cultures of Asia and Africa, 1987.

Anderson, June. *Return to Tradition: The Revitalization of Turkish Village Carpets.* Seattle: University of Washington Press, 1998.

Andrews, Walter G. *An Introduction to Ottoman Poetry.* Chicago: Bibliotheca Islamica, 1976.

———. *Poetry's Voice, Society's Song: Ottoman Lyric Poetry.* Seattle: University of Washington Press, 1985.

Andrews, Walter G., Najaat Black, and Mehmet Kalpaklı. *Ottoman Lyric Poetry: An Anthology.* Austin: University of Texas Press, 1997.

Aslanapa, Oktay. *Turkish Arts: Seljuk and Ottoman Carpets, Tiles, and Miniature Paintings.* Istanbul: Doğan Kardeş Yayınları, 1961.

———. "Turkish Ceramic Art." *Archaeology* 24 (1971): 204–13.

———. *Turkish Art and Architecture.* New York: Praeger, 1971.

Atasoy, Nurhan, and Filiz Çağman. *Turkish Miniature Painting.* Istanbul: Doğan Kardeş Yayınları, 1974.

Atıl, Esin, ed. *Turkish Art.* Washington, D.C.: Smithsonian Institute, 1980.

———. *The Age of Suleyman the Magnificent.* Washington, D.C.: National Gallery of Art and Harry Abrams, 1987.

Atis, Sarah G. "Turkish Literature." In *The Oxford Encyclopedia of the Modern Islamic World*, vol. 4. New York: Oxford University Press, 1995.

Baram, Uzi, and Lynda Carroll, eds. *A Historical Archaeology of the Ottoman Empire: Breaking New Ground (Contributions to Global Historical Archaeology).* New York: Kluwer Academic/Plenum, 2000.

Barmore, F. "Turkish Mosque Orientation and the Secular Variation of the Magnetic Declination." *Journal of Near East Studies* 44 (1985): 81–98.

Bartok, Béla. *Turkish Folk Music from Asia Minor.* Ed. Benjamin Suchoff. Princeton, N.J.: Princeton University Press, 1976.

Başgöz, İlhan, comp. *Turkish Folklore Reader.* Bloomington: Indiana University Press, 1971.

———. "Love Themes in Turkish Folk Poetry." *Review of National Literatures* 4 (1973): 99–114.

———. "Yaşar Kemal and Turkish Folk Literature." *Edebiyat* (Philadelphia) 5 (1980): 37–47.

Başgöz, İlhan, and Mark Glazer, eds. *Studies in Turkish Folklore: In Honor of Pertev T. Boratav.* Bloomington: Indiana University Turkish Studies, no. 1, 1978.

Bates, Ülkü. "The Impact of the Mongol Invasion on Turkish Architecture." *International Journal of Middle East Studies* 9 (1978): 23–32.

Bayraktar, E. "Music in Turkey." *Turkish Review* (Ankara), no. 32 (1993): 37–65.

Berk, N. "Painting in Turkey." *Turkish Treasures* (Istanbul) 1 (1978): 52–59.

Binyazar, A. "The Yaşar Kemal Phenomenon." *Edebiyat* (Philadelphia) 5 (1980): 23–36.

Birge, John Kingsley. "Yunus Emre: Turkey's Great Poet of the People." In *The Macdonald Presentation Volume: A Tribute to Duncan Black Macdonald.* Princeton, N.J.: Princeton University Press, 1933.

Bodrogligeti, A. "A Collection of Turkish Poems from the 14th Century." *Acta Orientalia* (Budapest, Hungary) 16 (1963): 245–311.

Book of Dede Korkut: A Turkish Epic, The. Trans. and ed. Faruk Sümer et al. Austin: University of Texas Press, 1991.

Bozdoğan, Sibel, Suha Özkan, and Engin Yenal. *Sedat Eldem: Architect in Turkey.* New York: Aperture, 1987.

Burrill, Kathleen R. F. *The Quatrains of Nesimi: Fourteenth-Century Turkish Hurufi.* The Hague: Mouton, 1972.

———. "Modern Turkish Literature." *Review of National Literatures* 4 (1973): 13–26.

———. "From Gazi State to Republic: A Changing Scene for Turkish Artists and Men of Letters." In *Studies in Art and Literature of the Near East in Honor of Richard Ettinghausen,* ed. Peter J. Chelkowski. Salt Lake City: University of Utah Press, 1974.

———. "The Prose Poem in Ottoman Literature: Halit Ziya Uşaklıgil and His Prototype Collection of Mensur Şiirler." *Journal of Turkish Studies* 8 (1984): 25–40.

Carretto, G. "Yakup Kadri (1887–1974)." *Oriento Moderno* (Rome) 55 (1975): 193–95.

Chambers, Richard L., and Günay Kut Alpay. *Contemporary Turkish Short Stories: An Intermediate Reader.* Chicago: Bibliotheca Islamica, 1977.

Clark, Richard. "Is Ottoman Literature Turkish Literature?" *Review of National Literatures* 4 (1973): 133–42.

Çelebi, Evliya. *Turkish Instruments of Music in the Seventeenth Century as Described in the Seyahatname of Evliya Çelebi.* Trans. and ed. Henry George Farmer. Glasgow: Civic Press, 1937.

Çelik, Zeynep. *Displaying the Orient: Architecture of Islam at Nineteenth-Century World's Fairs.* Berkeley: University of California Press, 1992.

Çizgen, Engin. *Photography in the Ottoman Empire, 1839–1919.* Istanbul: Haşet Kitabevi, 1987.

Danışman, H. H. Günhan. "Archaeological Perspectives: Anatolian Archaeology in the 1980s." *Current Turkish Thought* (Istanbul), nos. 54–55 (1983): 1–45.

Dankoff, R. "Penc-Beyt as a Synonym of Ghazal in Evliya Çelebi." *Turkish Studies Association Bulletin* 21, no. 2 (1997): 59–60.

Degh, L. "Politics Alive in Turkish Folklore." *Journal of American Folklore* 112, no. 4 (1999): 527.

Deleon, J. "Ballet in Turkey." *Current Turkish Thought* (Istanbul), no. 59 (1986): 2–22.

Delibaş, Selma. "Embroidery." In *Arts of Weaving, Traditional Turkish Arts*, ed. Nazal Ölçen. Ankara: Ministry of Tourism and Culture, 1987.

Demirtürk, E. L. "Teaching African-American Literature in Turkey: The Politics of Pedagogy." *College Literature* 26, no. 2 (Spring 1999): 166–75.

Denny, Walter. "Turkish Ceramics and Turkish Painting: The Role of Paper Cartoon in Turkish Ceramic Production." In *Essays in Islamic Art and Architecture: In Honor of Katharina Otto-Dorn*, ed. Abbas Daneshvari. Malibu: Undena, 1981.

———. "Atatürk and Political Art in Turkey." *Turkish Studies Association Bulletin* 6 (1982): 17–20. Illustrations.

———. "Textiles." In *Tulips, Arabesques, and Turbans: Decorative Arts from the Ottoman Empire*, ed. Yanni Petsopoulos. New York: Abbeville Press, 1982.

Denny, Walter B., Aileen Riberio, and Judy Levin, eds. *Court and Conquest: Ottoman Origins and the Design for Handel's 'Tamerlano' at the Glimmerglass Opera*. Kent, Ohio.: Kent State University Museum, 1998.

Derman, M. Uğur. *Letters in Gold: Ottoman Calligraphy from the Sakıp Sabancı Collection, Istanbul*. New York: Metropolitan Museum of Art, 1998.

Dijkema, F. T., ed. *The Ottoman Historical Monumental Inscriptions in Edirne*. Leiden: E. J. Brill, 1976.

Dor, Rémy. "Counting the Ages (Yaş): Examples from Turkish Folkloric Songs." *Eurasian Studies* (Ankara) 15 (1999): 2–21.

Dundes, Alan. "The Strategy of Turkish Boys' Verbal Dueling Rhymes." *Journal of American Folklore* 83 (1970): 325–49.

Eleazar, Birnbaum. "Turkish Literature through the Ages." In *Introduction to Islamic Civilization*, ed. R. M. Savory. Cambridge: Cambridge University Press, 1976.

Emre, Yunus. *The Humanist Poetry of Yunus Emre*. Trans. Talat Sait Halman. Istanbul: Istanbul Matbaası, 1973.

Erol, Sibel. "Güntekin's *Çalıkuşu*: A Search for Personal and National Identity." *Turkish Studies Association Bulletin* 15 (1991): 65–82.

———. "The Image of the Intellectual in Yakup Kadri Karaosmanoğlu's Works." *Turkish Studies Association Bulletin* 16 (1992): 1–19.

———. "Discourses on the Intellectual: The Universal, the Particular, and Their Mediation in the Works of Nazlı Eray." *New Perspectives on Turkey*, no. 11 (1994): 1–17.

———. *Turkish Miniature Painting*. Rutland, Vt.: Charles E. Tuttle, 1960.

———. ed. *Turkish Miniature Painting*. Tokyo: Charles E. Tutle, 1960.

Ettinghausen, Richard. *Turkey: Ancient Miniatures*. Greenwich, Conn.: New York Graphic Society, 1961.

———. *Turkish Miniatures from the Thirteenth to the Eighteenth Century*. New York: New American Library for UNESCO, 1965.

Evin, Ahmet. "Turkey." In *Modern World Drama*, ed. Byron Matlaw. New York: Dutton, 1972.

———. "A Poem by Nedim: Some Thoughts on Criticism of Turkish Literature and an Essay." *Edebiyat* (Philadelphia) 2 (1977): 43–55.

———. "Introduction: Yaşar Kemal." *Edebiyat* (Philadelphia) 5 (1980): 7–15.

———. "Seagull and the Fiction of Yaşar Kemal." *Edebiyat* (Philadelphia) 5 (1980): 198–204.

———. "Self and Society in the Turkish Novel." *Turkish Studies Association Bulletin* 6 (1982): 4–6.

———. *Origins and Development of the Turkish Novel.* Minneapolis, Minn.: Bibliotheca Islamica, 1983.

———. "Aziz Nesin." In *Encyclopedia of World Literature in the Twentieth Century*, ed. Leonard Klein. New York: Frederich Ungar, 1984.

———. "Ideology and Violence in Modern Turkish Literature." *Turkish Studies Association Bulletin* 8 (1984): 6–13.

———. *Nedim: Poet of the Tulip Era and the Origins of Turkish Westernization.* Weisbaden, Germany: Otto Harrassowitz, 1993.

Fazıl Hüsnü Dağlarca: Selected Poems. Trans. Talat Halman. Pittsburgh, Pa.: University of Pittsburgh Press, 1964.

Feldman, Walter. "A Musical Model for the Structure of the Ottoman Gazel." *Edebiyat* (Philadelphia) 1 (1987): 71–89.

———. "Mysticism, Didacticism and Authority in the Liturgical Poetry of Halveti Dervishes of Istanbul." *Edebiyat* (Philadelphia) 4, no. 2 (1993): 243–65.

———. "Imitation in Ottoman Poetry: The Ghazals of the Mid-Seventeenth Century." *Turkish Studies Association Bulletin* 21, no. 2 (1997): 41–58.

Fergar, Feyyaz Kayacan, ed. *Modern Turkish Poetry.* Ware, U.K.: Rockingham Press, 1992.

Finn, Robert P. *The Early Turkish Novel, 1872–1900.* Istanbul: ISIS, 1984.

Fuzuli. *Leyla and Majnun.* Trans. from Turkish by S. Huri. Leiden: E. J. Brill, 1970.

Germanus, J. "The Awakening of Turkish Literature." *Islamic Culture* 7 (1933): 177–94.

Gibb, Elias J. W. *A History of Ottoman Poetry.* Vol. 1–4. London: Luzac, 1900–1907.

———. *Ottoman Literature: The Poets and Poetry of Turkey.* London: M. Walter Dunne, 1901.

Goodwin, Godfrey. *A History of Ottoman Architecture.* Baltimore, Md.: Johns Hopkins University Press, 1971.

Gökalp, A. "Yaşar Kemal: From the Imaginary World of a People to an Epic of Reality." *Edebiyat* (Philadelphia) 5 (1980): 151–59.

Göksu, Saime, and Edward Timms. *Romantic Communist: The Life and Work of Nazım Hikmet.* New York: St. Martin's, 1999.

Halman, Talat Sait. "Turkish Poetry." In *Encyclopedia of Poetry and Poetics*, ed. Alex Preminger. Princeton, N.J.: Princeton University Press, 1965.

———. "Turkey." In *The Reader's Encyclopedia of Shakespeare*, ed. Oscar James Campbell and Edward G. Quinn. New York: Crowell, 1966.

———. "Two Modern Turkish Poets: Fazıl Hüsnü Dağlarca and Orhan Veli Kanık." *Literature East and West* 13 (1969): 377–85.

———. "Nazım Hikmet: Lyricist as Iconoclast." *Books Abroad* 43 (1969): 59–64.

———. "Islamic Themes in Turkish Poetry: Imitations and Mutations." *Yearbook of Comparative and General Literature*, no. 20 (1971): 67–71.

———. "Poetry and Society: The Turkish Experience." In *Modern Near East: Literature and Society*, ed. C. Max Kortepeter. New York: New York University Press, 1971.

———. "Turkish Literature in the 1960s." *Literary Review* 15 (1972): 387–522.

———. "The Ancient Ottoman Legacy." *Review of National Literatures Abroad* 48 (1974): 25–33.

———. "Comic Spirit in the Turkish Theatre." *Theatre Annual* 31 (1975): 16–42.

———. ed. *Modern Turkish Drama: An Anthology of Plays in Translation.* Chicago: Bibliotheca Islamica, 1976.

———. *Yunus Emre and His Mystical Poetry.* Bloomington: Indiana University Turkish Studies Series, 1981.

———. *Contemporary Turkish Literature: Fiction and Poetry*. East Brunswick, N.J.: Fairleigh Dickinson University Press, 1982.

———. "Yunus Emre's Humanism." *Turkish Review* (Ankara), no. 22 (1990): 13–31.

Helmecke, Gisela. "Embroideries." In *A Wealth of Silk and Velvet: Ottoman Fabrics and Embroideries*, ed. Christian Erber. Bremen, Germany: Temmen, 1995.

Hickman, W. "Said Faik: Three Stories and an Essay." *Edebiyat* (Philadelphia) 1 (1976): 71–92.

———. "Traditional Themes in the Work of Yaşar Kemal: İnce Memed." *Edebiyat* (Philadelphia) 5 (1980): 55–68.

Hoffman, D. S. "An Introduction to Music in Turkey." *Consort* 22 (1965): 54–61.

Holbrook, Victoria Rowe. "Diverse Tastes in the Spiritual Life: Textual Play in the Diffusion of Rumi's Order." In *The Legacy of Medieval Persian Sufism*, ed. Leonard Lewisohn. New York: Khaniqahi Nimatullahi, 1992.

———. "Originality and Ottoman Poetics: In the Wilderness of the New." *Journal of the American Oriental Society* 112 (1992): 440–54.

———. "A Technology of Reference? *Divan* and anti-*Divan* in the Reception of a Turkish Poet." *Edebiyat* (Philadelphia) 4, no. 1 (1993): 49–61.

———. "Philology Went Down to the Crossroads of Modernity to Meet Orientalism, Nationalism, and . . . Ottoman Poetry." *New Perspectives in Turkey*, no. 11 (1994): 19–41.

Holod, Renate, and Ahmet Evin. *Modern Turkish Architecture*. Philadelphia: University of Pennsylvania Press, 1984.

I Am Listening to Istanbul: Selected Poems of Orhan Veli Kanık. Trans. Talat Sait Halman. New York: Corinth Books, 1971.

İz, Fahir, ed. *An Anthology of Modern Turkish Short Stories*. Chicago: Bibliotheca Islamica, 1978.

———. "Mehmet Akif Ersoy: A Biography." *Erdem* (Ankara), no. 11 (1988): 311–38.

Jacobson, Joseph S., ed. *Turkish Folk Reader*. Salt Lake City: University of Utah, 1967.

Johnstone, Pauline. *Turkish Embroidery*. London: Victoria and Albert Museum, 1985.

Kafadar, Cemal. "Self and Others: The Diary of a Dervish in Seventeenth-Century Istanbul and First-Person Narratives in Ottoman Literature." *Studia Islamica* 69 (1989): 121–50.

Kahraman, Hasan Bülent. "'Je est un aurte': Turkish Literature in Transition between National and Global Self." In *Step-Mothertongue: From Nationalism to Multiculturalism: Literatures of Cyprus, Greece, and Turkey*, ed. Mehmet Yashin. London: Middlesex University Press, 2000.

Kalpaklı, M. "A Trial Reading of Neşati's *Taleb* Ghazal." *Turkish Studies Association Bulletin* 21, no. 2 (1997): 12–18.

Karabaş, Seyfi. "A Note on the Structural and Content Analysis of a Turkish Folktale." *International Journal of Turkish Studies* 5 (1990–91): 155–61.

Karpat, Kemal H. "Social Themes in Contemporary Turkish Literature." *Middle East Journal* 14 (1960): 29–44; 153–68.

Kent, Margery, trans. *Fairy Tales from Turkey*. London: George Routledge & Sons, 1946.

Key, Kerim Kâmi. "Trends in Modern Turkish Literature." *Muslim World* 47 (1957): 318–28.

Kunos, Ignâcz. *Turkish Fairy Tales and Folk Tales*. Trans. from Hungarian by R. Nisbet Bain. New York: Dover, 1969.

Kuran, Aptullah. *The Mosque in Early Ottoman Architecture*. Chicago: University of Chicago Press, 1968.

———. *Sinan: The Grand Old Master of Ottoman Architecture*. Washington, D.C.: Institute of Turkish Studies, 1987.

Levey, Michael. *The World of Ottoman Art*. New York: Scribner, 1975.

Lifchez, Raymond, ed. *The Dervish Lodge: Architecture, Art, and Sufism in Ottoman Turkey*. Berkeley: University of California Press, 1992.

Martinowitch, Nicholas N. *The Turkish Theatre*. 1933. Reprint, New York: Benjamin Blom, 1968.

McAfee, Helen. "The Turkish Drama." *Forum* 50 (1913): 230–38.

Meddâh, Yusuf. *Varga ve Gülşah: A Fourteenth-Century Anatolian Turkish Mesnevi*. Ed. and trans. Grace Martin Smith. Leiden: E. J. Brill, 1976.

Menemencioğlu, Nermin, ed. *The Penguin Book of Turkish Verse*. Harmondsworth, U.K.: Penguin, 1978.

Meredith-Owens, G. M. *Turkish Miniatures*. London: The Trustees of the British Museum, 1963.

Micklewright, Nancy. "Nineteenth-Century Images of Dervishes." In *The Dervish Lodge: Architecture, Art, and Sufism in Ottoman Istanbul*, ed. Raymond Lifchez. Berkeley: University of California Press, 1992.

Mizrahi, D. "The Sounds of Imagination: Language in the Turkish Shadow Theater." *Journal of Middle East Studies Society at Columbia University* 1 (1987): 17–37.

Necipoğlu, Gülru. *Architecture, Ceremonial, and Power: The Topkapı Palace in the Fifteenth and Sixteenth Centuries*. Cambridge, Mass.: MIT Press, 1991.

Nekimken, A. "The Impact of Bertolt Brecht on Society and the Development of Political Theater in Turkey." *Turkish Studies Association Bulletin* 4 (1980): 9–13.

Nesin, Aziz. *Istanbul Boy* [Böyle Gelmiş Böyle Gitmez]—*That's How It Was But Not How It's Going to Be: The Autobiography of Aziz Nesin*, part 1. Trans. Joseph J. Jacobson. Austin: University of Texas Press, 1977.

———. *Istanbul Boy—The Path: The Autobiography of Aziz Nesin*, part 2. Trans. Joseph J. Jacobson. Austin: University of Texas Press, 1979.

Oğuzertem, S. "Fictions of Narcissism: Metaphysical and Psychosexual Conflicts in the Stories of Ahmet Hamdi Tanpınar." *Turkish Studies Association Bulletin* 14 (1990): 223–33.

Olson, Emelie, and Kurtuluş Öztopçu. "Images of Women in the Poetry of Early Turkish Mystics." In *Humanist and Scholar: Essays in Honor of Andreas Tietze*, ed. Heath Lowry and Donald Quataert. Istanbul: ISIS and the Institute of Turkish Studies, 1993.

Otüş-Baskett, B. "Yaşar Kemal's Dream of Social Change: The Fable of the Hawk and the Goat-Beard." *Edebiyat* (Philadelphia) 5 (1980): 87–93.

Öz, Tahsin. *Turkish Textiles and Velvets: 14th–16th Centuries*. Ankara: Turkish Press, Broadcasting, and Tourism Department, 1950.

———. *Turkish Ceramics*. Ankara: Turkish Press, Broadcasting, and Tourism Department, 1953.

Özdoğru, Nüvit. "Turkey." In *The Reader's Encyclopedia of World Drama*, ed. John Gassner and Edward G. Quinn. New York: Crowell, 1969.

Patmore, Derek. *The Star and the Crescent: An Anthology of Modern Turkish Poetry*. London: Constable, 1946.

Petsopoulos, Yanni, ed. *Tulips, Arabesques, and Turbans: Decorative Arts from the Ottoman Empire*. New York: Abbeville Press, 1982.

Ramazanoğlu, Gülseren. *Turkish Embroidery*. New York: Van Nostrand Reinhold, 1976.

Rathbun, Carole. *Village in the Turkish Novel and Short Story, 1920 to 1955*. The Hague: Mouton, 1972.

Renda, Günsel. "An Illustrated 18th-Century *Hamse* in the Walters Art Gallery." *Journal of Walters Art Gallery* 39 (1981): 15–32.

————. "Traditional Turkish Painting and the Beginnings of Western Trends." In *A History of Turkish Painting*, ed. O. Grabar et al. Seattle: University of Washington Press, 1987.

Rice, E. "Representations of Janissary Music (Mehter) as Musical Exoticisms in Western Compositions." *Journal of Musicological Research* 19, no. 1 (1999): 41–88.

Robinson, Richard D. *Main Currents in Turkish Literature*. New York: American Universities Field Staff, 1954.

Robson, Bruce. *The Drum Beats Nightly: The Development of the Turkish Drama as a Vehicle for Social and Political Comment in the Post-Revolutionary Period from 1924 to the Present*. Tokyo: The Centre for East Asian Cultural Studies, 1976.

Schimmel, A. "Yunus Emre." *Turkish Review* (Ankara), no. 32 (1993): 67–90.

Signell, Karl L. *Makam: Modal Practice in Turkish Art Music*. Seattle: University of Washington School of Music, 1977.

Silay, K. "Ottoman Elitism Revisited: Buket Uzuner's *Balık İzlerinin Sesi* (B.İ.S) as a Recent Manifestation of (Post)modernis(tic) Discourse in Turkish Literature." *Turkish Studies Association Bulletin* 17, no. 1 (1993): 25–34.

————. *Nedim and the Poetics of the Ottoman Court: Medieval Inheritance and the Need for Change*. Bloomington: Indiana University Turkish Studies Series, 1994.

Siyavuşgil, Sabri East. *Karagöz: Its History, Its Characters, Its Mystic, and Satiric Spirit*. Ankara: Saim Toraman Basımevi, 1955.

Sofi, Huri. "Yunus Emre: In Memoriam." *Muslim World* 49 (1959): 111–23.

Soucek, Svat. "Sabahattin Ali." *Turkish Studies Association Bulletin* 5 (1981): 11–18.

Soysal, Sevgi. "Hanife." Trans. Nilüfer Mazanoğlu Reddy. *Southern Humanities Review* 26 (1992): 145–52.

Stokes, Martin. *The Arabesk Debate: Music and Musicians in Modern Turkey*. Oxford: Clarendon Press, 1992.

————. "Turkish Urban Popular Music." *Middle East Studies Bulletin* 33, no. 1 (1999): 10–15.

Stratton, Arthur. *Sinan*. New York: Charles Scribner's Sons, 1972.

Taylor, Roderik R. *Ottoman Embroidery*. London: Cassell, 1993.

Tekelioğlu, Orhan. "The Rise of a Spontaneous Synthesis: Historical Background of Turkish Popular Music." *Middle Eastern Studies* 32, no. 1 (1996): 194–216.

————. "Modernizing Reforms and Turkish Music in the 1930s." *Turkish Studies* 2, no. 1 (2001): 93–108.

Tietze, Andreas. *Turkish Literary Reader*. Bloomington: Indiana University Press, 1963.

————. *The Turkish Shadow Theater and the Puppet Collection of the L. A. Mayer Memorial Foundation*. Berlin: Gebr. Mann Verlag, 1977.

————. "The Study of Literature as the Cultural Manifestation of Socio-Economic Changes: Achievements and Potential of the Study of Ottoman Literature." *International Journal of Turkish Studies* 2 (1981): 44–56.

Turgay-Ahmad, Bedia. "Modern Turkish Theater." *Review of National Literatures* 4 (1973): 65–81.

Turkey: From Empire to Nation. Ed. Talat Sait Halman. *Review of National Literatures* 4 (1973): 1–142.

Turkish Literature: Comprising Fables, Belles-Lettres, and Sacred Traditions. Trans. Epiphanius Wilson. Freeport, N.Y.: Books for Libraries Press, 1970.

Uturgauri, S. "Folklore and the Prose of Yaşar Kemal." *Edebiyat* (Philadelphia) 5 (1980): 135–50.

Ünsal, Behçet. *Turkish Islamic Architecture in Seljuk and Ottoman Times, 1071–1923*. New York: St. Martin's, 1974.

Vogt-Göknil, Ulya. *Living Architecture: Ottoman*. New York: Grosset & Dunlop, 1966.
Walker, Barbara K. *Turkish Folk-tales Retold by Barbara K. Walker*. Oxford: Oxford University Press, 1993.
———. *The Art of the Turkish Tale*. Lubbock: Texas Tech University Press and Turkish Ministry of Culture, 1993.
Walker, Warren. "Triple-Tiered Migration in *The Book of Dede Korkut*." In *The Literature of Emigration and Exile*, ed. James Whilark and Wendell Aycock. Lubbock: Texas Tech University Press, 1992.
———. *A Turkish Folktale: The Art of Behçet Mahir*. New York: Garland, 1996.
———. "Extant Analogues of the 'Franklin's Tale' in the Turkish Oral Tradition." *Chaucer Review* 33, no. 4 (1999): 432–37.
Walker, Warren S., and Ahmet E. Uysal. *Tales Alive in Turkey*. Lubbock: Texas Technical University Press, 1966.
———. *More Tales Alive in Turkey*. Lubbock: Texas Technical University Press, 1992.
Wright, O. "Çargâh in Turkish Classical Music: History versus Theory." *Bulletin of the School of Oriental and African Studies* 52 (1990): 224–44.
Yetkin, Suut Kemal. *Turkish Architecture*. Ankara: Institute of History of Turkish and Islamic Arts, 1965.
Yücel, A. "Contemporary Turkish Architecture." *Mimar* (Singapore) 10 (1983): 59–68.
Zygulski, Zdzislaw. *Ottoman Art in the Service of the Empire*. New York: New York University Press, 1992.

Attitudes, Values, and Culture

Adıvar, Abdülhak Adnan. "Islamic and Western Thought in Turkey." *Middle East Journal* 1 (1947): 270–80.
———. "Interaction of Islamic and Western Thought in Turkey." In *Near Eastern Culture and Society: A Symposium on the Meeting of East and West*, ed. T. Cuyler Young. Princeton, N.J.: Princeton University Press, 1951.
Adıvar, Halide Edip. *The Turkish Ordeal*. New York: Century, 1928.
———. *Turkey Faces West: A Turkish View of Recent Changes and Their Origin*. New Haven, Conn.: Yale University Press, 1930.
———. *Conflict of East and West in Turkey*. Lahore: Ashraf, 1935.
Akgün, Seçil. "European Influence on the Development of the Social and Cultural Life of the Ottoman Empire in the Eighteenth Century." *Revues des études sud-est européennes*, (1983): 89–94.
Akural, S. M. *Turkic Culture: Continuity and Change*. Bloomington: Indiana University Press, 1987.
Balaman, A. "The Acculturation Process of Children in Rural Areas of Turkey." *Korean Journal of Middle East Studies*, no. 10 (1989): 171–96.
Bektaş, Y. "The Sultan's Messenger: Cultural Constructions of Ottoman Telegraphy, 1847–1880." *Technology and Culture* 41, no. 4 (2000): 669–96.
Bisbee, Eleanor. *The People of Turkey*. New York: East and West Association, 1946.
Büken, Gülriz. "Backlash: An Argument against the Spread of American Popular Culture in Turkey." In *Here, There, and Everywhere—The Foreign Politics of American Popular Culture*, ed. R. Wagnleiter and E. T. May. Hanover: University Press of New England, 2000.
Cansever, Gökçe. "Achievement Motive in Turkish Adolescents." *Journal of Social Psychology* 76 (1968): 269–70.

Davis, F. J. "Perspectives of Turkish Students in the United States." *Sociology and Social Research* 48 (1963): 47–57.

Devereux, Robert. "Society and Culture in the Second Turkish Republic." *Middle Eastern Affairs* 12 (1961): 230–39.

Dindi, Hasan, Maija Gazur, Wayne M. Gazur, and Ayşen Kırkköprü-Dindi. *Turkish Culture for Americans.* Boulder, Colo.: International Concepts, 1989.

Ege, Nezahat Nurettin. *Turgut Lives in Turkey.* New York: Longmans, Green, 1948.

Ekrem, Selma. *Turkey: Old and New.* New York: Charles Scribner's Sons, 1947.

Ergil, Doğu. "A Sociological Analysis of Honor Crimes in Turkey." *METU Studies in Development* (Ankara) 20 (1978): 26–64.

Esmer, Yılmaz. "Turkish Public Opinion and Europe." *Cambridge Review of International Affairs* 10 (1996): 79–87.

Field, G. "Religious Commitment and Work Orientations of Turkish Students." *Human Organization* 27 (1968): 147–51.

Frey, Frederick W. "Surveying Peasant Attitudes in Turkey." *Public Opinion Quarterly* 27 (1963): 335–55.

Gawrych, G. "The Culture and Politics of Violence in Turkish Society, 1903–1914." *Middle Eastern Studies* 22 (1986): 307–30.

Göçek, Fatma Müge. *East Encounters West: France and the Ottoman Empire in the Eighteenth Century.* New York: Oxford University Press, 1987.

Gülalp, Haldun N. "Turkey: Questions of National Identity." In *New Xenophobia in Europe,* ed. Bernd Baumgartl and Adrian Fawell. The Hague: Kluwer, 1995.

Güvenç, Bozkurt. "Secular Trends and Turkish Identity." *Perceptions* (Ankara) 2, no. 4 (1998): 46–70.

Helling, G., and B. Helling. "Values Implicit in Turkish Images of Human Types: An Empirical Approach." *Turkish Studies Association Bulletin* 10 (1986): 87–98.

Helvacıoğlu, Banu. "Allahu Ekber, We Are Turks: Yearning for a Different Homecoming at the Periphery of Europe." *Third World Quarterly* 17, no. 3 (1996): 503–23.

———. "Europe in Turkish Discourse: How Does One Conceive of Oneself?" In *Boundaries of Europe?* Ed. Rikard Larrson. Stockholm: Swedish Council for Planning and Co-ordination of Research, 1998.

Heper, Metin, Ayşe Öncü, and Heinz Kramer, eds. *Turkey and the West: Changing Political and Cultural Identities.* London: I. B. Tauris, 1993.

Hillenbrand, Carole, ed. *The Sultan's Turret: Studies in Persian and Turkish Culture.* Leiden: E. J. Brill, 1999.

Hyman, Herbert L., Arif Payaslıoğlu, and Frederick W. Frey. "The Values of Turkish College Youth." *Public Opinion Quarterly* 22 (1958): 275–91.

Itzkowitz, Norman. "The Ottoman Empire." In *The World of Islam: Faith, People, and Culture,* ed. Bernard Lewis. London: Thames and Hudson, 1976.

İçduygu, Ahmet, and Arif Payaslıoğlu. "Awareness of and Support for Human Rights among Turkish University Students." *Human Rights Quarterly* 21, no. 2 (1999): 513–34.

İçduygu, Ahmet, Yılmaz Çolak, and Nalan Soyarık. "What Is the Matter with Citizenship? A Turkish Debate." *Middle Eastern Studies* 35, no. 4 (1999): 187–208.

Jaquette, D., and S. Erkut. "Operative and Representational Social Thought: Some Categories of Social Experience in the Turkish Village." *Hacettepe Bulletin of Social Sciences and Humanities* (Ankara) 7 (1975): 70–92.

Johnson, Gordon, ed. *Turkey and Europe in a Cultural Context.* Cambridge: Centre of Middle Eastern Studies, University of Cambridge, 1988.

Kadıoğlu, Ayşe. "Paradox of Turkish Nationalism and the Construction of Official Identity." *Middle Eastern Studies* 32, no. 2 (1996): 177–94.

———. "Citizenship and Inviduation in Turkey: The Triumph of Will over Reason." CEMOTİ (Paris) 26 (1998): 23–43.

Kağıtçıbaşı, Çiğdem. "Social Norms and Authoritarianism: A Comparison of Turkish and American Adolescents." *Journal of Personality and Social Psychology* 16 (1970): 444–51.

———. "Psychological Aspects of Modernization in Turkey." *Journal of Cross Cultural Psychology* 4 (1973): 157–74.

———. "Psychological Approaches to Fertility Behavior in Turkey." *Boğaziçi University Journal* (Social Sciences Series, Istanbul) 2 (1974): 109–25.

———. "Cross-National Encounters: The Turkish AFS Study." *Boğaziçi University Journal* (Social Sciences Series, Istanbul) 4–5 (1976–1977): 15–34.

———. "The Effects of Socioeconomic Development on Draw-A-Man Scores in Turkey." *Journal of Social Psychology* 108 (1979): 3–8.

Kazamias, Andreas M. "Potential Elites in Turkey: Exploring the Values and Attitudes of Lise Youth." *Comparative Education Review* 11 (1967): 22–37.

Köksal, Duygu. "The Dilemmas of a Search for Cultural Synthesis: A Portrait of Cemil Meriç as a Conservative Intellectual." *New Perspectives on Turkey*, no. 21 (1999): 79–101.

Le Compte, William A. "Self Esteem and Trait Anxiety in Turkey: A New Bottle for Some Rare Old Wine." *Boğaziçi University Journal* (Social Sciences Series, Istanbul) 10 (1983): 65–79.

Le Compte, William A., and G. Le Compte. "Effects of Education and Intercultural Contact on Traditional Attitudes in Turkey." *Journal of Social Psychology* 80 (1970): 11–22.

Lengyel, Emil. *Turkey*. New York: Random House, 1941.

Lerner, Daniel, and David Riesman. "Self and Society: Reflections on Some Turks in Transition." *Explorations* 20 (1955): 67–80.

Lewis, Bernard. "Turkey: Westernization." In *Unity and Variety in Western Civilization*, ed. Gustave von Grunebaum. Chicago: University of Chicago Press, 1955.

Lewis, G. "Mother's and Father's Aspirations for Schooling: Contrasts between Daughters and Sons." *METU Studies in Development* (Ankara) 8 (1981): 453–86.

Magnarella, Paul J. "The Turkish Bride-Wealth Practice in Transition." *Muslim World* 59 (1969): 142–52.

———. "Turkish National Character and Turkish Townsmen." *Turkish Studies Association Bulletin* 7, no. 2 (1982): 17–19.

Malik, Iftilchar H. "Turkey at the Crossroads: Encountering Modernity and Tradition." *Journal of South Asian and Middle Eastern Studies* 24, no. 2 (2001): 1–32.

McClelland, David. "National Character and Economic Growth in Turkey and Iran." In *Communications and Political Development*, ed. Lucien W. Pye. Princeton, N.J.: Princeton University Press, 1967.

Meeker, Michael E. "The Black Sea Turks: Some Aspects of Their Ethnic and Cultural Background." *International Journal of Middle East Studies* 2 (1971): 318 45.

———. "Meaning and Society in the Near East: Examples from the Black Sea Turks and the Levantine Arabs." *International Journal of Middle East Studies* 7 part 1 (1976): 243–70; part 2 (1976): 383–423.

Melikian, L., D. Cüceloğlu, and R. Lynn. "Achievement Motivation in Afghanistan, Brazil, Saudi Arabia, and Turkey." *Journal of Social Psychology* 82 (1971): 183–5.

Meyering, H. R. "The Turkish Stereotype." *Sociology and Social Research* 22 (1937): 112–23.

Narlı, N., and S. Çiftçioğlu. "Do Differences in Political Socialization Cause Differences in Security-Related Expectations? The Case of Turkey." *Boğaziçi Journal* (Social Sciences Series) 9, no. 1 (1995): 113–33.

Neyzi, Leyla. "Gülümser's Story: Life History Narratives, Memory, and Belonging in Turkey." *New Perspectives on Turkey*, no. 20 (1999): 1–26.

Osborne, C. V. "Turkey's Westernizing Movement." *Great Britain and the East* 48 (1937): 694–95.

Öztürkmen, A. "The Role of the People's Houses in the Making of National Culture in Turkey." *New Perspectives on Turkey*, no. 11 (1994): 159–81.

Renda, Günsel, and Carl Cortepeter. *The Transformation of Turkish Culture: The Atatürk Legacy*. Princeton, N.J.: Kingston Press, 1986.

Roos, Leslie L., Jr. "Frustration and Attitude Change among Turkish Villagers." *Journal of Social Psychology* 74 (1967): 163–69.

———. "Attitude Change and Turkish Modernization." *Ekistics* (Athens) 27 (1969): 7–23.

Rustow, Dankwart A. "Turkey: The Modernity of Tradition." In *Political Culture and Political Development*, ed. Lucien W. Pye. Princeton, N.J.: Princeton University Press, 1969.

Selsky, J. W. "'Even We Are Sheep': Cultural Displacement in a Turkish Classroom." *Journal of Management Inquiry* 9, no. 4 (2000): 362–73.

Sencer, Ayata. "Continuity and Change in Turkish Culture." *New Perspectives on Turkey*, no. 9 (1993): 137–49.

Seufret, Günter. "The Sacred Aura of the Turkish Flag." *New Perspectives on Turkey*, no. 16 (1997): 53–61.

Shankland, David. *Customs and Etiquette in Turkey*. Kent: Paul Norbury, 1999.

Spencer, Robert F. "Culture Process and Intellectual Current: Durkheim and Atatürk." *American Anthropologist* 60 (1958): 640–57.

Stevenson, I. "Characteristics of Cases of the Reincarnation Type in Turkey and Their Comparison with Cases in Two Other Cultures." *International Journal of Comparative Sociology* 11 (1970): 1–17.

Stone, Frank A. *The Rub of Cultures in Modern Turkey*. Bloomington: Indiana University Press, 1973.

Sunar, D. G., and S. O. Aral. "Norms of Reciprocity and Compensation among Turkish Students." *METU Studies in Development* (Ankara) 7 (1975): 69–81.

Sümer, E. A. "Changing Dynamic Aspects of the Turkish Culture and Its Significance for Child Training." In *The Child and His Family*, ed. E. J. Anthony and C. Koupernik. New York: Wiley Interscience, 1970.

Tapper, Nancy. "Changing Wedding Rituals in a Turkish Town." *Journal of Turkish Studies*, no. 9 (1985): 305–13.

———. "'Traditional' and 'Modern' Wedding Rituals in a Turkish Town." *International Journal of Turkish Studies* 5 (1990–91): 137–54.

Tezcan, Semih. "The Tradition of Blood Feuds in Turkey." *Turkish Studies Association Bulletin* 6 (1982): 7–13.

Tomlin, E. W. F. *Life in Modern Turkey*. New York: Thomas Nelson, 1946.

Toğrol, Beyhan. "Goals Chosen by Turkish Students in Response to Hypothetical Situations." *Istanbul University Studies in Experimental Psychology* 6 (1968): 1–14.

Toynbee, Arnold J. *The Western Question in Greece and Turkey: A Study in the Contact of Civilisations*. London: Constable, 1922.

———. "The Turkish State of Mind." *Atlantic Monthly* 136 (1925): 548–60.

Turhan, Mümtaz. *Where Are We in Westernization?* Trans. David Garwood. Istanbul: Robert College Research Center, 1965.

Tweedy, Owen. "Turkey in Step with Twentieth-Century Civilization." *Current History* 29 (1928): 247–51.

Uğurel, Şemin. "Ecology of Attitudes in Adolescents in Rural Parts of Turkey." *Contributions to Human Development* (Switzerland) 1 (1974): 49–66.

Uysal, A. "Street Cries in Turkey." *Journal of American Folklore* 81 (1968): 193–215.

———. "Beliefs and Practices Regarding Hidden Treasure in Turkey." *Erdem* (Ankara) 1 (1985): 97–110.

Vorhoff, Karin. "Businessmen and Their Organizations: Between Instrumental Solidarity, Cultural Diversity, and the State." In *Turkish Society in the Grip of Nationalism: Studies on Political Culture in Contemporary Turkey,* ed. Stéphane Yerasimos, Günter Seufert, and Karin Vorhoff. Istanbul: Orient-Institut, 2000.

Demography

Akşit, Bahattin, Kayhan Mutlu, H. Ünal Nalbantoğlu, A. Adnan Akçay, and Mustafa Şen. "Population Movements in Southeastern Anatolia: Some Findings of an Empirical Research in 1993." *New Perspectives on Turkey,* no. 14 (1996): 53–74.

Beeley, Brian. *Migration: The Turkish Case.* Milton Keynes, U.K.: Open University Press, 1983.

Behar, C., Y. Courbage, and A. Günsoy. "Economic Growth or Survival? The Problematic Case of Child Mortality in Turkey." *European Journal of Population* 15, no. 3 (1999): 241–78.

Bhattacharayya, A. "Role of Rural-Urban Income Inequality in Fertility Reductions: Cases of Turkey, Taiwan, and Morocco." *Economic Development and Cultural Change* 26 (1977): 117–38.

Clark, John. "The Growth of Ankara, 1961–1969." *Review of the Geographical Institute of the University of Istanbul* 13 (1971): 119–39.

Clay, Christopher. "Labour Migration and Economic Conditions in Nineteenth-Century Anatolia." *Middle Eastern Studies* 34, no. 4 (1998): 1–32.

Collins, J. Walter. "The Turkish Census and What It Means." *Contemporary Review* 133 (1928): 194–200.

Cook, M. A. *Population Pressure in Rural Anatolia, 1450–1600.* New York: Oxford University Press, 1972.

Demeny, Paul, and Frederick C. Shorter. *Estimating Turkish Mortality, Fertility, and Age Structure: Application of Some New Techniques.* Istanbul: Sermet Matbaası, 1968.

Erder, Leila. "Population Rise and Fall in Anatolia, 1550–1620." *Middle Eastern Studies* 15 (1979): 322–45.

Fişek, Nusret, and Frederick H. Shorter. "Fertility Control in Turkey." *Demography* 5 (1968): 578–90.

Franz, Erhard. *Population Policy in Turkey: Family Planning and Migration between 1960 and 1992.* Hamburg: Deutsches Orient-Institut, 1994.

Hayasaka, M. "The Polish Emigration and the Ottoman Empire." *Annals of the Japanese Association of Middle East Studies,* no. 2 (1987): 166–86.

İçduygu, Ahmet. "Transit Migrants in Turkey." *Boğaziçi Journal-Review of Social, Economic and Administrative Studies* (Istanbul) 10, no. 2 (1996): 127–42

Jennings, Ronald C. "Urban Population in Anatolia in the Sixteenth Century: A Study of Kayseri, Karaman, Amasya, Trabzon, and Erzurum." *International Journal of Middle East Studies* 7 (1976), 21–57.

Kağıtçıbaşı, Çiğdem. "Psychological Approaches to Fertility Behavior in Turkey." *Boğaziçi University Journal* (Social Sciences Series, Istanbul) 2 (1974): 99–108.

Karpat, Kemal H. "Ottoman Population Records and Census of 1881/82–1893." *International Journal of Middle East Studies* 9 (1978): 237–74.

———. "The Ottoman Emigration to America, 1860–1914." *International Journal of Middle East Studies* 17 (1985): 175–209.

———. *Ottoman Population 1830–1914: Demographic and Social Characteristics.* Madison: University of Wisconsin Press, 1985.

Keyder, Çağlar, and Ayhan Aksu-Koç. *External Labour Migration from Turkey and Its Impact.* Ottawa: IDRC, 1991.

Kırışçi, Kemal. "Post–Second World War Immigration from Balkan Countries to Turkey." *New Perspectives on Turkey,* no. 12 (1995): 61–77.

Kostanick, Huey Louis. "Turkish Resettlement of Refugees from Bulgaria, 1950–1953." *Middle East Journal* 9 (1955): 41–52.

Lieberman, Samuel S. *An Economic Approach to Differential Demographic Behavior in Turkey.* New York: Garland, 1979.

McCarty, Justin. "Age, Family, and Migration in Nineteenth-Century Black Sea Provinces of the Ottoman Empire." *International Journal of Middle East Studies* 10 (1979): 309–23.

———. *Muslims and Minorities: The Population of Ottoman Anatolia and the End of the Empire.* New York: New York University Press, 1983.

———. "Muslims in Ottoman Empire: Population from 1800–1912." *Nationalist Papers* 28, no. 1 (2000): 29–44.

Munro, J. M. "Migration in Turkey." *Economic Development and Cultural Change* 22 (1974): 634–53.

Murphey, Rhoads. "Some Features of Nomadism in the Ottoman Empire: A Survey Based on Tribal Census and Judicial Appeal Documentation from Archives of the Prime Ministry in Istanbul." *Journal of Turkish Studies* 7 (1984): 189–98.

Mutlu, Servet. "Population and Agglomeration Trends in the Turkish Settlement System: An Empirical Analysis and Some of Its Implications." *METU Studies in Development* (Ankara) 16 (1989): 99–125.

———. "Population by Ethnic Groups and Provinces." *New Perspectives on Turkey,* no. 12 (1995): 33–60.

Orhonlu, C. "Some Thoughts on the Results of the Migrations and Deportations during the Greek Invasion of Anatolia." *Journal of Regional Cultural Institute,* nos. 2–3 (1974): 113–19.

Özbay, Ferhunde. "Education and Fertility in Rural Turkey." *METU Studies in Development* (Ankara) 6 (1979): 51–67.

Özbay, Ferhunde, and Frederic C. Shorter. "Turkey: Changes in Birth Control Practice, 1963 to 1968." *Studies in Family Planning* 51 (1970): 1–7.

Sarç, Ömer Celal. "Growth of the Turkish Rural Population." *Middle Eastern Affairs* 3 (1952): 71–80.

Schechtman, Joseph B. "Compulsory Transfer of the Turkish Minority from Bulgaria." *Journal of Central European Affairs* 12 (1952): 154–89.

Shaw, Stanford J. "The Ottoman Census System and Population, 1831–1914." *International Journal of Middle East Studies* 9 (1978): 325–38.

———. "The Population of Istanbul in the Nineteenth Century." *International Journal of Middle East Studies* 10 (1979): 265–77.

———. "Ottoman Population Movements during the Last Years of the Empire." *Osmanlı Araştırmaları/Journal of Ottoman Studies* (Istanbul) 1 (1980): 191–205.

Shorter, Frederic C. "Information on Fertility, Mortality, and Population Growth in Turkey." *Population Index* 34 (1968): 3–22.

———. "The Economics of Turkish Population Policy since the Founding of the Republic." *Hacettepe Bulletin of Social Sciences and Humanities* (Ankara) 1 (1969): 58–66.

———. "The Population of Turkey after the War of Independence." *International Journal of Middle East Studies* 17 (1985): 417–41.

———. "The Welfare Implications of Infant Mortality Trends in Turkey." *Journal of Economics and Administrative Studies* (Istanbul) 4 (1990): 89–104.

———. "The Crisis of Population Knowledge in Turkey." *New Perspectives on Turkey*, no. 12 (1995): 1–31.

———. "Turkish Population in the Great Depression." *New Perspectives on Turkey*, no. 23 (Fall 2000): 103–24.

Shorter, Frederic C., and B. Güvenç, eds. *Turkish Demography: Proceedings of a Conference.* Ankara: Hacettepe University Institute of Population Studies, 1969.

Srikantan, K. S. "Regional and Rural-Urban Socio-Demographic Differences in Turkey." *Middle East Journal* 27 (1973): 275–300.

Şahin, İ., Feridun M. Emecen, and Yusuf Halaçoğlu. "Turkish Settlements in Rumelia (Bulgaria) in the 15th and 16th Centuries: Town and Village Population." *International Journal of Turkish Studies* 4 (1989): 23–42.

Taeuber, Irene B. "Population and Modernization in Turkey." *Population Index* 24 (1958): 101–22.

Tanfer, K. "Internal Migration in Turkey: Socioeconomic Characteristics by Destination and Type of Move, 1965–1970." *Studies in Comparative International Development* 18 (1983): 76–111.

Tanoğlu, Ali. "The Recent Emigration of the Bulgarian Turks." *Istanbul Üniversitesi Coğrafya Enstitüsü Review*, no. 2 (1955): 3–35.

Tekeli, İlhan, and Leila Erder. "Settlement Distribution and Structural Change in Turkish Agriculture: A Key to Migration Models and Policy." In *Why People Move*, ed. Jorge Balan. Paris: UNESCO, 1981.

Toros, A. "How Compatible Is the Turkish Population Structure for the EU?" *Perceptions* 2, no. 3 (1997): 156–66.

Tuna, Orhan. "The Problem of Immigrants from Bulgaria to Turkey." *İstanbul Üniversitesi İktisat Fakültesi Revue* 13 (1951): 209–19.

Tuncer, Baran. *Turkey's Population and Economy in the Future.* Ankara: Development Foundation of Turkey, 1977.

———. *The Impact of Population Growth on the Turkish Economy.* Ankara: Hacettepe University Institute of Population Studies, 1988.

Tümertekin, Erol. "Gradual Internal Migration in Turkey: A Test of Rovenstein's Hypothesis." *Review of the Geographical Institute of the University of Istanbul* 7 (1973): 157–59.

Education and Health

Abadan-Unat, Nermin. "Educational Problems of Turkish Migrants' Children." *International Review of Education* 21 (1975): 311–22.

Ataöv, Türkkaya. "The Faculty of Political Sciences of Turkey [Ankara University]." *Middle East Journal* 14 (1960): 243–5.

Başgöz, İlhan, and Howard E. Wilson. *Educational Problems in Turkey, 1920–1940*. Bloomington: Indiana University Press, 1968.

Burroughs, Franklin. "Robert College and Turkish Advancement." *Muslim World* 54 (1964): 288–91.

Carter, W. L. "New Educational System of Turkey." *Life and Letters Today* 25 (1940): 10–18.

Davison, Roderic H. "Westernized Education in Ottoman Turkey." *Middle East Journal* 15 (1961): 289–301.

Dewey, John. "Foreign Schools in Turkey." *New Republic* 41 (1924–1925): 40–42.

Eren, Nuri. "The Village Institutes of Turkey." *Royal Central Asian Journal* 33 (1946): 281–88.

Ertürk, S. "A Comparative Study of Teacher Behaviors in 1960 and 1970." *Hacettepe Bulletin of Social Sciences and Humanities* (Ankara) 2 (1970): 158–205.

Eseniş, Adnan. *Education for Democracy in Turkey*. Ankara: Milli Eğitim Basımevi, 1950.

Fotos, Evan. "An Appreciation of Turkish University Life." *Middle Eastern Affairs* 6 (1955): 248–58.

Goodman, N. "Health Services in Afghanistan, Iran, and Turkey." *Royal Central Asian Journal* 53 (1966): 134–42.

Göçek, Müge. "Shifting the Boundaries of Literacy: The Introduction of Western Style Education to the Ottoman Empire." In *Literacy: Interdisciplinary Conversations*, ed. D. Keller-Cohen. Princeton, N.J.: Hampton Press, 1993.

Greenwood, Keith M. *Robert College: The American Founders*. Istanbul: Boğaziçi University Press, 2000.

Hekimkil, E. *Education in Turkey*. Geneva, Switzerland: 22nd International Conference on Public Education, 1959.

Heper, Metin. *Decision Making in the Middle East Technical University: Responsiveness of the University to the Socioeconomic Development Efforts in Turkey*. Ankara: Middle East Technical University, 1973.

———. "Decision-Making and the Information Flow Systems in the Middle East Technical University." In *Planning the Development of Universities-III*, ed. Victor G. Onushkin. Paris: UNESCO, 1974.

İpşirli, Mehmet. "Archival Education Turkey." *Studies on Turkish-Arab Relations* (Istanbul) 4 (1989): 117–19.

Karpat, Kemal H. "Reinterpreting Ottoman History: A Note on the Condition of Education in 1874." *International Journal of Turkish Studies* 2 (1981–1982): 93–100.

Kazamias, Adreas M. *Education and the Quest for Modernity in Turkey*. Chicago: University of Chicago Press, 1966.

Kortepeter, C. Max. "American Liberalism Establishes Bases: Robert College and the American University of Beirut." *Journal of the American Institute for the Study of Middle Eastern Civilization* 1 (1980): 22–37.

Lybyer, Albert H. "Reform of Turkish Education." *Current History* 37 (1932): 119–20.

Murphy, Karen. "Turkey's Open Education Faculty." *Educational Technology Research and Development Journal* 37 (1989): 122–25.

———. "The Motivation of Students in Distance Education Systems: The Case of the Turkish Open Education Faculty." *International Council for Distance Education Bulletin* 20 (1989): 26–30.

Oğuzkan, Turhan. *Adult Education in Turkey*. Paris: UNESCO, 1955.

Okyar, Osman. "Universities in Turkey." *Minerva* 6 (1968): 213–43.

Ötüken, Adnan. "General Education and Learning in Turkey." *Cultura Turcica* (Ankara) 1 (1964): 126–35.

———. "General Education and Learning in Turkey: Publications in Turkey." *Cultura Turcica* (Ankara) 1 (1964): 224–31.

Özdalga, Elisabeth. "Education in the Name of 'Order and Progress': Reflections on the Recent Eight-Year Obligatory School Reform in Turkey." *Muslim World* 89, nos. 3–4 (July–October 1999): 414–38.

Özdil, İlhan. "Education in Turkey." *Middle Eastern Affairs* 1 (1950): 285–90.

Özelli, M. "The Estimates of Private Internal Rates of Return on Educational Investment in the First Turkish Republic, 1923–1960." *International Journal of Middle East Studies* 1 (1970): 154–76.

Özsunay, E. "Participation of Students in University and Faculty Administration in Turkey." *American Journal of Comparative Law* 7 (1969): 378–84.

Paçacı, M., and Y. Aktay. "75 Years of Higher Religious Education in Modern Turkey." *Muslim World* 89, nos. 3–4 (July–October 1999): 389–413.

Patrick, Mary M. *A Bosporus Adventure: Istanbul (Constantinople) Woman's College, 1871–1924.* Stanford, Calif.: Stanford University Press, 1934.

Redden, Kenneth. *Legal Education in Turkey.* İstanbul: Fakülteler Matbaası, 1957.

Reed, Cass. "Education in the Turkish Republic." *Open Courts* 49 (1935): 225–35.

Reed, Howard A. "Hacettepe and Middle East Technical Universities: New Universities in Turkey." *Minerva* 13 (1975): 200–35.

Rodrigue, Aron. *French Jews, Turkish Jews: The Alliance Israélite Universelle and the Politics of Jewish Schooling in Turkey, 1860–1925.* Bloomington: Indiana University Press, 1990.

Roos, L., and G. Agnell. "New Teachers for Turkish Villages: A Military-Sponsored Educational Program." *Journal of Developing Areas* 2 (1968): 519–31.

Sassani, Abul H. K. *Education in Turkey.* Washington, D.C.: Department of Health, Education and Welfare, 1952.

Sey, Y., and M. Tapan. "Architectural Education in Turkey: Past and Present." *Mimar* (Singapore) 10 (1983): 69–75.

Shor, Franc. "Robert College: Turkish Gateway to the Future." *National Geographic Magazine*, no. 112 (1957): 399–418.

Stanley, Brian. "Turkish Schools Seen through the Eyes of an English Visitor." *School and Society* 40 (1934): 814–19.

Stone, Frank A. *Academies for Anatolia: A Study of the Rationale and Impact of the Educational Institutions Sponsored by the American Board in Turkey, 1830–1980.* Lanham, Md.: University Press of America, 1984.

Szyliowicz, Joseph A. "Atatürk and Educational Modernization." *Journal of the American Institute for the Study of Middle Eastern Civilization* 1 (Autumn–Winter 1980–1981): 118–26.

———. "Continuity and Change in Turkey's Educational Policies." *Journal of Turkish Studies* 8 (1984): 241–50.

Taylor, Carl E., Rahmi Dirican, and Kurt W. Deushle. *Health and Manpower Planning in Turkey: An International Research Case Study.* Baltimore, Md.: Johns Hopkins University Press, 1968.

Temelkuran, T. "The First Teacher Training College for Girls in Turkey." *Journal of Regional Culture Institute* 5 (1972): 37–44.

Tezel, H. "The Turkish Naval Academy: 220 Years of Naval Education." *U.S. Naval Institute Proceedings* 91 (1973): 73–85.

Tonta, Yaşar. "A Brief Look at Automation Activities in Turkish University Libraries." *Program* 24 (1990): 73–80.

———. "An Interlending Network for Turkish University Libraries." *Information Development* 6 (1991): 105–11.

Tütengil, Cahit. "A Turkish Experience: The Village Institutes." *Turkish Studies Association Bulletin* 4 (1980): 1–8.

Verschoyle, T. "Education in Turkey." *International Affairs* 26 (1950): 59–70.

Vrooman, Lee. "Recent Tendencies in Turkish Education." *Moslem World* 17 (1927): 370–74.

Weiker, Walter F. "Academic Freedom and Problems of Higher Education in Turkey." *Middle East Journal* 16 (1962): 279–96.

Whitten, Benjamin, and Thomas Minder. "Education for Librarianship in Developing Nations: The Hacettepe Experience." *Journal of Education for Librarianship* 14 (1974): 220–33.

Wilson, Lucy. "Education in the Republic of Turkey." *School and Society* 28 (1928): 601–10.

Yavaş, U., and D. Rountree. "The Transfer of Management Know-How to Turkey through Graduate Business Education: Some Empirical Findings." *Management International Review* 20 (1980): 71–79.

Language

Akkan, Suzan. "Turkish Abbreviations." *Turkish Studies Association Bulletin* 1 (1976): 16–19.

Alderson, Anthony, and Fahir İz, ed. *Concise Oxford Turkish Dictionary*. Oxford: Clarendon, 1959.

———. *Oxford English-Turkish Dictionary*. 3rd ed. New York: Oxford University Press, 1984.

Balim-Harding, Çiğdem, and Colin Imber, eds. *The Balance of Truth: Essays in Honour of Professor Geoffrey Lewis*. Istanbul: ISIS Press, 2000.

Balkan, K. "Similarities between the Language of Gutians in the Ancient Near East and Old Turkish." *Erdem* (Ankara), no. 16 (1990): 65–125.

Bayraktaroğlu, Sinan, and Arın Bayraktaroğlu. *Colloquial Turkish*. London: Routledge, 1992.

Bengisu, Rona. *Turkish Phrase Book*. London: BBC Publications, 1993.

Birnbaum, E. "The Transliteration of Ottoman Turkish for Library and General Purposes." *Journal of American Oriental Society* 87 (1967): 122–56.

Boeschoten, H. E., and L. Verhoeven. *Turkish Linguistics Today*. Leiden: E. J. Brill, 1991.

Bolman, J., and S. Bolman. "The Challenge of the Turkish Language." *Turkish Review* (Ankara), no. 31 (1993): 45–49.

Bulliet, R. "First Names and Political Change in Modern Turkey." *International Journal of Middle East Studies* 9 (1978): 489–95.

Burrill, Kathleen. "Turkish Language Instruction." *Middle East Studies Association Bulletin* 6 (1972): 1–26.

Clauson, Gerard. "The Initial Labial Sound in the Turkish Languages." *Bulletin of the School of Oriental and African Studies* 24 (1961): 298–306.

Edmonds, William A. "Language Reform in Turkey and Its Relevance to Other Areas." *Muslim World* 45 (1955): 53–60.

Erguvanlı, Eser Emine. *The Function of Word Order in Turkish Grammar*. Berkeley: University of California Press, 1984.

Fukumori, T. "Event-Related Potentials for Turkish Vowel Harmony." *Annals of the Japanese Association for Middle Eastern Studies*, no. 15 (2000): 73–90.

Galin, Müge. *Turkish Sampler: Writings for All Readers*. Bloomington: Indiana University Turkish Studies, no. 7, 1989.

Gilson, Erika H. *The Turkish Grammar of Thomas Vaughan: Ottoman Turkish at the End of the 17th Century According to an English "Transkiptionstext."* Wiesbaden, Germany: Harrossowitz, 1987.

Halman, Talat Sait. *201 Turkish Verbs Fully Conjugated in All Tenses*. Woodbury, N.Y.: Barron's Educational Series, 1981.

Heyd, Uriel. *Language Reform in Modern Turkey*. Jerusalem: Israel Oriental Society, 1954.

Hony, H. C. "The New Turkish." *Journal of Royal Asiatic Society* 3 (1947): 216–21.

———. ed. *A Turkish-English Dictionary*. With the advice of Fahir İz. Oxford: Oxford University Press, 1947.

Hrebicek, L. "Several Turkish Homonymous Constructions and Their Generative Description." *Archiv Orientalni* (Prague) 39 (1971): 146–54.

———. "The Turkish Language Reform and Contemporary Texts: A Contribution to the Stylistic Evaluation of Borrowings." *Archiv Orientalni* (Prague) 43 (1975): 223–31.

———. "The Turkish Language Reform and Contemporary Lexicon." *Archiv Orientalni* (Prague) 45 (1977): 132–39.

———. "The Turkish Language Reform and Contemporary Grammar." *Archiv Orientalni* (Prague) 46 (1978): 334–37.

Ishımaru, Y. "Terminology and National Identity in the Writings of Şemseddin Sami." *Annals of the Japanese Association for Middle Eastern Studies*, no. 15 (2000): 205–24.

İz, Fahir, ed. *English-Turkish Dictionary*. New York: Oxford University Press, 1952.

———. "Atatürk and Turkish Language Reform." *Turkish Review*, no. 23 (1991): 69–82.

İz, Fahir, and H. C. Hony, eds. *An English-Turkish Dictionary*. Oxford: Oxford University Press, 1957.

İz, Fahir, H. C. Hony, and A. D. Alderson. *The Oxford Turkish Dictionary*. London: Oxford University Press, 1992.

Johanson, Lars. *Structural Factors in Turkic Language Contacts*. Richmond, U.K.: Curzon Press, 1999.

Kahane, Henry, Renée Kahane, and Andreas Tietze. *The Lingua Franca in the Levant: Turkish Nautical Terms of Italian and Greek Origin*. Urbana: University of Illinois Press, 1958.

Karabaş, Seyfi. "A Note on Ideology in Some Turkish Idioms." *International Journal of Turkish Studies* 3 (1984–1985): 117–22.

Kennessy, M. "A Turkish Grammar from the 17th Century." *Acta Orientalni* (Prague) 28 (1974): 119–26.

Kramsky, J. "On the Oldest Stratum of Words in the Basic Lexical Fund of Modern Turkish." *Archiv Orientalni* (Prague) 24 (1956): 224–25.

Kreider, Herman H. *Essentials of Modern Turkish*. Washington, D.C.: Middle East Institute, 1954.

Kumbaracı, T. "Consonantaly Condition Alternation of Vocalic Morphophonemes in Turkish." *Anthropological Linguistics* 8 (1966): 11–24.

Landau, Jacob. "Language Policy and Political Development in Israel and Turkey." In *Language Policy and Political Development*, ed. Brian Weinstein. Norwood, N.J.: Ablex, 1990.

Langenscheidt's Standard Turkish Dictionary, by Resuhi Akdikmen. New York: Langenscheidt, 1986.

Lees, Robert B. *The Phonology of Modern Standard Turkish*. Bloomington: Indiana University Press, 1961.

Lewis, Geoffrey L. *Teach Yourself Turkish*. London: English Universities Press, 1953.
———. *Turkish Grammar*. New York: Oxford University Press, 1967.
———. "Oh, No! We Never Mention Her." *Asian Affairs* 12 (1981): 155–66. (Thoughts on Turkish language reform.)
———. *The Turkish Language Reform: A Catastrophic Success*. Oxford: Oxford University Press, 1999.
Mansuroğlu, Mecdut. "The Rise and Development of Written Turkish in Anatolia." *Oriens* 7 (1954): 250–64.
Mardin, Yusuf. *Colloquial Turkish*. London: Routledge & Kegan Paul, 1961.
———. *Turkish Phrase Book*. London: Routledge & Kegan Paul, 1970.
McQuown, Norman A., and Sadi Koylan. *Spoken Turkish*. Ithaca, N.Y.: Spoken Language Services, 1973.
Meskill, R. H. *A Transformational Analysis of Turkish Syntax*. The Hague: Mouton, 1970.
Mundy, C. S. "The 'clü gerund' in Old Ottoman." *Bulletin of the School of Oriental and African Studies* 16 (1954): 298–319.
Nash, Rose. *Turkish Intonation: An Instrumental Study*. The Hague: Mouton, 1973.
Németh, J. *Turkish Grammar*. (English adaptation of the German original by T. Halasi-Kun.) The Hague: Mouton, 1962.
———. *Turkish Reader for Beginners*. Trans. from German by T. Halasi-Kun. The Hague: Mouton, 1966.
Perry, John R. "-at and -a: Arabic Loan Words with the Feminine Ending in Turkish." *Turkish Studies Association Bulletin* 8 (1984): 16–25.
———. "Language Reform in Turkey and Iran." *International Journal of Middle East Studies* 17 (1985): 296–311.
Pierce, J. "Some Problems in Understanding Consonantal Conditioning of Turkish Vowels." *Anthropological Linguistics* 8 (1966): 25–29.
———. "Glottology and the Turkish Basic Vocabulary." *American Anthropologist* 68 (1966): 137–43.
Redhouse, James William. *A Turkish and English Lexicon Showing in English the Significations of the Turkish Terms*. Beirut: Libraire du Liban, 1974.
Redhouse English-Turkish Dictionary. Istanbul: Redhouse Yayınevi, 1974.
Robson, B. "Historical Notes on the Single Vowel Conspiracy in Turkish." *General Linguistics* 11 (1971): 145–50.
Sebüktekin, Hikmet. *Turkish-English Contrastive Analysis: Turkish Morphology and Corresponding English Styles*. The Hague: Mouton, 1971.
———. "Morphotactics of Turkish Verb Suffixation." *Boğaziçi University Journal* (Humanities Series, Istanbul) 2 (1974): 87–116.
Sheka, Y. "Shifting Meaning of Categorical Verb Forms in Turkish Colloquial Speech." *Sovyetskaya Tyurkologiya*, no. 5 (1985): 62–71.
Spearman, Diana, and M. N. Turfan. "The Turkish Language Reform." *History Today* 20 (1970): 88–97.
Strauss, J. "Language Modernization: The Case of Tatar and Modern Turkish." *Central Asian Survey* 12, no. 4 (1993): 565–76.
———. "The *Millet*s and the Ottoman Language: The Contribution of Ottoman Greeks to Ottoman Letters (19th–20th Centuries)." *Die Welt des Islams* 35, no. 2 (1995): 189–249.
Swift, Lloyd B. *A Reference Grammar of Modern Turkish*. The Hague: Mouton, 1963.
Thomas, Lewis V. *Elementary Turkish*. Ed. Norman Itzkowitz. Cambridge, Mass.: Harvard University Press, 1967.

Tietze, Andreas. "Some Recent Turkish Publications on Anatolian Dialects." *Oriens* (Frankfurt) 3 (1950): 316–8.

———. "Analysis of a Turkish Multiple Riddle." *Rocznik Orientalni* (Warsaw) 27 (1964): 91–110.

———. "Persian Loanwords in Anatolian Turkish." *Oriens* (Frankfurt) 20 (1967): 125–68.

———. *Advanced Turkish Reader: Texts from the Social Sciences and Related Fields.* Bloomington: Indiana University Press, 1973.

———. *Turkish Literary Reader.* Richmond, U.K.: Curzon Press, 1997.

———. *Advanced Turkish Reader.* Richmond, U.K.: Curzon Press, 1997.

Trix, F. "The Stamboul Alphabet of Shemseddin Sami Bey: Precursor to Turkish Script Reform." *International Journal of Middle East Studies* 31 (1999): 255–72.

Turkish at Your Fingertips. Comp. Lexus. London: Routledge, 1989.

Türkmen, F. "The Issue of a Common Turkish Script." *Eurasian Studies* (Ankara), no. 1 (1994): 85–90.

Underhill, Robert. *Turkish Grammar.* Cambridge, Mass.: MIT Press, 1976.

Vanici-Osam, U. "May You Be Shot with Greasy Bullets—Curse Utterances in Turkish." *Asian Folklore Studies* 57, no. 1 (1998): 71–86.

Waterson, Natalie. "Some Aspects of the Phonology of the Nominal Forms of the Turkish Word." *Bulletin of School of Oriental and African Studies* 18 (1956): 578–91.

Wittek, Paul. *Turkish.* New York: McKay, 1962.

Zimmer, K. E. "Psychological Correlates of Some Turkish Morpheme Structure Conditions." *Language* 45 (1969): 309–21.

Mass Media

Brummett, Palmira. *Image and Imperialism in the Ottoman Revolutionary Press, 1908–1911.* Ithaca, N.Y.: SUNY Press, 2000.

Dönmezer, Sulhi. "Evaluation of Legislation Regulating and Limiting the Freedom of the Press." *Annales de la Faculté de Droit d'Istanbul* 16 (1966): 119–37.

Finkel, Andrew. "Who Guards the Turkish Press? A Perspective on Press Corruption in Turkey." *Journal of International Affairs* 54, no. 1 (Fall 2000): 145–66.

Frey, Frederick W. *The Mass Media and Rural Development in Turkey.* Cambridge, Mass.: Center for International Studies, 1966.

Geray, H. "Turkey's Communications Boom." *Turkish Review* (Ankara), no. 31 (1993): 25–30.

Kaya, A. R. "A fait accompli: Transformations of Media Structures in Turkey." *METU Studies in Development* (Ankara) 21, no. 3, (1994): 384–404.

Korkud, Refik. *The Democratic Regime, the Press, the Opposition, the Abuse of Liberties.* Ankara: Türkiye Fikir Ajansı, 1959.

Levonian, Lutfy. *The Turkish Press, 1925–1932.* Athens: School of Religion, 1932.

———. *The Turkish Press, 1932–1936.* Beirut: n.p., 1937.

Ogan, Christine. "Dilemma for the Mass Media in Developing Countries: To Reach a Few or None at All." *Turkish Studies Association Bulletin* 4 (1980): 10–16.

Öncü, Ayşe. "Packaging Islam: Cultural Politics on the Landscape of Turkish Commercial Politics." *New Perspectives on Turkey*, no. 10 (1994): 13–36.

———. "The Banal and the Subversive: Politics of Language on Turkish Television." *European Journal of Cultural Studies* 3, no. 3 (2000): 283–310.

Press in Turkey, The. Washington, D.C.: Library of Congress, 1949.

Robinson, Richard D. *The Opposition and the Press.* New York: American Universities Field Staff, 1955.

Serez, Naci. "Radio in Turkey." *Middle East Affairs* 4 (1953): 127–31.

Sowerwine, Sema E. "The Turkish Press and Its Impact on Foreign Policy, 1961–1980." *Journal of South Asian and Middle Eastern Studies* 23, no. 4 (2000): 37–61.

Şahin, Haluk. "Legal Status of Broadcasting in Turkey." *Turkish Studies Association Bulletin* 5 (1981): 21–22.

Türkkan, R. Oğuz. "The Turkish Press." *Middle Eastern Affairs* 1 (1950): 142–49.

White, Jenny B. "Amplifying Trust: Community and Communication in Turkey." In *New Media and the Muslim World: The Emerging Public Sphere*, ed. Dale Eickelman and Jon Anderson. Bloomington: Indiana University Press, 1999.

Yalman, Ahmet Emin. *Development of Modern Turkey as Measured by Its Press.* New York: Columbia Studies in History, Economics, and Public Law, 1944.

Yavuz, M. Hakan. "Media Identities for Kurds and Alevis in Turkey." In *New Media and the Politics of Civil Soiety in Muslim Societies*, ed. Dale F. Eickelman and Jon Anderson. (Bloomington: Indiana University Press, 1999).

Religion

Abadan-Unat, Nermin, and Ahmet Yücekök. "Religious Pluralism in Turkey." *Turkish Yearbook of International Relations* (Ankara) 10 (1969–1970): 24–49.

Abu Manneh, Butros, "The Naqshbandiyya in the Ottoman Lands in the Early 19th Century." *Die Welt des Islams* 22 (1984): 1–35.

Ahmad, Feroz. "Islamic Reassertion in Turkey." *Third World Quarterly* 10 (1988): 750–69.

———. "Politics and Islam in Modern Turkey." *Middle Eastern Studies* 27 (1991): 3–21.

Alkan, Türker. "The National Salvation Party in Turkey." In *Islam and Politics in the Modern Middle East*, ed. Metin Heper and Raphael Israeli. London: Croom Helm, 1984.

Aras, Bülent. "Turkish Islam's Moderate Face." *Middle East Quarterly* 5, no. 3 (1998): 23–29.

Arnold, Thomas W. *The Caliphate.* Oxford: Oxford University Press, 1924.

Ayata, Ayşe. "The Turkish Alevis." *Innovation in Social Sciences Research* 5, no. 3 (1992): 109–14.

Ayata, Sencer. "Patronage, Party, and State: Politicization of Islam in Turkey." *Middle East Journal* 50, no. 1 (1996): 40–56.

Barnes, John R. *An Introduction to Religious Foundations in the Ottoman Empire.* Leiden: E. J. Brill, 1987.

Bellah, Robert N. "Religious Aspects of Modernization in Turkey and Japan." *American Journal of Sociology* 64 (1958): 1–5.

Benton, C. "Many Contradictions: Women and Islamists in Turkey." *Muslim World* 86, no. 2 (1996): 106–29.

Berkes, Niyazi. "Historical Background of Turkish Secularism." In *Islam and the West*, ed. Richard N. Frye. The Hague: Mouton, 1957.

———. *The Development of Secularism in Turkey.* Montreal: McGill University Press, 1964.

Birge, John K. *The Bektashi Order of Dervishes.* London: Luzac, 1937.

———. "Secularism in Turkey and Its Meaning." *International Review of Missions* 33 (1944): 426–32.

———. "Islam in Modern Turkey." In *Islam in the Modern World*, ed. Dorothea S. Franck. Washington, D.C.: Middle East Institute, 1951.

Bishku, Michael B. "Secularism and Islam in Turkey." *Mediterranean Quarterly* 3, no. 4 (1992): 75–93.

Bozkurt, G. "The Reception of Western European Law in Turkey from the Tanzimat to the Turkish Republic, 1839–1939." *Islam-Zeitschrift für Gesehichte und Kultur des Islamischen Orients* 75, no. 2 (1998): 283–95.

Bruinessen, Martin van. "Popular Islam, Kurdish Nationalism, and Rural Revolt: The Rebellion of Sheikh Said in Turkey." In *Religion and Rural Revolt*, ed. Jànos M. Bak and Gerhard Benecke. Manchester, U.K.: Manchester University Press, 1984.

Çınar, Alev İnan. "Refah Party and the City Administration of Istanbul? Liberal Islam, Localism, and Hybridity." *New Perspectives on Turkey*, no. 16 (1997): 23–40.

Dağlı, I. D. "Islam, Politics, and the Welfare Party." *Foreign Policy* (Ankara) 19, nos. 3–4 (1995): 17–28.

Davison, Andrew. *Secularism and Revivalism in Turkey: A Hermeneutic Reconsideration.* New Haven, Conn.: Yale University Press, 1998.

Deringil, Selim. "'There Is No Compulsion in Religion': On Conversion and Apostasy in the Late Ottoman Empire." *Comparative Studies in Society and History* 42, no. 3 (2000): 547–75.

Dumont, Paul. "Hojas for the Revolution: The Religious Strategy of Mustafa Kemal Atatürk." *Journal of the American Institute for the Study of Middle Eastern Civilization* 1 (Spring–Summer 1980–1981): 17–32.

Duran, Burhanettin. "Approaching the Kurdish Question via *Adil Düzen* [Just Order]: An Islamist Formula of the Welfare Party for Ethnic Coexistence." *Journal of Muslim Minority Affairs* 18, no. 1 (1998): 111–28.

Erdoğan, Mustafa. "Islam in Turkish Politics: Turkey's Quest for Democracy without Islam." *Critique* 15 (1999): 25–50.

———. "Religious Freedom in the Turkish Constitution." *Muslim World* 89, nos. 3–4 (1999): 377–88.

Ergil, Doğu. "Secularization as a Class Conflict: The Turkish Example." *Asian Affairs* 62 (1975): 69–80.

———. "Secularization of Islamic Law and Institutions in Turkey: A Socio-Historic Analysis." *Studies in Islam* 15 (1978): 71–142.

Fallers, Lloyd. *Turkish Islam*. Chicago: Aldine, 1971.

Fortna, Benjamin C. "Islamic Morality in Late Ottoman 'Secular' Schools." *International Journal of Middle East Studies* 32, no. 3 (2000): 369–94.

Friedlander, Ira. *The Whirling Dervishes, Being an Account of the Sufi Order Known as the Mevlevis and Its Founder the Poet and Mystic Mevlana Jalalau'ddin Rumi.* New York: Collier Books, 1975.

Garnett, Lucy Mary Jane. *Mysticism and Magic in Turkey: An Account of the Religious Doctrines, Monastic Organisation, and Ecstatic Powers of the Dervish Orders.* New York: Scribner, 1912.

Geyikdağı, Yaşar. *Political Parties in Turkey: The Role of Islam.* New York: Praeger, 1984.

Göle, Nilüfer. *The Forbidden Modern: Civilization and Veiling.* Ann Arbor: University of Michigan Press, 1996.

———. "Authoritarian Secularism and Islamist Politics: The Case of Turkey." In *Civil Society in the Middle East*, ed. A. R. Norton. Leiden: E. J. Brill, 1996.

———. "Secularism and Islamism in Turkey: The Making of Elites and Counter-Elites." *Middle East Journal* 51, no. 1 (1997): 46–58.

Gülalp, Haldun N. "Islamism and Kurdish Nationalism: Rival Adversaries of Kemalism in Turkey." In *Islamism and the Question of Minorities*, ed. Tamara Sonn. Atlanta: Scholars Press, 1996.

——. "Political Islam in Turkey: The Rise and Fall of the Refah Party." *Muslim World* 89, no. 1 (1999): 22–41.

——. "The Poverty of Democracy in Turkey: The Refah Party Episode." *New Perspectives on Turkey* 21 (1999): 35–60.

Heper, Metin. "Islam, Polity, and Society in Turkey: A Middle Eastern Perspective." *Middle East Journal* 35 (1981): 345–63.

——. "The State and Religion in the Ottoman-Turkish Polity: A Theoretical Perspective." *Etudes Balkaniques*, no. 3 (1988): 92–97.

——. "The State, Religion, and Pluralism: The Turkish Case in Comparative Perspective." *British Journal of Middle Eastern Studies* 18 (1991): 38–55.

——. "Islam and Democracy in Turkey: Toward a Reconciliation?" *Middle East Journal* 51 (1997): 32–45.

Heyd, Uriel. "Islam in Modern Turkey." *Journal of the Royal Central Asian Society* 34 (1947): 209–308.

——. *Revival of Islam in Turkey*. Jerusalem: Magnes Press, 1968.

Holdbrook, Victoria Rowe. "Ibn Arabi and Ottoman Dervish Traditions: The Melâmi Supra-Order." *Journal of the Muhyiddin Ibn Arabi Society* 9 (1991): 18–35.

Houston, Chris. "Islamic Solutions to the Kurdish Problem: Late Rendezvous or Illegitimate Shortcut?" *New Perspectives on Turkey*, no. 16 (1997): 1–22.

Howe, Marvin. *Turkey Today: A Nation Divided over Islam's Revival*. Boulder, Colo.: Westview, 2000.

Hurgronje, Snouck. "Islam and Turkish Nationalism." *Foreign Affairs* 3 (1924): 61–77.

İçduygu, Ahmet, and Lincoln H. Day. "The Effects of International Migration on Religious Observance and Attitudes in Turkey." *Journal for the Scientific Study of Religion* 37, no. 4 (1999): 596–607.

İnalcık, Halil. "Islam in the Ottoman Empire." *Cultura Turcica* (Ankara) 5–7 (1968–1970): 19–29.

——. "The Caliphate and Atatürk's İnkılâp." *Belleten* (Ankara), no. 144 (1982): 353–65.

Kadıoğlu, Ayşe. "Women's Subordination in Turkey: Is Islam Really the Villain?" *Middle East Journal* 48, no. 4 (1994): 645–60.

——. "Republican Epistemology and Islamic Discourses in Turkey in the 1990s." *Muslim World* 88, no. 1 (1998): 1–21.

Kadıoğlu, Ayşe, and Menderes Çınar. "An Islamic Critique of Modernity in Turkey: Politics of Difference Backward." *Orient* 40, no. 1 (1999): 53–69.

Kamrava, M. "Pseudo-Democratic Politics and Populist Possibilities: The Rise and Demise of Turkey's Refah Party." *British Journal of Middle East Studies* 25, no. 2 (1998): 275–302.

Karpat, Kemal H. "The Evolution of the Turkish Political System and the Changing Meanings of Modernity, Security, and Islam." *Islamic Culture* (Nyerabad, India) 59 (1985): 377–410.

——. *The Politicization of Islam: Reconstructing Identity, State, Faith, and Community in the Late Ottoman Empire*. New York: Oxford University Press, 2001.

Kasaba, Reşat. "Cohabitation? Islamist and Secular Groups in Modern Turkey." In *Democratic Civility: The History and Cross-Cultural Possibility of a Modern Ideal*, ed. R. Hefner. New Brunswick, N.J.: Transaction Publishers, 1998.

Kasuya, G. "Arguments on the Caliphate in Turkey and *Layiklik*." *Annals of Japanese Association for Middle Eastern Studies*, no. 9 (1994): 93–116.

Keyman, E. Fuat. "On the Relation between Global Modernity and Nationalism: The Crisis of Hegemony and the Rise of (Islamic) Identity in Turkey." *New Perspectives on Turkey*, no. 13 (1995): 93–120.

———. "Globalization, Islam, and Democracy in Turkey." In *Navigations in Globalization*, ed. Jane Jenson. London: Ashgate, 2000.

Khalid, D. "Atatürk's Concepts of Islamic Reformism and Muslim Unity." *Journal of Regional Culture Institute* 7 (1974): 39–52.

Kinzer, Stephen. *Crescent and Star: Turkey between Two Worlds.* New York: Farrar, Strauss & Giroux, 2001.

Kushner, David. "Turkish Secularists and Islam." *Jerusalem Quarterly*, no. 38 (1986): 89–106.

Landau, Jacob M. "The National Salvation Party in Turkey." *Asian and African Studies* 11 (1976): 1–57.

———. "Islamism and Secularism: The Turkish Case." In *Studies in Judaism and Islam.* Jerusalem N.e.: The Magnes Press, 1981.

Lewis, Bernard. "Islamic Revival in Turkey." *International Affairs* 38 (1952): 38–48.

———. "Why Turkey Is the Only Muslim Country." *Middle East Quarterly* 1, no. 1 (1994): 41–49.

Lewis, Geoffrey. "Islam in Politics—A Muslim World Symposium: Turkey." *Muslim World* 56 (1966): 235–9.

Linke, Lilo. *Allah Dethroned: A Journey through Modern Turkey.* London: Constable, 1937.

Ludington, Nicholas S. *Turkish Islam and the Secular State.* Washington, D.C.: American University, American Institute for Islamic Affairs, 1984.

Mango, Andrew. "Islam in Turkey." In *The Islamic Near East*, ed Douglas Grant. Toronto: University of Toronto Press, 1960.

Mardin, Şerif. "Religion in Modern Turkey." *International Social Science Journal* 29 (1977): 279–97.

———. "Bediüzzaman Said Nursi (1873–1960): The Shaping of a Vocation." In *Religious Organization and Religious Experience*, ed. J. Davis. London: Academic Press, 1982.

———. "Turkey: Islam and Westernization." In *Religions and Societies: Asia and the Middle East*, ed. Carlo Caldarola. The Hague: Mouton, 1982.

———. "Religion and Politics in Modern Turkey." In *Islam in Political Process*, ed. James A. Piscatori. Cambridge: Cambridge University Press, 1983.

———. *Religion and Social Change in Modern Turkey: The Case of Bediüzzaman Said Nursi.* Albany, N.Y.: SUNY Press, 1989.

———. "Just and Unjust." *Daedalus* 120 (1991): 113–29.

Mason, W. "The Future of Political Islam in Turkey." *World Policy Journal* 17, no. 2 (2000): 56–67.

Mehmet, Özay. *Islamic Identity and Development: Studies of the Islamic Periphery.* London: Routledge, 1990.

Miller, R. "The Ottoman and Islamic Substratum of Turkey's Swiss Civil Code." *Journal of Islamic Studies* 11, no. 3 (2000): 35–61.

Nereid, C. *In the Light of Said Nursi: Turkish Nationalism and the Religious Alternative.* London: C. Hurst, 1997.

Norton, John. "Bektashis in Turkey." In *Islam in the Modern World*, ed. Denis MacEoin and Ahmed Al-Shahi. London: Croom Helm, 1983.

Olson, Emelie. "Muslim Identity and Secularism in Contemporary Turkey: 'The Headscarf Issue.'" *Anthropological Quarterly* 58 (1985): 161–71.

———. "The Use of Religious Symbol Systems and Ritual in Turkey: Women's Activities at Muslim Shrines." *Muslim World* 84 (1994): 202–16.

Olsson, Tord, Elizabeth Özdalga, and Catharina Raudvere, ed. *Alevi Identity*. Richmond, U.K.: Curzon Press, 1998.

Öniş, Ziya. "Political Economy of Islamic Resurgence in Turkey." *Third World Quarterly* 18, no. 4 (1997): 743–66.

Özbudun, Ergun. "Islam and Politics in Modern Turkey." In *The Islamic Impulse,* ed. Barbara Freyer Stowasser. London: Croom Helm, 1987.

Özcan, A. *Pan-Islamism: Indian Muslims, the Ottomans, and Britain (1877–1924)*. Leiden: E. J. Brill, 1997.

Özcan, Yusuf Ziya. "Mosques in Turkey: A Quantitative Analysis." *Intellectual Discourse* 2, no. 1 (1994): 19–40.

Özdalga, Elisabeth, "Womanhood, Dignity, and Faith: Reflections on an Islamic Woman's Life Story." *The European Journal of Women's Studies* 4, no. 4 (1997): 473–97.

———. *The Veiling Issue: Official Secularism and Popular Islam in Turkey*. Richmond, U.K.: Curzon Press, 1998.

———. "Worldly Asceticism in Islamic Casting: Fethullah Gülen's Inspired Piety and Activism." *Critique* 17 (2000): 83–104.

Özdemir, Adil, and Kenneth Frank. *Visible Islam in Modern Turkey*. London: Macmillan, 2000.

Özyürek, Esra G. "'Feeling Tells Better Than Language': Emotional Expression and Gender Hierarchy in the Sermons of Fethullah Gülen Hocaefendi." *New Perspectives on Turkey*, no 16 (1997): 41–51.

Pears, Edwin. "Christians and Islam in Turkey." *Nineteenth Century* 73 (1913): 278–91.

Peters, R. "Religious Attitudes toward Modernization in the Ottoman Empire: A Nineteenth-Century Pious Text on Steamship, Factories, and the Telegraph." *Die Welt des Islams*, no. 26 (1986): 76–105.

Piricky, Gabriel. "Some Observations on New Departures in Modernist Interpretations of Islam in Contemporary Turkey: Fethullah Gülen Cemaati." *Asian and African Studies*, no. 8 (1999): 83–90.

Ramsaur, E. E. "The Bektashi Dervishes and the Young Turks." *Moslem World* 32 (1942): 7–14.

Reed, Howard. "A New Force at Work in Democratic Turkey." *Middle East Journal* 7 (1953): 33–44.

———. "Revival of Islam in Secular Turkey." *Middle East Journal* 8 (1954): 267–82.

———. "Turkey's New İmam-Hatip Schools." *Die Welt des Islams* 4 (1955): 150–63.

———. "The Faculty of Divinity at Ankara." *Muslim World* 46 (1956): 295–312; 47 (1957): 22–35.

———. "Secularism and Islam in Turkish Politics." *Current History* 32 (1957): 333–38.

———. "Atatürk's Secularizing Legacy and the Continuing Vitality of Islam in Republican Turkey." In *Islam in the Contemporary World*, ed. Cyriac K. Pullapilly. Notre Dame, Ind.: Riverside, 1980.

Robins, P. "Political Islam in Turkey: The Rise of the Welfare Party." *Japanese Institute of Middle Eastern Economies Institute Review*, no. 28 (1995): 71–80.

Robinson, Richard D. "Mosque and School in Turkey." *Muslim World* 51 (1961): 107–10, 185–88.

Sakallıoğlu, Ümit Cizre. "Parameters and Strategies of Islam-State Interaction in Republican Turkey." *International Journal of Middle East Studies* 28, no. 2 (1996): 231–51.

Saktanber, Ayşe. "Formation of a Middle-Class Ethos and Its Quotidian: Revitalizing Islam in Urban Turkey." In *Space, Culture, and Power: New Identities in Globalizing Cities*, ed. Ayşe Öncü and Petra Weyland. London: Zed, 1997.

Salt, Jeremy. "Nationalism and the Rise of Muslim Sentiment in Turkey." *Middle Eastern Studies* 31, no. 1 (1995): 12–27.

Sarıbay, Ali Yaşar. "Religion in Contemporary Turkish Society and Polity." *Current Turkish Thought* (Istanbul), no. 58 (1986): 2–24.

Sayarı, Sabri. "Turkey's Islamist Challenge." *Middle East Quarterly* 3, no. 3 (1995): 35–43.

Schimmel, Annemarie. "Islam in Turkey." In *Religion in the Middle East: Three Religions in Concord and Conflict*, ed. A. J. Arberry. Cambridge: Cambridge University Press, 1969.

Scott, R. "Turkish Village Attitudes toward Religious Education." *Muslim World* 55 (1965): 222–29.

———. "Qur'an Courses in Turkey." *Muslim World* 61 (1971): 239–55.

Sever, Ayşegül. "The Twilight of Refah: Turkey and the Islamist Welfare Party." *Scandinavian Journal of Alternatives and Area Studies* 18, no. 4 (1999): 31–49.

Shankland, David. "Social Change and Culture: Responses to Modernisation in an Alevi Village in Anatolia." In *When History Accelerates: Essays on Rapid Social Change, Complexity, and Creativity*, ed. C. Hann. London: Athlone Press, 1994.

———. *Islam and Society in Turkey*. Huntingdon, U.K.: Eothen Press, 1999.

Smith, Wilfred Cantwell. "Modern Turkey: Islamic Reformation?" *Islamic Culture* 25 (1951): 155–86.

Stirling, Paul. "Religious Change in Republican Turkey." *Middle East Journal* 12 (1958): 395–408.

Sunar, İlkay, and Binnaz Toprak. "Islam in Politics: The Case of Turkey." *Government and Opposition* 18 (1983): 421–41.

Tapper, Nancy, and Richard Tapper. "The Birth of the Prophet: Ritual and Gender in Turkish Islam." *Man* 22 (1987): 69–92.

———. "'Thank God We're Secular!' Aspects of Fundamentalism in a Turkish Town." In *Aspects of Religious Fundamentalism*, ed. Lionel Caplan. London: Macmillan, 1987.

Tapper, Richard, ed. *Islam in Modern Turkey: Religion, Politics, and Literature in a Secular State*. London: I. B. Tauris, 1991.

Thomas, Lewis V. "Recent Developments in Turkish Islam." *Middle East Journal* 6 (1952): 22–40.

———. "Turkish Islam." *Muslim World* 44 (1954): 181–85.

Tınaz, N. "Religion, Politics, and Social Change in Modern Turkey." *Hamdard Islamicus* 14, no. 4 (1991): 67–104.

Toprak, Binnaz. *Islam and Political Development in Turkey*. Leiden: E. J. Brill, 1981.

———. "Politicization of Islam in a Secular State: The National Salvation Party in Turkey." In *From Nationalism to Revolutionary Islam*, ed. Said Amir Arjomand. London: Macmillan, 1984.

———. "Islamist Intellectuals of the 1980s in Turkey." *Current Turkish Thought* (Istanbul), no. 62 (1987): 1–19.

Vorhoff, Karin. "Let's Reclaim Our History and Culture!—Imagining Alevi Community in Turkey." *Die Welt des Islams* 38, no. 2 (1998): 220–52.

———. "Alevism, or Can Islam be Secular?" *Les annales de l'autre Islam* 6 (1999): 135–51.

Wagstaff, Malcolm, ed. *Aspects of Religion in Secular Turkey*. Durham, U.K.: Centre for Middle Eastern and Islamic Studies, University of Durham, 1990.

Weiker, Walter F. "Turkey, the Middle East, and Islam." *Middle East Review* 17 (1985): 27–32.

White, Jenny. "Islam and Democracy: The Turkish Experience." *Current History* 94, no. 588 (1995): 7–12.

———. "Pragmatists or Ideologs: Turkey's Welfare Party in Power." *Current History* 96, no. 606 (1997): 25–30.

Williams, Kenneth. "Is Turkey Deserting Islam?" *Great Britain and the East* 50 (1938): 485.

Woolworth, William S., Jr. "The Moslem Mind in Turkey Today." *Moslem World* 17 (1927): 139–46.

Yalman, Nur. "Islamic Reform and the Mystic Tradition in Eastern Turkey." *Archives Européennes des Sociologies* 10 (1969): 41–60.

———. "Some Observations on Secularism in Islam: The Cultural Revolution in Turkey." *Daedalus* 102 (1973): 139–68.

———. "The Center and the Periphery: The Reform of Religious Institutions in Turkey." *Current Turkish Thought* (Istanbul), no. 38 (1979): 1–23.

Yavuz, M. Hakan. "Political Islam and the Welfare (Refah) Party in Turkey." *Comparative Politics* 30, no. 1 (1997): 63–82.

———. "Search for a New Social Contract in Turkey: Fethullah Gülen, the Virtue Party, and the Kurds." *SAIS Review* 19, no. 1 (1999): 114–43.

———. "The Assassination of Collective Memory: The Case of Turkey." *Muslim World* 89 (1999): 193–207.

———. "Towards an Islamic Liberalism: The Nurcu Movement and Fethullah Güven in Turkey." *Middle East Journal* 53, no. 4 (1999): 584–604.

———. "Cleansing Islam from the Public Space." *Journal of International Affairs* 54, no. 1 (Fall 2000): 21–42.

———. "Turkey's Fault Lines and the Crisis of Kemalism." *Current History* 99 (2000): 33–38.

Yeşilada, Birol. "The Refah Party Phenomenon in Turkey." In *Comparative Political Parties and Political Elites: Essays in Honor of Samuel J Eldersveld*, ed. Birol Yeşilada. Ann Arbor: University of Michigan Press, 1999.

Yocum, Glenn. "Notes on an Easter Ramadan." *Journal of the American Academy of Religion* 60, no. 2 (1992): 201–30.

———. "Islam and Gender in Turkey." *Religious Studies Review* 21, no. 3 (1995): 186–90.

Zubaida, S. "Turkish Islam and National Identity." *MERİP Reports* 26, no. 22 (1996): 10–15.

———. "Trajectories of Political Islam: Egypt, Iran, and Turkey." *Political Quarterly* 71, no. 1 (2000): 60–78.

Urbanization, Urbanism, and Housing

Aksoy, S. "The Housing Problems of Istanbul and the Gecekondu [Squatter Housing] Phenomenon." *Planning and Administration* 7 (1980): 39–48.

Baer, Marc David. "The Islamization of Ottoman Cities." *New Perspectives on Turkey* 20 (1999): 132–42.

Buğra, Ayşe. "The Immoral Economy of Housing in Turkey." *International Journal of Urban and Regional Research* 22, no. 2 (1998): 303–17.

Çelik, Zeynep. *The Remaking of Istanbul: Portrait of an Ottoman City in the Nineteenth Century*. Seattle: University of Washington Press, 1986.

Danielson, Michael N., and Ruşen Keleş. *The Politics of Rapid Urbanization: Government and Growth in Modern Turkey*. New York: Holmes & Meier, 1985.

Dicle, Attila. "Gecekondu [Squatter Settlement]: The Problems of Internal Migration and Squatter Settlement in Turkey." *Journal of South Asian and Middle Eastern Studies* 6 (1983): 48–61.

Eldem, Edhem. *The Ottoman City between East and West: Aleppo, İzmir, and Istanbul.* New York: Cambridge University Press, 1999.

Erdentuğ, Aygen, and Berrak Burçak. "Political Tuning in Ankara, a Capital, as Reflected in Its Urban Symbols and Images." *International Journal of Urban and Regional Research* 22, no. 4 (1998): 589–601.

Erder, Leyla, and Suraiya Faroqhi. "The Development of the Anatolian Urban Network during the Sixteenth Century." *Journal of the Economic and Social History of the Middle East* 22 (1980): 265–303.

Erman, Tahire. "The Meaning of City Living for Rural Migrant Women and Their Role in Migration: The Case of Turkey." *Women's Studies International Forum* 20 (1997): 263–73.

———. "Squatter (Gecekondu) Housing versus Apartment Housing: Turkish Rural-to-Urban Migrant Residents' Perspectives." *Habitat International* 28, no. 1 (1997): 91–106.

———. "Becoming 'Urban' or Remaining 'Rural': The Views of Rural-to-Urban Migrants on the 'Integration' Question." *International Journal of Middle East Studies*, no. 13 (1998): 541–61.

Geray, Cevat. "Urbanization in Turkey." *Ankara Üniversitesi Siyasal Bilgiler Fakültesi Dergisi* (Ankara) 24 (1969): 157–74.

Heper, Metin. *Gecekondu Policy in Turkey: An Evaluation with a Case Study of Rumelihisarüstü Squatter Area in Istanbul.* Istanbul: Boğaziçi University, 1978.

———. "Critical Factors Concerning Housing Policy in a Squatter Area in Istanbul, Turkey." In *The Residential Circumstances of the Urban Poor: An Overview of Housing and Its Improvement in Developing Countries.* New York: Praeger, 1981.

Inani, A. "Istanbul: City of Peace and Metropolis of Islam." *Islam Today*, no. 3 (1985): 26–33.

İbrahim, Yasa. "The Impact of Rural Exodus on the Occupational Patterns of Cities: The Case of Ankara." In *Social Stratification and Development in the Mediterranean Basin*, ed. Mübeccel B. Kiray. The Hague: Mouton, 1973.

Karpat, Kemal H. *The Gecekondu [Squatter Settlement]: Rural Migration and Urbanization.* New York: Cambridge University Press, 1976.

———. "Ottoman Urbanism: The Crimean Emigration to Dobruca and the Founding of the Mecidiye, 1856–1878." *International Journal of Turkish Studies* 3 (1984–1985): 1–25.

Keleş, Ruşen. "Urbanization and Balanced Regional Development in Turkey." *Ekistics* (Athens) 22 (1966): 163–68.

———. *Urbanization in Turkey.* New York: Ford Foundation, 1974.

Kongar, Emre. "Some Comparative Characteristics of Gecekondu [Squatter Settlement] Families in İzmir." *Studies in Development* (Ankara), no. 4 (1972), 643–56.

Keyder, Çağlar, ed. *Istanbul: Between the Global and the Local.* Lanham, Md.: Rowman & Littlefield, 1999.

Levine, Ned. "Old Culture-New Culture: A Study of Migrants in Ankara, Turkey." *Social Forces* 51 (1973): 355–68.

———. "Value Orientations among Migrants in Ankara, Turkey: A Case Study." *Asian and African Studies* 8 (1973): 50–68.

———. "Anti Urbanization: An Implicit Development Policy in Turkey." *Journal of Developing Areas* 14 (1980): 513–39.

Magnarella, Paul J. "From Villager to Townsman in Turkey." *Middle East Journal* 24 (1970): 229–39.

———. "Turkish Townsmen View Apollo." *Middle East Journal* 26 (1972): 181–83.

Namikawa, Ryo, and Banri Namikawa. *Istanbul: Tale of Three Cities.* Palo Alto, Calif.: Kodansha International, 1972.

Öncü, Ayşe. "The Myth of the 'Ideal Home' Travels across Cultural Borders to Istanbul." In *Space, Culture, and Power: New Identities in Globalizing Cities*, eds. Ayşe Öncü and Petra Weyland. London: Zed, 1997.

Reimer, M. J. "Urban Regulation and Planning Agencies in Mid-Nineteenth-Century Alexandria and Istanbul." *Turkish Studies Association Bulletin* 19, no. 1 (1995): 1–26.

Sanlı, İbrahim, Yücel Ünal, and İsmet Kılıçaslan. *International Migration and Metropolitan Development in Turkey*. Istanbul: Istanbul Teknik Üniversitesi, 1976.

Suzuki, Peter T. "Encounters with Istanbul: Urban Peasants and Village Peasants." *International Journal of Comparative Sociology* 5 (1964): 208–16.

———. "Peasants without Plows: Some Anatolians in Istanbul." *Rural Sociology* 31 (1966): 428–38.

———. "Community Development in an Urban Setting: Turkey's Peasants in Shantytowns." *Journal of Community Development Society* 6 (1975): 102–10.

Şenyapılı, T. "A Proposal for a Comprehensive Framework for the Marginal Sector and Squatter Housing." *METU Studies in Development* (Ankara) 6 (1979): 373–416.

Tekeli, İlhan. "The Evolution of Spatial Organization in the Ottoman Empire and the Turkish Republic." *Ekistics* (Athens) 31 (1971): 37–60.

———. "Evolution of Spatial Organization in the Ottoman Empire and Turkish Republic." In *Regional Policy*, ed. John Friedmann and William Alonso. Cambridge, Mass.: M.I.T. Press, 1975.

———. "Urban Patterns in Anatolia: Organization and Evolution." In *Conservation as Cultural Survival*, ed. Renata Holod. Geneva: Aga Khan Award for Architecture, 1978.

———. "On the Dynamics of Experience of Urbanization in Turkey." In *Urban Problems and Economic Development,* ed. Lata Chatterjee and Peter Mijkap. Alphen aan den Rijn: Sijthoff and Noordhoff International Publishers, 1981.

———. "Case Study of a Relocated Capital: Ankara." In *Urban Planning Practice in Developing Countries*, ed. John L. Taylor and David G. Williams. Brussels: Commission of the European Communities, 1982.

———. "Nineteenth-Century Transformation of Istanbul Metropolitan Area." In *Villes Ottomanes a la fin de l'empire*, ed. Paul Dumont and François Georgeon. Paris: L'Harmattan, 1992.

Tekeli, İlhan, and Gökhan Menteş. "Development of 'Holdings' in Turkey and Their Organization Space." In *Planning Industrial Development*, ed. David F. Walker. Chichester, U.K.: Wiley, 1980.

Weiker, Walter F. *Decentralizing Government in Modernizing Nations: Growth Potential of Turkish Provincial Cities*. Beverly Hills, Calif.: Sage, 1972.

Women and Family

Abadan, Nermin. *Social Change and Turkish Women*. Ankara: Ankara Üniversitesi Siyasal Bilgiler Fakültesi Yayını, 1963.

———. "Turkey." In *Women in the Modern World*, ed. Raphael Patai. Glencoe, Ill.: Free Press, 1967.

———. "The Place of Turkish Women in Society." *Ankara Üniversitesi Siyasal Bilgiler Fakültesi Dergisi* 4 (1968): 131–44.

Abadan-Unat, Nermin. "The Modernization of Turkish Women." *Middle East Journal* 32 (1978): 291–306.

———. "Movement of Women and National Liberation: The Case of Turkey." *Journal of the American Institute for the Study of Middle Eastern Civilization* 1 (Autumn–Winter 1980–1981): 4–16.

———. ed. *Women in Turkish Society*. Leiden: E. J. Brill, 1981.

Acar, Feride. "Turkish Women in Academia: Roles and Careers." *METU Studies in Development* (Ankara) 10 (1983): 409–46.

———. "Women in Academic Science Careers in Turkey." In *Token Women or Gender Equality*, ed. Veronica Stolte-Heiskanen, Feride Acar, Nora Ananieva, Dorothea Gaudart, and Ruza Fürst-Dilic. New York: St. Martin's, 1991.

———. "Higher Education in Turkey: A Gold Bracelet for Women." In *The Gender Gap in Higher Education*, ed. Suzanne Stiverlie, Lynda Malik, and Duncan Harris. London: Kegan, 1994.

Acar, Feride, and Ayşe Güneş-Ayata, eds. *Gender and Identity Construction: Women of Central Asia, the Caucasus, and Turkey*. Leiden: E. J. Brill, 2000.

Ahıska, Meltem. "Gender and National Fantasy: Early Turkish Radio Drama." *New Perspectives on Turkey*, no. 22 (Spring 2000): 25–60.

Ahmed, Leila. "Feminism and Feminist Movements in the Middle East, A Preliminary Exploration: Turkey, Egypt, Algeria, and People's Democratic Republic of Yemen." *Women's Studies International Forum* 5 (1982): 153–68.

Akgün, Seçil. "Women's Emancipation in Turkey." *Turkish Studies Association Bulletin* 10 (1986): 1–10.

Arat, Yeşim. "The Question of Suffrage in Turkey." *Current Turkish Thought* (Istanbul), no. 57 (1985): 1–15.

———. "Obstacles to Political Careers: Perceptions of Turkish Women." *International Political Science Review* 6 (1985): 355–66.

———. *The Patriarchal Paradox: Women Politicians in Turkey*. Rutherford, N.J.: Fairleigh Dickinson University Press, 1989.

———. "Islamic Fundamentalism and Women in Turkey." *Muslim World* 80 (1990): 17–23.

———. "Women's Movement and the Turkish State in the 1980–1990 Decade." In *Psychological Issues in the Political Transformation of Central and Eastern Europe*, ed. Klaus Helkama and Kirsi Tolonen. Helsinki, Finland: University of Helsinki, 1991.

———. "Women's Studies in Turkey: From Kemalism to Feminism." *New Perspectives on Turkey*, no. 9 (1993): 119–35.

———. "Toward a Democratic Society: The Women's Movement in Turkey in the 1980s." *Women's Studies International Forum* 17, nos. 2–3 (1994): 241–48.

———. "Women's Movement of the 1980s in Turkey: Radical Outcome of Liberal Feminism." In *Reconstructing Gender in the Middle East: Tradition, Identity and Power*, ed. Fatma Müge Göçek and Shiva Balaghi. New York: Columbia University Press, 1994.

———. "A Feminist Mirror in Turkey: Portraits of Two Activists in the 1980s." In *Challenges to Democracy in the Middle East*, ed. William Harris, Amatzia Baram, Ahmad Ashraf, Heath Lowry, and Yeşim Arat. Princeton, N.J.: Markus Wiener, 1997

———. "Feminists, Islamists and Political Change in Turkey." *Political Psychology* 19, no. 1 (1998): 117–32.

———. "A Woman Prime Minister in Turkey: Did It Matter?" *Women and Politics* 19 (1998): 1–22.

———. "From Emancipation to Liberation: The Changing Role of Women in Turkey's Public Realm." *Journal of International Affairs* 54, no. 1 (2000): 107–23.

Arat, Zehra. "Kemalism and Turkish Women." *Women and Politics* 14, no. 4 (1994): 57–80.

———. "Turkish Women and the Republican Reconstruction of Tradition." In *Reconstructing Gender in the Middle East: Power, Identity and Tradition*, ed. Fatma Müge Göçek and Shiva Balaghi. New York: Columbia University Press, 1994.

———. "Liberation or Indoctrination? Women's Education in Turkey." *Journal of Economics and Administrative Studies* (Istanbul) 8, nos. 1–2 (1994): 83–105

———. ed. *Deconstructing Images of "the Turkish Woman."* New York: St. Martin's, 1998.

Armstrong, Harold C. "The Turkish Women of Today." *North American Review* 228 (1929): 199–205.

Aswad, Barbara C. "Key and Peripheral Roles of Noble Women in a Middle Eastern Plains Village [in Hatay]." *Anthropological Quarterly* 40 (1967): 139–52.

Ayata, Ayşe. "Women in the [Turkish] Legislature." *Boğaziçi Journal-Review of Social, Economic and Administrative Studies* 8, no. 1–2 (1994): 107–20.

Baer, Gabriel. "Women and the Waqf: An Analysis of the Istanbul Tahrir of 1546." *Asian and African Studies* 17 (1983): 9–27.

Benedict, Peter. "Aspects of the Domestic Cycle in a Turkish Provincial Town." In *Mediterranean Family Structures*, ed. J. G. Peristiany. Cambridge: Cambridge University Press, 1976.

Berik, G. "State Policy in the 1980s and the Future of Women's Rights in Turkey." *New Perspectives on Turkey*, no. 4 (1990): 81–96.

Bing, Edward J. "Progress of Women in New Turkey." *Current History* 18 (1923): 305–11.

Brown, Demetra. *Some Pages from the Life of Turkish Women.* New York: Houghton Mifflin, 1909.

———. *The Unveiled Ladies of Stamboul.* New York: Houghton Mifflin, 1923.

Browning, Janet. "Some Aspects of the Portrayal of Women in Modern Turkish Literature." *British Society of Middle East Studies Bulletin* 6 (1979): 109–15.

———. *Atatürk's Legacy to the Women of Turkey.* Durham, U.K.: Center of Middle Eastern and Islamic Studies, University of Durham, 1985.

Coşar, Fatma M. "Women in Turkish Society." In *Women in the Muslim World*, ed. Lois Beck and Nikkie Keddie. Cambridge, Mass.: Harvard University Press, 1978.

Croutier, Alev Lytle. *Harem: The World behind the Veil.* New York: Abbeville Press, 1989.

Çağlı, Uğur, and Levent Durukan. "Sex Role Portrayals in Turkish TV Advertising: Some Preliminary Findings." *METU Studies in Development* (Ankara) 16 (1989): 153–75.

Çitçi, Oya. "Women at Work." *Turkish Public Administration Annual* (Ankara), no. 2 (1975): 155–92.

Daver, Bülent. "Political Rights of Women." *Ankara Üniversitesi Siyasal Bilgiler Fakültesi Dergisi* (Ankara) 24 (1969): 111–20.

Davis, Fanny. *The Ottoman Lady: A Social History from 1718 to 1918.* New York: Greenwood, 1986.

———. *Turkish Women.* New York: Turkish Information Office, n.d.

Delaney, Carol. *The Seed and the Soil: Gender and Cosmology in Turkish Village Society.* Berkeley: University of California Press, 1991.

———. "Untangling the Meanings of Hair in Turkish Society." In *Off with Her Head: The Denial of Women's Identity in Myth, Religion, and Culture*, ed. Howard Eilberg-Schwartz and Wendy Doniger, eds. Berkeley: University of California Press, 1995.

———. "Father-State [Devlet Baba], Motherland [Anavatan], and the Birth of Turkey." In *Naturalizing Power: Essays in Feminist Cultural Analysis*, ed. Sylvia Yanagisako and Carol Delaney. New York: Routledge, 1995.

Dengler, Ian C. "Turkish Women in the Ottoman Empire: The Classical Age." In *Women in the Muslim World*, ed. Lois Beck and Nikki Keddie. Cambridge, Mass.: Harvard University Press, 1978.

Dobkin, M. "Social Ranking in the Woman's World of Purdah: A Turkish Example." *Anthropological Quarterly* 40 (1967): 65–72.

Doğramacı, Emel. "Ziya Gökalp and Women's Rights." *Die Welt des Islams* 18 (1978): 212–20.

———. *Status of Women in Turkey*. 3rd ed. Ankara: Meteksan, 1989.

Ecevit, Yıldız. "Shop Floor Control: The Ideological Construction of Turkish Women Factory Workers." In *Working Women: International Perspectives on Labor and Gender Ideology*, ed. N. Redclift and T. Sinclair. London: Routledge, 1991.

Edip, Halide (Adıvar). "Women's Part in Turkey's Progress." *Open Court* 46 (1932): 343–60.

Ekrem, Selma. *Unveiled: The Autobiography of a Turkish Girl*. New York: Ives Washburn, 1942.

Ellis, Ellen Deborah, and Florance Palmer. "The Feminist Movement in Turkey." *Contemporary Review*, no. 105 (1914): 857–64.

Emerson, Mabel E. "The Outlook for the Women of Turkey Today." *Moslem World* 15 (1925): 269–73.

Erder, Türköz, ed. *Family in Turkish Society*. Ankara: Turkish Social Sciences Association, 1985.

Erginsoy, Güliz. "Global Encounters and Gender Hierarchies in the Community of 'Garipçe.'" *New Perspectives on Turkey*, no. 18 (1998): 131–46.

Erman, Tahire. "Women and the Housing Environment: The Experiences of Turkish Migrant Women in Squatter (Gecekondu) Housing and Apartment Housing." *Environment and Behavior* 28, no. 6 (1996): 764–98.

———. "The Impact of Migration on Turkish Rural Women: Four Emergent Patterns." *Gender and Society* 12, no. 2 (1998): 146–67.

Esim, Simel, and Dilek Cindoğlu. "Women's Organizations in 1990s Turkey: Predicaments and Prospects." *Middle Eastern Studies* 35, no. 1 (1999): 178–88.

Ewing, Katherine P. "The Violence of Non-Recognition: Becoming a 'Concious' Woman in Turkey." In *Cultures under Siege: Collective Violence and Trauma in Anthropological and Psychoanalytic Perspective*, ed. Antonius Robben and Marcelo Suarez-Orozco. Cambridge: Cambridge University Press, 2000.

Fallers, L. A., and M. C. Fallers. "Sex Roles in Edremit." In *Mediterranean Family Structures*, ed. J. Peristiany. Cambridge: Cambridge University Press, 1976.

Faroqhi, Suraiya. "From the Slave Market to Arafat: Biographies of Bursa Women in the Late Eighteenth Century." *Turkish Studies Association Bulletin* 25, no. 1 (Spring 2000): 3–20.

Garnett, Lucy M. J. *The Women of Turkey and Their Folklore*. London: David Nutt, 1891.

———. *Home Life in Turkey*. New York: Macmillan, 1909.

Gerber, Haim. "Social and Economic Position of Women in an Ottoman City, Bursa, 1600–1700." *International Journal of Middle East Studies* 12 (1980): 231–44.

Good, Del Vecchio M. J. "A Comparative Perspective on Provincial Iran and Turkey." In *Women in the Muslim World*, ed. Lois Beck and Nikki Keddie. Cambridge, Mass.: Harvard University Press, 1978.

Goodwin, Godfrey. *The Private World of Ottoman Women*. London: Al Saqi, 2000.

Göle, Nilüfer. "Islamism, Feminism, and Post-Modernism: Women's Movements in Islamic Countries." *New Perspectives on Turkey*, no. 19 (1998): 53–70.

Hearst, W. J. "Turkish Families." In *Ethnic Family Values in Australia*, ed. Des Storer. Melbourne: Prentice Hall of Australia, 1985.

Hefferman, T. "Feminism against the East/West Divide: Lady Mary Pirrepont's 'Turkish Embassy Letters.'" *Eighteenth-Century Studies* 33, no. 2 (2000): 201–15.

İçduygu, Ahmet. "Correlates of Timing of Induced Abortion in Turkey." *Demography India* 25, no. 1 (1996): 131–46.

———. "The Consequences of International Migration for the Status of Women: A Turkish Study." *International Migration* 35, no. 3 (1997): 337–71.

İmamoğlu, E. Olcay. "A Model of Gender Relations in the Turkish Family." *Boğaziçi Journal-Review of Social, Economic, and Administrative Studies* 8, no. 2 (1994): 165–76.

İnan, Afet. *The Emancipation of the Turkish Women.* Paris: UNESCO, 1963.

———. *The Rights and Responsibilities of the Turkish Women.* Trans. Ahmet E. Uysal. Ankara: Türk Tarih Kurumu Basımevi, 1981.

İncirlioğlu, Emine Onaran. "Marriage, Gender Relations, and Rural Transformation in Central Anatolia." In *Culture and Economy: Changes in Turkish Villages,* ed. Paul Stirling. Huntingdon, U.K.: Eothen, 1993.

Jenkens, Hester Donaldson. *Behind Turkish Lattices: The Story of a Turkish Woman's Life.* London: Chatto and Windus, 1911.

———. *An Educational Ambassador to the Near East: The Story of Marry Patrick Mills and an American College in the Orient.* New York: Fleming H. Revell, 1925.

Kabasakal, Hayat, Nakiye A. Boyacıgiller, and Deniz Erden. "Organizational Characteristics as Correlates of Women in Middle and Top Management." *Boğaziçi Journal-Review of Social, Economic, and Administrative Studies* 8 (1994): 45–62.

Kadıoğlu, Ayşe. "Impact of Migration Experiences on Gender Roles: Findings of a Field Research in Turkey." *International Migration* 32, no. 4 (1994): 533–60.

———. "Migration Experiences of Turkish Women: Notes from a Researcher's Diary." *International Migration* 35, no. 4 (1997): 537–57.

Kağıtçıbaşı, Çiğdem. "Modernity and the Role of Women in Turkey." *Boğaziçi University Journal* (Social Science Series, Istanbul) 3 (1975): 83–89.

———. "Rural Women and Development in Turkey." Proceedings of the International Seminar on Rural Women and Development. Cairo: Ain Shams University, 1980.

———. "Women and Development in Turkey." *International Journal of Turkish Studies* 2 (1981–1982): 59–70.

———. *The Changing Value of Children in Turkey.* Honolulu: East-West Center, 1982.

———. "A Model of Family Change through Development: The Turkish Family in Comparative Perspective." In *From a Different Perspective: Studies of Behavior across Cultures,* ed. I. R. Lagunes and Y. H. Poortinga. Lisse, Netherlands: Swets and Zeitlinger, 1985.

———. "Status of Women in Turkey: Cross-Cultural Perspectives." *International Journal of Middle East Studies* 18 (1986): 485–99.

———. "Child Rearing in Turkey: Implications for Immigration and Intervention." In *Different Cultures, Same School,* ed. L. Eldering and F. Kloprogge. Lisse, Netherlands: Swets and Zeitlinger, 1989.

———. "Child Rearing in Turkey and an Intervention Research." *Psychology and Developing Societies* 1, no. 1 (1989): 37–52.

———. "The Turkish Early Enrichment Project and the Mother-Child Education Program." *Journal of Adolescent and Adult Literacy* 41 (1997): 70–72.

Kağıtçıbaşı, Çiğdem, and Aykut Kansu. "Socialization of Sex Roles and Family Dynamics: A Cross-Generational Comparison." *Boğaziçi University Journal* (Social Science Series, Istanbul) 5 (1977): 35–48.

Kağıtçıbaşı, Çiğdem, and Diane Sunar. "Family and Socialization in Turkey." In *Parent-Child Socialization in Diverse Cultures,* ed. J. L. Roopnarine and D. B. Carter. Norwood, N.J.: Ablex, 1992.

Kandiyoti, Deniz. "Social Change and Family Structure in a Turkish Village." In *Kinship and Modernization in Mediterranean Society*, ed. J. G. Peristiany. Rome: The Center for Mediterranean Studies, 1976.

———. "Sex Roles and Social Change: A Comparative Appraisal of Turkey's Women." *Signs* 3 (1977): 57–73.

———. ed. *Major Issues on the Status of Women in Turkey: Approaches and Priorities*. Ankara: Turkish Social Science Association, 1980.

———. "Emancipated but Unliberated? Reflections on the Turkish Case." *Feminist Studies* 13 (1987): 317–38.

———. "Slave Girls, Temptresses, and Comrades: Images of Women in the Turkish Novel." *Feminist Issues* 8 (1988): 35–50.

———. "Women and the Turkish State: Political Actors or Symbolic Pawns." In *Woman-Nation-State*, ed. N. Yuval-Davis and A. Anthias. London: Macmillan, 1988.

Karpat, Kemal H. "The Ottoman Family: Documents Pertaining to Its Size." *International Journal of Turkish Studies* 4 (1987): 137–45.

Kıray, Mübeccel. "Changing Roles of Mothers: Changing Intra-Family Relations in a Turkish Town." In *Mediterranean Family Structures*, ed. J. G. Peristiany. Cambridge: Cambridge University Press, 1976.

Kırca, Süheyla. "*Kim* and *Kadınca*: Bridging the Gap between Feminism and Women's Magazines." *New Perspectives on Turkey*, no. 22 (Spring 2000): 61–84.

Kongar, Emre. "A Survey of Family Change in Two Turkish Gecekondu [Shantytown] Areas." In *Mediterranean Family Structures*, ed. J. G. Peristiany. Cambridge: Cambridge University Press, 1976.

Kudat, Ayşe. "Ritual Kinship in Eastern Turkey." *Anthropological Quarterly* 44 (1971): 37–50.

———. "Structural Changes in the Migrant Turkish Family." In *Manpower Mobility across Cultural Boundaries: Social, Economic, and Legal Aspects*, ed. R. K. Krane. Leiden: E. J. Brill, 1975.

———. *Stability and Change in the Turkish Family at Home and Abroad: Comparative Perspectives*. Berlin: International Institute of Comparative Social Studies, 1975.

Lott, Emmeline. *Harem Life in Egypt and Constantinople: The English Governess in Egypt*. 2nd ed., 2 vols. London: Richard Bentley, 1866.

Magnarella, Paul J. "Conjugal Role Relationships in a Modernizing Turkish Town." *International Journal of Sociology of the Family* 2 (1972): 179–92.

———. "The Reception of Swiss Family Law in Turkey." *Anthropological Quarterly* 46 (1972): 100–16.

———. "Turkish Family Law." *World and I* 3 (1988): 502–13.

Magnarella, Paul J., and Orhan Türkdoğan. "Descent, Affinity, and Ritual Relations in Eastern Turkey." *American Anthropologist* 75 (1973): 1626–33.

Marcus, Julie. *A World of Difference: Islam and Gender Hierarchy in Turkey*. London: Zed, 1992.

Micklewright, Nancy. "Public and Private for Ottoman Woman of the Nineteenth Century." In *Women, Patronage and Self-Representation in Islamic Countries*, ed. D. Fairchild Ruggles. Albany, N.Y.: SUNY Press, 2000.

Mirdal, G. "Stress and Distress in Migration: Problems and Resources of Turkish Women in Denmark." *International Migration Review* 18 (1984): 984–1003.

Müftüler-Baç, Melten. "Turkish Women's Predicament." *Women's Studies International Forum* 22, no. 3 (1999): 303–15.

Orga, İrfan. *Portrait of a Turkish Family.* New York: Macmillan, 1950.

Özar, Şemsa. "Some Observations on the Position of Women in the Labor Market in the Development Process of Turkey." *Boğaziçi Journal-Review of Social, Economic, and Administrative Studies* 8, no. 2 (1994): 21–43.

Özbay, Ferhunde, ed. *Women, Family, and Social Change in Turkey.* Paris: UNESCO, 1990.

———. "Women's Labor in Urban and Rural Settings." *Boğaziçi Journal-Review of Social, Economic, and Administrative Studies* 8, no. 2 (1994): 5–19.

Özbek, A., and V. D. Volkan. "Psychiatric Problems within the Satellite Extended Families of Turkey." *American Journal of Psychotherapy* 30 (1976): 576–82.

Paleczek, Rasuly, ed. *Turkish Families in Transition.* Frankfurt: Lang, 1996.

Parker, Lockie. "Women in New Turkey." *Asia* 34 (1934): 356–61.

Peirce, Leslie. *The Imperial Harem: Women and Sovereignty in the Ottoman Empire.* Oxford: Oxford University Press, 1993.

Penzer, Norman Mosley. *The Harem: An Account of the Institution as It Existed in the Palace of the Turkish Sultans with a History of the Grand Seraglio from Its Foundations to the Present Times.* Philadelphia: Lippincott, 1937.

Rustow, Rachel L. "Family Living in Modern Turkey." *Child Study* 32 (1955): 19–25.

Saktanber, Ayşe. "Becoming the 'Other' as a Muslim in Turkey: Turkish Women vs. Islamist Women." *New Perspectives on Turkey*, no. 11 (1994): 99–134.

———. *Living Islam: Women, Politics and Society in Turkey.* London: I. B. Tauris, 1998.

Saz, Leyla. *The Imperial Harem of the Sultans: Daily Life at the Çırağan Palace during the 19th Century: Memoirs of Leyla (Saz) Hanımefendi [1850–1936].* Istanbul: Peva, 1994.

Schwartz, A. "Atatürk's Daughters." *Wilson Quarterly* 19, no. 4 (1995): 68–79.

Sirman, Nükhet. "Feminism in Turkey: A Short History." *New Perspectives on Turkey* 3 (1989): 1–34.

Sönmez, Emel. *Turkish Women in Turkish Literature of the Nineteenth Century.* Leiden: E. J. Brill, 1969.

———. "Turkish Women in Turkish Literature of the 19th Century." *Die Welt des Islams* 12 (1969): 1–73.

———. "Turkish Women in Turkish Literature of the 19th Century." *Hacettepe Bulletin of Social Sciences and Humanities* (Ankara) 2 (1970): 123–57.

———. "The Novelist Halide Edip Adıvar and Turkish Feminism." *Die Welt des Islams* 14, nos. 1–4 (1971): 81–114.

Sunar, Diane G. "Female Stereotypes in the United States and Turkey." *Journal of Cross-Cultural Psychology* 13 (1982): 445–60.

Şenesen, Gülay G. "Female Participation in the Turkish University Administration: Econometric and Survey Findings."*Boğaziçi Journal-Review of Social, Economic, and Administrative Studies* 8 (1994): 63–81.

Tekeli, Şirin. "Emergence of the Feminist Movement in Turkey." In *The New Women's Movement*, ed. Drude Dahlerup. London: Sage, 1986.

———. ed. *Women in Modern Turkish Society: A Reader.* London: Zed, 1995.

Tokgöz, Oya. "Turkish Women: Voters and Consumers: Cases in Political and Consumer Socialization in Turkey." *Orient* (Hamburg) 26 (1985): 76–87.

Toynbee, Rosalind. "Turkish Women of Today." *Forum* 80 (1928): 412–20.

Tucker, Judith. "Revisiting Reform: Women and the Ottoman Law of Family Rights." *Arab Studies Journal* 4, no. 2 (1996): 4–18.

———. *In the House of the Law: Gender and Islamic Law in Ottoman Syria and Palestine.* Berkeley: University of California Press, 1997.

Tugay, Emine Fuat. *Three Centuries: Family Chronicles of Turkey and Egypt*. New York: Oxford University Press, 1963.

Tümertekin, Erol. "The Distribution of Sex Ratios with Special Reference to Internal Migration in Turkey." *Review of the Geographical Institute of the University of Istanbul* 4 (1958): 9–32.

Vaka, Demetra. *Haremlik: Some Pages from the Life of Turkish Women*. New York: Houghton Mifflin, 1909.

White, Jenny. "Linking the Urban Poor to the World Market: Women and Work in Istanbul." *MERIP Reports* 21 (1991): 18–22.

———. *Money Makes Us Relatives: Women's Labor in Turkey*. Austin: University of Texas Press, 1994.

———. "An Unmarried Girl and a Grinding Stone." In *Children in the Muslim Middle East*, ed. Elizabeth Warnock Fernea. Austin: University of Texas Press, 1995.

Yorgun, P. "The Women's Question and Difficulties of Feminism in Turkey." *Khamsin* (London) 11 (1984): 70–85.

Zeyneb, Hanum. *A Turkish Woman's European Impressions*. Ed. Grace Ellison. Philadelphia: Lippincott, 1913.

Zeytinoğlu, Işık Urla. "Employment of Women and Labour Laws in Turkey." *Comparative Labor Law Journal* 15, no. 2 (1994): 177–205.

Zilfi, Madeline. *Women in the Ottoman Empire: Middle Eastern Women in the Early Modern Era*. Leiden: E. J. Brill, 1997.

About the Author

Metin Heper (B.S. Istanbul University; M.A. Syracuse University; Ph.D. Syracuse University) is a professor of political science at Bilkent University in Ankara, director of the Center for Turkish Politics and History at the same university, and a founding member of the Turkish Academy of Sciences. Professor Heper has been a Fulbright Scholar and Visiting Professor at University of Connecticut, Lester Martin Fellow at the Hebrew University of Jerusalem, Simon Senior Research Fellow at the University of Manchester, U.K, a research associate at Harvard University, and a research fellow and visiting professor at Princeton University. His work focuses on the impact of the strong state tradition that the Turkish Republic inherited from the Ottoman Empire on the transition to and the consolidation and deepening of democracy in Turkey. He is the author of *The State Tradition in Turkey* and *İsmet İnönü: The Making of a Turkish Statesman,* and the editor of *Dilemmas of Decentralizing: Municipal Government in Turkey; Democracy and Local Government: Istanbul in the 1980s; Strong State and Economic Interest Groups: The Post-1980 Turkish Experience;* and *The State and Public Bureaucracies: A Comparative Perspective.* Metin Heper is also the co-editor of *Islam and Politics in the Modern Middle East; The State, the Military, and Democracy: Turkey in the 1980s; Political Parties and Democracy in Turkey; Political Parties in Turkey; Turkey and the West: Changing Political and Cultural Identities; Politics in the Third Turkish Republic; Political Leaders and Democracy in Turkey;* and *Institutions and Democratic Statecraft.*